English Football

A FANS' HANDBOOK 1999–2000

THE ROUGH GUIDE

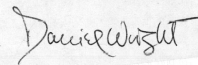

There are more than one hundred and fifty Rough Guide titles
covering destinations from Amsterdam to Zimbabwe

Forthcoming titles include

Cuba • Dominican Republic • Las Vegas • Sardinia • Switzerland

Rough Guide Reference Series

Classical Music • Drum 'n' Bass • European Football • House
The Internet • Jazz • Music USA • Opera • Reggae
Rock • World Music

Rough Guides on the Internet

www.roughguides.com

Editor: Dan Goldstein
Design and layout: Dan Goldstein
Production: Robert Evers, Susanne Hillen, Michelle Draycott
Commissioning editor: Jonathan Buckley
Rough Guides series editor: Mark Ellingham

This first edition published September 1999 by Rough Guides Ltd, 62–70 Shorts Gardens, London WC2H 9AB.
Distributed by the Penguin Group:
Penguin Books Ltd, 27 Wrights Lane, London W8 5TZ
Penguin Books USA Inc., 375 Hudson Street, New York 10014, USA
Penguin Books Australia Ltd, 487 Maroondah Highway, PO Box 257, Ringwood, Victoria 3134, Australia
Penguin Books Canada Ltd, 10 Alcorn Avenue, Toronto, Ontario, Canada M4V 1E4
Penguin Books (NZ) Ltd, 182–190 Wairau Road, Auckland 10, New Zealand
Typeset to an original design by Dan Goldstein.
Printed in England by Clays Ltd, St Ives PLC

624pp
A catalogue record for this book is available from the British Library
ISBN 1-85828-455-4

English Football

A FANS' HANDBOOK 1999–2000

THE ROUGH GUIDE

Written and researched by

Dan Goldstein

THE ROUGH GUIDES

Contents

Introduction

Every July and August, on the parched earth of Parker's Piece in Cambridge, a thousand voices ring out into the sky, in French, Italian, Greek, Turkish, Japanese, Cantonese or Urdu. They all sound different, but they are all saying the same things: offside; handball; get in there; goal! The foreign students come to learn English, the common language of the developed world. But before they have learned a word of it, they have already learned something capable of bringing them together – football, the game the globe plays.

Few of the overseas visitors who play on Parker's Piece realise that it was here, in 1848, that a group of Cambridge scholars posted up the first codified set of rules for the game. They have changed a fair bit since, but their basic principles remain, universally recognised, more likely to find consensus than any European Commission edict or United Nations resolution.

Over the past few years, English professional football has had its own foreign invasion to deal with. The Bosman judgement has made it easier for top clubs to sign overseas players, while satellite TV cash has given those players undreamt-of salaries. Imported styles and attitudes have had a huge effect on England's traditionally insular footballing outlook, much of it beneficial. The irony is that things used to be the other way round. In the early part of the twentieth century, it was the British who travelled the world, preaching football's gospel with an almost missionary zeal. England was the home of football – the first country to have a football association, the first to introduce a league competition, the first to play internationals (even if they were only against the Scots).

Today the debate is not about whether the English game is the best in the world (we know it isn't), but whether it will ever again come close. After all, the foreign invasion has also served to reduce the number of openings for fresh, homegrown talent, not just from England but from across the British Isles. Not even King Kev has a quick fix for that. And are the travails of the national team symptomatic of a wider problem – the inevitable consequence of the game selling its soul? With money from merchandising, sponsorship and TV rights pouring into the top clubs, the gap between rich and poor is widening, leaving some supporters pining for the 'good old days'.

This is understandable – football often seems more like business than sport now. But it is also simplistic. Leaving nostalgia to one side, the 'good old days' meant decrepit grounds; non-existent facilities for the young, the old or the disabled; tedious, route-one football; and a climate of fear and loathing engendered by persistent hooliganism. In any case, English football's greatest strength remains just about intact – its four-division, 92-team professional league structure, easily the biggest in Europe. For travelling supporters, most of whom now go to away games without fear of being attacked for the colour of their shirt, the English game's diversity is richer than ever.

This is where the **Rough Guide to English Football** comes in. It contains all the vital matchday information – how to get to each ground, ticketing details, tips on eating and drinking, and listings for local radio stations, newspapers and fanzines. But this guide goes deeper than that – into the soul of each club, tracing its history, assessing its impact on the game, plotting its contemporary agonies or ecstasies, and giving an insight into what its future may hold. So now you can put each of the 92 clubs in context – whether you're stuck on a train outside Reading, wondering how long it'll take to get to the Madejski, or are just an armchair fan dreaming of past glories, and hoping for fresh ones.

A book such as this can never be easy to write, but it would have been a whole lot harder were it not for the input of so many fans, whose wisdom, reminiscences and practical advice have played a vital part in giving each club's story an authentic feel. We hope this dialogue will continue, so if you see a date that's wrong, a vital player who's missing, a bus number that's changed or a website address that's out-of-date, then please write, c/o The Rough Guides, and tell us all about it. All the best contributions will be credited in the next edition.

Dan Goldstein, 1999

Acknowledgements

The following have all helped make this book what it is and are credited in no particular order:

Michael Kenrick, Michael Hesp, Tranmere Kev, Will Thornton, David Stephenson, Mike Hammond, Neal, Colin, Martin, Richard, Rachel and Scott at Empics, Richard Jones, Paul Hawksbee, the Ipswich Three, Stuart and Natasha Catterson, John Murphy, Andy Beill, Dave and Simon at Paragon, Chris Hull at the Football League, Simon Evans, Paul Muscutt, Bernard Gallagher, Matthew Vosburgh, Pete, Brian, Chris and Bridget at Poundbury, Andy C, Jeff King, Bill Borrows, Nigel Lord, Phil and Bob, Annette Wilby, Dave, Wimp and Gav, Paul Wilkinson, Jon Castell, Christian Jahnsen, Steve Pennycooke, Phil Morley, C J Morris, Trevor Gilchrist, Trish and Chris, the Chemical Brothers, the Copa America and UK Gold's *Doctor Who* re-runs for helping to keep me awake, and Janice, Marysia, Maxim and Sacha, with whom I hope to be able to spend a bit more time next year.

This book is dedicated to my father, who never stopped calling them Leyton Orient

Further reading and surfing

All newspapers, fanzines, books and websites used in the course of researching and writing this book are mentioned in the individual club chapters. The author is also indebted to the following sources.

Books

Club Colours, Bob Bickerton (Hamlyn, 1998)
Football Fans Guide, Janet Williams (CollinsWillow, 1998)
Football Memories, Brian Glanville (Virgin, 1999)
Purnell's Encyclopedia Of Association Football, Norman S Barrett (Purnell, 1972)
Rothmans Book Of Football Records, Jack Rollin (Headline, 1998)
Rothmans Football Yearbook, Jack Rollin (Headline)
The European Football Yearbook, Mike Hammond (Sports Projects, various years)
The FA Book For Boys – 25th Edition (Heinemann/Pan, 1972)
The FA Cup Final – A Postwar History, Ivan Ponting (TW, 1994)
The Football Grounds Of Britain, Simon Inglis (CollinsWillow, 1996)
The Guinness Football Encyclopedia, Graham Hart (Guinness, 1996)
The PFA Premier & Football League Players' Records 1946–1998, Barry J Hugman (Queen Anne Press, 1998)

Websites

e-soccer – an excellent source of football links: *www.e-soccer.com*
Football 365 – one of the few online news services with its own voice: *www.football365.co.uk*
Sportspages – the specialist sports book retailer online: *www.sportspages.co.uk*
The Football Fan's Good Pub Guide – speaks for itself: *www.users.globalnet.co.uk/~plaborne/*

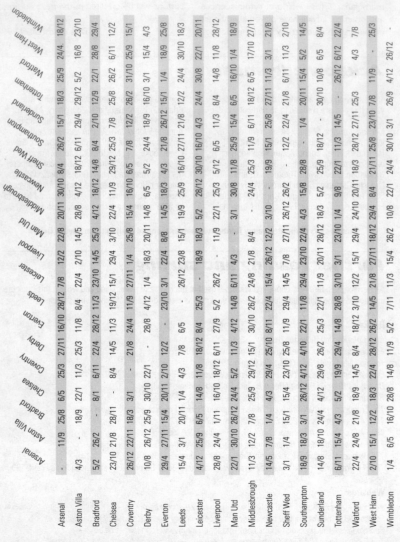

	Arsenal	Aston Villa	Bradford	Chelsea	Coventry	Derby	Everton	Leeds	Leicester	Liverpool	Man Utd	Middlesbrough	Newcastle	Sheff Wed	Southampton	Sunderland	Tottenham	Watford	West Ham	Wimbledon
Arsenal	-	11/9	25/8	6/5	25/3	27/11	16/10	28/12	7/8	12/2	22/8	20/11	30/10	8/4	26/2	15/1	18/3	25/9	24/4.	18/12
Aston Villa	4/3	-	18/9	22/1	11/3	25/3	11/8	8/4	22/4	2/10	14/5	28/8	4/12	18/12	6/11	29/4	29/12	5/2	16/8	23/10
Bradford	5/2	26/2	-	8/1	6/11	22/4	28/12	11/3	23/10	14/5	25/3	4/12	18/12	14/8	8/4	2/10	12/9	22/1	28/8	29/4
Chelsea	23/10	21/8	28/11	-	8/4	14/5	11/3	19/12	15/1	29/4	3/10	22/4	11/9	29/12	25/3	7/8	25/8	26/2	6/11	12/2
Coventry	26/12	22/11	18/3	3/1	-	21/8	24/4	11/9	27/11	1/4	25/8	15/4	16/10	6/5	7/8	12/2	26/2	31/10	25/9	15/1
Derby	10/8	26/12	25/9	30/10	22/1	-	28/8	4/12	1/4	18/3	20/11	14/8	6/5	5/2	24/4	18/9	16/10	3/1	15/4	4/3
Everton	29/4	27/11	15/4	20/11	2/10	12/2	-	23/10	3/1	22/4	8/8	14/5	18/3	4/3	21/8	26/12	15/1	1/4	18/9	25/8
Leeds	15/4	3/1	20/11	1/4	4/3	7/8	6/5	-	26/12	23/8	15/1	19/9	25/9	16/10	27/11	21/8	12/2	24/4	30/10	18/3
Leicester	4/12	25/9	6/5	14/8	11/8	18/12	8/4	25/3	-	18/9	18/3	5/2	28/12	30/10	16/10	4/3	24/4	30/8	22/1	20/11
Liverpool	28/8	24/4	1/11	16/10	18/12	6/11	27/9	5/2	26/2	-	11/9	22/1	25/3	5/12	6/5	11/3	8/4	14/8	11/8	28/12
Man Utd	22/1	30/10	26/12	24/4	5/2	11/3	4/12	14/8	6/11	4/3	-	3/1	30/8	11/8	25/9	15/4	6/5	16/10	1/4	18/9
Middlesbrough	11/3	12/2	7/8	25/9	29/12	15/1	30/10	26/2	24/8	21/8	8/4	-	24/4	25/3	11/9	6/11	18/12	6/5	17/10	27/11
Newcastle	14/5	7/8	1/4	4/3	29/4	25/10	8/11	22/4	15/4	26/12	12/2	3/10	-	19/9	15/1	25/8	27/11	11/3	3/1	21/8
Sheff Wed	3/1	1/4	15/1	15/4	23/10	25/8	11/9	29/4	14/5	7/8	27/11	26/12	26/2	-	12/2	22/4	21/8	6/11	11/3	2/10
Southampton	18/9	18/3	3/1	26/12	4/12	4/10	22/1	11/8	29/4	23/10	22/4	4/3	15/8	28/8	-	1/4	20/11	15/4	5/2	14/5
Sunderland	14/8	18/10	24/4	4/12	29/8	26/2	25/3	22/1	11/9	20/11	28/12	18/3	5/2	25/9	18/12	-	30/10	10/8	6/5	8/4
Tottenham	6/11	15/4	4/3	5/2	19/9	29/4	14/8	28/8	3/10	3/1	23/10	1/4	9/8	22/1	11/3	14/5	-	26/12	6/12	22/4
Watford	22/4	24/8	21/8	18/9	14/5	8/4	18/12	3/10	12/2	15/1	29/4	24/10	20/11	18/3	28/12	27/11	25/3	-	4/3	7/8
West Ham	2/10	15/1	12/2	18/3	22/4	28/12	26/2	14/5	21/8	27/11	18/12	29/4	8/4	21/11	25/8	23/10	7/8	11/9	-	25/3
Wimbledon	1/4	6/5	16/10	28/8	14/8	11/9	5/2	7/11	11/3	15/4	26/2	10/8	22/1	24/4	30/10	3/1	26/9	4/12	26/12	-

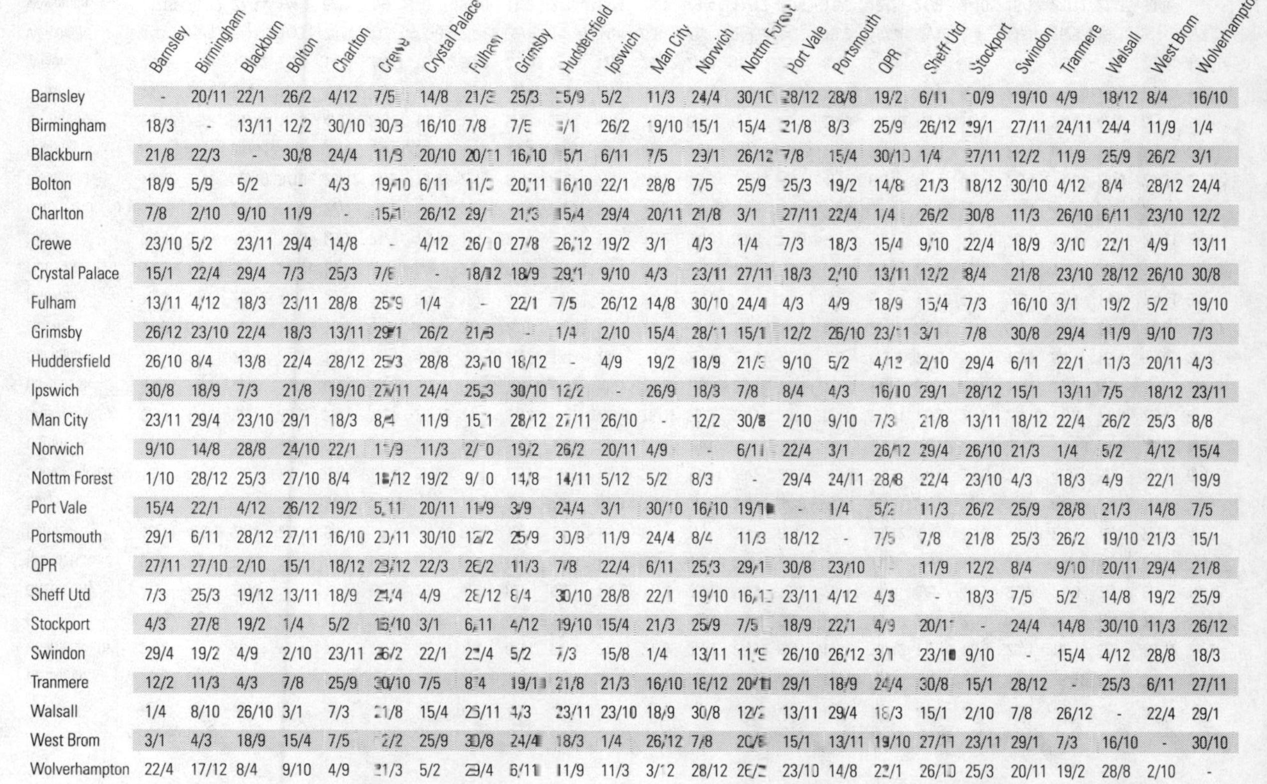

	Barnsley	Birmingham	Blackburn	Bolton	Charlton	Crewe	Crystal Palace	Fulham	Grimsby	Huddersfield	Ipswich	Man City	Norwich	Nottm Forest	Port Vale	Portsmouth	QPR	Sheff Utd	Stockport	Swindon	Tranmere	Walsall	West Brom	Wolverhampton
Barnsley	-	20/11	22/1	26/2	4/12	7/5	14/8	21/3	25/3	5/9	5/2	11/3	24/4	30/10	28/12	28/8	19/2	6/11	10/9	19/10	4/9	18/12	8/4	16/10
Birmingham	18/3	-	13/11	12/2	30/10	30/3	16/10	7/8	7/[illegible]	[illegible]/1	26/2	9/10	15/1	15/4	21/8	8/3	25/9	26/12	29/1	27/11	24/11	24/4	11/9	1/4
Blackburn	21/8	22/3	-	30/8	24/4	11/3	20/10	20/11	16/10	5/1	6/11	7/5	23/1	26/12	7/8	15/4	30/10	1/4	27/11	12/2	11/9	25/9	26/2	3/1
Bolton	18/9	5/9	5/2	-	4/3	19/10	6/11	11/3	20/11	16/10	22/1	28/8	7/5	25/9	25/3	19/2	14/8	21/3	18/12	30/10	4/12	8/4	28/12	24/4
Charlton	7/8	2/10	9/10	11/9	-	15/1	26/12	29/[illegible]	21/3	15/4	29/4	20/11	21/8	3/1	27/11	22/4	1/4	26/2	30/8	11/3	26/10	6/11	23/10	12/2
Crewe	23/10	5/2	23/11	29/4	14/8	-	4/12	26/10	27/8	26/12	19/2	3/1	4/3	1/4	7/3	18/3	15/4	9/10	22/4	18/9	3/10	22/1	4/9	13/11
Crystal Palace	15/1	22/4	29/4	7/3	25/3	7/8	-	18/12	18/9	29/1	9/10	4/3	23/11	27/11	18/3	2/10	13/11	12/2	8/4	21/8	23/10	28/12	26/10	30/8
Fulham	13/11	4/12	18/3	23/11	28/8	25/9	1/4	-	22/1	7/5	26/12	14/8	30/10	24/4	4/3	4/9	18/9	15/4	7/3	16/10	3/1	19/2	5/2	19/10
Grimsby	26/12	23/10	22/4	18/3	13/11	29/1	26/2	21/3	-	1/4	2/10	15/4	28/11	15/1	12/2	26/10	23/11	3/1	7/8	30/8	29/4	11/9	9/10	7/3
Huddersfield	26/10	8/4	13/8	22/4	28/12	25/3	28/8	23/10	18/12	-	4/9	19/2	18/9	21/3	9/10	5/2	4/12	2/10	29/4	6/11	22/1	11/3	20/11	4/3
Ipswich	30/8	18/9	7/3	21/8	19/10	27/11	24/4	25/3	30/10	12/2	-	26/9	18/3	7/8	8/4	4/3	16/10	29/1	28/12	15/1	13/11	7/5	18/12	23/11
Man City	23/11	29/4	23/10	29/1	18/3	8/4	11/9	15/1	28/12	27/11	26/10	-	12/2	30/8	2/10	9/10	7/3	21/8	13/11	18/12	22/4	26/2	25/3	8/8
Norwich	9/10	14/8	28/8	24/10	22/1	1/3	11/3	2/10	19/2	26/2	20/11	4/9	-	6/11	22/4	3/1	26/12	29/4	26/10	21/3	1/4	5/2	4/12	15/4
Nottm Forest	1/10	28/12	25/3	27/10	8/4	1[illegible]/12	19/2	9/[illegible]0	14/8	14/11	5/12	5/2	8/3	-	29/4	24/11	28/8	22/4	23/10	4/3	18/3	4/9	22/1	19/9
Port Vale	15/4	22/1	4/12	26/12	19/2	5/11	20/11	11/9	3/9	24/4	3/1	30/10	16/10	19/1[illegible]	-	1/4	5/2	11/3	26/2	25/9	28/8	21/3	14/8	7/5
Portsmouth	29/1	6/11	28/12	27/11	16/10	20/11	30/10	12/2	25/9	30/3	11/9	24/4	8/4	11/3	18/12	-	7/5	7/8	21/8	25/3	26/2	19/10	21/3	15/1
QPR	27/11	27/10	2/10	15/1	18/12	23/12	22/3	26/2	11/3	7/8	22/4	6/11	25/3	29/1	30/8	23/10	-	11/9	12/2	8/4	9/10	20/11	29/4	21/8
Sheff Utd	7/3	25/3	19/12	13/11	18/9	2[illegible]/4	4/9	26/12	8/4	30/10	28/8	22/1	19/10	16/1[illegible]	23/11	4/12	4/3	-	18/3	7/5	5/2	14/8	19/2	25/9
Stockport	4/3	27/8	19/2	1/4	5/2	15/10	3/1	6/11	4/12	19/10	15/4	21/3	25/9	7/5	18/9	22/1	4/9	20/1[illegible]	-	24/4	14/8	30/10	11/3	26/12
Swindon	29/4	19/2	4/9	2/10	23/11	26/2	22/1	27/4	5/2	7/3	15/8	1/4	13/11	11/[illegible]	26/10	26/12	3/1	23/1[illegible]	9/10	-	15/4	4/12	28/8	18/3
Tranmere	12/2	11/3	4/3	7/8	25/9	30/10	7/5	8/4	19/1[illegible]	21/8	21/3	16/10	15/12	20/[illegible]	29/1	18/9	24/4	30/8	15/1	28/12	-	25/3	6/11	27/11
Walsall	1/4	8/10	26/10	3/1	7/3	21/8	15/4	25/11	4/3	23/11	23/10	18/9	30/8	12/2	13/11	29/4	16/3	15/1	2/10	7/8	26/12	-	22/4	29/1
West Brom	3/1	4/3	18/9	15/4	7/5	[illegible]2/2	25/9	30/8	24/4	18/3	1/4	26/12	7/8	20/[illegible]	15/1	13/11	19/10	27/11	23/11	29/1	7/3	16/10	-	30/10
Wolverhampton	22/4	17/12	8/4	9/10	4/9	21/3	5/2	[illegible]3/4	6/11	11/9	11/3	3/12	28/12	2[illegible]/[illegible]	23/10	14/8	22/1	26/10	25/3	20/11	19/2	28/8	2/10	-

	Blackpool	Bournemouth	Brentford	Bristol City	Bristol Rovers	Burnley	Bury	Cambridge Utd	Cardiff	Chesterfield	Colchester	Gillingham	Luton	Millwall	Notts County	Oldham	Oxford Utd	Preston	Reading	Scunthorpe	Stoke	Wigan	Wrexham	Wycombe
Blackpool	-	18/9	29/1	12/2	24/4	21/3	16/10	27/11	11/3	6/5	3/1	21/8	15/1	23/11	4/3	19/10	30/8	1/4	11/12	15/4	26/12	6/11	7/8	25/9
Bournemouth	26/2	-	23/11	15/1	19/10	12/2	25/9	7/8	6/11	24/4	21/8	21/3	30/8	27/11	8/1	8/4	18/12	11/3	11/9	29/1	16/10	6/5	28/12	25/3
Brentford	28/8	18/3	-	26/12	4/12	24/4	22/1	4/3	4/9	11/12	6/5	19/10	18/9	15/4	5/2	14/8	16/10	25/9	2/11	13/11	3/1	1/4	7/3	19/2
Bristol City	4/9	14/8	25/3	-	17/10	25/9	28/8	6/11	8/1	5/2	19/10	11/3	28/12	11/9	19/2	23/11	24/4	6/5	4/12	26/2	21/3	22/1	8/4	18/12
Bristol Rovers	2/10	29/4	7/8	22/4	-	30/8	2/11	3/1	9/10	18/3	11/12	15/1	27/11	26/12	23/10	18/9	21/8	15/4	13/11	12/2	1/4	4/3	29/1	7/3
Burnley	13/11	4/9	2/10	23/10	5/2	-	25/3	29/4	18/12	14/8	18/9	8/1	7/3	22/4	8/4	22/1	28/12	4/3	18/3	10/10	28/8	19/2	2/11	4/12
Bury	22/4	23/10	21/8	29/1	11/3	26/12	-	11/12	2/10	15/4	30/8	7/8	12/2	3/1	9/10	4/3	21/3	27/11	29/4	1/4	6/11	23/11	15/1	18/9
Cambridge Utd	19/2	4/12	11/9	7/3	8/4	19/10	8/1	-	28/12	22/1	16/10	25/9	13/11	26/2	28/8	18/12	25/3	24/4	14/8	2/11	4/9	5/2	18/3	6/5
Cardiff	2/11	7/3	12/2	11/12	6/5	1/4	24/4	15/4	-	13/11	18/3	27/11	29/1	7/8	18/9	16/10	15/1	3/1	26/12	30/8	19/10	25/9	20/8	4/3
Chesterfield	9/10	2/10	8/1	30/8	23/11	15/1	28/12	21/8	21/3	-	7/8	18/12	25/3	29/1	29/4	6/11	27/11	12/2	26/2	23/10	11/9	11/3	22/4	8/4
Colchester	8/4	22/1	9/10	29/4	8/1	26/2	5/2	22/4	23/11	4/12	-	25/3	18/12	23/10	14/8	21/3	11/3	6/11	28/8	11/9	19/2	4/9	2/10	28/12
Gillingham	22/1	12/11	29/4	2/11	14/8	11/12	4/12	23/10	19/2	1/4	26/12	-	22/4	2/10	7/3	4/9	4/3	18/9	3/1	18/3	5/2	15/4	9/10	28/8
Luton	14/8	5/2	26/2	15/4	19/2	6/11	4/9	21/3	28/8	26/12	1/4	16/10	-	11/3	4/12	6/5	25/9	23/11	22/1	3/1	11/12	24/4	11/9	19/10
Millwall	18/3	19/2	28/12	4/3	25/3	16/10	8/4	18/9	4/12	28/8	25/9	24/4	2/11	-	18/12	5/2	6/5	19/10	4/9	7/3	22/1	14/8	13/11	8/1
Notts County	11/9	11/12	30/8	27/11	25/9	3/1	6/5	29/1	26/2	19/10	15/1	6/11	7/8	1/4	-	24/4	23/11	21/3	15/4	21/8	11/3	26/12	12/2	16/10
Oldham	29/4	3/1	15/1	18/3	26/2	21/8	11/9	1/4	22/4	7/3	13/11	12/2	9/10	30/8	2/10	-	29/1	7/8	23/10	26/12	15/4	11/12	27/11	2/11
Oxford Utd	5/2	1/4	22/4	2/10	22/1	15/4	13/11	26/12	14/8	19/2	2/11	11/9	23/10	9/10	18/3	28/8	-	11/12	7/3	29/4	4/12	3/1	26/2	4/9
Preston	18/12	2/11	23/10	9/10	28/12	11/9	19/2	2/10	8/4	4/9	7/3	26/2	18/3	29/4	13/11	4/12	8/1	-	5/2	22/4	14/8	28/8	25/3	22/1
Reading	8/1	4/3	11/3	7/8	22/3	24/11	20/10	15/1	25/3	18/9	29/1	8/4	21/8	12/2	28/12	25/9	7/11	30/8	-	27/11	6/5	16/10	18/12	24/4
Scunthorpe	28/12	28/8	21/3	18/9	4/9	6/5	18/12	11/3	5/2	25/9	4/3	23/11	8/4	6/11	22/1	25/3	19/10	16/10	19/2	-	24/4	4/12	8/1	14/8
Stoke	25/3	22/4	8/4	13/11	18/12	29/1	8/3	12/2	29/4	4/3	27/11	30/8	8/1	22/8	3/11	28/12	7/8	15/1	9/10	2/10	-	18/9	23/10	18/3
Wigan	7/3	9/10	18/12	21/8	11/9	27/11	18/3	30/8	23/10	2/11	12/2	28/12	2/10	15/1	25/3	8/1	8/4	29/1	22/4	7/8	26/2	-	29/4	13/11
Wrexham	4/12	15/4	6/11	3/1	28/8	11/3	14/8	23/11	22/1	16/10	24/4	6/5	4/3	21/3	4/9	19/2	18/9	26/12	1/4	11/12	25/9	19/10	-	5/2
Wycombe	23/10	26/12	27/11	1/4	6/11	7/8	26/2	9/10	11/9	3/1	15/4	29/1	29/4	11/12	22/4	11/3	12/2	21/8	2/10	15/1	23/11	21/3	30/8	-

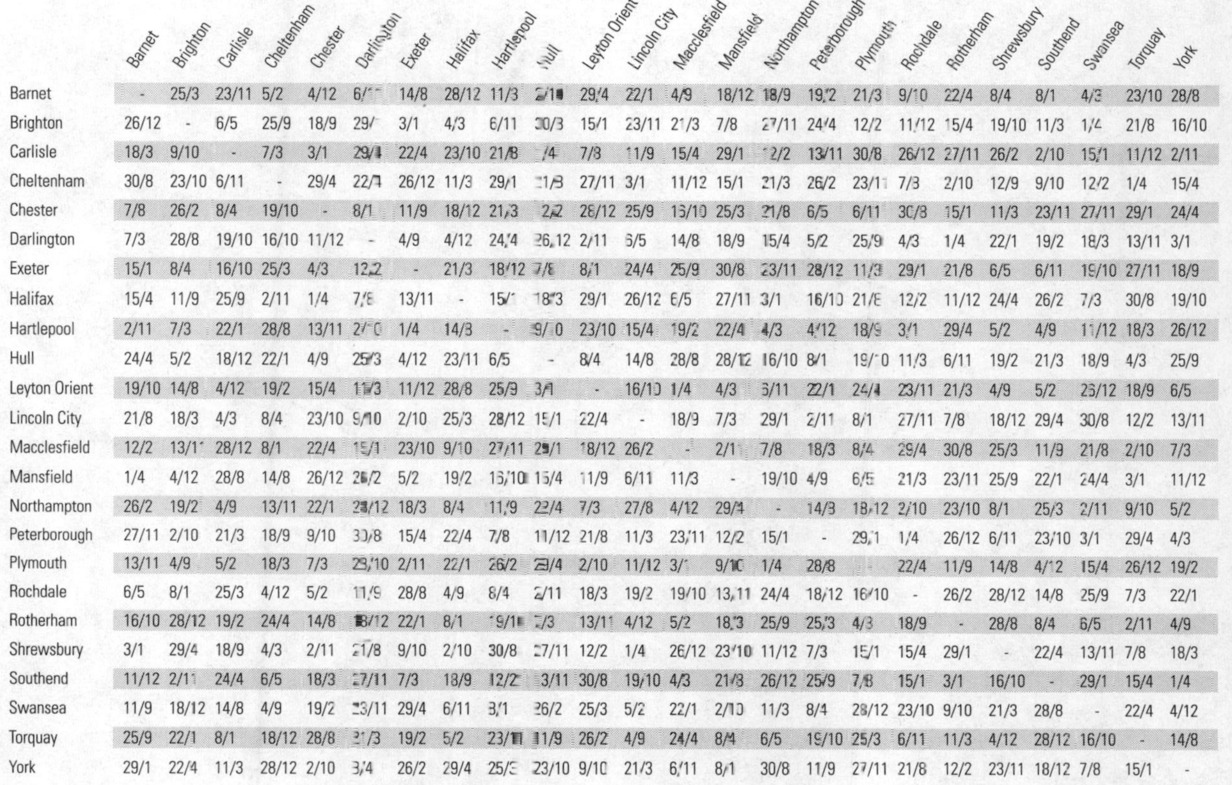

	Barnet	Brighton	Carlisle	Cheltenham	Chester	Darlington	Exeter	Halifax	Hartlepool	Hull	Leyton Orient	Lincoln City	Macclesfield	Mansfield	Northampton	Peterborough	Plymouth	Rochdale	Rotherham	Shrewsbury	Southend	Swansea	Torquay	York
Barnet	-	25/3	23/11	5/2	4/12	[illegible]	14/8	28/12	11/3	[illegible]	29/4	22/1	4/9	18/12	18/9	19/2	21/3	9/10	22/4	8/4	8/1	4/3	23/10	28/8
Brighton	26/12	-	6/5	25/9	18/9	[illegible]	3/1	4/3	6/11	30/3	15/1	23/11	21/3	7/8	27/11	24/4	12/2	11/12	15/4	19/10	11/3	1/4	21/8	16/10
Carlisle	18/3	9/10	-	7/3	3/1	29/1	22/4	23/10	21/8	[illegible]	7/3	11/9	15/4	29/1	12/2	13/11	30/8	26/12	27/11	26/2	2/10	15/1	11/12	2/11
Cheltenham	30/8	23/10	6/11	-	29/4	22/1	26/12	11/3	29/1	21/3	27/11	3/1	11/12	15/1	21/3	26/2	23/11	7/3	2/10	12/9	9/10	12/2	1/4	15/4
Chester	7/8	26/2	8/4	19/10	-	8/1	11/9	18/12	21/3	2/2	28/12	25/9	13/10	25/3	21/8	6/5	6/11	30/3	15/1	11/3	23/11	27/11	29/1	24/4
Darlington	7/3	28/8	19/10	16/10	11/12	-	4/9	4/12	24/4	26/12	2/11	6/5	14/8	18/9	15/4	5/2	25/9	4/3	1/4	22/1	19/2	18/3	13/11	3/1
Exeter	15/1	8/4	16/10	25/3	4/3	12/2	-	21/3	18/12	7/8	8/1	24/4	25/9	30/8	23/11	28/12	11/3	29/1	21/8	6/5	6/11	19/10	27/11	18/9
Halifax	15/4	11/9	25/9	2/11	1/4	7/8	13/11	-	15/1	18/3	29/1	26/12	6/5	27/11	3/1	16/10	21/8	12/2	11/12	24/4	26/2	7/3	30/8	19/10
Hartlepool	2/11	7/3	22/1	28/8	13/11	[illegible]	1/4	14/3	-	9/10	23/10	15/4	19/2	22/4	4/3	4/12	18/9	3/1	29/4	5/2	4/9	11/12	18/3	26/12
Hull	24/4	5/2	18/12	22/1	4/9	25/3	4/12	23/11	6/5	-	8/4	14/8	28/8	28/12	16/10	8/1	19/10	11/3	6/11	19/2	21/3	18/9	4/3	25/9
Leyton Orient	19/10	14/8	4/12	19/2	15/4	11/3	11/12	28/8	25/9	3/1	-	16/10	1/4	4/3	6/11	22/1	24/4	23/11	21/3	4/9	5/2	23/12	18/9	6/5
Lincoln City	21/8	18/3	4/3	8/4	23/10	9/10	2/10	25/3	28/12	15/1	22/4	-	18/9	7/3	29/1	2/11	8/1	27/11	7/8	18/12	29/4	30/8	12/2	13/11
Macclesfield	12/2	13/11	28/12	8/1	22/4	15/1	23/10	9/10	27/11	29/1	18/12	26/2	-	2/11	7/8	18/3	8/4	29/4	30/8	25/3	11/9	21/8	2/10	7/3
Mansfield	1/4	4/12	28/8	14/8	26/12	26/2	5/2	19/2	16/10	15/4	11/9	6/11	11/3	-	19/10	4/9	6/5	21/3	23/11	25/9	22/1	24/4	3/1	11/12
Northampton	26/2	19/2	4/9	13/11	22/1	28/12	18/3	8/4	11/9	22/4	7/3	27/8	4/12	29/4	-	14/3	18/12	2/10	23/10	8/1	25/3	2/11	9/10	5/2
Peterborough	27/11	2/10	21/3	18/9	9/10	30/8	15/4	22/4	7/8	11/12	21/8	11/3	23/11	12/2	15/1	-	29/1	1/4	26/12	6/11	23/10	3/1	29/4	4/3
Plymouth	13/11	4/9	5/2	18/3	7/3	23/10	2/11	22/1	26/2	23/4	2/10	11/12	3/1	9/10	1/4	28/8	-	22/4	11/9	14/8	4/12	15/4	26/12	19/2
Rochdale	6/5	8/1	25/3	4/12	5/2	11/9	28/8	4/9	8/4	2/11	18/3	19/2	19/10	13/11	24/4	18/12	16/10	-	26/2	28/12	14/8	25/9	7/3	22/1
Rotherham	16/10	28/12	19/2	24/4	14/8	18/12	22/1	8/1	[illegible]	[illegible]	13/11	4/12	5/2	18/3	25/9	25/3	4/3	18/9	-	28/8	8/4	6/5	2/11	4/9
Shrewsbury	3/1	29/4	18/9	4/3	2/11	21/8	9/10	2/10	30/8	27/11	12/2	1/4	26/12	23/10	11/12	7/3	15/1	15/4	29/1	-	22/4	13/11	7/8	18/3
Southend	11/12	2/11	24/4	6/5	18/3	27/11	7/3	18/9	12/2	3/11	30/8	19/10	4/3	21/3	26/12	25/9	7/8	15/1	3/1	16/10	-	29/1	15/4	1/4
Swansea	11/9	18/12	14/8	4/9	19/2	23/11	29/4	6/11	3/1	26/2	25/3	5/2	22/1	2/10	11/3	8/4	28/12	23/10	9/10	21/3	28/8	-	22/4	4/12
Torquay	25/9	22/1	8/1	18/12	28/8	21/3	19/2	5/2	23/11	11/9	26/2	4/9	24/4	8/4	6/5	19/10	25/3	6/11	11/3	4/12	28/12	16/10	-	14/8
York	29/1	22/4	11/3	28/12	2/10	3/4	26/2	29/4	25/3	23/10	9/10	21/3	6/11	8/1	30/8	11/9	27/11	21/8	12/2	23/11	18/12	7/8	15/1	-

Arsenal

Formation	1886 as Dial Square
Stadium	Highbury, London, N5 1BU. ☎0171/704 4000
Ground capacity	38,500
First-choice colours	Red shirts with white sleeves
Major honours	League champions 1931, 1933, 1934, 1935, 1938, 1948, 1953, 1971, 1989, 1991, 1998; FA Cup winners 1930, 1936, 1950, 1971, 1979, 1993, 1998; League Cup winners 1987, 1993; European Cup-Winners' Cup winners 1994; Inter-Cities Fairs' Cup winners 1970
Position 1998/99	Second in Premiership

Highbury is the first London football ground that many fans from outside the capital set eyes on. Clearly visible from the East Coast main line running into King's Cross, it rises regally from the serried ranks of terraced housing that surround it, one of the few English stadia to be as impressive from the outside as it is inside. Its prominence is appropriate. Both nationally and internationally, Arsenal is the best-known of all London's many professional clubs, its name a byword for pride and prestige. Never mind 'Lucky Arsenal' or 'Boring Arsenal' – today's club is above all healthy, wealthy and wise, sitting pretty on a stack of honours and achievements, and planning optimistically for the future.

A full set of marbles – Highbury on a matchday

The club's location, more inner-city than cosy commuter-belt, has been particularly handy in recent years. New money positively oozes from the vibrant Victoriana of nearby Islington, made fashionable by Tony Blair and a legion of media luvvies, many of them Arsenal supporters. At the same time, the council estates of Highbury and Finsbury Park provide a solid bedrock of working-class devotion, much of it initially Irish and Italian, but nowadays just as likely to be Caribbean, Greek or Turkish. The streets around the 'Arsenal Stadium' (as it's officially known) may be unpromising, but they give the club a sense of place.

What they don't provide is much room for expansion. Highbury as it stands now doesn't quite pass the 40,000-capacity line, and plans to build higher have met with bitter resistance from residents and conservationists alike. There was an outcry from fans when, a couple of years ago, Arsenal first mooted the idea of buying Wembley Stadium. But a move to an all-new arena, possibly in Finsbury Park or in among the disused works surrounding King's Cross, can't be ruled out.

Leaving behind such a historic and distinctive ground as Highbury would risk wrenching the heart out of the club. Yet look again at this palace of footballing perfection – the marbled East and West Stands date not from the Victorian era but from the Thirties, while the North Bank and Clock End, sympathetic though they may be, are very much products of the last decade. In between those glorious eras, the club has been in the shadows as often as the limelight, while prior to the Thirties Arsenal were pretty rootless, often penniless and, as far as the opposition were concerned, mostly harmless.

They began life a world away, in the outlying south-east London suburbs of Woolwich and Plumstead. A group of predominantly Scottish workers at the Royal Arsenal Armaments Factory in Woolwich formed a football team in 1886, calling themselves Dial Square after the location of one of the Arsenal's workshops. They played their first game on 11 December, trouncing the Eastern Wanderers 6–0 on a field that had an open sewer running through the middle of it. Suitably encouraged, members convened at the *Royal Oak* pub next to Woolwich Arsenal station on Christmas Day to map out the team's future. They had nowhere to play, nothing to wear and a name nobody liked. But one by one the issues were resolved. One member came up with the name 'Royal Arsenal', which met with immediate approval. Meanwhile two players, Morris Bates and Fred Beardsley, who had both turned out for Nottingham Forest in the past, agreed to write to their former club and ask for help with equipment – they received, by return of post, a complete set of red shirts and a new matchball. Finally it was agreed that an area of nearby Plumstead Common would be used as the club's first 'home' ground.

Arsenal were in business – sort of. Their first match on Plumstead Common, played in January 1887, was a 6–1 mauling of Erith. But the playing surface was badly cut up by horses on military manoeuvres, and it soon became clear the Common was not the ideal home it was meant to be. After a brief spell at a waterlogged former pig farm on the edge of Plumstead Marshes, the team settled at the nearby Manor Field. This was far from perfect – army wagons were used as stands, while players got changed in pubs along Plumstead High Street – but it did provide a base from which Royal Arsenal could capture their first silverware: the Kent Senior

Face in the crowd – full-back Tom Parker (centre) leads the team from a title-deciding game, 1931

Cup and the London Charity Cup, both won in 1890.

The following year Arsenal were on the move again, this time to a 'proper' venue with a stand, terracing and dressing rooms – the Invicta Ground, newly laid out on the other side of Plumstead High Street by mineral-water magnate George Weaver. Club members decided to turn professional and change their name again, this time to 'Woolwich Arsenal'. Big crowds were soon drawn to the Invicta Ground, culminating in a full house of 12,000 to see a friendly against the Scottish champions, Hearts, in 1893. By this time Woolwich Arsenal had applied to join the Second Division of the Football League, which was being expanded. The League, desperate to challenge the dominance of the rival Southern League in the London area, accepted them without hesitation. Weaver, who was already charging the club a hefty £200 per year in rent, anticipated rich pickings, and upped this figure to £350 at a stroke.

This simply could not be afforded, so reluctantly Woolwich Arsenal agreed to re-purchase Manor Field, financing the deal by forming themselves into a limited liability company with shareholders and a board of directors. Members and fans rallied round during the summer of 1893 to ensure the ground would be ready for League football, and it was – the 1893/94 season kicked-off with a 2–2 draw at home to Newcastle United on 2 September.

After all the trauma of getting there, life in the League turned out to be comfortable enough for Woolwich Arsenal, if fairly unexciting – mid-table finishes being the norm before the board appointed Harry Bradshaw as manager in 1901. After a couple of close things, Bradshaw engineered promotion to the First Division with a second-place finish behind Preston in 1904. This prompted the club to build a new Kop end at Manor Field, and during the team's first season in the top flight, crowds regularly topped 20,000.

The boom, however, was short-lived. In 1905 Woolwich Arsenal were given two London rivals in the League, as Chelsea and Clapton Orient were admitted. They were followed not long after by the defection of both Spurs and Fulham from the Southern League. Arsenal might have been playing First Division football but their ground was still way behind most other London clubs' in terms of amenity, while its location was notoriously inconvenient. George Allison, who would later become the team's manager, was often the only journalist onboard the suburban train that puffed its way slowly out to Plumstead from Charing Cross.

Faced with stiff competition for the first time in its short life, Woolwich Arsenal was brought to the brink of collapse. In March 1910, with average crowds of less than 10,000 and debts of £12,500, the club went into voluntary liquidation.

Enter Henry Norris, politician, successful property developer and chairman of Fulham FC. After assuming responsibility for the club's debts, Norris proposed merging Woolwich Arsenal with his 'other' club. The logic was obvious – Arsenal had the top-flight status which Fulham lacked, while the latter's Craven Cottage was an outstanding, newly built footballing arena. The merger, however, contravened League regulations and was instantly rejected, as was a later suggestion that Arsenal would merely ground-share at Fulham.

Suddenly lumbered with a football club nobody wanted to watch, Norris spent the next two years scouting around for a new home for Woolwich Arsenal. He wanted somewhere as easily accessible from central London as Fulham, and cared little for the sentiments of Arsenal's small, hardcore support on the south-eastern fringes. He eventually found what he was looking for in 1912 – a playing field owned by St John's College of Divinity in Highbury, directly opposite Gillespie Road tube station on the Piccadilly Line, just 15 minutes' ride from the West End. To move a professional club such a distance (ten miles separated Highbury from Plumstead) was unprecedented, but by 1913 Norris had managed to get his right-hand man William Hill onto the League's management committee, and Arsenal's switch won approval on the understanding that both men relinquished all interest in Fulham, which they were happy to do.

The intervening period since Norris' takeover had taken its toll on the club's football, however, and at the end of the 1912/13 season, Woolwich Arsenal were relegated after winning only a single home game all year. While there was a suspicion that Norris had deliberately run the club into the ground, relegation was not part of his plans – he'd invested thousands in the building of a new ground at Highbury and Second Division football threatened the viability of the whole enterprise. After World War I, therefore, Norris engineered promotion back up to the top flight. His team, now known simply as 'The Arsenal', had finished no better than fifth in the Second Division of 1914/15, but after the war it was decided both divisions would be expanded by two clubs, and this gave Norris the atmosphere of confusion he needed to enact his plan.

It was clear that the top two teams from the Second Division, Derby and Preston, should be promoted. And the club that had finished second from bottom in the First, Chelsea, were reprieved on the grounds that the team that had finished above them, Manchester United, had secured their survival only by bribing Liverpool in their notorious last game of the 1914/15 season. However, it was then decided that Tottenham, who'd finished bottom of the First Division, should still be relegated, while Norris successfully argued that The Arsenal should replace them to ensure proper representation for London in the top flight.

Spurs, who together with Orient had fought a desperate rearguard action against Arsenal's move to north London in the first place, were furious. But Norris, who'd had helping hands both from his ally Hill on the committee and from another close associate, Liverpool chairman and League president John McKenna, was unrepentant. After all, Arsenal had supported the League at a time when Tottenham were dead set against it – why shouldn't they be rewarded for their loyalty?

But if Norris thought the last piece in his great Arsenal jigsaw had fallen into place, he was mistaken. First Division matches were soon pulling big crowds to Highbury, enabling the chairman to buy the site outright from the Church for £64,000. But the team still hadn't won a major honour of any kind when, in 1925, Norris lured the Huddersfield Town manager Herbert Chapman south with the promise of a £2,000 annual salary (easily the highest in the League) and as much control over team affairs as he wanted.

This suited Chapman down to the ground. The traditional English view of a 'manager' was largely administrative, with team affairs being looked after by coaching staff. At Huddersfield Chapman had turned this wisdom on its head, involving himself with all aspects of tactics, team selection and transfers, as well as day-to-day business issues. The result was three League championships in a row from 1924.

At Highbury Chapman would be equally influential, if not more so. But Norris and Hall would not be around to see the fruits of his labours. In 1927, the year Chapman's side reached its first FA Cup final (lost 1–0 to Cardiff City), both men were suspended from football by the FA, which had had enough of their bullying and shady back-room deals. The new chairman was Samuel Hill-Wood, an altogether more 'correct' establishment figure, but one equally happy to let Chapman have his way.

Of all the manager's many innovations, the most immediately effective was tactical. In the early Twenties, the FA had been forced to change the laws to counter the 'offside traps' laid by defenders like Bill McCracken at Newcastle. Now a forward would be onside if there were three defenders between him and the goal, and offside if there were two. Eenterprising centre-forwards such as Everton's Dixie

The appliance of science – Chapman's classic kit

Arsenal had worn red shirts since **Nottingham Forest** sent the founder members a full set to get them started back in 1886. But when **Herbert Chapman** became the club's manager in 1925, he thought the strip looked undistinguished. A keen golfer, he was inspired by another player's outfit of a short-sleeved red jumper worn over a white undershirt, and resolved to make this the team's own shirt design.

There was more to Chapman's idea than mere aesthetics. He wanted to make sure his players could see each other quickly and, to this end, he introduced two further innovations. The first was to add **white hoops** to Arsenal's traditional navy-blue socks, so that, if a player was controlling the ball, he could spot a team-mate's movement without taking his eye off it.

The second was to **print numbers** on the back of his players' shirts, not so that fans could identify them, but so that the players could see which team-mates were around them, and adjust their own position accordingly.

Sixties revival – as worn by George Graham

The ground-breaking new outfit was introduced in 1933, and between then and World War II Arsenal won three League championships and an FA Cup wearing it. The strip survived the war and remained in use until the mid-Sixties, when the Arsenal board decided to adopt plain red shirts and socks in an attempt to emulate the success of Matt Busby's Manchester United. The experiment was a disaster, and Chapman's old combination was revived by **Bertie Mee** when he became manager in 1967. The white sleeves, at least, have been with us ever since.

Dean had a field day, and Chapman was determined to devise a way of stopping them. Together with Charles Buchan, the former Sunderland forward who'd been Chapman's first Highbury signing, and who became the manager's eyes and ears on the pitch, he evolved a system whereby a third centre-half would be deployed to mark the centre-forward wherever he went. To compensate for the loss of a midfield player, Chapman brought his inside-forwards in deeper, while the wing-halves were encouraged to be more mobile and full-backs were pushed wider to cover and overlap. Soon dubbed the 'W–M' formation, it was rigorously enforced by Buchan and Chapman's coach Tom Whittaker, with Charlie Roberts as the third centre-half, tough in the tackle and towering in the air.

While the team were beginning to look more purposeful on the pitch, Chapman also played a key role in making the club itself more attractive. Believing that 'The

Arsenal' sounded pompous, he shortened the name to plain 'Arsenal' and dreamt up a catchy new nickname, 'the Gunners'. He also persuaded *London Transport* to rename Gillespie Road tube station 'Arsenal'; had a 45-minute clock installed at Highbury for the players' reference (this was later converted to a normal 12-hour device and installed at what became the Clock End); and arranged for a fleet of vans to shine their headlights onto the pitch to test the feasibility of floodlit football.

Above all, Chapman won things. With a team featuring the unflappable Tom Parker at full-back, playmaker Alex James instigating the quick counter-attacks that were pivotal to the 'W–M' gameplan, and Cliff 'Boy' Bastin a predatory goalscorer who would swoop at his target from the left flank, Arsenal symbolically beat Chapman's former club, Huddersfield, 2–0 in the 1930 FA Cup final at Wembley. Chapman had told Henry Norris he would need five years to turn Arsenal into a first-class unit, and his prediction was spot-on.

What the manager did not predict, though, was the extent to which his team would go on to dominate English football for the remainder of the Thirties. Within a year of the first Cup triumph, there was a first League championship, Arsenal establishing a new record points total of 66 and scoring 127 goals to finish seven points clear of Aston Villa in second. Twelve months later there was an unlucky 2–1 Cup final defeat by Newcastle – whose equalising goal should never have been allowed to stand – but the club was confident enough to open a fabulous new West Stand at Highbury, built from the finest materials in the Art Deco style and designed with meticulous attention to detail by architect Claude Ferrier.

The stadium, like the team, was not cheap to build. But Arsenal were making a statement of intent, and their football matched their stylish new surroundings, with three titles being won in successive seasons from 1932/33. The second of these campaigns was notable for the debut of Ted Drake, a more conventional centre-forward who would take over from Bastin as the primary source of goals. Sadly, Herbert Chapman would not live to see Drake's abundant talent come to fruition. In January 1934, while suffering from a cold, Chapman went to a reserve match to look at an opposition player recommended to him by a scout, and caught pneumonia. He died a few days later, and Arsenal players were among the pall-bearers at his funeral.

How to replace the irreplaceable? Samuel Hill-Wood thought he had the answer in George Allison, the very journalist whose passion for the club was first ignited on those long railway journeys out to south-east London, and who had since become a well-known radio commentator. To the outside world it seemed a bizarre appointment, but such was Allison's easy rapport with the Highbury setup – and the precision with which Chapman had built his footballing machine – that the team scarcely missed a beat. Certainly the fans noticed little difference, more than 73,000 of them crowding into Highbury to see Arsenal take on Sunderland in a top-of-the-table clash in March 1935.

It was Sunderland who, after the 1934/35 title, finally wrested the League championship from Arsenal's grasp. Yet still the honours kept coming. There was another FA Cup in 1936, won 1–0 against Sheffield United courtesy of a classic Bastin-to-Drake move which ended with the latter scoring and then writhing in agony – he had injured his knee while stretching to reach Bastin's clearance, and played the rest of the game as a passenger.

Like Chapman, the architect Ferrier would not live to see his work completed, being killed in an accident before a new East Stand rose up to mirror the West one, its marble hall decorated with a noble bust of Chapman, and once again setting the club apart – not just from the rest of London, but from the rest of the country.

Nothing was won in 1936/37. But a year later, with established players like Drake, Bastin, goalkeeper Eddie Hapgood and half-back Wilf Copping augmented by younger talents like the Compton brothers, Les and Denis, the championship trophy was back on the boardroom table, won by four points from the club that had usurped it in 1937, Manchester United.

Highbury's last game before World War II saw Arsenal entertain Brentford, a game from which footage would be taken to make the film *The Arsenal Stadium Mystery*. But while several key figures at the club enjoyed their brief stint of fame in the glare of the movie lights, more serious issues would soon be on the agenda. On the eve of the war Arsenal were heavily in debt, crippled by interest payments on loans used to pay for Highbury's grandiose expansion. Wartime restrictions slashed the club's income at the gate, and after the North Bank was destroyed in the Blitz, Arsenal's future seemed to hang in the balance.

Happily, once hostilities were over and the North Bank had been re-roofed, the postwar attendance boom cured the club's financial ills almost at once. Tom Whittaker, who succeeded Allison as manager after the first postwar season, inherited a radically changed squad, but the tactics remained largely unaltered. In Ronnie Rooke, Whittaker had a goalscorer every bit as sharp as Drake had been, while wing-half Joe Mercer was a dominating yet always affable captain. In 1947/48, Arsenal won their first six games and went 17 matches unbeaten, while Rooke found the net 33 times – another title was in the bag.

Two years later, Mercer was voted England's footballer of the year. Despite being rejected by Everton as 'over the hill' prior to his move to Arsenal, he continued to live on Merseyside and trained during the week with Liverpool. With Arsenal due to meet Liverpool in the 1950 FA Cup final, Mercer was restricted to training at Anfield in the afternoons, while the Liverpool team used the ground in the mornings. Even so, there was a suspicion that inside information had somehow found its way to the Gunners' side, such was the superiority enjoyed on the day by Mercer, midfielder Jimmy Logie (who had succeeded Alex James as the team's creator-in-chief) and veteran target man Reg Lewis, who scored both the goals in a 2–0 win.

The double is done – George (left) and McLintock have fun in the Wembley sun, 1971

Logie and Mercer would again be at the heart of things when, three years later, Arsenal won the title again. Inside-forward Doug Lishman, signed by Whittaker from Walsall not long after the war, was top marksman this time, and had any one of his 22 goals not counted, the title would not have been won – Arsenal's eventual margin over runners-up Preston being 0.099 of a goal.

The statistics suggest that the team of 1952/53 were barely good enough to be champions, losing nine times, gathering only 54 points and shipping 64 goals – a rate that would have had old Herbert Chapman spinning in his grave. History, meanwhile, adds that the win marked the end of Chapman's influence on the club, and of a period of sustained success stretching back more than 20 years.

After Whittaker's death in 1956, the board began appointing former players to the manager's job, beginning with Jack Crayston, a member of the last prewar title-winning side, and continuing with goalkeeper George Swindin two years later. In 1962, Arsenal thought they'd pulled off a considerable coup in persuading Billy Wright to succeed Swindin. As a player he had won almost everything there was to win with Wolves, while he also had two years as manager of England's Under-23 team under his belt. Yet he was never cut out to be in charge of a club like Arsenal, and although he guided Highbury into Europe via the Inter-Cities Fairs' Cup in 1963, the mood at the club was heavy.

The man who lightened things up was Bertie Mee, the former club physiotherapist who took over from Wright in 1966, and who insisted on a clause in his contract that allowed him to go back to being physio after a year if he didn't make out as a manager. The clause was never invoked.

Mee had little truck with the team of celebrities assembled by Wright. Instead he put his faith in youth, giving the captain's armband to wily central defender Frank McLintock; signing another Scot, canny midfielder George Graham, from Chelsea; and entrusting goalscoring duties to emerging striker John Radford. With Bob Wilson establishing himself in goal and little George Armstrong providing fresh options on the flanks, Mee's Arsenal were at least a better unit than their immediate predecessors. What turned them into the finished item was the arrival of midfielder-

Last-gasp glory (1) – Alan Sunderland (far right) hails his finale to the 'five-minute Cup final', 1979

cum-striker Ray Kennedy and of a flashy Islington lad, Charlie George, to partner Radford upfront in 1968.

After the ignominy of watching his flu-ridden side lose the League Cup final to Third Division Swindon Town in 1969, Mee's first triumph came in Europe. Having thrashed Ajax 3–0 at Highbury in the semi-finals, the Gunners faced Anderlecht of Belgium over a two-leg Fairs' Cup final in 1970. They began disastrously, conceding three goals in Brussels. But toward the end of that first leg Kennedy grabbed a vital away goal, and Arsenal were back in it. The return, watched by a heaving crowd of more than 50,000, saw them score three without reply – the club's first continental honour was won.

The following season, showing a resilience and resourcefulness not seen in an Arsenal team since Chapman's day, Mee's side edged its way forward in both the League and the FA Cup. In the end they had the chance to win both within the space of five days. The title came first, courtesy of a solitary Kennedy goal at Spurs in front of another 50,000 crowd, on the Monday night before the Cup final. Yet by the time Arsenal strode out onto the Wembley pitch alongside Liverpool, the critics were suggesting they'd be easy meat – after all, a fixture backlog had forced them to play ten games since a replay win over Stoke in the semi-finals, and the heat was sweltering.

When Steve Heighway beat Wilson at his near post to open the scoring two minutes into extra time, Arsenal's double dream seemed to have ended. But the side's reserves of physical energy, honed by the exerience of Mee and his unforgiving coach Don Howe, were immense. Eddie Kelly snatched an equaliser, and then, with 111 minutes played, George worked a one-two with Radford on the edge of the box before letting fly from 20 yards. After scoring he could do no more than lie outstretched on the Wembley turf – Arsenal had done the double for the first time and, just as important, had equalled Tottenham's achievement of a decade earlier. And they had done it using only 16 players.

The following year, Arsenal lost their title to Derby and their FA Cup to Leeds. Don Howe left to take charge at West Brom, and without him the team lost much of their former consistency. As the Seventies wore on, it became clear that far from heralding the dawn of an era, Mee's double had actually been the end of one. The club he left in 1976 had just finished 17th in the First Division.

Mee's successor, Terry Neill, brought goalkeeper Pat Jennings with him from Spurs, sold the under-achieving Alan Ball and bought striker Malcolm Macdonald from Newcastle for £330,000. Just as significant, though, was the backbone of unheralded Irish players around which Neill built his team – elegant stopper David O'Leary, midfield schemer Liam Brady and target man Frank Stapleton. The side failed to live up to its billing in a 1978 FA Cup final defeat by unfancied Ipswich, but the following season, as the rest of the country toiled through the Winter of Discontent, Highbury's undersoil heating system allowed Arsenal to play on. This was just as well, since the Gunners needed five matches to despatch Sheffield Wednesday in the third round of the FA Cup, before progressing all the way to the immortal 'five-minute final' against Manchester United, won in the dying seconds by Alan Sunderland's counter-attack strike.

In 1979/80 Neill's side again indulged its taste for epic FA Cup-ties, taking four games to beat Liverpool in the semi-finals before losing the final to Second Division West Ham. There was disappointment, too, in Europe, where Juventus were beaten in the Cup-Winners' Cup semis but Arsenal lost the final to Valencia on penalties.

Having come so far but won so little, Neill's side broke up. Stapleton and Brady went to Manchester United and Juventus, respectively, and neither man was properly replaced. Denis Hill-Wood, son of Thirties chairman Samuel, died in 1982, and though he would be succeeded by his own son

Peter, a little of Highbury's invincible aura went with him. Two years later Terry Neill was sacked after a series of embarrassing Cup defeats, and his replacement, Don Howe, lasted less than two seasons.

While Peter Hill-Wood remained chairman, boardroom power now rested with Arsenal's MD Ken Friar and a recently appointed director, former sugar trader David Dein. It was Friar who approached Terry Venables with a view to bringing him back to English football as Highbury manager, and when Barcelona refused to release *El Tel* from his contract, Venables suggested Arsenal should talk to George Graham. The club's double-winning playmaker had worked with Venables as a coach at Crystal Palace, then become a successful manager in his own right at Millwall. Now he was to take Arsenal by the scruff of the neck and instill a never-say-die spirit once again. Out went 'Fancy Dan' strikers like Paul Mariner and Tony Woodcock. In came a new sense of discipline and solidity, courtesy of a back four containing the evergreen O'Leary, Kenny Sansom, Viv Anderson and a 19-year-old Tony Adams. Within a year Arsenal had won the League Cup for the first time, beating Liverpool 2–1 at Wembley, with Graham saying prophetically after the match: 'This is just the start'.

A year later Arsenal lost the League Cup final to Luton Town, but by now George Graham's sights were set higher. With John Lukic in goal, Lee Dixon and Nigel Winterburn as first-choice full-backs, David Rocastle and Michael Thomas linking in midfield, and Paul Merson and Alan Smith providing the perfect 'little and large' combination upfront, Arsenal fought Liverpool tooth and nail for the title in 1988/89. In the end it came down to the season's very last game on 26 May 1989 – a rescheduled meeting of the two sides at Anfield which Arsenal needed to win by two clear goals to snatch the championship. Liverpool had won their last ten home games and, with the FA Cup already in the bag, were at short odds for the double. Yet the title decider was notable for being played just six weeks after the Hillsborough disaster. Anfield was not quite the forbidding fortress it was hyped up to be, and once Smith had deflected Winterburn's free-kick inside Bruce Grobbelaar's far post to put Arsenal in front on 50 minutes, an uneasy quiet descended on the ground.

Two minutes into stoppage time, and with the Liverpool players doing high-fives on the pitch, Smith flicked Dixon's through pass into the path of Thomas, who played an inadvertent one-two off Steve Nicol's shin and calmly shot past Grobbelaar. There was scarcely time for the restart.

George Graham, who had told the Arsenal directors all along that he had a gameplan to beat Liverpool, paraded the League trophy around Anfield with as much dignity as he could manage in the circumstances, while from the away end the ironic chant of 'Boring, Boring Arsenal' rang out into the Merseyside air. Like George and Sunderland before him, Thomas had got his name into the history books by scoring late for a team that refused to admit they were beaten. Newspaper journalists who had already written their reports before his goal failed to do the game justice, so the moment belonged instead to television, showing the title decider live for the first time.

Another championship arrived in 1991, despite the club having two points deducted for an infamous 'brawl' at Old Trafford, and captain Adams serving four months in prison for a drink-driving conviction. By comparison with 1989 the side was little changed save for the replacement of Lukic in goal by David Seaman – Arsenal were more miserly in defence than ever.

English clubs had by now been readmitted to European competition after the lifting of the Heysel ban, but after going down 3–1 at home to Benfica, Arsenal failed to qualify for the Champions' League in 1991/92. It was a mistake Graham was determined not to repeat. After Ian Wright had arrived from Crystal Palace to lead the Gunners to a 'double' of League Cup and

Last-gasp glory (2) – Michael Thomas steers the ball goalward in stoppage time at Anfield, 1989

FA Cup final victories over Sheffield Wednesday in 1993, the club concentrated its energies on the Cup-Winners' Cup. Standard Liège were hit for ten over two legs early on, before a much-hyped Torino side were edged out by a single goal, and David Ginola's Paris St-Germain were beaten in the semi-finals. The final, against Parma in Copenhagen, was the Arsenal game Graham would recall with the most pride – a typically gritty performance, against one of the toughest sides Europe could offer. After Smith grabbed an opportunist early strike, the Gunners simply would not let their Italian opponents get into their stride and, if anything, finished playing the more accomplished football.

First England, now Europe – what else was left for Graham to conquer? The answer lay in a financial scandal which would ultimately prove a more stubborn opponent than any he had faced as a player or coach. On 21 February 1995, he was dismissed after allegedly receiving transfer 'bungs' from the disgraced Norwegian agent Rune Hauge (see panel p.13). He received no compensation, and was subsequently banned from football worldwide for a year after being found guilty by an FA tribunal. Meanwhile, Paul Merson had revealed his long-standing alcohol and cocaine addictions, and months later Real Zaragoza's Nayim destroyed the club's chances of retaining the Cup-Winners' Cup with his lob from the halfway line.

Arsenal was not used to being described as 'a club in crisis', but it most certainly was that now. Caretaker manager Stewart Houston, Graham's former assistant, made way for Bruce Rioch before the start of the 1995/96 season, but Rioch in turn would last no more than a year. As Highbury struggled to emerge from the long shadow of the Graham affair, vice-chairman David Dein became acutely aware that Arsenal were falling behind in the race to be the Premiership's glitziest attraction. While Manchester United were monopolising the honours, Tottenham and Chelsea were awash with exotic foreign stars, making a fortune from merchandising as a result. Highbury – and not least the rebuilt North Bank, where affluent bond-holders now rubbed shoulders with the club's traditional support – needed some glamour of its own. The club's tightly drawn wage structure was smashed to bring Dennis Bergkamp and David Platt to Arsenal from Italy. But this wasn't enough – Dein wanted a manager capable of getting the best from

A Gunner and his spoils – Tony Adams, 1994

the sort of star quality the club hadn't possessed since Liam Brady's time. He found just the man in Arsène Wenger, a much-admired French coach who'd shown he could handle big-money signings at Monaco, and whose work in the Japanese J-League had given him vital experience in dealing with a Premiership-style media circus.

Wenger was not released from his Japanese contract until November 1996, by which time Arsenal were already out of Europe for another season and labouring in the League. Yet he began his reign not with a clearance sale but by offering new contracts to the entire 'back five' (Seaman included). With Wright and Bergkamp showing signs of clicking in attack, the manager concentrated on midfield, buying Bergkamp's former Ajax team-mate Marc Overmars to operate on the flanks, and two Frenchmen, Manu Petit and Patrick Vieira, to shore up the centre-circle.

Yet even at the midway point of the following season, with Arsenal lying fifth, there was little indication of the glory to come. Some fans even called for Wenger's head. Luckily, the club wasn't listening. Between Boxing Day and May 1998, the team went 18 games unbeaten. A 4–0 win over Everton at Highbury, with skipper Adams netting the last, confirmed that Manchester United's title was coming south. Three weeks later, Newcastle were despatched 2–0 at Wembley with goals from Overmars and another of Wenger's French signings, Nicolas Anelka.

Contrary to all expectations, Arsenal had equalled Manchester United's 'double double', and with a team that had spent less than a season and a half together. The triumph spoke volumes for Wenger's management style – like Graham, he ruled his squad with an iron hand, while outwardly appearing the epitome of dignified calm. Also like Graham, however, his initial expeditions into Europe ended in failure: shock defeat by PAOK Salonika in the 1997/98 UEFA Cup, followed by a group-stage exit from the 1998/99 Champions' League, in which Arsenal chose to play their home games at Wembley, allowing thousands more fans to watch them but also, inadvertently, giving the brisk counter-attacking game of Lens and Dynamo Kiev the extra space it needed to hurt them.

With both domestic honours lost to United, 1998/99 was a let-down for many fans, albeit a glorious one. Had Bergkamp not missed his last-minute penalty in the FA Cup semi and Jimmy Floyd Hasselbaink not stolen in to take all three points from Arsenal at Elland Road, Highbury might have been celebrating a uniquely retained double.

As it is, while other Premiership managers import players on the strength of video evidence or recommendations from agents, Arsène Wenger's matchless continental scouting network has set the club well on the way to his stated goal of being 'the centre for all the best young talent in Europe'.

Not bad for a side that once played on a Plumstead pig-farm.

Here we go!

Most **motorists** will approach along the M1 motorway (junction 21 of the M25), exiting at junction 2 onto the A1. Keep following signs for 'City A1' and follow this road in toward central London. Go round the Archway one-way system, continuing to follow the A1 as it becomes Holloway Road. Pass underneath the railway bridge and the Hornsey Road turning on your left, and take the next left-turn into Drayton Park. Follow the road round and the stadium is on your right.

It's **street parking** for all around the ground and probably not that close to it, either. You may get lucky in the streets behind Highbury Corner (about a 10min walk away to the south), or you could consider parking near a tube station on the Piccadilly Line (see below) and training it in from there. Stops with decent street parking near to them include Caledonian Road (to the south) and Bounds Green (north).

Arsenal **tube station** is only a handful of stops out of central London on the Piccadilly Line. Allow 15–30mins depending on which main-line station you've arrived at.

Just the ticket

Visiting fans are, as ever, allocated the west side of the Clock End, with further space available in the adjacent West Stand for non-Premiership fixtures. Check availability with your own club as most Arsenal games are all-ticket and anything

Agents bearing gifts – the fall of George Graham

It all started just before Christmas 1991, in the lounge bar of London's *Park Lane Hotel*. Norwegian players' agent **Rune Hauge** dipped into his holdall, pulled out a series of plain brown envelopes, and handed them to **George Graham**. The Arsenal manager was bemused, but Hauge said: 'Please put this in your briefcase – it is an appreciation for all you have done to help me open up doors here in England.' When he got home, Graham opened the envelopes and found they contained £140,000 in £50 notes.

In August 1992, Graham received more money from Hauge – this time a banker's draft in the post for £285,000. He deposited both sums in an offshore Trust Fund for his children, and always claimed they were unsolicited gifts.

Before long, Arsenal Football Club, the Premier League and the Football Association would all beg to differ. They alleged that both payments were illegal 'bungs', the first given to Graham in connection with Arsenal's purchase of defender **Pål Lydersen** from the Norwegian club IK Start, the second linked to the subsequent arrival of Danish international **John Jensen** from Brøndby.

In 1994 Graham agreed to pay the money – together with the interest it had accrued – to Arsenal on tax advice. The club agreed it would terminate his contract at the end of the 1994/95 season and give the manager appropriate compensation. But when a Premier League inquiry into the affair found Graham guilty of taking a 'cut' from both transfers – after receiving damning evidence from three IK Start officials – he was sacked by Arsenal without receiving a penny.

A subsequent FA tribunal ruled that while Graham had not conspired with Hauge to make a personal profit from the transfers, he knew the payments were connected with them – he was banned from football for a year and made to pay all legal fees. The ban was extended worldwide by FIFA, who also barred Hauge from acting as an agent.

As a result of the Graham-Hauge case, the FA also launched a far-reaching inquiry into the whole question of 'bungs'. Yet after three years of deliberation it came up with little concrete evidence of wrongdoing, with only **Steve Burtenshaw** (Arsenal scout in Graham's time as manager) being fined for his part in the Hauge transfers.

Two months after his sacking, Graham walked into the *Mezzaluna* restaurant in Hampstead to be confronted by a private party of family, friends and former Arsenal colleagues. Among the guests was **Terry Venables**, who presented Graham with a cake in the shape of a football pitch. 'This, George,' he said, 'is an unsolicited gift'.

Dennis, you've scored – Dixon and Bergkamp

spare is sold up to two months in advance. Price in 1998/99 was adults £16, no concessions. **Disabled visitors** have limited space in the south-west corner of the ground. Advance booking essential on ☎0171/704 4040.

Swift half

Most pubs in the vicinity are obviously 'Arsenal houses' but many, including ***The Marquess Tavern*** on Canonbury Street, ***The World's End*** on Stroud Green Road and ***The Highbury Barn*** in Highbury Park also welcome well-behaved visitors; the *Barn*, with its big-screen TV and summer courtyard, is a good bet for families.

Club merchandise

While some clubs use the arrival of a new sponsor as an excuse to launch a new kit design after only a year, Arsenal resisted this temptation for 1999/2000, drafting new *Sega* and *Dreamcast* logos onto the existing *Nike* design.

There are two main outlets for this and the many hundreds of other branded items: ***The Gunners Shop*** on the Avenell Road side of the ground and the ***Arsenal World Of Sport*** next-door to the overground entrance of Finsbury Park station.

Barmy army

The gentrification of the North Bank saw off most of Highbury's hooligan element – as well as destroying much of the atmosphere that once rivalled Tottenham's Shelf and Chelsea's Shed.

These days the mood only occasionally turns nasty at Cup games where home tickets are sold on the day.

In print

London lacks a Saturday evening paper but the weekday ***Evening Standard*** devotes a lot of column inches to Arsenal and previews weekend games in its Friday edition.

Best-established of the fanzines are ***The Gooner*** (BCM Box 7499, London, WC1N 3XX), ***One-Nil Down, Two-One Up*** (PO Box 10794, London, N10 2DW) and ***Highbury High*** (PO Box 16198, London, N1 9WF).

Of the plethora of Arsenal books, three in particular stand out: George Graham's autobiography ***The Glory And The Grief*** (Andre Deutsch, £15.99), Tom Watt's North Bank history ***The End – 80 Years Of Life On The Terraces*** (Mainstream, £9.99), and Nick Hornby's seminal ***Fever Pitch*** (Orion, £6.99).

On air

The standard London choice of radio stations is between the BBC's ***GLR*** (94.9 FM) and ***Capital Gold*** (1548 AM).

In the net

Arsenal's **official site**, *Arsenal FC Interactive* or *AFCi* for short, has been maintained to a high standard for a number of years. With its exciting sci-fi graphics it appeals to kids, but it also has plenty of serious content including a stats database that covers every Arsenal game ever played, along with extensive news, multi-media and e-commerce sections. Find it all at: www.arsenal.co.uk/.

Online for even longer than the official site is the unofficial ***ArseWeb***, which boasts a simple, easy-to-use layout and a superb 'Links Farm' at: www.arseweb.com. Also worth a look are the great-looking ***Arsenal World*** at www.arsenal-world.com/. And ***Steve Gleiber's Homepage*** which includes an excellent fan's-eye history of the club at: www.users.fl.net.au/~steve/.

Aston Villa

Formation	1874
Stadium	Villa Park, Trinity Road, Birmingham, B6 6HE. ☎0121/327 2299
Ground capacity	39,300
First-choice colours	Claret and sky blue
Major honours	League champions 1894, 1896, 1897, 1899, 1900, 1910, 1981; Second Division champions 1938, 1960; Third Division champions 1972; FA Cup winners 1887, 1895, 1897, 1905, 1913, 1920, 1957; League Cup winners 1961, 1975, 1977, 1994, 1996; European Cup winners 1982; European SuperCup winners 1983
Position 1998/99	Sixth in Premiership

In an area of England known for conservatism, heavy industry, Spaghetti Junction, *Crossroads* and the Electric Light Orchestra, Aston Villa are extraordinary. In their early years, they were the game's most important innovators, helping to lead football into the professional era as well as playing to a more sophisticated standard than any contemporary rivals. In the modern age, the club has again been at the forefront of change, embracing the global transfer market and the needs of commerce with a gusto that would have impressed even those early Victorian visionaries.

Yet in between these two golden ages, the club almost died a slow, ignominious death, its heritage neglected by complacent directors, its (often Second and Third Division) football rejected by fans who voted with their feet – turning Villa Park, one of the country's leading sporting venues, into a theatre of ghosts.

As one of the Football League's founding members, Villa have more wise and ancient spirits looking down on them than most. In the West Midlands, however, the club was considered a latecomer when it was formed by members of the Villa Cross Wesleyan Chapel cricket club in 1874. In the neighbouring Black Country football was already well-established, but in Birmingham it was disorganised, and the new team had to wait more than a year for their first match. Even then, the opposition was not a football team at all, but Aston Brook St Mary's rugby club. When the two sides met in March 1875, they couldn't agree on a set of rules to play by. So they compromised – playing the first half under rugby rules with an oval ball, the second half under 'association' rules with a round one. Both teams fielded 15 men throughout, and after a goalless (pointless?) first half, Villa won 1–0 thanks to a goal from Jack Hughes.

Villa played the second half of that rugby-soccer match with half their outfield players in defence, the other half in attack, and no midfield at all. The strategy might have found favour with Villa's manager of more than a century later, Graham Taylor, and the team kept using it in matches (both halves soccer by now) against other emerging local sides for the next couple of seasons. But George Ramsay, a slightly built Scot who turned up and begged a game at a Villa training session in the winter of 1876, was less than impressed. By the end of the session, the other men were so taken with Ramsay's close control, passing and movement that they immediately elected him a member.

Two years later Ramsay became Villa's captain and persuaded another skilful Scot, Archie Hunter, to join him at the club. Hunter had come to Birmingham hoping to play for the town's biggest team of the day, Calthorpe, but couldn't find their ground. So he went to Villa instead. Like

Won and lost by Villa – the original FA Cup

Ramsay, Hunter based his passing game on that of the Glasgow club Queen's Park. The Scotsmen's ideas were a revelation in England where, up until this time, most players simply took the ball as far as they could until they were stopped by an opponent. Villa began to charge admission money at their Perry Barr ground – the first team in Birmingham to do so.

In 1880 Villa won their first trophy, the Birmingham Cup, and also entered the FA Cup for the first time. After beating Stafford Road Railway Works in the latter, Villa were drawn against Oxford University and, fearing a hefty defeat, withdrew. They continued to enter the competition in subsequent years, though, reaching the quarter-finals in 1883 and 1884. The first year they clawed their way back from 3–0 down only to lose 4–3 to Notts County. A year later they went to Queen's Park (many Scottish and Irish clubs entered the FA Cup back then), and were thrashed 6–1.

In 1886/87, Villa made their big Cup breakthrough. They destroyed Wednesbury 13–0; came through three replays against Wolves; shrugged off a half-time champagne binge to defeat Darwen; then at last beat the Scots at their own game in winning a semi-final against Rangers at Crewe. The final, against West Bromwich Albion, was played at Kennington Oval. Few fans of either side made the journey down to London, waiting for news instead via telegrams delivered to Birmingham pubs – not exactly big-screen television, but it kept the landlords happy. Dennis Hodgetts got Villa's first goal with a suspicion of offside, and in the last minute Archie Hunter surged through the Albion defence to wrap up the victory. Back home at the *Bell Inn* the following day, Hunter passed the Cup round to the lucky few who were able to get in. Precisely what time the pub closed is not known.

By the late 1880s, under the influence of another Scot, director William McGregor, Villa had become a professional club. Of the team that won the Cup against West Brom, only inside-left Howard Vaughton did not receive appearance money. After Villa had controversially lost the Cup to Preston in 1888 (the referee had told the players the third-round tie would be considered a friendly because the Perry Barr crowd kept spilling onto the pitch, but he was overruled by the FA), McGregor reflected bitterly that the club's season was effectively over, with only local honours to play for. Friendly matches attracted lower crowds than competitive games, and McGregor was worried he might not be able to pay players' wages. He wrote to the directors of Blackburn, Bolton, West Brom and Preston, suggesting they meet to arrange 'home and away fixtures each season' at a 'friendly conference'. His idea was that England's 10 or 12 leading teams would play each other, and he asked his fellow directors to nominate further clubs for inclusion in the scheme.

The 'friendly conference' was held on 23 March, the eve of the 1888 FA Cup final, and by 17 April the foundation of the Football League was announced, with

Accrington, Burnley, Derby, Everton, Notts County, Stoke and Wolves all joining McGregor's original shortlist. In May, a League committee met to arrange a fixture list, and it was agreed to award two points for a win and one for a draw.

There was no football equivalent of the League anywhere else in the world, and it took Villa a while to adjust to the new level of competitive football they had done so much to bring into being. They finished second to Preston in the League's first year, 1888/89, but midway through the following campaign Archie Hunter suffered a stroke on the pitch at Everton, and was forced to give up playing. (He died four years later, still serving Villa in an administrative role, aged 35.) Without Hunter's leadership the team drifted into mid-table for a couple of years, and lost the 1892 Cup final to West Brom – amid allegations that Villa goalkeeper Jimmy Warner had 'thrown' the game after betting on Albion.

While Villa's ruling committee acted quickly to suspend Warner, the saga rumbled on for months as members became increasingly uneasy about the way the club was being run. One of them, a Birmingham Corporation surveyor called Fred Rinder, held an extraordinary meeting at the city's New Gallery in February 1893, at which he accused the team of being a haven for drunks, and called on the entire committee to resign. The motion was carried, and Rinder was appointed financial secretary of an entirely new committee.

With Rinder at the helm, Villa developed a proper 'colts' team to encourage young talent in-house. George Ramsay was still at the club as secretary, overseeing

Two trophies in one day – Villa's early double

'I don't see why we should not bring off the double event in winning the League trophy and the English Cup,' Villa captain **John Devey** told reporters in February 1897. 'It has been done before [by Preston] and it will be done again.'

Devey had good reason to be confident. Villa themselves had come close to doing the double in 1893/94, and the bulk of the team that had won the title in 1896 was still together – Tom Wilkes in goal; full-backs Albert Evans and Howard Spencer; Jack Reynolds, James Cowan and Jimmy Crabtree at half-back; and Johnny Campbell, signed from Celtic as an outside left but used by Villa as an unusually quick (for the period) centre-forward.

Devey, a right-winger whose ability to cut inside and score goals was matched by **Freddie Wheldon** on the opposite flank, reckoned 42 points would be enough for Villa to retain the title. They ended up with 47, and when Derby County lost to Bury on the afternoon of Saturday 10 April, Villa were confirmed as champions. At the time, though, the players had other things on their minds – for 10 April was also the date of the FA Cup final, with Villa due to face **Everton** at Crystal Palace.

Earlier that day, dozens of Birmingham factories were forced to cancel their Saturday morning shift for lack of workers, as 10,000 Villa fans descended on London for the final. (The total crowd of 65,891 was a record for any football match anywhere, and brought the FA record receipts of £2,875.)

Campbell's low, wind-assisted drive from 25 yards put Villa in front after 15 minutes, but before the half-hour was up, Everton had scored twice. Wheldon equalised from a free-kick after 34 minutes, and the same player headed home from a corner two minutes later to put Villa back in front at 3–2.

There were no more goals in the second half, but supporters and reporters alike sensed they had witnessed the most exhilarating FA Cup final yet played.

Fittingly, Villa's first match after their 'double event' was played at their new home, **Villa Park**, against Blackburn Rovers a week later.

transfers and tactics, and it was he who assembled the new half-back line of Willie Groves, Jack Reynolds and James Cowan with which Villa would become League champions in 1893/94. With that trio providing the openings and Hodgetts, Charlie Athersmith and John Devey exploiting them with relish, Villa sealed their title with a 6–3 win at Bury on 7 April 1894.

In the summer of 1894, Groves contracted tuberculosis and was instructed never to play football again. Without him Villa finished third in the League, but at the end of the season there was another FA Cup final against West Brom to look forward to. This time the final was held at Crystal Palace, and hundreds of fans were still making their way into the ground from the adjacent funfair when Bob Chatt scored the only goal of the game for Villa after just 39 seconds.

The Cup was coming back to Birmingham. Where it went next, nobody knows. Sportswear manufacturer William Shillcock had won permission from his old friend, William McGregor, to put the trophy on display in his shop window. On the morning of 8 September 1895, Shillcock found a pile of rubble on the floor, a hole in his roof – and no Cup in the window. He offered £10 reward for its return, to no avail. The contract for a new Cup was won by *Vaughton & Sons*, family firm of the former Villa player Howard Vaughton.

The loss of the FA Cup embarrassed Villa, but Fred Rinder had been encouraged by the team's success, and turned the club into a limited company in 1896. Villa needed the share capital because Rinder felt the club needed a new home – at Aston Lower Grounds, former site of a pleasure park similar to that at Crystal Palace. A sports ground there was rented from *Flowers* brewery, a new grandstand was built, and the club's offices took the place of an earlier restaurant and aquarium. Compared with Perry Barr it was all very grand, and why not? By the time Villa played their first game there, on 17 April 1897, they had won the League and FA Cup double (see panel p.17) – only the second team ever to do so. A year later, their new home was named Villa Park.

After their double triumph, Villa lost Jack Reynolds and centre-forward Johnny Campbell to Celtic, and the team's grip on both trophies was loosened, too. In 1899, though, they regained the League title after walloping Liverpool 5–0 at Villa Park – the first time the title's destiny was decided by the top two clubs meeting on the final day of the season.

A late collapse in form by Sheffield United allowed Villa to begin the new century as they'd ended the last one – by being crowned League champions. But behind the scenes there was tension. Players were demanding higher bonuses than the ever-cautious Rinder was willing to grant, and with the exception of new centre-forward Billy Garraty, the squad was starting to resemble a private club for thirtysomethings – albeit lively ones.

Four trophyless seasons followed, and when Villa stepped out at Crystal Palace for the 1905 FA Cup final against newly crowned champions Newcastle, only three players remained from the 1900 League-winning side: Garraty, goalkeeper Billy George and veteran full-back Howard Spencer. To avoid any last-minute rush for the match, the Palace grounds were opened at 7.30am, for a game not scheduled to kick-off until 3.30pm. By that time there were 101,000 in the arena to see Villa win 2–0, with both goals coming from the opportunist Harry Hampton.

A man of formidable physique who knew how to throw his weight around, Hampton was still only a third of the way into his Villa career when his goals led the club to another League championship in 1909/10. That season the team performed poorly away from home, but famous Villa Park victories included a 7–1 mauling of Manchester United and a 5–0 defeat of Sheffield Wednesday in which all the goals were scored in the second half.

By now Villa's distinctive claret and blue shirts were being copied by other clubs,

Killing them softly – Brian Little takes the Norwich defence in his stride, Wembley, 1975

West Ham and Burnley among them. Rinder, never one to miss a new commercial opportunity, began selling replica jerseys for 26 shillings through a firm of Birmingham outfitters. These kits remained popular with amateur footballers until the outbreak of World War I.

Villa had time for one more trophy before the conflict, beating Sunderland 1–0 at Crystal Palace in front of a new record crowd of 121,000. Thousands more were locked outside in the pleasure park, and at one point a refreshment stall roof collapsed under the weight of people straining to get a view of the football. Miraculously, nobody was killed.

The resumption of professional football after the war saw the Villa team looking out of sorts and the club in serious debt. Thinking that the war would be a brief one, the board had ordered work to continue on improving Villa Park; the ground's concrete cycle track was removed to bring fans closer to the pitch, and both end terraces were banked up. Without gate receipts, Villa had no means of paying for these improvements – hence the debt.

Not surprisingly there was only one major signing for 1919/20, but former Barnsley centre-half Frank Barson would prove highly effective as Villa embarked on a run to another FA Cup final, against Huddersfield Town. The venue was Stamford Bridge, and the atmosphere was subdued. Few supporters could afford to travel south in an era of postwar austerity, while for Londoners, who had always made up a large percentage of Cup final crowds, the absence of a funfair or other attractions made the occasion less appealing. On a slippery surface, neither side got their game going and there were no goals after 90 minutes. Extra time was then played for the first time in an FA Cup final, enlivened by only a single goal. It was scored by Huddersfield – in their own net.

Back home in Birmingham, Villa paraded the trophy from a fleet of taxis before arriving at the *Holte Hotel*, behind the south terracing at Villa Park, for tea and cakes. Afterwards the players got changed for a League game against Manchester City in front of 45,000; they lost 1–0.

The 1920 Cup win should have signalled the start of another great era for Villa. Attendances were rising and the squad was confident and well-balanced. Yet a series of boardroom errors, compounded by a run of bad luck, allowed the club's affairs to descend into a state of tragic comedy by the middle of the decade. In 1921, four players left after refusing to settle in Birmingham to comply with Villa's residential rule. A year later Barson was sold to Manchester United for the same reason, and his battling spirit was sorely missed. His replacement, Tommy Ball, was shot dead by his landlord after an argument in 1923.

Ball's team-mates were shaken into action, and Villa reached their first Wembley Cup final, against Newcastle, in 1924. After dominating the match but failing to score, Villa conceded two soft goals in the last five minutes, prompting their captain Frank Moss to reflect afterwards: 'We had 20 chances; they had two.'

Meanwhile, a superb new stand had been built along the Trinity Road side of Villa Park under Fred Rinder's painstaking guidance. Magnificent though it was, however, the stand was also three times over budget. By July 1925, Villa were more than £50,000 in debt – a small fortune at the time – and Rinder was forced to resign.

The great man always maintained that his transformation of Villa Park would one day pay for itself, and that day arrived sooner than anyone else thought. The ground was soon hosting England internationals and, more importantly, becoming a favourite neutral venue for FA Cup semi-finals – a status it continues to enjoy to this day.

By 1928, Villa felt flush enough to spend £4,700 on the signing of centre-forward Tom 'Pongo' Waring from Tranmere. The perfect attacking partner for the more agile Billy Walker, Waring had immense aerial power and a finely honed goal-poacher's instinct. On the first day of the 1930/31 season he scored all four goals as Villa beat Manchester United 4–3. He went on to net 50 times during the campaign, part of a huge club total of 128 goals. The team's prodigious goalscoring, however, was betrayed by a creaking defence, and Villa finished seven points adrift of Arsenal in the final table of 1931.

Two seasons later, a crushing 5–0 defeat at Highbury gifted the title to Arsenal again, and in 1933/34 Villa finished a weak 13th. Like several of the League's founding clubs, Villa were struggling to adjust to the tactical innovations of Herbert Chapman's Arsenal. In fact, Villa had never employed a team manager until Jimmy McMullan was appointed in 1934. A year later George Ramsay, who had been the closest Villa had to a coach, died after 59 years' service, and to older supporters it seemed that a simpler, more innocent footballing era had passed with him.

But if Ramsay was gone, another of Villa's founding fathers, Fred Rinder, was now set for an astonishing comeback. The team were struggling at the wrong end of the table for much of 1935/36, and McMullan tried to buy his way out of trouble with a string of new signings. Totally disjointed, Villa were then humiliated 7–1 at home by Arsenal, for whom Ted Drake scored all seven goals. Five months later, Villa were relegated to the Second Division – the last of the League's founders to suffer this indignity. At an emergency meeting in July 1936, chairman Jack Jones was voted off the board and Rinder was re-elected to it, after 11 years in the wilderness.

Innovative as ever, Rinder persuaded Jimmy Hogan to bring his unique football vision to Villa Park. Born in Lancashire, Hogan had been an average player for Fulham at the turn of the century. He had done most of his coaching in Europe, having been an enemy prisoner in Budapest during World War I, and after an unsuccessful spell as manager of Fulham in 1934, he had left for Austria. Rinder coaxed him back to England, telling Hogan that his ideas would receive a warmer welcome at Villa. Hogan succeeded McMullan in November 1936, and was struck by the loyalty of fans turning up in vast numbers to watch Second Division football. He assured them he was 'a teacher and lover of constructive football, with every pass, every kick, every movement an object'. At the end of Hogan's first full season in charge, Villa had won the Second Division title. Crucially, they had done it conceding only 35 goals. The team had made the transition to the 'modern' game, while in Eric Houghton Villa possessed a player who could make the most of the more restricted space now afforded to forwards.

Back in the top flight, the team played before record crowds, 75,000 filling Villa Park for a Cup game with Manchester City in March 1938. Hogan put Frank Barson in charge of a new youth setup, and Rinder told the club's AGM that his manager had 'taught our players to play football'.

Fred Rinder died on Christmas Day 1938, and before long Hogan's plans for Villa would be history, too. World War II brought competitive football to a halt, and by the time hostilities had ceased, Hogan was at Celtic.

So began a long, painful process of decline. Villa's first two postwar managers, Alex Massie and George Martin, had plenty of talent on the books but lacked the vision to weld it into a real team. Eric Houghton, who had left the club in 1947, returned as manager six years later and appointed Hogan as his coach. He came close to being sacked after Villa escaped relegation with a 3–0 win over West Brom on the last day of the 1955/56 season, but the following year he brought the club its first piece of postwar silverware – the FA Cup.

After needing a replay to beat Albion in the semi-finals, Villa went into the final against Manchester United as outsiders. The tide turned their way after only six minutes, when their Irish winger Peter McParland collided with United 'keeper Ray Wood, and the latter had to be carried off with a fractured cheekbone, blood pouring from his head. McParland was not cautioned for his challenge (rushing headlong into a goalkeeper with the ball in his hands was deemed 'fair game' in 1957), and although Wood returned to play on the wing, McParland scored twice past stand-in 'keeper Jackie Blancflower, and the final score of 2–1 did not begin to suggest Villa's dominance.

Houghton's side had denied the Busby Babes a League and Cup double to emulate Villa's achievement of 60 years earlier, but theirs was a hollow victory which served only to foster complacency, as the board allowed Houghton to lead the club to the brink of relegation before replacing him with Joe Mercer in 1958. Mercer's team boasted a smattering of fine individuals, including centre-forward Gerry Hitchens and wing-half Bobby Thomson, and after running away with the Second Division title in 1960, Villa reached the final of the fledgling League Cup competition, beating Rotherham 3–2 over two legs. They reached the same final two years later, but were beaten by Birmingham City in a match that was to assume symbolic significance for the club's fans.

Between 1962 and 1966, Villa hovered nervously around the relegation zone, finally dropping down in 1967 after Mercer's replacement, Dick Taylor, had rashly sought sanctuary by signing a number of

Good discipline – Saunders lifts silverware

veteran 'battlers'. Taylor in turn was replaced by Tommy Cummings, whose only achievement was to avoid relegation to the Third Division. He was sacked in November 1968, and within a month Villa's board of directors had gone, too.

In a curious echo of the events that brought Fred Rinder's committee to power in 1893, a thousand disenchanted Villa fans met at Digbeth Civic Hall on 21 November to vent their exasperation at the board. Villa's share structure had remained exactly as it was when Rinder formed his limited company in 1896, and this was crippling cashflow. Eventually the directors accepted a buyout scheme hatched by merchant banker Pat Matthews, who installed Doug Ellis as chairman (see panel p.25) and Tommy Docherty as team manager. With their club refreshed and recapitalised, the fans returned to Villa Park. Docherty brought in the Rioch brothers, Bruce and Neil, and Chico Hamilton to boost the forward line, but his real work lay in getting the team fit and organised again – four years after the club had been forced to sell

Steak, sand and Saunders – the European Cup

In 1981/82 Villa survived a frozen pitch in Iceland, a trip to East Berlin, the shock resignation of their manager, hooliganism in Brussels and an injury to their goalkeeper in the final to win the **European Cup** at the first attempt. If it all sounds unlikely now, it scarely seemed real then, either – the players involved say the enormity of their achievement only hit home weeks after they had shown off the trophy from the balcony of Birmingham's Council House.

The saga began with a routine 5–0 win over **Valur Reykjavik** at Villa Park in September 1981. Gary Shaw, nursing an ankle injury, made his first start of the season on a frozen, pockmarked surface in the return leg, but confounded the doctors to score both Villa's goals in a 2–0 victory.

Next up were **Dynamo Berlin**, the team of the East German secret police. In the away leg, Jimmy Rimmer saved a penalty to prevent the Germans taking a 2–1 lead, and with five minutes left Tony Morley ran half the length of the pitch to score an unexpected winner. Dynamo silenced Villa Park with a goal after only 15 minutes of the return, but Villa's defensive organisation saw them through on away goals. Before the quarter-finals, manager **Ron Saunders** resigned after a row with the club's ruling Bendall family, and was replaced by his assistant **Tony Barton**. 'European experience is irrelevant,' Barton told a sceptical media. 'The players believe they can win.'

That belief was shaken when the away leg against **Dynamo Kiev** was moved to the Black Sea port of Simferopol at the last minute, Kiev being iced over. Villa brought their own food supplies – steak, egg and chips – and were happy to draw 0–0. They won the return 2–0 in front of 38,500 at Villa Park.

So to the semi-finals and **Anderlecht**. After Morley had found a way through the Belgians' offside trap to give them the lead at home, Rimmer kept Villa in the tie. The return leg was marred by crowd trouble, started by Villa fans high on duty-free booze from their cross-Channel ferry trip. Play was suspended for seven minutes while Villa's players appealed to the fans for calm. Anderlecht then appealed – without success – to get Villa thrown out after the game had ended scoreless.

Alcohol was banned from sale before the final in Rotterdam against **Bayern Munich**. Villa began nervously, Rimmer limping off after nine minutes to be replaced in goal by Nigel Spink, making only his second appearance. Spink went on to make a string of acrobatic saves before Cowans and Morley combined to find striker Peter Withe unmarked on the Bayern six-yard line. As the ball came to him it bobbled on sand in the goalmouth – yet somehow his miscued shot crept in off the post. The only goal of the game.

European winner – Peter Withe beats a bobble in the Bayern six-yard box, Rotterdam, 1982

its training ground to raise funds, 'the Doc' introduced a pre-match warm-up ritual to Villa for the first time.

The revival was brief. Docherty's team were playing 'too much football' for the Second Division, and in January 1970, with Villa bottom of the table, the Doc was dismissed. His replacement, former Villa player Vic Crowe, was as demure as Docherty was outspoken. He could not prevent relegation to the Third Division, but within a year Villa were at Wembley for a League Cup final against top-flight Tottenham. Hamilton, Bruce Rioch and Andy Lochhead all went close as Crowe's side bossed the game, but two late Martin Chivers goals prevented an upset.

Visibly reeling from the defeat, Villa failed to win promotion in 1971, but there was to be no mistake 12 months later after Crowe and his assistant, Ron Wylie, made two crucial signings in central defender Chris Nicholl and goalscoring winger Ray Graydon. Also in 1972, Villa beat Liverpool over two legs to win the FA Youth Cup, their stars being full-back John Gidman and a bustling forward called Brian Little.

It took time for the club's younger talents to blossom in the first team, however, and after two seasons of Second Division football Villa's board lost patience with Crowe and Wylie. The new boss, Ron Saunders, made only a couple of signings in midfielders Frank Carrodus and Leighton Phillips. But the manager's influence on the team was immense. Under Saunders, the emphasis was on discipline and patience – the players worked hard for each other and the ball went forward in its own time. Initially the style was unpopular with fans, but after only a year at the helm, Saunders had taken Villa back into the First Division and won the League Cup thanks to a 1–0 win over Norwich, earned by Graydon's follow-up from a missed penalty.

Villa's first season back in the top drawer was best forgotten, as was the club's first foray into Europe that year. But in 1977 Saunders' side recaptured the League Cup after a twice-replayed final against Everton; the winner was scored by Little but Villa's real star was midfielder Dennis Mortimer, whose energy kept the team ticking throughout the three games.

Saunders claimed his young side would reach 'the very top' within three or four years, but in fact wholesale changes were made before the pinnacle was climbed in

Say that again – Vengloš (left) bewilders Platt

1981. The midfield partnership of Mortimer (now club captain) and Gordon 'Sid' Cowans remained intact, but Little was forced to retire through injury, and other players, such as Gidman and striker Andy Gray, were sold after falling out with their manager. For 1980/81, in came Peter Withe as a new target man, backed up by two youngsters, Gary Shaw and Tony Morley.

For much of the season, Villa were involved in a two-way race for the title with Bobby Robson's Ipswich Town. With their elegant, almost continental-style football, Ipswich were the media darlings. But Villa, if more workmanlike, were also less prone to mistakes. Needing a point to secure the club's first championship in 71 years, Villa lost their last match 2–0 at Arsenal. But Ipswich also lost, 2–1 to Middlesbrough, and Villa were champions. In addition to its enormous historic significance, the win was a personal triumph for Saunders, whose emphasis on teamwork and fitness had enabled Villa to win the League using only 14 players.

The following season should have seen Saunders lead Villa to glory in Europe, but while the club was successful in that arena (see panel p.22), the manager wasn't there to celebrate – midway through the campaign he walked out, after the club's ruling Bendall family had tried to re-negotiate the terms of his contract.

The loss of Saunders was a blow that would be felt only after Villa had lifted the European Cup in 1982. After earlier selling his stake to the Bendalls, Doug Ellis bought them out and returned as chairman. He had little faith in Saunders' successor, Tony Barton, who he claimed was a better scout than a first-team boss, and replaced him with Graham Turner in 1984. On paper Turner's record was decent, but he looked out of his depth in the top flight, and made way for Billy McNeill a month into the 1986/87 season. McNeill had the big-league experience Turner lacked, but inherited a poor side – Villa were bottom when he took over, and bottom when he left at the end of the season. Next up was Graham Taylor, the man who'd worked wonders at Watford but whose uncompromising long-ball style was initially anathema to the Villa squad. Taylor sold some of the team's less consistent players such as Paul Elliott and Tony Dorigo, and brought in Alan McInally as the main striker.

Taylor's Villa were promoted at the first attempt but needed last-day defeats for Bradford City and Middlesbrough to ensure they finished in second place on goals scored. Had it not been for McInally's 22 goals, the team would have gone straight back down again in 1989. The striker was sold to Bayern Munich at the end of the season, but Villa didn't miss him. Instead a radically reshaped side including stoppers Paul McGrath and Kent Nielsen, wingers Tony Daley and Ian Ormondroyd and, most significant of all, young midfielder David Platt, made a surprise bid for the title. In the end, Villa ran out of steam to gift the

League to Liverpool, but the FA had been keeping an eye on Taylor's progress, and after Bobby Robson quit at the end of the 1990 World Cup, Taylor was put in charge of England.

Ellis' next move was to bring in Jozef Venglоš, who'd coached Czechoslovakia to the quarter-finals at Italia '90, as Taylor's replacement. Quietly spoken, with an old-fashioned politeness which seemed quite

Deadlier than the mail – Doug Ellis

When Herbert Douglas Ellis became chairman of Aston Villa in December 1968, the club was technically insolvent. The previous board had resigned *en masse* and merchant banker Pat Matthews invited new directors to put £25,000 each into the club. One of them was Ellis, a former **Birmingham City** director who left St Andrew's disenchanted with boardroom bickering and determined to do things his way in future, or not at all.

This single-mindedness had already made Ellis, the son of a World War I widow, a self-made millionaire by the time he was 40. Among his many enterprises was an early package-tour company running flights from Birmingham Airport to Mallorca. His mother cut the crusts off the sandwiches while Doug called in at the off-licence each day to buy alcohol to serve on the plane – it hadn't yet occurred to anyone to sell duty-free drinks to package tourists.

Blind man's bluff – 'Deadly' and Big Ron

Ellis arranged a £2,500 overdraft to set up his travel business but never touched it and claims never to have borrowed a penny since. As Villa chairman he was given the nickname 'Deadly' (reportedly by Jimmy Greaves) because of his reputation for dismissing managers. Yet many of the men supposedly sacked by Ellis had decided to leave, and Villa's most infamous bust-up with a first-team boss, the **Ron Saunders** affair, occurred at a time when he was not involved with the club.

After leading **Wolves** into the voluntary liquidation which would ultimately save them in 1982, 'Deadly' returned to Villa, buying out the Bendall family's controlling interest four years after he had been voted off the board. Since then his cosmopolitan outlook (Ellis has a German wife and a string of associates across the globe from his travel industry days) has led Villa to the forefront of moves toward a European league, while his instinct for innovation has brought executive boxes and advanced retail operations to Villa Park, way ahead of their acceptance by the footballing mainstream.

Always publicly amiable, Ellis has retained an autocratic grip on the club, even after Villa's stock-market flotation in 1997. He is in his office six days a week, often working until everyone else has gone home, and insists on signing every cheque himself – a task he likens to 'a footballer keeping his eye on the ball.' Many fans, though, say his caution has prevented Villa from challenging for the game's highest honours.

The plain facts are these. Thirty years ago Villa were £20,000 in debt, playing in the Second Division and attracting average crowds of 12,000. In 1999 the club was a publicly quoted company worth £120 million, with plans to extend Villa Park to a 50,000 all-seater arena. Best keep that cheque-book in your drawer, Doug.

'The sort of goal he'd scored in the video' – Milošević wins the League Cup for Villa, 1996

out of place in the England of the early Nineties, Vengloš was always struggling to impose his tactical ideas on Taylor's personnel – and on the latter's last signing, striker Tony Cascarino, especially. It was no surprise when 'Doctor Jo' resigned after his only season had ended with Villa in 17th place. Only later, when other Premiership clubs began to adopt such thinking, did Villa appreciate that the good Doctor's ideas on diet, exercise and personal training had benefitted the club in the long run.

Villa's next manager, Ron Atkinson, couldn't have been more different. Unlike Vengloš, Big Ron was a consummate media operator who could turn almost any shortcoming into a PR victory. He insisted on working with his own players, spending most of the £5.5million Villa had received from Bari of Italy for Platt before his team had kicked a ball. Under Atkinson, Villa finished seventh in the League in 1991/92 and, when the club joined its top-flight rivals to leave William McGregor's Football League and form the Premiership the following season, his side pushed Manchester United all the way for the title, their progress powered by the attacking combination of Dean Saunders and Dalian Atkinson.

In 1993/94 Villa could only finish tenth in the Premiership but found consolation in the League Cup final, where a 3–1 win over United was secured by goals from Saunders and Atkinson, and engineered by Andy Townsend, dominating a midfield which his manager had packed with bodies to knock United out of their stride.

Behind the scenes, however, Ellis was becoming frustrated by what he saw as Big Ron's casual attitude to his job. When Villa struggled at the start of 1994/95, the chairman had the excuse he needed to sack Atkinson and bring Brian Little, former hero of the Holte End, back to Villa Park as manager. Little steered the side away from the drop, but Atkinson's legacy was an ageing squad which the new manager decided should be drastically overhauled for 1995/96. Villa began the season with a new strikeforce of Dwight Yorke, bought by Ellis for £10,000 after a club tour of Trinidad & Tobago in 1990, and Savo Milošević, on whom Little was persuaded to spend £3.5million after seeing a video of goals he had scored for Partizan Belgrade in the Yugoslav league. The duo never really hit it off, but did combine brilliantly when Villa regained the League Cup with a 3–0 win over Leeds at Wembley – the first goal a spectacular solo effort from Milošević, the third a result of the Yugoslav going through on goal but then rolling the ball wide for Yorke, better placed, to finish.

With Mark Bosnich in goal and Gareth Southgate and Ugo Ehiogu firmly established in front of him, Villa looked poised for another title challenge in 1996/97. But it never materialised, and the team's sixth-place finish flattered them. As if to prove the point, Villa were at the wrong end of the table for much of the following season, despite Little smashing the club's transfer record to bring striker Stan Collymore from Liverpool for £7million. After a 2–1 defeat at Wimbledon in February 1998, Little quit, to be replaced by his former coach John Gregory, another Villa old boy.

In contrast to the reticent Little, Gregory displayed a gritty sense of humour rare in English football management. It soon spread to the players, who visibly relaxed under his guidance. Villa didn't just survive in 1997/98 – they qualified for Europe.

In 1998/99, with Milošević finally despatched to Zaragoza and Yorke sold at a modest profit to Manchester United for £12.5million, Gregory's Villa began the campaign as front-runners, only to fall away badly in the spring, suffering injuries and a lack of verve in front of goal – the latter attributable to the off-field problems of Collymore and his would-be attacking foil, Paul Merson.

Still, Gregory ended the season feeling as comfortable as any recent manager at Villa Park has been. Villa are European regulars, making tidy profits for their shareholders, and planning grand new extensions to their stadium. Those old ghosts should be proud, after all.

Here we go!

Aston is a couple of miles from Birmingham, and sufficiently near motorways to render driving through the city centre unnecessary. **Motorists** should approach on the M6 motorway and exit at junction 6 (Spaghetti Junction) onto the A38(M) Aston Expressway, toward the city centre.

After leaving the Expressway at the first exit, you have two choices: either follow a signpost to one of the many matchday **car parks** provided by local schools and businesses (the safest bet, though it may involve a fair walk to the ground) or attempt street parking nearer Villa Park. For the latter, turn right into Victoria Road, first right into Bevington Road, then third right into Trinity Road – the ground is on your left.

Witton **train station** is only a 2min walk from the ground and is served by trains running from Birmingham New Street to Walsall. However, the stop before it, Aston, gets both Walsall trains and those headed for Lichfield, and is still no more than 10mins walk away – it might be a better bet if kick-off is looming or you need to get back to New Street in a hurry.

Thousands of Villa fans use these local trains, rendering detailed directions unnecessary – just follow the claret and blue.

New Street itself has fast onward connections for London Euston, Manchester, Sheffield, Derby, Leeds and Bristol, with feasible late-evening departures for midweek games. For the latest timings call ☎0345/484950.

Just the ticket

Visiting fans are accommodated in the Lower North Stand – turnstiles in Witton Lane, at one end of the Doug Ellis Stand. Ticket price here in 1998/99 was a flat £17, with no concessions for visitors. Once inside, the view of the enormous Holte End, opposite, will fair take the breath away, even if the football doesn't.

Disabled visitors have some spaces at the back of the Lower North Stand, but a bigger allocation is planned for the extended Trinity Road Stand when this is built. In the meantime, advance booking is essential through the club on ☎0121/327 5399.

Unlike some Premiership grounds, Villa Park is not booked out for the season. However, many games *are* all-ticket. Check with your club in advance, rather than turning up on the off-chance – nobody wants to brave Spaghetti Junction for nothing.

Swift half

Close to the ground, ***The Harriers***, at the junction of The Broadway and Davey Road, welcomes both home and away fans, with the added advantage of a fish-and-chip shop almost next-door. A little further afield, the ***Faculty & Firkin***, just inside the Aston Science Park close to the Aston University campus, is a good bet before the match – you may even meet the Villa internet mailing list football team quaffing a quick one.

Birmingham is the **birthplace of the balti** so if you're in need of serious sustenance before or after the game, there are a couple of curry-house options along Witton Road, the other side of Witton train station from Villa Park.

Club merchandise

The impressive ***Villa Village*** (open Mon–Sat 9am–5.30pm, later on matchdays, ☎0121/327 2800) is conveniently located just behind the North Stand. Villa's trend-setting claret-and-blue colour scheme is hard to avoid, but its latest incarnation is controversial, the club having moved to an 'annual cycle' for home shirt designs – a common practice in Europe but rare here, even among profit-driven Premiership clubs. The new shirts are £42.99 (kids' sizes £32.99), but for £7 less you can choose from a wide range of older replicas, including the (mainly blue) 1957 FA Cup final shirt and the (mainly white) 1982 European Cup model.

Doug Ellis, a former wine merchant among many other things, doubtless approves of Villa's latest move into fine wine and champagne, which should be on sale during the 1999/2000 season.

Barmy army

Villa Park's North Stand somehow remained unsegregated for much of the Seventies and Eighties, and the terracing which once stood where visiting fans are now seated witnessed some ugly scenes, particularly when Birmingham or West Brom were the visitors. Villa fans' behaviour in Europe (see panel p.22) was also frequently less than saintly.

Today the boot is on the other foot. Villla's hardcore element is renowned for anti-fascism, and the club's broad-mindedness reflects the rich ethnic mix in the surrounding area, as well as the team's recent exploits in continental Europe.

In print

The ***Birmingham Post*** and ***Evening Mail*** offer comprehensive coverage of Villa six days a week. After the final whistle on Saturdays, the ***Sports Argus*** carries match reports on all West Midlands teams – it's normally available around Villa Park from 6pm.

The official club magazine is ***Claret & Blue***, published by Sports Projects and one of the more readable of its kind.

Of the fanzines, Dave Woodhall's ***Heroes & Villains*** (PO Box 1703, Perry Barr, Birmingham, B42 1UZ) is one of the better-established, but don't miss also ***The Witton Wag*** (PO Box 26, Wednesbury, WS10 9YT) or ***The Holy Trinity*** (216 Brandwood Road, King's Heath, B14 6LD).

Graham McColl's ***Illustrated History of Aston Villa*** (Hamlyn, £17.99) is meticulously researched and divertingly well written – probably the best all-round book about the club. Sports Projects publishes a number of fine Villa books including Doug Ellis' pinch-of-salt autobiography, ***Deadly!*** (£14.95), and Simon Inglis' essential ***Villa Park – 100 Years*** (£24.95).

On air

BBC Radio WM (95.6 FM) tends to cycle through the local sides in its matchday coverage, while commercial ***X-tra AM*** (1152 AM) is more likely to offer live commentary on a single game – very often Villa. The former's after-match phone-ins are good for a giggle.

In the net

Villa's **official website** is a little graphic-heavy but has all the essentials, including an excellent news archive (many stories have *RealAudio* interviews), a detailed history and the expected, comprehensive e-commerce section. You'll find it at: www.astonvilla-fc.com.

Of the unofficial sites, ***VillaWeb*** claims to have been the first Villa presence on the web and is very efficiently run from Denmark by Christian Jahnsen. It's at: www.gbar.dtu.dk/~c937079/AVFC/.

For a rootsier perspective, try the online fanzine ***Well Prepared*** at: www.toppa.demon.co.uk/well_prep.html; or 15-year-old Alan Bates' ***Villa Island*** at: www.villaisland.freeserve.co.uk/index2.htm.

Barnet

Formation	1912 as Barnet & Alston
Stadium	Underhill, Westcombe Drive, Barnet, Herts, EN5 2BE. ☎0181/441 6932
Ground capacity	4,000
First-choice colours	Amber and black
Major honours	Conference champions 1991; FA Amateur Cup winners 1946
Position 1998/99	16th in Third Division

There are three things every football fan knows about Barnet. That they have the smallest ground in the League. That John Motson supports them. And that their former manager, Barry Fry, once woke the neighbours up while cutting the grass by moonlight. In this sleepy, well-settled area of suburban North London, if you don't support Arsenal or Tottenham you probably don't follow football at all. Yet it says a lot about Barnet that, in less than a decade of League football, they've built up as colourful a history as their bigger neighbours have managed to accumulate in a century or more.

Open access – you can still wave to the PA bloke at Underhill

By no means all of the Barnet story makes for wholesome, family reading. The chairman whose cash injection powered the club out of the non-League game was a self-confessed ticket tout, and one of the club's sponsors in the early Nineties had to withdraw his backing when he was arrested for fraud. Barnet have been threatened with expulsion from the League, with relegation, and with having their ground closed down by the local council. In the past couple of seasons the team have been sponsored by *Loaded*, the magazine for men who like everything about women except meeting them.

Small wonder the nimbys and the non-football types of the *Mill Hill Preservation Society* are doing their best to block the club's move to Copthall Stadium, an under-used arena near their current Underhill ground which Barnet want to develop into a multi-purpose stadium for football, rugby union and athletics. Underhill itself, meanwhile, is decaying by the week, its capacity restricted by safety concerns, its infrastructure starved of any serious investment since the club's Conference days.

What would Barnet's founding fathers, with their strict ethos of sportsmanship, fair play and 'stiff upper lip', have made of it all? While Arsenal and Spurs were embracing professionalism and flying the flag for London in the Football League well before World War I, Barnet were still resolutely amateur, recruiting their footballers from local factories and competing in the Olympian, London and Athenian Leagues.

Even in those early days, though, football in the area was suffering the instability of closures, mergers and shifting venues. The first club to take play under the name of Barnet FC was forced to disband by an FA inquiry, just three years after it was

'Psycho' – Conference survivor Paul Wilson

founded in 1888. A rival team, Barnet Avenue, took over the name in 1903, while four years later, a third team began playing at Underhill as Barnet Alston. In 1912 they merged with the 'Avenue' Barnet to become Barnet & Alston – plain Barnet FC from 1919.

Seven years later the club finally got around to building a stand at Underhill (seldom has anyone ever done anything quickly at this ground), and during the Thirties, with former England winger Lester Finch in the side, Barnet began to dominate the local amateur scene. Finch was still wearing the now moderately famous amber and black stripes when the team won their first major honour, the FA Amateur Cup, by beating Bishop Auckland 3–2 at Stamford Bridge in 1946.

Two years later Barnet were Amateur Cup finalists again, losing 1–0 to one of their many London rivals, Leytonstone. In 1952, a record Underhill crowd of more than 11,000 turned up for the Amateur Cup visit of Wycombe Wanderers, but while local interest in the team was at a high, Barnet's football soon failed to live up to its billing – the team finished bottom of the Athenian League in 1957. George Wheeler, one of the heroes of the 1946 side, took over as manager and coaxed the team to a third Amateur Cup final appearance, at Wembley, two years later, but Barnet were beaten 3–2 by Crook Town.

In the early Sixties, as Barnet celebrated taking a record seventh Athenian League title, it became clear the club would have to shake off its purist approach if it was to capitalize on the support it still enjoyed over and above that of local amateur rivals. The board agreed to pay players appearance money for the first time, installed a set of floodlights and built a new Main Stand at Underhill. The team responded by reaching the third round of the FA Cup for the first time in 1965, and six months after that, Barnet took a crucial step towards professionalism by applying to join the semi-pro Southern League.

Barnet won the Southern title in their first season, 1965/66, and won it again 11 years later, when a handful of appearances from an ageing Jimmy Greaves briefly brought a media circus to Underhill. The serious business came a year later, though, when the appointment of Barry Fry as manager led to a top-half finish in 1978/79 – good enough for Barnet to gain admittance to the Alliance Premier League as founder members.

From a footballing point of view, the club was comfortable at this new level. But by the mid-Eighties, the cost of travelling to games in what was a national league competition, coupled with the reluctance of the Football League to set up any kind of automatic promotion and relegation between the Fourth Division and the Alliance Premier, was giving several of the latter's members money worries – not least Barnet. In 1984 Fry, who had temporarily given up the manager's role but effectively still ran the place, put a second mortgage on his house to solve a cashflow crisis. But the club was still servicing a six-figure debt, and a year later Fry sought help from Stan Flashman. 'Fat Stan' had made his money selling tickets to *Evita* and other West End shows at way over face value, to tourists and business parties who would pay any price. Attracted by the prospect of taking Barnet into the Football League (which finally agreed to allow its bottom club to swap places with the Alliance champions when the latter became the Conference in 1986), Flashman gave Fry the money he needed to bring players with League experience to Underhill. Now amateurism was well and truly out; designer suits and BMWs were in.

Barnet finished runners-up in three of the first four Conference seasons, until a last-day win over Fisher Athletic finally landed the title – and promotion to the League – in 1991. The achievement was all the greater because Fry, under pressure from Flashman to keep the till ringing, had sold four of his best players – Phil Gridelet, Paul Harding, Andy Clarke and David Regis – to League clubs during the season. Among the heroes who stuck around were goalkeeper Gary Phillips, the reliable defensive pairing of Mickey Bodley and Gary Poole, midfield anchor Paul Wilson and striker Gary Bull, whose 30 goals made him Conference top scorer by a mile.

Both Bull and the forward Fry had signed to replace Clarke, Mark Carter, scored twice in the club's first-ever League game, at home to Crewe in August 1991, but Barnet lost 7–4 – a typically brash debut. Fry immediately set about fixing the defence, and a month later his team won 6–0 at Lincoln City; they ended the season in seventh place.

If that was creditable, the side's performance the following season was even better, culminating in a third-place finish and promotion to what was now the Second (formerly Third) Division. Once again, though, Barnet were in danger of overreaching themselves. New safety regulations, courtesy of the Taylor Report, reduced Underhill's capacity to less than half the 9,000 it was capable of holding when Barnet entered the League – gate receipts plunged accordingly. At the end of the 1992/93 season Flashman quit, his legacy a string of debts, the prospect of a winding-up order from the Inland Revnue, and a motion (not sustained) to have the club expelled from the League because of their perilous financial state.

Barry Fry, too, had had enough, and when he moved to Southend United, he took many of Barnet's promotion-winning squad with him. Edwin Stein, Fry's assistant from the Conference era, took over as first-team boss, but the club's new board couldn't afford to pay his wages, and he was replaced by goalkeeper Phillips as player-manager before the 1993/94 campaign had really got started. The team lost their first nine Second Division games and finished bottom, having won only five times all season.

Barnet turned to another goalkeeper, former England man Ray Clemence, to turn the tide in 1994/95, and the team managed decent finishes in the middle of the Third Division over the next two seasons. Clemence's side was a well-balanced mix

Hats off – Barry Fry survived being sacked three times

of journeyman pros (Alex Dyer, Alan Pardew) and promising youngsters (Dougie Freedman, Linvoy Primus). But as well as getting the playing staff sorted out, Clemence also encouraged a capable back-room team including Terry Bullivant as first-team coach and Terry Gibson as boss of the youth team.

On the first day of the 1996/97 season, however, Clemence was poached by Glenn Hoddle to be the England goalkeeping coach and, rather than promote any of his existing staff, chairman Tony Kleanthous (who'd taken over the club two years earlier) persuaded Alan Mullery to come out of retirement and become director of football, with Bullivant again as coach. The result was a dismal 15th place and the loss of much of the good work done by Clemence; Mullery quit before the end of the season, and Bullivant also left in the summer to take charge of Reading. Kleanthous' next appointment, John Still, got Barnet into the play-offs in 1997/98, where they lost to Colchester in the semi-finals.

Yeeess! – Gary Phillips hails a rare point, 1993

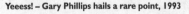

The team then hovered worryingly close to the bottom of the Third Division for much of 1998/99. What was left of the crowd became disenchanted with Still's long-ball tactics, and the cut-price sale of striker Sean Devine to Wycombe was similarly unpopular. Barnet's final 16th placing was their lowest since the club entered the League.

Perhaps more important, however, the club was given a second (and probably last) reprieve from the League which enabled the team to carry on playing at Underhill, even though it falls below the required standard in several respects – not least of which is its size. With the outcome of the public inquiry into Copthall still not known in the summer of 1999, Barnet were in limbo and Tony Kleanthous freely admitted to becoming 'a bit emotional' about the impasse. Not that there's anything new in that – this is a club that has always worn its heart on its sleeve, and often paid a high price for doing so.

Here we go!

Unless coming from elsewhere in London, **motorists** will approach on the M25. Exit at junction 23 and follow the A1081 to Barnet, turning right at the T-junction into the High Street. Go straight on at the next lights down Barnet Hill, pass High Barnet underground station on your left, then turn right at the lights into Underhill and immediately left into Barnet Lane – the ground is on your left. Street parking is plentiful, but beware car crime.

Fans travelling by **train** have two options. The first is to catch the notorious Northern Line tube to High Barnet and walk from there – allow 1hr from central London for the tube journey, then 5mins to walk down Barnet Hill to the ground (see above) and 15mins to walk back up it again. The alternative is New Barnet station, slightly further from Underhill but only a 20min suburban train ride from King's Cross (service half-hourly). Call ☎0345/484950 for the latest timings.

From New Barnet station, turn left along Station Road, right at the T-junction onto the Great North Road/Barnet Hill, then left into Fairfield Way – the ground is on your right. Allow 20mins.

Just the ticket

The 'temporary' uncovered South Stand where **visiting fans** are seated has been at Underhill since 1995 and will probably be there until the ground is closed. Visitors are sometimes allocated a standing area at the south end of the East Terrace, depending on the numbers expected. Either way it was £10 to get in during 1998/99, with no concessions for visiting fans.

There are facilities for **disabled fans** in front of the Family Stand, but the view from here across Underhill's sloping pitch is one of the worst in the League. Book if you must on ☎0181/441 6932.

Swift half

Until 1926, Barnet held regular club meetings at ***The Old Red Lion*** just across the road from the ground. The pub is justly proud of its football heritage and continues to welcome fans of both the home side and visiting teams – don't let the doorman put you off. There's food on matchdays before and after kick off.

Families are welcome at ***The Weaver*** (☎0181/449 9292), down Great North Road beyond the fork with Station Road.

For serious food, the *Barnet FC Curry Club* (see below) recommends ***The New Barnet Curry Centre*** on Station Road, on the route back to New Barnet. ***The Fresh Fry*** fish-and-chip shop on Great North Road does plaice and skate to order – they're worth the wait.

Club merchandise

Barnet's **club shop** (Mon–Sat 9.30am–5.30pm, ☎0181/440 0725) is not actually at Underhill at all, but at 40 High Street – a 5min walk up the hill beyond High Barnet tube. The club's first shirt to bear the *Loaded* logo was a tasteful black, amber and white affair, but a revised version introduced for 1998/99 grew stripes that made the magazine's name read *oadeo*.

Barmy army

The East Terrace does what it can to raise Barnet from their anxieties. Fans here approached the club's near-extinction in 1993 with overwhelmingly good humour, but the arrival of Alan Mullery three years later tested their patience; the campaign to oust him soon got its required result. Barnet's big rivals are Enfield – a stormy relationship dating back to pre-Conference days.

In print

The weekly ***Barnet Times*** newspaper will provide the latest on the Copthall Stadium development – back pages supporting the plan, letters pages rubbishing it. As with all London clubs, the absence of a Saturday evening paper of any kind continues to surprise visitors from other major English conurbations.

Fanzine ***Two Together*** is disarmingly honest and to the point, when the editors can get it together. Order a copy from 5 Trellis Drive, Lychpit, Basingstoke, RG24 8YU.

On air

Fans say the choice is between two BBC stations: ***GLR*** (94.9 FM) and ***Three Counties Radio*** (103.8 FM).

In the net

In the absence of an offficial website, Tim and Phil Webb produce the most ambitious offering at: members.aol.com/TWebb 25681/Barnet.htm. The site won't win any awards for graphic style but there's plenty going on.

Two Together fanzine can be found at: www.twotogether.demon.co.uk. And ***The Barnet FC Curry Club***, which includes current 'keeper Lee Harrison among its membership, has a site at: www.geocities.com/Colosseum/Bench/7319.

Barnsley

Formation	1887 as Barnsley St Peter's
Stadium	Oakwell, Grove Street, Barnsley, S71 1ET. ☎01226/211211
Ground capacity	18,800
First-choice colours	Red and white
Major honours	Third Division (North) champions 1934, 1939, 1955; FA Cup winners 1912
Position 1998/99	13th in First Division

Over the years, Barnsley FC have meant many different things to the wider world. In the early part of this century they were Battling Barnsley, a team whose never-say-die spirit enabled them to survive a dozen games to win the FA Cup in 1912. In the early Eighties they were Brilliant Barnsley, a side of huge attacking energy that captured the public's imagination with a series of Cup runs, some mounted from the murky depths of the Third Division. And at the end of the millennium we've had Brazilian Barnsley, a team whose insistence on playing precise, measured football did not prevent them from winning the club's first promotion to the top flight of the English game.

It was not, of course, *Just Like Watching Brazil*, as Fleet Street was happy to brand Barnsley's football once the media bandwagon had rolled into town at the end of the 1996/97 promotion season, and found a section of the Oakwell crowd singing that very refrain to the tune of *Blue Moon*. For one thing, there was none of the preening and pouting associated with the stars who wear those famous yellow shirts (unless you count Macedonian striker Georgi Hristov's complaint that Barnsley girls weren't as good-looking as the ones he'd left back in Belgrade). The players just knuckled down and got on with it, and the fact that they were relegated after only a season ultimately mattered little to supporters who, deep down, had always known Premiership life was going to be a struggle. The crucial thing was that Barnsley had made their point – the town was on the map, famous at last for something other than miners' strikes, pit closures, Arthur Scargill and Michael Parkinson.

To the people of Barnsley, this is what the club is really about. Plenty of other English teams symbolise their town, but few do it with as much pride, as little compromise, or as scant consideration for what outsiders may think. Typical Yorkshire, you might say – though even that would be an over-simplification.

If Brazilian Barnsley's story was unlikely, then that of Battling Barnsley has an equally fairytale quality to it. Like many of today's professional clubs, Barnsley's origins lie with the church, the Rev Tiverton Preedy having founded a team as Barnsley St Peter's in 1887. Their first pitch was a sloping field in Oakwell Lane, and within a year the club had persuaded the landowner to let them have an adjacent, more level pitch – where the current ground now stands. At the same time the club decided to turn fully professional, a bold and controversial move but, ultimately, the right one.

The side was successful enough in local South Yorkshire leagues for the Football League to admit them to the Second Division in 1898. The club simplified its name to 'Barnsley FC', and also dispensed with the brown-and-white striped shirts the players had been wearing, in favour of plain red ones.

Barnsley ended their first season third from bottom of the Second Division, and were obliged to seek re-election. But after being spared an identical fate by goal average the following year, they gradually got to grips with life in the League. They began performing well in the FA Cup, too, reaching the quarter-finals in 1907, and the final itself three years later, when they held Newcastle to a 1–1 draw at Crystal Palace before losing the replay, 2–0, at Goodison Park.

All's well at Oakwell – Danny Wilson in the dugout, April 1997

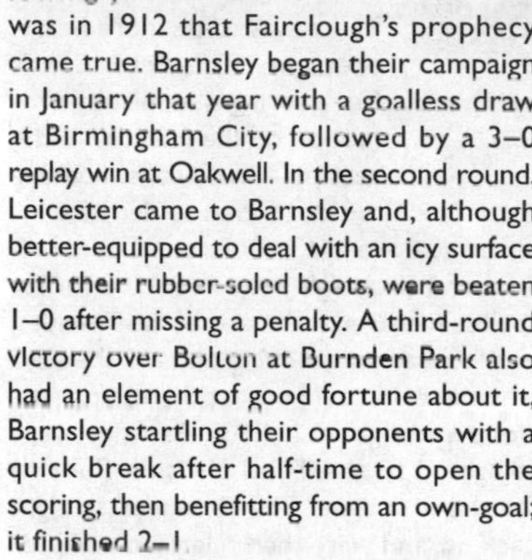

Barnsley's manager Arthur Fairclough, who as club secretary had negotiated admission to the League, now told the local *Evening Chronicle* that if he could keep his team together, there was no reason why they couldn't go all the way and win the Cup the following year. In fact it was in 1912 that Fairclough's prophecy came true. Barnsley began their campaign in January that year with a goalless draw at Birmingham City, followed by a 3–0 replay win at Oakwell. In the second round, Leicester came to Barnsley and, although better-equipped to deal with an icy surface with their rubber-soled boots, were beaten 1–0 after missing a penalty. A third-round victory over Bolton at Burnden Park also had an element of good fortune about it, Barnsley startling their opponents with a quick break after half-time to open the scoring, then benefitting from an own-goal; it finished 2–1.

It was a Yorkshire derby against Bradford City in the quarter-finals that really caught the country's attention, and prompted the first description of Fairclough's side as 'Battling Barnsley'. Seldom has the Cup thrown together two teams as well-matched and as well-drilled – there were four games in all, with the first three all ending goalless.

Around 25,000 were at Oakwell for the first match and nearly 32,000 at Bradford for the first replay. The official attendance at Elland Road for the second replay was 37,000 but there were probably many more, some fans making the journey on foot because train services were restricted by a (you guessed it) miners' strike. The referee blew the final whistle five minutes early, and refused to play extra time because the crowd kept spilling onto the pitch. Bramall Lane, Sheffield, saw some goals at last, Barnsley coming back from 2–1 down to win 3–2 with Harold Lillycrop's last kick of the game in extra time.

There were two more games on neutral soil for Barnsley's semi-final against Swindon Town. The first game, at Stamford Bridge, was goalless, and Barnsley won the replay at Notts County 1–0, the opposition again conveniently missing a penalty.

There wasn't a football fan in the land surprised to learn that the final against West Brom had finished 0–0 but, for once, Barnsley's stubborn, tightly drawn strategy couldn't be blamed – the Crystal Palace pitch was rock hard and high temperatures made it impossible for the game to be played at anything higher than waltz tempo.

As the seconds ticked away toward the end of extra time in the replay at Bramall Lane, thousands of fans began to drift away, convinced it would be another goalless draw. But with two minutes left, Barnsley's Harry Tufnell went on a solo run from inside his own half, evaded two tackles, and placed the ball to the right of the West Brom 'keeper. 'Altogether a cool piece of business,' gushed the *Evening Chronicle* the following day, adding without a trace of

Palmed off – Andy Rammell feels the pinch at Sheffield United

and Derby, the top two Second Division sides in 1915, went up anyway, while Spurs, who'd finished bottom of the First that year, were given a reprieve. The League committee in its wisdom then decided to ask for nominations for the remaining place. Arsenal, who'd finished the 1914/15 season in fifth, four points behind Barnsley, got 18 votes to the Yorkshiremen's five. Enraged Oakwell officials refused to appeal, stormed out of the committee hearing and boarded the next train home.

There was to be more heartbreak in 1922, Peter Sant's free-scoring side missing promotion on the final day of the season, when Stoke, needing to win by three clear goals to deny Barnsley on goal average, beat Bristol City…3–0. Arthur Fairclough returned for another spell as manager at the end of the Twenties, but football was moving on, and the days when a team could make progress on guts alone were gone. In 1932 Barnsley were relegated to the Third Division (North) for the first time. They bounced straight back up, and were then relegated and promoted again on the eve of World War II.

The man who engineered that last promotion, manager Angus Seed, remained in the job after the war. In 1949 Seed signed a skilful, unusually articulate wing-half, Danny Blanchflower, from the Ulster club Glentoran. The fee of £6,500 seemed high for a player who was not yet a full international, but Seed was assembling a subtle blend of speed and skill in his team, and Blanchflower was the missing ingredient. In 1950/51, the Irishman's understanding with nippy centre-forward Cecil McCormack brought the latter a Barnsley season record of 33 goals, while Blanchflower's compatriot Eddie McMorran picked up the scraps. In March 1951, however, Aston Villa

hyperbole that it was 'one of the best goals ever scored on a football field'.

Barnsley's Cup-winning side had cost only £250 to put together, and the club had used only 12 players – Jimmy Moore coming in for Bert Leavey after the latter had broken his leg against Bradford City. No club had taken so much money at the turnstiles on its way to the Cup, yet the players got only £25 each in bonuses, with Moore and Leavey having to divide their money in half.

Two other records were set that year. Barnsley became the only club ever to have won the Cup on Yorkshire soil – a record that still stands. And they became the first FA Cup-winning League side never to have had experience of the top flight – a record that stood until the promotion of 1997.

Barnsley had come close to breaking it much earlier. In 1914/15, the last League season before World War I, they finished third in the Second Division, three points shy of a promotion place. After the war, however, the League decided to expand the First Division to 22 clubs, and Barnsley seemed natural candidates for it. Preston offered Barnsley £14,500 for Blanchflower, and the club could not refuse.

Within two years Barnsley were relegated and Seed resigned. His successor, Tim Ward, could do no more than maintain the status quo, and the complacency that set in led directly to the club's nadir – relegation to the Fourth Division in 1965. In September 1966, English football was bathing in the afterglow of World Cup success. But the euphoria passed Oakwell by. Barnsley lost their first five games of the season and sat sullenly at the bottom of the League. Attendances for League games plunged to around 2,000, and with his bankers getting itchy feet about a company overdraft of more than £40,000, club chairman Sir Joseph Richards warned that Barnsley would close unless more fans could be tempted through the turnstiles. The directors then put up £10,000 of their own money to invest in new players and stave off the threat of re-election, and support came trickling back – though only in real numbers for cup-ties.

Barnsley finished 16th in 1967 and were promoted to the Third Division a year later, but by 1972 they were down in the basement again, and they would stay there for the rest of the Seventies.

The man who pulled the team (and the town) up by the boot-straps was Allan Clarke. 'Sniffer' had been a key member of Don Revie's Leeds United side in the early Seventies but was coming to the end of his career as a forward and eagerly accepted Barnsley general manager Johnny Steele's offer of a player-manager's role in the summer of 1978. Leading from the front, Clarke managed a goal every three games, constantly out-witting Fourth Division defences while lifting his team-mates with his thoroughly professional outlook, cultivated over seven years of subjugation by Revie.

Clarke won promotion at the end of his first year, and stayed long enough to consolidate Barnsley's place in the Third Division before being tempted away by the chance to manage Leeds in 1980. His successor was another former Elland Road idol, Norman Hunter, who carried on where Clarke had left off. On paper the squad was workaday, but in Mick McCarthy Barnsley had a stopper who could distribute intelligently from the back (as well as roar at his team-mates in a broad Yorkshire brogue), in Joe Joyce a right-back who captained the side with character, in Ronnie Glavin an industrious midfielder of rare goalscoring prowess, and in Trevor Aylott a powerfully elusive target man. Brilliant Barnsley, indeed.

Few of the players had any experience of life in the upper half of the League, but in 1981 they won promotion to the Second Division, reaching the fifth round of the FA Cup along the way, and the following year Barnsley finished sixth, just four points shy of promotion to the top flight. They also reached the quarter-finals of the League Cup, where they held Liverpool to a goalless draw at Anfield before losing the replay 3–1. As the Eighties wore on and Margaret Thatcher sucked the industrial

French champagne, Brazilian beat – Redfearn and Marcelle, 1997

life out of the town, Oakwell lost its impetus. Aylott and McCarthy moved on, as did Hunter, to be replaced by yet another former Leeds man, Bobby Collins, who in turn made way for the returning Clarke. The team drifted aimlessly into mid-table, and the club's fan base – much of which was now either on strike or on the dole – shrank with each passing season.

'Mad Mel' Machin took Barnsley to the brink of relegation with a series of bewildering transfer deals at the turn of the Nineties, but his successor Viv Anderson restored some of the panache with the help of Andy Rammell's goals, before leaving to join Bryan Robson at Middlesbrough in 1994. Anderson's former assistant, Danny Wilson, then took over. As an ageing midfielder hesitantly playing out the last days of his career in a Barnsley shirt, Wilson had been vilified by a section of the Oakwell crowd. As soon as he'd moved into the dugout, the hecklers were silenced.

Pursuing Anderson's policy of thoughtful football infused with gritty top-level experience, Wilson led the team to within four points of the play-offs in his first year, and a year later made a string of signings – John Hendrie, Paul Wilkinson and Trinidadian Clint Marcelle – to cure the goal drought which had pushed Barnsley down into mid-table in 1995/96. By May 1997, Wilson's side had done more than merely finish second to guarantee a place in the top division for the first time in Barnsley's 110-year history; they'd done it playing a brand of football that was supposed to be the sole province of the Premiership, and probably only the top third of that.

Unable to compete at the upper end of the domestic market, Wilson broke the club's transfer record to buy striker Hristov from Partizan Belgrade and the national captain of Slovenia, Ales Krizan, to bolster the defence. Neither gamble paid off, and though Barnsley reached the quarter-finals of the FA Cup with a famous defeat of Manchester United and also won at Anfield in the Premiership, the trap door of relegation was always opening too wide for comfort.

Barnsley fans were disappointed but not dismayed, even though a string of refereeing decisions had gone against them in crucial games. What upset them more was the sale of inspirational skipper Neil Redfearn to Charlton and Wilson's departure for Sheffield Wednesday at the end of the season, and the failure of Wilson's successor, Hendrie, to keep the dream alive – Barnsley never came close to play-off places in 1998/99.

The board were not amused, either. Having diverted the club's Premiership TV income from ground improvements to player transfer fees and salaries, they'd expected better things, and sacked Hendrie at the end of the season.

The appointment of Dave 'Harry' Bassett, self-confessed long-ball lover and a former Sheffield United boss to boot, received a mixed reaction from fans. He may be the man to get Barnsley back into the Premiership. But at what cost to Oakwell's greatest asset – its pride?

Here we go!

Motorists should avoid Barnsley town centre as far as possible, though Oakwell's location does make it difficult.

Approaching on the M1 motorway (as travellers from most directions will do), exit at junction 37 onto the A628 Dodworth Road toward Barnsley. Turn left at the lights into Pogmoor Road, then after about a mile go right at the lights into Gawber Road. and follow this around a sharp bend into Victoria Road. Continue straight on until the *B&Q* roundabout, at which turn right (signposted Pontefract A628). Take next left into Queen's Road, at the end of which you'll find the spacious **visitors' car park** on the right-hand side.

Barnsley Interchange **train station** is served by local trains running between Sheffield and Leeds (half-hourly, journey 30mins from Sheffield, 50mins from Leeds). The station is no more than a 10min walk from Oakwell along Kendray Street and Queen's Road. There are late departures in both directions but no onward connections for London after a midweek game. For the latest timings call ☎0345/484950.

Just the ticket

Ray of light – Oakwell's enclosed viewing gallery for the disabled

Barnsley's plans for developing Oakwell took a back seat to their fight to stay in the Premiership and the construction of a new Football Academy, and **visiting fans** are located in one of the bits that isn't finished – the as yet uncovered Spion Kop, once a vast bank of terracing and now home for around 2,000 away fans – more for cup-ties. Enter via the footpath that runs from the Queen's Road car park and the end of Grove Street. Tickets in 1998/99 were £15, with concessions £9 only if your club offers them to visitors. Oakwell's superb enclosed gallery for **disabled fans** was built in 1986 and is deservedly popular – book early through your own club.

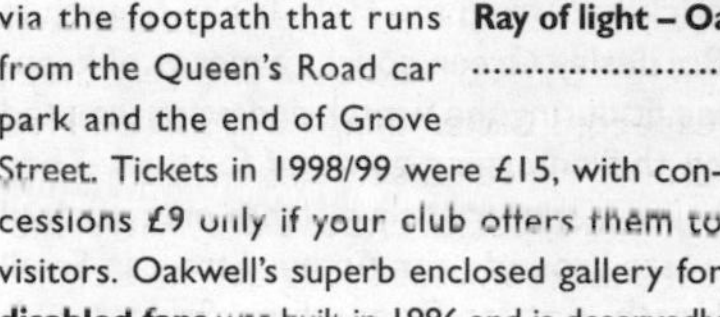

Swift half

Many of Barnsley's town-centre pubs are 'home only' and in any event, police advise against anyone wearing away colours in town either before or after the match. ***The Fealty & Firkin*** on Market Hill welcomes supporters of all hues, as does ***The Outpost*** on Sheffield Road. Best bet for families is ***The Prince Of Wales*** on Eldon Street.

Club merchandise

The ***Reds Superstore*** (open Mon–Fri 9am–5pm and on matchdays until 30mins after whistle, ☎01226/211211) is behind the impressive Ora Stand, the other end of the ground from the Kop. There's also a ***Reds In Town*** store (Mon–Fri 9am–5pm) in the Alhambra shopping centre.

Barmy army

The club has held season-ticket prices for the second successive year since relegation – an indication of how keen the board are to ensure Oakwell attendances don't plummet as they have historically when Barnsley's status has dipped. So far there's little sign of that, and the prevalence of *We'll Be Back* T-shirts during 1998/99 underlined fans' confidence. Trouble is rare inside Oakwell, with any tension likely to surface in town after the game.

In print

The ***Evening Chronicle*** keeps as close an eye on Barnsley's progress today as it did during the great FA Cup run of 1912. Look out for the ***Green'Un*** after the final whistle, with reports from other Yorkshire clubs as well as Barnsley.

Barnsley FC – The Official History 1887-1998 (Yore, £21.95) is as comprehensive as its title suggests and includes graphic detail on the club's sole Premiership season. A more unorthodox book is ***Barnsley: A Study In Football 1953-59*** (Crowberry, £9.99), a tautly drawn, fly-on-the-wall insight into Oakwell's tribulations of the period, with no stone left unturned.

On air

Choose between ***BBC Radio Sheffield*** (88.6 FM) and the independent ***Hallam*** (97.4 FM), both of which also feel obliged to cover the Sheffield clubs in detail. The club has its own matchday station, ***Oakwell 1575 AM***, offering live commentary within a rather restricted radius of the ground.

In the net

The official website is a *Planet*-run affair but, happily, is one of their better efforts, tidily maintained and with a proper fans' forum. Find it at: www.barnsleyfc.co.uk. The first unofficial Barnsley site was *Wilson Is God* (now ***Wilson Is Gon***, for obvious reasons) which features an entertaining section on past Oakwell greats and not-so-greats. Travel back in time to: www.fortunecity.com/wembley/oakwell/142/bfc.htm.

Birmingham City

Formation	1875 as Small Heath Alliance
Stadium	St Andrew's, Birmingham, B9 4NH. ☎0709/111 25837
Ground capacity	30,000
First-choice colours	Blue and white
Major honours	Second Division champions 1893, 1921, 1948, 1955, 1995; League Cup winners 1963; Associate Members' Cup winners 1991, 1995
Position 1998/99	Fourth in First Division (eliminated in play-off semi-finals)

Dozens of senior English football clubs wear blue, but mention of 'the Blues' leads inevitably to only one – Birmingham City. The team have never sported any other colour at St Andrew's, the club's home for nearly a century, and where the PA anthem *Singin' The Blues* is belted out, loud and proud, by thousands of Brummie voices. The lyrics are sung with feeling, and for good reason – the club's story is as melancholy as anything Muddy Waters could have written, a tortured tale of chances half-taken, resources squandered, hopes falsely raised and silverware spurned. Yet still they come, the section of the Birmingham public for whom the club symbolises their city, their background, their life. Forever devoted, forever hopeful. Forever Blue.

The club was formed a year after its city neighbour Aston Villa and, judged from the record books alone, it seems it has been playing catch-up ever since. Happily for Blues fans, it is not as simple as that.

City have enjoyed significant spells of dominance in Birmingham, not least in the late Sixties and early Seventies when Villa were on the brink of oblivion and City were a glamour club *par excellence*. When the team subsequently plunged into the wrong half of the League for the first time, fans displayed greater loyalty than their Villa counterparts had done in similar circumstances. And today, despite Blues' inability (so far) to reach the Premiership, there's a sense of purpose at St Andrew's that's somehow absent from Villa Park, where the players are less consistent and the boardroom regime is less popular.

Like Villa, Birmingham City have their roots in the church. In 1875, a group of cricketers from the Holy Trinity Church in Bordesley Green sought a means of keeping fit during the winter, and were tempted by the emerging game of football. They began playing friendly matches on a patch of waste ground near Arthur Street in Small Heath, not far from where St Andrew's stands today, and formalised their club as the Small Heath Alliance. The team soon acquired the nickname 'Heathens' and in 1877 moved to a ground in Sparkbrook where admission money could be charged. This was quickly outgrown, however, and within months it was back to Small Heath and a field on Muntz Street, rented from the aristocratic Gressey family for the princely sum of £5 a year.

On 27 September 1879, Aston Villa came to Muntz Street for the first-ever derby match between the two clubs. As is so often the case with such occasions, the result has since been thrown into doubt, but contemporary accounts record it as a win for Small Heath by 'one goal and a disputed goal to nil'.

Symbolic though that victory was, there were even more momentous times ahead. In 1885 the club turned professional, with the players receiving half the gate money in lieu of regular wages – the more successful the team, the more people would be drawn to Muntz Street and the fatter the players' pay-packets would be. Three years later Small Heath formed itself into a limited company – the first in England to do so – and dropped the 'Alliance' bit from its name. Such innovations found little favour with the new Football League, however, with Villa (whose idea the League was) ignoring Small Heath's claims to founder membership in favour of the Black Country clubs, Wolverhampton Wanderers and West Bromwich Albion.

Undeterred, Small Heath entered the FA Cup for the first time in 1889, and helped to form a rival league tournament, the Football Alliance, with 11 other clubs – among them two further West Midlands sides, Birmingham St George's and Walsall Town Swifts. They remained there for three seasons until the League decided to admit Alliance members into an expanded, two-division competition. Under the restructuring, three clubs went straight from the Alliance into the First Division of the League but, despite finishing third in 1892, Small Heath were overlooked in favour of the team that had finished just beneath them, Sheffield Wednesday. They then became the first winners of the Second Division title the following year, but failed to gain promotion after losing a test match to their near-namesakes Newton Heath – forerunners of Manchester United. In 1894 Small Heath finally made it up, scoring 103 goals in 28 games to finish as runners-up in the Second Division, and beating Darwen in the resultant test match.

The next ten years were spent floating between the divisions, with forwards Freddie Wheldon and Walter Abbott doing their best to bail out an often shaky defence, and the team proving hard to beat at Muntz Street, where the playing surface was so poor that some of Small Heath's opponents offered them money to swap venues. It wasn't the pitch, however, that persuaded the club to build a new ground for itself in 1906. Muntz Street wasn't equipped to deal with the rising crowds the team were attracting, and thousands of supporters were regularly getting in for free by storming the turnstiles, depriving the club (not to mention the players, of course) of much-needed extra income.

Director Harry Morris relied heavily on the voluntary work of supporters to

Born to be Blue – Trevor Francis, 1973

design and build the club's new home, St Andrew's, on the unpromising site of a former brickworks. But the result was an impressive ground capable of holding 75,000, and built in only ten months – during which time the board approved a name change from Small Heath to Birmingham, in an attempt to broaden the team's appeal. Despite the change, the club never quite managed to sell the place out to capacity, but the turnout of 36,000 for the ground's inaugural fixture, against Middlesbrough on Boxing Day 1906, wasn't bad considering the heavy snowfalls of the day before.

These off-the-pitch advances failed to inspire Birmingham's team, however, and the club endured an extended spell of Second Division football either side of World

War I. Birmingham won the Second Division title in 1921 and, inspired by the dogged goalkeeping of Harry Hibbs and the goalscoring of Joe Bradford, they then remained in the top drawer until the last full season before World War II. While the team never made a credible challenge for the League championship, they did manage a first FA Cup final appearance, against West Brom in 1931 – Blues lost 2–1 despite a heroic performance from Hibbs and a goal from Bradford, now nearing the end of a Birmingham career that would see him amass 267 goals in 445 games.

The team's left-back at Wembley that day, George Liddell, was made first-team manager in 1933 and remained in the post until the outbreak of war. Under Liddell, Birmingham's football became more adventurous and attendances soared, more than 67,000 going through the St Andrew's turnstiles for an FA Cup tie against Everton in 1939. Yet Liddell's strategy was also risky – his constant chopping and changing of the line-up unsettled the players, and just three months after the euphoria of the Everton tie, Birmingham were relegated.

During the war, *Luftwaffe* bombers hit St Andrew's 20 times, the Main Stand and Railway End being destroyed outright, while the roof over the Spion Kop – the largest of its kind in England – collapsed, leaving great lumps of twisted metal and concrete in its wake. Yet out of adversity the club emerged stronger and more optimistic. The board added 'City' to the Birmingham name and authorised rebuilding of the ground to begin as soon as the appropriate materials were available.

In the first FA Cup competition after the war, the team reached the semi-finals, losing only to the eventual winners, Derby County, after a replay. There was a run to the quarter-finals the following year, and a Second Division title in 1948. In contrast to the prewar side, this Birmingham was a more disciplined entity, closely marshalled by manager Harry Storer and containing two outstanding defensive players: left-back Ken Green, who made every tackle look like a well-rehearsed manoeuvre, and goalkeeper Gil Merrick, whose unshakeable self-confidence was as frustrating to opposing forwards as it was reassuring to his own team-mates. In those first three postwar seasons, the newly christened 'City' lost only eight home matches and conceded less than a goal a game – an achievement almost unheard of at the time.

Promotion coincided with Storer's departure, however, and his replacement Bob Brocklebank did not reinforce the Blues' squad sufficiently for life in the top flight. Birmingham were relegated after just two seasons, and there were to be five frustrating years of knocking on promotion's door before the Second Division title was won again in 1955. New manager Arthur Turner had assembled a side every bit as efficient as Storer's, with Trevor Smith a commanding presence in the heart of the defence and Jeff Hall, an immaculate reader of opposition attacks, at right-back. But Turner's team could also move forward with purpose, the momentum generated by an energetic half-back line and brought to a conclusion by eccentric target man Eddy Brown, who would celebrate goals by shaking hands with corner-flags and fire quotes from Shakespeare at journalists after matches.

With Merrick and Green still playing and lending their experience to proceedings, Turner's Birmingham achieved the club's best League finish – sixth in the First Division – in 1956, and reached the FA Cup final, only for their dreams to be shattered by the bravery of Manchester City 'keeper Bert Trautmann; Blues were beaten 3–1.

Birmingham never quite scaled the same heights again. Jeff Hall tragically died from polio in 1959, and Gil Merrick retired a year later after playing 551 games for the club, becoming team manager soon after. City remained a First Division side until the mid-Sixties, and in the meantime beat Villa over two legs to win the League Cup in 1963, inspired by the instinctive playmaking of Jimmy Bloomfield. The club also enjoyed a period in the European limelight, entering the first Inter-Cities Fairs Cup (forerunner of the modern UEFA Cup), and reaching the semi-finals before losing to Barcelona. They were then beaten by the same club in the 1960 final, and by Roma at the same stage a year later. There was time for one more campaign in 1961/62 before the format of the competition was changed to allow clubs from cities not hosting trade fairs to enter – thus depriving Birmingham of a lucrative and character-building annual diversion.

It took City seven years to escape the Second Division after the relegation of 1965, but life had its consolations. For one thing, there was the discovery of the club's most potent strikeforce in years: Trevor Francis, a stylish and deceptively quick forward who made his Birmingham debut at the age of 16, and Bob Latchford, a local lad who was a more conventional but no less skilful goal-poacher. For another thing, Villa's plight was far worse than Blues' – at the time City were winning promotion to the First Division in 1972, their great rivals were only just clambering out of the Third.

Manager Freddie Goodwin, the man Blues fans credited with their club's revival, also took City to two FA Cup semi-finals (the second, in 1975, was lost to Fulham only in the last minute of extra time) and dressed his players in blue shirts with a

Blue hats on Blue days – Birmingham's riot act

Hooliganism came relatively late to **St Andrew's** but, once there, evolved into as dangerous a culture of violence as any in the country, stubbornly refusing to die out until the ground began to be rebuilt.

Feeling down – Roger Wiseman takes a direct hit, 1992

While the team's form didn't help matters, events off the pitch also played a crucial role in fostering City fans' resentment. From the optimism of the **Bullring** and Trevor Francis in the late Sixties, by the mid-Eighties the town was in the grip of post-industrial depression and City were threatened by a merger with Walsall, proposed by despised chairman **Ken Wheldon**. In May 1985, on the same day as the Bradford fire, Blues fans used the St Andrew's pitch as a battlefield for a clash with **Leeds United**'s infamous travelling support. More than 100 police were injured and one fan was killed when a wall collapsed.

Four years later, with the club £3million in debt, about 9,000 City fans descended on **Crystal Palace** to 'celebrate' relegation to the Third Division. Many were in fancy dress, wrong-footing police (and, initially, each other) by meeting up at Crystal Palace athletics stadium rather than Selhurst Park. Once at the match, a section of the visiting support invaded the pitch and, though the sight of Andy Pandy, Father Christmas and (inevitably) the Blues Brothers doing battle with the Metropolitan Police was comical, the resulting bloodshed was anything but.

The last serious incident was in 1992, when City fans, already enraged by the Kumar brothers' misguided card membership scheme, again stormed the St Andrew's pitch during a game against **Stoke**, assaulting referee **Roger Wiseman** and prompting dozens of arrests. Sadly, the animosity between the two clubs simmers to this day.

From takeover to makeover – Sullivan and Brady at St Andrew's

white vertical panel down the front – a style classic that immediately marked Birmingham out as dynamic and different.

Goodwin's departure in 1975 had few immediate effects, but the team gradually lost its way, his successors Willie Bell and Jim Smith unable to inspire the same dedication from either players or supporters. Smith's signing of the outstanding defender Alberto Tarantini from Argentina's 1978 World Cup-winning squad created a bubble of anticipation, but this was swiftly pricked by relegation the following year, after Brian Clough had tempted Trevor Francis to Nottingham Forest by making him Britain's first £1million player. After relegation Tarantini also quit, and Smith's response was to sign a string of seasoned professionals – former Clough acolytes Archie Gemmill and Colin Todd among them – to haul Birmingham straight back up again. With midfielder Alan Curbishley playing the passes and striker Frank Worthington tormenting Second Division defences, Smith's plan worked in the short term. A new wave of talent was also emerging at this time – including goalkeeper Tony Coton, uncompromising defender Mark Dennis, midfielder Kevin Dillon and another Blue who was to die tragically young, winger Ian Handysides. But the old guard moved on before the side could establish itself in the First Division, and before long Smith had gone, too. The arrival of the disciplinarian manager Ron Saunders, 'on the rebound' from Villa in 1982, was just what the youngsters didn't need.

Saunders got Birmingham relegated, promoted, then relegated again, and this time there was no going back. Mass unemployment in the motor industry, which had provided City with the bedrock of their support for decades, was hitting attendances hard and fostering a resentment which would aggravate an already serious hooliganism problem (see panel p.43). The fabric of St Andrew's was visibly crumbling after years of neglect by the club's ruling Coombes family, and a succession of high-profile managers were unable to work miracles with a team comprising tired old pros and untried YTS players. In 1989, Birmingham were relegated to the Third Division for the first time in their history – the darkest Blue day of all.

Salvation appeared to come quickly in the shape of the Kumar brothers, who used cash from their Manchester-based retail empire to buy out the previous board at the turn of the Nineties. The Kumars, however, had built their businesses on loans guaranteed by the *BCCI* banking group, and when the latter went belly-up after a fraud scandal in 1992, Birmingham City nearly went with it. At the end of the year the club was in receivership, threatening the slender progress the team had made in managing to climb out of the old Third Division – and winning the Leyland Daf Cup at Wembley – under the management of Terry Cooper.

In early March 1993 Blues fans woke to the news that David Sullivan, proprietor of the *Sunday Sport* newspaper and a premium-rate sex line business that had made him one of the 100 richest men in Britain, had bought a controlling interest in City from the receivers. As if that news wasn't stunning enough, Sullivan then appointed former glamour model Karren Brady as the club's managing director, and brought in the Gold brothers, millionaire owners of the *Ann Summers* chain of sex shops, as co-directors. After a sticky start in which Brady had a much-publicised liaison with City striker Paul Peschisolido (who she later married after he was transferred from St Andrew's) and the team were relegated again, the fans began to warm to their unlikely new masters.

The Gold brothers, reasoning that football fans were no different from sex-shop punters in wanting amenable surroundings in which to spend their money, pressed ahead with plans to rebuild the Kop and Tilton Road stands, regardless of Birmingham's League position. And Brady's choice as manager, Barry Fry, delivered both the Second Division title and the Auto Windscreens Shield in 1995.

At the end of the 1995/96 season, as Fry's management style became increasingly haphazard, Sullivan dispensed with his services and appointed Trevor Francis in his place. Francis' record as a manager was chequered (dressing-room spats at QPR, regular jaunts to Wembley with Sheffield Wednesday), but as far as Blues fans were concerned, this was the return of the prodigal son.

So it has proved – up to a point. Though it took him a while to sift through the huge squad bequeathed to him by Fry, who had bought and sold 61 players in three years at the helm, Francis gradually imposed himself, taking City to within one goal of the play-off zone in 1998, and to a consistent spot in those positions for most of 1998/99. Once in the play-offs, however, City allowed themselves to be muscled out of their passing game by Watford, and went out on penalties in an emotional semi-final second leg at St Andrew's.

Afterwards, Francis admitted he was 'very depressed' while Brady calculated that the club's continued absence from the Premiership was costing City a potential doubling of annual turnover. The two have since agreed that the manager should have a new long-term contract, and with the new Railway Stand opening in 1999, a resourceful and richly talented squad, and supporters who are starting to believe once again, the top flight may not have to wait much longer. That is only as it should be – these Blues deserve to finish the millennium on a high note.

Here we go!

Small Heath is about a mile east of the centre of Birmingham. **Motorists** should approach on the M6 motorway and exit at Junction 6 (Spaghetti Junction) onto the A38(M) Aston Expressway, toward the city centre. Leave at the second exit off the Expressway, then take the first exit off the roundabout onto Dartmouth Middleway. St Andrew's Street is a turning on the left after a mile or so, but **car parking** at the ground itself and in the surrounding streets can be tricky, so you may want to leave at an earlier roundabout to park up.

The nearest **train station** is Birmingham New Street (see Aston Villa for connections), a 20min walk away via the Bullring (currently in the process of being redeveloped) and Digbeth. If you get lost in the rabbit warren of underpasses in front of the station, follow signs for Digbeth and you can't go too far wrong. The ground is visible from the Bordesley Circus roundabout at the end of the High Street.

Just the ticket

Visiting fans are accommodated in the superb new Railway Stand, opened by Jasper Carrott (but don't let that put you off) in March 1999. Around half the 8,000 seats are allocated to visitors, with a separate galleried area for families. Ticket prices in 1998/99 were adults £14, concessions £8. Matches at St Andrew's are never all-ticket, but concessions *must* be booked in advance through the visiting club.

Disabled visitors have a few spaces in the Main Stand – booking essential on ☎0709/111 25837, ext 247.

Swift half

Police advise against drinking in the pubs close to St Andrew's, so the best bet is to buy a few tins from an off-licence and head for a BYO balti house for supper. The ***Birmingham Internet Balti Guide*** (see *In The Net* below) recommends, among others, the ***Lazzat Kadah*** at 592 Coventry Road in Small Heath, close to St Andrew's, and the ***Shama*** at 17 Moseley Road in Digbeth, between the ground and New Street station.

Bear in mind that authentic balti houses are often very small and could not accommodate huge groups of football supporters, even if they wanted to. Be discreet and respectful of their traditions – your tastebuds will thank you for it.

Club merchandise

The St Andrew's **club shop** (open Mon–Sat 9.30am–5.30pm, later on matchdays, ☎0709/111 25837, ext 8) is behind the new Kop Stand in Cattell Road. There's also a **city centre shop** in Dale End (open Mon–Sat 9am–5.30pm, ☎0121/212 0873). Both sell a wide range of good-looking leisurewear from *Le Coq Sportif*, but the company's latest shirt design for 1999/2000, which attempts another revival of the vertical white facing (which staged an earlier comeback three years ago) but adds narrow blue stripes into the mixture, has not proved popular with fans – some say it reminds them of West Brom.

The club is hoping to re-negotiate its kit supply contract so that it can have more say over future designs. Quite right too.

Barmy army

Anyone who hasn't visited St Andrew's for a while would be amazed at the transformation. Not only has the ground now been three-quarters rebuilt, but the whole surrounding area has been given a facelift as part of an inner-city regeneration plan. The result has been a long-overdue softening of the hooligan element which plagued Birmingham for years (see panel p.43), but trouble does occasionally resurface, particularly at Midlands derbies.

Tears before bedtime – St Andrew's, May 1999

In print

The ***Birmingham Post*** and ***Evening Mail*** offer good coverage of City six days a week. After the final whistle on Saturdays, the ***Sports Argus*** carries match reports on all West Midlands teams – normally available around St Andrew's from 6pm.

City's ground-breaking fanzine ***Tired And Weary***, which campaigned fearlessly through the neglect of the late Eighties and early Nineties, is sadly no more. Look out instead for ***Wake Up Blue***, ***The Zulu*** and ***Singin' The Blues***.

The best City history books are currently out of print, but there's always ***Good As Gold***, the story of the Gold brothers' rise to fame and-fortune (£9.95), and ***Brady Plays The Blues*** (£14.99), the MD's diary of the 1994/95 season. Ms Brady has also penned a couple of football novels, ***Trophy Wives*** and ***United!*** – but Booker Prize nominees can rest easy in their beds.

On air

BBC Radio WM (95.6 FM) tends to cycle through the local sides in its matchday coverage, while commercial ***X-tra AM*** (1152 AM) is more likely to offer live commentary on a single game – sometimes City's.

In the net

City's **official website** is typical *Planet* fare, with plenty of *RealAudio* interviews and commentary (plus an unusually solid news service and archive) but no real insight into the club. Keep your plug-ins primed for: www.bcfc.co.uk.

The most appealing of the unofficial sites is ***A View From The Tilton***, which has the 'alternative' feel many fan-run sites aim for but also delivers on up-to-date content Star features are the *Birmingham Balti Guide* (see *Swift Half* above) and a link to the *Internet Football Ground Guide* run by the same webmaster, Duncan Adams. Find him at: dspace.dial.pipex.com/town/park/yfh45/index.html.

Blackburn Rovers

Formation	1875
Stadium	Ewood Park, Blackburn, BB2 4JF. ☎01254/698888
Ground capacity	31,300
First-choice colours	Blue-and-white halved shirts
Major honours	League champions 1912, 1914, 1995; Second Division champions 1939; Third Division champions 1975; FA Cup winners 1884, 1885, 1886, 1890, 1891, 1928; Full Members' Cup winners 1987
Position 1998/99	19th in Premiership (relegated)

Before Blackburn's penultimate home game of 1998/99 against Nottingham Forest, the club's multi-millionaire owner, Jack Walker, made an impassioned plea to fans to get behind the team in their hour of need. A victory would do wonders for Rovers' chances of saving their Premiership bacon. A draw would be bad news. A defeat would be a disaster. Blackburn lost, 2–1, to a sde that had already been relegated. And Rovers' own relegation was confirmed four days later, when they failed to beat Manchester United at Ewood Park.

Walker's appeal was, perhaps, an understandable reaction. After all, he had sunk more than merely a sizeable chunk of his personal fortune into Blackburn Rovers. The loss of Premiership status would not only hit his wallet but hurt his pride, for this is the club he supported from the terraces as a boy. In helping to raise Rovers from mid-League mediocrity to the very pinnacle of the English game, Walker had been engaged not in a business investment but in a personal crusade. Now the heart that had driven that crusade was aching, and he wanted the fans to show their hearts were aching, too.

Heartfelt appeal – Walker addresses the fans

Yet the question remains – why did he deem the appeal necessary? At any other club, such a gripping end to the season would be enough to whip up a frenzy of support, whether the issue was 'Lancashire's Premier Pride' or survival in the Football League itself. What gave Rovers' owner cause to feel that Ewood Park would be quiet, on this day of all days?

Cynics would say the answer lies in the large number of latter-day converts to the Rovers cause – the fans who stayed away when the chips were down in the Eighties, but who have since helped to triple Ewood Park's average gate from 8,000 to 24,000. These supporters, the theory goes, don't have hearts as big as Jack Walker's. (They also don't have his dosh, but that's another

Familiar pose – Simon Garner, Rovers' record goalscorer

story.) When relegation loomed, they were not kept awake at night by the imminent death of a footballing dream. They would see it more as the end of a fun few years, and maybe stick to the shopping mall next season – unless Manchester United should happen to pay a visit, of course.

In reality, if the atmosphere at Ewood Park wasn't all it might have been at times last term, it had little to do with the commitment of the fans, and more to do with that of the players they were paying good money to come and watch. After the defeat by Forest, Rovers manager Brian Kidd raged publicly at the indifferent attitude of some of his squad. Lack of application was totally unacceptable, to manager, supporters and millionaire benefactor alike.

Such is the price, however, of trying to acquire footballing prosperity through use of the cheque-book alone. In the short term, money probably can buy love – there was no lack of pride or passion about the Blackburn side Kenny Dalglish led to the Premiership title in 1995. Yet as Kidd discovered when he arrived at Ewood Park three-and-a-half-years later, there were too many players whose contracts contained get-out clauses enabling them to move on should Rovers be relegated. As the pressure mounted, their loyalty seemed to be increasingly to themselves, rather than to the club. Pulling on that famous blue-and-white halved shirt no longer made them feel special – and on the pitch, it showed.

Such ambivalence is an insult to Rovers fans of whatever vintage, whether their allegiance dates back to the 1992 play-off final or through seven decades, as Jack Walker's does. For even the most recent of Blackburn's admirers is dimly aware that the shirt symbolises nearly 120 years of professional football, and a history which legitimately portrays Rovers not just as one of the leading lights in the development of the game, but as perhaps its first true dominant force.

The Football League wasn't so much as a twinkle in the eye of Aston Villa director William McGregor when Rovers first saw the light of day in November 1875. The club was brought into existence at a meeting in the town's *St Leger Hotel*, at which the prime movers were John Lewis and Arthur Constantine. Both were prominent figures in the local community – though Lewis, a God-fearing Special Constable, was originally from Market Drayton in Shropshire – and since many of the new club's members were ex-public schoolboys who'd been introduced to football in their youth, they chose the colours of Malvern School, Cambridge blue and white halves, as the uniform of their team.

Rovers played their first fixture as guests of the neighbouring Church club on 11 December, and drew 1–1. Between that game and the summer of 1876 they played all matches away from home, until a field with a drainage pool in the middle of it (covered with turf laid on planks for matches) became available at the appopriately named location of Oozehead, on

Preston New Road. A year later they moved on to the more promising surroundings of Pleasington Cricket Ground, and from there to another cricket field at Alexandra Meadows, where crowds soon topped 6,000 and would have been higher still if so many hadn't been able to watch for free from the neighbouring hills.

Football had become so popular so quickly in this corner of the north-west that a rival club, Blackburn Olympic, was formed in 1878. Both Blackburn sides entered the FA Cup for the first time the following year, and in 1880 Rovers turned professional. With players' wages to be paid for, the club couldn't afford any more freeloaders among its fan base, and in October 1881 moved to a completely enclosed ground on Leamington Road.

It was from Leamington Road that Rovers launched their first great FA Cup run, becoming the first club from the north to challenge the supremacy of the southern public-school sides by reaching the final in March 1882. Although they lost that game at the Oval, 1–0 to the Old Etonians, and rivals Olympic beat the same opponents 2–1 to lift the Cup the following year, Rovers would not be denied their moment of glory for long.

On 29 March 1884, they were back at the Oval to face Queen's Park in the final. Scottish and Irish clubs regularly entered the FA Cup at this time and the Glasgow side arrived in London with a big reputation for their flowing football. Rovers, however, had a brilliant playmaker of their own in Jim Forrest, and he was the decisive influence in a 2–1 win.

The two sides met again the following year when Rovers won more comfortably, 2–0, and in 1886 they held West Bromwich Albion to a goalless draw at the Oval before completing their hat-trick of Cup wins with a 2–0 victory in a replay at the Baseball Ground, Derby.

In 1888, when William McGregor decided to invite a number of clubs to discussions about the formation of a Football League, the name Blackburn Rovers simply couldn't be ignored. The team played their first League game at home to Accrington on 15 September 1888, drawing 5–5 with two goals from centre-forward William Townley. They finished the season in fourth place, and the following year, with Forrest still pulling the midfield strings, beat Sheffield Wednesday 6–1 to lift the FA Cup for the fourth time, Townley becoming the first player to score a Cup final hat-trick. A 3–1 win over Notts County made it five FA Cups, and provided a fitting end to an 1890/91 season which had seen Rovers inaugurate yet another new ground, this time at Ewood Park.

It could be argued that after their final house move Blackburn never quite enjoyed the same dominant position over the English game. Yet while the turn of the century was indeed a quiet time at Ewood Park, the side that emerged toward the end of the Edwardian era was probably more gifted than the Cup-hogging version. World

The title at Anfield – Dalglish (centre) is in his element

War I may have been approaching, but football was a far more competitive business than it had been in Blackburn's earlier heyday when right-back Bob Crompton led the club to a first League championship in 1912, and to a second two years later. Crompton, who would go on to be capped 41 times by England (a remarkable figure given how few internationals the English played at the time), had joined Rovers in 1896 and would go on playing through the outbreak of war, before retiring in 1916 with more than 500 League appearances to his name. A professional plumber who possessed a formidable bulk, Crompton chose not to go in too hard in the tackle, preferring a game based on anticipation that was way ahead of its time.

While Crompton's was the key influence on the pitch, Rovers' inspiration off it came from a local textile magnate, the aptly named Laurence Cotton, who had become club chairman in 1905 and spent thousands on both upgrading Ewood Park and improving the squad. Thanks to Cotton's cash, Rovers consolidated after their first title win by doubling the British transfer record to buy centre-forward Danny Shea from West Ham for £2,000. Shea would prove as crucial to the 1914 championship in attack as Crompton was in defence, scoring 27 of Blackburn's 78 goals.

Rovers finished third in 1914/15, the last full season before the war, and never really recovered their momentum once peace had returned. Laurence Cotton died in 1921, and as the textile industry out of which both he and the town had built their riches declined, so Blackburn's influence on the English game declined with it. The prolific goalscoring of Ted Harper kept the team respectably in mid-table in the First Division, and in 1928, with Bob Crompton now manager as well as a director, Rovers managed one more FA Cup triumph, beating Huddersfield Town 2–1 at Wembley.

In 1936, the club lost top-flight status for the first time. Promotion was attained when Crompton resumed management duties on the eve of World War II, but war again disrupted Rovers' flow, and they were down again by 1948. This time they would spend a decade playing Second Division football, not all of it unattractive, especially once Johnny Carey had taken over as manager in 1953, and encouraged fresh talents such as wing-half Ronnie Clayton and striker Tommy Briggs. Four years later Blackburn were back in the top flight, and in 1960 they managed an FA Cup final appearance – albeit one destined for disaster once maverick striker Derek Dougan handed in a transfer request on the eve of the match. Rovers lost 3–0 to Wolves.

Dougan's main complaint had been unimaginative coaching, and Cup final defeat was the signal for change at Ewood Park. Under the inventive management of Jack Marshall, Blackburn spent the first half of the Sixties in the First Division, with young defenders Mike England and Keith Newton making national headlines. Locally, though, Marshall's side were very much in the shadow of the great Manchester United and Burnley teams of the era, and few in Lancashire were surprised when Rovers were relegated in 1966. The drop did not seem too serious at the time, yet it was to herald the beginning of a malaise which would all but wipe the club off the map over the next two decades. In 1971 Rovers tasted life in the Third Division for the first time, after a brief but disastrous return to the manager's chair by Carey. Gordon Lee got them back up as champions in 1975, only to then leave for Newcastle.

Another relegation in 1979 saw the appointment of Howard Kendall as player-manager. Like Lee he concentrated on the less glamorous aspects of the game, assembling a no-nonsense defence in which Glenn Keeley and Derek Fazackerley were key components, while giving the midfield anchor role to Tony Parkes and handing Duncan Mackenzie, like Kendall enjoying his last years as a player in the lower half of the League, free rein upfront. Kendall's Rovers won the Third Divsion title at the first time of asking and, though he would soon be tempted away by Everton, his

The stand that Jack's steel built – a new Ewood Park rises under the lights, 1993

legacy would prove more lasting than Lee's. Sadly, fewer and fewer members of the Blackburn public seemed interested. Economic recession was exacting a heavy toll on the local community and as the cotton mills shut one by one, so Ewood Park crowds declined, too. In 1984 part of the ground was gutted after an arson attack, and two years later, the arrival of Wimbledon for a League Cup tie only just managed to lure 2,000 souls through the turnstiles.

Rovers began to turn the corner in 1987, when chairman Bill Fox replaced long-serving manager Bobby Saxton with the genial Scot, Don Mackay. With Tony Parkes as his assistant, Mackay knew the first priority was to reclaim popular suppport. He had little money for big-name signings, yet managed to persuade the likes of Frank Stapleton, Steve Archibald and (briefly) Ossie Ardiles to play out the twilight of their careers at Ewood Park, while also getting the best out of long-serving Rovers stars such as midfielder Nicky Reid and striker Simon Garner.

Meanwhile, Fox asked a friend of his in the steel business, Jack Walker, to donate the metalwork needed for a new Riverside Stand. This Walker duly did, and the stand was named after his company, *WalkerSteel*.

By 1990, Blackburn had managed three fifth-place finishes on the spin, always threatening to get back into the First Division but never quite managing it, losing in the play-off semi-finals each time. More significantly for the future of the club, however, 1990 also saw Jack Walker's company, which was still a family business, being sold to *British Steel* for £350million.

In January 1991, Walker acquired a majority stake in Rovers – though he turned down the chance to be chairman and even refused a seat on the board. What he did demand was a say in who to appoint as manager. In September 1991, Walker edged Mackay out, replacing him with Kenny Dalglish, the former Liverpool manager who'd been working on his golf handicap since walking out on Anfield earlier in the year.

With a sprinkling of astute signings (striker Mike Newell, re-signed stopper Colin Hendry and midfielder Tim Sherwood), Dalglish's team looked certain to go up automatically for much of the campaign, only for a late loss of form to force them to enter the play-offs once again. They needed a disputed penalty against Leicester at Wembley to haul them up.

Once in the newly formed Premiership, however, there was no stopping either

A Rover for a decade – Jason Wilcox

Dalglish or Walker. Blackburn broke the British transfer record to buy Southampton striker Alan Shearer for £3.3million, while full-back Graeme Le Saux and wingers Stuart Ripley and Kevin Gallacher were among the other new arrivals. A fourth-place finish, for a side that scored more goals than any other in that first Premiership season, was no more than Rovers deserved.

The team's expansive style owed much to Dalglish's time at Anfield – a flat back-four, solid but also mobile and superbly marshalled by Hendry, coupled with a midfield that used the full width of the pitch and an attack that needed only the faintest whiff of goal. For the first time in two generations, Blackburn were going places.

But how far, exactly? In 1993/94, with David Batty added to the midfield mix, Rovers mounted a late surge for the title but failed to unseat Manchester United. Second place got the club into Europe for the first time in its history, but as the 1994/95 campaign got under way, defeat by the unknown Swedish side Trelleborgs in the UEFA Cup first round seemed like a bad omen. It was anything but. With new £5million signing Chris Sutton giving Shearer additional space upfront, Blackburn were irrepressible in the Premiership. They went into their last game at Liverpool knowing that victory would secure the title. They lost, 2–1, but Manchester United's inability to beat West Ham the same day meant the championship was heading for Ewood Park for the first time in 83 years.

With almost indecent haste, Dalglish announced his intention to become 'director of football' (was he running away from the pressure again, as at Anfield?), while his assistant Ray Harford took over day-to-day management. Without Dalglish's vital European experience, a disastrous Champions' League debut ensued, and although Rovers finished a reasonable seventh in the Premiership, they couldn't resist the £15million Newcastle offered for Shearer in the summer of 1996.

In October that year, with Blackburn toiling at the wrong end of the table, Harford was removed and Tony Parkes took temporary charge, while Walker, convinced his club needed a coach with top European credentials, tried to tempt Sven Göran Eriksson up to Ewood. When Eriksson demurred, Walker plumped for Roy Hodgson, who'd just taken Inter Milan to the UEFA Cup final. Hodgson's impact was immediate – Rovers were a breath of fresh air in the Premiership of 1997/98, playing smart, confident football and heading back into Europe with a sixth-place finish.

In the summer of 1998, Hodgson lavished £7.5million on the untried striker Kevin Davies, while simultaneously allowing the talismanic Hendry to move to Rangers. Uncertain in front of goal, vulnerable in defence, torn apart by injuries, Blackburn rather unluckily went out of the UEFA Cup to Lyon – and nosedived in the Premiership. In November 1998, Hodgson departed after some well-publicised differences of opinion with his captain Sherwood, and while his successor Brian

Kidd did more than £20million of transfer business (including the sale of the restless Sherwood and the purchase of promising forward Matt Jansen), Rovers finished the season as a ragbag of individuals who appeared to deserve their fate. With Gallacher and Jason Wilcox (a survivor of the Mackay era) still onboard, youngsters like Damien Duff and £10million in the bank from the sale of Sutton, Blackburn were optimistic in the summer of 1999. Jack Walker's faith will not waver, but then, he has the club running through his blood. How many of his players can say the same?

Here we go!

Most **motorists** will approach on the newly completed M65. Exit at junction 4 onto the A666 Bolton Road. Turn right into Kidder Street after about a mile and a half for the ground. There are various secure **car parks** around Ewood Park.

Blackburn **train station** is on the cross-country line from Leeds to Blackpool (hourly, journey time 1hr 30mins from Leeds), and also has direct trains from Manchester via Bolton. You can get back to Leeds or Manchester after an evening game, but there are no late connections for London. Check times on ☎0345/484950.

The station is a fair hike from Ewood Park but any Darwen-bound service from the adjacent bus station will drop you off along the Bolton Road, a 2min walk from the ground.

Just the ticket

Visiting fans are located in either the upper or lower tier of the Darwen End. Ticket prices are adults £18, concessions £10. **Disabled visitors** have spaces in front of this stand – book in advance ☎01254/263794.

Swift half

You can get a pint at the ground but the nearby pubs are more atmospheric and welcome visiting fans. Try ***The Fernhurst*** on Bolton Road or ***The Fox & Hounds*** on Ewood Triangle, the latter possibly a better bet for families.

Club merchandise

Rovers' shirt is a design classic, of course, though the shade of blue used has changed quite a bit over the years. The original Cambridge blue was revived in the late Eighties, and Blackburn won promotion to the Premiership wearing cobalt – the *WalkerSteel* house colour. See the latest shade, along with *G+D* (for *Gallacher + Duff* – no, honestly) branded leisurewear at the **club shop** (open Mon–Sat 9.30am–5.30pm, later on matchdays) behind the Blackburn Stand, opposite the Darwen End.

Barmy army

The arsonist has put his matches away and there's been no serious trouble at Ewood Park for a long time… Now what were we saying about a lack of passion?

In print

The ***Lancashire Evening Telegraph*** previews fixtures with a Saturday lunchtime edition and also covers Burnley. Its more locally focused stablemate is the ***Blackburn Citizen***.

There were two fanzines at the last count: ***4000 Holes*** (PO Box 609, Ribchester, PR3 3YT) and ***Loadsamoney*** (44 Tiverton Drive, Blackburn, BB2 4NR).

For the full story of the club up until 1995 try ***Blackburn Rovers – An Illustrated History*** by Mike Hackman (Breedon, £14.99).

On air

Blackburn was the first club in England to have its own radio station, ***Radio Rovers*** (1413 AM), which broadcasts on matchdays within a ten-mile radius of Ewood. Alternatively try ***BBC Radio Lancashire*** (95.5 FM).

In the net

The **official website** *They Think It's All Rovers* (formerly *Park Life*) boasts innovative graphic design, excellent links and a cool e-commerce section. Above all, though, it actually belongs to Blackburn, rather than an outside company. See for yourself at: www.rovers.co.uk/.

There's a vibrant Rovers fan culture spread right across the globe, though two of the best sites are locally maintained. **Jeff Whitfield**'s site has impressive stats and history archives at: www.blackburn.demon.co.uk/brfc.html. And **Lee Grooby** has a nice, busy, newsy offering at: www.brfc-supporters.org.uk/.

Blackpool

Formation	1887
Stadium	Bloomfield Road, Blackpool, FY1 6JJ. ☎01253/405331
Ground capacity	11,250
First-choice colours	Tangerine and white
Major honours	Second Division champions 1930; FA Cup winners 1953; Anglo-Italian Cup winners 1971
Position 1998/99	14th in Second Division

A few weeks shy of his 84th birthday, Stanley Matthews returned to Wembley to be given an *AXA*-sponsored FA Cup Legends Award – the first man to receive one. The award itself was of little consequence but, as the star of one of the immortal FA Cup finals – and one of the most famous matches ever to be played at the stadium, in any competition – it was fitting that Matthews should be nominated for it.

At the ceremony, Matthews was reunited with two other surviving members of the Blackpool side that came back from 3–1 down to beat Bolton 4–3 in 1953, Cyril Davidson and Bill Perry. But as well as recalling the events of that sunny Saturday afternoon 46 years ago, the great man also looked forward to the rebuilding of Wembley, and gave nostalgia short shrift.

'Of course the Twin Towers have got to go,' Matthews told reporters. 'But the most important thing is that Wembley is still Wembley, the position is still there, the stadium is still there. If you played Cup finals in Manchester or Birmingham it wouldn't be the same. They wouldn't have the atmosphere.'

If that is true of Wembley, is it also true of Bloomfield Road, the arena where Matthews and his contemporaries first made the tangerine shirts of Blackpool FC famous? Again, it seems nostalgia will have no part to play. Blackpool have been trying to escape their old ground for much of the Nineties, to a greenfield site on the edge of town that can accommodate not just a new football stadium but a vast new retail and commercial development, including a hotel, conference facilities and a concert hall.

Like Wembley, however, Blackpool's proposed new home at Wyndyke Farm has been fraught with contractual haggles, planning disputes, and all the attendant grim publicity that such problems generate. For the past four seasons, stop-start negotiations over the site have overshadowed events on the pitch – adversely affecting the team's performance, some say.

In describing the plight of their club, Blackpool fans often make reference to events at Bournemouth and Brighton earlier in the decade. The comparisons are easy to draw, given Blackpool's seaside location and the team's inability to draw large support from transient elements in the town's population – a headache these Seasiders share with their South Coast equivalents. In other key respects, though, Blackpool is very different. The club's owners, the Oyston family, have pumped millions into keeping Bloomfield Road open for business since saving Blackpool from bankruptcy in 1987. If they were going to asset-strip the club, as Brighton's directors attempted to do, they'd have started long ago. As for the consortium that has spent the last year or two trying to buy the Oystons out (on the back, it must be said, of a well-orchestrated media campaign), they derive a position of strength from owning the land the Oystons want to build on, but concede that if Blackpool's planning applications are finally rejected, then the whole deal is off. In other words, no new arena, no takeover – hardly the 'Community Football Club' spirit shown at Bournemouth.

Much of the momentum behind Blackpool's move was lost when Owen Oyston, minor media baron and self-styled socialist

Beaten at the byline – Stanley Matthews (left) gets the better of the Bolton defence, 1953

millionaire, was jailed for rape in 1996. Unable to conduct business while at Her Majesty's Pleasure, he has confined himself to issuing statements from his prison cell while his wife Vicki, son Karl and associate Gill Bridge have kept the club solvent by the well-trod Nineties route of expanding commercial activities.

Bloomfield Road, alas, becomes steadily more decrepit with each passing season, the club paying only for essential safety work to be carried out while the real money goes into pursuing the new stadium. The barriers are rusting, the advertising boards fading, and half the famous old Kop is closed altogether, probably for good. Attendances hover around the 5,000 mark – enough to make a decent noise, but not enough to put any cash in the bank.

It's a far and increasingly bitter cry from the club's heyday in the Forties and Fifties, when 30,000 would pack into the ground (12,000 on the Kop alone) for the visit of the English game's elite clubs – and see them beaten in style. The excitement was all the more feverish because, unlike near neighbours such as Blackburn, Burnley and Preston, Blackpool had never approached such heights before. The club was officially formed only a year before the foundation of the Football League, while top-flight football didn't arrive until the Thirties.

The game was played in the town from an early stage, however. Victoria FC, the club to which historians normally trace Blackpool's roots, started out in 1877 as a church club with a ground in Caunce Street. Within a few years the team had disbanded, but some of its members are believed to have then joined forces with old boys from St John's School to form a new club, Blackpool St John's. The different factions were never properly united, though, and in 1887, at a meeting in the *Stanley Arms*, members resolved to wind up their club and start a new one under the less parochial name of Blackpool FC.

A year later Blackpool became founder members of the Lancashire League, playing at a ground inside the Victorian pleasure park of Raikes Hall Gardens. Two years after the team had won the Lancashire title for the first time in 1894, Blackpool became a limited company and made a successful application to join the Second Division of the Football League.

Sunny by the sea – Blackpool get ready to bounce back from the Second Division, 1968

Within three years, however, Blackpool were booted out after finishing third from bottom of the Second Division. The club's League status had failed to capture the local imagination in the way the board had envisaged, partly because a rival club, South Shore, was attracting a following of its own. At the end of 1899 the two clubs decided to merge, taking Blackpool's name but using South Shore's ground at Bloomfield Road. Months later Blackpool were re-elected to the League.

Crowds at the club's new home were still modest but at least the team were able to consolidate their position in the middle of the Second Division table. Blackpool plodded anonymously on until the outbreak of World War I, when fire destroyed Bloomfield Road's only stand of note, prompting a rebuilding programme that would eventually result in the ground being constructed along the lines visitors see today. On the pitch, though, the team continued to tread water through to the early Twenties, their solid, fuss-free football illuminated by the occasional character, such as inside-forward George Mee, who played 195 consecutive matches to set a club record that stands to this day, and full-back Peter Fairhurst, who paid the ultimate price for his courage, going into a coma after heading a rain-soaked ball in a League match, and later dying in hospital.

In 1923, the board appointed Major Frank Buckley as team manager and, though he was unable to get Blackpool promoted before departing for Wolves four years later, his contribution to the club was immense. It was Buckley who dressed the players in tangerine for the first time, instituted a proper youth system, and invested greater resources in Blackpool's scouting network – all initiatives that would serve the club well for decades to come. One of Buckley's last contributions at Blackpool was the signing of Jimmy Hampson, an energetic centre-forward who came from Nelson for a moderate £2,000. Once at Blackpool, Hampson scored 31 goals in his first full season, 1927/28, then 40 the following year and 45 the year after that, the last enough to bring the Second Division title to Bloomfield Road. Blackpool struggled in their first spell in the top flight, but

Hampson kept on scoring, netting 32 times in 1930/31 and making his England debut the same season. He would go on to score 247 goals in 360 games for Blackpool, and would almost certainly have enjoyed a post-war career had he not drowned while on a fishing trip off Fleetwood in January 1938. His body was never found.

The team were in the First Division at the time of the Hampson tragedy, but there had been another spell in the next drawer down after relegation in 1933, with promotion not achieved again for another four years. Even with Major Buckley's scouts performing miracles and money coming in from a series of transfers, Blackpool were still striving to shake off their reputation for mediocrity as World War II loomed.

Strangely, almost uniquely among English senior clubs, Blackpool were to find the war an invigorating experience. Bloomfield Road was used as a training ground by the RAF, who established a major base in the town. This brought many pilots and other RAF personnel to Blackpool who had been professional footballers in peacetime. Thus, when 'Blackpool' won an English wartime championship by beating Arsenal 4–2 in 1943, their team contained 'guest' players who were on the books of Bolton, Leeds, Tottenham and Hearts – and an effortlessly skilful outside-right from Stoke by the name of Stanley Matthews.

Two years after the war, Matthews was happy to sign for Blackpool after the club had offered Stoke £11,000 for his signature. The price was low but Matthews was already 32 and, in the opinion of many critics, past his prime. How wrong they were. Matthews' obsession with physical fitness – rare among English footballers at the time – had ensured he was as fast down the flank as he'd been when first capped by England 13 years earlier. At Blackpool, he quickly struck up a rapport with centre-forward Stan Mortensen, either crossing early or holding the ball up before beating his full-back to deliver the killer pass.

Together with players such as full-back Eddie Shimwell, captain Harry Johnston and centre-half Eric Hayward, and managed by the extrovert, cigar-toting Joe Smith, Matthews and Mortensen took Blackpool to their first FA Cup final in 1948. There they were unlucky to meet Matt Busby's Manchester United at their hungriest, but still put up a decent fight before conceding two late goals to lose 4–2.

Three years later Blackpool were back at Wembley for a second Cup final, with a side enhanced by the addition of Jackie Mudie and Bill Perry to its forward line. They were well-beaten by Jackie Milburn's Newcastle, but Matthews was unbowed. 'There's always next year,' he said, without a trace of irony. Actually, it was to be another two years befor Blackpool lined up against Bolton for what will forever be known as the 'Matthews final'. Nat Lofthouse put Bolton ahead with a mis-hit shot as early as the second minute, and after an hour in which Matthews, now 38, had scarcely touched the ball, they were 3–1 up. Sparking into life as if he had suddenly realised this really was his last chance of a Cup-winner's medal, Matthews then embarked on a series of his trademark dribbles down the right flank, crossing for

No cell-out – the pre-prison Owen Oyston

Mortensen to pull one back, then laying on a string of further chances before Mortensen, completing the first Cup final hat-trick at Wembley, equalised direct from a free-kick with a minute to go.

Bolton were beaten now, physically and mentally, and they offered scant resistance when, deep into stoppage time, Matthews danced his way down to the byline and pulled the ball back, not for the tightly marked Mortensen but for the South African, Perry, to fire home unstoppably.

It was a fairytale ending to the match, but Matthews' Blackpool career was far from over. In 1956 the team finished as runners-up to Manchester United in the League (albeit 11 points adrift), and there were four more top-half finishes before Stoke called him back in 1961.

Manager Smith had also moved on in 1958, but his successor Ronnie Stuart oversaw a period of sustained if unspectacular stability. While never really threatening to win anything, Blackpool continued to produce accomplished players including Tommy Hutchison, Gordon Milne, Tony Green and the masterful full-back Jimmy Armfield.

Brilliant at the back – skipper Tony Butler

However, with the exception of Armfield, who would go on to make a record 568 appearances for the club, these players tended to produce their best football after leaving Bloomfield Road.

When World Cup-winning midfielder Alan Ball moved to Everton for a British record £112,000 in 1966, Blackpool had made a sale too far. A year later they finished bottom of the First Division and were relegated, prompting Stan Mortensen to move into the manager's chair, with Harry Johnston as his assistant. They failed to get the team promoted, but laid a decent foundation for Les Shannon and Bob Stokoe to build on. Blackpool were back in the First Division by 1970.

Within a year they'd finished bottom again, however, after winning only four games all season – and this time there was to be no return. The Seventies were characterised by upper-to-mid-table finishes in the Second Division, further outgoing transfers and steadily dwindling support. A boardroom coup resulted in another of Blackpool's postwar heroes, Allan Brown, taking charge as manager, and he seemed to be settling in well before walking out midway through the 1977/78 season. His departure proved a turning point – the team went from promotion contenders to relegation material within months, and while they completed their fixtures early and went on a post-season tour of America, a freak combination of results saw them dropping to the Third Division *in absentia*.

By the start of the Nineties Blackpool had fallen further to the Fourth Division, but they were promoted back up again via the play-offs in 1992, and only an unlikely comeback by Bradford City prevented another play-off final appearance in 1996.

Nigel Worthington succeeded Gary Megson as manager after the latter was poached by Stockport in 1997, but his lot is a familiar one – plenty of young talent, but not enough money to keep them once they have matured. Meanwhile, Bloomfield Road is in not so much a Tangerine dream, more a red rage.

Here we go!

Motorists have an easy time of it once they've negotiated the traffic on the M62 or M6. Exit the M6 at Junction 32 onto the M55, and follow this to its end. Follow signs for the town's main car parks along Blackpool's new 'spine' road, the A5230 Yeadon Way. Go straight on at the first roundabout and at two mini-roundabouts – you'll see a large car park in front of you at the end of Seaside Way, with the ground on your right.

This being Blackpool, the **car parks** are cheaper in winter – less than £1 a day, in fact.

The town has two **train stations**. Blackpool North is the end stop on a line plied by direct services from Manchester, Preston, York, Leeds and Bradford; Blackpool South is one stop from the end of the same line, but not all trains call here.

Fans coming from London or the Midlands should change at Preston, which has stopping trains for Blackpool South every hour (journey time 25mins). Call ☎0345/484950 for the latest timings.

Blackpool South is a 5min walk from the ground – you'll see the floodlights from the top of the bridge. Blackpool North is nearly 2miles away – take bus #22 or #22A from the adjacent bus station to Bloomfield Road.

Just the ticket

Visiting fans are accommodated in the Kop, the end nearest Blackpool Tower. As well as being partially out-of-bounds for safety reasons, the Kop is now roofless and can be extremely bleak in winter – umbrellas and/or warm clothing essential.

For games against bigger visiting sides, additional space is opened up in the adjacent East Paddock. Ticket prices in 1998/99 were adults £10, concessions £5.

Disabled visitors have a few spaces in the West Stand – booking not normally necessary.

Swift half

The pub nearest the ground, the ***Bloomfield*** on Bloomfield Road, welcomes away fans but can get very busy. There's a huge range of both eating and drinking options along the seafront, so long as you don't mind plastic decor and – in some cases – plastic glasses, too.

Club merchandise

The **club shop** (open Mon–Sat 9am–5.30pm, later on matchdays, ☎01253/405331) is behind the South Stand – entrance in Bloomfield Road. Blackpool have recently opened another store on Church Street in the town centre. Both outlets sell a small but perfectly formed range of goods, with those distinctive tangerine shirts at £36.95 (kids' sizes £26.95) and – very appropriately, given the winter weather at the ground – some tasteful heavy jackets.

Barmy army

Blackpool fans are generally a peace-loving lot, yet the town is a hooliganism black spot. Fans from other clubs descend on the seafront after watching matches elsewhere in the north-west, and combine with off-season tourists, stag-party weekenders and nightclubbers to create a potent cocktail of violence and visits to casualty.

That said, plenty of visiting supporters have a perfectly wonderful weekend away here – any trouble is easy enough to avoid.

In print

Local paper the ***West Lancashire Evening Gazette*** has been vitriolic in its criticism of the Oystons. For once, you may get a more balanced few from the fanzines – ***Another View From The Tower*** (PO Box 106, Sale, Cheshire, M33 7AA) and ***Do I Like Tangerine*** (89 South Park, Lytham, FY8 4QU).

For the ultimate book on the Matthews Cup run, look no further than Gerry Wolstenholme's ***Cup Kings – Blackpool 1953*** (Bluecoat, £21).

On air

Both ***BBC Radio Lancashire*** (103.9 FM) and ***Red Rose Radio*** (999 AM) manage a fair amount of Blackpool programming in a corner of the country crowded with senior clubs.

In the net

Blackpool's **official website** is a tidy affair, smartly laid out and well-organised with an excellent history, a news archive and a wide range of links. Find it at: www.blackpoolfc.co.uk. Most impressive of the unofficial sites is the huge ***Seasiders.net*** which plugs any gaps the official one may have left Head for: www.seasiders.net.

Bolton Wanderers

Formation	1874 as Christ Church FC
Stadium	Reebok Stadium, Burnden Way, Lostock, Bolton, BL6 6JW. ☎01204/673673
Ground capacity	25,000
First-choice colours	White shirts, navy-blue shorts
Major honours	First Division champions 1997; Second Division champions 1909, 1978; Third Division champions 1973; FA Cup winners 1923, 1926, 1929, 1958; Associate Members' Cup winners 1989
Position 1998/99	Sixth in First Division (beaten play-off finalists)

Founder members of the Football League, in the vanguard of the fight to legalise professionalism, participants in the first-ever Wembley Cup final and pioneers in the rush to build new stadia in the Nineties, Bolton Wanderers are living proof that, in football, a willingness to innovate is not enough. As the fans trooped away from the Twin Towers following Bolton's 2–0 play-off final defeat by Watford in May 1999, the obvious question for them to ask was: where did we go wrong? The side had been playing decent football all season, clearly feared nobody in the First Division and looked, too all intents and purposes, like Premiership material. But Bolton have looked this good before, perhaps better, and still not quite delivered the goods. Both their Nineties excursions into the top flight have ended after a single season and, for all that the Reebok Stadium is an impressive piece of engineering and design, the club itself looks no better equipped for the elite than it did in the days of Burnden Park.

None of this is really Bolton's fault. Like so many other great footballing names from the north-west, their reputation soared in an earlier, simpler era, and began to diminish with the abolition of the maximum wage in 1961. Since then it's been a case of muddling along on the fringes, with a tradition of spectacular Cup giant-killing – and often, it must be said, admirable football – ensuring that the mass media still have some space for the Wanderers, even if Manchester United are on the doorstep.

If following Bolton over the past few years has been a distinctly bittersweet experience, then the same could be said for much of their history. The club has courted trouble of one kind or another for most of its 125-year existence – even, in fact, in the days before it was known as Bolton Wanderers.

It began life, in fact, as the football club of Christ Church in Blackburn Street, Bolton, where the Sunday school teacher, Thomas Ogden, decided to form a team for some of his pupils to play the newly popular game in 1874. The club's president was the Vicar of Christ Church, and once he had given his blessing, as it were, to the club following a trial match in July of that year, the team began playing regularly, first at the Park Recreation Ground and subsequently at Cockle's Field on Pike's Lane.

After a while, though, it became clear that the church and the football club would have to go their separate ways. The Vicar kept changing his mind about which premises members could use for meetings, and in 1877 a large number of them broke away to form a new club, which they named Bolton Wanderers to commemorate their long search for a permanent headquarters. They were by no means the only footballing attraction in the town at the time, but with a new base at the *Gladstone Hotel* and the recruitment of a handful of Scottish players with greater tactical awareness, Wanderers soon became the team to watch. In 1880 they turned professional (those Scots needed some

The eyes don't have it – Eidur Gudjohnsen can't believe Bolton have blown it, Wembley, 1999

incentive to move south, after all) and a year later they moved to a more enclosed ground in Pike's Lane, where gate money could be charged for the first time. Alas, Bolton's desire to pay players landed them in trouble with the FA, to whom the idea of anyone playing the game for profit was still anathema. Bolton reasoned that if a club was attracting paying customers at the gate, it should be allowed to reward players out of the proceeds – and that paying players directly made more sense than arranging full-time work for them elsewhere, as had been the previous practice. The row rumbled on for years, and it wasn't until the FA finally legitimised professionalism in 1885 that the club was in the clear.

Wanderers had entered the FA Cup for the first time in 1882, and in Bolton as elsewhere the competition proved immensely popular with the public – hence the necessity to keep on the right side of the FA. Still, the club's stand on professionalism had caught the eye of Aston Villa director William McGregor, who numbered Bolton among the clubs to be invited to the first meetings formulating the new Football League. Wanderers duly became founder members and played their first League game at Pike's Lane on 8 September 1888, losing 6–3 to Derby County.

Bolton finished that first League season in fifth place and reached the FA Cup semi-finals a year later. But like many of the early League pioneers, they were very nearly victims of their own success. With gates rising as high as 20,000 at the turn of the 1890s, the landlord at Pike's Lane increased the club's rent every year, until Wanderers reached the point where it made more sense to strike out on their own and build a new ground for themselves. This ground would be Burnden Park, and to finance its construction the club turned itself into a limited company in 1895. The team played their first game there on 11 September that year, but there were more problems ahead – notably with the pitch, which was prone to flooding and had to be relaid with a pronounced slope to aid drainage, and with hooliganism, which almost caused Bolton to be thrown out of the FA (again) before the 19th century was out. Still, former club secretary J J Bentley, a prime mover in the fight for professionalism, was now president of the

Lostock and barrel – it may not quite be in Bolton but 'the Reebok' is a sight for sore eyes

Football League and helped to ensure that the ground was used for major events aside from Bolton games, including the FA Cup final replay between Sheffield United and Tottenham in 1901.

So much for the ground – what of the team? Bolton had reached their first Cup final in 1894, losing 4–1 to Notts County in front of 37,000 at Anfield. They were to reach another ten years later, losing 1–0 to the Manchester City side that would subsequently be investigated (and severely punished) for match-fixing. City's pain was of no comfort to Bolton, for not only was the Cup final result allowed to stand, but Wanderers were also relegated the same year, for the second of what would be three brief spells of football outside the First Division in the years prior to World War I.

Greater glories, however, would come to Bolton after the war. On 28 April 1923, Wanderers and West Ham United were paired to meet in the Cup final – the first to be played inside the newly built 'Empire Stadium' at Wembley. The organisers knew there would be huge interest in the game (and in the venue), but nothing prepared them for the heaving mass of humanity, a quarter of a million strong, that descended on north-west London in the hope of seeing the game. While 126,000 fans passed legitimately through the turnstiles, it's estimated that between 70,000 and 100,000 more probably 'rushed' their way in past hopelessly inadequate barriers.

Enormous though it was, the crowd was essentially good-natured and it was this, coupled with the famous appearance of a policeman on a white horse and the arrival of the King, that prevented serious injury (or worse) in the crush. The match kicked-off 40 minutes late, but Bolton made up for lost time by taking the lead after two minutes through inside-forward David Jack. After half-time, the referee awarded Wanderers a second goal after John Smith's shot appeared to go in before bouncing back out of the netting. Contemporary match reports described Bolton's 2–0 win as 'the most unsatisfactory match ever decided in the history of the competition', such was the frequency with which the crowd encroached onto the pitch.

But Bolton didn't care, and nor should they have, for they would soon prove that the West Ham result was no freak. Three years later Jack was again on target, as Wanderers gained belated revenge over Manchester City with a 1–0 win to take the Cup for a second time. As before, Jack and his fellow inside-forward Joe Smith were the team's key performers, ably supported from the flanks by the long-serving Ted Vizard.

Controversially, Jack was then sold to Arsenal in October 1928, the first player in Britain to be transferred for more than £10,000. Burnden Park was being extensively rebuilt at the time and fans complained that the club was more interested in having a nice, neat ground than a good team. Yet at the end of the 1928/29 season, with six survivors from the 1926 Cup-winning side and a magnificent display from the injured Dick Pym in goal, Wanderers beat Portsmouth 2–0 at Wembley. That made it three FA Cups in seven years.

Relegation followed in 1933 but the club's veteran manager Charles Foweraker, in his job since the end of World War I, refused to be panicked. Bolton were back up within two years, continuing their Cup fighting tradition along the way. World War II saw the end of Foweraker's reign but the club was in a stronger position than many in the immediate postwar period. Bolton's run in the first FA Cup competition after the war, however, is remembered for all the wrong reasons. In March 1946, thirty-three people lost their lives at Burnden Park when barriers collapsed under the weight of a huge crowd that had gathered for the Cup visit of Stoke City – Britain's worst football tragedy until the Ibrox disaster of 1971.

It took a while for the club to recover from its sense of loss, but after the appointment of Bill Ridding as manager in 1951, Wanderers became quite a force in the First Division. While many of the most enduring qualities in Ridding's line-up were defensive, it did possess a matchless personality in attack by the name of Nat Lofthouse.

A compact, muscular centre-forward who was born in Bolton in 1925 and signed schoolboy forms with the club on the eve of World War II, Lofthouse had already made his England debut by the time Ridding arrived at Burnden Park. In 1952, his battling performance in England's 3–2 win over Austria earned him the nickname 'Lion Of Vienna', but Bolton fans would remember him best for his role in the club's two postwar FA Cup finals.

In 1953, it was Lofthouse's snap-shot that opened the scoring for Bolton against Blackpool after just 75 seconds – an aspect of the 'Matthews Cup final' often overlooked in retrospect, given the dramatic way in which Wanderers were to throw away their 3–1 lead before losing 4–3.

Perhaps there was an element of professional jealousy about it, but when Bolton again reached the Cup final five years later,

A man who never left Bolton – Nat Lofthouse

Sideline smirks – Rioch and Todd, 1993

Lofthouse was determined not to be edged out of the limelight again. He and manager Ridding told the Wanderers players to ignore the wave of sentimental feeling whipped up by the media for their opponents, Manchester United, who had been decimated by the Munich air crash. Again, Lofthouse was quickest out of the blocks, stabbing the ball home after only three minutes. Bolton expected a backlash, but it never came. After 57 minutes, United 'keeper Harry Gregg fumbled the ball and Lofthouse, jumping with him as he tried to gather at the second attempt, bundled both ball and goalkeeper over the line. Referee Sherlock saw no clue as to any wrongdoing, and gave a goal without hesitation. Bolton had won the Cup for the first time in nearly 30 years.

Two years later Lofthouse retired, his knees and ankles riddled with injuries picked up from opposition tackles. But he refused to leave Burnden Park, becoming reserve-team coach even though the job description included cleaning boots and sweeping the floors. Bill Ridding remained in charge, but without his inspirational captain was unable to motivate Bolton in the same way. The team flirted with relegation for a couple of seasons before finally dropping down in 1964. Ridding soldiered on for another four years, but with young talents such as Francis Lee and Wyn Davies being sold to pay mounting bills, couldn't win promotion. In 1968 Nat Lofthouse stepped into the breach. He would later declare he was 'the worst manager in the world', though even after he resigned in 1970, he would serve two stints as caretaker boss as first Jimmy McIlroy and then Jimmy Meadows made quick departures from the manager's seat. The latter's reign ended with relegation to the Third Division, but two years later Bolton bounced back under Jimmy Armfield, and when Ian Greaves took over from Armfield in 1974, the revival continued.

With a side in which the young Peter Reid and experienced Roy Greaves were the perfect combination in midfield, Bolton won the Second Division title in 1978. At the time they were reckoned a better prospect than the two sides that came up with them, Spurs and Southampton. But while those two clubs were building on a firm financial base, Ian Greaves' Bolton had succeeded despite a chronic lack of cash. Within two years they were down again, and this time they were in for an even longer fall – all the way to the Fourth Division by 1988.

Bolton were in good company – Wolves, Burnley and Sheffield United were among the other great clubs from England's industrial heartland languishing in the wrong half of the League during the mid-Eighties. Yet none of those took the drastic step Wanderers had been forced to take in 1986, when half the Railway End of Burnden was sold to a supermarket chain, effectively cutting the old ground's spectator areas in two. Nat Lofthouse, now back at the club in an administrative role after a brief absence in the Seventies, must have wept at the sight.

While the superstore paid off the club's overdraft, Phil Neal got Bolton straight out of the Fourth Division as player-manager. Neal's team were efficient rather than extravagant, but had come close to a second promotion on a number of occasions before the former Liverpool and England full-back made way for Bruce Rioch and his assistant Colin Todd in 1992. The new regime put the emphasis firmly on attack and, with Tony Philliskirk leading the line, Bolton won immediate promotion to what had become the First Division. There the progress continued, as Rioch and Todd got the best from youngsters such as stopper Alan Stubbs and playmaker Jason McAteer, along with an array of goalscoring talent that included Owen Coyle, Andy Walker and John McGinlay.

In 1994 Bolton reached the FA Cup quarter-finals after beating Arsenal and Aston Villa, and a year later there were two visits to Wembley. The first was for a League Cup final meeting with Liverpool, at which Wanderers were unlucky to find Steve McManaman on a particularly inspired day. The second was for a promotion play-off final, won 4–3 thanks to a spirited fightback against Reading.

Bolton were in the Premiership, but they were there without Rioch, who'd been tempted away by Arsenal. His replacement Roy McFarland lasted only half of the 1995/96 season before being dismissed in favour of Colin Todd, who was powerless to prevent the club from finishing bottom of the table.

Relegation had not been part of the board's plans when Bolton signed up to build a new multi-purpose stadium as part of an out-of-town leisure complex in Lostock in 1995 – the very year that Burnden Park was celebrating its centenary. So it was vital that as work on the stadium got under way, Todd's team gained immediate promotion back to the elite. This they duly did, ending the 1996/97 season as First Division champions and scoring 100 goals in the process.

Sportswear company *Reebok*, a local firm with a global outlook, agreed to sponsor the new stadium in addition to Bolton's shirts, giving what was now a £35million project a vital additional source of income. Yet while the arena itself was beautifully designed in both practical and aesthetic

Villa killers – (from left) Lee, Patterson, Stubbs and McAteer celebrate a Cup upset, 1994

terms, it failed to inspire Todd's injury-hit squad until it was too late – five wins in the last ten games wasn't enough to prevent another instant relegation, this time on goal difference from a mightily relieved Everton.

With no instant promotion this time, Wanderers' millennium season looked set to tell fans a lot about their club. Could Todd's squad of expressive youngsters and cheap Scandinavian imports bounce back from their Wembley disaster? And if not, would it be another case of Bolton having a handsome ground, but not enough good players to complete the picture?

Here we go!

The Reebok is one of those new arenas sited deliberately next to a motorway junction. **Motorists** need simply exit the M61 at junction 6, follow the A6027 Burnden Way, and the ground is on the left. The visitors' **car park** (£5) at the ground is the only realistic option unless you like a long hike from a bleak industrial estate.

A **railway line** runs right past the stadium but plans for a 'Reebok Halt' are still on the drawing board. In the meantime, the local Lostock station is served only by stopping trains from Bolton, from where you may be better off catching a shuttle bus.

Bolton station is served by direct trains from Manchester – change there for all other destinations, but don't expect late connections for evening games. Double-check on ☎0345/484950.

Just the ticket

Visiting fans are housed in the South Stand, where ticket prices in 1998/99 were upper tier adults £17, lower tier £14, concessions £11 in both areas. There's space for 5,000 fans in all and few games are all-ticket.

Disabled visitors enjoy excellent facilities in the South Stand – booking is essential on ☎01204/673601.

Swift half

The chain pubs and restaurants on modern retail complexes are often suspicious of visiting fans and those around the Reebok are no exception. The best bet, therefore, is to have a pie and a pint **inside the ground**, where the quality is fine and prices are not too high, either.

Club merchandise

As you'd expect from a club so closely associated with its kit manufacturer (*Reebok*), the Bolton **club shop** at the stadium has a vast range of well-designed if rather heavily branded leisurewear. To its credit, though, the store also stocks *TOFFS* vintage replicas of Forties, Fifties and Sixties shirts.

Barmy army

The hooliganism that got Bolton into trouble in the late 19th century was still plaguing Burnden Park on and off 100 years later. Since the move to the Reebok, however, the atmosphere has calmed considerably.

In print

The ***Manchester Evening News*** gets its Saturday evening *Pink* to Bolton at around 6pm.

The fanzines are ***White Love*** (PO Box 150, Bolton, BL2 1GY) and ***Tripe 'n' Trotters*** (Bolton Enterprise Centre, Washington Street, Bolton, BL3 5EY), while the essential book about the club is ***The Trotters – The Concise Post-War History Of Bolton Wanderers*** by Ivan Ponting and Barry J Hugman.

On air

Bolton is lucky enough to get a choice of two local BBC stations: ***GMR*** (95.1 FM) and ***BBC Radio Lancashire*** (103.9 FM).

In the net

Bolton's **official website** is run by *Planet Internet* but is one of the company's more complete efforts, with a particularly full historical archive containing an extensive A-to-Z of past players, along with the usual news, multi-media and e-commerce areas. It's at: www.bwfc.co.uk/.

On the unofficial side, ***Wandering On The Web*** has a nice light-hearted feel to it at: www.netcomuk.co.uk/~cjw/football.html. Two other sites should be worth a look after being rebuilt during the summer of 1999. ***Wanderers Web*** is at www.wanderersweb.freeserve.co.uk/; while the ***Tripe 'n' Trotters*** fanzine is online at: pages.eidosnet.co.uk/~danny.nuttall/index.html.

Bournemouth

Formation	1899 as Boscombe FC
Stadium	Dean Court, Bournemouth, BH7 7AF. ☎01202/397777
Ground capacity	11,000
First-choice colours	Red-and-black stripes
Major honours	Third Division champions 1987; Associate Members' Cup winners 1984
Position 1998/99	Seventh in Second Division

After watching their side escape relegation from the Second Division in a season when they'd entered the Christmas period with only nine points to their name, followers of AFC Bournemouth referred to the drama as *The Great Escape*. Little did they know that within 18 months, their club would be called upon to perform a Houdini Act every bit as spectacular and, in its own way, even more terrifying. This time it wasn't just a question of status; the very future of professional football in Bournemouth was at stake. At one stage, the club was five minutes from being wound-up, with the Inland Revenue, Customs & Excise and Lloyd's Bank owed an estimated £2million between them – not so much *The Great Escape*, more like *Mission Impossible*.

Tree's a crowd – Dean Court's Cherry Orchard in winter

Of course, Bournemouth were not wound-up. But they certainly would have been, were it not for an extraordinary life-saving campaign mounted by fans between January and June 1997, when the town was alive with fund-raising auctions, celebrity matches, concerts, sponsored cycle rides and cake-stalls (this is Bournemouth, remember). From the word go, however, the fans wanted to do more than simply bail the club out – they wanted to take it over, lock, stock and cider barrel.

In the summer of 1997, after a rescue package had been put together and agreed by the official receivers, the club was reborn as AFC Bournemouth Community Football Club – the only one of its kind in Britain, or Europe for that matter. A club run by the people of Bournemouth, for the people of Bournemouth. A red revolution, for the team they call the Cherries, played out against a social and political backdrop that couldn't be a truer shade of blue.

In a sense, it was about time something exciting happened to Bournemouth, a side whose first 70 years of football were almost irretrievably dull. Not for the good denizens of Dean Court was there to be anything as gripping as a run to the semi-finals of the FA Cup, as diverting as a long search for a new home, or as sordid as a spell outside the League. Once the club had been elected to the Third Division of the Football League in 1923, it stayed there – for longer than anyone else in history.

There was at least a whiff of change in the air on the eve of the club's admission to the League. At a meeting in the *Portman*

Hotel public house, where the players used to get changed, it was suggested that the club change its name to reflect its new position in the game's national hierarchy.

The new name, Bournemouth & Boscombe Athletic, didn't exactly trip off the tongue. But prior to 1923 the club had been known simply as Boscombe FC, after the district (historically smarter than Bournemouth) in which it was situated. Members wanted to incorporate 'Bournemouth' into the name to encourage wider support, while at the same time retaining the loyalty of the existing fan base. Even in those days, it seems, local football fans had a knack for happy compromise...

Boscombe FC, themselves formed in 1899 from the ashes of the Boscombe St John's Institute club, had quickly emerged as the main soccer event in town. In 1910, a Mr J E Cooper-Dean granted the club a long lease on some waste ground next to King's Park – this would become Dean Court in honour of the benefactor. The same year, Boscombe signed their first professional player from Southampton for £10.

In 1920, the club turned fully professional and entered the Southern League, from which entry to the Third Division (South) of the Football League was almost a formality. The team struggled there at first, finishing second from bottom at the end of their first season. Once they'd got the measure of the competition, however, Bournemouth settled in for the long haul, with centre-forward Ronnie Eyre arriving from Sheffield Wednesday to cure the side's goal-shyness.

Eyre left in 1933, having scored more than 200 League goals, and several of the team's older players departed with him. The youngsters they left behind finished sixth in 1937 – Bournemouth's best League placing thus far. To celebrate the achievement, manager Charlie Bell took his players on a tour of Holland, where they were unlucky to lose 1–0 to the Dutch national side. Within two years, sadly, many of those players would be called up by the military as World War II enveloped the continent – and Bell's squad was cut down in its prime.

The club recovered quickly, though. Harry Lowe's side were runners-up in the Third Division (South) of 1947/48 – not enough for promotion but a fair reward to a team known for defensive solidity, if not always flair. Yet Lowe failed to turn that side into champions, and by 1955, the board admitted the club was in serious financial trouble at its AGM.

A star in stripes – Ted MacDougall stoops to conquer Walsall at Fellows Park, 1971

Bournemouth needed somebody to fire the public imagination, and in new manager Freddie Cox they had just the man. Cox hurled a bunch of local kids into the first team, and told them to go out and attack. A stirring FA Cup run in 1956/57 saw Swindon Town, Wolves and Spurs all beaten, before Manchester United's 'Busby Babes' escaped from Dean Court with a 2–1 win, courtesy of one goal from a suspiciously offside position and another from a controversial penalty – almost 29,000 roared their disapproval.

Cox was poached by Portsmouth in 1958, and without him the team managed decent League finishes without ever quite looking the part. He returned to Dean Court in 1965, but the magic had gone. In 1969 Cox signed the predatory Scottish striker Ted MacDougall from York City, but his impact was minimal initially – the team began the Seventies by being relegated to the Fourth Division for the first time, on goal average.

Cox then made way for a thoroughly modern manager, John Bond. Persuaded by MacDougall to sign his old striking partner from York, Phil Boyer, Bond built a team whose attacking power was always too strong for the division. Bournemouth were promoted at the first attempt, with MacDougall scoring 49 goals – including six in one game against non-League Oxford City, a new FA Cup scoring record.

Neither manager nor goalscorer were done just yet. In 1971, the club changed its name to AFC Bournemouth and adopted a red-and-black striped kit inspired by AC Milan. It was a brilliant PR move, and the media's attention was snared with the writing of another chapter in the 'SuperMac' legend, MacDougall surpassing his own record by scoring nine times in an 11–0 FA Cup win over Margate. The TV cameras became regulars for League games at Dean Court, too, as Bournemouth were drawn into an entertaining three-way battle for promotion to the Second Division. Crowds of 20,000 or more jostled among the trees for a view of Bond's dazzlers.

Favourite son – Mel Machin, Mr Motivator

Ultimately, though, media and public alike were disappointed – Bournemouth lost out to the other two promotion contenders, Aston Villa and Brighton, and MacDougall was sold to Manchester United for £200,000.

Bond followed him out in 1973, to take charge of Norwich City. The TV crews packed their vans and the vast majority of fans drifted away with them. Before long Bournemouth were back playing in front of 3,000 after relegation to the Fourth Division in 1975. They still looked like Milan, but Dean Court was as far removed from the San Siro as it was possible to imagine.

Alec Stock restored some pride to the club in the late Seventies before David Webb pushed Bournemouth back up into the Third Division following a 17-game unbeaten run in 1982. The next two years were eventful if not particularly productive. Webb was dismissed and replaced by Harry Redknapp as caretaker-manager, before Don Megson took over full-time. Megson brought an overweight George Best to Dean Court to consolidate Bournemouth's Third Division status, but by the start of the 1983/84 season both men had gone, and Redknapp was back in charge. His team beat Manchester United 2–0 in the FA Cup third round, and became the first winners of the Associate Members' Cup. The manager's eye for a bargain saw the signing of defender Paul Morrell, midfielder Sean O'Driscoll and target man Trevor Aylott – three men experienced enough to take Bournemouth into the Second Division for the first time in their history in 1987, after winning the Third Divsion title with a record 97 points.

In 1988 Redknapp made some more smart signings, bringing Ian Bishop, Luther Blissett, Shaun Teale and John Bond's son Kevin (for a second spell) to the club. The team finished 12th in 1989 (the club's best-ever League position), but a year later, despite the emergence of Harry Redknapp's son Jamie, a last-day defeat at home to Leeds consigned them to relegation.

Redknapp quit in 1992, and his successor, Tony Pulis, had few resources to work with. Bournemouth lost all seven of their opening games in 1994/95 and, with five clubs being relegated that season due to League reorganisation, the team seemed doomed to drop when Mel Machin – scorer of one of Bournemouth's other goals against Margate all those years ago – took over just before Christmas. What followed wasn't just a *Great Escape*, sealed with a last-day win over Shrewsbury; it marked a sea change in Bournemouth's outlook, with Machin putting the emphasis on young players who were cheap to buy, open to ideas and hungry for success.

By Christmas 1996, however, the full extent of Bournemouth's problems was becoming evident. As at so many other lower-division sides, the board had been concealing the scale of the club's debt in the hope that a run of form on the pitch would bring the money flooding back in. They resigned *en masse* in early 1997, but there were still six months of frantic fund-raising and negotiating to be done before Bournemouth could be sure their 3,000th League game at the end of the season was not their last.

In the close season Manchester United came to Dean Court for a friendly to help the cause, and there were no complaints about the refereeing this time. Trevor Watkins, the local solicitor who had set up a Trust Committee to co-ordinate the club's rescue, became chairman of the reconstituted Bournemouth and immediately threw his weight behind Machin and his assistant John Williams. Some 34,000 fans made the trip to Wembley for the 1998 Auto Windscreens final against Grimsby, and although that game was lost and the play-offs were just missed for the second time in a row in 1999, the team was looking in rude health.

The debts are still huge, however, and Watkins must find a way of drawing more of that 34,000 to League football on a regular basis. Perhaps a new 'community stadium', which the club plans to build on the site of Dean Court, will do the trick.

Here we go!

Most **motorists** will approach Bournemouth (or rather, Boscombe) from the A31 at Ringwood, having either come along the A338 via Salisbury (from the north/M4) or the M27/M3 via Southampton (from the north-east and east). Just beyond Ringwood, exit the A31 at the Ashley Heath interchange, signposted A338 Bournemouth. Follow this into the outskirts of Bournemouth, over the Cooper-Dean flyover, then get in the left-hand lane, go up a slight incline and take the first left. At the mini-roundabout take the second exit into King's Park, which is where Dean Court is located.

The club **car park** is first left but if you miss it, there's a council-owned one just after. Both charge £1.

The nearest **train station** is Pokesdown, served only by local trains between Bournemouth Central and Southampton. Long-distance trains (direct services to London Waterloo, Reading, Birmingham and Manchester, call ☎0345/484950 for the latest timings) will deposit you at Bournemouth Central where you can change. If no local train is imminent, catch bus #25, #33 or #68 from the stop on the bridge over the railway line – ask the driver for the *Queen's Park* pub, a 5min walk from the ground.

From Pokesdown station, turn right and take the first right into Gloucester Road. This leads into King's Park and the floodlights should be visible on the left. Allow 15mins.

Just the ticket

Visiting fans are housed in the Brighton Beach end, so-called not because it's by the sea but because it's built on a stony bank (they're proud of their sand down here). Alternatively, there are some visitors' seats in Block A of the adjacent Main Stand – enter through turnstile #25. Ticket prices in 1998/99 varied according to the match, and whether sitting or standing – between £8.50 and £15, concessions around half that. The club has dramatically improved its facilities for **disabled fans** with 30 spaces now available in front of the South Stand – book in advance on ☎01202/395381.

Swift half

The ***Portman*** on the corner of Ashley Road and Tower Road is where the club adopted the name Bournemouth & Boscombe Athletic in 1923. You no longer run the risk of bumping into a player fitting his jock-strap, and the local Eldridge Pope ales are fine. To get there, walk through King's Park and over the railway bridge.

Back at the ground, the AFC Bournemouth ***Supporters' Club*** is listed in the *Good Beer Guide* and welcomes visiting fans (guest admission £1 – book well in advance on ☎01202/398313). The Club is behind the South Stand and serves good **food** on matchdays.

Club merchandise

Bournemouth's ***Red & Black Shack*** (open matchdays 12.30–3pm and after the game) offers a range of items made specifically to raise funds for the Trust, including a *Pick Of The Cherries* video featuring actor Buster Merryfield and a CD of the new club anthem *We're Here To Stay*. Luckily, the Trust also accepts straight cash donations.

Barmy army

Bournemouth's hardcore support makes a lot of noise, goes on a lot of sponsored walks and bakes exceedingly good cakes. They showed admirable restraint in May 1990 when, as well as seeing their team relegated, they also saw their town smashed up, burned and looted by Leeds fans 'celebrating' promotion.

In print

The fanzine ***Community Service*** (Ground Floor Flat, 2 Heron Drive, Green Lanes, London, N4 2FX) tries to offer an alternative perspective, but don't expect criticism of the board.

Speaking of which, Trevor Watkins' book ***Cherries In The Red*** (Headline, £16.99) offers an insight into how an 'ordinary' fan – though Watkins is far from being one of those – helped to save his club and ended up being chairman.

On air

BBC Radio Solent (96.1 FM) devotes a lot of airtime to Southampton but is worth a listen.

In the net

The fan-run **official website** is a joy to behold at: www.afcb.co.uk. No nonsense, just a friendly, efficiently maintained site that puts many Premiership offerings to shame. Then again, can you imagine a Premiership club giving fans the chance to view the accounts, read the programme's contents for free, or send an e-mail greeting to the chairman? The original Bournemouth site is **Ray Brown**'s offering at www.maths.soton.ac.uk/rpb/AFCB.html, while **Dave Rose**'s site, at www.homeusers.prestel.co.uk/rose220/afcb1.htm, contains fine history and memorabilia areas.

Cup upset – Mark Stein leads Wolves a merry dance, 1998

Bradford City

Formation	1903
Stadium	Valley Parade, Bradford, BD8 7DY. ☎01274/773355
Ground capacity	18,000
First-choice colours	Claret and amber stripes
Major honours	Second Division champions 1908; Third Division champions 1985; Third Division (North) champions 1929; FA Cup winners 1911
Position 1998/99	Second in First Division (promoted to Premiership)

Stuart McCall spent the evening of 11 May 1985 driving from Bradford to Pinderfields Hospital in Wakefield, 15 miles away. He was wearing his Bradford City kit under his club blazer. With him in the car was his brother, Les. McCall remembers the drive as the longest of his life – he and Les were looking for their father, in the hours after the Valley Parade fire.

With the rest of the family accounted for, they'd gone first to Bradford Royal Hospital, only to be told that those who had suffered the most serious burns had been transferred to Wakefield. Andy McCall had been a professional footballer himself, a winger in the great postwar Blackpool side of Mortensen and Matthews. Now here he was, in the special burns unit at Pinderfields, his hands and head heavily bandaged, his face so thickly covered with ointment as to render it unrecognisable.

A few days later, Stuart McCall returned to the ward to show his father and the dozen or so other patients the Third Division trophy whose capture Bradford City should have been celebrating on 11 May. He had thought twice about doing so, aware of how crassly insignificant a piece of silverware might seem against a backdrop of intense human tragedy. Yet the sight of the trophy had a remarkable effect, bringing the victims together, reminding them of the common cause which had brought them all to Valley Parade on that fateful afternoon – to share in what was then City's finest hour in the modern era.

After that, McCall resolved to bring top-flight football to Valley Parade, not for himself but for the supporters who had suffered so much – either because they counted friends or relatives among the 56 people who died in the fire, or because of the trauma they'd suffered simply by being there. Yet it was to be 14 years before McCall fulfilled his promise, playing in the 3–2 win at Wolves which guaranteed City promotion to the Premiership in May 1999.

During those 14 years, the Main Stand – and much else at Valley Parade – had been rebuilt, the club had gained two new chairmen, and McCall had become a Scottish international, playing the best years of his career at Everton and Rangers, before returning 'home' to City in 1998. Yet, while the club's resilience in the face of suffering received its just reward with the 1999 promotion, the full story of City's return to the elite after decades of obscurity is more remarkable still.

The club's heyday, in the years leading up to World War I, was the culmination of a rapid rise to prominence. Bradford had been a hotbed of rugby, and one of the local sides, Manningham, became founder members of the Northern Union in 1895. They enjoyed a few fairly successful years playing at their Valley Parade ground, but gradually diversified into other sports. Archery was particularly popular by 1903, and it was while shooting arrows that members hit on the idea of playing football as a more lucrative alternative to rugby. The Football League, keen to establish their game in the West Riding of Yorkshire, cynically admitted Manningham's proposed soccer side, Bradford City AFC, before it had kicked a ball.

City won the Second Division title within five years thanks to the potent goalscoring trio of George Handley, James McDonald and Frank O'Rourke. Off the pitch, however, things were still in a state of chaos. The club had been formed into a limited company following mounting losses in 1908, while a year earlier, another rugby club, Bradford, had formed a soccer team and proposed a merger. This was rejected two-to-one by City members, so Bradford went off to form their own football club, Bradford Park Avenue, which itself gained admission to the League in 1908. (Just to complicate the issue, Bradford members who disapproved of the switch to soccer then quit to found Bradford Northern rugby league club – today's Bradford Bulls.)

At first, City's football remained gloriously unaffected by these distractions. They came fifth in the League at the end of the 1910/11 season, and also reached an FA Cup final. Their opponents Newcastle were the holders and strong favourites, but City's defence held firm to produce a goalless draw in front of nearly 70,000 at Crystal Palace, and in the replay at Old Trafford, O'Rourke distracted the Newcastle 'keeper in a goalmouth scramble, allowing a header from James Speirs to loop into the net for the only goal of the game. The trophy Speirs received was a brand-new one, ordered by the FA after the theft of the original, and forged, appropriately enough, in Bradford. The city turned out in force to hail its heroes although, truth to tell, there wasn't much local about the team – eight of them, in fact, were Scots.

While attempting to defend the Cup the following year, City met Park Avenue for the first time in a competitive fixture, winning 1–0 away in front of nearly 25,000. They were then knocked out by Barnsley, after three replays.

In the summer of 1914, City ignored the clouds of war gathering over Europe to tour Belgium, Switzerland and Germany, playing ten games and losing only one – at Frankfurt, where their defeat was blamed on a Zeppelin airship flying over the ground

Captain on Parade – McCall returns, 1998

during the match. The players, of course, had every right to be fearful. No senior English club would be unaffected by World War I, but Bradford City's loss was acute. Eight players died in the fighting, including the club's first England international, Jimmy Conlin; towering centre-half Bob Torrance; and Cup-winner Speirs.

The war did lasting damage to the club's morale. The promotion of Bradford Park Avenue to the First Division led to three seasons of top-flight rivalry which, while entertaining at the time, also served to divide loyalties and weaken City's fan base. Park Avenue were relegated in 1921, and City followed them down a year later, after losing all their last five games.

There followed five seasons of flat, Second Division football, in which City never finished above 15th in the table. In 1927 they were relegated to the Third Division (North) after losing 8–0 at Manchester City on the last day. At the end of the 1927/28 season, City's bankers refused to

A smile between friends – Richardson and Kamara, 1996

George Swindin to Arsenal led to the drop in 1937, the team finishing one place below Park Avenue, who survived. City remained in their rivals' shadows during World War II, with Park Avenue's Len Shackleton playing for both clubs in two separate games on Christmas Day 1940 – even scoring for City with a rare header. After hostilities the club was crippled by debts incurred in the rebuilding of a war-damaged Valley Parade, and in 1949 City had to apply for re-election after finishing bottom of the Third Division (North). Park Avenue's relegation the same year brought local derbies back onto the fixture calendar, but the 25,000-plus crowds who watched them were very much the exception for both clubs, as the postwar attendance boom seemed largely to pass Bradford by.

The two sides were separated in 1958, when City made the cut into the new national Third Division and Park Avenue dropped into the Fourth. Within three years they had swapped places, City having been relegated at the end of 1960/61. From 1963 to the end of the decade, both sides toiled in the Fourth Division and, with crowds dwindling at both grounds, something had to give.

City applied for re-election twice in this period, but Park Avenue's form was even more wretched – between 1967 and 1970 they won just 15 out of 138 League games, and their fourth successive application for re-election fell on deaf ears. For 1970/71 they were replaced in the Fourth Division by Cambridge United, and by 1974, after leaving their impressive ground at Park Avenue for one season of Northern Premier League football at Valley Parade, the club folded.

Park Avenue's demise was not celebrated by City fans, for whom the rivalry had always been friendly. (The Park Avenue

allow the club any more credit, and while the board resigned *en masse*, fans were asked to prop up the club by means of public subscription. To make matters worse, Park Avenue won the Third Division (North) title.

The new board appointed Peter O'Rourke, architect of the 1911 FA Cup triumph, as secretary-manager. His task was enormous – many of City's players had sought employment elsewhere after their wages had gone unpaid at the end of the previous season, and the club began the new campaign with a squad of only 14. But what a way to begin it. Rotherham were thrashed 11–1 at Valley Parade on the opening day, and as if that record victory weren't enough, the team then won 8–2 at Ashington in October to register a best-ever away win, too. City finished the season top of the table, with the same points total as Park Avenue had amassed a year before, but after scoring 128 goals, compared with their rivals' 101.

City now looked to be back in business. Promotion to the First Division was reckoned to be only a couple of seasons away, and the mood at Valley Parade was more hopeful than for two decades. But that optimism was misplaced. City avoided immediate relegation by only a point in 1930, and though they hung around in the Second Division for another seven seasons, the sale of their talismanic goalkeeper club's revival in 1987 attracted support from across Bradford.) Yet the way was now clear for City to rise as the sole professional club in a metropolitan area which, despite the decline of its once-famous wool industry, was still growing. In an attempt to kick-start the process, City's directors proposed to rename the club 'Bradford Metro', believing it might encourage ex-Park Avenue fans to change allegiances. The plan was dropped after an outcry from fans, leaving City's climb from obscurity to take its natural, leisurely course.

In 1976/77, City won promotion to the Third, having gone the entire season unbeaten at Valley Parade. But they were relegated again the following season, and it wasn't until the arrival of George Mulhall as manager at the tail-end of 1978 that the club began to stir from its slumber. In 1979 Mulhall signed Bobby Campbell, an Ulster-born target man whose legendary short fuse had led him to flee Britain for spells in Canadian and Australian football. With Campbell's more destructive urges tamed, former Park Avenue playmaker Terry Dolan running the midfield and the defence in the capable hands of West Indian full-back Ces Podd, Mulhall's side were a formidable unit.

City missed out on promotion only on goal difference in 1980, and while Mulhall left to join Bolton the following year, his successors Roy McFarland and Mick Jones inherited a solid, experienced first team which had little trouble getting promoted to the Third Division in 1982. Later that year, McFarland and Jones were poached (illegally) by Derby and City got themselves another player-manager and coach combination, maintaining the Leeds connection by appointing Trevor Cherry and Terry Yorath. They immediately put the emphasis on youth, drafting former apprentices such as Stuart McCall, Peter Jackson and Mark Ellis into the first team as City consolidated in mid-table in the Third Division.

Off the field, it was time for another of the club's habitual cashflow crises. Leeds still hadn't received their nominal £10,000 fee for Cherry, and slapped a winding-up order on City. The club went into receivership and was reconstituted as Bradford City (1983) Ltd, led by local businessmen Stafford Heginbotham and Jack Tordoff.

Money remained tight, but Cherry and Yorath were smooth transfer market operators, selling Campbell to Derby then taking him back on loan, and bringing John Hendrie, Dave Evans and goalkeeper Eric McManus in to reinforce the squad for another promotion push. City hadn't been in the Second Division since 1927, yet they played with such confidence during the 1984/85 season that there was an almost an air of anti-climax when they won the Third Division title with a game to spare.

Chairman Heginbotham authorised the replacement of the Main Stand's old wooden roof, to comply with more stringent Second Division safety standards. Work was due to begin the Monday after City's last game of the season at home to Lincoln. A game too far... A cigarette was casually dropped, litter under the wooden floors ignited, and within seconds a huge

A Jewell not a clown – Paul as a player, 1993

fireball had engulfed the stand, the heat intensified by the design and materials of the roof. What should have been a celebration had become a tragedy of barely imaginable proportions.

If the fire tore at the heart of the club, it was only by stealth at first. City began a nomadic existence as Valley Parade was rebuilt, playing at Leeds, Huddersfield and Bradford Northern's Odsal ground. Stafford Heginbotham, very much the people's chairman, stepped down in early 1988 after a heart attack, and his successor, Tordoff, refused manager Terry Dolan the cash to buy the one extra player he felt would take City into the top flight; the team finished fourth, and were knocked out of the play-offs by Middlesbrough.

The squad that had served City well for much of the Eighties was broken up, and relegation followed in 1990. Managers John Docherty, Frank Stapleton and Lennie Lawrence came and went, the last dismissed by Geoffrey Richardson, who acquired a controlling interest in the club from Tordoff in 1994. On his arrival, Richardson announced a five-year plan to get City into the Premiership. He was dismissed as a joker, but he had the money, the vision and the courage to pull it off.

Chris Kamara got the team into the First Division after epic play-off wins over Blackpool and Notts County in 1996, only to be sacked (amid allegations that his dismissal was racially motivated, furiously denied by Richardson) two years later.

The man Richardson now chose to put in charge of his expensive squad was Kamara's first-team coach Paul Jewell, who'd been at the club for a decade as a player. Again, it was a move that raised eyebrows, yet Jewell's straightforward, laid-back approach allowed signings such as McCall, Peter Beagrie, Lee Mills and Dean Windass to let their talent do the talking. After Sunderland had raced away with the First Division title in 1998/99, City ended a two-way battle for second place one point above Ipswich – thanks to that last-day win at Wolves.

'This is a bond that links everyone in the town,' said Stuart McCall after the game. He was talking about the fire – but he might just as well have been referring to City's return to top-flight football for the first time in 77 years.

Here we go!

Motorists will likely as not approach Bradford on the M62 – allow as much time as you can for traffic. Exit the M62 at Junction 26 onto the M606, and follow this to its end. Get into the right-hand lane and you'll find Valley Parade well-signposted from here. If you lose the signs, the district to look for is Manningham.

There's a **car park** at the ground but this fills up quickly. Street parking is possible along Midland Road but not in the side streets off it, where residents' schemes are rampant. More impromptu car parks are expected to open up at nearby schools and businesses following City's promotion to the Premiership.

The city has two **train stations**, Bradford Interchange and Forster Square, with direct trains to Leeds, Manchester and Sheffield. Fans travelling from London should change at Leeds. Call ☎0345/484950 for the latest timings.

Bradford Interchange is a good 30min walk from the ground through the city centre – best jump on a Manningham bus from the adjacent bus station. Forster Square station is much nearer. Just cross the dual carriageway and head straight along Midland Road – Valley Parade is on your left after 10–15mins.

Just the ticket

Today's Valley Parade is unrecognisable from the pre-1985 version. As well as a new Main Stand, the shallow Midland Road Stand opposite was replaced in 1996, while the historic Kop terrace was finally pulled down in 1998, with a new stand scheduled to open in its place during 1999/2000.

Visiting fans are accommodated at the 'Bradford End', which has around 1,800 seats. In the past, a further allocation has been available on Midland Road but there seems little prospect of this with season-ticket sales surging to record levels for Premiership football. **Disabled visitors** have spaces in the Midland Road Stand – advance booking essential on ☎01274/770022.

Swift half

The are plenty of pubs near the ground which, while well-used by City fans, also welcome discreet visitors. ***The Cartwright*** near the junction of Midland Road and Queen's Road, just to the north of the ground, and ***The Oakleigh*** in Oak Avenue a little further north still, both do a fine range of real ales. For families, ***The New Beehive*** on Westgate has a separate children's room.

There's a large Asian community in Manningham but, strangely, a broader range of Bradford's famous **curry houses** is to be found in the city centre, towards the Interchange.

Club merchandise

While Park Avenue adopted the Bradford Corporation colours of red, yellow and black, City went off at a tangent and adopted claret and amber. The colours reminded people of bantams and the team have been stuck with that nickname more or less ever since.

The distinctive colour scheme covers anything and everything at the ***Bantam Leisure Megastore*** (open Mon–Sat 9.30am–5.30pm, later on matchdays, ☎01274/773355) at one end of the Main Stand. The *JCT600* logo emblazoned across the shirt in recent seasons belongs to former chairman Jack Tordoff's car dealership.

Barmy army

The hooligan element which once plagued City – particularly during Yorkshire or trans-Pennine derbies – was stopped in its tracks by the fire. Today the club has a well-earned reputation for friendliness, although police advise against visiting fans wearing colours in the city centre after the match.

In print

The ***Bradford Telegraph & Argus*** has the most detailed coverage of City, and on Saturday evenings is accompanied by the 'pink' ***Yorkshire Sport***.

The ***City Gent*** (PO Box 56, Bradford, BD13 4YU) is the oldest surviving football fanzine in England, having been publishing continuously since October 1984. Now much more than a fanzine, it has infiltrated conventional media such as local newspapers and radio, and has also become a leading source of historical material on the club. Volunteer salespeople at Valley Parade also offer the Park Avenue fanzine ***Wings Of A Sparrow.***

There are two recommended history books. ***City Memories*** (True North, £9.99) by John Dewhirst of the *City Gent* is an evocative pictorial chronicle, while ***Of Boars & Bantams***, though out of print, is being continued online by author Don Gillan (see below).

Stuart McCall's ***The Real McCall*** (Mainstream, £9.99) is, for obvious reasons, a more human tale than most player autobiographies.

On air

The club has its own station, ***Bantams*** (1566 AM), on matchdays. Otherwise it's ***BBC Radio Leeds*** (92.4 FM) – not popular with City folk.

In the net

Inexplicably there is no **official website** but the ***City Gent*** has stepped into the breach at: www.legend.co.uk/citygent/. Far more than just an online version of the fanzine, the site contains a detailed archive of both City and Park Avenue, and also offers a gateway to Don Gillan's work-in-progress (see *In Print* above).

For a sideways view, try ***The Boy From Brazil & Other Stories*** at www.boyfrombrazil.freeserve.co.uk

Awaiting the whistle – nails bitten to the bone at Wolves, 1999

Brentford

Formation	1889
Stadium	Griffin Park, Braemar Road, Brentford, Middx, TW8 0NT. ☎0181/847 2511
Ground capacity	12,750
First-choice colours	Red-and-white stripes
Major honours	Second Division champions 1935; Third Division champions 1992, 1999; Third Division (South) champions 1933; Fourth Division champions 1963
Position 1998/99	Promoted as Third Division champions

They're unaccustomed to change down at Griffin Park. Traditionally this is London's sleepiest senior footballing venue, where time doesn't seem to pass so much as amble amiably by, as if it were being borne by the nearby river Thames. So when Ron Noades came purring in in his silver Mercedes in the summer of 1998, the place was in for a bit of a shock.

Flush with cash – though not, perhaps, as much as he'd originally envisaged – from the sale of Crystal Palace to Mark Goldberg, the former Selhurst Park chairman took control of Brentford FC and set about shaking the old place up in his own, inimitable style. The quest to re-house the club in a new stadium further out toward the edge of west London would continue apace. There would be a massive overhaul of the playing staff – eleven players to come or go in the close season, to be followed by 16 further moves once the campaign had got under way. And there would be a new, big-name manager: Noades himself.

Like John Reames at Lincoln, Brentford's new chairman saw no point giving the manager's job to anyone he wasn't sure about. When nobody suitable materialised to replace Micky Adams, Noades decided to take over team affairs personally – albeit backed by a formidable array of coaches including Ray Lewington, Terry Bullivant and Brian Sparrow. With managing director Gary Hargraves supervising day-to-day business matters, Noades would have enough time to select the team, supervise transfers and talk tactics with his coaches, while still being in overall charge of the club. That was the theory, anyway.

And if Brentford supporters were not exactly dancing in the streets at the prospect of their new chairman cutting the wage bill by trying to run the team himself, they were not really in a position to argue. Their club had just been relegated to the Third Division, less than 12 months after reaching the Second Division play-off final. Morale was at a low ebb, and money, before Noades' arrival, had always been tight anyway. Palace fans gave their former chairman decidedly mixed reviews, but what did they know?

What, indeed. With Icelandic defender Hermann Hreidarsson a new club record signing from Palace, young midfielder Ijah Anderson lively in midfield and another newcomer, striker Lloyd Owusu, irresistible in attack, Brentford were always too good for the rest of the basement in 1998/99. Seldom out of the play-off places, they came even stronger during the closing weeks and eventually sealed the title with a typically assured 1–0 win at Cambridge United, the divisional leaders up to that point. After the match, Noades cut an unusually shy figure in the centre of the team's celebration photos, as if reluctant to take too much of the credit. Was this dramatic turnaround really down to him?

Some of it indubitably was. Noades had shaken up a demoralised squad with a new sense of purpose (and with much bigger pay packets for those who were kept on). But he had also had a remarkable effect at club level, bringing a fresh, fighting 'can-do'

Abbey crunch – Andy Scott celebrates the Third Division title win at Cambridge, May 1999

attitude to a corner of London's footballing landscape that had often appeared dangerously content with its lot. Noades allowed no room for complacency at Brentford, and it showed.

The worry for supporters is that they have witnessed these bright, promising dawns before, and too many of them have turned out to be false – brought to a premature end by a culture of safety-first survival. And Brentford's traditional tendency to muddle along is perfectly expressed by the story of the club's foundation. When members of a Brentford rowing club met in a boathouse at Kew Bridge to decide on an activity that would keep them fit during the winter months, football beat rugby by only one vote. Football or rugby? Innovation or inertia? The choices these football clubs have to make…

Another tradition was also set early on – that of Brentford surprising themselves. Considering that they had few members who had played organised football regularly, the rowing club's new team did remarkably well in local amateur circles. Playing on a rough field covered today by Clifden Road, and using the *Griffin* pub in which to change into the rowing club's fetching colour scheme of pink, claret and light blue, the team soon gained a following of their own.

In 1891 Brentford moved a mile or so north to Benn's Fields on Little Ealing Lane, and it was from there that they won their first accolade, the West London Alliance title of 1893. The players were now dressed in yellow, black and blue and had been given the nickname 'the Bees'. Local opposition continued to find their sting painful – Brentford won the West Middlesex Junior Cup in 1894 and the Senior edition a year later.

Crowds at Benn's Field were disappointing, however, and over the next nine years the club tried out three further grounds with varying degrees of success, before leasing an orchard from the *Fuller, Smith & Turner* brewery on which to build a new home in 1904. The orchard was next to the *Griffin* pub. In other words, Brentford were right back where they'd started.

Umbrella and coaching badge – Ron Noades

Restless though the club had been in terms of its location, the honours had kept coming. After triumphing in both the London Senior Amateur Cup and the Middlesex Senior Cup in 1898, Brentford were invited to join the Second Division of the Southern League, and accordingly turned professional the following year. Now that the club was enjoying such an elevated status, there was no shortage of volunteers from the public to help cut down the trees in the *Fullers* orchard so that Brentford's new ground, Griffin Park, could be made ready for the start of the 1904/05 season.

Within a year, however, Brentford were unfortunate to have the newly formed Chelsea club join the Football League right on their doorstep, and further progress was slower than it had been in the first 15 years of their existence. Still, they managed to get voted into the First Division of the Southern League after World War I, and in 1920 they joined the mass exodus of Southern League clubs to join the newly formed Third Division (South) of the Football League.

Initially, the signs were that Brentford's heart wasn't quite in the new competition. They opened their League account with a 3–0 defeat at Exeter, and in the morning before their first home game against Millwall, goalkeeper Jack Durston was busy taking five Surrey wickets as a bowler for Middlesex at Lord's Cricket Ground. Perhaps not surprisingly, Brentford finished the season second from bottom. Happily, there was no relegation at the time.

In an effort to prove that they were serious, Brentford adopted a new, more purposeful-looking strip of white shirts and black shorts. Manager Harry Curtis took the club to the fifth round of the FA Cup within a year of his appointment in 1926, and after another quick colour-change to today's red-and-white stripes in 1929, Brentford finally began to make their mark. With pacy winger Idris Hopkins putting crosses on a plate for centre-forward John Holliday, the team won every one of their 21 home games in the 1929/30 season. By 1933 they'd won the Third Division (South), and two years after that they'd won the Second.

It seemed inconceivable that Brentford's innocent, cavalier approach to football would thrive in a First Division dominated by rigidly defensive tactics, yet Curtis' side managed to finish fifth in 1935/36 – to this day the club's highest position in the League. Two sixth-places and further Cup runs followed, and fans could only speculate on what their club might have achieved had World War II not intervened to break Brentford's spell. As it was, the team were relegated at the end of the first postwar season and Curtis' reign ended in 1949.

By 1954 Brentford were in the Third Division and, despite the efforts of long-serving defender Ken Coote and tireless goalscorer Jim Towers, this seemed for a long while to be the club's natural level. A first drop down into the Fourth Division in 1962 was instantly corrected, but when Brentford hit the basement again five years later, chairman Jack Dunnett proposed that the club should be taken over by Queen's Park Rangers – the first of many proposed mergers between the various west London clubs and, like all subsequent ideas, swiftly kicked into touch by the fans.

Brentford spent much of the Seventies in the Fourth Division, as Chelsea, Fulham and QPR took it in turns to draw the serious crowds. Yet somehow the club managed to keep its overdraft to manageable proportions, picking up the odd bargain player here, selling a bit of spare land there – survival honed into a fine art.

The Eighties saw Brentford comfortably into mid-table in the Third Division, with Frank McLintock and then Steve Perryman bringing the no-nonsense approach they'd shown as players to the management of the team. With a solid base upon which to build and the physical presence of young striker Dean Holdsworth, Phil Holder pulled the Bees into the old Second Division just as it was being renamed the new First in 1992. But the club couldn't afford to refuse Wimbledon's record offer of £720,000 for Holdsworth, and without their prime source of goals Brentford were relegated within a year.

In 1995, with rumours abounding that the club was seeking a site for a new multi-purpose sports arena elsewhere within the boundaries of the local Hounslow Council, David Webb's well-disciplined side finished runners-up in the Second Division. But that was League reorganisation year and, denied the usual automatic promotion, Brentford lost their play-off semi-final to Huddersfield Town on a penalty shoot-out. They went one stage better two years later, but on a hot Wembley afternoon in May 1997 Brentford's bluster was no match for the culture of Dario Gradi's Crewe, and another promotion opportunity had been spurned.

Former Fulham manager Micky Adams oversaw a disastrous 1997/98 campaign which saw the club relegated on the final day of the season. A boardroom power vacuum ensued but, happily for Brentford fans, while their team had been toiling Ron Noades had been busy negotiating the sale of Crystal Palace – a sale that would have big consequences for both clubs, in ways neither of them expected.

Here we go!

Motorists have few problems reaching Griffin Park as it is handily placed for the M4 motorway (junction 15 off the M25). Leave the M4 at junction 2 and go straight on to the Chiswick Roundabout. Go all the way around this and back under the M4, following signs for A4 The West. Stay in the middle lane until past the slip road for the M4, then move over to the left-hand lane and turn left into Ealing Road at the next roundabout. The ground is on your right.

Arrive early for the best **street parking** spaces as there's no alternative at Griffin Park itself. Besides which, you wouldn't want to miss the area's pub life (see below).

Brentford overground **train station** receives services from London Waterloo and Vauxhall

Wilting at Wembley – after the play-off defeat, 1997

which call on their way to Weybridge. Service is only half-hourly but is still a better bet than the **tube** to Gunnersbury or South Ealing, both of which are a fair hike from the ground.

Just the ticket

Visiting fans can either sit or stand at the Brook Road end. Ticket prices in 1998/99 were adults £14 (concessions £11) for a seat, £9 (£6) for a spot on the terrace.

Disabled supporters have spaces in the Main (Braemar Road) Stand – book in advance on ☎0181/847 2511.

Swift half

Griffin Park famously has a pub on each corner, and all of them welcome the well-behaved visitor. The ***Griffin*** on the corner of New Road and Brook Road has obvious connections with the club, but has less of a football feel to it than the ***Princess Royal*** at the junction of Braemar Road and Ealing Road, where the club continued to maintain its offices until forced to leave by the League in 1929. Both pubs serve the excellent local *Fullers* ales.

The other two Griffin Park pubs are the ***Royal Oak*** on the corner of New Road and Brook Road, and the ***New Inn*** where New Road meets Ealing Road. Why not arrive early and take in all four…?.

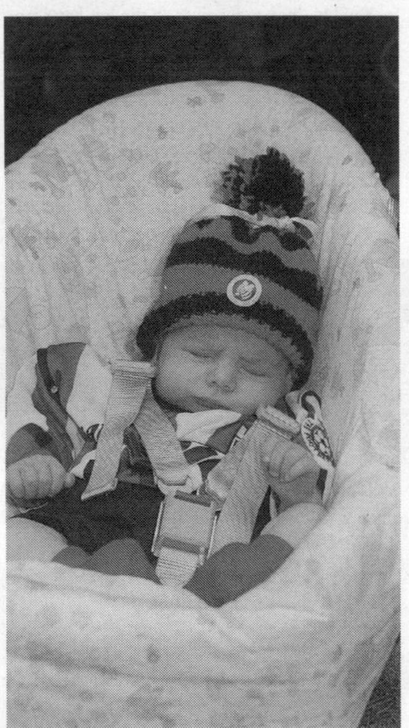

Baby Bee – this is London's 'family club'

Club merchandise

The ***Bees Fan-Attic*** behind the Main Stand in Braemar Road has home shirts at £34.99 (kids' sizes £24.99), along with the usual range of leisurewear, books, clocks and key-rings. Sadly, the club's original pink, claret and light-blue strip is still awaiting its contemporary revival.

Barmy army

Most disputes in this neck of the woods are settled over a pint of *Fullers London Pride* and a game of dominoes. On the rivalry front, Fulham are envied for their money (Mr Noades not being quite able to match Mr al-Fayed in that department), while QPR have never been forgiven for trying to swallow Brentford up in the Sixties.

In print

As usual for London there's no Saturday evening paper, but there are two fanzines to choose from: ***Beesotted*** (19A Stanley Road, Teddington, TW11 8TP) and ***Thorne In The Side*** (25 Shaftesbury Crescent, Laleham, TW18 1QL).

Dan Jackson's ***Positively Brentford*** (Polar, £22.95) is a lavish collection of photographs from 1896 to 1996.

On air

GLR (94.9 FM) may offer a little more Brentford coverage than ***Capital Gold*** (1548 AM).

In the net

Brentford's **official website** is extremely slick and thoroughly commendable, with rich content matched only by refreshing speed. Be amazed at: www.brentfordfc.co.uk/.

Both Brentford fanzines have an online presence. ***Thorne In The Side*** has an award-winning site at: www.channel-a.com/bfc/; while ***Beesotted*** is at: brentfordfc.cjb.net/.

Brighton & Hove Albion

Formation	1901 as Brighton & Hove United
Stadium	Withdean Athletics Stadium, Eldred Road, Withdean (office: 118 Queen's Road, Brighton, BN1 3XG. ☎01273/778855)
Ground capacity	6,000
First-choice colours	Blue and white striped shirts, blue shorts
Major honours	Third Division (South) champions 1958; Fourth Division champions 1965
Position 1998/99	17th in Third Division

The stereotyped portrait of Brighton as a sleepy Sussex seaside town, populated by pompous retired colonels and their blue-rinsed wives, is out of date. Today the place buzzes by day and swings by night, thanks to a large student population, thousands of foreign tourists and a thriving gay community. Norman Cook (aka Fatboy Slim) chooses to live here when he could live anywhere he wants, and even the crumbling Victorian edifice of the West Pier is being restored with National Lottery cash.

Floral tribute – the Goldstone's last day had the ambience of a wake

In one key respect, though, Brighton hasn't changed one bit – its relationship with football is as bittersweet as ever. Brighton & Hove Albion, the team that have flown the flag of League football here for nearly 70 years, inspire a devotion that would not seem out of place at Anfield or St James' Park. But the devoted have always been in the minority. Opposing them has been a wealth of vested interests, from local councillors keen to protect the sanctity of the town's Green Belt, to residents worried about car parking on the grass verges in front of their semis…the retired colonels haven't gone away, after all.

In the Nineties, these passions were brought to boiling point, as fans rallied (in vain) to prevent the loss of the club's Goldstone Ground, then tried (successfully) to oust the boardroom regime responsible for its sale. Thanks to a succession of sit-ins, marches, pitch invasions and other exploits, Brighton's hardcore following did more than simply challenge the notion that their town was a football backwater; they struck a blow for ignored, oppressed, deceived and otherwise put-upon fans everywhere. Whether all the campaigning will yet have its desired effect – the return of the club to a new home in Brighton or Hove – is another story.

Why did the Goldstone arouse such emotion in the first place? It's a question many visiting fans must have been asking themselves as the protests gathered force. It wasn't pretty, or comfortable, or even particularly atmospheric. But it was home. And it had been home for a long time.

It was in 1902 that the team first began playing at the Goldstone. At the time they shared it with Hove FC (the ground was actually in Hove, Brighton's smaller, more genteel neighbour to the west). But within two years the Hove club had taken its football elsewhere, having sold its Goldstone lease to Albion.

This was ironic, given the story behind Albion's formation. When a certain John Jackson held a meeting at the *Seven Stars Hotel* with a view to starting a new football club in June 1901, he knew that a place in the Southern League was up for grabs – a club called Brighton & Hove Rangers had been offered it, but then gone to the wall. Jackson had been team manager of another now-defunct outfit, Brighton United, and wanted to combine the two names together to form Brighton & Hove United. Hove FC objected, however, on the grounds that it sounded like they had been merged into the new club. So Brighton & Hove Albion it became.

Albion won the Southern League title for the first time in 1910 with a team that included international Charlie Webb. The championship gave Brighton the chance to contest the FA Charity Shield, then played for by the winners of the Southern League and the Football League. Albion beat Aston Villa 1–0 at Stamford Bridge, and local fans declared them (not unreasonably) 'Champions of England'.

During World War I, Webb was appointed manager. Unable to start work immediately (he was a prisoner of the Germans at the time), he took office in 1919 and remained there until 1947. His team spent the entire period in the Third Division (South), into which the Southern League had been absorbed.

If League life was dull, along the way there were some stirring FA Cup runs. In the 1932/33 competition, the club's secretary forgot to apply for exemption from qualifying and Albion had to play in the preliminary rounds. They then went on to beat Crystal Palace, Wrexham, Chelsea and Bradford Park Avenue before holding West Ham 2–2 in the fifth round, in front of more than 32,000. Brighton lost the replay but the club was back on the map.

Albion finally won promotion to the Second Division under Billy Lane in 1958. The championship was sealed with a 6–0 win over Watford in which a local 20-year-old, Adrian Thorne, scored five. Brighton lost their first Second Division game 9–0 at Middlesbrough, for whom a certain Brian Clough matched Thorne's scoring feat, and the club never established itself at this level. Still, interest among the locals soared – the Goldstone attendance record of 36,747 was set on 27 December 1958, when Brighton beat Fulham there, 3–0.

And Smith has scored – Gary Bailey can't stop Brighton's opening goal at Wembley, 1983

Relegation followed Lane's departure in 1961, and within a year Albion had fallen into the recently created Fourth Division. Archie Macaulay hauled them back up to the Third in 1965, and seven years later, with Pat Saward at the helm, Brighton were promoted again. They were relegated immediately following a run of 13 successive defeats, and the board decided it was time for some fresh managerial blood. Who better than Clough, the motivator extraordinaire who had just walked out on Derby County?

Cloughie's first month in charge was a disaster. Brighton were crushed at home 4–0 by Walton & Hersham in the FA Cup, and 8–2 by Bristol Rovers in the League. 'Things will get better,' Clough assured the fans. And they did – but only to the extent that Brighton avoided the drop. Clough then fled to Leeds, leaving his assistant Peter Taylor to pick up the pieces.

In 1975 Taylor signed Peter Ward, an inexperienced but cultured striker from Burton Albion, and Brian Horton, a combative midfielder from Port Vale. A year later Brighton came within three points of promotion, and though Taylor then left to rejoin Clough at Nottingham Forest, his replacement, Alan Mullery, won promotion at the first attempt. Ward scored a club-record 36 goals that season, but just as important were the experienced men at the other end Mullery had acquired in the summer: 'keeper Eric Steele and defenders Graham Cross and Chris Cattlin.

Mullery's side missed out on a second successive promotion only on goal difference, and the following year they won their last game 3–1 at Newcastle to earn a place in the top flight. The 'Seagulls', as the team had become known in Taylor's time, had never flown so high. Mullery, again putting the accent on defence, signed two young, quick-thinking stoppers, Steve Foster and Mark Lawrenson, to ensure that vertigo didn't set in. Brighton managed to finish in 16th place in 1980 and, after selling Ward to Forest, they avoided relegation the following year by winning their last four

Band of old – Steve Foster, Seagull stalwart

games. Mullery was becoming frustrated, however, and resigned soon after.

The new manager, Mike Bailey, was if anything even more defence-minded than Mullery. Lawrenson was sold to Liverpool for £900,000, but another young centre-back, Gary Stevens, was coming up through the ranks to replace him. Albion finished 13th in 1981/82 – their highest-ever League placing. The fans, though, were not amused, and there was a collective sigh of relief when Bailey was dumped in favour of Jimmy Melia in December 1982. Under Melia, a wisecracking, nightclubbing Scouser who had been a playmaker in Bill Shankly's first Liverpool side, Albion's football became watchable again. Okay, so they finished bottom and were relegated. But there was also the small matter of almost beating Manchester United in the FA Cup final...

Brighton began their Cup campaign that year with a modest 1–1 draw at home to Newcastle. Then a 1–0 win in the replay, secured by a re-signed Ward, set them on the road to Wembley. Manchester City were walloped 4–0 at the Goldstone, with

Michael Robinson scoring twice against his old club, then Jimmy Case hit a 25-yard screamer past his former employers as Brighton snatched an unlikely 2–1 win at Liverpool. The same player got winning goals against Norwich and Sheffield Wednesday, and before the town had really come to grips with the idea, Melia was leading Brighton out at Wembley alongside Ron Atkinson's United.

Albion were at the final without their captain Foster, who'd gone to court in an attempt to get his suspension overturned, and lost. But Tony Grealish made a fine stand-in skipper, and Steve Gatting, filling in for Foster, marked Norman Whiteside out of the game. Brighton richly deserved their 2–2 draw, secured by Stevens near the end of normal time. And they should have won the match when, in the last minute of extra time, Robinson laid the ball square to Gordon Smith, scorer of Albion's first, unmarked in the opposition box. But Smith shot tamely at Gary Bailey and United's goalkeeper beat him to the ricochet. Even today, the scene is black enough to wake a Brighton fan from the deepest sleep. But it also haunted United – Big Ron described it as 'the moment we died a thousand deaths'. They won the replay 4–0.

After relegation, Albion had no option but to sell Robinson, Foster and Stevens. Chris Cattlin replaced Melia as manager, and his sacking in 1986, to clear a path for the returning Mullery, angered fans. Mullery in turn was replaced by Barry Lloyd, and although Albion were relegated to the Third Division in 1987, Lloyd's passion for the club, coupled with Garry Nelson's instinctive goalscoring, hauled them straight back up again.

In 1990/91, Lloyd anticipated the soon-to-come obsession with imports by signing a Belarussian, Igor Gurinovich, and a Romanian, Stefan Iovan. Brighton's football was fun to watch, and the players were funny to look at – wearing blue-and-white striped shorts to match their shirts at home, and a shocking crimson tie-dye away. The pretty boys were no match, however, for Neil Warnock's hard-hitting Notts County in the 1991 play-off final at Wembley, and Brighton's 3–1 defeat that day marked the end of the club's flirtation with the English football elite.

The following season, Brighton were relegated from the old Second Division to the new one. The club was now two levels of football away from the top flight, but nobody had told Lloyd, who was now MD as well as manager, and trying to sustain a Premiership-style squad. By the end of 1993 the club was £3million in debt, and faced a series of winding-up orders – despite the fact that chairman Greg Stanley was reckoned to be one of the 300 richest men in Britain. Between them, Stanley and his business partner Bill Archer put together a 'rescue package'. In reality this was nothing of the kind – they merely arranged for a new loan to clear Albion's immediate debts, in exchange for a controlling interest in the club. They appointed a new chief executive, the former Liberal Democrat MP David Bellotti, and a new first-team boss, Liam Brady.

For a while, a fragile optimism returned. Then, on the eve of the 1995/96 season, it emerged through the pages of the *Brighton Evening Argus* that the board had secretly sold the Goldstone site to developers for £7.4million. The Seagulls would have to fly by the end of the season, and there was nowhere for them to fly to. Far from having been rescued from oblivion, the club was now heading inexorably closer to it. The supporters were incensed, their anger boiling over into a full-scale pitch invasion at the last game of the season against York City, which had to be abandoned. Brighton would be relegated anyway, regardless of the result.

The developers were persuaded to let Albion stay at the Goldstone for another year. But the fans knew this was only a temporary reprieve, and took to the pitch again in October 1996 – a disturbance for which the club was deducted two points. Brady resigned after his takeover bid was rejected, and his successor Jimmy Case lasted only a few months, during which Bellotti was literally driven from the ground by supporters.

The resistance movement culminated on 8 February 1997 with *Fans United*, when supporters of almost every League club in the country descended on the Goldstone to protest about the club's position. Within a month, the FA had hammered out a survival plan which involved Stanley and Archer leaving the board (though the latter would retain his shareholding), Dick Knight taking over as chairman, and a guarantee that in future no single individual would be allowed to take control of the club.

Suitably inspired, and with Steve Gritt now in charge, Albion battled to ensure League survival, sending Hereford down in their place by drawing 1–1 at Edgar Street on the last day of the 1996/97 campaign.

A two-year enforced exile at Gillingham's Priestfield Stadium was enlivened by a second *Fans United* event for a 'home' game against Doncaster Rovers – the club which, ironically, was now suffering in much the same way as Albion had done, and whose relegation in 1998 would keep the Seagulls in the League for another year.

Gritt was replaced by Brian Horton, who pulled Brighton up into a mid-table position in 1998/99 before being poached by Port Vale. His replacement, Jeff Wood, lasted only three months before Dick Knight persuaded Micky Adams to take charge for 1999/2000 – when the team will return to the Brighton area, playing home matches at Withdean Athletics Stadium. This is only a temporary home, however – on 6 May 1999 the people of Brighton gave a resounding 'Yes' vote in a referendum on the development of a new stadium at Falmer, a few miles north-east of town.

Albion also have a new sponsor for 1999/2000, lifelong fan Norman Cook having stumped up £100,000 of his record company's money. Since gate receipts at Withdean will be no guarantee of long-term financial survival, however, fans may reflect ironically on the name of Fatboy Slim's label – *Skint*.

Here we go!

Well, for a start, **motorists** can't go all the way. Parking in the vicinity of the Withdean Athletics Stadium is discouraged by the club, which wants to ensure good relations with its neighoburs in this leafy suburb. Hence the setting up of a **park and ride scheme**, with buses running to and from a car park in Mill Road, a mile from the ground.

To get to Mill Road, head for the junction of the A23 London Road and the A27. From here take the A23 toward Brighton (or stay on it if coming from London or the north). Turn right at the service station into Mill Road.

An alternative, if you fancy seeing something of the town, is to park at one of the many multistoreys in the centre, and catch a **train** from Brighton station to Preston Park. This station is also served by direct trains to and from London

Salvation – Robbie Reinelt (#9) keeps Albion in the League, 1997

Victoria (every 30mins, journey time 1hr), with several departures to choose from after an evening game. Brighton's main station (a 5min ride from Preston Park) also has direct services along the south coast to Portsmouth and Southampton. For the latest timings call ☎0345/484950. From Preston Park station, head straight down Clermont Road, then left at the T-junction with the A23 London Road. Turn left again into Tongdean Lane, go straight under the railway bridge, and the ground is at the junction with Eldred Avenue ahead.

Just the ticket

Space for **visiting fans** is severely limited at Withdean, with no more than 325 seats likely to be available. All matches will be all-ticket, with prices not surprisingly high at £14 for adults, £10 concessions. There should be some facilities for **disabled fans** – book through Albion on ☎01273/778855.

Swift half

Near Withdean Stadium, ***The Preston Brewery Tap*** (open all day every day, ☎01273/508700), on the A23 at 197 Preston Road, serves good food, has a beer garden and welcomes families.

The club is also trying to negotiate with the landlords for use of the ***Withdean Sportsman*** pub at the stadium itself.

In Ship Street in the centre of town, the *Seven Stars* where Brighton & Hove United was formed is now ***O'Sullivans*** bar.

Club merchandise

The club is hoping to open a small **shop** inside the North Stand at Withdean Stadium. Alternatively there is another shop **in town** at 6 Queen's Road (Mon–Sat 9.30am–5pm, ☎01273/778855), which also acts as a box office for match tickets.

Barmy army

The campaigning spirit shown by Brighton fans in recent years has been thoroughly commendable, but there was sometimes a fine line between full-blooded protest and bloody violence.

There were some unsavoury incidents at Gillingham during 1998/99, and the board is understandably nervous that trouble at Withdean during 1999/2000 will undo much of the good work that has been done in 'selling' Albion to the town's soccer-sceptical tendency.

In print

The ***Evening Argus***, which did so much to expose the boardroom shenanigans of the mid-Nineties, is the best place to look for Albion news and reports – look out for the ***Sports Argus*** on Saturday afternoons.

Albion's fanzine industy has thrived amid all the chaos. ***Build A Bonfire*** (22 Harding Avenue, Eastbourne, BN22 8PH) and ***Scars And Stripes*** (10 Greenland Close, Durrington, Worthing, BN13 2RP) have both retained their independent spirit, and Albion's **matchday programme** has been taken over by the latter – talk about a revolution.

Build A Bonfire is also the title of an excellent book about Albion's recent problems by Steve North and Paul Hodson (Mainstream, £14.99). The book uses pictures from the lens of Stewart Weir, whose own book reflecting the same era, ***More Than Ninety Minutes*** (self-published, £21.95), is one of the most powerful collections of football photography you will see.

For those who want to go back further than 1995, ***Seagulls – The Story of Brighton & Hove Albion*** by Tim Carder and Roger Harris (Goldstone Books, £19.95) is the seminal history.

On air

BBC Southern Counties Radio (95.3 FM) does battle with ***Capital Gold*** (1323 AM) for the moral high ground over the future of the club.

In the net

Albion's **official site** is at: www.seagulls.co.uk. It features regular news updates and an in-depth history section, but doesn't quite have the campaigning feel you expect. For the real supporters' spirit try ***Seagulls – The View From The Net***, at: www.domtech.co.uk/Seagulls/seagulls.nsf. This is where you'll find all the latest news on Withdean, Falmer and other pressing issues.

Also well worth a look is a small but perfectly formed site belonging to **Tim Carder**, chairman of the Supporters' Club, at: www3.mistral.co.uk/timc/index.html. It includes reports from club meetings as well as providing a repository for Carder's formidable Albion archive.

Bristol City

Formation	1894 as Bristol South End
Stadium	Ashton Gate, Bristol, BS3 2EJ. ☎0117/963 0630
Ground capacity	21,500
First-choice colours	Red and white
Major honours	Second Division champions 1906; Third Division (South) champions 1923, 1927, 1955; Welsh Cup winners 1934; Anglo-Scottish Cup winners 1978; Freight Rover Trophy winners 1986
Position 1998/99	24th in First Division (relegated)

Ah, Bristol. The last great underachieving metropolis of English football, as the legend has it. Hardly has a word been written to describe the city's contribution to the game without reference to its curious inability to produce successful teams, or to its vast, untapped potential. Yet it's as true today as it's ever been – Bristol is still a footballing nerve-centre waiting to happen. The question is: why are we still waiting?

The popular answer is that Bristol, along with its immediate hinterland, is essentially rugby country, where the round-ball game has enjoyed only brief periods of supremacy, and where the egg-chasers have had things their own way for most of the modern era. Added to this has been the culture clash between the city's two senior football clubs, City and Rovers – an intense, at times downright unpleasant rivalry that has consistently robbed the less committed elements of Bristol's soccer support of a single cause to rally around.

There's an element of truth in all this. But closer scrutiny reveals that the area's major rugby union force, Bath, are not what they were, while the local Bristol club has spent the last couple of seasons teetering on the edge of oblivion – a situation that has had particular ramifications for Bristol Rovers. As for the rivalry, with no other professional sides for miles around there should be plenty of room for both clubs. Besides which, there's nothing like single-minded support to keep the turnstiles ticking and the cash-tills ringing.

Jordan's Gate – Joe waves to the faithful

What can't be denied, though, is that sport in general has traditionally been pretty low down on Bristol's list of priorities. Even today, as the city's great railway and dockyard heritage is being re-invented to provide new leisure amenities, as new hi-tech developments gleam confidently around the periphery, and as the mellow-mood sounds of Massive Attack and Portishead give local pop culture a richly

If the cap doesn't fit – Benny Lennartsson ponders his fate

to enter the professional world of the Southern League. At a meeting in Bedminster's Albert Hall, the proposal was accepted and it was agreed to form a limited company under the name of Bristol City. At the same meeting, members decided to recruit the manager of Woolwich Arsenal, Sam Hollis, and to give him a transfer budget of £40 with which to buy new players. Three years later, the slow process of rationalisation of Bristol football began when City absorbed their near neighbours, Bedminster FC.

deserved audience in the wider world, Bristolians seem reluctant to shout out loud for the sportsmen (and sportswomen) who represent their town.

Such reticence is particularly frustrating for Bristol City, the club recent history suggests would have most to gain from a mass galvanisation of the city's missing thousands. With a large, decently appointed ground, a long history of football in the upper half of the League, a broad base of support and an ambitious chairman in Scott Davidson, City should be going places. Instead, at the end of the 1998/99 season the only place they went was down – to the Second Division, where they could re-acquaint themselves with Rovers but where, in all other respects, the outlook was obviously less promising.

Given the present climate of indifference, one of the great ironies for City is that in the year they turned professional, 1897, football was becoming so popular in Bristol that four other clubs took the same step at roughly the same time. City had started out three years earlier as Bristol South End, playing their football at a ground in St John's Lane in the district of Bedminster. They soon gained admission to the largely amateur Western League, but in 1897 some members expressed the desire

The attraction of Bedminster was that their ground, about a mile away at Ashton Gate, was better-equipped than City's. Yet during the merged club's first year of existence, the team shared home games more or less equally between Ashton Gate and St John's Lane.

Admission to the Second Division of the Football League in 1901 forced City to choose a single home ground. Initially this was St John's Lane, but with the directors unable to agree the terms of a new lease in 1904, the club switched permanently to Ashton Gate.

Perhaps relieved at finally possessing a settled home, the team excelled themselves in 1905/06, winning 30 of their 38 games (including 14 in succession in the early part of the season) to win the Second Division title. With Billy Wedlock, the so-called 'India Rubber Man' and an England international at the heart of their defence, City then finished as runners-up to Newcastle in their first season of First Division football, and although they subsequently drifted into mid-table, they also reached the 1909 FA Cup final, losing to Manchester United by the only goal.

Within two years the club had been relegated, and City were destined not to reach the same pinnacle of achievement again. They were a regular Second Division outfit either side of World War I, and after reaching the FA Cup semi-finals in 1920, they dropped into the Third Division (South). With cash becoming increasingly scarce, they bounced between those two divisions for the remainder of the Twenties before settling in the lower of the two for the bulk of the Thirties, crashing to a 9–0 defeat by Coventry, the club's biggest-ever loss, along the way.

It was much the same story after World War II, but attendances rose on the back of the post-austerity boom, and the goalscoring of Don Clark and, later, John Atyeo kept the crowds entertained if not always inspired. A local lad from nearby Westbury, Atyeo was to become something of a phenomenon, winning six England caps despite spending his entire career with City, much of it in the Third Division. He finally retired in 1966, having played more than 600 games for the club and averaged more than a goal every other game.

Atyeo's goals had helped City into the Second Division in 1955, and after relegation five years later, they would do so again in 1965. On this second occasion, the club was better prepared to consolidate its position, all the more so with the arrival of Alan Dicks as manager in 1967.

Compared with the teams of the Atyeo era, Dicks' City weren't always enthralling to watch. But they were undoubtedly effective, and after years of steadily building Second Division security, City scratched their 65-year itch and rejoined the top flight in 1976. The side's fighting spirit was typified by the tigerish Gerry Gow in midfield, but there was also a lighter side to their game, much of it revolving around energetic young striker Kevin Mabbutt – City had won many friends by the time they were relegated in 1980.

Inevitably, the drop resulted in the departure of Dicks and many of his stars. As it transpired, they were well out of it. Two more relegations followed in successive seasons, and in 1982, with City in the Fourth Division for the first time in their history, the receivers were called in. Gate income had plummeted, but the club's directors, hoping against hope for a turn in the tide, had been trying to maintain a First Division squad. The net result was insolvency, and while senior players ripped up their contracts and offered to play for nothing so that City could at least fulfil their fixtures, the former Leeds full-back Terry Cooper succeeded a young Roy Hodgson as manager. Cooper had been player-boss at Bristol Rovers earlier in the decade, but had also played briefly for City – his experience of 'mucking in' at both clubs stood him in good stead for what was to come.

With the club re-formed as Bristol City (1982) plc, Cooper joined a reconstituted board of directors. But money was still too tight to mention, and while Cooper gave first-team berths to 16-year-old YTS boys, he also continued to play himself, despite turning 40 by the time City scraped their way out of the Fourth Division in 1984.

Coming and going – record buy Ade Akinbiyi

Two years after that, Cooper brought a former Leeds team-mate, Scottish striker Joe Jordan, to Ashton Gate to play out the last years of his career. A strong-willed motivator but also an astute reader of the game, Jordan was the obvious choice to replace Cooper when the City revival stalled in 1988. Jordan's side, with the experienced John Bailey and Rob Newman in defence and Mark Gavin and Alan Walsh supporting the manager in upfront, reached the 1989 League Cup semi-finals – where they played Nottingham Forest off the park for much of the tie before losing 2–1 over two legs. A year later they got a more permanent reward for their efforts with promotion to the Second Division, and for a while the sky seemed to be City's limit.

But then Jordan was tempted back to Scotland to manage Hearts, and his former assistant Jimmy Lumsden couldn't match his mentor's authority. City maintained a presence in the Second Division as it was renamed the First – an uneventful era, but one enlivened by the arrival of striker Andy Cole, rejected by Arsenal for not pulling his weight, but a goalscorer perfectly suited to the languid Bristol style.

Further Cup runs under Russell Osman followed Cole's club-record £1.75million sale to Newcastle in 1993, but an ill-advised return by Jordan culminated in relegation two years later. Two more ex-Rovers men, John Ward and Terry Connor, got City back up again in 1998 after a play-off failure the previous year. Ward's side had given Graham Taylor's Watford a run for their money at the top of the Second Division table, and with the £1.2million signing of Gillingham striker Ade Akinbiyi in the close season, City's future again looked bright.

But after a run of poor results in the first part of the 1998/99 season, Ward was dismissed by an impatient board and replaced by Swedish coach Benny Lennartsson. He promptly made a series of foreign signings including Hungarian defender Vilmos Sebök and the first Moldovan ever to play English football, Ion Testimitanu. They were undoubtedly skilful, but their talents never gelled with the rest of the team, and City, after promising so much, finished bottom of the First Division.

In the summer of 1999, Gillingham's Tony Pulis – yet another man with Rovers connections – was recruited as successor to Lennartsson, while the club had to deal with a transfer request from Akinbiyi. The long wait goes on…

Here we go!

Motorists coming from either the M5 (north) or the M4/M32 (east) should follow signs for the A370 Weston or A38 Taunton. The ground is in

Derby day disturbance – mounted police approach the Atyeo Stand, 1996

Ashton Road, off the A3029 Winterstoke Road which joins the A370 as Brunel Way. Winterstoke Road is not a bad area for **car parking**, which is just as well as there are no formal facilities at Ashton Gate itself.

Bristol Temple Meads **train station** gets regular direct trains from Birmingham, Manchester, Leeds and London Paddington among many other places, but late trains for midweek games are thin on the ground. For the latest timings call ☎0345/484950.

The station is too far away from Ashton Gate to walk, but the #528 bus will take you all the way. If you've just missed one, taxis are plentiful – budget for a £5 fare.

Just the ticket

Visiting fans are allocated seats in sections of the Covered End, opposite the Atyeo Stand, the size of the allocation depending on the match. Tickets also vary according to the fixture, but are around £15 for adults, £9 concessions.

Disabled visitors are accommodated in one corner of the Covered End, advance booking essential on ☎0117/963 0630.

Swift half

The ***Ship & Castle*** on Ashton Vale Road is a small, family-friendly pub and a good place to escape the occasionally intimidating atmosphere before matches. Alternatively, for the contemporary Bristol experience try the **Hotwells area** of town, to the north of Ashton Gate, where cool pubs, plentiful **food options** and dockside vistas await.

Club merchandise

The ***City Supershop*** at one end of the Atyeo Stand (☎0117/963 0609) will sell you anything you like so long as it's not blue. The club's new 1999/2000 shirts are £39.99 (kids' sizes £29.99).

Barmy army

City's reputation for trouble stems almost entirely from the rivalry with Rovers, which resulted in pitch invasions in both the last two seasons in which the clubs were in the same division. Arson attacks, running battles with police and brawling in pubs all come with this most disputed of football territories.

Meanwhile, fans of many other teams marvel at the wall of noise (for a city that's supposed to be out of love with football) that emanates from the Cider'Eds in the Atyeo Stand.

In print

You'd never know Bristol wasn't a sporting town from the local ***Evening Post***, which publishes the excellent *Green'Un* after final whistle on a Saturday. There were at least two fanzines at the last count: ***One Team In Bristol*** (PO Box 12, Burnham On Sea, TA8 2YZ) and ***The Cider'Ed*** (3 Ravenswood Road, Redland, BS6 6BN).

The essential City book is ***Bristol City FC – The First 100 Years*** (£18.95), by Leigh Edwards and David Woods, published in 1997.

On air

BBC Radio Bristol (94.9 FM) is the place for local sport, with a Saturday afternoon show between 2pm and 6pm.

In the net

The **official site** is run by the club's media department and includes a tidy potted history, a news archive and online shopping, with more features promised for the future. See how far they've got at: www.bcfc.co.uk.

Of the unofficials, one of the most original is ***Bristol City ZybeReds***, which boasts smart graphics, witty content and that rare but always welcome feature, a proper site map. Again, more holes being filled all the time, at: www.bcfc.org.uk.

Bristol Rovers

Formation	1883 as Black Arabs
Stadium	Memorial Stadium, Filton Avenue, Horfield, Bristol, BS4 5BF. ☎0117/977 2000
Ground capacity	9,200
First-choice colours	Blue-and-white quarters
Major honours	Third Division champions 1990; Third Division (South) champions 1953
Position 1998/99	13th in Second Division

When Bristol Rovers returned to their city of origin after a decade-long exile in nearby Bath, their first match was attended by the city's Mayoress. A nice touch, you might think. But the lady in question chose to wear red for the occasion – adding further fuel to the argument, long-held by Rovers fans, that the local council is stuffed full of Bristol City supporters who have done everything in their power to prevent the Rovers' return to town, and will now do everything they can to make that return as unprofitable as possible.

Thousands of football fans have a persecution complex, but the Rovers faithful bear bigger chips on their shoulders than most, and for good reason. Quite aside from their antipathy toward the local council (of which more anon), their club has suffered two stadium fires, had two players banned for life for their involvement in a bribery scandal, come worryingly close to extinction on several occasions, and never played a single season of top-flight football. Yet, football being what it is, Rovers also inspire tremendous support that has, if anything, been made more enthusiastic by each tragic reverse.

The club was formed in 1883 by a group of schoolteachers after a meeting at a restaurant in Stapleton Road, in the Eastville district of Bristol. They played on a pitch at Purdown in the east of the city, alongside a field used by a rugby club known as The Arabs. The footballers copied the Arabs' black shirts with a yellow diagonal sash, and called themselves the Black Arabs for a season before opting for the more conventional-sounding Eastville Rovers. For the first few years the club was arranged on an informal basis, playing only friendly matches and moving from ground to ground. But in 1892 Rovers joined the Bristol & District League, the forerunner of the Western League, and five years later they moved to the Eastville Football & Athletic Ground, purchased for £150 from the Bristol Harlequins rugby club.

To reflect the improved facilities of its home patch, the club turned professional before the start of the 1897/98 season, and changed its name to Bristol Eastville Rovers at the same time. A year later the 'Eastville' bit was dropped, and a year after that the team joined the Southern League, acquitting themselves with surprising ease and winning the championship in 1905.

By this time, neighbours Bristol City had been admitted to the Second Division of the Football League. Rovers, in contrast, remained loyal to the Southern League up to and after World War I. But in 1920 they were unable to resist the mass exodus of clubs to the newly formed Third Division (South). They finished tenth in their first season of League football, but found the going much tougher than the old Southern League, and after a decades of toil in mid-table, manager Albert Prince-Cox decided that drastic measures were needed. In an attempt to make his players look larger than life, he dressed them in blue-and-white quartered shirts. It made no difference whatsoever, and in 1932 the club was forced to adapt the Eastville for greyhound racing in an attempt to generate

Moving the goalposts – football takes over from rugby at the Memorial Stadium

extra revenue. On the eve of World War II Rovers were forced to seek re-election to the League, and by 1940, with Hitler's bombs falling on Bristol and the club facing bankruptcy, chairman Fred Ashmead sold the Eastville ground to the greyhound company. The rest of his board complained bitterly that the £12,000 Rovers were offered for the stadium didn't cover their existing debts, but they were too late…

After the war, a manager with a less eccentric approach finally turned Rovers into a team to be feared for reasons other than the design of their shirts. His name was Bert Tann, and his appointment in 1950 resulted in the team adopting a simple yet effective approach to the game. Tann's squad was decidedly average-looking with the exception of its two menacing centre-forwards, Alfie Biggs and Geoff Bradford. Reasoning that Rovers should play to their strengths, Tann told his players to get the ball forward early. They did, and while footballing purists might have scoffed at this early incarnation of the 'long-ball game', the Eastville fans weren't complaining. In 1953 Rovers won the Third Division (South) title to gain promotion for the first time. They then established themselves as a useful Second Division side, and in 1956 Manchester United, featuring all the 'Busby Babes' apart from Duncan Edwards, were humbled 4–0 in the third round of the FA Cup.

Rovers remained in the right half of the Second Division – though never really challenging any higher – until Biggs departed for Preston in 1961. He was back at Eastville in a little over a year, but by then Rovers had returned to the Third Division. Bradford retired a year later, his record as the only man ever to be capped by England while playing for Rovers remaining to this day. Biggs soldiered on until 1967, while Bert Tann and the playing style he favoured hung around until 1972, his last four years having been spent as a less involved but still committed general manager.

Within two years Rovers had won promotion again under the guidance of Don Megson, and they would spent the rest of the Seventies in the Second Division, at

Check this out – player-coach Gary Penrice (centre) tries a shot against Leyton Orient, 1999

times playing neater football than in Tann's time but, significantly, always hovering dangerously above the drop zone.

Relegation finally came at the end of the 1980/81 season, but in many ways that was the least significant event of the campaign for Rovers. On 16 August 1980, the South Stand at Eastville was gutted by fire, destroying all the club's records as well as its dressing rooms and other facilities. At the time, rumours were rife that the blaze had been started deliberately by City fans (it was subsequently attributed to an electrical fault), and while Rovers were forced to play a handful of home games at City's Ashton Gate ground, the club was determined to move back to Eastville at the earliest opportunity.

Alas, the greyhound company was equally determined to make life for the football club difficult. With the dogs bringing in more money than football, the stadium's owners raised Rovers' rent to a level they knew the club could not afford. Reluctantly, Rovers agreed to ground-share at Ashton Gate but, just as they were about to pen to paper on the deal, Bristol City went into receivership. When the City board was reconstituted, the directors decided to double Rovers' agreed rent. Now there was no option but to go back to Eastville, but after four loss-making years there, the club decided enough was enough and agreed a ground-sharing deal with non-League Bath City for the use of Twerton Park, 13 miles east of Bristol.

While the new arrangement had obvious disadvantages, initially the escape from Eastville seemed to have a cleansing effect on the team. Under new manager Gerry Francis, a classic line-up including Nigel Martyn in goal, Geoff Twentyman in the heart of the defence, Ian Holloway on the right flank and a goal-hungry strikeforce of Devon White and Gary Penrice began thrilling the small but dedicated band of Rovers followers who made the regular trip out to Bath, with an entertaining (and surprisingly successful) brand of football.

After a play-off final loss to Port Vale in 1989, Rovers made no mistake the following year, winning the Third Division title and also making a historic first trip to Wembley for the Leyland Daf final, lost with honour to Tranmere Rovers. Sadly, Gerry Francis left for Queen's Park Rangers the following year, and took Ian Holloway with him. Even more sadly, in September 1990 the Main Stand and social club at Twerton Park were destroyed by fire, and this time there was no doubt as to who was to blame. A group of Bristol City fans had stopped off in Bath to start the blaze on their way home from an away game – seven were later convicted of arson.

The ground was quickly (if expensively) restored, but as the Nineties wore on, Rovers became increasingly restless at Twerton, all the more so after relegation to what was now the Second Division in 1993. Yet all attempts at finding a site for a new stadium closer to Bristol ended in blind alleys. One, at Hallen Marsh, came with the recommendation of the city council, who neglected to tell Rovers that it was too close to a local chemical works to be considered safe. (By the time they found out, chairman Denis Dunford and his son Geoff had already shelled out £300,000 on the project.) Another, at Pilning, conveniently outside city council jurisdiction but still within reasonable distance of Bristol, had to be abandoned after the land's owners, *ICI*, had a change of heart.

Finally, in 1996, Rovers agreed to move in with Bristol RFC at the rugby club's Memorial Ground. The ground had only two small stands and no spectator accommodation at all at one end, but at least it was in Bristol. Scarcely had Rovers managed a season of football there, however, than the rugby club hit money trouble and were forced to sell half the Memorial Ground to Rovers for £2.3million. Not long after, Bristol RFC went into receivership, and the Dunfords invoked a clause in their buyout contract that enabled them to purchase the remaining 50% share in the Memorial Ground for £100,000. Needless to say, the rugby club was not best pleased, while Rovers fans, stunned that the pendulum of fortune had finally swung their way, were overwhelmed with joy.

Now all the club needs is First Division football to go with its new-found security. Ian Holloway and Gary Penrice, who returned to Rovers as manager and player-coach respectively in 1996, steered the team into the play-offs within two seasons. They were beaten by Northampton after winning their home leg 3–1, and although 1998/99 contained an enjoyable Cup run, the side's inconsistency and inexperience combined to shackle them in mid-table in the League. But, then again, fans may breathe a sigh of relief at the prospect of their club going nowhere fast.

Here we go!

Coming from the east, **motorists** should exit the M32 at junction 2 and turn right onto the B4469 toward Horfield. After about a mile and a half, turn left at the lights into Filton Avenue, and left again for the club **car park**.

From the north or south, exit the M5 at junction 16 and take the A38 in toward Bristol city centre. After five miles turn left at the lights onto the B4469, then right at the next lights into Filton Avenue. If the car park is full, you're probably too late for convenient street parking as well – best arrive early.

Not gone, but forgotten – Twerton Park, Bath, home for too long

A Rover returns – Ian Holloway leads the charge against City, 1996

Bristol Parkway **train station** (see Bristol City for services, which are similar but not identical to those for Temple Meads) is the nearest to the ground but still about 2miles away – catch bus #73 to Filton Avenue, or take a cab (£6).

Just the ticket

Visiting fans are accommodated in the small terrace alongside the Centenary Stand – entrance in Alton Road. Ticket prices in 1999/2000 are adults £10, concessions £5. For Cup-ties and other big games, some seating is made available to visitors in the Centenary Stand.

The club can increase the amount of space allocated to **disabled visitors** by prior arrangement, so booking is essential on ☎0117/977 2000.

Swift half

The area around the A38 Gloucester Road positively brims with football-friendly pubs, including the ***Wellington*** and the ***John Cabot***. Both of these also welcome families.

When it comes to food, this is Bristol's curry-land so it seems daft not to sample a biryani or two. Again, Gloucester Road is the place to be.

Club merchandise

After a nasty moment three seasons ago when the players wore striped quarters, the plain blue-and-white affair is now back for what fans hope is a permanent return.

Barmy army

While Rovers fans have never resorted to arson attacks on Ashton Gate, the hardcore element within the 'Gasheads' (so-called because of the gasworks which once spread noxious odours across Eastville) support is far from blameless in the ongoing feud with City. That said, those supporters who fought local council elections under the *Bristol Party* banner in 1994 were campaigning for a healthier political attitude to city sports in general, not just for Rovers' return to Bristol.

In print

The ***Evening Post*** publishes the excellent *Green'Un* on Saturday evenings.

The established fanzines are ***Black Arab*** (PO Box 1740, Chipping Sodbury, BS37 6BF) and ***The 2nd Of May*** (17 Glyn Road, London, E5 0JB).

Pirates In Profile (£6.99) by Mike Jay and Stephen Byrne is a who's who of Rovers players covering the years 1920 to 1994.

On air

BBC Radio Bristol (94.9 FM) once boasted a vocal *Bristol Party* supporter in presenter Colin Howlett, who initially led the political campaign but stepped down due to a conflict of interest.

In the net

Rovers' **official website** is a superb collection of audio, video, information and supporter comment, free of frills and much the better for it. Be astounded at: www.bristolrovers.co.uk. Also excellent are two of the many unofficial offerings – ***The Temple Of Bristol Rovers*** at: www.geocities.com/Colosseum/Stadium/5022; and ***Pride Of The West*** at: www.btinternet.com/~uk/BRFC/.

Burnley

Formation	1881 as Burnley Rovers
Stadium	Turf Moor, Burnley, BB10 4BX. ☎01282/700000
Ground capacity	22,500
First-choice colours	Claret and sky blue
Major honours	League champions 1921, 1960; Second Division champions 1898, 1973; Third Division champions 1982; Fourth Division champions 1992; FA Cup winners 1914
Position 1998/99	15th in Second Division

Of all the Lancashire mill towns to spawn successful football clubs in the latter half of the 19th century, Burnley was the smallest. Even in the heyday of the cotton industry, fewer than 100,000 souls lived here. Yet the teams which represented the town did so with irrepressible pride. More than that, they possessed a spirit and a style distinctive enough to make Burnley a household name, not just in Britain but across Europe and the world. Today, most of the mills have gone, as have the coal mines which also once employed thousands in the town and surrounding area. Even the *Burnley Building Society*, a market leader two decades ago, is no more. But if both heavy industry and the service sector have gone, and not yet been replaced by much, the football team plays on – at a ground which has been home since 1883, in front of fans who are as knowledgeable as they are loyal, and dropping the occasional hint that maybe, just maybe, another glorious era may yet beckon Burnley.

If that sounds fanciful, it's worth remembering that even the club's early history was something of a mixed bag, consistency having eluded Burnley for most of their 118-year existence. In the team's formative years, after the Burnley Rovers rugby club had decided to swap codes, they were given hard lessons in the art of the round-ball game by better-established sides from nearby Accrington, Darwen, Nelson and elsewhere. Initially the team played at Calder Vale, but in February 1883 the local cricket club invited them to use a patch of land next to their ground called Turf Moor.

The town's love affair with football began soon after, the club having to excavate soil around the pitch in order to accommodate spectators for what were still essentially exhibition matches against local opposition. If 12,000 fans could be attracted to Turf Moor for a friendly, what could competitive football achieve? Burnley were soon to find out, embarking on a couple of FA Cup runs before being invited to join the Football League as founder members in 1888. Joining the League was a big leap, perhaps too big – Burnley had never managed better than mid-table anonymity before being relegated in 1897.

The team were too good for the Second Division, however, bouncing straight back with the help of Jimmy Ross' goals to win promotion as divisional champions a year later. Locally, too, the club had consolidated its position – Accrington had already dropped out of the League, while Darwen, thumped 9–0 by Burnley in 1892, would also depart the scene not long after.

By 1900, however, Burnley were back in the Second Division and apparently going nowhere fast. The turning point came in 1911 when a female fan advised the team that their green shirts were unlucky. The search was on for a new colour scheme, and Burnley drew inspiration from the great Aston Villa side of the era, copying their claret shirts with sky-blue sleeves. The effect was all but immediate – Burnley were back in the top flight by 1913, and a year later, they beat Liverpool 1–0 at Crystal Palace to win the FA Cup.

The team then finished fourth at the end of the last League season before World

Ill-starred all-stars – Burnley's class of '68 were unfortunately dubbed 'Team of the Seventies'

War I, and once the war was over Burnley recovered their shape with surprising ease. They were League runners-up in 1920 before being crowned champions for the first time the following year. The key to Turf Moor's triumph lay in its half-back line. At a time when a good 'half' could turn a game, Burnley had not one but three – George Halley, Tommy Boyle and William Watson, majestic individuals all and, having played together since before the 1914 Cup final, also a formidable unit. Two other men also played a pivotal role: goalkeeper Jerry Dawson, who'd been an indispensable last line of defence since making his Burnley debut in 1907 (and who would remain at the club for another seven years after the championship season), and John Haworth, whose appointment as the club's first modern 'manager' in 1911 coincided with the club's change of colours – and probably had a much more significant effect.

Between them, these disparate but complementary talents enabled Burnley to go 30 League games unbeaten at one point during the 1920/21 season – a record then and now. But if Haworth thought he was on the brink of creating an invincible team for the brave new decade, he was mistaken. Burnley would be no match for the Liverpool side that was to take a grip on the championship for the next two seasons, and by the time Herbert Chapman's Huddersfield began to revolutionise the way English teams were coached in the mid-Twenties, Turf Moor was struggling to keep pace. After Haworth's departure in 1925, Burnley took up residence in the wrong half of the First Division table, shipping 100-odd goals per season before finally dropping to the Second Division in 1930.

There Burnley remained until the outbreak of World War II. In contrast to the 1914–18 conflict, this pause in competitive football gave the club a welcome chance to rebuild, with Cliff Britton as new first-team boss. In the first full season of postwar action, 1946/47, Burnley returned to their most deftly disciplined ways, keeping 25 clean sheets on their way to a runners-up spot and promotion back to the First Division.

Just before that promotion was achieved, however, there was a first Wembley FA Cup final to look forward to, against top-flight Charlton Athletic. Going into the game as marginal underdogs, Burnley set their stall out early with captain Alan Brown organising a well-manned defence and inside-forwards Harry Potts and Billy Morris given few chances to express themselves. The scoresheet stayed predictably blank for 90 minutes and, once Burnley had gone a goal down in extra time, they found Charlton 'keeper Sam Bartram an unbreakable barrier.

While safety-first tactics had deprived Brown and Potts of a Cup-winner's medal, both men would subsequently get the chance to adopt bolder strategies in the manager's seat. Brown's spell in charge from 1954 to 1957 saw the team confirm their status as respectable occupants of the First Division's upper half. Behind the scenes, meanwhile, developments were taking place which were to shape the club's destiny for the next quarter-century. In 1951, local sausage-maker and wholesale butcher Bob Lord joined the board of directors. Within four years he had become chairman – a role he would occupy until his retirement through ill health in 1980. Lord reasoned that, even though a third of the town's population were regularly cramming into Turf Moor for home games, Burnley would always struggle to compete with the likes of Liverpool and Manchester United on gate receipts alone. He sought an alternative source of income and, in those innocent days before mass merchandising, there was only option – transfer revenues. Together with Brown, Lord negotiated the purchase of a 79-acre site at Gawthorpe Hall, an ideal location for a football academy. Before long young players were flocking to Burnley from across England and beyond, attracted by the club's training facilities and the long contracts offered them by Lord.

While Brown departed for Sunderland in 1957, the youth setup he'd instigated would soon deliver the goods for his former Burnley team-mate, Harry Potts, who took over as manager when Billy Dougal stepped down on health grounds in 1958. Given overall responsibility for the club's entire playing staff, Potts set about ensuring that every Burnley side, from the youngest apprentices to the first team, played to the same system, so that a teenager could be called up to the senior side at short notice and not feel out of place. He also preached fluidity players were encouraged to swap roles on the field at will, covering for each other repeatedly in training until it came naturally.

Today it all sounds like Ajax and the Dutch obsession with 'total football'. But this was north-east Lancashire at the end of the Fifties – nobody had heard of Ajax, and 'total football' hadn't yet been invented, not in Holland or anywhere else for that matter. Whatever it was called, the rest of the League weren't ready for it. Bob Lord had predicted Potts' side would take the title in 1962; they actually captured it two years earlier, winning 2–1 at Manchester City to pip Wolves, the long-time leaders, by a point.

Of the 18 players Potts used during the 1959/60 season, half had come through Burnley's youth scheme, and only two – inside-forward Jimmy McIlroy and full-back Alex Elder, both bought from the Ulster club Glentoran – had cost the club any money to sign. As well as the two Irishmen, there were pivotal players in the half-back line, just as there'd been in 1921: Tommy Cummings, Brian Miller and captain Jimmy Adamson. John Connelly provided pace, vision and goals from the wing, while centre-forward Ray Pointer was an able target on those occasions that Connelly chose not to go for goal himself.

With no other English club even close to assembling a talent factory as sophisticated and single-minded as Burnley's, Potts' side were expected to dominate the game throughout the early Sixties. Alas, they were quickly eclipsed by Bill Nicholson's 'push-and-run' Tottenham, coming close to a League and Cup double in 1962, but failing

Burnley's bullying butcher – Bob Lord

to win either – that year's Cup final defeat by Spurs would be the swansong for the ageing Adamson and Cummings, while McIlroy would soon depart for Stoke, much to the dismay of fans, as Bob Lord went on a selling spree to balance the books.

And yet Burnley continued to poke fun at the football establishment for the remainder of the decade. They finished third in the League in 1963, and again in 1966, while in European competition, Stade de Reims, VfB Stuttgart, Lausanne and Napoli were all well-beaten at Turf Moor.

The mid-Sixties side, in which the experienced Miller, Elder and Andy Lochhead underpinned emerging talents such as midfielders Ralph Coates and Dave Thomas and forward Frank Casper, looked as well-balanced as any Potts had crafted. When another two cultured midfielders, Martin Dobson and Leighton James, were added to the mix, Burnley were dubbed the 'Team of the Seventies' – despite achieving only modest placings in the League. Media hype was never really Burnley's style (Bob Lord frequently banned journalists from the Turf Moor press box), and all the talk backfired on them. At the end of the 1970/71 season, the club's first with Potts as general manager and Jimmy Adamson as first-team boss, Burnley were relegated.

They were back up again within two years, and reached the FA Cup semi-finals in 1974. Two years after that, however, Burnley went down again, and this time there was no going back. Those stars who had remained loyal were sold off as Lord, losing his touch perhaps, needed the cash to pay for an expensive new main stand that would bear his name.

By the time the old pork butcher died in 1981, Burnley were playing Third Division football for the first time in their history. In the cruellest of ironies, the club's ability to compete had been destroyed by the abolition of the minimum wage, players' freedom of contract, and other innovations which Lord had done his utmost to encourage in his younger days. Meanwhile, economic recession was gripping the town, throwing many of the most loyal Clarets fans onto the dole. As their prospects dimmed, so did those of their beloved football team.

In 1982 Brian Miller guided an innovative side, with Dobson playing as sweeper behind the likes of Trevor Steven, Brian Laws and Mike Phelan, to the Third Division title. Yet within a year Miller's work had been undone by John Bond, who replaced him as manager, sold Laws to Huddersfield for peanuts and released his understudy, one Lee Dixon, on a free transfer. Bond soon departed after relegation and by 1985 Burnley had sunk into the Fourth Division. Two years later, only a last-day victory over Leyton Orient prevented them from slipping out of the League altogether. Just up the road, a tiny club called Colne Dynamoes was powering its way toward League status, with Harry Potts (who else?) at the helm.

Happily, the mood at Turf Moor has lightened since then, if only in fits and starts. The Dynamoes were stopped in their tracks when their millionaire backer pulled the plug in 1990. Manager Jimmy Mullen pulled Burnley up with a Fourth

Division title in 1992, followed by another promotion, via the play-offs, two years later. Burnley were relegated again immediately but have since found stability, of a kind, in the nether reaches of what is now the Second Division. Bob Lord would be proud of the redeveloped Turf Moor, which boasts new stands on two sides and is only one step away from Premiership standard. Even the old Gawthorpe grounds have been given a fresh lease of life, with all-weather pitches to help the stars of tomorrow train through the Lancashire rain.

Which is not to say that the fans are happy. Nor should they be. Burnley have had three managers – Adrian Heath, Chris Waddle and Stan Ternent – in the last three years, and none has managed anything more meaningful than a holding operation. Barry Kilby and Ray Ingleby, former rivals in the battle to take control of the club, are now united on a reconstituted board, but the fans will want to see any new money spent properly.

That's the trouble with Burnley. The geography is too small to sustain grand plans – but the history is too big to excuse anything less.

Here we go!

Most **motorists** will approach Burnley via the M6 and M65. Exit the latter at junction 10 and follow the A671 into town. Follow this road onto the Centenary Way dual carriageway, then turn right at the roundabout into Yorkshire Street. There is **street parking** in this area, the ground itself being a little further up on left-hand side, after Yorkshire Street has become Brunshaw Road. Alternatively, the cricket club has a **car park** on the corner of Brunshaw Road and Belvedere Road. Coming from the south-east, there is an alternative, cross-country route, running along the Calder Valley from junction 24 of the M62 (see Halifax Town) and approaching Burnley on the A646 from Todmorden. Beware, though, that while this route looks much more direct on the map – and is also very picturesque – it is painfully slow and prone to hard winter weather.

Burnley has two **train stations** – Burnley Manchester Road on the cross-country line from York, Leeds and Bradford to Blackpool, and Burnley Central, confusingly, for trains to Manchester. There are no midweek evening connections beyond Manchester or Leeds. Check the latest timings on ☎0345/484950.

Neither station is more than a 15min walk from Turf Moor. From Burnley Manchester Road, turn right at the roundabout onto Centenary Way and follow the directions for motorists above. From Burnley Central, follow signs for the Town Centre, walk through the Market Square and continue onto the opposite dual carriageway – turn right, then left at the roundabout into Yorkshire Street (see above).

Just the ticket

Visiting fans are housed at the Cricket Field end – enter via Brunshaw Road. There are more

The harder they fall – losing at home to Preston, 1999

than 4,000 seats here so space isn't usually a problem. Burnley raised its admission prices for the first time in three years in 1999 – visitors now pay £13, concesions £6.50.

Disabled visitors have their own enclosure in the Cricket Field Stand. Book through the club on ☎01282/700010.

Swift half

Police advise visiting fans to sup up out of town. Try the Blackburn area if approaching on the M65, or Hebden Bridge on the A646.

Alternatively, you can get a pint at the ground for reasonable money.

Club merchandise

The **club shop** (open Mon–Sat 9.30am–5.30pm, later on matchdays) is next-door to the Bob Lord Stand on Brunshaw Road. For 1999/2000 the club has a new kit supplier – *Glory Years*, owned by former Clarets player Frank Casper.

Barmy army

The old terraces may have gone but the Burnley faithful are exploiting the fine acoustics of the new James Hargreaves Stand (formerly the celebrated Longside) to excellent effect. Local police are edgy, advising visitors not to display colours on torsos or in cars. But there's nothing to stop you enjoying the noise and imagining what Turf Moor was like when there were 25,000 in.

In print

The ***Burnley Express***, which once had Jimmy McIlroy on its reporting staff, is the locals' choice for Turf Moor news but only publishes on Tuesdays and Fridays.

Alternatively, the ***Lancashire Evening Telegraph*** normally has a back-page lead on the Clarets and previews fixtures with a Saturday lunchtime edition.

Fanzine ***The Claret Flag*** (9 Romney Avenue, Burnley, BB11 2PG) tells it like it is, while Ray Simpson's ***The Clarets Collection 1946–1996*** (£16.95) is a readable postwar who's who.

On air

BBC Radio Lancashire (95.5 FM) has the ear of Burnley fans despite its obligation also to cover the dreaded Blackburn Rovers.

In the net

Burnley's **official site** is a credit to the Second Division, with clear layout and an unusually diverse links area. The club is also set to become an internet service provider with its ***Clarets Online*** operation. Head for: www.clarets.co.uk.

The ***Burnley FC Email Group*** are at: www.geocities.com/Colosseum/7075/index.html. As well as the expected chat and messageboard pages, the site also hosts the ***Clarets Archive***, a fascinating trawl through Turf Moor history as seen through the eyes of those who were there.

Picture postcard – Bob Lord Stand, club shop, and supporters sheltering under umbrellas

Bury

Formation 1885
Stadium Gigg Lane, Bury, BL9 9HR. ☎0161/764 4881
Ground capacity 11,800
First-choice colours White shirts, blue shorts
Major honours Second Division champions 1895, 1997; Third Division champions 1961; FA Cup winners 1900, 1903
Position 1998/99 22nd in First Division (relegated)

After the end of the 1998/99 season, unheralded and largely unnoticed, the Football League announced a change in its rules. As from the following season, 1999/2000, the League would be reverting to goal difference as its means of separating two or more clubs equal on points. Partly, the League explained, this was to achieve harmony with the Premiership. Mostly, though, it was because the experiment with 'goals scored', rather than goal difference, had failed to produce the wildly attacking football initially expected of it.

But while the rest of the footballing world was either too busy (doing its end-of-term housekeeping) or too lazy (on holiday) to remark on the change, it did not go unnoticed down Gigg Lane, Bury way. A cursory glance down the final tables for 1998/99 reveals that only one promotion or relegation issue would have been different had goal difference been applied a year early. Bury would have stayed up.

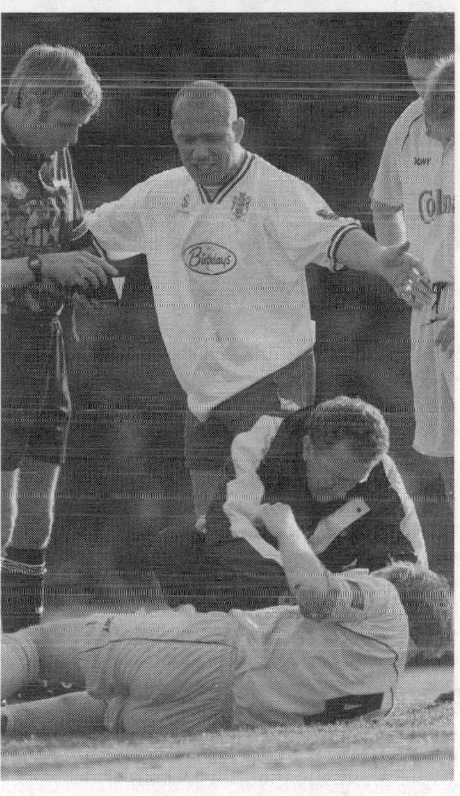

Famous last words – Darren Bullock pleads his innocence

Down at the wrong end of the First Division table, four clubs had finished level on 47 points, but only one of them had to drop. The club's goal-difference score of –25 was one better than Portsmouth's and five better than that of Port Vale, the team Bury beat 1–0 on the last day of the season. But Neil Warnock's side, always tough to break down and never knowing when they were beaten, had been struggling to score goals all season. Their final tally was just 35 from 46 games – easily the worst ratio in the entire League. As rule changes go, this one couldn't have been worse-timed for Bury.

The 'keeper who couldn't be kept – Dean Kiely, bound for Charlton Athletic

In the cold light of day, however, the Gigg Lane faithful knew deep down that Bury, for all their admirable fighting qualities, just didn't have the right resources to stay up. Had Oxford United (who went down) and Portsmouth not been going through crippling financial crises, then the lack of funds that is a fact of everyday life for Bury would probably have condemned the club to relegation much sooner. And in that respect, at least, little had changed since the team last dropped out of the upper half of England's senior footballing ladder, exactly three decades earlier.

This, after all, is a club which struggles to make ends meet in the long shadow cast by Old Trafford. Neville Neville and his wife Jill may do sterling work as the club's commercial manager and secretary, respectively, but their sons Gary and Philip, proud members of that other contemporary sporting family, *Fergie's Fledglings*, could probably draw as many local fans to a supermarket opening as Bury do to a League Cup tie on a Tuesday night. The town may have its own individual heritage and identity, but the *Metrolink* tram can whizz United (or City) fans into the centre of Manchester in a brace of shakes – leaving the Shakers, as Bury FC are nicknamed, a club in search of a constituency.

It hasn't always been this way. A century ago, when Manchester United were still Newton Heath and City had only just rid themselves of the name Ardwick, Bury had about as much trouble scoring goals as the Old Trafford shop has selling replica shirts. And not just any old goals, either – FA Cup final goals, the kind from which early reputations (and long-lasting records) are made.

In 1900, a Bury side led from the front by the likes of Charles Sagar and Jack Plant thrashed Southampton 4–0 in the final at Crystal Palace. It was the biggest winning margin in the history of the fixture, yet within three seasons Bury themselves had topped it. En route to the 1903 final, the Shakers went through every round without conceding a goal. At the final itself, there were mitigating circumstances. Their opponents, Derby County, fielded an injured goalkeeper, Jack Fryer. In the second half, Fryer took a further knock, and had to leave the field altogether. Even so, Bury's 6–0 winning margin – a Cup final record that's unlikely ever to be broken – did not flatter them. And it could easily have been more, for they hit the Derby woodwork twice, and had what looked a perfectly good penalty appeal turned down.

How gratifying these results must have been to the club's founding fathers, who in 1885 had got together with the intention merely of merging two church teams in order to create a united side to represent the town. The two original clubs were Bury Unitarians and Bury Wesleyans, and their members first came face to face with each other at a meeting in the *Waggon & Horses Hotel*. They got on better than they'd imagined, and at a second meeting in the *White Horse Hotel* on 24 April, it was agreed that the new club should be known simply as Bury FC.

It was also agreed that the club should pay its players wages, a common enough practice in the north-west for some years, but a concept only just legalised by the FA in London, which had up until this time regarded professionalism with suspicion. The new team also needed somewhere to play, and a plot of land on Gigg Lane was rented from the Earl of Derby, who owned the surrounding estate.

In 1887 Bury built their first stand at Gigg Lane, but the crowds didn't really turn up in numbers for another two years after that, when the club became a founder member of the Lancashire League. It was while playing in this League that Bury are thought to have earned their nickname, after the chairman predicted his team were going to give another local side 'a good shaking'. They probably did – Bury had played a key role in forming the League and were very much at home in it, winning the title in two successive years from 1892. Clearly in need of a new challenge, they were elected to the Second Division of the Football League, then promptly won it at the first attempt in 1895. (For the record, Newton Heath came third that year, ten points adrift of Bury, while Manchester City finished ninth.) After beating Liverpool 1–0 in a test match at Blackburn, Bury were promoted to the First Division.

While the team's Cup exploits would soon overshadow their League displays, Bury were by no means outclassed in the top flight, finishing fifth in 1901, seventh the following year and seventh again in 1908. Before long Gigg Lane could hold 20,000, and while there would be no more Cup finals, the club's star was still firmly in the ascendant.

Relegation arrived in 1912, however, and it wasn't until Earl Derby's unexpected decision to present the Gigg Lane freehold to the club as a gift in 1922 that the mood picked up again. Bury won promotion back to the top flight two years later, and finished fourth two years after that – the club's highest-ever League position.

The team stayed in the First Division until 1929, after which Bury settled on the next rung down for an extended period

Puffed away – Stan Ternent before his departure to Burnley

that would take them up to and beyond World War II. But the next move, in 1957, was down rather than up, as Gigg Lane tasted football in the lower half of the League for the first time. Manager Bob Stokoe led an inexperienced side to the Third Division title in 1961 and, augmented by the midfield prompting of a young Colin Bell, Bury clung grimly on to Second Division status, only for Bell to be sold to Manchester City and the club to drop down in 1966/67. The arrival of diminutive inside-forward Bobby Collins from Leeds helped to lift the team straight back up, but they came straight back down again, and by 1971 they had fallen into the Fourth Division – a slide that signalled an almost terminal decline in the club's fortunes.

For the next 20 years, Bury would hover listlessly between the bottom two divisions, discovering few new players of any great worth and winning few new friends within Greater Manchester's football community. Crowds which had averaged nearly 20,000 before World War II slid to around a fifth of that, which in a way was just as well because Gigg Lane, crippled by new safety regulations, could only hold 8,000 now anyway. In 1992, with £300,000 needed to make the ground safe and property developers breathing down Bury's neck, the club launched a supporters' bond, the *Shakers' Incentive Scheme*, and this, combined with a fortuitous third-round FA Cup draw away to Manchester United, kept the club afloat and playing at the only ground it had ever used.

In 1998/99, there was another Cup tie at United. Like the previous one, it was lost, but it provided a similar opportunity for Bury fans to contrast their modest, homely footballing experience with the Old Trafford mega-dream. By now, Gigg Lane itself was well on the way to becoming an all-seater venue, but the supporters weren't complaining. Stan Ternent and Sam Ellis had worked a minor miracle, taking the club from the basement to the First Division in two successive seasons. And if the team were struggling now, that wasn't altogether surprising – star player David Johnson had been sold to Ipswich for £1.1million, while Ternent and Ellis, frustrated by the lack of money available for players, had fled to Burnley in the summer of 1998. A year later, there was a further exodus, with two more players leaving Gigg Lane for seven-figure sums: impressive young goalkeeper Dean Kiely to Charlton, captain Chris Lucketti to Huddersfield.

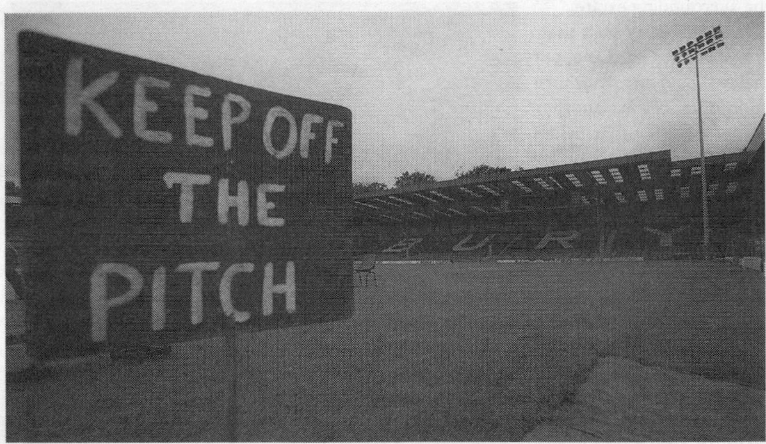

Message in a bottle-top – protecting the green, green grass of Bury's home

Their sales were a grim reminder of the consequences of Bury's relegation. And all because the League didn't change its rules in time…

Here we go!

Most **motorists** will probably approach on the M66 motorway. Exit at junction 3 and turn left (right if heading south) onto Pilsworth Road. Go straight over the roundabout and continue for about a mile before turning right at the lights onto Manchester Road. Gigg Lane is on the right after the playing fields on the left. There's no car park but **street parking** around Gigg Lane is in reasonable supply if you arrive early.

Bury's ***Metrolink* station** offers direct connections for Manchester Piccadilly mainline station (see Manchester City for services). It's about a 15min walk from the tram station to Gigg Lane, with some friendly pubs along the way. Turn left out of the station, left again at the T-junction into Knowlsey Street, then left into Manchester Road – Gigg Lane is a left-turning off this road.

Just the ticket

Visiting fans are allocated the whole of the Manchester Road end of the ground, where there are more than 2,000 seats. Ticket prices in 1998/99 were adults £14, concessions £8.

Disabled visitors have six spaces at the Manchester Road end – book in advance through your own club. **Visiting families** are also welcome in Bury's Family Stand, located at the Cemetery end of the Main Stand.

Swift half

The ***Bury FC Social Club***, just outside the ground on Gigg Lane itself, will admit away fans in small groups (guest admission £1) if it has room – arrive early to stand any chance. Alternatively, the ***Swan & Cemetery*** is the unofficial away fans' favourite on Manchester Road, while the ***Staff Of Life*** and the ***Pack Horse***, also on Manchester Road, both serve food and are happy to accommodate families.

Club merchandise

The **club shop** (☎0161/705 1244) is next-door to the *Social Club* but a new *Megastore* is planned for the Main Stand in the near future. An outlet for Bury town-centre is also planned.

Barmy army

With the Cemetery End due to be made all-seater for the 1999/2000 season, Bury fans will lose their last vestige of terracing and Gigg Lane, the detractors say, will never be the same. Whether the atmosphere really will be diminished is another matter, since supporters have already shown themselves to be a pretty hardy (not to say noisy) bunch.

Trouble is rare unless visiting fans – often from local sides – bring it with them.

In print

The ***Manchester Evening News*** produces its excellent *Pink* after the final whistle on Saturdays, with full coverage of Bury as well as the area's bigger clubs. For match previews there's also the ***Bury Times***.

Fanzines are ***The Hatchet*** (38 George Street, Sedgley Park, Prestwich, Manchester) and ***Where Were You At The Shay?*** (10 Andrew Close, Radcliffe, M26 1GQ).

Peter Cullen's Bury book in the ***Images Of England*** series (Tempus, £9.99) offers a pictorial account of the rise, fall and rise of the club.

On air

As is so often the case with smaller teams, Bury fans don't get much joy out of their local commercial station – in this case ***Piccadilly Radio*** (1152 AM) – which means it's back to the Beeb at ***GMR*** (95.1 FM).

In the net

The club's **official site** finally appeared at the end of the 1998/99 season, then disappeared again shortly after. Find it if you can at: www.buryfc.co.uk

Biggest of the unofficials is Gordon Sorfleet's site, but this has suffered a number of URL changes and was under reconstruction at press time. It should soon be back at: www.shakers-on-line.co.uk.

For an entertaining but thoughtful Gigg Lane perspective, take a peek at ***Dr P's Bury Diary*** at: www.geocities.com/Colosseum/Field/6751/bfcdiary.html.

Cambridge United

Formation	1919 as Abbey United
Stadium	The Abbey Stadium, Newmarket Road, Cambridge, CB5 8LN. ☎01223/566500
Ground capacity	9,600
First-choice colours	Amber with black trim
Major honours	Fourth Division champions 1977; Third Division champions 1991
Position 1998/99	Second in Second Division (promoted)

Professional football came late to Cambridge, and even today, there are those who say the game is not as important to the city as it might be. Historically this ambivalence was blamed on the city's student population, with its large rugby contingent and traditional indifference toward anything connected with 'the Town', as Cambridge United inevitably were. Today, student attitudes are changing (Nick Hornby used to go regularly, after all). But the once dependable working population is now increasingly transient, and feels no more loyalty to the local football club than all those ex-public schoolboys of yesteryear. And then, there are those diehard fans who continue to insist that it is Cambridge City, not United, who should have been elected to the League in 1970…

For decades, City were the elite team in Cambridge, with a ground near the centre of town and a long tradition of high-quality Southern League football. United, by contrast, played on the edge of the surrounding fenland countryside, on a pitch so bumpy it was known as 'the Celery Trenches', and attracting support mainly from outlying villages, rather than Cambridge itself. (In this respect, if in no other, local fans point to a parallel between the football scenes of Cambridge and Manchester. A comparison with Oxford would be nearer the mark.)

In the Celery Trenches days, the club was known as Abbey United, a name it retained until after World War II, when it turned professional and changed its name to Cambridge United. The team were by now playing at the Abbey Stadium, still some way from the city centre, but on a playing surface which did more to encourage good football. However, it wasn't until 1958, when United joined the Southern League, that City's local supremacy was threatened.

Throughout the Sixties the two clubs were at each other's throats, with City finishing one place above United, after an epic struggle, to win the Southern League Premier Division title in 1963. Four years later, United appointed Bill Leivers, a former Manchester City full-back, as manager, and in 1969 the team did a Southern League 'double' of Premier Division title and League Cup. Twelve months later they were champions again, retaining the title on 2 May, just 24 hours after playing Chelsea in a friendly at the Abbey, in front of a club-record 14,000. On 30 May, United were elected to the Football League by 31 votes to 17, in place of Bradford Park Avenue.

Like several freshly promoted non-League sides before and since, United found life in the Fourth Division more to their liking than they'd expected. Already a fully professional outfit, and backed by Leivers' knowledge of the top-flight game, they were promoted to the Third Division in 1973. This new status was much harder to maintain, though, and the team were relegated after only a season, in which they'd been beaten 6–0 by Darlington and Aldershot.

Leivers was replaced by a youthful, ambitious manager called Ron Atkinson, who quickly decided the club needed a complete overhaul of its playing staff. Out went almost all the players who'd brought

United out of the Southern League. In came two former Arsenal men, goalkeeper Malcolm Webster and full-back Brendon Batson; lanky central defender Steve Fallon; Steve Spriggs, a slight ball-winner from Huddersfield, and in attack, a Rod Stewart lookalike of a striker called Alan Biley, who arrived on a free transfer from Luton Town.

Dublin's fair pretty – Dion celebrates at Wembley, 1990

With only a modest playing career (most of it spent at Oxford United) and limited managerial experience (Kettering Town) behind him, 'Big Ron' had huge reserves of optimism and enthusiasm which quickly spread to the squad. United won the Fourth Division title in 1977, playing a brand of football that would not have seemed out of place two levels higher, and scoring 87 goals.

The following season, United were riding high at the top of the Third when Atkinson was approached by West Brom and left the Abbey, taking Batson with him. Big Ron maintained, though, that the team were good enough to be in the Second Division, and that the club could sustain that level of football 'if only we could persuade half the town to stop supporting City'. Atkinson's successor, John Docherty, duly took United up again, and the team finished their first Second Division season, 1978/79, in 12th place.

When Docherty brought George Reilly from Northampton to partner Biley in attack, United looked briefly to be heading for the top flight. But Biley was losing patience and at the start of 1980, he was sold to Derby for £350,000. Still, Cambridge finished eighth, and confirmation that the club was holding its own in this higher company came the following season, when Wolves and Aston Villa were both beaten in a run to the fourth round of the League Cup.

Three more mid-table finishes followed but, despite a decent FA Cup run in 1983, Docherty's side were beginning to break up. Reilly left for Graham Taylor's Watford and was not replaced, and Cambridge went a record 31 games without a win in 1983/84. Docherty was sacked and his replacement, player-manager John Ryan, could not prevent the side from being relegated.

Ryan stopped playing the following season, and might as well have quit the dugout, too – after United had won only three of their first 20 Third Division games, he was dismissed and replaced by Ken Shellito. Old stagers such as Fallon and Spriggs were still at the club, but they were powerless to prevent Cambridge going into freefall: under Shellito, the team went on another bizarre winless streak, this one running from Boxing Day 1984 to May Day 1985. They finished bottom, 25 points adrift of Preston, Orient and Burnley, the three clubs who went down with them.

Chris Turner, who'd played in central defence for Cambridge in the early Eighties, returned as manager. His first season ended with the club applying for re-election, but after the departure of Fallon and Spriggs (who'd made more than 800 appearances in a United shirt between them) had severed the last links with the Big Ron era, Turner set about rebuilding the team. There was little spare cash but the manager had an eye for a bargain, picking up strikers Dion Dublin and John Taylor as trainees from Norwich and Colchester respectively. Both scored hat-tricks within weeks of their debuts in early 1989, and that summer Turner added winger Lee Philpott to supply crosses for his promising strikeforce.

Even so, the team began 1989/90 in patchy form and Turner resigned halfway through. His assistant, John Beck, stepped in. Using the same line-up but crucially instructing his players to close the ball down in midfield and get it forward more quickly, Beck got instant results. Cambridge reached the quarter-finals of the FA Cup and, after winning seven of their last nine League games, they beat Maidstone United over two legs to qualify for the first promotion play-off ever to be played at Wembley. Their opponents, Chesterfield, were more experienced but, on a hot May afternoon, Beck's long-ball tactics drained them. Dublin headed home from a corner near the end, and Cambridge were up.

The following season, the same formula paid even richer dividends. In the prevailing, uneasy post-Hillsborough atmosphere, Cambridge were a refreshing novelty. The media loved Dublin's and Taylor's knock-about humour (their fathers had played together in Showaddywaddy, *The Sun* revealed) and Beck's unorthodox motivational tactics – cold showers and loud music were now *de rigueur* at the Abbey.

Beck's side reached the quarter-finals of the FA Cup again, before losing 2–1 at Arsenal. In the League they faced another absurd fixture backlog, but fitness levels and optimism were sky-high: after playing 18 games in 57 days, Cambridge finished the season as Third Division champions.

Like the Atkinson-Docherty side of the Seventies, they couldn't quite make it three promotions in a row. United finished fifth in the Second Division of 1991/92, above Blackburn and good enough for a play-off berth. But they were crushed 5–0 at Leicester, in a game that seemed to knock

On the spot – John Taylor, the club's record scorer, seals a three-goal comeback at Forest, 1998

The Abbey – everybody loves it except Cambridge themselves

the stuffing not just out of the team but out of the club's sense of ambition.

That summer Dublin was sold to Manchester United for £1 million, while Steve Claridge, another striker whose goals had been precious, went to Luton. The squad was further weakened by injuries and in October 1992, John Beck was sacked. At the end of the season Cambridge were relegated under Ian Atkins, and while his replacement Gary Johnson attempted to introduce a passing game in 1993/94, the squad wasn't strong enough to sustain it. Tommy Taylor replaced Johnson in April 1995, by which time United were in trouble again – they finished fifth from bottom of what was now the Second Division and, as that was being reduced in size, they found themselves relegated to the basement again.

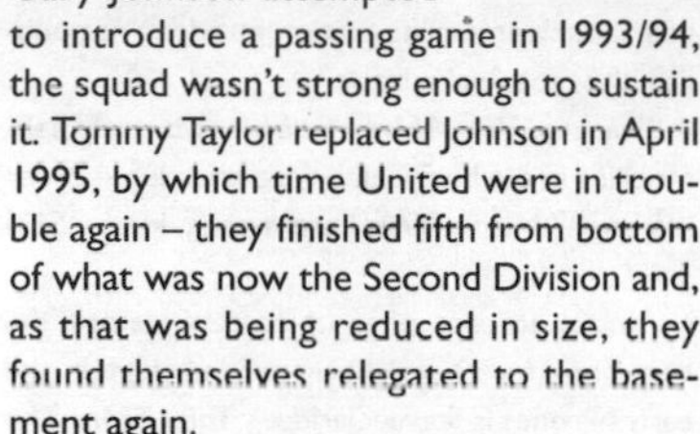

The acrimonious departure of Taylor to Leyton Orient in November 1996 opened the door for Roy McFarland to take charge, and gradually the former Derby captain's quiet, confident approach began to pay off.

In 1998/99, McFarland's young side – bolstered by the returning John Taylor – embarked on a fine League Cup run and took up near-permanent residence at the top of the Third Division table. Cambridge eventually lost the title after a 1–0 home defeat by Brentford on the season's final day, but promotion had long since been assured. The city, or at least some of it, waits with baited breath.

Here we go!

Motorists should avoid the centre of Cambridge at all costs, and beware that a new bus lane has turned Newmarket Road, in which the Abbey is situated, into a state of almost permanent gridlock.

From London and the south, take the M11 motorway and exit at junction 9 (signposted A11 Norwich), and stay on this road until the A604/A1307 exit (signposted Linton). Turn left at the roundabout onto the A1307 toward Cambridge, go straight on at the first roundabout, then right at the next one into Queen Edith's Way. Go straight on at the next roundabout and follow the Ring Road across one more roundabout and several sets of lights before you come to a *Sainsbury* supermarket on your right. At this roundabout, go straight over into Barnwell Road (signposted A14 Ely). Park where the United fans do, in the side streets off this road, then walk along Newmarket Road to the ground.

From the north and west, take the A14 toward Felixstowe as far as the B1047 exit (signposted Fen Ditton, Cambridge). Turn right at the lights and continue through Fen Ditton, then right at the T-junction into Newmarket Road. Get into the left-hand lane and turn left at the roundabout into Barnwell Road (see above).

From the east, exit the A14 at the A1303 (signposted Cambridge), turn left at the roundabout onto Newmarket Road, and follow this as far as the Fen Ditton traffic lights. Go straight on here, then immediately left at the roundabout into Barnwell Road for street parking.

Cambridge **train station** is served by non-stop trains from London King's Cross (half-hourly), and by slower cross-country services from Birmingham, Nottingham, Manchester and Liverpool – change at Peterborough for the East Coast main line to Leeds and Newcastle. For the latest timings call ☎0345/484950.

From the station it's a good 45min hike to the ground and the indirect **bus** connection could take you longer than your train ride. A **taxi** (£5) is worth every penny. If you must walk, go straight down Station Road, turn right into Tenison Road, then right again into Devonshire Road. Follow this round to the left and turn right at the crossroads into Mill Road. Walk over the bridge, then take the third left into Sedgewick Street. Follow this past a set of traffic-calming barriers and a row of shops into Cromwell Road. At the T-junction with Coldhams Lane, go straight over and walk across the fields to the ground.

Just the ticket

Visiting fans are housed in the celebrated Allotment End, on the far side of the ground from Newmarket Road. In 1998/99 all tickets were £8, no concessions. Seats are available for the same price in the covered Habbin Stand, just around the corner. **Disabled supporters** have spaces at the Newmarket Road end – book in advance on ☎01223/566500.

Swift half

One of the most appealing things about the Abbey is the warm welcome it extends to away supporters. For £1 guest admission, visiting fans can avail themselves of cheap beer and some surprisingly tasty bar snacks at the ***Supporters' Club*** behind the Newmarket Road terrace.

The best pub close to the ground is ***The Wrestlers*** on the opposite side of Newmarket Road, about half a mile towards the city centre. It offers the local Greene King ales and authentic Thai foot to eat in or take away.

Families or anyone with their own transport can enjoy the riverside location of ***The Plough*** in Fen Ditton; follow signs for The River from the B1047 in the village, then turn right into Green End and the pub is on your left.

Club merchandise

The **club shop** (☎01223/566500) is in front of the club offices facing Newmarket Road. The team have been forced to wear all sorts of amber-and-black combinations in recent seasons, with fans consistently saying they'd prefer something simpler. You pays yer money, you gets no choice.

Barmy army

After years of trying to relocate to a new stadium out of town, United are now reconciled to remaining at the cramped and uncomfortable Abbey. Fans must hope any rebuilding doesn't damage the atmosphere, as the covered Nemarket Road terrace makes as much noise as any in the lower divisions. The passion seldom leads to violence unless Peterborough are the visitors – there were some ugly scenes when 'Posh' came to town at the end of the 1998/99 season.

In print

The main local paper is the ***Cambridge Evening News*** which, despite its name, previews matches in a Saturday morning edition but does not publish after the final whistle.

Fanzine ***The Abbey Rabbit*** is bitterly self-mocking in the best Cambridge tradition – order it from 27 Martin Way, Letchworth, Herts, SG6 4XU.

In the absence of an up-to-date history, the best book for an insight into Cambridge in the early Nineties is Steve Claridge's ***Tales From The Boot Camps*** (Victor Gollancz, £5.99).

On air

BBC Radio Cambridgeshire is the fans' choice on 96 FM, 1026 AM. Community TV station ***Cambridge Red*** offers sporadic coverage of Abbey matters, but you'll need to find a pub with cable television to see it.

In the net

There is no **official website** but the impressive ***U's Net*** enjoys a certain amount of backing from the club. It's at: www.cambridgeunited.com.

This is one of the most detailed and efficiently maintained unofficial sites in the lower divisions – download a spreadsheet version of United's profit-and-loss accounts and find out what running a club at this level is really about – and includes comprehensive links.

More informal are ***Chris Mason's Web Pages*** at: www.freeyellow.com/members6/ chrismason. Not as informative as *U's Net*, but still worth a peek.

Cardiff City

Formation	1899 as Riverside FC
Stadium	Ninian Park, Cardiff, CF1 8SX. ☎01222/398636
Ground capacity	14,600
First-choice colours	Blue and white
Major honours	Third Division champions 1993; Third Division (South) champions 1947; FA Cup winners 1927; Welsh Cup winners 21 times
Position 1998/99	Third in Third Division (promoted)

Celebrations greeted Cardiff City's escape from the basement of the Football League at the end of the 1998/99 season. But they had an indefinably muted air about them. Partly this was because, after blazing something of a trail at the top of the Third Division for much of the campaign, City's form had stuttered toward the end, starved of goals and the ability to stay the course. The club finished well clear of the play-off places but, even so, a third-place finish was a little disappointing. In the overall scheme of things, however, it doesn't matter how promotion from the Third Division is achieved – as far as City fans are concerned, their club has no business being down there in the first place, and climbing one rung up the League ladder is only a small step on a much bigger and more ambitious crusade. Despite the fact that top-flight football hasn't visited the Welsh capital since 1962, the club's most dedicated supporters believe the Premiership is an attainable goal – maybe not now, maybe not in five years, but eventually.

Pressure point – Kevin Nugent assails Swansea City, 1999

To the cynic, the notion is fanciful. City's home at Ninian Park, for all that it once played host to dramatic nights of European football involving the likes of Porto, Hamburg, Standard Liège and Real Madrid, today looks rundown and ragged – a pale shadow of its former glorious self, and a wretched contrast with Cardiff's stunning new Millennium Stadium, which looms large as a potent reminder of what rugby union (and *National Lottery* cash) can achieve in this corner of South Wales. City have so far resisted the temptation to ground-share at the new arena, while a possible move to a new multi-sports and entertainment complex in the Cardiff Bay area is also on the back-burner. If the club is to remain at

Right to look worried – Terry Yorath in the hot seat, 1994

Ninian Park, then the ground will have to be substantially rebuilt, and this raises the familiar dilemma faced by lower-division clubs in the Nineties. With finances tight, which should come first? The stadium, or the squad that plays in it?

One thing is for sure – Cardiff City can't afford to do both. Even during the 1998/99 promotion run-in, the club was selling players to balance the books, and while supporters' confidence in the board may have been increased slightly by the summer departure of the former Birmingham City chairman Samesh Kumar, there is no sugar-daddy waiting in the valleys to replace him.

So it is that a city of more than 300,000 souls, economically prospering after years of decline and proclaiming itself to be a European capital, is lucky if its only major football club can survive in the third tier of the (English) national game. But if fans need a precedent on which to build their dreams of a new golden age, they can find it in the period immediately before and after World War II, when Cardiff City fell from the very top of the League to the ignominy of having to apply for re-election, yet managed to claw their way back to the top within a decade or two. If it could be done then, it could happen again now. Or so the optimists believe.

Even in its earliest days, the club fought a hard and sometimes acrimonious battle for recognition. Formed in 1899 as the football-playing section of Riverside cricket club, the team owed their existence to vision of Bartley Wilson, who believed that cricketers like himself needed a pastime to keep them fit during the winter, and who ignored contemporary warnings that football would never attract sufficient followers from rugby for him to put out 11 players for every game. Wilson's side began life in local leagues, playing on pitches in Sophia Gardens (where Glamorgan CCC now play).

In 1902 they changed their name to Riverside Albion, and three years after that, when Cardiff was officially given the status of a city, the club applied to the South Wales FA to adopt the name 'Cardiff City'. This application was denied, on the grounds that the club did not play in a high enough League. In 1908, having gained admission to the South Wales League, Riverside tried again on the name front, and this time permission was granted. Two years after that the club turned professional, forming itself as a limited company with Wilson as its first secretary, joining the Second Division of the Southern League, and moving into the newly built Ninian Park.

Promotion to the First Division of the Southern League was attained on the eve of World War I, and in 1920 Cardiff were elected to the Football League – not to the Third Division (South), where so many former Southern League teams had ended up, but to the Second Division. Even this level was not strong enough to hold the club, however, and City were promoted after only one season, finishing runners-up to Birmingham in 1920/21. That same year, they also reached the semi-finals of the FA Cup before losing to Wolves.

It had been a meteoric rise, and the names of the men responsible – manager

Fred Stewart, captain Fred Keenor and goalscoring winger Len Davies – have passed into City folklore. And yet their finest hours were still to come. They finished their first season of top-flight football in fourth place, and in 1924 missed out on the League championship by 0.024 of a goal – had City not missed a penalty in their final game of the season, they would have won the title.

But if there was to be no championship for Wales, there would at least be glory in the FA Cup. In 1925 Cardiff reached their first Cup final, losing 1–0 to Sheffield United. Two years later, though by now a less effervescent mid-table side, they were back at Wembley to beat Arsenal 1–0, with an effort from Hugh Ferguson that somehow squeezed under the body of Gunners goalkeeper Dan Lewis and bobbled over the line. It was the first (and only) time that the Cup had left England. It was also a timely piece of revenge over the Arsenal manager Herbert Chapman, whose Huddersfield side had denied Cardiff the title on goal average three years earlier.

In retrospect, the Cup final win was the swansong of an ageing side. By 1929 City had been relegated, and two years later they'd dropped into the Third Division (South) for the first time. Despite a brief stint in the manager's chair from the club's mentor, Bartley Wilson, Cardiff would remain at the wrong end of the League until after World War II, when a euphoric first postwar season ended with the Third Division (South) title, secured by a nine-point margin.

In 1952, City won promotion back up to the First Division on goal difference, and although there would be no repeat of the title-challenging of the Twenties, this new side, with its menacing twin strikeforce of Trevor Ford and Gerry Hitchens, could be every bit as entertaining as the earlier incarnation. Cardiff clung doggedly to their top-flight status until 1957, then managed another promotion two years later before finally taking their leave of the First Division in 1962.

For two seasons in a row in the late Sixties, Cardiff escaped relegation to the Third Division by a single place. But there was still plenty going on at Ninian Park, with manager Jimmy Scoular giving a debut to a gentle giant of a striker, John Toshack, in March 1966. Over the next five seasons 'Tosh' would come to symbolise the club, not just in the League but also in Europe, to which the club had regular access thanks to its frequent victories in the Welsh Cup.

City had begun the first of what would be 14 Cup-Winners' Cup campaigns by putting out the holders, Sporting Lisbon, in 1964/65. Three years later, with Toshack leading from the front, they reached the semi-finals, where SV Hamburg edged them out on a 4–3 aggregate. And in 1970/71, with Scoular having rebuilt the side into genuine promotion challengers, Toshack scored five goals in the first two rounds as Cardiff set up a quarter-final meeting with Real Madrid.

Then, in November 1970, the board sold Toshack to Liverpool. The sale sparked

Ready for anything – 'keeper Jon Hallworth

a furore, fans seeing it as a tacit admission that their club was no longer serious about rejoining the elite. Madrid were beaten 1–0 at Ninian Park but won the second leg 2–0, while in the Second Division, City finished third – not high enough for promotion. Twelve months later they were at the other end of the table, and Scoular had quit long before the club dropped down to the Third Division in 1975.

City bounced between the Second and Third Divisions for the next decade, before two successive relegations from 1985 hurled them into the Fourth. From having been muddling along in its own sweet way, the club was now in crisis. Over the next few years Ninian Park, much of it closed off for safety reasons, suffered not just a drop in crowd levels for Cardiff games (from a peak of almost 60,000 in the Fifties to 1,600 for the visit of Aldershot in 1991), but also the loss of revenue from Welsh internationals, which the local FA was increasingly obliged to stage at Cardiff Arms Park because of FIFA's minimum seating requirements.

In 1991, with just 48 hours to go before the club was wound-up with debts of nearly £2million, City were taken over by Rick Wright, owner of a vast leisure empire that included the Barry Island holiday resort. Under Wright's colourful leadership, the club embarked on a number of schmes designed to woo the punters back to Ninian Park, including refunds if Cardiff failed to win promotion. The fans returned, albeit in unspectacular numbers, and in 1992/93, with Eddie May in the manager's chair and a well-balanced strikeforce comprising the veteran Chris Pike and a young Nathan Blake, City won the Fourth Division title. A run to the fifth round of the FA Cup followed a year later, but both Pike and Blake (the latter sold for a paltry £300,000 to Sheffield United) had gone before the season's end, and shortly after it May made way for Terry Yorath.

There was to be no happy return to Welsh football for the former national-team manager, and at the end of Yorath's only season in charge City were relegated again. Rick Wright, whose interest in the club had been – by his own admission – more about business than football, sold out to Samesh Kumar, and over the next three seasons the club's Third Division finishes read 22nd, seventh, and 21st.

The return of Frank Burrows as manager (he'd had an earlier spell in charge at the end of the Eighties) in early 1998 prompted a recovery which culminated in the 1999 promotion, with a patchwork side of which few great things were expected the following season. But while expectation may be in short supply, there is no lack of hope.

Here we go!

Motorists have a fairly easy time of it once they've made their way down to South Wales. Exit the M4 at junction 33 onto the A4232 toward Cardiff. Leave this road at the second exit. Stay in the left-hand lane after the slip road and you will automatically join Leckwith Road. Follow this to the traffic lights, turn right into Sloper Road, and the ground is on the left.

Best bet for parking is the **car park** at the Cardiff Athletics Stadium opposite Ninian Park.

Cardiff Central **train station** gets direct services from London Paddington, Bristol, Birmingham and Manchester, among other cities (London service hourly, journey time 2hrs). Note that you'll struggle to get back anywhere from an evening game if a lot of stoppage time is played. Call ☎0345/484950 for the latest timings.

Cardiff Central is over a mile from Ninian Park and although it is walkable, the obvious thing to do is to change on to a local train and take it one stop to Ninian Park station, which is at the junction of Leckwith Road and Sloper Road, a 2min walk from the ground.

Just the ticket

Visiting fans usually have the choice between seats in Block A of the Grandstand and terracing at the Grange End, though the latter is sometimes given over to home fans for bigger games. Ticket prices in 1998/99 were £10 for a seat (£6 concessions), £8 standing (£4). **Disabled visitors** rub shoulders with their home counterparts

In the shadow of the Millennium Stadium – Ninian Park, City's home since 1910, and showing it

in the Family Enclosure at the front of the Grandstand. Best book in advance on ☎01222/222857.

Swift half

There are few welcoming pubs in the vicinity of Ninian Park and those there are can get absurdly busy. As an alternative, try the St Mary Street area in the city centre near the station – but keep away colours covered.

Club merchandise

The **club shop** (entrance in Sloper Road) is a quiet haven of *Bluebirds* regalia, with 1999/2000 design home shirts for £37 (kids' sizes £25) and a range of leisurewear that includes rugby tops (!).

Barmy army

Cardiff's hooligan problem refuses to die in spite of strenuous efforts by the club and local police. Things get particularly nasty at local derbies with Swansea, the Bristol clubs and any other team from the M4 corridor, but just because you've arrived from Darlington, doesn't mean it's guaranteed not to kick off.

All of which makes life doubly frustrating for the vast majority of City fans, whose patience has been stretched enough as it is in recent years.

In print

The excellent local ***Western Mail*** produces a *Sports Echo* after the final whistle on a Saturday – well worth hanging around for.

Fanzine ***Watch The Bluebirds Fly!*** (10 King Street, Abercynon, CF45 4UW) has been commenting on City for a decade and is worth a few bob of anyone's money.

On air

The local *BBC* station ***Radio Wales*** (882 AM) does a fair job of covering City despite a wide catchment area with a lot of other tastes to please. Alternatively there's the local commercial offering ***Red Dragon*** (97.4 FM).

In the net

City's **official site** is getting its act together after an uncertain start. It's now maintained by *BT* and will shortly offer e-commerce as well as the expected news and results areas. Go to: www.cardiffcityfc.co.uk. The unofficial ***Cardiff City Online*** boasts outstanding graphics, classic video to download and much more besides, at: www.cardiffcity.co.uk. Also worth a peek is ***CCFC Net***, which includes a fine history file at: www.virtualcardiff.co.uk/bluebirds/.

Carlisle United

Formation	1903 as Shaddongate United
Stadium	Brunton Park, Carlisle, CA1 1LL. ☎01228/526237
Ground capacity	16,600
First-choice colours	Blue shirts, white shorts
Major honours	Third Division champions 1965, 1995; Auto Windscreens Shield winners 1997
Position 1998/99	23rd in Third Division

'I believe in alien beings. I believe in Frankenstein. I believe in God.' The Carlisle chairman Michael Knighton was almost lost for words. But not quite. 'Most of all,' he went on, 'I believe in on-loan goalkeepers who can score goals in the 91st minute.'

His manager, Nigel Pearson, added: 'If I could write scripts like that, I wouldn't be in this game. I'd have a very good publishing contract.'

It was, of course, a fairytale to end all footballing fairytales. Fantastic enough, even, to stretch the imaginations of those Carlisle-supporting *literati*, Hunter Davies and Melvyn Bragg. Their team, needing a goal to avoid slipping out of the League, had thrown their goalkeeper Jimmy Glass into the Plymouth penalty box for a corner. After it was swung over, the ball was parried out by the visiting 'keeper, only for Glass to lash it home on the volley.

It was the last meaningful kick of the game – and of the season. It meant Carlisle were safe, while Scarborough, whose last match had already finished and whose fans had been celebrating, thinking Carlisle were doomed, were relegated to the Conference. Scarborough launched an appeal, claiming that Carlisle's post-deadline day signing of Glass on-loan from Swindon Town had been illegal. The appeal was rejected (Scarborough themselves had been party to the League agreement that a club could sign a goalkeeper after the deadline if suffering a backlog of injuries in that position, as Carlisle were), and England's most isolated professional club, 58 miles from its nearest senior rival, could celebrate in earnest.

The irony was that within six weeks of this *Roy Of The Rovers* drama being played out, all the main protagonists had left Carlisle. Glass was the first to go, back to Swindon for the start of the next season, after wishing the Cumbrian club well and selling hundreds of T-shirts for charity. Then Pearson was sacked, after only six months in the job, even though it had been his idea to wave Glass forward for that decisive corner. And finally, in the last act of an epilogue that was proving just as diverting as the main event, Knighton quit as chairman, following his family to London in the wake of an increasingly hostile campaign against him by fans.

Knighton, the man who had once juggled a ball on the Old Trafford pitch prior to an aborted takeover of Manchester United at the end of the Eighties, had settled on Carlisle in 1992. On his arrival at Brunton Park he had told supporters that within ten years their club would be 'among the 10 wealthiest in the country, competing in Europe in one of the best stadiums around'. Seven years later he was telling those same fans it would be better for Carlisle to be making money in the Conference than losing it in the League – exactly the kind of boardroom platitude guaranteed to get up the noses of supporters, for whom League status is almost a matter of life and death.

With three years to go before Knighton's predicted arrival of European football, Carlisle fans are not dreaming of Juventus coming to Cumbria. For them, a few years of stability and gradual ascent up the League ladder would be enough. The problem is that life has rarely been that

Art of Glass – Carlisle's on-loan 'keeper is about to be submerged under a mountain of bodies

simple at Carlisle, a club that seems to revel in making life complicated. In the year Knighton arrived, the team finished bottom of the League and would have been relegated to the Conference then, had it not been for the collapse and expulsion of Aldershot. In between times there have been two promotions, two relegations and two appearances at Wembley, the second bringing victory over Colchester in the final of the 1996/97 Auto Windscreens Shield.

Complicated times indeed for a club which, just to add a further sub-plot to the tale, has been fighting a rearguard action to keep League football in this far corner of north-west England since both Barrow and Workington failed to gain re-election in the Seventies. If Carlisle go, the professional game in Cumbria goes with them.

Perhaps because of its geographical isolation, Carlisle was a latecomer to senior football. Various local sides had been playing the game since the early 1880s, but it wasn't until Shaddongate United absorbed Carlisle Red Rose in 1903 that the city had something approaching a representative side. As if to prove their point, a year later Shaddongate changed their name to Carlisle United, and in 1905 the team entered their first major league competition, the Lancashire Combination.

A crowd of nearly 14,000 turned up at United's Devonshire Park ground to watch a Cup tie against Workington in 1907, but two years later the club was ordered to leave its home by the Duke of Devonshire's estate. So Carlisle moved a little way east to what would become Brunton Park, an 18-acre site next to the Warwick Road rugby ground. The team played their debut fixture there in 1909, and the following year took a step up into the Northern League.

Further progress on the pitch, though, had to wait until after World War I. Carlisle won the Northern League title for the first and only time in 1922, and six years later the club was elected to the Third Division (North) of the Football League, after the League had shown a rare sense of geographical balance in seeking a replacement for the ailing Durham City.

Top drawer, final act – Bobby Parker (right) at Derby, 1975

Carlisle began their League career with a 3–2 win at Accrington Stanley on 25 August 1928, and a week later thrashed Hartlepool 8–0 at Brunton Park – to this day the club's biggest winning margin in the League. The euphoria surrounding such results soon ebbed away, however, and with the exception of a solitary application for re-election in 1935, the club would spend the whole period up to World War II in mid-table.

During the war, while many professional sides continued to play in specially arranged regional competitions, Carlisle were forced to withdraw totally, playing only local friendlies as travel to any other senior club was not practicable. After the war, though, the club took the bold step of recruiting skilful inside-forward Ivor Broadis from the reserve team at Tottenham. The move was a culture shock for Broadis, who said it was 'like stepping down from the *Savoy Hotel* to the *Jungle Café*'. But he overcame his misgivings to become the youngest player-manager in League history at the age of 23, and had won many friends in Carlisle before effectively arranging his own £18,000 transfer to Sunderland in 1949.

Broadis' replacement would be equally colourful but in a vastly different way. Bill Shankly thought long and hard when Carlisle approached him to be their new manager, believing he still had plenty to offer as a player. But these were the days before freedom of contract and Preston, who held Shankly's registration, refused to release him. So in March 1949 he entered Brunton Park for the first time, and immediately set about turning the city's isolation to his advantage. He instigated a massive PR campaign, urging local people to support United as a symbol of their region, and frequently taking the tannoy before games to address fans with the now immortal words: 'This is your manager speaking.' Worried that the club was finding it hard to attract players because of its location, Shankly also persuaded the board to acquire a large house which was converted into flats in which new arrivals could live together. It was all revolutionary stuff, and it paid off. As season-ticket sales rose to record levels, Carlisle finished third in 1950/51, and also held Arsenal to a goalless draw in the FA Cup at Highbury.

The club should now have gone from strength to strength. Instead, the board reneged on a promise of bonus payments to be paid in the event of Carlisle finishing in the top three. Shankly resigned and moved on to Grimsby Town, while the club he left behind drifted back into mid-table before dropping into the Fourth Division, despite the return of Broadis as player-coach, in 1958.

The next turning point came with the appointment of Alan Ashman as manager in early 1963. As a centre-forward with more than 100 Carlisle goals to his name in the Fifties, Ashman knew how to 'work' the club, if not as extravagantly as Shankly, then just as effectively. In 1963/64 his team won promotion after scoring 113 goals, 39 of them from striker Hughie McIlmoyle, top scorer in the League that year.

Twelve months later, United sealed the Third Division title with a 3–0 defeat of

Mansfield in front of more than 18,000 at Brunton Park.

Carlisle were lying third in the Second Division when Ashman left the club in 1967, and thanks to the efforts of Bob Stokoe among others, they were still a solid Second Division outfit when he returned five years later. In the interim, they had reached the semi-finals of the League Cup and won 3–2 at Roma in the Anglo-Italian Cup. Now Ashman would top all that by taking the club into the top flight in 1974, the team's football as brash and ebullient as ever, the fans rubbing their eyes in disbelief. On seeing his former charges join Liverpool in the First Division, Shankly described Carlisle's rise as 'the greatest achievement in the history of football'.

United won their opening three top-flight matches, and the first *Match Of The Day* table of 1974/75 showed them top of the First Division. By season's end they were bottom, and one of the happier chapters in the Carlisle saga was over. Ashman's side had been experienced but, ultimately, lacking in star quality once the likes of Stan Bowles and Bob Hatton were sold, ironically before promotion had been achieved. Now the most influential players who'd remained, like striker Bobby Owen and the county cricket-playing Chris Balderstone, also bade farewell to Brunton Park.

The club's decline was slow but emphatic – back to the Third Division in 1977 and, after a Stokoe-inspired revival in the early Eighties, no more forays into the upper half of the League after 1986.

Michael Knighton's arrival in 1992 shored up Carlisle's increasingly precarious financial position, but while Brunton Park got new stands, a plush restaurant and other niceties, stability on the pitch was as distant a prospect as ever. Fans were enraged when the chairman decided he could do the manager's job himself in 1997, and frustrated by the sale of emerging talents like Rod Thomas, Rory Delap and Matt Jansen, all at crucial times in the team's development.

A cynic would point out that Jimmy Glass only joined Carlisle because Knighton had sold regular first-team 'keeper Tony Caig to Blackpool for £5,000 on transfer-deadline day. That particular story, however, turned out to possess the most miraculous of happy endings.

Here we go!

The good news for **motorists** is that once the marathon journey to Carlisle has been negotiated, the ground itself is easy to find. Simply exit the M6 at junction 43, take the A69 toward the city centre, and Brunton Park is on your right after about a mile, with the new East Stand clearly visible. There's a large **car park** (£1) at the rear of the ground.

Carlisle **train station** is on the West Coast mainline, with fast(ish) trains from London Euston or Birmingham New Street via Crewe (every 2hrs, journey times 4hrs from Euston, 3hrs 15mins from New Street). There are also cross-country trains from Newcastle (hourly, journey 1hr 30mins), but no destinations are accessible after an evening game. For the latest timings call ☎0345/484950.

Rare rapport – Knighton milks the applause after promotion, 1995

From the station, catch a #70, #74, #75, #99 or #685 bus to the ground along Warwick Road.

Just the ticket

Visiting fans are allocated 1,900 seats in the new East Stand – enter through turnstiles #17–21. Ticket prices in 1998/99 were adults £11, concessions £6.

Disabled visitors and their helpers are also accommodated in the East Stand – book in advance on ☎01228/526237.

Swift half

The best area for eating and drinking is around the train station in the city centre. Try the ***Friars Tavern*** on Devonshire Road, which does food and welcomes famillies.

Visiting supporters are advised to keep club colours hidden in town, and to steer clear of the Botchergate area.

Club merchandise

The **club shop** (☎01228/524014) sells the usual clobber but hasn't had a home-shirt design worth shouting about since the Birmingham-inspired, blue-with-white-facing-and-red-trim affair which Carlisle wore in their sole season of top-flight football 25 years ago. Of more interest recently have been the endless variety of green, red and gold away shirts that have been designed to reflect the corporate colours of the club's main sponsor, the *Eddie Stobart* trucking firm.

Eddie's Wembley stripes – Rod Thomas, 1997

Barmy army

The pitch invasion that followed Jimmy Glass' goal in May 1999 was eminently understandable, but while trouble in Brunton Park itself is rare, the city centre can be a bit tense at times (see *Swift half*, above). Don't let that put you off, though – Carlisle is an extremely welcoming place and well worth the haul, so long as you've plenty of time on your side.

In print

The picture desk at the local ***News & Star*** was indundated with calls after Carlisle's great escape, but although the paper runs an excellent United website (see below), there is insufficient demand for it to publish a Saturday evening edition.

The fanzines are ***Olga The Fox*** (24a Wetheriggs Lane, Penrith, CA11 8PE) and ***Hit The Bar*** (14 Hartland Road, London, N11 3JJ), while the essential history of the club is Paul Harrison's ***Lads In Blue*** (Yore, £18.99), which covers the period up to 1995.

On air

BBC Radio Cumbria (95.6 FM) got the lion's share of interviews after Carlisle's big day in '99, and continues to have the edge over its commercial rivals.

In the net

Carlisle's **official website** contains a decent level of historical and other background information about the club, but fell into disrepair after the Knighton clan departed in June 1999. See if it's back to its best at: www.carlisleunited.co.uk

Best of the unofficial sites is ***Carlisle United Online***, run by the *News & Star* newspaper and including a complete stats archive going back to 1904, as well as the expected rolling news. You'll find it at: www.cufconline.org.uk.

Finally there's the online fanzine ***Reeves Is Offside Again*** at: www.kynson.demon.co.uk/Reeves.is.offside.again/.

Charlton Athletic

Formation	1905
Stadium	The Valley, Floyd Road, London, SE7 8BL. ☎0181/333 4000
Ground capacity	20,000
First-choice colours	Red shirts, white shorts
Major honours	Third Division (South) champions 1929, 1935; FA Cup winners 1947
Position 1998/99	18th in Premiership (relegated)

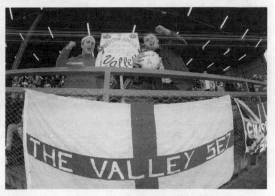

Victory is ours – back to The Valley, December 1992

No other club personifies the spirit, resourcefulness, loyalty and sheer bloody-mindedness of the English football fan better than Charlton Athletic. With the forces of greed, corporate insensitivity and political posturing all ranged against them, fans of the 'Addicks' have done more than simply fight their corner – they've waged a concerted and well-organised series of campaigns to ensure their club has what it deserves: its own ground, in its own part of south-east London, free from the predatory fingers of developers, and ready to be enjoyed again by thousands of like-minded souls for whom 'Charlton' means 'London SE7' and nowhere else.

Most impressive of all, the fight to bring Charlton back to The Valley in the late Eighties and early Nineties was taken up with remarkable good humour as well as indomitable spirit. The fans may have hogged the headlines, hijacked the airwaves, and got up the noses of local government by forming their own political party – but that was about as abusive as it got. There were no threats, no personal violence, no arson attacks. Just good old-fashioned debate, mixed with a liberal dose of thoroughly modern public relations.

When Charlton finally moved back to The Valley in 1992, after a six-year exile at Crystal Palace and a further 18-month stint at West Ham, it was the end of a long and deeply symbolic battle. But it was not the end of the war. In 1999, as the local council began to mutter ominously about The Valley not being an 'appropriate' location for a modern football ground and of there being development 'opportunities' on the site of the Millennium Dome nearby, fans began to think they would have to take up arms – albeit reluctantly – once again.

The commitment shown by Charlton fans in doing what has to be done deserves credit from their counterparts at other clubs, not just in London but across the country. They have been an inspiration to others (notably at Bristol Rovers), and their legacy will live on wherever and whenever business interests clash with football's natural order of things.

But Charlton Athletic is not just about its supporters. The audacity of the team, too, demands attention. While they have

The happy Valley – Charlton's ground as it was in 1970, with the East Bank to the right

spent much of their life in relative obscurity, Charlton have made several major assaults on the national football consciousness, from their 1947 FA Cup final triumph at Wembley, to the scarcely credible play-off final win at the same venue 51 years later.

There is always something appealing about a football team making an impact against the odds, and in Charlton's case there is even something charmingly innocent about the side's foundation. Unlike so many of England's senior clubs, which were the products of establshment entities such as Victorian cricket clubs or the Church, Charlton Athletic is a creation of the community – a team formed by nothing more sophisticated than a group of lads playing football in the streets.

The streets in question were on the south bank of the river Thames, close to where London's great flood barrier is today. The team soon found a patch of waste ground on which to play but, while this was preferable to the streets, it had an obvious problem – people kept dumping waste on it. After moving home a couple of times the club settled on the Angerstein Athletic Ground in Horn Lane, not far from where the Millennium Dome has since sprung up. They remained there until World War I, when the ground was commandeered by the military, forcing Charlton to seek a new home once hostilities had ceased.

They found what they were looking for at The Valley, initially no more than a marshy field surrounded by steep banking created from excavated rubble, but before long a venue whose topography was so obviously suited to expansion that the club could not help but prosper there. And prosper Charlton certainly did, joining the Kent League in 1919, turning professional and moving up to the Southern League a year later, and a year after that gaining admission to the Third Division (South) of the Football League.

Such a rapid rise brought predictable problems. The departure of Woolwich Arsenal north of the river on the eve of World War I had created a large catchment area of support for Charlton. The club was desperate to increase spectator accommodation at The Valley to cater for this local interest, but in doing so ended up massively in debt to its building contractors, *Humphreys*. In an attempt to recoup their losses, in 1923 *Humphreys* tried to engineer a merger between Charlton and and a nearby amateur side, Catford Southend, for whom the firm was also due to build a new ground called The Mount. The idea, apparently, was that if Charlton could be moved to The Mount, The Valley would then be free to become a venue for fairs, exhibitions and other, non-football sporting events.

Yet Catford was far enough away from Charlton to present a significant barrier to fans, who were also not impressed by the decision to dress their heroes in the dark and light blue stripes of Catford Southend, rather than their traditional red. Facilities at The Mount were also poor compared with those at The Valley, and crowds had slipped to little more than a 1,000 by the time this proposed south-east London superclub played its last match there at the end of the 1923/24 season.

Back at The Valley, and without Catford Southend (who struggled on for a few years before going to the wall in 1927), Charlton made steady but unspectacular progress, gaining promotion to the Second Division at the start of the Thirties before dropping down again a few years later. In 1931, however, the old *Humphreys* debt was taken over by new investors Albert and Stanley Gliksten, who in addition to improving the stands at The Valley, recruited Jimmy Seed as manager in 1933.

Like most visionary football bosses, Seed refused to accept that it was his club's destiny merely to tread water. Like the Glikstens – and a host of other dreamers before and since – he was inspired by the vast East Bank of terracing at The Valley and wondered what the atmosphere might be like if the ground were even two-thirds full. Before long, he would find out.

With a young Sam Bartram in goal and Ralph Allen's goalscoring upfront, Charlton won two promotions in a row from 1935. In 1936/37, the club's first-ever in the top flight, the team finished runners-up to Manchester City, and they remained in the top four until the outbreak of World War II. Though the side's strengths were primarily in defensive organisation, local crowds couldn't get enough of it, and more than 75,000 were at The Valley to see an FA Cup tie at home to Aston Villa in February 1938.

World War II disturbed Charlton's flow but not their ability to capture the public imagination. If anything Seed, who remained in charge, allowed his team greater freedom

Keeping it up in the air – veteran striker Carl Leaburn (right) gets ahead against Newcastle, 1997

of movement to match the nation's mood of postwar euphoria. With no League competition in 1945/46, attention was focused clearly on the FA Cup and Charlton did not disappoint their supporters, reaching a first-ever final.

There they would meet Derby County at Wembley, but not before adding two quirky footnotes to footballing history. The unique two-legged structure prior to the 1946 semi-finals allowed Charlton to become the only club ever to lose a game on the way to the final (they were beaten 2–1 at Fulham but won the tie 4–3 on aggregate). And in Welsh full-back Bert Turner they had a man who had illegally guested for Barry Town in a qualifying round – a fact the player himself might have wished had not been overlooked once the final got under way.

With five minutes of the match remaining, Turner deflected a Dally Duncan shot into his own net to put Derby ahead. Sixty seconds later, Turner's own-free kick was deflected in for a Charlton equaliser. Derby then ran out 3–1 winners in extra time, but Charlton would be back at Wembley the following year to have another crack at the Cup, this time against Burnley. Their 1947 side was much-changed, but three key protagonists remained from the defeated team of the previous season – goalkeeper Bartram, whose acrobatics kept Burnley at bay for two heat-soaked hours; captain and centre-forward Don Welsh, who somehow got his head to a hopeful cross six minutes from the end of extra time; and Scots winger Chris Duffy, whose stunning volley from Welsh's header crashed into the net and won Charlton their first and only FA Cup...

There would be no more trips to Wembley for a while, but Charlton remained a side to be reckoned with in the First Division throughout English football's postwar boom. The club had completed 13 successive seasons of top-flight football when, in 1956, Steed and Bartram both decided to step down. Both men, despite their advancing years, had wielded a decisive influence on the club, and within a year Charlton had been relegated to the Second Division.

By comparison with what had gone before, the late Fifties and Sixties were unremarkable times, spent entirely in the Second Division. They were brightened only by the goalscoring of Stuart Leary and by the extrovert forward Eddie Firmani, who arrived with his full-back brother Peter from South Africa in 1950, served a second spell at Charlton after a lengthy career in Italy, then had a third as player-manager toward the end of the Sixties.

There were two brief periods of Third Division football in the Seventies and early Eighties, and it was during the second of these that The Valley first began to be a burden rather than a blessing. In 1981 Michael Gliksten, son of Stanley, sold his majority shareholding in Charlton to young entrepeneur Mark Hulyer, while retaining ownership of the ground. Hulyer spent thousands attracting the former European footballer of the year Allan Simonsen from Barcelona, but neglected The Valley as it belonged to somebody else.

By early 1984 Charlton had called in the receivers with debts of £1.5million, and were saved only by the last-minute intervention of property developer John Fryer. Having spent so much on clearing the club's debts, Fryer too was reluctant to lavish extra funds on The Valley, and once local council inspectors had declared the East Bank unsafe, he had the excuse he needed to move Charlton lock, stock and Portakabin to Crystal Palace.

Selhurst Park had a south-east London postcode, but there the similarity with Charlton's neighbourhood ended. Geographically, it was twice as far away as the old Catford Mount had been. Culturally, it was a world away – an area of London most Charlton fans wouldn't travel to if somebody paid them. But Fryer appeared determined to take Charlton there, and on Saturday 21 September 1985, the team played what everyone assumed would be their last-ever game at The Valley, former

Penalty cause – Saša Ilić saves from the spot and Charlton are in the Premiership, May 1998

turnstile operator Rob Lee scoring the second in a 2–0 win over Stoke City.

Ironically, despite the upheaval of moving grounds – felt just as keenly by the players as by the fans – Charlton enjoyed a successful first season at Selhurst, finishing second to earn a place in the top flight for the first time in 30 years. For the supporters, though, his only hardened the blow. The cream of English football should have been coming to Charlton; instead, they were being directed to a ground that took fans of the 'home' team at least an hour to get to, whether they drove, hopped on a bus, took the train or jogged six-abreast. There was another, even harder pill for fans to swallow. Rather than simply being bulldozed to make way for the property development everyone assumed Fryer was planning, The Valley was simply left to rot, the pitch a jungle of weeds, the East Bank a brooding mass of crumbling concrete, like a vast, elaborate war memorial to the dead of a forgotten country.

Over the next few years, both on and off the pitch, Charlton defied all logic. Under the uncompromising and disarmingly honest management of Lennie Lawrence, a team of unlikely heroes such as goalkeeper Bob Bolder, defenders Steve Gritt and John Humphrey and midfielder Andy Peake somehow kept the club in the First Division, surviving a play-off with Leeds in 1987 before rising to the giddy heights of 14th place two years later.

Meanwhile, the fans were getting the first sniff that a return to The Valley might not be the impossible dream most had assumed it to be. In 1987 John Fryer stood down as chairman due to ill health, clearing a path to power for pro-Valley directors such as Roger Alwen and Michael Norris. Then Norris got together with the builders *Laing* to buy the freehold to the ground from Michael Gliksten. Initially, it seemed likely that *Laing* would simply redevelop the Valley site and build a new stadium for Charlton elsewhere. But industrial contamination around the Blackwall Tunnel approaches (again, today's Millennium Dome territory) persuaded them to go for a smaller development that would allow the club to take possession of its former ground, albeit on a much smaller scale.

Then came another obstacle – the club's plans for a new all-seater ground at

A fate writ large – Alan Curbishley, May 1999

The Valley, perfectly timed to coincide with the publication of the Taylor Report, were thrown out by the planning committee of Greenwich Council. Thus was born the *Valley Party* which, with the help of an inspired poster campaign and other innovations, won 10% of the vote in the local elections of May 1990. Suitably shamed – and clearly surprised at the level of public feeling over the issue – Greenwich's ruling Labour group finally approved Charlton's plans in April 1991.

By now the inevitable had happened and Lawrence's side, resolutely keeping the ball on the deck until the end, had been relegated at the end of 1989/90. But the fans didn't care which division their team were in – so long as they were playing at The Valley. Charlton duly said farewell to Selhurst Park in April 1991, only for delays in the Valley clear-up programme to force them into another ground-share at Upton Park (Wimbledon having since taken their place at Selhurst) before the great day finally arrived on 5 December 1992.

By now the team had new co-managers in Steve Gritt and Alan Curbishley, and while the former would soon part company with the club, Curbishley remained to instill his own attitude of pragmatic optimism into the players. As the new-look Valley began to take shape (the East Bank was covered over by a new stand in 1994), so the squad was also being rebuilt, with one eye on a place in the Premiership.

In 1996 Curbishley's side reached the play-offs, only to lose – what a cruel game football can be – to Crystal Palace in the semi-finals. Two years later, however, Charlton beat Ipswich at the same stage, and although they were outsiders against Sunderland in the final, their supporters were quietly confident. They had every right to be. In what will go down as one of the most extraordinary games Wembley has witnessed, Charlton took a first-half lead before equalising three times after the break and in extra time. With the score at 4–4 after 120 minutes of breathless football, Charlton netted seven out of seven penalties, and after Sunderland missed one, top-flight football was on its way back to The Valley after an absence of 41 years.

The team's two most obvious heroes – hat-trick man Clive Mendonca and Serbo-Australian 'keeper Saša Ilić, who had offered himself for a trial at Charlton after being tipped off about the club in a bar – took centre-stage as the players rode on an open-top bus through the streets of SE7. It was as if the FA Cup had been won all over again, though few of the fans who lined the route were old enough to remember what that had been like.

The reality, of course, was harsher. With little money to spend in the close season, Curbishley could only watch frustrated from the sidelines as his charges threw away lead after lead in the Premiership, eventually going down – after a gallant fight – following a last-day home defeat by Sheffield Wednesday.

But who's to say Charlton won't be back to reclaim a more permanent place among the elite, just as their predecessors did before World War II? The club is in decent financial health, Curbishley has built an admirable team spirit (and has a new four-year contract in his top drawer), and for as long as Charlton continue to produce talented youngsters like Rob Lee, Scott Minto and Lee Bowyer, the outlook must be bright.

Above all, the club is at one with itself, at ease, and at home. Though it has risen on their front doorstep, Charlton fans don't need the Millennium Dome. They have their own vision of the future, and it's called The Valley.

Here we go!

Motorists should exit the M25 at junction 2 and head in toward London on the A2. Continue on this road for about 10miles – ignore exit signs for 'A2 Central London' and continue on the dual carriageway, which is now the A102(M) Blackwall Tunnel approach road. Leave at the junction after the A2 exit and turn right at the roundabout under the flyover onto the A206 Woolwich Road. Turn right at the sign for Charlton train station into Charlton Church Lane, and the ground is in Floyd Road, first turning on the left.

When it comes to **parking**, the *Controlled Parking Zone* (*CPZ*) being imposed on the area by Greenwich Council is set to take effect from 1 December 1999. Its purpose is to deter people from parking in Charlton on their way to the Millennium Dome, but its effect on football matchdays could be devastating – arrive early.

Charlton overground **train station** is a 2min walk from the ground. Trains run half-hourly from Charing Cross, Waterloo East and London Bridge (journey 25min from Charing Cross).

Just the ticket

Visiting fans are usually allocated the whole of the South (Jimmy Seed) Stand, with seats for at least 2,000.

Disabled supporters have a few spaces at the back of the East Stand. Book in advance on ☎0181/333 4010.

Swift half

Most of the pubs along the A206 Woolwich Road welcome well-behaved visiting fans; the stretch of Charlton Church Lane around the junction with Floyd Road is a good area for take-aways and other **food options**. Those who've had to park their cars on the heights above The Valley have further pubs to choose from in Charlton Village.

Club merchandise

The ***Superstore*** (☎0181/333 4035) in behind the East Stand sells the expected range of red-and-white goods, and also – unusually for a club shop – stocks replica international shirts.

Barmy army

Apart from the odd spot of bother with neighbouring Millwall, trouble is exceedingly rare here, the fans' aggressive instincts being channelled firmly in the right direction.

In print

Fanzine ***Voice Of The Valley***, which played a key role in the debate over the future of Charlton's ground after its launch in 1988, is now produced in association with the club but should still be worth a read.

Two quirky books about the club are Richard Redden's history ***Valley Of Tears, Valley Of Joy*** (£18.95), which was published to coincide with Charlton's return to The Valley; and ***The Greatest Team On Earth – Poetry In Motion*** (£3.99), poet Ted Orr-Smith's tribute to the club's 1998 play-off final win at Wembley.

On air

In addition to London standards ***GLR*** (94.9 FM) and ***Capital Gold*** (1548 AM), the club runs its own station, ***Charlton Live*** (106.8 FM), broadcasting on matchday Saturdays from 1.30pm.

In the net

As with fanzines, so with the web – the club has taken over the former unofficial *Addicks Online* and transformed it into its official site, at: www.charlton-athletic.co.uk. The site contains a link to an *Addicks* archive which has all the reports carried by the former fan-run site between 1995 and 1998.

Of the remaining unofficial sites, one of the best is ***Forever Charlton***, with an excellent range of links and a fan-orientated news area, all at: forever.charlton.net.

Chelsea

Formation	1905
Stadium	Stamford Bridge, London, SW6 1HS. ☎0171/385 5545
Ground capacity	32,000
First-choice colours	All blue with white trim
Major honours	League champions 1955; Second Division champions 1984, 1989; FA Cup winners 1970, 1997; League Cup winners 1965, 1998; Full Members' Cup winners 1986, 1990; European Cup-Winners' Cup winners 1971, 1998
Position 1998/99	Third in Premiership

History has turned full circle at Chelsea. From the mid-Sixties to the early Seventies, the club's Stamford Bridge home was the place to see and be seen, famous as much for its glamorous supporters as for the achievements of its team, which were themselves pretty considerable – high League placings, Wembley almost a second home, Europe likewise. Today's picture is uncannily similar. Britain's new political class may have replaced the actors and pop musicians, and the team may, if anything, be capable of even more than the vintage of a generation ago. Argue over the details all you like – the fact remains, Chelsea are chic again.

Nor should we expect anything less, of course, from a corner of central south-west London that's been famous for fashion ever since the team's earlier era of glory. When Peter Osgood, Charlie Cooke, Alan Hudson and the rest were strutting their stuff at the Bridge, the boutique tills in the surrounding streets were ringing to the tune of 'Swinging London'.

Today, the wave of frenzied, fashion-conscious shopping has given way to an atmosphere of refined affluence. Smart cars may still waft purposefully about the place, but the biggest boutique on the King's Road is now just another branch of *Next*, while the old Chelsea Indoor Market, former haven of the weird, the wild and the wonderful, is a *Marks & Spencer* food hall.

There is nothing off the peg, however, about the modern Chelsea FC. Its players are hand-picked from the elite clubs of Europe. Its stadium, though by no means complete, is being resurrected amidst the gleaming plate-glass optimism of the Chelsea Village complex of hotels, apartments, restaurants and shops. Even the pitch has been re-laid, its specification tailored to suit the precise micro-climate of London, SW6.

It's important to consider the whole Stamford Bridge site, rather than merely the team, because – perhaps more than any club in England, certainly in London – the story of Chelsea's football has been inextricably linked with the fate of the club's real estate. This was particularly true in the calamitous period between the mid-Seventies and the late Eighties, when the club was nearly driven to the wall under pressure from property developers. And it was true right at the start of the Chelsea story, as the ground was built long before before there was a team to play on it.

Stamford Bridge began life in 1877, as a new home for the London Athletics Club. Its initial rival was the Lillie Bridge ground nearby – which had hosted the second FA Cup final in 1873. Right from the word go, however, there were problems. Only 6,000 turned up for the Bridge's opening, and within six years the developers who'd built it, the Waddell brothers, had fled the country under a mountain of debt.

The ground continued to be used for athletics, though, and one of the London AC's starters, Fred Parker, thought it could become something much bigger. Together with his friends the Mears brothers, Gus and Joe (whose father, as luck would have it, was a builder himself), he set about trying to turn Stamford Bridge into a grand multi-sports arena, similar to the Crystal Palace stadium in south London which had since taken over as the main venue for FA Cup finals.

Gus Mears duly bought the freehold to the Bridge in 1904, and invited the established Fulham FC to move in as tenants from their home at Craven Cottage. The Fulham board were divided, however, and ultimately declined Mears' offer. This was a devastating blow – without football, Mears could see no future for Stamford Bridge. Fred Parker maintained that a new club could be formed to play the game there, but Mears was sceptical and decided to sell up to the *Great Western Railway*, which ran trains along a line adjacent to the ground and wanted to build a coal yard on the site.

What happened next has been well-chronicled but is worth repeating. Apparently Mears invited Parker to the Bridge to tell him of his decision to sell. As the two men walked across the pitch, Mears' dog bit Parker's leg and, according to Parker, Mears' reaction was: 'Scotch terrier – bites before he speaks!' Blood was pouring from Parker's leg but, as he hopped about in pain, he couldn't stop himself laughing at his friend's quip. Mears, meanwhile, was so impressed by Parker's reaction he decided that maybe his instincts were to be trusted after all.

While Mears gave the go-ahead for a new stand to be built at the Bridge, Parker was charged with assembling a new team to play under the name of Chelsea. He applied to the Southern League for membership, but established London-based members Fulham and Tottenham were outraged at the idea of a club gaining admission before it had played a match, and Parker was rebuffed.

Undaunted, Parker then approached the Football League, which wanted to expand by four clubs and was also keen to make further inroads into the game in London, where only Woolwich Arsenal flew

Bates' hotel – the expansive frontage of Chelsea Village, 1998

Stinging the Blues – Tommy Docherty, 1964

the flag. The odds were still stacked against Chelsea but, in a stirring speech to the League's AGM in June 1905, Parker convinced members they should give his side a chance. It was agreed the club could play in the Second DIvision for 1905/06 (along with another London newcomer, Clapton Orient), and so Chelsea became the first and only team to be admitted to the League without kicking a ball.

During the summer Parker assembled a formidable squad including two prolific goalscorers, Jimmy Windridge and George Hilsdon, and Sheffield United's former goalkeeper, the giant Billy Foulke. Parker recruited John Tait Robinson as the team's first manager, while Gus Mears dressed the players in Lord Chelsea's official colours of pale blue, white and black.

Chelsea lost their first League game 1–0 at Stockport County, but soon got the measure of Second Division football and finished third in the table.

The following season, Mears' and Parker's faith was rewarded both on and off the pitch. The team were scoring goals as if they were going out of fashion, with Hilsdon netting five against Glossop North End in the League and six against Worksop Town in the FA Cup. The crowds, meanwhile, were coming through the Stamford Bridge turnstiles in unprecedented numbers – only 6,000 had turned up for the first home League game against Hull City in 1905, but by the end of the 1906/07 campaign Chelsea were averaging 18,000, making them the most popular team in the Second Division.

What they'd all come to see was promotion to the top flight, and this was duly attained with nine points to spare in 1907. David Calderhead succeeded Roberton as manager and Chelsea maintained their First Division status for three seasons, with crowds reaching record levels – the Stamford Bridge average of 32,000 in 1907/08 was the highest in the land.

In just four years, Chelsea had gone from being a speculator's idle dream to the most popular football team in England. There was something almost unreal about it, and ultimately – on what would be the first of many occasions – the side failed to live up to their star billing. Chelsea were relegated in 1910, promoted again two years later, then spent three seasons in more relegation trouble before World War I put them out of their misery.

There'd been some successes in the Cup, however, and after a run to the semifinals in 1911, Chelsea made it to the final four years later. Britain was now at war but the FA insisted the game, against Sheffield United, should go ahead, although they were forced to move it from Crystal Palace to Old Trafford because of fears that a local club playing in a London final would encourage absenteeism from the capital's war effort. The match became known as 'the Khaki Cup final' because of the number of soldiers in the crowd, their trenchcoats interspersed with the red of Sheffield supporters who made the short journey to Manchester, despite wartime restrictions. With the conflict spreading across Europe, newspapers devoted little attention to the match, the *Daily Mirror* previewing it with a single sentence.

There wasn't much to say after the game, either, as Chelsea were utterly outplayed and lost 3–0. As the man from the *Mirror* put it: 'If they [Chelsea] had played all day, they wouldn't have scored.'

The team's captain that day, full-back Jack Harrow, remained with the club during the war and led Chelsea to another FA Cup semi-final in 1920, along with a third-place finish in the League – albeit a long way behind the all-conquering champions West Bromwich Albion. After that it was mainly downhill, with relegation striking again in 1924, followed by an extended spell of trying to escape the Second Division.

The pattern for the inter-war years had been set. Chelsea often fielded some extravagantly talented teams, yet these somehow added up to less than the sum of their parts. Promotion was finally achieved in 1930, whereupon the club signed two established Scots goalscorers, Hughie Gallacher and Alex Jackson. The arrival of Irishman Joe Bambrick in 1932 completed a forward line in which all five players were internationals, but none of them could lift Chelsea back into the limelight they'd occupied before World War I.

After World War II, the club again went shopping, buying centre-forward Tommy Lawton from Everton, inside-forward Len Goulden from West Ham and Welsh full-back Danny Winter from Bolton. But Lawton, like Gallacher before him, never settled at Chelsea and was sold to Notts County within two years, to be replaced by Newcastle's Roy Bentley. Still the team

Gone to the dogs – the decline of Stamford Bridge

When Chelsea's founder **Gus Mears** acquired Stamford Bridge in 1904, he envisaged a 70,000-seater sports arena to rival the best in Europe. Eight decades later it was voted the worst football ground in London. So what happened?

Gus Mears died in 1912, leaving the Bridge to his brother, Joe, who continued to develop a range of sports at the ground without investing much in its facilities. At one stage **cycling, athletics, rugby, baseball** and **speedway** all rubbed shoulders with the footballers of Chelsea FC. But the athletics soon rendered the pitch unplayable, while the speedway cut up the athletics track. By the mid-Thirties there were only two sports left – football and **greyhound racing**, with the latter apparently holding sway.

Two of the Bridge's landmark edifices were built with the dogs in mind. The shallow roof over the back of the Fulham Road terracing, soon to be nicknamed **'the Shed'**, was designed to keep the rain off bookies' heads at greyhound meetings, while the weird stand-on-stilts in the north-east corner was positioned to give punters a grandstand view of the finishing line. Neither was of much use to football. It didn't matter how much noise Chelsea's hardcore support made under the Shed roof – the players were too far away to hear them. And the north-east stand offered such a poor view of the pitch that it was closed off long before being demolished in 1977.

The greyhounds ran their last race in 1968, when the new mood of optimism generated by the Docherty and Sexton teams prompted new chairman **Brian Mears** to lay extravagant plans for a new 11,000-seater **East Stand**. This was to be part of an all-new Stamford Bridge, but its construction coincided with falling crowds and massive inflation that caused a doubling of its cost to £2million.

The stand had almost bankrupted the club, but it was to be eight years before the Mears family came to terms with Chelsea's ruin. **Ken Bates** bought the club from them in 1982, but by then it was almost too late...

was under-achieving, reaching two FA Cup semi-finals in 1950 and 1952, but losing both to Arsenal. Far from being the glamour club Gus Mears and Fred Parker had envisaged all those years ago, Chelsea were now a standing joke – all dressed up with nothing to win.

The man who wiped the smile off the nation's faces was Ted Drake, the former Arsenal centre-forward who took over from long-serving Billy Birrell as manager at the end of the 1951/52 season. Prior to Drake's arrival, Chelsea had usually entered the transfer market looking to buy established stars. The club felt it was above the bargain-basement bartering indulged in by other sides, and had no real youth policy of its own. Together with his scout Jimmy Thompson and Dickie Foss, who made Chelsea one of the first senior clubs to have a junior football scheme, Drake changed the culture of Stamford Bridge, replacing the club's old symbol of the Pensioner with a heraldic lion, aggressive, determined and ready for anything.

Within three years, Chelsea had won the League. Roy Bentley was the star of the show, scoring a quarter of the team's 81 goals, ably assisted in attack by John McNichol, a typical Drake signing from Brighton, and right-winger Eric Parsons. The team were workmanlike and efficient, their points total of 52 the lowest of any title-winning side since the war. Even Drake himself regarded his champions as an interim side, and it says a lot about the club's outlook that while no future Chelsea team would match the 1955 championship, club historians have tended to concentrate on subsequent, more attractive line-ups.

The first of these would be 'Drake's Ducklings', London's answer to the 'Busby Babes' and every bit as beguiling in their own way. This was the team that Foss and Thompson built – either signed on apprentice forms by the club or transferred for little money from the lower divisions or Scotland – and it was led from the front by Jimmy Greaves, a young centre-forward from London's East End whose cool, economic approach to finsihing left defenders standing and journalists lost for words.

While the Babes would be decimated at Munich, the Ducklings would quack their last of natural causes, petering out as a force after Greaves was sold to AC Milan in 1961, having scored 124 goals in 157 League games for Chelsea. Ted Drake left soon after but, fortunately for the club, his legacy of a strong youth structure and first-team work ethic remained for the man who succeeded him, Tommy Docherty, to exploit. It was Drake who had recruited Docherty as player-coach earlier in the year, and he had made an immediate impact on the players with his fresh ideas and even fresher wit. The media, too, loved him for his quotability and his knack for turning being able to turn the smallest Chelsea story into news. In complete contrast to Drake, 'the Doc' was a thoroughly modern manager capable of dealing with thoroughly modern pressures. Docherty always made sure he had a lot to tell the world about. Unable to prevent Chelsea's relegation in 1962, he got them back up again within a year, building a new team around Peter 'the Cat' Bonetti in goal; the Harris brothers,

The Cat pounces – Bonetti follows the ball out, 1967

Alan and 'Chopper' Ron, in defence; midfield artisans John Hollins and Terry Venables; and forwards George Graham and Bobby Tambling. All except Graham were products of the Chelsea youth scheme.

Playing ruthlessly attacking football, Docherty's side beat Leicester over two legs to lift the League Cup in 1965. Graham and Venables left soon after but were more than adequately replaced by Charlie Cooke and Tommy Baldwin. Having reached a 1967 FA Cup final against a Tottenham side containing Greaves and Venables, Chelsea could – and should – have put one over them, but never got going and lost 2–1.

By the time Chelsea reached their next Cup final, against Don Revie's Leeds in 1970, Docherty had fled to Rotherham and been replaced by Dave Sexton, a manager whose objectives were similar but whose methods of achieving them couldn't have been more different. Exuding an air of calm authority, Sexton was capable of conducting a press conference without insulting anyone and, more important, struck up an instant rapport with the players. His was to be the classic among all Chelsea's fine teams of the period, with Peter Osgood and Ian Hutchinson now the first-choice strikers, the maverick Alan Hudson as playmaker and Peter Houseman (who was to die tragically in a car crash in 1977) an underrated presence on the flanks – though still with Bonetti, Ron Harris and Hollins as a backbone of steel.

Steel was the quality Sexton's team had which Docherty's had lacked. Twice behind against Leeds on a peat-bog of a Wembley pitch, they clawed their way back to force a replay at Old Trafford – scene of Chelsea's 'Khaki Cup final' 55 years earlier. Again they went behind, but Osgood's flying header from Cooke's inviting cross levelled matters again 12 minutes from time. Just before the break in extra time, Hutchinson launched a trademark long throw into the Leeds box, Jack Charlton could do no more than flick it on, and

Leeds in the lead – Wembley, 1970

David Webb, tormented as a full back by Eddie Gray in the first game but switched to central defence by Sexton for the replay, bundled the ball home. The FA Cup was Chelsea's.

The following year, Sexton's side surpassed that achievement by lifting the European Cup-Winners' Cup. After routine wins over Aris Salonika and CSKA Sofia in the early rounds, Chelsea came from two down to beat Belgium's Club Bruges in the quarter-finals, then beat the holders Manchester City 1–0 home and away, to set up a final encounter with Real Madrid. At the Olympiakos stadium in Athens, it seemed as though Osgood's goal would be enough until Zoco's equaliser in stoppage time. With no provision for penalty shootouts, the 1–1 draw forced a replay, to be held at the same venue just two days later. By rights Chelsea should have been demoralised and dead on their feet, yet if anything

Life's a Butch – Ray Wilkins' good hair day

their football was sharper than in the first game, and were worthy winners, 2–1.

A year later Chelsea were back at Wembley but lost the League Cup final to Stoke, 2–1. In Europe they beat Jeunesse Hautcharage of Luxembourg 21–0 on aggregate, with Osgood netting eight goals in the tie as a whole. But they then unaccountably lost to Atvidaberg of Sweden on away goals.

Nobody at the Bridge knew it at the time, but Chelsea wouldn't get back into Europe for another 23 years. The old guard aged and were not replaced, while others such as Hudson, Cooke and Osgood decided to pursue their careers elsewhere. Sexton left for QPR in 1974, leaving Ron Suart and Eddie McCreadie to pilot the ship as it headed for the rocks of relegation a year later.

The club continued to throw up new talent, including the giant central defender Mickey Droy; the Wilkins brothers, Graham and Ray (or 'Butch' as he was known then); and the promising striker Teddy Maybank. But debts incurred in the building of a new East Stand at Stamford Bridge (see panel p.135) had turned Chelsea from a 'buying' club into a 'selling' one, and the best players of the mid-Seventies would spend the prime time of their careers with other clubs. Ken Shellito, Geoff Hurst and Danny Blanchflower all had spells as manager, but none could arrest Chelsea's newly acquired tendency to yo-yo between the First and Second Divisions.

It was to a Second Division club that Ken Bates arrived in 1982. Like a lot of senior clubs, Chelsea had remained in the hands of a single family for generations. The chairman was Brian Mears, son Gus Mears' nephew, Joe Mears junior. Brian ran the club with his half-brother, David, but at the dawn of the Eighties both seemed oblivious to Chelsea's increasingly parlous state. After an FA Cup tie against Spurs in 1982, the bank manager phoned the board saying he had two cheques, one for the FA's share of the gate money and the other to pay the players' wages. 'Which one should I bounce?' he asked. Yet the following week, Lord Chelsea hosted a pre-match banquet for the Mears family at which top-of-the-range brandy and cigars were consumed and the bill came to more than £500.

In between those two events, Bates, a self-made millionaire with a wide range of business interests who'd had a brief spell as chairman of Oldham Athletic in the Sixties, had bought the club for £1, inheriting £2million of debts. He embarked on a round of rigorous cost-cutting, ridding Stamford Bridge of a redundant tier of 'hangers-on' and agreeing to lease the ground for six years from a property company controlled by the Mears family, *SBP*, to ease cashflow.

So began a long-running saga over the fate of both the club and its ground that would rumble on for the best part of two decades. David Mears enraged Bates by selling his majority stake in *SBP* to developers,

Marler Estates, who soon evolved a plan to bulldoze Stamford Bridge and replace it with luxury flats. *Marler* then added neighbouring Fulham and QPR (along with their grounds) to their portfolio, and for a while it seemed that all three would be moving in together at QPR's Loftus Road ground.

The man who stood in the way was Bates. He managed to extend Chelsea's lease using a combination of populist campaigning ('Save The Bridge') and a series of High Court actions against *Marler* and the company that bought them out in 1988, *Cabra Estates*. In theory he was ready to exercise Chelsea's right to buy the freehold to the Bridge, where he had his own redevelopment plans (crucially, including a football stadium). In reality, he couldn't afford the inflated price brought about by the Eighties boom – hence the need to stall and stall again.

At the start of the Nineties, a solution appeared to present itself in the shape of a groundshare with Fulham; at one point Bates even authorised the building of a third dressing-room at the Bridge to accommodate the Cottagers. But by 1992 the property slump had rendered such a move unnecessary – *Cabra* had collapsed and both Fulham and Chelsea had new freeholders, the *Royal Bank Of Scotland*. Bates agreed a 20-year lease with the bank but, although the team had consolidated a position in the lucrative new Premiership under Glenn Hoddle, the chairman still lacked the money he needed to develop 'Chelsea Village' – his vision of the Stamford Bridge site that would not only subsidise the rebuilding of the ground, but also offer the long-term stability that would keep Chelsea prospering regardless of the team's notoriously unpredictable form.

In June 1993, Bates placed an advert in the *Financial Times* asking for backers. One man who saw it was Matthew Harding, the multi-millionaire owner of the *Benfield* insurance group who agreed to loan Chelsea £7.5million towards stand and squad rebuilding, convertible into shares if not repaid. Bates and Harding seemed the ideal partnership to take the club forward, but the former was not used to sharing power and resented Harding's access to ready cash. In fact, the two men could not have been further apart, and soon embarked on a bitter PR battle for the hearts, minds and wallets of Chelsea's fans.

While Bates insisted his 'Chelsa Village' masterplan was the only way forward, Harding wanted more emphasis on the football, with a 60,000-capacity stadium (as opposed to Bates' 42,000) and a smaller hotel complex. Bates brought Ruud Gullit to the club, then Harding went behind his back to buy the freehold to Stamford Bridge from the *Royal Bank Of Scotland* for £16.5million. Bates repaid Harding's loans and banned him from the boardroom; Harding responded by reaching out to the fans with pre-match pints of Guinness and oysters at the *Imperial Arms* in the King's Road. While Bates entertained John Major and David Mellor in the VIP box at Stamford Bridge, Harding donated £1million to Tony Blair's election war chest.

Scoring but drawing – Eighties idol Kerry Dixon

An uneasy truce between the two men had broken out when, on 22 October 1996, a helicopter carrying Chelsea fans to London from a League Cup tie at Bolton crashed, killing all those onboard. One of them was Matthew Harding.

The following Saturday, the Chelsea team held hands around the centre-spot at the Bridge, where a symbolic pint of *Guinness* stood in memory of a man whose 'one of the lads' persona had made him as popular with the players as he'd been with the fans. Over the next few months, the star-studded team that had been financed partly by Harding's money rode a tidal wave of emotion and landed the FA Cup, won 2–0 at Wembley at the expense of another costly assemblage of talent, Middlesbrough.

Making friends with the ball – the Hoddle years

Before the debate over incarnation, before Eileen Drewery, before David Batty's missed penalty and Gazza's missed World Cup...**Glenn Hoddle** taught Chelsea how to play football again. Arriving as player-manager from **Swindon Town** in 1993, Hoddle inherited a mish-mash of a side whose identity had been kicked between the differing personalities of his many predecessors, including **John Neal, John Hollins, Bobby Campbell** and **Ian Porterfield**. Chelsea were in the newly formed Premiership but that was where the good news ended.

Hoddle's impact was immediate. Playing as a sweeper, he instigated many of Chelsea's moves with his precise passing, just as he had done for Tottenham a decade earlier. Just as important, he taught journeyman players such as **Dennis Wise, Gavin Peacock** and **John Spencer** to do the same. Only poor away form prevented Chelsea from finishing higher than 14th in 1993/94, and they also reached the FA Cup final. Their 4–0 drubbing by Manchester United might have broken lesser teams but Hoddle was defiant, insisting it was the beginning of a new era, not the death of a dream.

Crucially, Chelsea were back in Europe for the first time in 22 years. With Norwegian defender **Erland Johnsen** and Russian 'keeper **Dimitri Kharine** fronting the first wave of Stamford Bridge imports and youngsters such as **Eddie Newton** and **Michael Duberry** progressing at an astonishing rate, Chelsea reached the semi-finals of the 1994/95 Cup-Winners' Cup, where they were unlucky to lose to the eventual winners **Real Zaragoza**. This run, achieved with a squad costing a fraction of Luca Vialli's 1998 team, deserves at least an equal place in the club's recent history.

Blue period – Hoddle thinks it through

In the summer of 1995, Hoddle persuaded Chelsea chairman Ken Bates to sign former Dutch international captain **Ruud Gullit**, along with former Manchester United striker **Mark Hughes** and the versatile Romanian **Dan Petrescu**. This was the start of the glamorous new Chelsea but Hoddle did not hang around long to see it. He had already clashed with Bates about the width of the pitch proposed in the Chelsea Village plans, and the chairman shed no tears when Hoddle was appointed England manager to succeed **Terry Venables** after Euro '96...

Hear no evil – Mellor, Harding and Bates in the directors' box

As Bates' Chelsea Village rose from the rubble, a bold new era beckoned. But there was to be another twist. Midway through the 1997/98 season Bates sacked his player-manager, Gullit, and installed veteran Italian striker Gianluca Vialli in his place. Gullit, like Hoddle before him, had found Bates increasingly difficult to deal with, and as with all personality clashes at the Bridge since 1982, there was only ever going to be one winner.

The squad's morale should have been hit hard but in fact the reverse happened, the less up-tight but still ambitious Vialli leading Chelsea to no fewer than four trophies in 1998: the League Cup, the Cup-Winners' Cup, the European SuperCup and the Charity Shield.

Twelve months later there was no silverware in the cabinet and Vialli admitted he was 'not at all happy' after a season in which Chelsea had been in contention for the League Cup, FA Cup, Cup-Winners' Cup and Premiership, and ended up with nothing. On the other hand, the club was edging closer to membership of the European elite via the Champions' League, the development of Chelsea Village was almost complete and, for once, the boardroom was tranquility personified. Is it the calm before a storm? Or is it a sign that Chelsea FC, like the King's Road nearby, has shed its pretensions to be a fashion icon, found a more comfortable niche in life, and finally grown up?

Here we go!

Stamford Bridge is actually in Fulham, rather than Chelsea. **Motorists** should take the M4 in toward London from Junction 15 of the M25. The M4 in turn becomes the A4 and this should be followed as far as the Hammersmith Flyover. Turn right at the lights into the B317 North End Road, go straight over two mini-roundabouts, then left at the next one into Fulham Broadway. Turn left at the lights into the A308 Fulham Road, and Stamford Bridge is on the left, just after Fulham Broadway tube.

The underground **car park** at the ground is a rip-off, so try the streets off to the right between Fulham Road and King's Road. Watch out for ravenous meters, residents' schemes, rampant wheelclamping and chrome-plated *Shogun* bullbars.

Fulham Broadway **tube station** is on the Wimbledon branch of the District Line – be sure your train has either Wimbledon or Parson's Green on the front. Allow 45mins from most London mainline stations.

The club plans to open a new overground train station, on the land Gus Mears nearly sold for coal sidings in 1905, behind the East Stand.

Just the ticket

Visiting fans are allocated a portion of the East Stand lower tier, normally the north end. Ticket prices here in 1998/99 were adults £23, no concessions. For Cup games away clubs are allocated the uncovered West Stand opposite, but this may change if the club gets the go-ahead to add a further tier to the stand – construction was subject to the outcome of a public inquiry in 1999.

Disabled visitors have just six spaces in the East Stand – advance booking essential through your own club.

Swift half

Most of the pubs around the Bridge are 'home only', so visiting supporters tend to sup up in the West End, or at pubs close to stations on the District Line.

Of the latter, ***The Blackbird***, next-door to Earl's Court tube, has a nice mix of home and away support and is a 20min walk (or 5min tube ride) from the ground.

There's a bewildering range of upmarket **food options** within the Chelsea Village complex, of which the bistro in the new ***Court Hotel***, scheduled to open in summer 1999, promises to be relatively affordable.

Club merchandise

The ***Chelsea Megastore*** (open Mon–Sat 10am–6pm, later on matchdays, ☎0171/565 1490), to the left of the Chelsea Village entrance, is the biggest club shop in the country. The range of goods is simply staggering, as is the number of 'virtual' photo opportunities supporters can indulge in thanks to instant digital photography.

Chelsea's shirt for 1999/2000 is one of the simplest (and most popular) for years – adults £42.99, kids £32.99, but add a whopping £13.99 for personalisation. Alternatively there are excellent replicas of the club's Fifties, Sixties and Seventies styles, as well as some smart leisure tops from £23.99.

Barmy army

'The Shed' gave birth to some of the most obstinately violent supporters in English football history. Chelsea fans, many of them not locals at all but hailing from dormitory towns in Surrey and Hampshire, were behind sophisticated gangs of thugs that haunted England internationals abroad as well as their own team's away games in the League and in Europe – 300 alone were deported from Belgium prior to a game against Club Bruges as recently as 1995.

Ironically, Stamford Bridge was often a perfectly safe place to visit, its police presence the heaviest in London, its fencing higher than anywhere else (and, if Ken Bates had had his way, it would have been electrified too).

The worst scenes followed Chelsea's play-off final against Middlesbrough in 1988, when a 1–0 win was insufficient to prevent the club from being relegated. Fans scaled the fencing in front of the Shed (maybe Bates was right) and charged across the pitch at the visiting contingent as the 'Boro players were attempting a lap of honour.

Today the Shed has become the *Chelsea Village Hotel* and the silent majority, encouraged by new stands that are less than half-a-mile from the pitch, have found their voice. Stamford Bridge is no longer merely safe but sociable, too.

In print

As usual with London clubs there's no Saturday evening paper, but the weekday ***Evening Standard*** did a fine job of covering the Bates–Harding war of the mid-Nineties. The paper previews all major London games on Friday evenings.

The official **club magazine** is nothing to write home about but fanzine ***The Chelsea Independent*** (PO Box 4027, London, W9 3ZF), voice of the club's independent supporters' association, continues to ask pertiment questions of the Bates regime.

The *doyen* of Chelsea historians, Ron Hockings, produced the excellent ***Ninety Years Of The Blues*** in 1995 – worth the effort of tracking a copy down. Neil Henderson's ***Chelsea – Feeling Blue*** (People's History, £9.99) tells the story of the club through the eyes of its supporters, while ***A View From The Bridge*** (More Than Ninety Minutes, £21.95) is a mainly photographic recollection of life in the Shed.

The only way to get both sides of the Bates–Harding saga is to buy both the former's ***My Chelsea Dream*** (Virgin, £16.99) and Alyson Rudd's posthumous biography of the latter, ***Pursuing The Dream*** (Mainstream, £15.99).

On air

Chelsea fans have more than just ***GLR*** (94.9 FM) and ***Capital Gold*** (1548 AM) to choose from, with the club's own station ***Radio Chelsea*** (1494 AM) also broadcasting on matchdays.

In-house TV station ***Channel Chelsea*** broadcasts throughout the North (Matthew Harding), East and South Stands before and after matches, starting at 11.30am on Saturdays.

In the net

Chelsea's **official website** is a real lesson in what can be achieved if a Premiership club throws a bit of thought and money behind developing its own site, rather than just paying for a branded version of someone else's. The signposting could be better but there's a lot going on here, so be patient.

Highlights include an unusual (for an official site) amount of subjective comment from fans in the *Blue Is The Colour* section, an outstanding online shopping area (an *IBM e-business*, naturally) that puts *Planet*-run offerings to shame, and a large multi-media area with sections devoted to both *Chelsea Radio* and *Channel Chelsea*. Be impressed at: www.chelseafc.co.uk.

Of the unofficial sites, ***Priesty's Chelsea Refuge*** has a wicked sense of humour and comprehensive links at: www.btinternet.com/~alexc/chelsea.htm. The ***Chelsea Supporters' Registry*** acts as a forum for fans across the world at: fans-of.chelsea-fc.com/csr/. And ***Singing The Blues*** offers an excellent news wire (courtesy of the *NewsNow* service) which pools stories together from several major sources; it's at: www.tonann.dircon.co.uk/.

A gentleman of Cremona – Gianluca Vialli

'The players have all warmed to Luca in the short time he has been here and we are all desperately disappointed that things have not worked out for him here at Chelsea.' These were the words of striker **Mark Hughes** on the eve of the club's 1997 FA Cup final against Middlesbrough. Of all **Ruud Gullit**'s signings the previous summer, Vialli had been the least successful, struggling with a series of injuries and apparently being earmarked for a transfer after the 'Boro game.

Reunited with an old friend – Vialli and *Recopa*

Yet Vialli stayed, and six months later, when Gullit was sacked while trying to negotiate a lucrative new playing contract despite being obviously past his prime, it was Vialli's rapport with the players that made the Italian striker the obvious choice to take over.

Born into a wealthy Cremona family in 1964, Vialli could afford to approach the game with a detachment rare among top European players. It has always served him well, first as a young goal-poacher at **Sampdoria** (with whom he first won the Cup-Winners' Cup in 1990), then as a member of a 'trident' of forwards at **Juventus** which ultimately brought home the European Cup in 1996.

It was at Juve that Vialli learned how to deploy the 'rotation' system of squad management without upsetting players (a speciality of coach **Marcello Lippi**), and also the importance of physical training under the club's legendary fitness coach, **Gianpietro Ventrone.** Both lessons were vigorously applied in his first 18 months as manager at Stamford Bridge, where team spirit survived the creation of a potentially lethal cocktail of nationalities and the most gruelling fixture schedule the club had ever faced.

No manager works alone, however, and Vialli has been particularly indebted to his assistant manager **Gwyn Williams** and his coach **Graham Rix**. It was Rix's idea to send on goalscorer **Gianfranco Zola** in the Cup-Winners' Cup final win over **VfB Stuttgart** in 1998 (Vialli's finest hour as a manager so far), and Chelsea's loss of form at a key point in the 1998/99 season coincided with Rix being imprisoned for having sex with an under-age girl – the kind of incident for which not even the most cultured and wide-ranging Italian upbringing can legislate.

Cheltenham Town

Formation	1892
Stadium	Whaddon Road, Cheltenham, Glos. ☎01242/573558
Ground capacity	6,100
First-choice colours	Red-and-white stripes
Major honours	Conference champions 1999; Southern League champions 1985; FA Trophy winners 1998
Position 1998/99	Promoted to Football League as Conference champions

The Football League has welcomed (if that's the word) a number of new clubs since promotion from the Conference was formalised in the late Eighties, but none, perhaps, as brave as Cheltenham Town. A modest football club from a rugby stronghold, beset by obscure local rivalries and public apathy, Cheltenham had achieved very little until three years ago. There was no stack of non-League silverware on the mantelpiece, no great FA Cup giant-killing tradition, no vast stadium waiting to be filled. The town was well-known for its horse racing, its tourist-magnet spa and *GCHQ*, but football? Come again…?

Yet on the morning of Friday 23 April 1999, club director Paul Roberts came into his office, tired and hungover after a night of celebrations that had run long into the early hours, to find 50 or 60 faxes spilling onto the floor. The previous evening, Cheltenham had beaten Yeovil 3–2 to secure the Conference championship. Now the eyes of a nation's media were on the team. Who were they? Who was the manager? What did they wear? Did any of them have quirky day-jobs, you know, traffic warden or undertaker or roof-thatcher, something like that? For Cheltenham Town, fame had come suddenly, and with a vengeance.

That the club had come so far owed much to its unassuming, insurance-selling chairman Paul Baker and its no-nonsense team manager Steve Cotterill. While Baker set about ensuring that Cheltenham's Whaddon Road ground would meet League requirements, Cotterill made the most of the experienced Conference hands, local lads and free transfers from Hereford that made up his haphazard but somehow tightly knit squad. With no fat-walleted benefactor to aid them, no history of challenging for League status and few star names in their line-up, Cheltenham were nobody's favourites to win the Conference in 1998/99. But winning the FA Trophy at Wembley the previous year had kick-started a much-needed ground-swell of local support, and Cotterill, once a striker at Wimbledon and Bournemouth but Cheltenham born and bred, knew how to turn it to his advantage.

His team began the season brightly. By Christmas they were embroiled in a four-way battle for top spot with Kettering, Stevenage and Rushden. By March they were so far clear it was almost embarrassing – even if they hadn't beaten Yeovil, there would have been four more chances to tie up the title.

Then, of course, came the hard part. Until 1999 Cheltenham had been the essence of a part-time club. Many of the squad's senior players had good day-jobs that simply wouldn't be compatible with full-time football in the League, and were loath to give them up. Among them were strikers Jimmy Smith and Jason Eaton, the team's main sources of goals since the early Nineties, players for whom winning the Conference marked the end of a love affair with the club, rather than the start of one. Also on his way was Clive Walker, the 42-year-old former Chelsea winger who had done so much to give the team a professional outlook, but whose personal ambitions remained outside the League.

Other members of the squad were happy to turn professional, but with a transfer budget firmly in five, rather than six, figures, manager Cotterill was anxiously waiting by his phone for news of bargains as the kick-off to the 1999/2000 season approached.

And yet, if Cheltenham don't quite manage to 'do a Macclesfield' and use winning the Conference as the springboard for another promotion in the League, the pause for breath will do no more than restore the historical status quo to Whaddon Road. Prior to 1997, the club had made gradual, considered progress, as befits the measured tempo of life touted by the town's tourist literature.

The club was founded in 1892, but spent the first 30 years of its existence playing in local amateur leagues. The county of Gloucestershire was as much a football backwater then as it is now, and most of Cheltenham's toughest opponents hailed from the Birmingham area. The early years played in grounds at Whaddon Road Lane (about half a mile from the club's contemporary home) and Carter's Field were not without their successes, but decent crowds weren't attracted to the team until they moved to their current ground in 1932.

FA Trophy fever – Michael Duff and Russell Milton hail victory

At the same time, the club embraced a form of professionalism, joining the Birmingham Combination and abandoning its traditional, foppish-looking ruby-coloured shirts in favour of a more purposeful red-and-white. In 1933/34 Carlisle United were knocked out of the FA Cup second round at Whaddon Road, and with 10,000 expected for the third-round visit of First Division Blackpool, the venue was hastily switched to the (now demolished) Cheltenham Athletic Ground. The crowds duly arrived, but Town lost 3–1.

In 1935, the club began what would be a 50-year spell in the Southern League. In the first line-up was wing-half Tim Ward, a local lad who would soon be sold to Derby County and who would go on to become the only ex-Cheltenham player to be capped by England. After World War II, Peter Goring starred at centre-forward before being lured away by Arsenal. Without him, the club struggled to make an

A pilgrimage along the A40 – some 18,000 Cheltenham fans made their way to Wembley in 1998

impact until the mid-Fifties, when under the managership of Bill Raeside and, later, Arch Anderson, Cheltenham forged a regular presence for themselves in the top six of the Southern League. Their best finish of the period was a runners-up spot behind Guildford City in 1955/56, inspired by dependable centre-half Joe Hyde, who would go on to play more than 450 games for the club.

A Southern League Cup triumph put some serious silverware in the safe for the first time in 1958, and although Cheltenham were relegated from the Premier to the First Division four years later, they were back up again by 1964. In 1968 they came within four points of winning the championship, yet within a year had been relegated again, this time by 0.002 of a goal. (In contrast Cambridge United, the team that beat Cheltenham in the Southern League Cup final that year, would be in the Football League within 12 months.)

The Seventies were distinguished by mediocrity as much as anything, with former Southampton and England winger Terry Paine failing to raise the club from its slumbers during a stint as manager. A seemingly interminable nightmare of poor-quality football played in front of low three-figure crowds was finally ended in 1983, when Alan Wood's side won promotion back to the Premier Division of the Southern League. Wood immediately made way for John Murphy, and within two years Cheltenham had won the Southern League title for the first time, gaining automatic entry into the non-League game's upper echelon, the Conference.

Over the next seven seasons, the club consolidated its position without really threatening to climb higher. There were good runs in the FA Trophy and the odd foray into the first round of the FA Cup, but in the Conference the team remained stuck in the lower half of the table. For the 1989/90 season the club boasted the former Aston Villa, Wolves and Everton striker Andy Gray as a new signing, but after an FA Trophy defeat by Kingstonian he decided he'd had enough of bobbing along with the Robins at Whaddon Road, and left to take up the microphone at *Sky Sports*. While Gray's contribution to the team had been modest, his presence had been a focal point for fans, and his departure seemed to signal a loss of ambition at the club. Swingeing cuts in the wage bill followed, and Cheltenham were relegated back to the Midland Division of the Southern League in 1992.

The mid-Nineties were frustrating. With Murphy returning for a second spell as manager and advocating all-out attack, Cheltenham were good to watch but not consistent enough to win promotion back to the Conference. In the absence of a quick return, support ebbed away again until the 1996/97 season, when Chris Robinson's side found themselves in a nip-and-tuck race for promotion with Gresley Rovers, Halesowen Town and their bitterest rivals, Gloucester City. As Gresley pulled away from the pack, Robinson was replaced by Steve Cotterill. But Gresley's ground was not up to Conference standard, and Cheltenham's eventual second place was enough to see them up.

The club had enjoyed a stroke of good fortune, and Cotterill resolved to make the most of it. In 1997/98, with Clive Walker enjoying the umpteenth Indian summer of his career, captain Chris Banks in assured form and Neil Grayson, Dale Watkins and Jason Eaton all getting among the goals, Cheltenham went 17 Conference games unbeaten. Crowds at Whaddon Road doubled, and although the side could ultimately do no better than finish a distant second to Halifax Town, there was ample compensation elsewhere in a run to the third round of the FA Cup, where Cheltenham took Reading to a replay.

There was also the small matter of the FA Trophy, in which Enfield, Rushden, Ashton United and Dover Athletic were all beaten en route to a Wembley final against the former League side Southport. The game wasn't a classic, but the pilgrimage of 18,000 fans down the A40 to London proved an inspiration, and their devotion was rewarded 11 minutes from time when Eaton headed the only goal of the game.

The town had not seen celebrations like it, and again, Cotterill was determined to make the most of his opportunity, using the euphoria of Wembley as a springboard to launch an assault on the Conference title in 1998/99. On 22 April 1999, his task reached fruition. In front of a capacity 6,000 crowd at Whaddon Road, Cheltenham needed to beat Yeovil to make the title theirs. The score was 2–2 when, in the seventh minute of stoppage time, Michael Duff headed home from a free-kick. From out of the pandemonium which broke loose, Gloucestershire gained its first-ever professional football club.

Here we go!

Motorists will approach Cheltenham on either the M5 motorway or, if coming from the south-east, the A40. From the M5, exit at junction 10 onto the A4019 toward Cheltenham. Take the left exit at the roundabout, go straight over two mini-roundabouts, then turn right and follow signs for Prestbury. Turn right into Albert Road, the left at the roundabout into Prestbury Road and right into Whaddon Road – the ground is on the left.

Local lad made good – manager Steve Cotterill

On the A40, go straight through the outlying village of Charlton Kings, straight on at the junction with the A435 Cirencester Road, then right at the next lights into Hales Road. Follow this road for about 1.5miles, then turn left after the left-hand bend into Whaddon Road – the ground is on the right after about half a mile.

The club **car park** is large and cheap (£1), and certainly preferable to street parking in the Whaddon area, where car crime is a problem.

Cheltenham Spa **train station** receives direct services from Bristol, Birmingham, Sheffield, Doncaster and Newcastle, as well as irregular trains from London Paddington (otherwise change at Bristol Parkway for Cheltenham from London). For the latest timings call ☎0345/484950. From the station there should be a plentiful supply of **taxis** to take you out to Whaddon (£4–5).

Just the ticket

It seems certain that the non-League tradition of fans gaining entry to Whaddon Road and then moving around wherever they please will end as Cheltenham enter the League. Also likely to end is the era of low ticket prices – **visiting fans** will pay £11 to sit (concessions £8), £9 to stand (£6) in 1999/2000. The club plans to build a new 3,000 all-seater stand on the Wymans Road side of the ground, which among other things will have improved facilities for **disabled supporters.** Call the club for the current situation on ☎01242/573558.

The ultimate answer at 42 – Clive Walker

Swift half

You can get a pie and a pint in the **club bar** at the ground, and this is probably the best bet locally. Otherwise try the Bath Road area in the town centre, which is lined with welcoming pubs. If you fancy hanging around, Cheltenham's thriving **nightclub scene** attracts visitors from as far afield as Birmingham and Bristol.

Club merchandise

There is the inevitable new kit to 'celebrate' the club's arrival in the League, available at the **club shop** adjoining the Main Stand.

Barmy army

The club's traditional rivalries with Gloucester City, Forest Green Rovers and Hereford United have been put on what the fans hope is permanent hold by Cheltenham's promotion to the League. Visitors from further afield should find a warm welcome.

In print

Look out for the ***Pink 'Un*** sports special from around 6pm on Saturdays – always a worthwhile read even though Cheltenham fans are frustrated by its extensive coverage of rival clubs, not to mention Gloucester's rugby union side.

On air

BBC Radio Gloucestershire (94.9 FM) has the edge over local commercial station ***CAT FM*** (102.6 FM), though again, Cheltenham have to share airtime with other local sporting interests.

In the net

Cheltenham's **official website** is smart-looking and has the feel of a fan-run site. There's a good history section and the expected squad details and news, with e-commerce promised for the future at: www.cheltenhamtown.co.uk.

Two unofficial sites which give the fans' view are ***Super Dale's Boots*** at www.thekop.demon.co.uk; and the ***Robins Fanzine*** at: www.angelfire.com/ct/cheltenhamrobins.

Chester City

Formation	1884 as Chester FC
Stadium	Deva Stadium, Bumpers Lane, Chester, CH1 4LT. ☎01244/371376
Ground capacity	6,000
First-choice colours	Blue-and-white stripes
Major honours	Welsh Cup winners 1908, 1933, 1947
Position 1998/99	14th in Third Division

In 1986, Chester City were served a winding-up petition for unpaid tax. The club was more than £1million in debt, a crisis that was only resolved by the sale of its historic Sealand Road ground for development in 1990. The team then spent two years in enforced exile, sharing grounds with Macclesfield Town, before moving back to Chester at the newly built Deva Stadium in 1992. It had been a long and painfully drawn out saga, but at least, at the end of it, the club had a new home which complied fully with the requirements of the Taylor Report, a team holding their own in the old Third Division, and a balance sheet free of debt.

Autumn collection – shaking the bucket at Brentford, 1998

Seven years on, and football's wheel of fortune has played a cruel trick on the team and their long-suffering supporters. On the eve of the 1998/99 season, chairman Mark Guterman, a young Wilmslow-based businessman who'd bought a majority shareholding in City from *Morrison*, the firm that built the Deva Stadium, in 1995, announced that the club was up for sale. When no buyer stepped forward, Guterman successfully applied to the courts to have the club put in administration, effectively granting City a stay of execution from creditors who between them were owed an estimated £500,000.

With the PFA stepping in to pay players' wages and the Crown's officially appointed administrator David Acland cutting huge swathes through the club's off-the-field overhead, Chester somehow contrived to play through to the end of the season, despite threats of expulsion from the Football League and continuing attempts by creditors – who included City's former lawyers and the company that once printed the matchday programme – to get the administration order revoked.

While the club continued to live this hand-to-mouth existence, an *Independent Supporters' Association* was formed to co-ordinate

The border of night and day – Chester's Deva Stadium, partly in England, mostly in Wales

an action plan and collection buckets were passed around at Chester's away games. Yet the question remained – why hadn't anyone stepped in to acquire Guterman's shares? One local consortium, led by David Pickering, backed down after discovering that *Morrison*, as guarantors of City's £20,000-a-year rent for the Deva Stadium to the city council, still held a so-called 'special share' which theoretically would allow the company to veto boardroom decisions. Another interested party was *Total Network Solutions*, the hi-tech firm that already backed the League Of Wales side Llansantffraid – but they took one look at Chester's financial projections and backed out. Reg Brealey, chairman of Grantham Town and a man formerly associated with Sheffield United, Lincoln City and Darlington, also entered the frame but was fighting a court battle of his own over an allegedly unpaid solicitors' bill.

In November, Guterman stepped down as chairman but continued to own 94% of the shares. The *ISA* launched a Trust Fund in the hope of being able to buy the club out in partnership with a business consortium, and their prayers were answered with the emergence of Terry Smith as the administrator's favoured candidate to be the new chairman. A former coach of the Great Britain American Football team who enjoyed the backing of his Florida-based businessman father, Smith claimed he and his 'associates' had been looking to buy a British football club for a while. So why Chester?

'Americans love history and Chester is steeped in history,' came the reply. 'The football club has 114 years of history and you cannot take that away from fans.'

Indeed not – although, as it happens, the history of football in this ancient Roman town straddling the border between England and Wales goes back far beyond the club's formation in 1884. An old street version of the game, with hundreds of players on either side and with handling of the ball very much allowed, was played every Shrove Tuesday from medieval times, though it was subsequently banned by a number of monarchs who feared it was a threat to public order. Once the laws of the modern game had been formalised in the mid-19th century, a number of clubs sprang up in the Chester area, but none was big enough to make much of an impact before 1884, when Chester Rovers merged with King's School Old Boys to form Chester FC.

The team played their first games on a pitch at Faulkner Street in Bishopfield, today's Hoole area. There were enough facilities for spectators to be charged admission, but the pitch was poor – something that was to afflict all Chester's grounds until the club moved to Sealand Road in 1906. Local MP Lord Melchett persuaded the site's owner, the Earl of Crewe, to grant the club a lease on the land, and shortly afterwards Chester was floated as a limited company, with Melchett becoming the majority shareholder.

Yet in addition to the obvious rival attractions of Liverpool and Everton not far away, Chester were also playing in the shadow of better-established Cheshire clubs such as Crewe Alexandra, Northwich Victoria and Stockport County. All three had tasted League football and, while Northwich had soon returned to the non-League game, Crewe and Stockport were thriving. The event that finally put Chester on the local football map took place on Good Friday 1931, when senior Football League official Charles Sutcliffe officially opened a new grandstand at Sealand Road. He was so impressed by the large crowd that had turned up for what was, after all, only a game against Port Vale reserves, that he recommended Chester for membership of the Third Division (North) that very summer.

Chester duly played their first League game on 29 August, when 13,000 turned up for the visit of Wigan Borough. Little did they know that the match they were witnessing would soon officially be declared never to have been played, for Borough subsequently resigned from the League and all their matches that season were expunged from the records. Today, most history books list Chester's League debut as the Anglo-Welsh derby at Wrexham which was played the following week.

Playing in Wales was nothing new to Chester, who had won the Welsh Cup as early as 1908, and who would win it twice more in the years before and after World War II. But in the English game, major honours were to prove more elusive. Charles Hewitt, the manager who led the club from Cheshire League obscurity into national competition, took Chester to runners-up spot in the Third Division (North) in 1936, but this was insufficient for promotion and he departed for Millwall soon after.

There was another close shave in the first season after World War II, when Chester finished third under Frank Brown. Yet within a year the team had dropped to 20th place, and the next decade would be spent exclusively in the lower half of the Third Division (North) until the Fourth Division was created in 1958 and Chester, almost inevitably, were sent straight down into it.

After a third-place finish in 1959 (again, not enough for promotion then), the club plumbed new depths, finishing bottom of the League two years in a row from 1961, and making three (successful) applications for re-election. Somehow, Sealand Road youth product Ron Davies managed to average a goal every other game during this period, but when he was sold to Luton Town, Chester's destiny appeared to be

Back to Macc – Chester at Moss Rose in the Third Division, 1998

At the sharp end – Kevin Ratcliffe takes a much-needed break

sealed. While Davies went on to score 150 goals for Southampton and earn 29 caps for Wales through the late Sixties and early Seventies, his former club toiled aimlessly on in the League's lower reaches.

Until 1975, that is, when long-serving manager Ken Roberts managed to pull the team up to the Third Division with a fourth-place finish. Chester were promoted by the narrowest of margins – on goal average – but Roberts' team had already made its potential plain by reaching the semi-finals of the League Cup, where only a narrow two-leg defeat by Aston Villa deprived them of a trip to Wembley.

Roberts was succeeded prior to the start of the 1976/77 season by a player-manager, the ex-Manchester City midfielder Alan Oakes. By 1978 he had taken Chester to within two points of a berth in the Second Division, and was also coaxing a young striker from Flint by the name of Ian Rush through the club's youth scheme. Rush earned his debut the following season and made an immediate impact, not just on Chester's opponents but on the Liverpool scouts sitting in the stands – in April 1980 he was transferred to Anfield for £300,000. After that, Chester never really looked like entering the top half of the League again. Oakes departed after relegation to the Fourth Division and an FA Cup defeat at non-League Penrith in 1982, and a procession of managers left the club – under its newly adopted name of 'Chester City' – bottom of the League again by 1984. However, the arrival of Harry McNally as manager in 1985 brought the spirit of ambition back to the club. Ignoring the meddling of chairman Eric Barnes, McNally assembled a bold side around the talents of midfielder Milton Graham and striker Stuart Rimmer, the latter an Everton reject who would go on to score more than 150 goals in two spells at Chester.

McNally's team won promotion to the Third Division in 1986, and remained there throughout the crisis surrounding the fate of Sealand Road and the exile at Macclesfield. The popular Ray Crofts succeeded Barnes as chairman and the club appeared to have a rosy future when the Deva Stadium opened its doors in August 1992.

As so often happens, though, the football failed to live up to its bold new surroundings. Chester were relegated at the end of the 1992/93 season, and although manager Graham Barrow got them straight back up, the retirement of Crofts for health reasons led to another crisis of confidence within the club. After an argument over resources with new chairman Graeme Wilkes, Barrow resigned and Chester were relegated once again in 1995.

The appointment of former Everton and Wales captain Kevin Ratcliffe as manager at the end of that relegation season brought stability to the playing side, but financially the club's position was sliding almost from the moment Mark Guterman walked through the doors of the Deva. Over-spending on players in the face of falling crowds is an easy formula by which football clubs can lose money quickly. It might have been the reverse of Chester's problem in the Eighties (when lack of investment stopped the club in its tracks), but that was no comfort to the supporters who marched 400-strong from the town hall to the last game of 1998/99, not so much in protest, but in celebration that their beleaguered club had managed to see out the campaign…

Here we go!

Motorists coming from the south or east should approach Chester on the A55 ring road, exiting onto the A483 toward the town centre. Carry straight on over three roundabouts and turn left at the fourth into Nicholas Street, then left at each of two sets of lights into Bumpers Lane – the Deva Stadium is at the end of this road on the right. Coming from the north, exit the M56 at junction 15 onto the M53 – this in turn becomes the A55, then follow directions above.

After a six-year wait, Chester finally got some road signs pointing travellers in the direction of the Deva Stadium in 1998, so you shouldn't go too far wrong.

The large **car park** at the ground (£1.50) rarely fills up and is preferable to street parking on the surrounding industrial estate.

Chester **train station** receives direct services from Birmingham New Street, Manchester and Liverpool; if coming from London Euston, change at Crewe. Getting back from an evening kick-off shouldn't present a problem but check the latest timings on ☎0345/484950.

From the station, which is a good mile and a half from the ground, you can either take the shuttle bus to the bus station and a regular bus #28 along Sealand Road from there, or hail a **taxi** (about £4 one-way).

Just the ticket

Visiting fans can either stand on the South Terrace or sit at the south end of the West Stand. Ticket prices in 1998/99 were £10 to stand and £7.50 to sit, with no concessions for visitors.

Disabled supporters have areas allocated to them in both East and West Stands, with fans of visiting teams normally allocated the latter. Advance booking essential on ☎01244/371376.

Swift half

Aside from the (theoretically members-only) **supporters' club bar,** the area around the Deva Stadium is a bit of a food and drink desert. Ignore the adjacent retail park and head into town, where the Chester City *ISA* recommend the Irish bar ***Scruffy Murphy's*** on Northgate Street.

Alternatively, the ***Boathouse Inn*** off Dee Lane has one of the few family rooms in town.

Club merchandise

Chester are going retro for 1999/2000, with a replica of the 1965 pinstriped design as the team's home shirt and a return to green-and-yellow (the club's early Sixties colours) for the away kit. See them both at the **club shop** in the East Stand.

Barmy army

There's not normally any trouble at the Deva unless Wrexham are the visitors.

In print

Local newspapers the ***Cheshire Chronicle*** and (especially) the ***Evening Leader*** have had a field day with all the takeover and administration talk and are worth picking up. Liverpool's ***Football Echo*** normally makes it to Chester at around 6pm on a Saturday.

The ultimate Chester history book is Chas Sumner's ***On The Borderline*** (Yore, £18.95), while the main fanzine is ***Hello Albert*** (96 Romsley Road, Bartley Green, Birmingham, B32 3PS)

On air

Liverpool stations ***BBC Radio Merseyside*** (95.8 FM) and ***Radio City*** (96.7 FM) both squeeze in some Chester coverage from time to time.

In the net

The club has relaunched its **official site** with the help of Rob Ashcroft, who has added his existing results archive to an already impressive site with smart graphics and a good history at: surf.to/ccfc-net. He faces competition, though, from the **unofficial offering** at: www.chester-city.co.uk. This hosts the *ISA* and *Hello Albert* sites, and has a detailed site map to help you around.

Chesterfield

Formation	1866 as Chesterfield Town
Stadium	Recreation Ground, Saltergate, Chesterfield, S40 4SX. ☎01246/209765
Ground capacity	8,800
First-choice colours	Blue and white
Major honours	Third Division (North) champions 1931, 1936; Fourth Division champions 1970, 1985; Anglo-Scottish Cup winners 1981
Position 1998/99	Ninth in Second Division

From the outside looking in, Chesterfield would appear to have a lot going for them. One of the oldest clubs in the League has a solid, dependable team secure in the right half of the Second Division, a homely, attractive ground steeped in tradition, a loyal and innovative manager, and a recent run of form that includes coming within minutes of the FA Cup final in 1997. Look a little harder, though, and a different, rather gloomier picture emerges.

The town's geographical location, sandwiched between the conurbations of Derby and Sheffield, may have been instrumental in giving Chesterfield its position in early English football history, but it also places an obvious barrier around the team's supporter base. The Recreation Ground at Saltergate, a venue almost as quaintly appealing as the crooked spire of St Mary's All Saints Church that gives the town its fame (and the team their nickname of 'Spireites'), needs millions lavished on it to bring it up to the standards required by the Taylor Report – money the club would rather spend on a new stadium out of town. And John Duncan, in the manager's hot seat since February 1993, is beginning to face a backlash from supporters aggrieved at the club's apparent lack of ambition, following yet another narrow but decisive failure to make the promotion play-offs in 1999.

Fans point to both the 1997 Cup run and the club's extensive history as evidence that they, and the town, deserve better than the predictable fare currently being served up at Saltergate. Yet prior to 1997 Chesterfield had made little impression on the English game's broader picture, save for a widely recognised ability to produce great goalkeepers. Apart from a brief spell in the Second Division in the late Forties, the club has spent the entire postwar period in the lower half of the League. As for the ancient history, while it is true that only Stoke City and the two Nottingham clubs are older than Chesterfield in the League, it is also true that for much of its early existence the club was run on a purely casual basis, and that even after entry to the League was granted at the turn of the century, the town then had to endure another decade of non-League football after an application for re-election was turned down.

The club spent the first 53 years of its life, from formation in 1866 to the end of World War I, as Chesterfield Town. At first the team played only friendly matches, at a variety of venues around the town, very possibly including Saltergate itself. In 1871 two of the club's founding fathers, town clerk John Cutts and treasurer C W Robinson, drew up a set of rules which are still in existence today. Thirteen years later the club settled at Saltergate for good, though in those early days the ground was little more than an enclosed field with a simple covered stand on the Compton Street side. Visitors included the likes of Sheffield Wednesday and Notts County among other local sides, and it was success in these games that prompted the club to turn professional in 1891.

Milking the moment – celebrating against 'Boro, 1997

As well as paying players, Chesterfield adopted a more purposeful outlook in other ways. At the instigation of manager Russell Timmeus, the team were dressed in bold white shirts with a large union jack emblazoned across the front, and the club won the first formal competition it entered – the Barnes Cup, a regional tournament named after local colliery owner and Chesterfield MP Alfred Barnes.

In 1892 the club not only retained the Barnes Cup but also won the Derbyshire Minor Cup and the Sheffield Cup. In addition Chesterfield entered the FA Cup for the first time, and joined the Sheffield League. It was during this period that the club acquired their first of many colourful goalkeepers – one Charlie Bunyan, who'd been between the sticks for Hyde in their record-breaking 26–0 defeat by Preston in 1887, but whose regular forays into the opposition half, so costly then, would continue at Saltergate.

In 1896 Chesterfield joined the more competitive Midland League, and three years later they successfully applied for membership of the Second Division of the Football League, the club becoming a limited liability company at the same time. Around 2,500 Chesterfield fans made the short trip to Sheffield Wednesday for the team's League debut, and although that game was lost 5–1, the club finished its first season of League football in a creditable seventh position, aided by the goalscoring of centre-forward Herbert Munday.

Toward the end of the 1902/03 season, Chesterfield made another goalkeeping discovery – this time an effortlessly consistent figure, Sam Hardy. By 1904/05 he had become the club's first choice, helping the team to a fifth-place finish in a League season in which they conceded just 35 goals in 34 games. At the end of the campaign he was sold to Liverpool, and although the huge (for the time) transfer fee of £500 was a significant boost to the Saltergate coffers, Hardy would go on to prove what a loss he was to Chesterfield, helping his new club to the League title in 1906, and going on to become the most celebrated 'keeper in Edwardian England.

Without Hardy, Chesterfield's form nosedived. They'd finished in the bottom three of the Second Division four years running when, in 1909, the League decided to kick them out, welcoming back Lincoln City in their place.

Out but not down, Chesterfield rejoined the Midland League and became regular top-half finishers in that competition, while continuing to enter the FA Cup, claiming the odd Football League scalp along the way. Local interest in the side had waned after the loss of League status, however, and after World War I, the borough council was forced to step in and purchase not just the freehold to Saltergate, but the club itself. The idea was that the team would represent the town in an official capacity, and for a brief period they even played under the name Chesterfield

Keeping it neat and tidy – but Saltergate's days as a Football League venue are surely numbered

Municipal FC. However, in 1921, when the club attempted to rejoin the League by becoming a founder member of the Third Division (North), it was found that municipal ownership of teams contravened League rules, and members were obliged to buy the council out – and the club to change its name to plain 'Chesterfield' – before League status was granted.

The buy-back placed a strain on the club's resources, and the first few seasons back in the League were tough going. After making a lengthy journey to Darlington for a game in December 1923, Chesterfield were dismayed to find that the pitch was frozen, so they asked referee Bert Fogg if the match could be played on an adjacent cricket field to avoid a postponement – Fogg agreed, but Darlington won 2–1.

As so often happens, it took the arrival of an open-minded manager to give the club a sense of ambition again. In Chesterfield's case, his name was Ted Davison, a plain-speaking but perceptive figure whose appointment at the end of 1926 signalled an upturn in the club's fortunes. Together with new chairman Harold Shentall, who was appointed in 1928, Davison steered Chesterfield toward promotion with a hard-running, free-scoring side. The Third Division (North) title was finally won in 1931, Albert Pynegar top-scoring with 27 of the team's 102 goals, three of them in the 8–1 demolition of Gateshead which sealed the championship on the final day.

Chesterfield had problems adapting to Second Division life and were relegated in 1933, but three years later, with Bill Harvey in the dugout and Davison continuing to oversee team affairs as general manager, they'd won the Third Division (North) title again. This time the team were good enough to hold their own at the higher level, and while Shentall's over-ambitious rebuilding of Saltergate resulted in many of the club's best players having to be sold, there was enough fresh talent coming through to keep Chesterfield up as World War II approached.

In the first full season after the war, 1946/47, Chesterfield managed their best-ever League position, finishing fourth in the Second Division, eight points shy of promotion to the top flight. Alas, in the following close season several key players, including goalscoring forwards Tom Swinscoe and Syd Ottewell, were sold, and their departure knocked the stuffing out of a side that could, conceivably, have challenged for a further promotion in later years.

As it was, Chesterfield were relegated in 1951, and they would spend the remainder of the decade in the Third Division (North) before becoming part of the new national Third Division in 1958/59. As well as being historic for the obvious reasons, that campaign was also notable for the debut of a former Sheffield coal-bagger by the name of Gordon Banks in goal. Banks had joined Chesterfield's junior side earlier in the decade, helping them to the FA Youth Cup final in 1955/56. After that he completed his National Service in Germany before returning to Chesterfield, where he seized on an injury to long-standing 'keeper Ron Powell and made his first-team debut against Colchester on 29 November 1958. He quickly became the club's first-choice goalkeeper, but news of his extraordinary reactions soon spread, and at the end of the season Leicester City bid £7,000 for his signature. Ted Davison, still taking the club's big decisions as secretary-manager but more pragmatic now, felt he couldn't turn the money down.

It was another case of a short-term expediency costing the club dear in the long run. By 1961 Chesterfield were in the Fourth Division for the first time, entering a barren patch that would not be ended until manager Jimmy McGuigan and locally born striker Ernie Moss helped the club to the divisional title in 1970. Fifteen years of solid and occasionally sophisticated Third Division football followed, with Moss returning for two further spells at the club, the last coinciding with relegation back to the basement and an immediate championship. More pertinently, Chesterfield's demotion and promotion coincided with yet another cash crisis, perhaps the most serious the club had ever faced.

Despite another bail-out from the local council 70 years after the last, the training ground where Gordon Banks had been shown the goalkeeping ropes (and which another famous 'keeper, Bob Wilson, had been able to watch from the house of his wife-to-be before joining Arsenal in the early Sixties) had to be sold to clear the debts. Another relegation followed in 1989, and after a play-off final defeat by Cambridge United in 1990, the team struggled in mid-table of what was now the Third Division until John Duncan's arrival lifted both sights and spirits. In the 1994/95 play-offs, a 5–2 semi-final drubbing of local rivals Mansfield was much-enjoyed by fans and was followed by a comfortable 2–0 win ovre Bury at Wembley.

Two years later, Chesterfield supporters would claim they should by rights have been back at the Twin Towers, this time in an FA Cup final against Chelsea. Had the referee in their semi-final with top-flight Middlesbrough given a goal after the ball came down off the 'Boro bar and crossed the line, they might well have done. But he waved play on, the game finished 3–3, and Chesterfield lost the replay.

The 1996/97 Cup run, which also saw Nottingham Forest humbled at Saltergate, gave the club the kind of national exposure

Football focus – John Duncan adjusts his set

it had not enjoyed in decades. But it also alerted bigger clubs to the talents buried deep within Duncan's squad, and young striker Kevin Davies was soon sold to Southampton for £750,000.

Today, with chairman Norton Lea intent on taking Chesterfield into a 10,000-seater stadium on the site of the former *Markham's* works out of town, planners raising objections and fans reluctant to say farewell to their beloved Saltergate, the passion and purpose which accompanied that Cup run seem like a distant memory. How fickle this game can be.

Here we go!

Many Chesterfield fans walk to Saltergate and, surprisingly, its town-centre location presents few problems for visiting **motorists.** Simply exit the M1 at junction 29, approach Chesterfield on the A617, then follow signs for the A619 Bakewell. This becomes Markham Road, with a roundabout at the end at which you should turn right into Foljambe Road – the ground is straight ahead. There's **street parking** off Ashgate Road to your left.

Chesterfield **train station** is very well-served with direct services from London St Pancras, Bristol, Birmingham, Leeds and Newcastle among other places. Nearby Derby and Sheffield have late departures for evening games, but more distant destinations do not. Call ☎0345/484950 for the latest timings.

Saltergate is a 20min walk from the station through the town centre and across Tapton Lane.

Just the ticket

Visiting fans have standing spaces in the Cross Street End and an allocation of seating at that end of the Main Stand. Prices in 1998/99 were £8.50 and £9.50 respectively, no concessions.

Disabled supporters have spaces in front of the Main Stand – book in advance on ☎01246/209765.

Swift half

On Saltergate itself between the ground and the town centre is the ***Barley Mow*** with a fine range of real ales and excellent food at low prices. Those with their own transport should consider heading out along the B6057 toward Sheffield for the ***Derby Tup***, about a mile out of town at Whittington Moor, with yet more real-ale choices and hearty food.

Club merchandise

The **club shop** is located conveniently behind the area of the Main Stand allocated to visiting fans – but there's no sign of that union jack shirt being revived just yet.

Barmy army

Chesterfield fans are a good-humoured bunch and trouble is rare at Saltergate unless Mansfield are visiting. In the town centre, be discreet with your colours.

In print

The ***Derbyshire Times*** is produced in the town but for Saturday evening match reports Chesterfield relies on the Sheffield ***Green'Un***, normally in town by about 6pm.

Sadly, fanzine ***The Crooked Spireite*** is no more and the best Chesterfield **books** are likewise out of print. Shame.

On air

Again, it's Sheffield that provides the coverage, with ***BBC Radio Sheffield*** (104.1 FM) offering some Chesterfield bits and bobs.

In the net

There's no **official website** and the only unofficial offering still around in the summer of 1999 was ***Aspire*** at: www.spirenet.demon.co.uk. Luckily, this is a very thorough site with a detailed history, the latest on Chesterfield's new stadium and the unique *Spireola* internet jukebox of football songs old and new.

Colchester United

Formation	1937
Stadium	Layer Road, Colchester, Essex, CO2 7JJ. ☎01206/508800
Ground capacity	8,200
First-choice colours	Blue and white stripes
Major honours	Conference champions 1992; FA Trophy winners 1992
Position 1998/99	18th in Second Division

The Colchester United story is punctuated by two momentous events – the first almost impossibly good, the second almost indescribably bad. Nearly 20 years separated the team's FA Cup defeat of Don Revie's Leeds and relegation from the Football League in 1990, yet as the Conference loomed, commentators couldn't help but refer to the giant-killing, so great and enduring was its impact on the nation. Yet in its own way, the shrewd, unflappable manner in which Colchester have bounced back from non-League football to the Second Division during the Nineties deserves at least as much credit as their Cup exploits of two decades earlier, perhaps more. Layer Road, the archetypal tight lower-division ground, may not have been the centre of the country's attention as it was in 1971, but Colchester fans aren't bothered – what matters to them is status, not celebrity.

More to life than Leeds – the Watney Cup is won, 1971

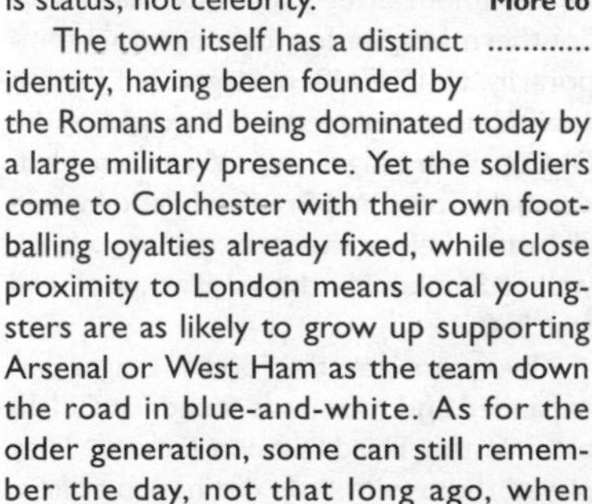

The town itself has a distinct identity, having been founded by the Romans and being dominated today by a large military presence. Yet the soldiers come to Colchester with their own footballing loyalties already fixed, while close proximity to London means local youngsters are as likely to grow up supporting Arsenal or West Ham as the team down the road in blue-and-white. As for the older generation, some can still remember the day, not that long ago, when Colchester United didn't exist at all, the club's foundation in 1937 making it the youngest of all current League members.

Prior to that, football had been played at a reasonably high level by the amateur side Colchester Town. Founded in 1874, the team appears to have had a somewhat haphazard attitude to its commitments. Town's first recorded game, against Braintree in October 1882, saw the team take

Culture at Colchester – Mark Kinsella, 1994

the field without their goalkeeper, who'd been 'accidentally left behind'. Rather than put an outfield player in goal, Town decided the best form of defence was attack – and won 3–1.

After that, Town players did their best to ensure the club could always put out a full team. In 1886, star player Ernie Goby was forbidden to play in an away game against Ipswich because his father, an undertaker, had an important funeral to carry out. Goby junior accompanied the hearse until his father was out of sight, then pulled his kit-bag out from alongside the coffin and legged it to the station to catch the train to Ipswich.

In the early days, many of Town's games were against army sides, including representative teams from the Irish Fusiliers, the Scottish Rifles and other regiments while they were stationed at the local garrison. Colchester's relationship with its military population was ambivalent (and remains so to this day), and these matches were occasionally marred by violence, either on or off the pitch. In 1909, however, Town had cause to be grateful when the 4th Battalion King's Royal Rifle Corps vacated the Layer Road site, and the footballers moved in. The ground was briefly re-occupied by the army during World War I, but after hostilities Town bought the place outright in 1919.

During the Twenties and Thirties the club remained resolutely amateur, in common with several other East Anglian clubs including Ipswich Town nearby. Yet enough money was earned from playing in the Spartan League for a Main Stand to be built at Layer Road in 1933, and plans for further expansion were on the drawing board when the club's mentor, secretary Charles Clark, died the following year. Without him, a vacuum was created within Town's hierarchy. Some insisted that professionalism was the only way forward, and at a crowded meeting in February 1937, they received overwhelming support from the Colchester public. Town loyalists agreed to sell Layer Road to the new club, Colchester United, but only with the proviso that they be allowed to continue to use the ground for their own matches.

This arrangement did not last long. While United fired the local imagination after being immediately admitted to the Southern League, Town struggled on at Layer Road for only a year before being wound-up, after which their players formed the backbone of United's reserve side in the Eastern Counties League.

World War II put a block on United's development after just three seasons of Southern League football, but only temporarily. In 1947/48, manager Ted Fenton took Colchester to the fifth round of the FA Cup, with League clubs Wrexham, Huddersfield Town and Bradford Park Avenue all beaten before the team ran into a brick wall at Stanley Matthews' Blackpool, and lost 5–0.

Two years later the Football League was expanded and room was found for Colchester in the Third Division (South). They played there with little distinction at first, but managed a third-place finish in 1957, missing promotion to the Second Division by only a point. A year later they made the cut into the newly formed national Third Division. Relegation followed in 1961 but United were back up again within the year, local lad Bobby Hunt scoring 37 of the team's 104 goals in the 1961/62 season.

For the remainder of the Sixties the club bounced between Third and Fourth Divisions, and had just been relegated for the third time in seven years when Dick Graham took over as manager in 1968. Two years later his side, with veteran ex-England international striker Ray Crawford and the combative Dave Simmons forming a bustling partnership in attack, beat Ringmer Town, Barnet, Cambridge United and Rochdale to set up a fifth-round FA Cup meeting with Leeds, then top of the League. Don Revie's team were at full strength, and with a capacity 15,000 expected through the Layer Road turnstiles, temporary scaffolding was hastily erected over the Main Stand to accommodate the *Match Of The Day* cameras.

From the word go, Leeds were never allowed to get into their stride. Clearly upset by the compact pitch, the closeness of the Essex crowd and the energy of Dick Graham's players, they allowed Crawford to score two goals unmarked in the first half, and were then caught appealing for a throw-in as Simmons raced through to make it 3–0 just after the interval. Leeds pulled two back as Colchester tired, but inspired goalkeeping by Graham Smith – accompanied by some equally inspired commentary from David Coleman up in the gantry – prevented them from getting back on terms.

Just as they'd been in 1948, Colchester were the toast of the nation. There were 50,000 at Goodison Park for the quarter-final meeting with Everton, and although the First Division side won 5–0, there was to be another televised triumph that summer in the Watney Cup, a quintessentially Seventies competition into which teams were invited on the basis of how many goals they'd scored the previous season. Colchester reached the final at Wembley, and beat top-flight West Brom on penalties after the match had finished 4–4.

There was a feeling that Graham was starting something big. And yet, strangely, his team of seasoned campaigners were less well-equipped to deal with the hurly-burly of the Fourth Division than with the nervous niceties of top-flight defences. Crawford retired, Jim Smith replaced Graham, and United went back to their old obscurity, hopping up and down between Third and Fourth during the Seventies, before enduring a sustained and increasingly miserable spell in the basement during the Eighties.

After the Bradford fire in 1985, much of Layer Road's old wooden terracing was closed off and Colchester faced mounting losses. A Luton-style ban on away fans resulted only in a further fall in attendances, which barely passed the 1,000 mark on occasions during 1987/88. Two years later, despite fielding a side with experienced

Tough on the touchline – coach Steve Whitton

professionals such as Billy Gilbert, Tommy English and Ian Allinson, Colchester finished bottom of the League, and were relegated to the Conference.

Chairman Jonathan Crisp had no choice but to sell the freehold to Layer Road to the local council for £1million, and while the sale would have unfortunate consequences later on, at the time it cleared Colchester's debts and, crucially, allowed the team to remain full-time professional. With the ban on away supporters now lifted and United playing neat football under player-manager Ian Atkins, local interest rose again. More than 7,000 were at Layer Road for the visit of Altrincham in April 1991, and though Barnet just pipped Colchester to the Conference title that year, there was no mistake 12 months later. Atkins had left to coach Birmingham, but his replacement Roy McDonough kept the team intact and won the Conference after a nip-and-tuck battle with Wycombe. Just to put the icing on the cake, Colchester then won the FA Trophy, beating Witton Albion in front of 30,000 at Wembley.

After a reasonably successful first term back in the League in 1992/93, Colchester flirted dangerously with the drop again the following year and McDonough was replaced by George Burley, who took the side to fourth in the table by the end of 1994. On Boxing Day, however, Burley resigned to take over at his former club Ipswich Town, and before long caretaker boss Dale Roberts had fled up the A12 to join him. While the two clubs haggled over compensation, Steve Wignall, a former Anfield apprentice who'd played nearly 300 games for Colchester in the late Seventies and early Eighties, was appointed manager.

Wignall's team narrowly missed out on the play-offs on three occasions, and in 1996/97, despite selling star midfielder Mark Kinsella to Charlton (for a useful, club-record £300,000), United reached the Auto Windscreens final at Wembley, unluckily lost on penalties to Carlisle.

Disappointment that day became jubilation at the same venue a year later when Colchester, having beaten Barnet after extra-time in the semi-finals, won the play-off final against Torquay – thanks to a Dave Gregory penalty and some goalkeeping heroics from Carl Emberson.

The club was now on the third rung of England's professional ladder for the first time in nearly 20 years, and a little bit dizzy at the view. After some indifferent League form and a calamitous FA Cup defeat at Northern League side Bedlington Terriers, Wignall resigned in March 1999, to be replaced by the experienced Mick Wadsworth, whose combination of club stalwarts and last-gasp loan signings managed to keep Colchester up.

Meanwhile Layer Road, for all its cosiness, can't house United for much longer. The 10-year lease agreed by the club and the local council expires in 2002, and both parties are jointly funding feasibility studies aimed at securing a site for a new, 10,000-seater stadium out of town. The question is, where will Colchester move to next? A new division? Or a new home?

Here we go!

Motorists will find Colchester without any difficulty but the residential area which surrounds Layer Road isn't known to locals as 'the Crystal Maze' for nothing. From the A12, leave at the A604 Cambridge exit and head toward Colchester along Essex Yeomanry Way. At the next roundabout, take the second exit onto London Road – the ground is well-signposted from here.

There's no **car park** at the ground and many of the surrounding roads don't need residents' schemes – all those driveways already do the job. If you arrive early enough you should find a space on Layer Road itself. The army barracks opposite the ground is strictly out of bounds.

There are two **train stations** but unless you're on a local stopping service, you'll wind up at Colchester North rather than Colchester Town. Colchester North is on a fast line between London Liverpool Street and Ipswich/Norwich (service hourly, journey time 1hr from London). Call ☎0345/484950 for the latest timings.

From Colchester North, take any bus one stop to the High Street. From the bus stop, go back to the top of North Hill, cross the road, turn left and go along Head Street to Headgate. Turn right here for bus *Eastern National* bus #64 or #64A to the ground. This service is very frequent during the day but half-hourly in the evenings – last bus 2159. There are plenty of evening buses from Head Street back to Colchester North station, however, and feasible late connections from there back to London.

Play-off pressure – Colchester's Steve Forbes restrains his man

Just the ticket

Unusually, **visiting fans** have a number of choices at Layer Road. The visitors' terrace is at the Layer Road End (adults £9, concessions £5), but there are also some seats allocated in Block E of the Main *East Coast Cable* Stand (£11/£7). Additionally, visiting **families** have both seats and standing room at their disposal in the Family Stand, by reciprocal agreement – booking essential through your own club.

Disabled supporters have a small area at end of the Main Stand. Book in advance on ☎01206/508802.

Swift half

There's only one pub close to the ground – ***The Drury Arms***, on the corner of Drury Road and Layer Road. It normally welcomes both home and away fans but has been known to turn away large groups of visitors wearing colours. ***The Dragoon***, on Military Road, 10mins' walk toward the town centre, comes *Good Beer Guide* recommended and does decent food, too.

Families are welcome at ***The Sun*** on the A1124 Lexden Road, which has table football outside if weather permits.

Club merchandise

The **club shop** (matchdays only, ☎01206/508809) is behind the Barside Terrace – enter via Layer Road. Home shirts are £34.99, kids' sizes £27.99. Fans are hoping for a more conventional striped design after questionable efforts in recent years.

Barmy army

Aside from Southend (just up the road), Ipswich (the Burley affair) and Wycombe (Conference-era rivalry), few teams travel to Layer Road expecting trouble. The other 'barmy army' across the way causes its fair share of problems in town-centre pubs of an evening, however.

In print

The Colchester fanzine is ***The Blue Eagle*** (22 Silverdale Avenue, Westcliff-on-Sea, SS0 9BA), while exiled fans have their own monthly magazine, ***U's From 'Ome*** (110 Northfield Park, Soham, CB7 5XA).

On air

Local commercial station ***SGR*** (96.1 FM) has a long association with United, having sponsored the team in the mid-Nineties, and tends to be first with the big stories.

As ever, the local *BBC* station, ***Radio Essex*** (103.5 FM) is also worth a try.

In the net

Colchester's **official *Coluweb* site** is not much to look at but is a decent size and is very well-maintained. Unusually for an official site, it has a real fans' feel – perhaps because it's run by volunteers. See for yourself at: www.cufc.co.uk.

Fanzine ***The Blue Eagle*** is also online at: wkweb5.cablenet.co.uk/skinners/.

Coventry City

Formation	1883 as Singer's FC
Stadium	Highfield Road Stadium, King Richard Street, Coventry, CV2 4FW. ☎01203/234000
Ground capacity	23,500
First-choice colours	Sky-blue
Major honours	Second Division champions 1967; Third Division champions 1964; Third Division (South) champions 1936; FA Cup winners 1987
Position 1998/99	15th in Premiership

Highfield Road Stadium, one of the least talked-about football grounds in the Premiership, was celebrating its centenary in 1999. As stadium centenaries go, it was pretty quiet – no TV documentaries, no five-hour radio specials, no tearful reunions of past players and backroom staff. It was as if the ground's owners, Coventry City, had forgotten there was an important birthday to mark. If a card, cake and present were delivered, they were probably late.

In fact, Coventry had not forgotten. The club did, however, have its mind elsewhere – on the former site of a gasworks at Foleshill, to the north of the city. This unpromising parcel of land, dotted with rusting gas-holders and crossed by polluted pipework, is where Coventry are to build 'Arena 2000', the club's home for the new millennium. They were given the green light for the project in the early part of 1999, and are due to play their first game at the new stadium in August 2001.

The stadium will seat 40,000, but it will be far more than just a football ground. A retractable pitch will allow the venue to be used for live music and other events, for which the capacity will rise to 45,000. The huge cost of building the arena – estimated at more than £60million – will be met partly by the sale of Highfield Road for housing and partly by retail chains which are expected to move in to new superstores as part of adjacent developments on the same site.

In the normal run of things, such a scheme might reasonably be expected to attract a long, drawn-out public inquiry. But the Government, keen to add the new arena to the roster of venues for England's 2006 World Cup bid, waved the plans through without so much as a furrowed brow. For once, the city of Coventry, laid waste by Nazi bombing in World War II, reduced to the *Ghost Town* of popular song by mass unemployment in the early Eighties, seemed to be in the right place at the right time.

The news of Coventry City moving to a new stadium is hardly earth-shattering. But the idea that their new home might be bold enough (and big enough) to put the likes of the Riverside, the Reebok and the Britannia firmly in the shade still takes a little getting used to. After all, this is Coventry – past masters at survival on the edge of the nation's footballing elite, the top flight's escapologists *par excellence*, a team whose ability to dodge the drop is the stuff of legend (not to mention a fair smattering of controversy). A club can't just go from being borderline Premiership material to owners of the most modern football stadium in the country. Right?

Wrong. Five years ago, Coventry City's turnover was £4million a year. Now it's more like £19million, and the club's ebullient, infectiously enthusiastic chairman, Bryan Richardson, wants to double that figure again over the next four years. Arena 2000, with its state-of-the-art design, removable roof and seven-day trading potential, is the means by which he might do it. Of the 20 clubs currently in the Premiership, only Arsenal, Everton and

Liverpool can boast a longer continuous stay in the top drawer of the English game. The club, like the city, has put up with being the butt of a thousand jokes. Now it's payback time, and the area south-west of the M1/M6 interchange – not to mention the shape of the Premiership – may never be the same again.

This isn't the first time that City have sought to re-invent themselves in time for the dawning of a bold new area. In the early Sixties another visionary chairman, Derrick Robbins, and his young team manager Jimmy Hill hauled a little-regarded, underachieving Midlands football club up the League table in a whirlwind of commercial innovation, supporter euphoria and PR hype. By 1967 Coventry had their hands on a place in the top flight for the first time in their history and, having waited so long, they were not going to release their grip lightly. If the Arena 2000 development proceeds according to plan, that grip will soon be tighter than ever.

All this talk of World Cups, removable roofs and £40million turnovers is a far cry from the club's origins which, as Robbins and Hill were made to feel all too aware, are almost romantically humble. With no one football club emerging as a major force in Coventry as the game began to take a hold elsewhere in the West Midlands in the mid-19th century, it was left to workers at the *Singer* cycle factory to form their own team in 1883. Early matches were played against other works sides at Dowell's Field off Binley Road, and in 1887 the venue was shifted to a properly enclosed ground at Stoke Road, just south of the club's present home.

In 1891 the team lifted their first piece of silverware, the Birmingham Junior Cup, and three years later were admitted to the Birmingham & District League. There they continued to play in the black and red corporate colours of the *Singer* firm, but in 1898 the club severed the last of its links with the factory and changed its name to Coventry City, in the hope of becoming the area's *de facto* representative side.

Within a year the club had moved into Highfield Road, kicking off the 1899/1900 season with a 1–0 win over Shrewsbury. A contemporary newspaper report described the ground's only stand as 'a gigantic structure'. In fact it could hold only 2,000 souls, and City's attendance for that first game numbered barely half that again.

When survival is victory – fans mob 'keeper Steve Ogrizovic after another Coventry escape, 1996

A passion for fashion – Steve Hunt (left) models Coventry's classic late Seventies *Admiral* kit

Progress continued to be slow, but by 1908 Coventry had been admitted to the Southern League, and two years later the team reached the quarter-finals of the FA Cup – quite an achievement for a non-League side, even then.

It wasn't until after World War I, however, that the club got its first big break. In 1920 many members of the Southern League defected to form the Football League's new Third Division (South). But, rather than go in at that level, Coventry were elected – perhaps a little fortunately – directly to the Second Division.

This should have brought some stability to the club's finances, which up until this point had always been rather precarious, but far from it. A procession of different boardroom setups and secretary-managers struggled to keep City solvent, while on the pitch, the team lost their opening League game 5–0 at home to Tottenham and didn't win a match until Christmas Day. For six seasons Coventry avoided the drop, never finishing above 18th place, before finally succumbing in 1925. Six years later the club acquired a new manager, Harry Storer, who assembled a new-look side around dangerous centre-forward Clarrie Bourton – to this day the most porlific scorer in City's history. Storer's team was almost recklessly enterprising, and didn't win promotion until the Third Division (South) title came their way in 1936. Before then, though, they'd scored 100 goals in four seasons out of five, with Bourton alone netting 49 in 1931/32. Crowds rose to the 20,000 mark, and Storer kept the momentum going right up until the eve of World War II, with Coventry missing promotion to the First Division by only a point in 1938.

The Blitz of 14 November 1940 didn't just reduce the old centre of Coventry to rubble; it gouged gigantic holes out of the Highfield Road pitch and, while the local populace clearly had more pressing matters to consider, it fatally undermined the progress of Storer's team. After the war Storer himself left for Birmingham City, and when he returned in 1951 he could do little with an ageing team that had forgotten how to run, pass and take the other guy on. It was as if the air of postwar depression that swept over the ruined city had also descended on its football club – by 1958, Coventry were in the Fourth Division, having finished 19th in the Third Division (South) the previous season. Better times, however, were just around the corner for both city and City. As the Sixties dawned and the centre of Coventry was belatedly rebuilt amid a mass of agressive, futuristic concrete, the newly rationalised local motor industry (the proud *Singer* name had become just another brand within the giant *Rootes* group) was working overtime to meet the demands of a national consumer boom. As for the football, promotion from the Fourth Division had been won at the first attempt in 1959, and two years later Derrick Robbins appointed the former Fulham inside-forward Jimmy Hill as his new first-team manager.

As chairman of the PFA, Hill's impact on the game had already been immense. The minimum wage had been abolished and professional football in Britain, not to mention elsewhere, would never be the same again. Now, while chairman Robbins' building firm re-fashioned Highfield Road with sections of pre-formed concrete to reflect the style of the born-again city, the man with the pointed beard and endless chit-chat put his instinct for innovation at the service of the club's commercial activities. Out went City's dull royal-blue strip; in its place came a return to the pale blue the players had worn prior to the Storer years. This was not the retrograde step it sounded – Hill also dispensed with the team's old-fashioned nickname of 'Bantams', replacing it with 'Sky Blues', a more up-to-the-minute sounding title that would soon act not just as a convenient standby for headline writers but as a fully fledged corporate brand, spawning such developments as *Radio Sky Blue* and the *Sky Blue Tavern*, where fans were encouraged to have a prematch pint – all proceeds to the club, naturally. There were hoots of derision from the football establishment at the idea of this Third Division club trying to market itself as a modern-day, all-inclusive leisure industry package. And, in truth, not all of Robbins' and Hill's ideas were successful.

But, like Herbert Chapman and Bill Shankly, two other managers who took it upon themselves to change the way their clubs were perceived by their public, Hill also saw to it that Coventry delivered on the pitch, too. In March 1963, top-flight Sunderland arrived at Highfield Road for an FA Cup fifth-round tie, and with three entrance gates broken down in the rush to see the match, as many as 50,000 fans entered the ground. Five minutes from time, a John Sillett cross was headed powerfully home by City's iron-man centre-half George Curtis, and the home side were 2–1 up. As Hill's *Sky Blue Song* rang around the ground, there was an unmistakable whiff of revolution in the Coventry air.

A year later, with winger Ronnie Rees and striker George Hudson encouraged by their manager's adventurous tactics, City won promotion from the Third Division, the title being sealed with a 1–0 home win over Colchester, in a game which Hill had arranged to kick-off 15 minutes after those involving Coventry's promotion rivals. By 1967, with goalkeeper Bill Glazier solid as a rock and Ernie Machin playing the passes in midfield, City had won the Second Division championship – top-flight football had come to town at last.

The club's pub – City fans outside the *Sky Blue Tavern*

By now the *Rootes* group had become a European bridgehead for America's *Chrysler Corporation* and, riding a wave of late Sixties optimism, Coventry City and their fans felt ready to take on the world. It didn't quite work out that way. While the *Chrysler* factory became bogged down by industrial unrest, a fire destroyed Highfield Road's Main Stand and the Second Division trophy that was housed within it. Jimmy Hill became chairman and recruited Noel Cantwell as manager but, aside from a sixth-place finish in 1970, Coventry struggled to make an impact at the highest level.

So began the legend of the last-day escape – no fewer than ten of them over the next 28 seasons, some truly glorious, other tainted by controversy, as Coventry somehow managed to ensure delayed kick-offs so that others' results could be known before their own games were over.

The most notorious incident came in 1977, when thousands of Bristol City fans were delayed by traffic on their way to Highfield Road for the last game of the season, and Jimmy Hill delayed kick-off by five minutes on police advice. Both teams were in danger of going down but, with the score at 2–2 and five minutes left on the clock, Coventry were on the rack. Then word came through that Sunderland had lost their match at Everton, which had begun on time – allowing both teams to relax and play out the game as if it were a practice match. While Sunderland appealed in vain to the FA, the champagne corks were popping again in the Coventry boardroom.

As the Seventies became the Eighties, however, chairman Hill began to lose his popular touch. A plan to rename the club 'Coventry Talbot', as part of a sponsorship deal with the division of the *Peugeot* empire that had taken over the city's troubled *Chrysler* plant, was bitterly opposed by fans and ultimately vetoed by the League.

Then, in an attempt to stem a rising tide of hooliganism, Hill decided to turn Highfield Road into England's first all-seater football ground in 1981. Ironically, much of the atmosphere Hill himself had done so much to generate in the Sixties was now lost. And, as every match was now all-ticket, casual support fell away alarmingly. Almost overnight, average crowds crashed from 19,000 to more like 11,000. All it needed was for local band the Specials to record a new version of their #1 hit single as *Ghost Ground*, and the image would

Reaching for the Sky – Coventry's victorious Wembley line-up, 1987

have been complete. Reluctantly, Hill agreed to remove some of the seats from the Highfield Road Kop to create a small standing area. Then he resigned, ending a 21-year association with the club which had, for the most part, amply rewarded both parties. The team's long-serving manager Gordon Milne also departed at around this time, and for the next four seasons Coventry would finish no higher than 17th in the table.

Both club and town were at a low ebb, but in 1986/87, they got a huge and totally unexpected lift. Under the joint managership of George Curtis and John Sillett, and almost entirely unnoticed by the national media, Coventry trod a confident path through that season's FA Cup campaign. Even when the semi-final draw pitched them against Second Division Leeds, they were considered the underdogs. Yet Leeds were beaten 3–2 after extra time and so, in the final at Wembley, were Tottenham – victory being sealed by Gary Mabbutt's own goal, but better remembered for the flying header from Keith Houchen which made it 2–2 in the second half.

It was the first major honour the club had won, and the irony was that it arrived at a time when Coventry had few stars. By comparison with the Seventies and early Eighties, there was no elegant Danny Thomas or Mick Coop in defence, no Willie Carr bossing the midfield, no Tommy Hutchison weaving his magic on the wings and no Ian Wallace turning it all into goals. Instead, there was a sense of teamwork Coventry had lacked since Milne's time, coupled with a burning desire, encouraged by the extrovert Sillett, to go out there and have fun.

It was certainly fitting that Sillett and Curtis, the two men who had combined as players to launch Coventry's giant-killing Cup career in the Fifties, should now bask in a moment of reflected Wembley glory. Afterwards, Curtis stepped up to become the club's managing director, but Sillett never recovered from City's defeat at non-League Sutton United in the Cup the following year, and was on his way by 1990. A succession of managers, not to mention boardroom coups, saw Coventry heavily in debt and again at the wrong end of the table in 1992. The players may now have been wearing *Peugeot* on their shirts but the team were not, as the car firm's adverts would have put it, going from strength to strength. All that changed, however, when Bryan Richardson completed his takeover of the club in 1993, bringing fresh cash and ideas to the party just at the time when the formation of the Premiership was about to make survival in the top flight more critical than ever.

Wee wonder – Gordon Strachan, miracle man

Richardson's most inspired decision was to bring Ron Atkinson and Gordon Strachan to Highfield Road as a new management partnership in 1995. While Big Ron would soon depart amid some acrimony, he had kept Coventry up for another year while Strachan, setting a fine example to his players in the areas of diet, attitude and outlook, also learnt a few tricks of the transfer-market trade from the old master. The Scotsman's ability to pluck useful talent from the bigger clubs' unwanted bins (Dion Dublin, Noel Whelan, Darren Huckerby) eventually lifted City above the relegation fray and into mid-table respectability. And Coventry weren't just respectable – on their day they could be effortlessly stylish, too.

Today the club is sposnored by a Japanese car maker, *Subaru*, and new signings are as likely to come from Holland, Belgium or Morocco as from elsewhere in the Premiership. While City remain a focal point (and a continuing source of pride) for the town, they now believe they can accomplish more than that.

This, really, is what the Arena 2000 project is all about. To turn the notion of being 'sent to Coventry' from a punishment into a privilege. And who's to say, after so many years of battling successfully against the odds, that the club will not achieve its goal?

Here we go!

Most **motorists** will approach on the M6 and, as ever, extra time should be allowed for rush-hour traffic if attending a midweek game. Exit the M6 at junction 3 onto the A444 and follow this road toward Coventry – the ground is well-signposted. It's **street parking** for all and the roads in the immediate vicinity of the ground are, inevitably, coned off. Allow time for a 15min walk once you've parked up.

Coventry **train station** is served by almost all trains running from London Euston to Birmingham (half-hourly, journey 1hr 15mins from Euston), and also has direct cross-country trains to and from Leicester and Nottingham. For evening kick-offs, there are late trains for Birmingham and London but stations further afield could be a problem. Check on ☎0345/484950.

The station is a long walk from Highfield Road, so catch a #17 or #27 bus instead.

Just the ticket

Visiting fans are housed in a section of the Sky Blue Stand – entrance in Thackhall Street. Prices in 1998/99 were adults £20, with concessions £10, bookable in advance and available only if the visiting club also offers them. **Disabled visitors** have their own area in the Clock Stand, in one corner between the visitors' seating and the *McDonalds* Family Stand. Booking essential on ☎01203/234020.

Swift half

The ***Sky Blue Tavern***, in Swan Lane on the east side of the ground, has separate rooms for home and away fans and offers beer from *Mitchell & Butlers*, a division of *Bass* and sponsor of Highfield Road's Sky Blue Stand. The pub charges £1 admission but, as Basil Fawlty might say, this keeps the riff-raff out.

Club merchandise

In addition to **club shops** at the ground and in the West Orchards area of town, Coventry have also begun operating concessions in local branches of *Safeway*. The idea is to control sales of the new home shirt so that prices (£39.99, kids' sizes £29.99) can be kept down by cutting out the middle-man.

Barmy army

Despite a long history of trouble and plentiful Midlands rivalries ranging from Wolves to Nottingham Forest via the inevitable Villa, the atmosphere at Highfield Road is now both lively and friendly – just as Jimmy Hill would claim he always intended.

In print

As well as the ***Sports Argus*** from Birmingham, Coventry has its own Saturday evening ***Pink***.

Fanzine *Sent To Coventry* re-invented itself as ***Lady Godiva Rides Again*** but this is now only available in electronic form (see *In the net* below). Others still publishing using dead trees include ***Sky Blue Army*** and ***Twist & Shout***.

Club historian Jim Brown is the man behind ***Coventry City: The Elite Era*** (Desert Island, £16.99), while a less conventional look at City is provided by Rick Gekoski's year-in-the-life study ***Staying Up*** (Little, Brown, £16.99).

On air

BBC Radio Coventry (94.8 FM) is preferred to the broader-based ***Radio WM*** (95.6 FM).

In the net

City's **official website** is run by *Planet Internet* and can be hopelessly slowed by grahpics. Be patient, though, because there's a lot going on at: www.ccfc.co.uk.

The unofficial ***CWN*** site is a better bet for impartial news at: www.cwn.org.uk/skyblues. And ***Lady Godiva Rides Again*** fanzine is online at: www.webforums.co.uk/lgra/index.html.

Crewe Alexandra

Formation	1877
Stadium	Gresty Road, Crewe, Cheshire, CW2 6EB. ☎01270/213014
Ground capacity	10,500 (when new Main Stand completed)
First-choice colours	Red and white
Major honours	Welsh Cup winners 1936, 1937
Position 1998/99	18th in First Division

Crewe Alexandra are the exception that disproves every modern rule of English football. The rulebook says a club this size can't hope to survive as the gap between rich and poor widens, yet Crewe are prospering, thanks to their proactive approach to wealthier neighbours such as Liverpool, with whom they have a ground-breaking player development deal. The rulebook says loyalty among managers is a thing of the past, but Dario Gradi has been in the Gresty Road dugout since June 1983, and has a contract that will keep him there until 2007. The rulebook says a team can't keep playing a passing game after promotion to the First Division – yet that's exactly what Gradi's team have done, finishing 11th in their first season up, and escaping the drop in 1999 with three wins on the spin in May.

The League's longest-serving manager – Dario Gradi, MBE

It says a lot about Crewe that when their First Division survival was assured, fans all over the country breathed a sigh of relief. Such is the club's achievement that its presence in the upper half of England's professional setup has acquired an almost talismanic quality – not least among younger players, some of whom have been known to take pay cuts in the hope of improving under Gradi's expert tutelage.

For the club itself, too, First Division survival has far-reaching implications. Over the past two years, almost every League fixture at Gresty Road has been all-ticket, the ground's tiny capacity preventing Crewe from reaping the full financial rewards of their new-found status. Now a new Main Stand is rising confidently into the sky to almost double that capacity in the 1999/2000 season, and First Division games will mean First Divsion gate receipts at last.

It's appropriate that the new stand is to be sponsored by *Railtrack*, since the football club, like the town itself, has always been associated with the railways. They may no longer employ a majority of the local populace but, even in decline, the sleepers and ballast are having a beneficial effect – the demolition of redundant railway sheds is allowing the club to build a car park behind the new stand, as well as providing enough space for the enlarged shopping and catering facilities which Crewe also need if they are to thrive.

Another constant is the fans' antipathy to the railway association and any puns

Football is the winner – Adebola, in plain-ish shirt, keeps the ball on the deck at Wembley, 1997

resulting from it. Even the club's official nickname *The Railwaymen* is spurned (though it's hardly the only football moniker to suffer this fate) in favour of *The Alex*, which sounds much friendlier as well as emphasising the precious originality of the club's name.

Precisely what prompted the team to be called Crewe Alexandra is still being debated. Some say the club's founders, who originally got together to play cricket, were inspired by Princess Alexandra of Denmark, who married Queen Victoria's eldest son (later King Edward VII) in 1863; others that the name was derived from a meeting in the *Alexandra Hotel* – wherever that might have been. Either way, within a decade of the club's foundation in 1865, football was on the agenda as a winter pursuit for members, most of whom (surprise, surprise) worked on the railways. The establishment of Crewe Alexandra FC in 1877 coincided with the club moving to the newly built 'Alexandra Recreation Ground', encompassing cricket field, football pitch and cycling track, on an expanse of land not far from the club's present home.

For the first ten years the ground was better-known nationally than the football team, but that all changed in 1888 when, having apparently been knocked out of the FA Cup by Burton Swifts, Crewe complained that their opponents' crossbars were too low. The FA agreed and ordered a replay which Swifts refused to take part in; Crewe were given a walkover and went on to reach the semi-finals (where they lost to Preston), their best performance in the competition to this day. The furore over the Swifts game refused to go away, however, prompting the FA to change its Cup regulations – no such retrospective appeals have been allowed since.

There was to be a further brush with authority eight years later. Crewe had been admitted as founder members of the Football League Second Division in 1892, and after losing their first League game 7–1 (to Burton Swifts – who else?), they had theoretically turned professional the following year. Yet the club's sporting culture was still essentially amateur – an attitude more in keeping with the public school ethos of the south than with the commercially minded north-west – and a second application for re-election was turned down by the League in 1896; Crewe were replaced by Gainsborough Trinity.

There followed 25 years in the wilderness of the Birmingham League and Central League before the club returned to the Football League as part of the newly formed Third Division (North) in 1921. Yet despite finishing consistently mid-table for most of the period before World War II, Crewe were still giving the impression of being fish out of water. Many of their best players, including Bill Lewis and Fred Keenor, were Welsh, and the team actually lifted the Welsh Cup twice in the mid-Thirties.

After the war, not even a young Harry Catterick could lift Crewe from the soft underbelly of the Third Division (North). Yet Catterick's era of stability in the early Fifties would soon be looked upon fondly, as under his successors Ralph Ward and Maurice Lindley the team's confidence plummeted. The Alex finished bottom of the table three seasons in a row from 1955/56, at one stage going 30 games without a win, and more than three years without a victory away from Gresty Road.

By 1960 Crewe's League form had picked up a little, and only a stunning last-minute save by Bill Brown prevented an FA Cup victory at home to Tottenham that year; Spurs just edged the replay, 13–2.

Finally, with Jimmy McGuigan at the helm, left-winger Ron Smith providing the crosses and centre-forward Frank Lord nodding them home, Crewe were promoted to the Third Division in 1963. The club then sold both Smith and Lord, and the team were relegated immediately. Crewe's next stint in the Third, after promotion in 1968, was equally brief, despite the best efforts of manager Ernie Tagg and accomplished defender Tommy Lowry.

Tagg would remain at the club in a number of capacities for another six years, while Lowry played on for four years after that to break the Alex's League appearance record. Yet while Crewe remained a model of tidy administration and sensible finance in the lower divisions, the team were going nowhere fast. In the decade after Tagg's second spell as manager had ended in 1974, they finished no Fourth Division campaign higher than tenth and failed to reach even the third round of the FA Cup.

When Dario Gradi arrived in June 1983, Gresty Road had made four applications for re-election in five years – all of them, somehow, successful. Born in Milan and

Face of youth – Seth Johnson in the bootroom

raised on the culture of Italian *calcio*, Gradi had turned down the chance to play the English game professionally, preferring to coach from the sidelines before he turned 30. Though he'd managed Crystal Palace in the top flight, he arrived at Crewe with lower-division experience from an earlier spell at Wimbledon. Just as he had insisted the Dons turn fully professional at the end of the Seventies, so Gradi was appalled at the lack of ambition evident on his arrival at Gresty Road.

Crewe had always been good at poaching unwanted players from bigger neighbours (Smith and Lowry were both ex-Liverpool), but Gradi wanted the club to develop its own youngsters. In a move that was years ahead of its time – and which would stand the club in excellent stead when it came to seeking partnerships among the footballing elite – he set up a School of Excellence. At the same time, he scouted around for some young professionals to improve Crewe's immediate League position; David Platt, Geoff Thomas and Rob Jones, future England internationals all, fell into this category.

A first promotion, to the old Third Division in 1989, was reversed two years later after all the above-mentioned players had been sold. But by now Gradi's School of Excellence was starting to bear fruit of its own, and Crewe were in the newly renamed Second Division by 1994.

This was followed by three successive appearances in the promotion play-offs, inspired by the likes of Rob Savage, Neil Lennon, Dele Adebola and Danny Murphy. Promotion to the First Division was achieved after a 1997 play-off final against Brentford in which the team's thoughtful, passing style was threatened by determinedly physical opposition – but won the day, 1–0.

Once again, Gradi was obliged to sell his best Academy graduates, yet Crewe managed a fine 11th-place finish in 1998, and with the club's latest prodigy, Seth Johnson, deliberately delaying a £3million transfer to Derby to help keep the club in the First Division – and Murphy unexpectedly returning on loan after being sold to Liverpool – Alex miraculously beat the drop in 1999. A glorious exception indeed.

Here we go!

Motorists coming from the north-west, Midlands or south will almost certainly approach Crewe along the M6 motorway, while the main road into town from the east is the A500/A5020.

From the north, exit at junction 17 and turn right at the T-junction onto the A534 towards Crewe. Continue along this road for about 6miles and go straight across two roundabouts; turn left at the third, then first left after the train station into Gresty Road – note, however, that on matchdays this turning is blocked off and you may be redirected to the next left, South Street.

From the south, leave the M6 motorway at junction 16 and take the A500 toward Crewe (those coming from the east will already be on this road). After a couple of miles turn right at the roundabout onto the A5020, left at the next, straight on at the next and left at the next. This last takes you into Nantwich Road, with the train station on your left. Gresty Road is on your left as above.

The new **car park** behind the Railtrack Stand will hold about 800 cars – get there early if you want a space. Alternatively, street parking is available but watch out for residents' schemes planned for the 1999/2000 season.

Crewe **train station** is 2mins' walk from the ground. Trains run along the West Coast mainline from London Euston (service half-hourly, journey time 2hrs 15mins), terminating at Liverpool (journey 45mins), or Glasgow via Preston. There are also direct connections for Birmingham, Manchester, Stoke-on-Trent and Derby. Even with all these trains, though, getting home after an evening kick-off can be problematical. For the latest timings call ☎0345/484950.

Just the ticket

There will be some wholesale changes at Gresty Road once the Railtrack Stand is completed, possibly not quite in time for the start of the 1999/2000 season. **Visiting fans** will be moved from the Gresty Road end to the Ringway Stand ('The Pop' to Alex fans), roughly doubling the number that can be accommodated to around 2,000. Ticket prices at the Gresty Road end in 1998/99 were adults £13.50; concessions (OAPs £10.50, juniors £6) on a reciprocal basis only.

Facilities for the **disabled** should also be greatly improved (though Crewe have already won a Football Trust award for their service in this respect), with around 170 spaces along the front edge of the new Railtrack Stand – book in advance through the club on ☎01270/252610.

Swift half

Nantwich Road is well-endowed with fan-friendly pubs. Most will welcome visiting supporters but some may close after the final whistle of a game involving one of Crewe's (many) local rivals.

The Brunswick is a big, friendly place with a wide range of ales and lagers, and an upstairs bar to retreat to if the ground floor is packed out.

For families, ***The Bank***, also on Nantwich Road but closer to the ground, is a recently built pub with (friendly) doormen, a beer garden and decent food.

Club merchandise

The **club shop** (open Mon–Sat 9am–5pm, later on matchdays, ☎01270/213014) is moving from the 'Pop' Stand to the new Railtrack Stand, where it will double in size. Home shirts are £35 (children's sizes £27), but whether fans succeed in persuading the club to 'keep it red' (Crewe have worn some particularly odd combinations of red and white recently) remains to be seen.

Barmy army

Alex fans pride themselves on their friendliness, with only Wrexham, inspiring a warped kind of nationalism perhaps, prompting recent trouble.

As well as their sense of humour, the supporters also have a well-earned reputation for music on the terraces, laying claim to being the originators of *Blue Moon* in a football context, and with one group of supporters forming dance-crossover band ***Dario G*** (named after guess who?) – their 1998 hit *Carnaval de Paris* featured a solo from the Gresty Road trumpeter.

In print

Potteries-based paper ***The Evening Sentinel*** is gradually waking up to the importance of Crewe,

Loan ranger – Danny Murphy returns, 1999

though its Saturday *Green'Un* rarely reaches the town before 6.30pm on matchdays.

The Alex's ground-breaking fanzine ***Super Dario Land*** is sadly no longer with us. Its spiritual successor is ***1842***.

The first complete statistical record of the club is Marco Crisp's ***Crewe Alexandra – Match By Match*** (£8.99), but this will be supplemented in late 1999 by Harold Finch's new history, ***Crewe Alexandra FC, 1877-1999*** (Tempus, £9.99).

On air

BBC Radio Stoke (94.6 FM) and commercial ***Signal Radio*** (102.6 FM) both tend to focus on Stoke City and Port Vale, though the former does have a dedicated Alex reporter.

In the net

In the absence of an official site, the best starting point is ***The Alexandra Extravaganza*** at: www.crewealex.u-net.com. Properly maintained with a nice line in ironic humour by Paul Wilkinson, it includes an *Alex News* section, updated daily.

Appropriately enough, the club's ***Football In The Community*** programme has its own site, at: www.s-chesire.ac.uk/cafc. You'll find details of Crewe's outside coaching schemes here, too.

Crystal Palace

Formation	1905
Stadium	Selhurst Park, London, SE25 6PU. ☎0181/768 6000
Ground capacity	26,500
First-choice colours	Red and blue
Major honours	First Division champions 1994; Second Division champions 1979; Third Division (South) champions 1921; Zenith Data Systems Cup winners 1991
Position 1998/99	14th in First Division

Every football supporter needs a sense of humour now and again, but for the faithful of Crystal Palace, it is practically a 24-hour requirement. A club which has regularly threatened to become South London's answer to Arsenal or Tottenham yet failed to mature on every occasion, a team that have turned snatching relegation from the jaws of top-flight survival into an art form, and a succession of back-room personalities who have been by turns recklessly colourful and obstinately dull – all this has forced Palace supporters to see the funny side, or not bother seeing the team at all.

Even to this traditionally most ironical view of the game, however, the events of the 1998/99 season were not funny. At first, the majority of fans welcomed Mark Goldberg's £23million takeover of Palace from the incumbent chairman Ron Noades. The fact that negotiations had dragged on through the first half of 1998, distracting the team as they were engaged in their habitual attempt to avoid relegation from the Premiership, didn't seem to matter. The side probably weren't good enough to stay up anyway. And once Noades, the club's saviour in the early Eighties but long since perceived as a man whose dour pragmatism was holding the club back, was out of the way, a bold new era could begin.

Only later did people begin to question why the takeover had been delayed in the first place. In reality, Goldberg was struggling to meet Noades' asking price for the club, to the extent that the latter offered to lend his would-be successor some of the shortfall. By the time the deal was finally completed in the summer of 1998, Palace had indeed been relegated, yet Goldberg appeared not to consider that a First Division club might not be worth the same as a Premiership one. He proudly announced a five-year plan to bring European football to Selhurst Park, and offered Terry Venables, who'd begun his coaching career at Palace in the mid-Seventies, a lavish contract to ensure that the plan was followed.

Then it all started to go wrong. Off the pitch, shares in Goldberg's hi-tech recruitment business, from which he derived much of his financial clout, collapsed. On it, Venables' expensively assembled team were lacking balance and, as results started to go against them, confidence too – Palace were not, as everyone had assumed, going to win promotion at the first attempt.

As Goldberg's reserves of cash ran dry, so the debts began to pile up. Venables was released, reportedly owed £2million. It emerged that the club also owed millions in unpaid transfer fees, mainly to overseas clubs. And Ron Noades, now sitting pretty as chairman (and manager) of Brentford, was also owed an undisclosed amount.

Depending on which newspaper you read, Palace's liabilities were anywhere between £9million and £25million. In March 1999, in an effort to protect the club from its many creditors, Goldberg successfully applied to have Palace placed in the hands of administrators. While the players threatened to go on strike over unpaid wages, some 46 members of Selhurst's back-room staff lost their jobs overnight.

The real drama, however, was still to come. While Steve Coppell, now in his fourth stint as Palace manager, somehow kept a demoralised team in mid-table despite a wave of outgoing transfers, the Football League announced that any club still in a form of receivership (including administration) at the end of July 1999 would be kicked out of the competition. The administrator, Simon Paterson, got a number of bites on his bait as he sought a consortium willing to take on Palace's debts, but all were put off by the fact that, while he had sold his majority stake in the club to Goldberg, Ron Noades had retained the freehold to Selhurst Park and to Palace's training ground at Mitcham.

As the time ticked away to the League deadline, not even Palace's large cast of celebrity comedian fans – Jo Brand, Sean Hughes and Eddie Izzard among them – could raise a laugh from the club's desperate plight. No, this was not funny at all.

Before Palace's last game of the 1998/99 campaign (a 6–0 lashing at QPR, themselves not exactly flush with cash, but at least solvent), fans unfurled a banner which read: 'An iceberg sank the Titanic; don't let a Goldberg sink the Palace.' And yet, faced with the opportunity to buy the club he had supported as a boy, Palace's hapless chairman had merely done what any self-respecting fan would do. His mistake – the first of many – was to reveal to Ron Noades just how keen he was to do the deal. The result, as Noades later admitted, was a sale the terms of which were not only bad for Goldberg personally, but ruinously bad for the club.

And if Goldberg was paying a high price for dreaming, then again, he was doing no more than the average fan does with the dawning of each new season. For this is Crystal Palace, a club named after a huge, dazzling, dream-like structure that no longer exists, followed by a vast groundswell of support that seldom bothers to turn up, pursuing a vision of joining the footballing elite that is no closer to being achieved now than it was when it first surfaced, nearly a century and a half ago, before the current club was even founded.

Students of the history of the game will testify that, among the clubs represented at the first meeting of the Football Association at the *Freemasons' Tavern* in Great Queen

Pride before a fall – Terry Venables salutes the Holmesdale on his return to Palace, August 1998

The 'Barcelona look' – Don Rogers, 1972

Street, London on 26 October 1863, was one going by the name of Crystal Palace. While most of the teams in attendance were from public schools, gentlemen's clubs or military regiments, Palace were a working men's team, founded by staff employed at the Crystal Palace itself, which had been built in Hyde Park as the centrepiece of the Great Exhibition of 1851, but which was moved to Sydenham Hill in South London shortly afterwards. The team were formed in 1861 and played in the first-ever FA Cup of 1871/72, drawing 0–0 with Hitchin in their opening fixture and going on to reach the semi-finals.

Not long after that, however, the club disbanded, and there would be no team playing under the name Crystal Palace until the present version was founded some 30 years later. By this time, the grounds surrounding the Palace itself had been turned into a fully fledged pleasure park containing, among other things, a vast, open arena that had become the venue of choice for the FA Cup final. When the company that ran the Palace grounds decided to form a football club, the FA rejected its application for membership because it was suspicious of the notion that any team might have home advantage in a Cup final. Palace's founders, however, sidestepped the issue by forming a separate company to run the club, and the FA duly admitted the new team as members in 1905.

With a capacity conservatively estimated at 120,000, the Crystal Palace arena was never going to come close to being filled by the fledgling club. Still, the surrounding area was poorly served by professional football, and Palace were soon attracting five-figure crowds despite playing in the Southern League, which was already beginning to lose some of its most prominent London members to the Football League. The team's record in the Southern League was modest, but there were some decent FA Cup runs to serve as a distraction – 35,000 turned up for the first-round visit of Everton in 1911.

During World War I, the Crystal Palace grounds were commandeered by the Admiralty and, though they did not know it at the time, the team were destined never to play there again. In 1915 they moved to the velodrome at Herne Hill, and three years later to a ground known as 'The Nest', on land now occupied by the Selhurst railway depot. This was where Palace began their Football League career, having migrated, along with much of what remained of the Southern League, to the newly created Third Division in 1920.

The team couldn't have got off to a better start, either, winning the Third Division title with a five-point margin to spare over second-placed Southampton. Veteran club secretary Frank Goodman could only reflect sadly on what might have been, had the team still been playing at their former home.

A few years later, Palace moved to Selhurst Park. Like the Sydenham grounds, this was a huge, natural bowl, one which the club had acquired in 1922 and which became home for the team two years later. Palace ended their first season at Selhurst by being relegated to the Third Division (South). Yet the crowds continued to turn up in numbers for the remainder of the Twenties and throughout the Thirties, despite Palace's inability to win promotion. (Meanwhile, in 1936, the old Palace itself burned to the ground in an inferno of shattering glass and molten ironwork; the stone steps that led up to it can still be seen in Crystal Palace Park.)

After World War II it was a similar story, with the club being obliged to seek re-election after finishing bottom of the Third Division (South) in 1949. When the regional Third Divisions were scrapped nine years later, Palace narrowly missed the 'cut' and found themselves in the new Fourth Division. Even this proved harder to escape than the club was expecting until, in 1961, the goalscoring of Johnny Byrne and the quietly assured managerial style of Arthur Rowe combined to bring Palace a runners-up spot behind League newcomers Peterborough.

As the Sixties progressed and South London shook itself out of the torpor of postwar austerity, so Palace moved with the times, becoming more brashly confident with each passing season. Byrne was capped by England. Chairman Arthur Wait persuaded Real Madrid, Puskás, di Stefano and all, to inaugurate new floodlights at Selhurst Park. Dick Graham, who succeeded Rowe in 1962, got Palace promoted to the Second Division within two years. Finally, in 1969, wearing claret shirts with sky-blue pinstripes and primrose collar and cuffs, the team managed one more promotion – entering the top flight for the first time. The manager responsible for the latest rise, former Bury boss Bert Head, had assembled a side whose football was not, perhaps, quite as attractive as the shirts they wore. Yet once in the First Division, Palace continued to be in expansive mood, Head's apparently limitless chequebook bringing the likes of Alan Birchenall, Steve Kember and Don Rogers to the club.

In 1972, ambitious new chairman Raymond Bloye pushed Bert Head 'upstairs' into a general manager's role to make way for the former Manchester City coach Malcolm Allison. Given more elbow room than he'd been allowed at Maine Road, Allison decided Palaces needed another PR makeover for the Seventies. He ditched the claret and sky-blue in favour of red-and-blue stripes, 'to make us look like Barcelona'. Out, too, went the old nickname of 'Glaziers'. From now on Palace were the 'Eagles', and woe betide any team that dared to swoop down on their nest.

In December 1972, Rogers scored twice as Manchester United were torn apart, 5–0, in front of a disbelieving Selhurst. But the euphoria lasted only a matter of weeks. Allison had put more emphasis on youth development than big signings. The problem was that Palace's cavalier football had consistently landed them in relegation trouble, and youth was not a quick fix. At the end of 1972/73 they were down, and 12 months later they were relegated again, to the Third Division.

Incredibly, Bloye kept faith with Allison. In 1975/76, prompted by the former Everton midfielder Alan Whittle and with young winger Peter Taylor outstanding, Palace

In the 'Team of the Eighties' – Peter Nicholas

won at Leeds, Chelsea and Sunderland to reach the semi-finals of the FA Cup. With his Havana cigars and 'lucky' Panama hat, Allison made the club the focus of media attention again. But he could not get Palace past Southampton in the semis, and by the end of the season he was on his way. Taylor, who like Byrne before him was capped by England as a Third Division player, also moved on.

The new manager was Allison's former player-coach, Terry Venables, whose footballing philosophy was much the same – keep the ball on the floor, and trust in youth. Yet Venables was more single-minded than his predecessor, and his less wayward approach to team selection got Palace up to the Second Division at the end of his first season. Two years later, with a young but confident side for which defenders Kenny Sansom, Jim Cannon and Billy Gilbert provided a solid foundation, Palace won another promotion, sealing the Second Division title with a 2–0 win over Burnley in front of 51,000 at Selhurst.

Top-flight football was coming back to South London, and the media, again seduced by the club's jocular charm, dubbed Venables' side the 'Team of the Eighties'. A 13th-place finish in their debut First Division season wasn't bad, but despite the tricky wing play of Vince Hilaire, scoring goals was always a problem.

In the summer of 1980 Venables swapped Sansom, now an England player, with Arsenal for the young striker Clive Allen. Also arriving were the former England captain Gerry Francis and ex-Charlton forward Mike Flanagan. Yet instead of giving Palace drive, the new arrivals slowed the team down. After only one win in six games at the start of 1980/81, Venables jumped ship to QPR, taking many of the club's best players with him. Chairman Bloye's big spending was catching up with the club, and while one end of the ground was sold off to become a *Sainsbury* supermarket, a brief return by Malcolm Allison to the manager's chair served only to land Palace deeper in the relegation mire.

So it was that in the spring of 1981, the former Wimbledon chairman Ron Noades arrived at Selhurst Park, telling the press the club's problem was 'cashflow, not insolvency',

The Wright stuff – super-sub Ian salutes the Palace contingent at Wembley, 1990

and installing Dario Gradi as new manager. Alas, this was not the calm, confident Gradi who would later emerge at Crewe, and Palace finished bottom of the 1980/81 First Division.

The club spent the mid-Eighties treading water. When former Manchester United winger Steve Coppell arrived as manager in 1984, he had to plan away trips carefully, after consulting a list of hotels across the country to whom Palace still owed money for their previous visit. Luckily, the club soon began to receive extra income from Charlton Athletic as tenants.

In 1985, Coppell signed an untried but promising striker, Ian Wright, from non-League Greenwich Borough. Wright was a latecomer to professional football but now that he had arrived, his energy, enthusiasm and willingness to work spread like a welcome infection through the squad. With his terrific acceleration and intelligent movement, Wright wanted the ball played early and in front of him, so Coppell built his own version of the 'long ball' game around his star player. When the taller Mark Bright arrived from Leicester to add flick-ons and knock-downs to Palace's repertoire, the team had a strikeforce capable of terrorising the most comfortable Second Division defence.

In 1988/89, Palace finished third and beat Swindon and Blackburn in the play-offs to win promotion. Was this, perhaps, the 'Team of the Nineties'? After a 9–0 defeat at Anfield in the early part of the season, it seemed emphatically not. Coppell responded by making Nigel Martyn Britain's first £1million goalkeeper, and by the time Palace met Liverpool again in an FA Cup semi-final at Villa Park in April 1990, the team's First Division safety was all but assured. Wright was absent injured, but the team shrugged it off, coming from behind twice to beat Kenny Dalglish's favourites 4–3 after extra time.

For the final against Manchester United, Wright was still unfit but included on the bench. With Palace 2–1 down and time ticking away, Coppell told him to get

Four times a manager – Steve Coppell

stripped off – Wright came on, scored twice, and would have won the Cup for Palace had Mark Hughes not plundered an equaliser deep into extra time.

Palace lost a drab replay 1–0, but drew sufficient strength from their Wembley adventure to finish third in the League the following season – enough for a place in Europe, they thought, until UEFA withdrew its ban on second-placed Liverpool. The 1991/92 season also began well. Wimbledon had replaced Charlton as tenants at Selhurst, and with the club making money at last, Palace looked forward to a place in the newly formed Premiership.

Then, in September 1991, thousands of Palace fans watched their televisions in horror as Ron Noades criticised black players in a *BBC* documentary. The club had prided itself on its multi-ethnicity. Now Ian Wright vowed never to play for Palace again. He was swiftly sold to Arsenal, and within 18 months he was scoring one of the goals at Highbury that sent his former club down.

So began the mid-Nineties rollercoaster ride. Palace were promoted twice – as champions of what was now the First Division in 1994, then via David Hopkin's wonder-goal in the play-off final of 1997. After his plan to relocate the club close to its spiritual home in Crystal Palace Park was rebuffed by Bromley Council, Noades agreed to the spectacular rebuilding of Selhurst's Holmesdale banking – but was then criticised for not spending money on the team as relegation loomed in 1994/95. Three years later, cash was made available to bring the likes of Attilio Lombardo, Tomas Brolin and Saša Ćurčić to Selhurst Park – but by this time the takeover drama had begun, and again, Palace went down…

In July 1999, Jo Brand and Eddie Izzard were among the stars who turned out for *Glad All Over*, an evening of comedy at Croydon's Fairfield Halls in aid of the 'Selhurst 46' who had been made redundant by Palace's administrators. Sadly, in the latest and deepest of the club's many crises, it was unclear who, exactly, would have the last laugh.

Here we go!

To avoid the maze of South London suburbia that makes Selhurst the hardest ground in Britain to find, the best bet for **motorists** is to follow the M25 round to junction 5 and take the M23 and then A23 in toward Croydon. Follow the signs for 'Crystal Palace' until the junction with the B266. This will take you into Thornton Heath High Street, at the end of which is a roundabout; turn left here into Whitehorse Lane and the ground is on the right.

The large **car park** at Selhurst gets filled up with supermarket shoppers on a Saturday, but street parking isn't too difficult as long as you don't set your heart on being next to the ground.

There are three overground **train stations** within a short stroll of the ground but the one that receives the fastest, most frequent service is Norwood Junction, served by trains from Victoria and London Bridge (allow 25mins from either). Walk up the station approach, turn left into South Norwood High Street and right into Park Road – the ground is on the left.

Just the ticket

Visiting fans are allocated the Holmesdale end of the Arthur Wait Stand – buy your ticket at the office, not the turnstiles. Prices in 1998/99 were £20 adults, £12 concessions.

Disabled visitors enjoy excellent facilities in both the Arthur Wait and Holmesdale Stands – booking essential on ☎0181/771 8841.

Swift half

The ***Goat House*** close to Norwood Junction station in Penge Road, is a favourite of both home and away fans and has a family room. Closer to the ground itself is the ***Selhurst Arms*** which also welcomes visitors.

Club merchandise

The **club shop** next-door to the supermarket in Whitehorse Lane has replicas of many of Palace's classic kits of the past, in addition to the latest red-and-blue incarnation.

Barmy army

Unless you count Palace fan Matthew Simmons' altercation with Eric Cantona in 1994, trouble rarely rears its head at Selhurst Park these days.

In print

The ***Croydon Advertiser*** is the best of several local papers for Palace news, but there's no Saturday evening edition.

Ground-breaking fanzine *Eagle Eye* has been succeeded by the equally witty ***Palace Echo*** (PO Box 6172, London, SW11 6LH), but the former lives on in the shape of ***We All Follow The Palace*** (£11.95), a compilation book of its best writing. The Rev Nigel Sands is the man behind the official ***History Of The Club*** (£17.95).

On air

In addition to London standards ***GLR*** (94.9 FM) and ***Capital Gold*** (1548 AM), the club runs its own station on 1278 AM. (Or at least, it did.)

In the net

The **official website** became ominously unavailable after the administrators moved in, but it might be worth a try at: www.cpfc.co.uk.

Of the unofficial sites, the most comprehensive is run by the ***Independent Supporters' Association*** at: www.palace-eagles.com. Also worth a look is the extensive historical archive at: members.aol.com/cparc1/cp_home.html.

Darlington

Formation	1883
Stadium	Feethams Ground, Darlington, DL1 5JB. ☎01325/240240
Ground capacity	8,500
First-choice colours	Black and white
Major honours	Third Division (North) champions 1925; Fourth Division champions 1991; Conference champions 1990
Position 1998/99	11th in Third Division

On the last day of the 1989/90 season, a fair percentage of the male population of Darlington found itself adrift in an anonymous High Street somewhere deep into south-east London suburbia. None had ever been there before, and it's a fair bet than none will ever be back. Yet, here they were, nervously supping their pints in front of the local pubs on a swelteringly hot day in May, awaiting arguably the most important day in the history of their football club.

In the thick of it – Kubicki and Tutill at Rotherham, 1998

Darlington needed only a draw at the tight, unwelcoming ground of Welling United to seal that year's Conference title, and secure promotion back to the Football League at the first attempt. They won 1–0, with a goal three minutes from time, rendering Barnet's 4–1 win over Chorley the same day irrelevant, and sending their supporters off on the long journey home weary, bemused but, ultimately, satisfied.

It was a triumph not just for the players, not just for the team's young manager Brian Little and his hard-working assistant, Frank Gray, but also for the club itself, which after relegation in 1989 had gambled on remaining full-time professional when the easy option would have been to slash the wage bill by becoming, like much of the rest of the Conference, part-time. And the gamble paid off in more ways than one. Not only did the team's confidence come back, but so did the crowds – up 50% on average, to 3,500, by comparison with that last year in the Fourth Division. They went even higher as, over the course of the following year, Darlington kept the momentum going and won the Fourth Division title for the first time in their history.

Darlo debate – director of coaching David Hodgson (right) makes a point to Ian Butterworth

It couldn't last. At the end of the 1990/91 season, Little was poached by Leicester City, and Gray, though able enough as a motivator, never had enough resources to make a go of it in the Third Division – Darlington finished bottom in 1992, and have not been back since.

This tale of two relegations and two promotions in four years deserves telling because, generally speaking, this is a corner of England's footballing map that is unaccustomed to such upheavals. With its trim market square, lush greenery and well-tended Victorian villas, the town of Darlington is the antithesis of clichéd northern gloom. The town's industrial heritage (the first railway line in the world was laid between here and Stockton in 1825) has been safely locked away for posterity in a museum, the air is fresh, and the football club shares its quaint, appealing ground, Feethams, with the local cricket team. The pace of life is gradual, more in keeping with the West Country than with the north-east, and by and large, that's how the locals seem to like it. No wonder those faces on Welling High Street looked bewildered.

Darlington FC's progress, likewise, has been steady as she goes. There had been a club in the town as early as 1861, but the present one wasn't formed until July 1883, after a meeting at the local grammar school. In their first season the team reached the final of the Durham Senior Cup, losing to Sunderland in a replay after complaining they'd been intimidated in the first match. The following year the two sides met again in the final, and this time Darlington weren't taking any winding-up from anybody – they won.

The side acquired their nickname 'the Quakers' because their ground at Feethams was rented from a prominent member of the local Quaker community, John Pease – a Quaker hat remains on the club's badge to this day, together with Stephenson's *Rocket*, one of the original locomotives on the Stockton-to-Darlington line.

In 1889, the club became a founder member of the Northern League, winning it for the first time in 1896 and again in 1900. Darlington remained resolutely amateur, however, until 1908, when they joined the North-Eastern League. A mighty FA

Cup run in 1910/11 saw the team reach the last 16 after playing 11 games – one a victory over First Division Sheffield United at Bramall Lane. The club hoped such exploits would grant them admission to the Football League's Second Division but, though it was never officially admitted, Darlington's geographical isolation undoubtedly worked against them, and a long succession of applications for membership fell on deaf ears.

In 1913 the team were crowned champions of the North-Eastern League, but then World War I, the pressure of having to pay players' wages and the absence of Football League status all conspired to send the club to the brink of bankruptcy. Salvation appeared in the form of a rival side, Darlington Forge Albion, who agreed to clear all outstanding debts in exchange for the old club's name and its lease at Feethams. The new club also completed building the East Stand at the ground and, suitably boosted and equipped, Darlington finally entered the League via the newly created Third Division (North) in 1921.

Within four seasons they had won the title and promotion to the Second Division. Relegation followed in 1927, however, and the club was destined not to taste life in the upper half of the Football League again.

Practically the whole of the Thirties, Forties and Fifties were spent in the Third Division (North), the only highlights being a fourth-place finish in 1949 and another excellent Cup run in 1957/58, which included a 4–1 thrashing of Chelsea at Feethams after Darlington had drawn 3–3 at Stamford Bridge, having taken a 3–0 lead.

When the Fourth Division was formed the following year, Darlington inevitably fell into it, not to emerge until 1966, when Lol Morgan's innovative management earned them a runners-up spot behind Doncaster Rovers. Again, the Third Division was a bridge too far and the team beat a hasty retreat. And whereas, in the preceding decades, Darlington had hovered in mid-table of the basement, now they spent far too much time at or near the bottom of it. As the Seventies wore on, applications for re-election became an almost annual occurrence. Gates which had reached a high of more than 20,000 for a Cup tie against Bolton in 1960 were now as little as a tenth of that, and in January 1982, the board announced that unless £50,000 was found within six weeks, Darlington would be wound-up.

The way we were – the poplars still line Feethams but the barrel-roofed East Stand is no more

Sunderland came to Feethams for a friendly, free of charge, as did Southampton, led by then England captain Kevin Keegan. The locals were roused, and bit by bit the target was met.

Thus saved, Darlington briefly prospered. Cyril Knowles, the former Spurs left-back who had inspired the *Nice One, Cyril* record of Seventies chart infamy but a player whose career had begun in the Durham pit team of Monckton Colliery, returned to the north-east to become manager at Feethams in 1983, the club's centenary year. Within two years Middlesbrough had been knocked out of the FA Cup and the team had won promotion. This time Darlington managed two seasons of Third Division football before being relegated, and Knowles was on his way out by 1987 – a mistake, in retrospect, since he would soon be doing more fine work at Darlo's local rivals Hartlepool (before his untimely death in 1991), while without him the team's morale plummeted still further. Relegation to the Conference was just reward for a team that had managed only eight wins out of 46 games in 1988/89. How fortunate Darlington would be to have Messrs Little and Gray on hand to stop the rot…

Once their era was over, the club returned to obscurity in what was now the Third Division. David Hodgson, who took over the management of the team with a former Middlesbrough team-mate Jim Platt in 1995 and has since assumed become director of coaching with Ian Butterworth as his assistant, has built a solid if unspectacular team around experienced men such as Marco Gabbiadini, Dariusz Kubicki and Carl Shutt. Meanwhile the club has its own *Centre of Excellence* and a commitment to encourage young talent in the area – if Darlington didn't quite have the right mix to make the play-offs in 1998/99, it may not be that far off.

As for Feethams, chief executive Mike Peden has been the driving force behind a thorough rebuilding programme, which has seen the distinctive old East Stand replaced and the West Stand and South Terrace also demolished – although the Darlo faithful's much-loved 'Tin Shed' terrace at the north end of the ground is to remain.

That's how they like things in this part of the world. Change, by all means, but not for change's sake.

Elland Road excellence – Leeds get a run for their money, 1996

Here we go!

Most **motorists** will approach Darlington on the A1(M) and then the A66(M). This in turn becomes the A66 at its end, after which you should follow the A67 toward the town centre. At the Grange Road roundabout, take the fourth exit into Victoria Road – the ground is on the right. There are pay-and-display car parks in the town centre but **street parking** shouldn't present too many problems if you arrive early enough. Darlington **train station** is on the East Coast mainline with direct services from London King's Cross, Peterborough, Doncaster,

York and Newcastle (service half-hourly, journey 2hrs 45mins from King's Cross). There are also local trains to and from Middlesbrough. Call ☎0345/484950 for the latest timings. The station is a pleasant, well-signposted 10min walk from Feethams.

Just the ticket

Visiting fans were scheduled to be relocated back in the South Stand in time for the start of the 1999/2000 season. Ticket prices should be around £11 adults, £8 concessions.

Disabled supporters have their own area of the excellent new East Stand. Book in advance on ☎01325/240240.

Swift half

The centre of Darlington is a riot of traditional and welcoming pubs, many of them also serving good food. Try the ***Tap & Spile*** on Bondgate with a fine range of real ales, or ***Hogan's*** nearer to the station.

Club merchandise

Darlington revived their classic Sixties narrow-hooped home shirt in 1997/98, but this has now given way to something more 'modern'. Happily, the new **club shop** in the East Stand has plenty of other black-and-white items to choose from.

Barmy army

Feethams deserves its reputation for friendliness, with only the local derby against Hartlepool likely to lead to any grief.

In print

The ***Evening Gazette*** publishes a Saturday evening 'pink' from Middlesbrough but this may not reach Darlington until after you've left town. Otherwise the ***Northern Echo*** is good for previews and other Darlo news.

Best-established of the fanzines is ***Mission Impossible*** (PO Box 232, Darlington, DL3 7YQ).

On air

BBC Radio Cleveland (95 FM) and commercial ***Century Radio*** (100.7 FM) manage to squeeze Darlo coverage in between all the 'Boro stuff.

In the net

Darlington's **official site** is a bit like the town – a place for everything and everything in its place. There's plenty of background info, some history, a video archive and squad details, but surprisingly no e-commerce as yet. Find it at: www.darlingtonfc.force9.co.uk.

The unofficial ***Quakers Online*** is run by the *Evening Gazette* newspaper and is well worth a surf at: www.eveninggazette.co.uk/dl/index.htm.

Derby County

Formation	1884
Stadium	Pride Park Stadium, Derby, DE24 8XL. ☎01332/667503
Ground capacity	33,250
First-choice colours	White shirts, black shorts
Major honours	League champions 1972, 1975; Second Division champions 1912, 1915, 1969, 1987; Third Division (North) champions 1957; FA Cup winners 1946
Position 1998/99	Eighth in Premiership

Derby County approach the millennium caught uncomfortably between two stools. Are they a mega-team in the making, one step away from the Champions' League and a place among the European elite? Or are they a jumped-up, provincial First Division side, sustained only by Premiership TV money and the memory of two League championships a generation ago, and ready to drop back down the moment a run of bad form blows their way?

Nobody is keener to know the answer than the club's own supporters. Over the past couple of seasons, the largesse of Derby's chairman and soaring season-ticket sales at their magnificent (and recently expanded) Pride Park stadium have brought both results on the pitch and financial stability off it – the first time those two desirables have come together since the last title was won, back in 1975. But the English top flight is barely recognisable from the one Brian Clough's Derby took by storm in the early Seventies, and in the 21st century, it is surely going to take more than some sharp half-time team talks and a couple of astute signings to turn County into true title contenders.

On the other hand, Derby have made the most of the cash bonanza that has come their way since Lionel Pickering took over the club in the early Nineties and promotion to the Premiership was achieved in 1997. The club currently enjoys a position of strength that would have been unthinkable at the start of the decade, and if it were to be squandered now, the fans would want some pretty good answers.

It would certainly be a turn-up if 'the Rams' were to tread water for a few years. The club's last 30 years have been as dramatic as any in the English game, and its earlier history was also pretty rapid-fire.

Within just four years of being formed as the football-playing branch of Derbyshire County Cricket Club in 1884, Derby were being invited to join the Football League as founder members. They'd started as they meant to go on, entering the FA Cup in their first year of existence, and allowing their patch of the cricket ground (which itself was in the middle of the city's racecourse) to be used as a venue for Cup semi-finals from 1886.

The club's membership was initially divided between those who saw it as a mere revenue-raising exercise for the real business of cricket, and those who believed the emerging game of football would soon prove a bigger draw to local people for the nine months of the year that the sun didn't shine on Derby. It was the latter group who were correct, of course, and the moment of truth came in 1895, when the football team were forced to cancel a lucrative Easter fixture because a race meeting was already scheduled for the same day. The club decided to move to Francis Ley's Baseball Ground (see panel p.191), and as the team left cricket behind physically, so they became independent from it legally – Derby County FC became a limited company a year later.

Derby celebrated their freedom by adopting a new strip, dispensing with the cricket club's old chocolate, amber and sky-blue colour scheme and replacing it with

Second time around – David Nish and Kevin Hector lead a Championship lap of honour, 1975

white shirts and black shorts – an outfit more in keeping with footballing convention, and one which would serve the club, with one notable exception, for more than a century.

The club's independence also had a liberating effect on its players. Derby came second to Aston Villa in the League (their best finish yet) and reached the semi-finals of the FA Cup in 1896. Two years later they went one better in the Cup, but lost the final, 3–1 to their near-neighbours Nottingham Forest. (There has been little love lost between the two clubs ever since.)

Derby's goalscorer against Forest was Steve Bloomer, a sallow, slightly built forward whose ability to shoot with little or no backlift had made him, perhaps, the professional game's first real star. Bloomer had signed for Derby in 1892, and earned his first England cap three years later. He would go on to score in all of his first ten internationals, and appear for Derby in a second Cup final (lost again, 4–1) against Sheffield United in 1899. By the time the club had reached its third and most infamous Cup final, against Bury in 1903, Bloomer had been sold to Middlesbrough for £750. It's doubtful, though, whether even his scoring power would have made much difference – Derby were smashed 6–0, a record winning margin in Cup finals which stands to this day, and which eventually persuaded the team's first manager, Harry Newbould, that enough was enough.

Newbould's successor, Jimmy Methven, had played at centre-half in all three of the club's unsuccessful Cup finals, and might have been considered an odd choice to run the team – all the more so when Derby were relegated to the Second Division after his first full season in charge in 1907. Yet Methven remained in his post until well after World War I, coaxing Bloomer back to the club in 1910, and landing the Second Division title two years later.

Incredibly, there was time for another round of relegation and promotion before war overtook football, Derby having finally said their farewell to Bloomer – after 331 goals, still a club record – as he embarked on a new career as a coach in Germany. (He was interned there during World War I, and died in Derby in 1938.)

The club survived only two postwar seasons of First Division football before being relegated again in 1921, and aside from a run to the semi-finals of the FA Cup in 1922/23, the fans had little to cheer them until George Jobey took over as manager and led Derby back into the top drawer in 1926. Off the pitch, meanwhile, the board were taking a series of landmark decisions, declining an invitation from Derby Corporation to turn the club into a municipally run entity, and buying the Baseball Ground from Ley for £10,000. Before long, work had begun on almost doubling the ground's capacity to 38,000 – and Jobey's side, featuring a succession of internationals including defender Tom Cooper, centre-forward Jack Bowers, and wingers Sammy Crooks and Dally Duncan, served the crowds with a sustained spell of stylish, top-flight football until the outbreak of World War II.

After being briefly suspended from wartime football when the FA discovered the club had been making illegal payments to players, Derby resumed playing after the war as if there had been scarcely a break. In 1945/46 there was no League competition, so the third, fourth, fifth and sixth rounds of the FA Cup were played over two legs to satisfy the postwar public's hunger for football. With inside-forwards Raich Carter and Peter Doherty both arriving in December 1945 and arch-goalscorer Jackie Stamps returning to the club after being signed by Jobey before hostilities had begun, Derby were irrepressible, using the extra games simply as an excuse to score more goals. Luton Town were hit for nine over two legs in the third round, Brighton for ten in the fifth. More than 80,000 were at Maine Road to see Birmingham beaten 4–0 in a semi-final replay, after the first game at Hillsborough had finished 1–1.

Derby's first Wembley Cup final (their only one so far, as it's turned out) would be against Charlton Athletic, who'd surprisingly beaten Bolton in their semi at Villa Park. The Londoners had been scoring almost as freely as Derby en route to Wembley, and the final did not disappoint the 98,000 who turned up expecting to

The gamble pays off – Taylor (far left), Clough and Mackay shake hands on promotion, 1969

Mud and malleable castings – the Baseball Ground

Mob rules – the final pitch invasion, May 1997

When Derby industrialist **Francis Ley** returned home from a business trip to America in 1889, he'd fallen in love with baseball and resolved to convert his homeland to it. At great expense, Ley converted the sports ground he'd laid out for his workers so that the American game could be played on it.

For a time, after Derby County had moved in as tenants in 1895, baseball co-existed with soccer at the grounds, which staged a baseball tournament each summer – won by Derby in 1897, with the football club's legendary pale-faced goalscorer **Steve Bloomer** at first base.

Ley was fighting a losing battle, however, and baseball had not been played at the ground for decades when County bought the arena from him in 1924. The club quickly built a new Main Stand, then added further stands at the Normanton and Osmaston ends – the latter where a terrace known as ***Catcher's Corner*** had stood on the site of Ley's baseball home plate.

Ley had allegedly driven a gipsy community from the grounds when he'd first laid them out, and this story fed the idea that a curse had been placed on County, preventing them from winning a trophy. Club captain **Jack Nicholas** crossed a gipsy's palm with silver for the benefit of the press prior to the 1946 FA Cup final – and Derby won.

If it was free of one curse, however, the Baseball Ground still had two others to contend with. Noxious smells from the adjacent ***Leys Malleable Castings*** foundry would occasionally be belched across the ground, stopping top European sides like **Benfica** and **Juventus** in their tracks in the mid-Seventies. And the ground's notoriously muddy pitch, which Derby manager **Brian Clough** had deliberately over-watered prior to key matches, wasn't ripped up until after the club's second League title in 1975.

By the early Nineties, the foundry and the terraced housing which once surrounded the Baseball Ground were gone, giving County the chance to totally rebuild the arena at a cost of £12million. This they planned to do until early 1996, when an about-turn by the board resulted in the club moving to Pride Park for the start of the 1997/98 season.

As of spring 1999, however, the Baseball Ground site had still not been redeveloped and the pitch was even being used for **England Under-21** training sessions. Back to first base, you might say…

see a fast, flowing game. That said, there were no goals until five minutes before time, when Charlton right-half Bert Turner diverted a Dally Duncan shot into his own net. Sixty seconds later, Turner's own 25-yard free-kick took a deflection off Doherty and went in. (Both Derby players later claimed 'credit' for their goals but their appeals were dismissed by the FA.) In extra time, the class of Carter and Doherty began to tell. Stamps' cross-shot was parried into the path of Doherty who slotted home, then Carter set up Stamps for a fine solo goal, before Doherty found the same player in space to make the final score 4–1 to Derby.

The team had done more than simply win the FA Cup. They had disproved the fanciful notion that a gipsy curse would prevent the club from ever lifting a trophy,

Bloody painful – Deano takes it on the nose

and given the town a much-needed shot in the arm after six years of war.

The stage seemed set for Derby to reclaim their place among the perennial title-chasers. But Doherty, an unsettling influence on the squad despite his Cup final heroics, was sold to Huddersfield at the end of 1946, while Carter had begun playing first-class cricket for Derbyshire. In the summer of 1947, manager Stuart McMillan broke the country's transfer record to sign winger Billy Steel from Morton, and the team finished the 1947/48 season in fourth place, as well as reaching the FA Cup semi-finals where they lost to the newly emerging Busby Babes.

Carter was sold to Hull City, and in March 1949, the transfer record was broken a second time when Johnny Morris arrived from Manchester United as a replacement for Carter. Derby came third in the League, but that was as good as it got for McMillan, who saw his side slip into mid-table for three seasons before relegation forced him out in 1953.

Jack Barker came in as manager, sold Jackie Stamps to Shrewsbury after the big man had scored his 100th League goal for Derby, and after an 18th-place finish in 1954, took the club into the Third Division (North) for the first time a year later. Later in 1955, the Baseball Ground witnessed perhaps the most embarrassing game in its history, when non-League Boston United knocked Derby out of the second round of the FA Cup, 6–1. Barker was dismissed, to be replaced by Harry Storer, who encouraged his players to attack, and whose faith in adventurous football was rewarded by the divisional title in 1957.

Storer and his successor, Tim Ward, presided over a spell of consolidation in the Second Division that would ultimately last more than a decade. Ward assembled a promising squad that included the unspectacular but rock-solid Colin Boulton in goal, assured full-backs Peter Daniel and Ron Webster, midfield anchorman Alan Durban, free-scoring inside-forward Ian Buxton and striker Kevin Hector. But the team were under-performing and, after Derby survived a brush with relegation in 1967, club chairman Sam Longson dismissed Ward, replacing him with the young management duo of Brian Clough and his assistant Peter Taylor. The two had known each other since their playing days at Middlesbrough in the Fifties, but had spent no more than two moderately successful years in management at Hartlepool before Longson approached them.

It was a gamble, and for a time it looked as if it wouldn't pay off. Clough and Taylor went through the Baseball Ground like a tornado, tearing pictures of the 1946 Cup-winning side off the walls, sacking Sammy Crooks from his post of chief scout, and selling Ian Buxton because, like Raich Carter before him, he insisted on playing cricket for Derbyshire until after the football season had begun. They also went shopping, big time, signing centre-half Roy McFarland, midfielders Alan Hinton and Willie Carlin, and forward John O'Hare.

And all for what? Clough and Taylor had set themselves on a collision course with the club's traditions and, after their first season, the team had finished 18th in the Second Divsion – one place lower than Ward had managed a year earlier. Longson stood by his men, however, and gave them more money to spend. Dave Mackay, a double-winner with Tottenham in 1961 and a player who could motivate an entire team from left-half, turned down the chance to manage Hearts in favour of joining Derby, and quickly became Clough's eyes and ears on the pitch, along with another key man in midfield, John McGovern. The new line-up carried all before them in 1968/69, winning the Second Division title by seven points and losing only five times all season.

Once in the top flight, Clough replaced Derby's black shorts with navy-blue ones and told his players: 'Now you look like England – go and play like them.' It may have sounded fatuous but few of the squad had tasted First Division life before, and Clough wanted to ensure they feared nobody. They didn't.

Derby quickly found a niche for themselves in the top half of the table, and after throwing stopper Terry Hennessey and ball-winner Archie Gemmill into the mix in 1970, Clough told Longson he needed one more player – central defender Colin Todd, who Clough had known since his days as youth coach at Sunderland – to win the title. Longson didn't believe him, but gave him the £175,000 he needed to prise Todd away from Roker Park, anyway. Derby County were crowned champions in 1972.

In 1972/73 Clough concentrated on the European Cup. Derby overran Zeljeznicar Sarajevo, Spartak Trnava and (famously) the Portuguese champions Benfica at the Baseball Ground, before losing to a cynically hard-tackling Juventus side in the semi-finals. (Roger Davies, County's big yet effortlessly skilful striker, was so incensed by the kicking he received in the home leg that he punched an opponent into the goalmouth; his sending-off tilted the balance of the tie Juve's way.)

The team finished third in the League that year, but behind the scenes, tension was simmering between Clough and Taylor on the one hand, and Longson and his board on the other. Longson was worried that his management team were trying to take control of the club, and when Clough appeared to stick two fingers up to the Manchester United directors after Derby had won at Old Trafford in October 1973, he had the excuse he needed to bring matters to a head. Clough and Taylor resigned, sending shockwaves not just through Derby but across the whole of English and, to an extent, European football.

Dave Mackay took over as manager and found that the players had, if anything, been less adversely affected by the trauma than the wider public. Under Mackay, Derby just got on with it, and after Bruce Rioch and Francis Lee had arrived to widen the range of goalscoring options, the team won the title again in 1975. Come the summer, the club embarked on yet another shopping spree, buying Arsenal striker Charlie George and Burnley's clever Welsh winger Leighton James. George scored a hat-trick as Real Madrid were humbled 4–1 at the Baseball Ground in the European Cup, but in the return leg Mackay fatally allowed

Survival, then revival – Arthur Cox

complacency to creep in – Derby's 5–1 defeat and consequent death of the club's European dream were to prove an unwanted turning point.

County finished fourth in 1975/76 – good enough for one last, brief continental adventure in the UEFA Cup, but not good enough for Mackay, who resigned midway through the following season with the team stuck firmly in mid-table. He had brought some wonderfully cultured players to the club but, unlike Clough, had tended to favour experienced pros over young innocents. As a result, Derby's large and costly squad aged fast.

When Kevin Hector left for Canada in 1978, the last link with Clough's Second Division title-winning side was severed (Hector would return to break the club's all-time appearance record in the early Eighties), and after a disastrous two years under Tommy Docherty, Derby were relegated in 1980. From having been on the threshold of European greatness, the club was sinking back into the mediocrity that had dogged it in the Fifties and Sixties – with the danger that, once again, nostalgia for past achievements would help to keep it there.

There were plenty of other problems, too. Derby's star players were sold off one by one but, with an almost non-existent youth policy, the club did not have any way of nurturing replacements. The Baseball Ground, subject of grandiose rebuilding plans during Clough's reign, was falling apart under the parallel burdens of old age and rampant hooliganism. Not that the club owned it anymore, anyway – County's bankers had seized the deeds as collateral for loans on which the club had defaulted after the 1980 relegation.

Peter Taylor, striking out on his own after taking Nottingham Forest to the top of the European tree with Clough, returned to Derby as manager in 1982, worked for two years with a zero budget, and got the team relegated again. The club was celebrating its centenary in 1984, but for a time it looked as though Derby's 100th year would be their last.

Then down came media mogul Robert Maxwell in his helicopter in September 1984 (see panel) to bail Derby out and set the club back on the straight and narrow. With Arthur Cox as manager and Roy McFarland as his assistant, the team won promotion from the Third Division in 1986, and the Second Division title 12 short months later.

Cox's gritty approach to man management, together with McFarland's knowledge of the club and Maxwell's millions, had put Derby back on the map in double-quick time. England goalkeeper Peter Shilton, highly rated young defender Mark Wright and Welsh striker Dean Saunders were among the players who moved to the Baseball Ground at this time, and between them they took Derby to fifth place in the League in 1989 – a position from which, had it not been for the Heysel ban, the club could have mounted another assault on Europe. The Rams were riding high on late-Eighties optimism but, like

Royal flush – Pickering, Smith and the Windsors open Pride Park

The man in the helicopter – Maxwell at Derby

Derby County were on the brink of bankruptcy when, in September 1984, media mogul **Robert Maxwell** descended on the Baseball Ground in his own private helicopter and pledged to save the club from extinction. He was as good as his word, but alarm bells should have been ringing among the Derby faithful even then – Maxwell left the match before the end, and rarely managed to sit through the full 90 minutes during his entire seven-year association with the club.

With officialdom turning a blind eye to the fact that he already owned Oxford United (and was also sniffing around Reading, Watford and Spurs at the time), Maxwell used his huge borrowing power to reschedule Derby's debts and also purchased the Baseball Ground from the club's bankers.

Fat and round – not even the hat and scarf fitted

Though he seldom had time to make much impact on the day-to-day running of the club, Maxwell installed **his son Ian** as vice-chairman to ensure he was kept informed, and had another crucial ally in managing director **Stuart Webb**. It was Webb and Ian Maxwell who negotiated most of manager Arthur Cox's transfer deals, promising untold riches to players who were reluctant to sign. If that didn't work, Maxwell Senior could always lean on the sports desk at his paper, the ***Daily Mirror***, to run a story that might swing the deal – as **Lee Chapman** found when he became the object of a tug-of-war between Derby and Brian Clough's Nottingham Forest.

Yet, unlike his great rival **Rupert Murdoch** and his subsequent attempt to buy Manchester United, Maxwell had no coherent strategy for Derby. Initially a personal plaything, the club stuck out like a sore thumb as his media empire began to fall apart. On the eve of the economic recession that would destroy both himself and his business, Maxwell spent barely an hour of the 1989/90 season watching Derby – prompting fans to invent the message: 'He's Fat, He's Round, He's Never At The Ground'.

Maxwell's mysterious death coincided with Derby's relegation in 1991 – and it took the accountants months to sort out the mess he'd left behind at the Baseball Ground. He may have saved the club, but his legacy was another mountain of debt.

so many boom businesses of the era, their foundations were built on sand. As Maxwell's empire began to crumble around his ears, so severe cash restrictions were placed on Cox. After a close shave in 1990, Derby were relegated the following year. Wright and Saunders were sold to Liverpool, while Shilton bowed out soon after, never to play at the top level again. Maxwell's death the same year put the club in a surreal form of limbo. Manager Cox continued to command the respect of fans, but was powerless to expand the squad while there was nobody around to sign any pay-cheques. A consortium of local businessmen bought Derby from the Maxwell

Racing uncertainty – Paulo Wanchope in full flow

estate, only to find they'd inherited more debt than they'd bargained for.

The club was in need of another life-raft, and found it when Lionel Pickering acquired a controlling interest at the end of 1991. Like Maxwell, Pickering had made his fortune in the media. Unlike Maxwell, his business had been in local news agencies rather than the national press. Crucially, Pickering was also a Derby man, through and through.

Pickering pumped millions into strengthening the squad for promotion, and felt let down when first Cox and, after his departure, McFarland failed to clinch it, Derby twice failing to get through the play-offs in 1992 and 1994. In June 1995, Pickering sacked McFarland and recruited Jim Smith. Like Cox, Smith was an archetypally English manager, preferring old-style motivation methods to endless discussions over tactics. But he was also a shrewd operator in the transfer market, aware that his chairman's money could be well-spent abroad. One of Smith's first moves was to buy the accomplished Croatian defender Igor Štimac from Hajduk Split for £1.5million – not a bad piece of business for a player who would go on to perform a key role for his country at Euro '96 and France '98. Meanwhile the board, having authorised work to begin on the total refurbishment of the Baseball Ground, dramatically switched horses in the spring of 1996, joining the *Derby Pride* consortium aiming to construct a new community arena for the region. The result was Pride Park Stadium, an impressive new ground built at a cost of £24million and since added to at yet more expense. The arena was opened by Her Majesty The Queen and the Duke Of Edinburgh on 18 July 1997, with a match between County and Sampdoria. Such a stadium clearly demanded Premiership football and, as luck would have it, Smith's side had won promotion a year earlier, having gone 20 games unbeaten after Štimac's arrival. Once in the top flight, the club began to flaunt its new-found cosmopolitan attitude, buying Estonian goalkeeper Mart Poom; another Croatian, Aljoša Asanović; two Italians, Stefano Eranio and Ciccio Baiano; and two Costa Ricans, Mauricio Solis and Paulo Wanchope. The latter, a prodigious if haphazard talent, quickly became a crowd favourite and helped the club to achieve record season-ticket sales as the team, very much against the odds, consolidated their Premiership position.

In the summer of 1998, Jim Smith broke the club's transfer record to bring the Argentinian defender Horacio Carbonari to Pride Park for £2.75million. But if, in 1997/98, Derby had conceded too many goals, in 1998/99 they scored too few. With Smith transfer-listing club captain Štimac and Wanchope at the end of the season, and the club investing heavily in a new youth academy and training centre, there are signs that Derby are poised for another change of direction.

So will it be up, or down?

Here we go!

Unlike some new stadia, Derby's home is not 'out of town'. In fact, it's closer to the centre of Derby than the old Baseball Ground. However, car parking at Pride Park itself is limited and the best bet for **motorists** is to park at one of the multi-storeys in town. Among these, the car park on the Cock Pitt roundabout is well-placed for the M1 motorway, being on the inner ring road just off the A6 London Road (junction 24 on the M1) and the A52 (junction 25). Regular **shuttle buses** run between the bus station at the roundabout and Pride Park on matchdays.

Derby **train station** gets direct services from London St Pancras, Leicester and Sheffield (hourly, journey time 1hr 45mins from London, 35mins from Sheffield), with cross-country trains also serving Nottingham, Stoke and Manchester. There are no connections for London after an evening game, but check times on ☎0345/484950.

From the station, turn right onto Railway Terrace, go through the walkway under the railway line and turn right onto Pride Park Way – the stadium is along here on the right.

Just the ticket

Visiting fans are accommodated in a section of the South (Mansfield Bitter) Stand. Ticket prices here in 1998/99 ranged from £19 to £21 (concessions £10 to £11). The same stand has plentiful space for **disabled visitors** – book in advance on ☎01332/667531.

Swift half

Around Pride Park there's not much alternative to the concourse **bars** inside the stadium, which serve a range of draught bitter and lager up to 15mins before kick-off.

A cluster of pubs near the train station are worth a visit, including ***The Merry Widows*** (directly opposite), ***The Brunswick*** toward the pedestrian passageway under the railway line, and ***The Alexandra*** a little further on still.

Club merchandise

The sleek and shiny ***Rams Superstore*** (open Mon–Sat 9.30am–5.30pm, later on matchdays, ☎01332/209000) built into the rear of the North Stand offers a huge range of products including some unusually (for football!) stylish leisurewear courtesy of the club's kit supplier *Puma*. Like many teams, Derby are returning to a plainer style of shirt for 1999/2000 and this has already found favour with fans.

Barmy army

The days when local residents used to fear for their property (not to mention their lives) on matchdays in Derby are long gone. Trouble is rare now outside local grudge matches against Forest or Leicester.

In print

The local ***Evening Telegraph*** can be relied upon for detailed and objective news – its reporter Gerald Mortimer has been watching the Rams for more than 50 years. The paper publishes a Saturday evening ***Green'Un*** at around 5.30pm.

The club's own press and communications department produces the official magazine ***Rampage***, while fanzine ***Hey Big Spender*** (13 Walsham Court, Derby, DE21 4SB) has tended to focus on the team rather than the more common targets of dugout and boardroom, and is none the worse for that.

Anton Rippon's ***The Derby County Story*** (Breedon, £16.99) was updated in 1998, while the same author and publisher are responsible for ***Images of Derby County*** (£14.99), which makes fine use of the photo archive at Lionel Pickering's *Raymonds* news agency.

On air

There's little to choose between ***Ram FM*** (102.8 FM) and ***BBC Radio Derby*** (92.4 FM).

In the net

Derby's **official site** is maintained in-house and, as a result, conveys an authentic feel of the club. Find it at: www.dcfc.co.uk. Interestingly, the club is offering free internet access for fans from 1999.

The ***Evening Telegraph*** is in the process of assembling a complete Derby County player and match-report database at: www.therams.co.uk.

Everton

Formation	1878 as St Domingo
Stadium	Goodison Park, Liverpool, L4 4EL. ☎0151/330 2200
Ground capacity	40,200
First-choice colours	Blue shirts, white shorts
Major honours	League champions 1891, 1915, 1928, 1932, 1939, 1963, 1970, 1985, 1987; FA Cup winners 1906, 1933, 1966, 1984, 1995; European Cup-Winners' Cup winners 1985
Position 1998/99	14th in Premiership

For longer than many fans care to remember, Everton have taken the field at Goodison Park to the accompaniment of the *Z-Cars* theme. To an outsider the tune suggests dependability: these players, like the other boys in blue who once featured on Britain's TV screens, will always be there or thereabouts, getting the job done solidly and responsibly, and asking for little in return other than, perhaps, a nice hot cuppa. To Evertonians in the Sixties, the theme suggested innovation – *Z-Cars* was set in a fictional Merseyside town, and was infinitely more modern than its plodding London equivalent, *Dixon Of Dock Green.*

Today there is another sense, though, in which the choice of club anthem seems strangely appropriate. Like a Sixties re-run stuck in the middle of Saturday prime-time, recent Everton sides have looked anachronistic – their players struggling to come to terms with the tastes of modern audiences, their management locked in disagreement as to how to halt tumbling ratings. While the rest of the Premiership has glamourised itself into a footballing *NYPD Blue*, Goodison is only just graduating to *Softly Softly Task Force*. The result? Five relegation battles in the past six seasons.

Everton's salvation could yet come from television if, as Goodison half-expects, the former *Coronation Street* actor and theatre luvvie Bill Kenwright gets to run the club the way he wants to. Kenwright, who has a blue 'shrine' at one end of his Shaftesbury Avenue office dedicated to his heroes, maintains an unflinching grasp on the club's place in English football history. Whether he has the vision – or the clout – to help write another chapter in that history is another matter. The club's youngest fans, meanwhile, can be forgiven for wondering what all the fuss is about. They have had little to shout about other than the FA Cup win of 1995. They need some hotter, more action-packed storylines to feed their dreams, and they need them fast.

Keeping youngsters amused was the club's original *raison d'être*, more than a century ago. The Rev B S Chambers, Minister of St Domingo's Methodist Church in the Everton district of Liverpool, had started a cricket team for pupils of his Sunday School in 1876. The team was a roaring success, so Chambers sought a way of firing the kids' imagination outside the summer months. A football team was the obvious option, and St Domingo FC was duly formed in 1878.

The club quickly attracted members from outside the St Domingo's parish, so in November 1879, at a meeting in the *Queen's Head Hotel* near *Ye Anciente Everton Toffee House*, its name was changed to Everton FC. Stanley Park had been opened nearby in 1870, and the first Everton teams played on a patch of turf with homemade goalposts in the south-east corner.

In theory, anyone could come along and watch for nothing, but by 1882 crowds were as high as 2,000, and the club needed a proper home. It thought it had found one at Priory Road, where gate money was collected for the first time for a game against Walsall in 1883. But the benefactor who had donated the land, J Cruitt, objected to the disturbance caused by Everton's fans when the team beat Earlestown 1–0 to win their first trophy, the Liverpool Cup, and withdrew his support after little more than a season.

By September 1884 Everton had moved again, this time to a better-equipped ground in Anfield Road (see panel p.201). The team were indebted to John Houlding, sometime Tory MP and Mayor of Liverpool, for arranging use of the land, which he co-owned with the *Orrell Brothers* brewery. Houlding's largesse provided the stability Everton needed to become a force in what was now a rapidly growing pastime. The club turned professional in 1885, and within three years became one of the 12 founder members of the Football League.

The first League season, 1888/89, was dominated by Preston, but the following year Everton ran them a close second, and in 1891 they turned the tables by finishing two points above Preston to take the title. No other side came close to Everton's haul of 63 goals that season – despite the fact that the team launched almost all their attacks down the left, where winger Alfred Milward and inside forward Edgar Chadwick were too sharp for their rivals' slow-witted defences.

Off the field, meanwhile, it became clear Houlding was exploiting his position as both president of Everton and the club's landlord. To pacify critics of his high-rent regime, he offered to sell Anfield to the club for £6,000. Everton refused, sacked Houlding, and moved to a new ground on the north side of Stanley Park called Mere Green. The site was unpromising, but the Everton board were as visionary as they were affluent. The new ground, quickly renamed Goodison Park after the road in which it stood, was to have three stands housing a total of 11,000 people, together with proper turnstiles and all mod cons. In essence, this was the first proper football ground in England.

The players were given a bold new uniform to match their surroundings: salmon pink shirts with blue stripes and blue shorts. A century later this kit would be cynically revived, much to the chagrin of fans. Everton's players didn't like it first time around, either, and in 1901 the club adopted an altogether more tasteful strip of royal blue shirts and white shorts.

By this time the team had featured in two FA Cup finals, losing them both. But in the 1906 semi-finals Everton beat Liverpool, the rival club launched from Anfield by Houlding, 2–0, and in the final at Crystal Palace, Newcastle were beaten 1–0 with

Grim Goodison – too nervous to watch, 1998

Leaping to conquer – Dixie Dean (far left) puts Southampton to the sword, Goodison, 1930

a goal by Sandy Young, running on to a pass by right-winger Jack Sharp. The team returned to Merseyside by train and were met at Lime Street station by a four-in-hand carriage, from which captain Jack Taylor showed off the Cup to thousands of cheering fans – an early foray into mass adulation that pre-dated the open-top bus routine by decades.

Everton returned to defend the Cup in the 1907 final but lost 2–1 to Sheffield Wednesday, and fans had to wait another eight years for the next serious piece of silverware. The club, though, was forging ahead under the motto *Nil satis nisi optimum* – 'Only the best will do'. The profits from those FA Cup runs were ploughed into a spectacular new Main Stand, designed by Archibald Leitch and featuring his trademark criss-cross steelwork across the front of its balcony; it would be a Goodison landmark for 60 years.

In 1914/15, Everton won their second League championship. The side was physically tougher and tactically less predictable than the 1891 vintage, with half-back Harry Makepeace, a veteran of the 1906 Cup campaign, the man who kept the machine turning. Right-winger Sam Chedgzoy supplied the crosses, and striker Bobby Parker knocked them in, finishing the season with 36 goals, equalling an earlier League record set by another Evertonian, Bertie Freeman.

World War I stopped the team's evolution in its tracks. Chedgzoy returned to delight Goodison with his trickery, and Everton's football was as attractive as any in the League. The side lacked a cutting edge, however, and in 1925, club chairman Will Cuff instructed his secretary, Tom McIntosh, to buy an 18-year-old from Tranmere Rovers, William Ralph Dean. Born in Birkenhead, 'Dixie' Dean, to use the musical nickname he always hated, had scored 27 goals in as many games for Tranmere, who wanted £2,500 'plus some players' for his signature. McIntosh offered £3,000 cash, and got his man – though the fact that Dean had supported Everton as a boy probably helped swing the deal.

Dean made his debut for Everton at Arsenal on 21 March 1925, and a week later marked his home debut with the opening goal in a 2–0 win over Aston Villa. By the following autumn, Dean was well into his goalscoring stride, hitting successive hat-tricks against Burnley and Leeds in October, and thriving on the service from Chedgzoy and the man on the opposite flank, tiny Scotsman Alec Troup.

On 10 June 1926, however, Dean fractured his skull in a motorbike accident and lay unconscious for 36 hours. Doctors feared for his life, but he made a remarkable recovery, and by October he was back in Everton's reserve team, throwing himself at high balls with all his old fearlessness.

It wasn't just that Dean was brave. His technique of 'hanging' in mid-air was something few centre-forwards of the era had even attempted, let alone perfected with the same devastating majesty. Nor was he merely an aerial threat – of the record-breaking 60 League goals he scored in 1927/28, only a third came from headers.

Wherever the goals came from, there was a certain inevitability about Everton's title win that year. Only two points separated them from Huddersfield at the end of the season, but with Dean's help the team had scored 102 goals, 11 more than the runners-up. On the last day of the season, Dixie needed to score a hat-trick against Arsenal to break the 59-goal record set by Middlesbrough's George Camsell the previous year. When his third goal went in from a Troup corner with eight minutes left, the entire Arsenal team came up to shake his hand.

Dean's top-flight scoring record will never be beaten, not least because the size of the division has since been reduced, and because he took spectacular advantage of a newly relaxed offside law. Dean kept on

Grassroots of a rivalry – Everton at Anfield

It took the greed of a local brewer, the passion of a church organist and the financial clout of a doctor to give the city of Liverpool two professional football clubs. The original Everton club had been in existence for six years when it was offered a site for a new ground by brewer **John Houlding** in 1884. The field in question was in **Anfield Road**, and Houlding co-owned it with another firm of brewers, Orrell Brothers. He also owned the *Sandon Hotel*, which the players used to get changed in and where club meetings took place.

Everton beat Earlestown 5–0 in their first game at Anfield on 27 September 1884. And, in footballing terms at least, they never really looked back. The team recruited their first professional players, entered the FA Cup for the first time in 1886, became **founder members** of the Football League two years later, and won the title in 1891.

Thousands of supporters were now watching Everton every week, and Houlding, by now club president, knew a business opportunity when he saw one. He **doubled Everton's rent** in four years and insisted that all on-site catering be provided by his company. A group of club members led by **George Mahon**, organist at St Domingo's Church, had always been unhappy about the team's close links with the beer trade. Now Mahon joined forces with a wealthy medic, **Dr James Baxter**, to propose that the club move to a new ground in Goodison Road, on the other side of Stanley Park.

Mahon and Baxter clearly enjoyed majority support among grassroots members, but Houlding, furious that his business plan had been scuppered, registered the name 'Everton' as a **limited company** without telling the rest of the board, and vowed to set up a new club under that name to play at Anfield.

On 15 March 1892, 'King John' Houlding, as he'd become known to supporters, was officially 'kicked' from the board of Everton FC. The FA ruled there could **only be one Everton** and sided with Mahon and Baxter – forcing Houlding to change the name of his new club to **Liverpool**.

Reacting to the split, the *Liverpool Review* commented wryly: 'The fat is in the fire now.' Sizzle, sizzle.

Reaching for the skies – Joe Royle, 1962

scoring throughout the Twenties and Thirties, but the side had come to rely too much on him, and in 1930 Everton were relegated to the Second Division. Twelve months and 128 League goals later the team were promoted, and in 1932 they were League champions again, Dean notching up 45 goals while Ted Sagar, starting an Everton career that would extend to 463 games, made his name as an unflappable goalkeeper.

The following year, Everton reached their first Wembley FA Cup final, where they beat Manchester City 3–0 with goals from Dean, Jimmy Stein and Jimmy Dunn. The same carriage that had greeted the victorious 1906 Cup-winning side was at Lime Street to collect the players, and half a million turned up to see them ride in it.

There were to be no more trophies until the end of the Thirties but, throughout the intervening period, Everton's football won many friends, with Albert Geldard and Jackie Coulter continuing the Goodison tradition of quick, tricky play along the flanks. In 1936, Everton bought a 17-year-old centre-forward called Tommy Lawton from Burnley for £6,500. Like Dean before him, Lawton was bought on the instructions of Will Cuff, who promised the new boy he would play for England by his 20th birthday if he signed for Everton. Lawton signed, and did.

Surplus to requirements, Dean was sold to Notts County in 1938, after scoring 349 goals in 399 games for the club. Lawton, meanwhile, was to become the star of the side that would win England's last League championship before World War II. Supplied by the ingenious midfielder Joe Mercer, Lawton scored 34 goals as Everton took all before them, finishing four points clear at the top in 1939.

Though the club had been known as *The School Of Science* since the turn of the century, the coaching revolution of the Thirties had largely passed Everton by, and it wasn't until that title-winning season of 1938/39 that Goodison finally appointed a full-time team manager, Theo Kelly. He had little chance to make an impact – the country was soon at war and, even more than the last one, this conflict would wreak havoc with the team's development.

After the war, Lawton was sold to Chelsea while Mercer fell out with Kelly and joined Arsenal. More than 78,000 fans packed into Goodison for the Merseyside derby of September 1948, but the Everton they saw had only Ted Sagar left from the prewar title-winning side. Cliff Britton, a playmaker with the 1933 Cup-winning team, became manager and succeeded only in getting Everton relegated for the second and last time in 1951.

Goodison didn't witness top-flight football again until 1954, and it was to be another seven years before Everton clambered back into the top six. Ian Buchan and Johnny Carey both struggled to impose their will as managers, and in 1961 the club's new chairman, the *Littlewoods* pools and mail-order millionaire John Moores, famously sacked Carey in the back of a London taxi, replacing him with Harry Catterick from Sheffield Wednesday. 'The Cat' had been an undistinguished striker in the undistinguished Everton side of the early postwar years. But as a manager he was a cool disciplinarian – exactly the kind of man Moores needed to marshall an expensive but thus far inconsistent squad.

Within two years Everton had won the title, Goodison's heated pitch having allowed them to play through the hard winter of 1962/63 as their rivals for the championship kicked heels. Catterick's side went the entire season unbeaten at home, the first Everton team to do so. Always hard to break down, the side featured two expert goalscorers in captain Roy Vernon and Alex Young. Vernon, club captain and a Welsh international, was the classical target man, while Scotsman Young, *The Golden Vision*, did most of his damage around the edge of the box. Stop one, and you let the other off the hook – between them the pair netted 47 goals. The title was sealed with a 4–1 crushing of Fulham at Goodison, and as a crowd of 60,000 shouted Moores' name, the players stood swigging champagne and puffing cigars in front of the directors' box – with Catterick, even now, making sure they stayed in line.

Increasingly confident in his powers of selection, Catterick kept Everton's momentum going by introducing fresh talent at unlikely moments. When the team bowed out of the European Cup at Inter Milan in 1963/64, their best performer was an 18-year-old debutant called Colin Harvey. Later that season, the manager enraged fans by favouring an orthodox centre-forward, Fred Pickering, over the terrace hero Young. In fact, *The Golden Vision* was seen only fitfully over the next couple of seasons, and at Blackpool in 1965, Catterick was kicked to the ground by fans after again leaving out Young, this time preferring to give a debut to a 16-year-old by the name of Joe Royle...

Young was back in the side when Everton reached the 1966 FA Cup final, and this time the victim of Catterick's caprice was Pickering. His surprise replacement, Mike Trebilcock, scored twice as Everton came back from 2–0 down to beat Sheffield Wednesday 3–2. Trebilcock's inclusion caused consternation at BBC TV, who thought the player's name vulgar; their commentator Kenneth Wolstenholme pronounced it 'Trebilco' throughout.

Surprisingly, only left-back Ray Wilson represented the club in England's World Cup-winning side that year. Another disappointment for Everton fans came when the FA switched England's semi-final against Argentina from Goodison to Wembley – though the former ground did host five other games in the tournament, including Portugal's epic 5–3 defeat of North Korea in the quarter-finals.

Watching the World Cup, Catterick was particularly impressed by England's midfield anchorman Alan Ball. After the finals he paid Blackpool a new English record fee of £110,000 to bring Ball to Goodison, and six months later another gifted young midfielder, Howard Kendall, arrived from Preston. Catterick fielded these two alongside Harvey to create 'Los Tres Magnificos', a centre-circle trio that was as combative as it was creative. The 1968 FA Cup final was to have been their finest hour, but Everton inexplicably lost

Championship cheer – Labone, Ball and champers, 1970

1–0 to West Brom after extra time. Catterick stuck with the threesome, however, and after finishing third in the League the following season, Everton regained the title in 1970. With centre-half Brian Labone and goalkeeper Gordon West surviving from the 1963 title-winning side, Royle now the first-choice striker, and Ball and Kendall grabbing goals from midfield, Everton were playing the best football in England. They won the title with something to spare, finishing nine points clear of Don Revie's Leeds, and after beating every team in the division at least once.

The Seventies should have been a glorious decade for Everton. But Catterick's grip on the squad was fading, along with his own health. The troublesome Ball was sold to Arsenal at the end of 1971, and 18 months later *The Cat* himself 'moved upstairs' into an administrative role. His replacement, Billy Bingham, had the same knack for talent spotting, bringing striker Bob Latchford and creative midfielders Martin Dobson and Andy King to Everton. But he lacked Catterick's air of authority, and was sacked in January 1977 after three trophyless seasons.

Bingham's successor, Gordon Lee, was brasher and bolder but just as ineffective.

The lion from Llandudno – Neville Southall

Everton reached the League Cup final of 1976/77, but lost to Aston Villa after two replays. They also lost an FA Cup semi-final to Liverpool that year – a symbolic defeat by a team that had stolen the limelight of a decade from their rivals. In 1980, Dixie Dean died at Goodison after watching a Merseyside derby, and for some Everton fans, it seemed as though the club's spirit had died with him.

The obituaries were premature. The following year, club chairman Philip Carter decided he needed an Everton man to run the team, and appointed Howard Kendall as manager. Kendall's early progress was suffocatingly slow. But he was determined to create a team in the image of the Catterick side he had played in at the end of the Sixties. Gradually the pieces fell into place: Neville Southall was to be Kendall's Gordon West in goal; another Welshman, Kevin Ratcliffe, was a towering yet elegant stopper in the Labone mould; Peter Reid was the midfield tiger, as hungry for the ball as Ball ever was; and Graeme Sharp was the new Royle, a threatening target man but useful on the deck, too.

Kendall's philosophy differed from Catterick's in one important respect. 'Wingless wonders' had been all the rage in the Sixties, but Kendall wanted his team to use the full width of Goodison's pitch, and in Trevor Steven and Kevin Sheedy he had two of the quickest, most accurate crossers of a ball in their day.

The team's first success came in the FA Cup, when Graham Taylor's Watford were beaten 2–0 at Wembley in 1984. Victory was sweet, not least because Everton had lost the League Cup final to Liverpool on the same pitch two months earlier.

There was to be revenge for that defeat in the Charity Shield of 1984/85 and, more poignantly, in a 1–0 win at Anfield that autumn – the first time Everton had won at Liverpool since 1970. A few weeks later, Big Ron's Manchester United were whipped 5–0 at Goodison, and after Boxing Day 1984, Kendall's side went the rest of the League season unbeaten. In fact they won

Rugby, not football? – Gray is fêted for heading the ball out of the Watford goalie's hands, 1984

their last ten games, with Sharp and his fellow Scot Andy Gray scoring goals for fun. Everton finished 13 points clear of second-placed Liverpool, and the title was back at Goodison for the first time in 15 years.

There was more to come in what many Everton fans still regard as their finest-ever season. Europe had never been the club's favourite arena, and the team struggled to overcome University College Dublin in the first round of the 1984/85 Cup-Winners' Cup. After that, however, the campaign gradually gathered speed, until Bayern Munich were beaten 3–1 in the semi-final second leg at Goodison. After the game, Bayern coach Uli Hoeness claimed Everton were 'the best team in Europe', but added: 'Gray should be playing rugby, not football'.

In truth, Kendall had little time for the slow-motion sweeper systems deployed by the Europeans, and in 1985, at least, they were no match for his royal-blue steamroller. Rapid Vienna succumbed 3–1 to goals from Gray, Sheedy and Steven in the final in Rotterdam, and Everton had won their first European trophy. Within a fortnight, the Heysel tragedy resulted in all English clubs being banned from Europe for five years – an irony not lost on Evertonians, who would forever blame Liverpool fans for stifling their club's European ambitions at birth.

On the other hand, the absence of European distractions allowed Kendall to concentrate on domestic honours. He replaced Gray with Leicester's Gary Lineker, and Everton matched Liverpool all the way through the 1985/86 campaign – only to see their rivals snatch a League and Cup double from under their noses.

After the 1986 World Cup, Lineker was sold to Barcelona for £2.75million, and fans feared for the team's future. They needn't have worried. With cash in the bank from the Lineker sale, Kendall brought in reinforcements such as central defender Dave Watson, midfielder Ian Snodin and striker Wayne Clarke. Everton struggled with injuries for much of 1986/87, but the squad was now big enough to cope and, though their style was less adventurous than two years earlier, the team were still worthy champions, finishing nine points ahead of Liverpool.

By this time, Kendall was becoming frustrated at not being able to test his expertise in Europe. In the summer of 1987, he stunned Everton by resigning to coach in Spain, at Athletic Bilbao. The board thought they had a ready-made replacement in Kendall's assistant, Colin

Trouble with foreigners – Goodison's grey imports

For all its friendliness, Goodison Park has seldom **smiled on the exotic**. For decades Everton's idea of a foreign import was a Welshman, and in recent years the club's record of importing successfully has been about as dire as they come.

Swedish winger **Stefan Rehn** set the tone when he arrived from Djurgårdens in 1989. He made only **one full appearance** before returning home, where he went on to win 45 caps for his country.

In 1991 Howard Kendall signed another foreign flankman, **Robert Warzycha**. By Rehn's standards, 'Rob The Pole' was a success, playing more than 50 games. His highlight was a solo goal against Crystal Palace in the 1991 Zenith Data Systems Cup final at Wembley; Everton lost 4–1.

Another Kendall signing, **Preki Radosavljevic**, arrived from America in 1992. Yugoslav-born, he had been raised on US Indoor League soccer and, though undeniably skilful, he was usually out of breath after an hour. Of the 46 games he played for Everton, 24 were as a second-half substitute.

Daniel Amokachi became Everton's first black player when Mike Walker signed him from Club Bruges for a club record £3million in 1994. Amokachi had had a superb World Cup with Nigeria that summer but, though he became an FA Cup semi-final hero against Tottenham in his first season, he spent most of his Everton career on a different wavelength from the rest of the team. The only player who seemed capable of reading his movements was another import, Swedish winger **Anders Limpar**. Amokachi was sold in 1996, and Limpar, unfit and unwilling, followed soon after.

Pretty in pink – Rob 'The Pole' Warzycha

To replace Limpar, Everton bought the unsettled Russian international **Andrei Kanchelskis** from Manchester United for £5million. The transfer was held up when the player's former club, Shakhtar Donetsk, revealed a hitherto unknown **sell-on clause** in their contract with United, and claimed an extra £1million. Neither English club wanted to pay it – guess which one backed down. After a promising first year and a bit at Goodison, Kanchelskis declared himself tired of English football and was sold to Fiorentina.

Finally, suffering the now familiar threat of relegation in 1997, Everton signed French striker **Mickæl Madar** from Deportivo La Coruña to cure their goal drought. Madar had a reputation for **assaulting his own team-mates**, but while there was no repeat of that at Goodison, there was little aggression about his football, either. He was sold to Paris Saint-Germain within a year.

Harvey. But while Harvey's coaching credentials were not in question, he lacked Kendall's selection skills. Even the greatest achievement of his three-and-a-half year reign, a run to an FA Cup final defeat by Liverpool in 1989, was overshadowed by the Hillsborough disaster a month earlier.

Harvey was sacked in October 1990, only to be back at Goodison days later – as assistant to the returning Kendall. The threat of relegation was soon lifted, and Kendall's second spell in charge would include a number of highlights, including an immortal 4–4 FA Cup draw with Liverpool in 1991, and the subsequent transfer of Peter Beardsley across Stanley Park.

Off the field, though, events were starting to catch up with Everton. The old Gwladys Street terrace, home of the team's most vocal fans, was torn up to comply with the Taylor Report. Attendances at Goodison began to crumble, along with the atmosphere.

The Premier League began in 1992/93, and Everton, despite having played a key role in its formation, weren't ready for it. Within a year, John Moores (whose family still held a majority shareholding in the club) died aged 97, leaving a power vacuum in the boardroom. In December 1993 Kendall resigned, after the board told him the club couldn't afford his £1.7million bid for striker Dion Dublin. Kendall's replacement, Mike Walker, had no experience of running a club of Everton's size, and the team needed an unlikely three-goal comeback at home to Wimbledon to avoid relegation.

A month later, the Tranmere chairman Peter Johnson won a takeover battle against Bill Kenwright, who then surprised everyone by joining Johnson's 'dream team' board. Also appointed to the board was Clifford Finch, the man who had run Johnson's *Park Foods* hamper business with an iron hand. As the team lurched from one crisis to the next, constantly starved of funds and leadership, Finch brought his commercial 'knowledge' to bear, launching dozens of new Everton-branded products from lounge suits to lemonade, and building a kitsch new club shop in Walton Road from which to sell them.

Johnson sacked Walker three months into the 1994/95 season, replacing him with the fans' choice, Joe Royle. The former Oldham manager was fulfilling a boyhood dream to manage Everton, and his first year could not have gone better. Relegation was again a worry, and Royle, reasoning that Walker's side had been playing 'too much football', put the emphasis on defence. They weren't pretty to watch, but Royle's *Dogs Of War* knew how to dig in and get a result, particularly at Goodison. In the FA Cup, too, they were a force to be reckoned with, and when Paul Rideout poached a goal half an hour into the 1995 final at Wembley, not even Manchester United could find a response.

On paper, Everton now had it all: a trusted and talented manager, a decent squad, an ambitious board and a trophy in the cabinet. In reality, money was still tight. Improving Goodison was turning out to be a costly business, as was the £4million purchase of Duncan Ferguson, the Gwladys Street idol, from Rangers. In the summer of 1995, Royle spent a further £18million on Andrei Kanchelskis, Nick Barmby, Craig Short and Gary Speed. Everton finished 1995/96 in a creditable sixth place. Yet the squad still wasn't strong enough for a title push, and Royle knew it. Midway through the following season he tried to sign two Norwegian internationals, Tore André Flo and Claus Eftevåg. Johnson vetoed the deal, and Royle resigned – to be replaced, incredibly, by Kendall.

The great man was returning for a third stint at Goodison only because Johnson had failed to persuade a string of other candidates to join Everton. Kendall stepped up from the First Division, where he'd been in charge of Sheffield United, only to find that Premiership football had moved on without him; his team, flat-footed and one-dimensional, needed another last-day escape, a 1–1 draw at home to Coventry, to evade the drop in 1998.

Dour in the dugout – Kendall, Highbury, 1998

Kendall resigned, leaving Johnson with another long, hard summer of trying to lure top foreign coaches to Goodison. He finally settled on the former Rangers boss Walter Smith, who'd been in the job for barely four months when he was apparently undermined by his chairman in the sale of *Big Dunc* to Newcastle. Johnson, who earlier in the year had received a surprising level of support from fans for a move to a new stadium, now stepped down as chairman – though he remained the majority shareholder at both Everton and Tranmere, in flagrant breach of FA rules. Smith carried gamely on with a team which, without Ferguson, seemed almost incapable of scoring, eventually finding salvation in the form of Kevin Campbell, signed on loan from Trabzonspor.

Whether the club could afford to sign Campbell permanently from Turkey would depend on a lot of things – almost of all them financial.

Here we go!

Goodison Park is about 2miles north of Liverpool city centre. Coming from the north, **motorists** should exit the M6 at junction 26 onto the M58, continue to the end of this motorway, then turn left at the gyratory onto the M57. Leave this at junction 4, turn right onto the A580 Lancashire Road, and follow this across Queen's Drive into Walton Road. Goodison Road is a short way along, on the right.

From the south, follow the M6 as far as junction 21a, onto the M62 westbound toward Liverpool. Exit at junction 6 onto the M57 and follow this to junction 4, the A580 Lancashire Road. Then follow the directions above.

From the east, simply take the M62 as far as junction 6 onto the M57, and follow the directions above.

Best bet for parking around Goodison is the **car park** in Stanley Park, actually closer to Liverpool's ground than Everton's, but still no more than 10mins away.

Liverpool Lime Street **train station** is served by direct trains to and from London Euston (hourly, journey time 3hrs), with additional cross-country services to Manchester, Leeds and Birmingham. Passengers for Manchester and Leeds can catch a late train midweek; Londoners aren't so lucky. For the latest timings call ☎0345/484950.

From Lime Street, bus #19 runs from Queen's Square, right opposite the station, along Walton Lane, the road that divides Goodison from Stanley Park. Buses run every 10mins daytime, 20mins evenings. Other suitable routes from the centre of Liverpool are #20, #30, #F1, #F2 and #F9.

Just the ticket

With plans for a new stadium now on hold following Peter Johnson's withdrawal, **visiting fans** are going to have to put up with the wretched view from one end of the Bullens Road Stand (diagonally opposite the famous St Luke's church) for the foreseeable future. Ticket prices in the lower tier in 1998/99 were adults £17, OAPs £11, juniors £9. An extra £2 gets you into the upper tier, which at least offers a half-decent view, but there are no concessions here.

Disabled visitors have 13 spaces in front of the Bullens Road Stand, alongside Everton season ticket holders – book through your own club, not Goodison.

Swift half

Nobody with a sense of history should take a trip to Liverpool and miss the chance to have a pint at ***The Sandon***, across Stanley Park on Anfield Road. The famous hostelry where John Houlding's Everton got changed for matches endured a hideous existence in the Eighties as the *Picture House* theme pub, and was then allowed to become derelict. It was restored as *The Sandon* in 1997.

For a drink closer to Goodison, try ***The Spellow***, at 79 Goodison Road, a family-friendly place with good food and a big-screen TV.

Club merchandise

Everton's 'white castle' ***Megastore*** (open Mon–Sat 9am–5pm and evenings for midweek games, ☎0151/330 2333) is a 5min walk from the ground in Walton Road. The club's latest home shirt (£42.99; children's sizes £32.99) marks a welcome return to proper 'royal' blue, with a vestige of the white 'yoke' favoured by Kendall's successful mid-Eighties teams. You'll also find a vast range of other merchandise too nauseating to mention – as a rule, Everton fans don't buy it.

Barmy army

Even when football hooliganism was at its most dangerously potent, trouble was rare at Goodison. Many of the thousands who packed into the Gwladys Street terrace are still there now, sitting instead of standing but making just as much noise, albeit much of it in despair rather than celebration.

In recent years, fans have dedicated most of their energy to, variously, trying to get Peter Johnson to take over the club, trying to get him kicked out again, and blocking any move from Goodison. Maximum effort, minimum refreshment.

In print

The morning ***Daily Press*** and evening ***Liverpool Echo*** are produced by the same company; the latter has a reputation for some of the best football writing of any provincial English paper, and was the first to break the story that Everton was up for sale in 1993.

A pink ***Sports Echo*** is produced on Saturday afternoons after the final whistle, and the same firm also publishes the rather bland ***Evertonian*** magazine on behalf of the club.

Best-established of the fanzines is ***When Skies Are Grey*** (PO Box 226, Liverpool, L69 7LE), bitterly critical of the club's management, but always logically so. ***Speke From The Harbour*** (146 Woolton Rd, Allerton, L19 5NH) is more irreverent.

Perhaps the most evocative of all Everton books is ***Goodison Glory*** (Breedon, £16.99), lovingly researched and written by *Liverpool Echo* sports editor Ken Rogers. Also worth a look are Ivan Ponting's ***Everton Player By Player*** (£14.99) and ***Everton: School Of Science*** (£7.95), Mark Platt's detailed account of how Harry Catterick assembled a team of League-beaters during the Sixties.

On air

Both ***BBC Radio Merseyside*** (95.8 FM) and ***Radio City*** (96.7 FM) offer as much Everton programming as any fan could reasonably expect, given the presence of Liverpool in the same town. For saturation coverage, try the club's own ***Radio Everton*** (1602 AM), available within about a 10-mile radius of Goodison.

You'll see ***TV Everton*** on monitors around the ground on matchdays, but this is a purely closed-circuit venture so far.

In the net

Everton's **official website** is steadily becoming a serious endeavour after a slow start. You'll find it at: www.evertonfc.com. It's fast and efficient, but although comment is invited from fans, little is published.

Of the unofficial sites, ***ToffeeWeb*** stands out from the crowd, at: www.toffeeweb.org. It's informal, approachable and utterly comprehensive – everything the official site isn't, in fact. The *What's New* area is a lesson to all footie webmasters everywhere.

Elsewhere, the ***Speke From The Harbour*** fanzine is online at: evertonfc.merseyworld.com/sfth/.

The opposing sides in the 'New Goodison' debate each have their own websites – pro-movers at www.geocities.com/Colosseum/Stadium/6381; anti-movers at www.geocities.com/Colosseum/Stadium/9408/index.htm.

Exeter City

Formation	1904
Stadium	St James' Park, Exeter, EX4 6PX. ☎01392/254073
Ground capacity	10,500
First-choice colours	Red and white stripes
Major honour	Fourth Division champions, 1990
Position 1998/99	12th in Third Division

Exeter is the kind of place that reaffirms your faith in the West Country. If your abiding memory of England's supposed holiday paradise is of sitting in a hot, stuffy car for five hours, only to find that your destination is asleep by the time you get there, the city comes as a refreshing change: lively, cosmopolitan and, thanks to the proximity of the M5, reasonably accessible.

Likewise with the local football team. Those whose confidence in the English game's strength in-depth has been shaken by Premiership excesses should take a trip to the 'other' St James' Park. Small, friendly and idiosyncratic, it's the sort of venue the last decade is supposed to have made obsolete. But after several brushes with demolition, the ground is now safe – as are its occupiers, Exeter City FC.

The club's history doesn't exactly glitter with glory. City have never played in the top half of the League, never been beyond the quarter-finals of a major Cup competition, never been to Wembley. Even their most famous old boy, Stanley Rous, is seldom associated with Exeter – by the time he became president of FIFA in the Fifties, his footballing origins as a goalkeeper for City reserves in the months after World War I had been all but forgotten.

None of this should be altogether surprising. This is rugby union country, after all, and the fact that City have survived as a professional outfit, with their pride and good humour intact, should be considered an achievement in itself.

The oval ball was being passed around St James' Park long before a soccer team calling themselves Exeter United began using it in 1894. It was known as Bradford's Field then and, as if sharing it with a rival code wasn't enough, United also had to put up with pigs grazing on the pitch – though not on matchdays, apparently. Maybe the patchy playing surface contributed to the club's lack of progress, maybe not. Either way, United had disbanded within ten years, and their place was taken by St Sidwell's United, a team formed by old boys from St Sidwell's School and members of the local Wesleyan church.

St Sidwell's re-christened themselves Exeter City before they had kicked a ball at Bradford's Field, but if the new name was intended to garner wider support among the locals, it had minimal success initially. Only 600 souls turned up to watch City's first home game, a 1–0 win over the 110th Battery of the Royal Artillery. But with the goals of the Rev Edward Reid (the club's links with the church were still strong), Exeter won the East Devon League at the first attempt, and transferred to the Plymouth & District League.

In 1906 Albert Bradford, the Sidwell Street butcher who owned City's ground, sold it to the club for £40, and the place was officially renamed St James' Park. City had to wait another five years, though, before the acquisition of some adjacent land allowed them to lay a pitch long enough to comply with the FA's minimum of 100 yards. By this time, the team had turned professional and become members of the Southern League. The players had also abandoned their 'unlucky' green-and-white quartered shirts (always too close to Plymouth Argyle's for comfort) in favour of today's red-and-white striped affair.

Red, white and redbrick – Victorian grandeur bears down on City at the St James' Road end

Exeter's ability to be as far removed from the action as possible was first shown in the summer of 1914. As Europe braced itself for war, City were on a boat halfway across the Atlantic, their manager, Arthur Chadwick, having decided to take them on a character-building tour of South America. Once there, they reputedly provided Brazil with their first international opposition, holding them to a 3–3 draw in Rio. Overall they lost only once in eight games.

One of the heroes of the tour was Dick Pym, whose nine-year tenure of City's goalkeeping jersey would encompass 186 consecutive appearances, and a change in status from Southern League to the Third Division (South) of the Football League, of which Exeter were founder members. City's level of popularity had changed, too; their first home game in the division, a 3–0 win over Brentford in 1920, was watched by 6,000.

A year later, the sale of Pym to Bolton Wanderers for £5,000 set an unwelcome precedent, but the club put the transfer fee to good use, buying out a lease over St James' Park which had been taken out to ease cashflow when the team had turned professional. While the club was now an owner-occupier once again, however, its place in the Third Division (South) was by no means secure – despite a last-day win at Aberdare in May 1922, City finished 21st and had to make the first of many applications for re-election.

In March 1925, Exeter travelled to Amsterdam for another foreign tour, and beat Ajax 5–1. But in the previous season they'd gone 13 away games without scoring, and poor form 'on the road' in England plagued them throughout the Twenties. As the decade drew to a close, though, City made another great local discovery in striker Cliff 'Boy' Bastin, who made his debut as a 16-year-old at the end of the 1927/28 season. Within a year he would be sold to Arsenal for £2,000 – then a huge amount for such an inexperienced player. Bastin's subsequent haul of 176 goals for the Gunners indicated that, if anything, Exeter had sold themselves short.

In 1929, Billy McDevitt took over as team manager and ushered in a more optimistic era. A crowd of more than 51,000 – the highest attendance ever to watch Exeter – saw McDevitt's side get an unlikely 2–2 draw at Roker Park in the 1931 FA Cup quarter-finals; Sunderland won an epic

A head for lows – striker Darran Rowbotham

replay 4–2, in front of a St James' Park record crowd of nearly 21,000. Two years later, with centre-forward Fred Whitlow chalking up a club record 33 goals in 32 games and the team as a whole scoring 88 times, Exeter finished second to Brentford in the Third Division (South) – still not enough for promotion, alas.

McDevitt's successor, Jack English, presided over a return to the bad old ways. In 1936, City won just once in their last 21 games and finished bottom, and a year later only Aldershot were beneath them. On 2 September 1939, City won 2–0 at Port Vale to go second in the table – only for the season to be curtailed by Neville Chamberlain's announcement the following day that Britain was at war with Germany.

After World War II, Exeter continued where they'd left off before the aborted 1939/40 season – muddling along in mid-table. By 1952 the club was applying for re-election again, and three years later City were forced to sell their latest prodigy, 18-year-old wing-half Maurice Setters, to West Brom after he had played only ten League games for the club.

In 1958, City became founder members of the new Fourth Division. After a close thing in 1959, the club finally won its first League promotion five years later, finishing fourth with the help of prolific scorers Dermot Curtis and Alan Banks. Curtis was the first City player to be capped by his country (Ireland), while Banks would go on to score 105 goals for the club. Oddly, both would return to Exeter after brief spells with Devon rivals – Curtis at Torquay, Banks at Plymouth. By the time they'd returned in the late Sixties, though, City were firmly back in the Fourth Division, having survived just two seasons in the next tier up.

Things didn't pick up again until 1976, when manager Johnny Newman signed a raw Cornish striker called Tony Kellow from non-League Falmouth Town. Kellow marked his debut with both goals in a 2–2 draw at Hartlepool in August, and when Newman was replaced by player-manager Bobby Saxton five months later, the stage was set for one of the club's best-ever runs of League form. After losing only three of their last 28 games, City were promoted again after finishing runners-up to Cambridge United. The club couldn't resist Blackpool's offer of £105,000 for Kellow in 1978, but within 18 months he'd been re-signed for £65,000, and in 1980/81 Exeter embarked on another great FA Cup run. Kellow hit a hat-trick to put out Leicester City, and then Newcastle, playing a cup-tie at 'the other St James' for the first time, were thrashed 4–0 in a fifth-round replay. Tottenham, the eventual winners, were given a few scares in the quarter-final at White Hart Lane before Exeter went down 2–0.

Kellow finished that season as the Third Division's top scorer but, as ever, bad times were just around the corner. In the summer of 1983 the club appointed Gerry

Francis as player-manager; almost his first act was to sell Kellow to Plymouth. City were knocked out of the FA Cup by non-League Maidstone United, and between January and April 1984, they went 18 League games without a win. Relegation inevitably followed, and Francis was sacked.

Kellow was coaxed back for a third and final spell with Exeter, but it wasn't until the appointment of Terry Cooper as manager in 1989 that the tide was turned again. Crucially more experienced in the ways of lower-division survival than Francis, Cooper assembled a classic combination of old pros (Steve Neville, Clive Whitehead) and fresh youngsters (Scott Hiley, Darran Rowbotham). In 1989/90, City won the Fourth Division title with ten points to spare, after going the entire season unbeaten at St James' Park – this despite losing defender Chris Vinnicombe to Rangers in November, and top scorer Rowbotham missing the last 14 games injured.

Had it not been for a boardroom power struggle that led to Cooper's resignation a year later, City might have enjoyed a sustained spell in the Third (soon to be Second) Division. As it was, by the time he'd returned to take over from Alan Ball in 1994, Exeter were as good as relegated.

Twelve months later, they almost disappeared altogether. The team finished bottom of the League and, had Macclesfield Town not been denied promotion from the Conference because of 'inadequate facilities', Exeter would have swapped places with them. And while the club's League status received an unexpected reprieve, chairman Ivor Doble was struggling to balance the books as the City Council blocked his plan to sell St James' Park and build a new stadium out of town. On 16 April 1995, fans gathered to watch what they feared was not just City's last game at the historic ground, but their last game ever.

Happily, Doble managed to sell the ground to developers Beazer Homes, who allowed City to play at St James' for another year while the club looked for a new home. Then the Council, in a U-turn typical of local government's ambivalent attitude to football in England, stepped in to buy the freehold from Beazer, and St James' was saved.

The arrival of Peter Fox as manager in 1995, together with the return of the fans' favourite goal-poacher Rowbotham after six years away at as many clubs, heralded a new era of stability. And it couldn't have happened to a nicer club.

Here we go!

Motorists will almost certainly approach Exeter on the M5. Exit at Junction 30, then follow signs for Middlemoor – fourth exit from the motorway roundabout, then left at the next one. At the Middlemoor roundabout take the second exit (signposted Heavitree) and follow signs for City Centre. At the bottom of the hill turn right at the roundabout into Western Way, then take the second exit at the roundabout at the top of the hill – this is Old Tiverton Road. Take the first left into St James' Road.

There is no **car park** at the ground but there are plenty of others en route and in the city centre, a 15min walk away. **Street parking** is possible but watch out for residents' schemes.

The railway line runs so close to St James' Park that the club has had to plant trees to stop wayward clearances from bouncing onto the track. **St James' Park halt** is on the local line between Exeter St David's and Exmouth (service half-hourly, journey time 6mins).

Mainline trains run between St David's and London Paddington (hourly, journey time 2hrs 30mins), but there are no late departures for evening games other than the overnight service at 0125. There is also a service between St David's, Bristol and Cardiff, with connections for the Midlands and North at Bristol.

Just the ticket

Visiting fans are housed either at the St James' Road end of the Grandstand or, if there are enough of them, in the terrace around the corner. Ticket prices in the Grandstand for 1998/99 were adults £10, concessions £7; knock £2 off if the terrace is open. **Disabled supporters** have 18 spaces at the front of the Grandstand – book in advance on ☎01392/254073.

Swift half

Forget the pubs near the ground and make tracks instead for ***The Centre Spot***, the Exeter City social club bar (guest admission 50p). It contains, among other things, a replica of the Jules Rimet World Cup trophy – presented by Peter Lorimer to the Norwegian branch of the supporters' club in 1994, after they'd won a local cup competition for fans of English teams.

Families and anyone seeking more of a pub atmosphere should head for ***The Jolly Porter*** on St David's Hill, in front of the mainline train station. There's a range of real ales on tap, bar snacks, and a separate restaurant for those in need of serious **food** before the long haul home.

Club merchandise

The **club shop** is refreshingly unpretentious. It'll sell you a home shirt for £35 (children's sizes £27.50), bars of ECFC chocolate or fudge for £1, and a tube of red face paint (Plymouth fans need not apply) for 50p.

Barmy army

City's beloved 'Big Bank' was built over the fields the club bought to extend the pitch in 1911, and has been the scene of much good-natured singing (and sobbing) ever since. Thanks to a record £1.5million grant from the Football Trust, the terracing is to be covered for the first time, while the hardcore fans' other favoured spot, the equally characterful Cowshed, is to be turned into an all-seater stand. While fans hope the alterations don't harm the St James' Park atmosphere, the club reckons the grant award has probably saved City from going out of business.

In print

Football battles for space with rugby union in the local ***Express & Echo*** paper, of which there is no Saturday evening edition. There are no fanzines but the **matchday programme** is not a bad read at all.

The definitive book about the club is ***Exeter City FC 1904-1994*** (Tempus, £9.99) by Dave Fisher and Gerald Gosling. The same authors are also responsible for the City book in the ***Images Of England*** series (Tempus, £9.99), which includes photos of many of the club's early stars.

On air

The choice is between ***BBC Radio Devon*** (95.8 FM) and ***Gemini FM*** (97 FM), but don't expect blanket City coverage from either. No football phone-ins, either.

In the net

There are two main websites, with confusingly similar URLs. ***GreciaNet*** has the official endorsement of, but is not run by, the club; find it at: www. ecfc.demon.co.uk.

A more ambitious unofficial site is ***ExeWeb***, which lives at: www.ecfc.co.uk. It has some straightforward, elegant graphics and lively content, but its star feature is a vast online music store, from which profits are donated to the club. Buy a CD, save a City.

Cheating at history – fans head home after City's 'last game', 1995

Fulham

Formation	1879 as Fulham St Andrew's
Stadium	Craven Cottage, Stevenage Road, London, SW6 6HH. ☎0171/384 4700
Ground capacity	19,000
First-choice colours	White shirts, black shorts
Major honours	Second Division champions 1949, 1999; Third Division (South) champions 1932
Position 1998/99	Promoted as Second Division champions

For more than a century, Fulham have played their football on the banks of the river Thames. But in recent times the club has appeared to be on the brink in more ways than that. When the team plunged to the depths of the lowest division in the mid-Nineties, they looked on the verge of dropping out of the League. When a succession of developers laid out grandiose plans to exploit the property boom of the late Eighties, it was the club's historic home, Craven Cottage, that was threatened with oblivion. And when the first of those developers, David Bulstrode, announced his plan to create 'Fulham Park Rangers' earlier in that decade, the whole club itself seemed likely to become a posthumous entry in footballing history books.

Yet none of those apparently likely eventualities has come to pass. After what has been – even by the standards of this most idiosyncratic of London clubs – a highly eventful last couple of seasons, Fulham have acquired a charismatic, visionary and deep-pocketed backer; gained (and lost) two potentially inspirational managers; embarked on the total rebuilding of Craven Cottage; and, almost as an afterthought, climbed two rungs of the League ladder to stand one step from the Premiership.

The excitement is far from unprecedented. On at least two other occasions in its history, this likeable, almost innocent club has had the audacity to take on the elite of English football at its own game, and has not looked out of place. Internationals aplenty have worn the club's simple strip of white shirts and black shorts, watched by crowds comfortably into five figures. And while Fulham have not played top flight football since 1968, the club has won friends and admirers across the country for the feisty way in which it has consistently stood up to the forces of commercial greed – and won.

It's only right that the broader football community, in London especially, should like, respect and sympathise with Fulham. Followers of Chelsea, Arsenal and QPR, to name but three, owe the very existence of their clubs in their current form to the historic stubbornness of the Cottagers.

In fact, none of the names mentioned above – or any other of today's senior London teams – were around when the club came into the world as Fulham St Andrew's in 1879. The team's full title was Fulham St Andrew's Church Sunday School FC – a pretty good clue as to the club's origins, if a bit of a mouthful for supporters to chant. Not that there were many of those initially. The idea that the public might want to pay money to watch football seemed outlandish in London at the time, and as St Andrew's drifted aimlessly from field to field, they did so not because they wanted to attract more followers, but because they needed a decent playing surface – and kept being kicked off whenever they found one.

It wasn't until 1891 that the team played at a proper enclosed ground for the first time, and even this was shared with Wasps rugby club. It was an unholy alliance, then as now, and not just because it involved sharing a home with egg-chasers – the ground, next to the *Half Moon* pub in Putney, was on the other side of the Thames

The house that Archie built – Craven Cottage

from Fulham itself, a particularly inappropriate location as the club had only recently removed the 'St Andrew's' suffix from its name. For Fulham truly to represent their own sleepy, suburban area of west London (as it was then), the club had to move back north of the river. When they were offered the chance to redevelop the site of Craven Cottage in 1894, Fulham jumped at it.

The original Cottage had been built in 1780 by Baron Craven, and had been home to – among others – the author Edward Bulwer-Lytton, the exiled French Emperor Napoleon III, an American businessman, a farmer and a retired policeman. It burned down in 1888, and the grounds surrounding it had become completely overgrown by the time Fulham took up residence. At first, the club did little more than clear the site, lay a new pitch and build a single, tiny stand – the 'Rabbit Hutch'.

Still, Fulham won their first game at the ground (a Middlesex Senior Cup tie against Minerva in October 1896) 4–0, and seemed to draw new reserves of confidence from having their own home at last. Two years later the club had turned professional and joined the Southern League, and by 1903 it had become a limited company with a reconstituted board and sizeable share capital of £7,500.

One of Fulham's new directors, local property tycoon Henry Norris, would turn out to have a profound influence not just on the future of Craven Cottage but on the development of professional football right across London. It was Norris who, in 1905, turned down an invitation from another local developer, Gus Mears, for Fulham to move into Mears' intended new arena at Stamford Bridge. This in turn led Mears to start his own club (Chelsea), while Norris hired the renowned Scottish stadium designer Archibald Leitch to improve Fulham's ground – the result was the building of today's 'Cottage' to house the players' dressing rooms and club offices, along with the ornate Main Stand along Stevenage Road.

Now the crowds turned up in earnest, and they were treated to increasingly high levels of football. Under the guidance of their first proper manager, Harry Bradshaw, Fulham won the Southern League two years in a row from 1906, after which they were invited to join the Second Division of the Football League. At the end of their first League season they came fourth, three points shy of promotion, and also reached the semi-finals of the FA Cup, where Newcastle edged them out, 6–0.

What seemed an irrepressible rise was soon checked by outside competition. Mears' Chelsea, by now a First Division side, were attracting bigger crowds, while Norris, impatient at Fulham's inability to gain promotion, took over another top-flight London side, Woolwich Arsenal, in 1910, with the intention of merging the two clubs. The League would have none of it, so Norris turned his back on Fulham and, on the eve of World War I, moved Arsenal north of the river...

Deprived of Norris' ambition, Fulham settled for the gentle, good-humoured anonymity which was to become a club hallmark. After World War I, the team spent nine seasons in the Second Division before being relegated to the Third Division (South) for the first time in 1928 – ironically with Harry Bradshaw's son, Joe, in the manager's chair.

Fulham managed to keep the backbone of their team together, despite the drop, and in the best Craven Cottage tradition the side oozed character. Inside-forward Frank Osborne had been capped by England earlier in the decade, as had left-back Johnny Arnold, who also played Test cricket for his country. Another fine cricketer was outside-left Jim 'Galloping Hairpin' Hammond, who combined aerial power with tremendous acceleration to become the first man to score 100 goals for Fulham. Yet even Hammond's exploits were eclipsed during the club's promotion season of 1931/32 by those of centre-forward Frank 'Bonzo' Newton, whose physical presence and utter fearlessness netted him 43 of the 111 goals the team scored in their 42 League games.

Now back in the Second Division, Fulham had an inconsequential season under innovative coach Jimmy Hogan (see Aston Villa) in 1934/35, before reaching another FA Cup semi-final – again lost, this time to Sheffield United – the following year.

Jack Peart had succeeded Hogan as manager and remained in his post after World War II, but it wasn't until Frank Osborne combined his secretary's job (he'd retired as a player before the war) with that of manager that the team started to go places. With another loyal former player, Frank Penn, as his coach, Osborne took Fulham to the Second Division title 1948/49. Osborne then became general manager and appointed Bill Dodgin to look after the first team. Dodgin shared Osborne's and Penn's enthusiasm for developing young talent, and although Fulham were relegated after only three top-flight seasons, the back-room staff used the club's drop in status to their advantage. From 1952 they began clearing out the dead wood to make way for less experienced but more promising players, like full-back Tom Wilson, outside-left Tosh Chamberlain, centre-forward Beddy Jezzard and an outstanding array of inside-forwards – Bobby Robson, Jimmy Hill and Johnny Haynes. 'The ball is round, so pass it round,' Dodgin told his pupils, and they obeyed, much to the delight of comedian Tommy Trinder, Fulham's chairman at the time.

Trinder's personal magnetism ensured there were always plenty of showbiz personalities among the 25,000-odd who would turn up to watch this young Fulham strutting their Second Division stuff. And as the Fifties went on, so the number of style merchants increased, with Gibraltarian goalkeeper Tony Macedo, full-backs George Cohen and Jimmy Langley, wing-half Alan Mullery and Graham Leggat, a Scottish international winger with a taste for sublime solo goals, all bringing the house down at the Cottage.

While Robson, Hill and centre-half Ron Greenwood set about acquiring the tactical knowledge that would make them three of the English game's most influential managers, the star of the show on the pitch

A luvvie supreme – Johnny Haynes

Taking Stock – Fulham's winding road to Wembley

After Fulham had beaten **Birmingham City** with a last-minute goal to reach the 1975 FA Cup final, their veteran midfielder **Alan Mullery** climbed on to a table and raised a champagne toast to his team-mates 'for taking two old men back to Wembley'. The other 'old man' in Fulham's line-up was England's 1966 World Cup-winning captain **Bobby Moore**, who like Mullery would now enjoy one last big game in the spotlight.

All shook up – Bonds (left) and Mullery

But there was a third – even older – figure at the heart of Fulham's run: manager **Alec Stock** who, despite a long record of FA Cup success dating back to non-League **Yeovil Town**'s giant-slaying of Sunderland in 1949, had never before led a team out at an FA Cup final. In those days before penalty shoot-outs, it took Stock's side 11 games to reach Wembley, including three to remove **Hull City** from the third round and four against **Nottingham Forest** the round after. As Second Division opponents for top-flight West Ham, Fulham were clearly the underdogs in the final, but in addition to Moore and Mullery they also possessed predatory striker **Viv Busby**, who'd already scored six goals in the Cup that year, and an underrated goalkeeper, **Peter Mellor**, whose heroics had kept out Everton in the fifth round.

Cometh the hour, however, and the Cottagers' house came tumbling down. Busby was marked out of the game by **Kevin Lock**, Mullery was shackled by West Ham's captain **Billy Bonds**, and Moore was powerless to prevent little-known striker **Alan Taylor** from scoring twice in five minutes to put the game beyond Fulham's reach – both goals, alas, at least partly attributable to errors by Mellor.

While Mullery would gain some consolation in being named footballer of the year at the age of 33, Stock would not get another chance to lead a side to the Cup. Bobby Moore, meanwhile, was entitled to feeling ambivalent after seeing his former club West Ham lift silverware again. He left Fulham's post-match reception early and went to bed without realising he'd been burgled. The following morning, he found the culprit had returned and left Moore's **football memorabilia** in a neat pile on his front lawn...

was the 'Maestro' Haynes, who would soon be captain not just of Fulham but also of England. Haynes' precise, practised approach to the game set a fine example to his fellow internationals, while his exaggerated, hands-on-hips admonishment of team-mates who had failed to read his intentions suited the theatrical pretensions of Craven Cottage to a tee.

In 1958, Haynes led Fulham to the semi-finals of the FA Cup, where they held a patchwork, post-Munich Manchester United 2–2 at Villa Park before losing a Highbury replay, 5–3, after Macedo had uncharacteristically gifted the opposition two goals. A year later, Fulham's lyrical performances finally got the stage they deserved when Jezzard took over as manager and won the club promotion at the first attempt.

Fulham somehow clung on to top-flight status for most of the Sixties, but while the standard of football played at the Cottage may have been higher, much of the wit and spontaneity had gone. A fourth FA Cup semi-final appearance in 1962 ended in a fourth defeat – at the hands of double-chasing Burnley – and the team's 20th-place finish that year was typical of their First Division achievements (or lack of them).

Trinder was still the public face of the club, wisecracking in the face of adversity and inspiring huge loyalty in his players. Like Jezzard before them, Cohen, Chamberlain and Haynes would all spend their entire professional careers at Fulham, the last after playing more than 600 games and also – once Jimmy Hill's PFA had helped abolish the minimum wage in 1961 – becoming Britain's first £100-a-week footballer. Meanwhile Robson, Mullery and another great midfield find, Rodney Marsh, would all return to the club after being sold for fat transfer fees.

Yet it was the sale of Mullery and Marsh in the mid-Sixties that gave the biggest clue to Fulham's future direction. The financial muscle behind Trinder now belonged to Eric Miller, a successful businessman and would-be politician who wanted to rebuild Craven Cottage into a venue fit for European football. Miller made no bones about the need to sell players to finance the construction of a new Riverside Stand. But by the time work began on the project in 1969, Fulham had been relegated – twice.

The rot had set in 18 months earlier, when Miller sacked Bobby Robson from the manager's job after less than a year. Returning to Fulham for a second time after an abortive entry into management in Canada, Robson had given Miller's construction fund a £150,000 boost by selling striker Allan Clarke to Leicester, while buying a raw youngster by the name of Malcolm MacDonald from Tonbridge for just £1,000. Yet he could not prevent the team from dropping out of the top flight in May 1968, and after a poor start to the 1968/69 season, Miller panicked, replacing Robson with Haynes. Inspiring though he may have been as a player, Haynes was not cut out for management and quit within a month. His successor, Bill Dodgin junior, had the misfortune to take Fulham down into the Third Division, but did at least ensure that by the time Miller's precious stand had finally opened in 1972, the team were back in the Second.

Ironically, Mullery had by now returned to Fulham after winning almost everything there was to win with Spurs, and over the next few years, with the dignified Alec Stock taking charge and a procession of vintage talents following Mullery to the Cottage, Fulham drew the attention of a nation the Second Division, just as they'd done in the Fifties. An old England team-mate of Mullery's, Bobby Moore, helped the team reach the 1975 FA Cup final (see panel), and a year later, it was the turn of Rodney Marsh and George Best to take centre-stage, both returning to England from America to bring 20,000 crowds flocking back to Fulham.

In retrospect, the veterans' antics were little more than an entertaining cameo which served only to divert attention from the much darker overall scenario. Best and Marsh may have been great to watch, but they couldn't get Fulham promoted to the First Division, and without promotion the club's debts mounted to dangerous levels.

In 1977, engulfed by a series of scandals, Eric Miller committed suicide. The Dean family, who had run the club for a generation but had often been reliant on Miller's money, renamed the Riverside Stand after him, then sold out to a new chairman, Ernie Clay. In 1980 Fulham were relegated to the Third Division and, after a vain attempt to clear the debts by launching a rugby league club, Clay in turn sold out (at a not inconsiderable personal profit) to developers *Marler Estates* in 1986.

Marler already owned Stamford Bridge and within a year would also acquire QPR and their ground at Loftus Road. The mid-Eighties property boom was sweeping west London and *Marler* chairman David Bulstrode declared his intention to merge Fulham and QPR into 'Fulham Park Rangers', with Loftus Road as its home. This would free up the Craven Cottage site for a huge development of luxury flats. But Bulstrode hadn't reckoned on the

Football League, which vetoed the merger just as it had blocked Henry Norris' plans 75 years earlier; on the Department of the Environment, which gave Fulham's Main Stand and the Cottage itself a form of protection by assigning them Grade II listed status; or on the groundswell of opposition to his plans from supporters, which culminated in a fan-led consortium fronted by Jimmy Hill – and backed by businessman Bill Muddyman and a contemporary of Hill's in Fulham's Fifties team, Tom Wilson – buying the club's name in 1987.

Hill's group had saved the club but, in buying Fulham for a nominal fee, they'd also taken on its debts. And they had no say over the future of Craven Cottage, ownership of which was transferred to *Cabra Estates* when they purchased *Marler* in 1989. Knowing that they couldn't demolish the Cottage, *Cabra* unveiled plans to turn it into a pub – the centrepiece of another new development which, once again, would require Fulham to leave the ground.

Had *Cabra* not subsequently collapsed under the weight of the early Nineties recession, Craven Cottage would almost certainly not exist as a football ground today. As it was, the Muddyman family and Hill managed to keep the club there despite not having enough money to buy the site.

The dilemma was finally resolved in the summer of 1997, when the Muddymans persuaded *Harrods* owner Mohammed al-Fayed to acquire a majority shareholding in the club, and to buy the freehold to Craven Cottage from *Cabra*'s main creditors, the *Royal Bank Of Scotland*. At last, Fulham had a chairman who was not intent on making a killing by selling the club's desirable piece of real estate for development. At last, too, they had a man capable of financing major rebuilding of the playing staff – the need for which had been thrown into sharp relief when Fulham were relegated to the League's basement for the first time in 1994.

Al-Fayed, however, wanted to be sure his cash would be wisely spent. He dismissed Fulham's popular manager Micky Adams, who'd just pulled the club back into the Second Division, and appointed Kevin Keegan as 'chief operating officer'. Keegan in turn recruited Ray Wilkins as first-team coach, but that arrangement lasted less than a full season, Keegan taking over coaching duties himself before Fulham tried – and failed – to reach the First Division via the play-offs in 1998.

In 1998/99, with a squad now containing the likes of Chris Coleman, John Salako, Geoff Horsfield, Paul Bracewell and Paul Peschisolido, Fulham romped to the Second Division title, knocked Aston Villa out of the FA Cup, and came surprisingly close to doing the same to Manchester United. Everything in the garden was rosy, until Keegan accepted the post of England coach – initially on a short-term basis because he didn't want to 'let Fulham down', but ultimately full-time.

As Keegan bid farewell to a mixed reaction at the Cottage, there was no knowing how Fulham would perform in the First Division under new manager Bracewell, how the club might be affected by the rebuilding of the ground into a 26,000-capacity all-seater stadium, or how far al-Fayed was prepared to pursue his dream of bringing Premiership football to the banks of the Thames within five years. The plot thickens – as the fans have always liked it. But will it produce a happy ending?

Here we go!

For **motorists**, Craven Cottage is one of the easier London grounds to find but one of the worst to park at. Approach London from the M25 along the M4 (junction 15) which becomes the A4 at its end. Exit this at the Hammersmith Flyover (this is signposted Hammersmith A306). Follow this road to the Hammersmith Roundabout, then turn left under the A4 onto Fulham Palace Road. After about a mile turn right into Bishop's Park Road, and Craven Cottage is round to the right.

It's **street parking** for all, probably on a meter. If you can't find anything, head across Putney Bridge and walk back over the Thames – the ground is clearly visible from the south side of the river. The nearest **tube station** is Putney Bridge on the District Line, which has three branches – look for Wimbledon on the front of the train. Allow 30mins for the ride from central London, and another 10mins to walk from Putney Bridge, away from the river and up Fulham Palace Road to Bishop's Park Road on your left.

The shopkeeper's revenge – al-Fayed celebrates promotion, 1999

Just the ticket

After work on the Main and Riverside Stands, the latest bit of Craven Cottage to receive Mr al Fayed's attention is the Putney End, which should be converted to seating in time for the start of the 1999/2000 season. **Visiting fans** previously had this end of the ground to themselves but from now on it will be divided between home and away support.

Disabled supporters have their own enclosure between the Riverside Stand and the Hammersmith End. Book through the club on ☎0171/384 4700.

Swift half

Many pubs around the Cottage are now 'home only' but ***The Crabtree*** in Rainville Road, a 10min walk to the north, has a wide range of beers, a garden and food service. Alternatively, motorists parking up on the other side of the river have a range of drinking options in Putney, with the ***Duke's Head*** on Lower Richmond Road a deservedly popular, family-friendly choice.

The centres of Fulham and Putney offer a vast range of eating possibilities including pizzas, tapas, bagels and Turkish *meze*. Time to flex that credit card.

Club merchandise

The **club shop** (open Mon–Sat 9.30am–5.30pm, later on matchdays) is behind the Main Stand – entrance in Stevenage Road. Like many clubs, Fulham were obliged to change kits in 1999/2000 after their suppliers *Adidas* decided to confine themselves to the Premiership.

Barmy army

As at many clubs threatened in the past with closure, fans here have had more important things on their minds than doing battle with rivals. Trouble is exceedingly rare.

In print

Long-established fanzine ***There's Only One F In Fulham*** (11 Johnson's Close, Carshalton, SM5 2LU) has seen it all but remains fresh nonetheless. Speaking of people who've seen it all, Jimmy Hill's ***Autobiography*** (Hodder & Stoughton, £17.99) includes chapters on both his Fulham playing career and his time as chairman in the Nineties.

The ultimate history of the club is ***Fulham*** by Dennis Turner and Ken Coton (Ashwater, £27).

On air

GLR (94.9 FM) may offer a little more Fulham coverage than ***Capital Gold*** (1548 AM).

In the net

As you'd expect from a club sponsored by an internet service provider (*Demon*), Fulham's **official site** is pretty smart, with a completely new design from summer 1999. The club is also offering a customised browser for *Windows* users. Head for: www.fulham-fc.co.uk.

Online fanzine ***The Fulham Independent II*** runs a popular fans' message board at: members.tripod.com/~cravencottage/index.html.

Gillingham

Formation	1891 as Excelsior FC
Stadium	Priestfield Stadium, Gillingham, Kent, ME7 4DD. ☎01634/300000
Ground capacity	10,600
First-choice colours	Blue-and-black stripes
Major honours	Fourth Division champions 1964
Position 1998/99	Fourth in Second Division (beaten play-off finalists)

It was 5.30 in the morning and the Gillingham manager, Tony Pulis, found himself pacing about his home near Bournemouth, unable to sleep. Twelve hours earlier, his side had come within 30 seconds of winning promotion to the upper half of the League for the first time in their history. Two goals up against the runaway favourites Manchester City in the 1999 Second Division play-off final, and with the clock apparently ticking toward the 90-minute mark, Gillingham were coasting, their contingent of 35,000 fans giving one end of Wembley, at least, the proverbial carnival atmosphere.

Even when Kevin Horlock pulled one back for City, it had an air of consolation about it. But then, in the fifth minute of stoppage time, City's Paul Dickov found himself unmarked in the Gillingham box. Calmly, almost in slow motion, he turned and lifted the ball over 'keeper Vince Bartram, a former Arsenal team-mate and best man at Dickov's wedding. Two apiece.

In extra time, Gillingham had a decent penalty appeal for handball turned down – though whether it would have done them any good is a matter for conjecture, since they could manage only one goal out of four spot-kicks in the shoot-out that followed. City were up, and Gillingham – emotionally at least – about as far down as it is possible for a team to go.

Unknown to Gillingham's fans, however, Tony Pulis had another reason for his sleepless night after the match. Even before the club's first-ever visit to the Twin Towers, the manager had become embroiled in a bitter contractual dispute with chairman Paul Scally – a dispute which, once the play-off drama was over, became very public property. After a month of bickering, cooling off and more bickering, Pulis was dismissed, turning up a week later as the new manager of Bristol City. Meanwhile, Scally moved with similar speed to appoint a successor, plumping for former England Under-21 boss Peter Taylor, recently rendered surplus to the FA's requirements by Kevin Keegan's new broom.

Wisely, Taylor began by paying tribute to Pulis' efforts – although, in truth, the part played by Scally in Gillingham's remarkable late-Nineties revival was equally crucial, and it seems unlikely that either man could have lifted the club so far without the other's influence.

In June 1995, Gillingham were two hours away from extinction when Scally, a local thirtysomething millionaire and self-confessed Millwall fan who'd given up trying to invest in his own team, offered to take the club out of receivership. As well as pacifying Gillingham's many creditors, one of Scally's first moves was to appoint Pulis as manager in place of Neil Smillie.

The task ahead was formidable. Just two years earlier, Gillingham had only averted relegation to the Conference by beating Halifax Town in the penultimate game of the season, and they'd been firmly in the wrong half of the Third Division table ever since. But Scally gave his new manager money to spend on transfers and Pulis, rather than splash out on a couple of stars, set about building a large squad of versatile, experienced professionals.

With the giant Jim Stannard in goal and the lively Leo Fortune-West and Dennis Bailey upfront, Gillingham had such a good season in 1995/96 that older fans had to keep rubbing their eyes in disbelief. After Stannard had kept 29 clean sheets out of 46, Pulis' team finished as runners-up to Preston. It was only the third promotion in the club's history.

The fairytale continued through the next three seasons, with Gillingham first consolidating in mid-table in the Second Division, then missing out on the play-offs on goal difference in 1998, and finally clearing their route to Wembley by finishing fourth and beating Preston in a stirring play-off semi-final second leg at Priestfield in May 1999. And, if match referee Mark Halsey had not added so much stoppage time to the regulation 90 at Wembley, who's to say Gillingham would have looked out of place in the First Division?

Though unable to hide his disappointment at the club's play-off failure and clearly ruffled by his run-in with Pulis, chairman Scally remained in bullish mood. He believes he can bring Premiership football to Gillingham and, while the Priestfield Stadium gets a complete overhaul with new stands on three sides of the ground, the chairman also has his eye on a long-term future in a new, multi-usage stadium out of town, complete with retractable roof, movable seats and other 21st-century innovations. That, of course, would require substantial financial help from outside, but where there's a will, Scally reckons he can find a way. Gillingham's history of almost total mediocrity makes it easy to dismiss him as a dreamer, but Scally says the club's untapped potential is 'enormous', and logic dictates that he has a point.

For much of their life, the 'Gills' have been the only professional football team in Kent. The Medway towns – principally Gillingham, Chatham and Rochester – offer a promising local catchment area, while the wider county was effectively opened up by the untimely demise of Maidstone United, just three years after they'd achieved promotion to the Football League, in 1992. And for those who labour under the misapprehension that this is not really a footballing part of the country, it should be pointed out that one of the English game's most successful early teams, the Royal Engineers, hailed from Chatham.

Just give me five minutes – Gillingham's Paul Smith (centre) wants his time again, Wembley, 1999

Victorian values – tea and terraced housing at the Gillingham End of Priestfield, 1995

Indeed, it was the success of the Royal Engineers – four FA Cup final appearances between 1872 and 1878, including one victory over Old Etonians after a replay – that inspired the formation of several more local clubs in the latter part of the 19th century. One of these was Excelsior FC, who began life in 1891, playing on a patch of common land in Gillingham known as the Great Lines. In 1893, after winning the Kent Junior Cup and the Chatham District League, the club's members decided to turn their organisation into a limited company. After a meeting in the *Napier Arms* in the suburb of Brompton, they settled on the name New Brompton FC and agreed to buy the patch of land on which the Priestfield ground would be built.

Thanks to the unstinting efforts of founding fathers such as the club's first chairman, Alderman J Barnes, and long-serving secretary-manager W Ironisde Groombridge, New Brompton survived a series of early financial crises, entering the FA Cup for the first time in 1899, but remaining in non-League football until after World War I. In 1913 the name was changed to Gillingham FC, and two years after the end of hostilities the team became founder members of the Football League Third Division, opening their account with a 1–1 draw at home to Southampton on 28 August 1920. From there it was downhill all the way, Gillingham finishing bottom of the table at season's end, and being thankful that, with the Third Division due to be expanded into separate South and North sections the following year, their application for re-election was waved through by the League.

On the eve of World War II, after 17 seasons of mediocrity in the Third Division (South), Gillingham were not so lucky. They'd finished bottom of the pile again in 1937/38, and the League, keen to extend its influence into the hitherto amateur hotbed of East Anglia, decided to replace them with Ipswich Town.

Gillingham went into liquidation, but re-formed a year later and began playing in the Southern League. Travelling restrictions obliged them to move to the Kent League for a couple of seasons toward the end of World War II, but after that it was back to the Southern League before the club was finally re-elected to the Football League in 1950, the year both regional Third Divisions were expanded to 24 clubs.

Gillingham celebrated their return to League football by conceding 101 goals in their first season back, and when the regional Third Divisions were scrapped in 1958, the club inevitably found itself in the newly created Fourth Division. Even this was a struggle initially, before Freddie Cox guided the club to the championship in 1964 with a side which, like Pulis' three decades later, had its quality anchored firmly in defence.

Unspectacular though Gillingham were, however, they were solid enough to make a better fight of Third Division life than critics had predicted, remaining there until 1971, and bouncing back from relegation under Andy Nelson three years later. With the celebrity support of *Big Match* TV commentator Brian Moore and an increasingly confident, attacking attitude to the game, the Gills were almost fashionable as the Seventies wore on. And while the Medway dockyards were not immune from the effects of recession in the early Eighties, the team retained their Third Division status, reaching the height of their powers after the arrival of Keith Peacock as manager in 1981.

Peacock, a thoroughbred 'man of Kent' who'd spent his entire professional career playing career with Charlton Athletic, had a knack of developing unpredictable talents from the likes of left-back Mickey Adams, young central defender Steve Bruce, former Middlesbrough winger Terry Cochrane and, most colourfully of all, a recklessly courageous striker from Orpington by the name of Tony Cascarino. Despite being forced to sell most of his finds, Peacock guided Gillingham to the Third Division play-offs in 1987. In the days of two-leg, home-and-away finals, the Gills were 11 minutes from victory over Swindon when they conceded an equaliser, and a replay at neutral Selhurst Park was lost 2–0.

Within six months, Peacock had been dismissed after a run of poor results, much to the dismay of fans who'd witnessed the creation of arguably the most attractive team in Gillingham's history. While Peacock would go on to lead Maidstone into the League, the Gills lost their way, dropping back into the Fourth Division in 1989.

Six years later, the club's long-standing benefactor Tony Smith declared that he'd had enough, and placed the club in the hands of receivers. The first six months of 1995 were a rollercoaster ride of supporter campaigning, mystery buyers, beautiful sunsets and false dawns. Then along came Paul Scally – a Millwall fan the Gills could trust, and a man whose seemingly preposterous vision of the club's future so nearly became a reality in 1999. Referees' watches permitting, it may yet do so.

Here we go!

Motorists should exit the M2 at junction 4 onto the A278 toward Gillingham. Go straight over two roundabouts and turn left at the third toward the town centre, then take the first right into Woodlands Road. Go straight on at the lights

Thanks, lads – Pulis wins promotion, 1996

and then next left into Chicago Avenue – you'll see the ground up ahead from here, and **street parking** should be feasible in this area.

Gillingham **train station** gets fast trains from London Victoria (half-hourly, journey time 50mins, beware stopping services which can take up to 30mins longer), which in turn is about 30mins from other London termini by tube. Check the latest overground times by calling ☎0345/484950.

From the station, turn left into Balmoral Road, then right into Linden Road and the ground is straight in front of you – allow about 10mins.

Just the ticket

Exactly how much of the Priestfield is redeveloped during 1999/2000 will depend on how much Paul Scally can raise from the Football Trust and other sources, but **visiting fans** probably won't be affected for the time being, as the corner terrace between the Main Stand and the Gillingham End is one of the last scheduled for demolition. Tickets in 1998/99 were adults £10, concessions £8 – add £2 for a seat.

Disabled visitors will be moved to the new Gordon Road Stand if the Main Stand is being rebuilt – booking essential on ☎01634/851854.

Swift half

Home and away fans mix in a convivial pre-match atmosphere at ***The Cricketers*** in Sturdee Avenue, a couple of streets behind the Gordon Road Stand. Also worth a visit, for historical reasons as much as anything, is the ***Napier Arms*** in Britton Street, the other side of town from the station, where New Brompton FC was founded in 1893.

Few of Gillingham's football-friendly pubs serve **hot food** but the High Street, just across from the train station, has a range of takeaways and pricier sit-down options.

Club merchandise

The **club shop** is due to be relocated as part of the Priestfield rebuilding plans. The black stripes introduced by Paul Scally to make an Inter Milan-style shirt out of Gillingham's more usual plain blue actually have their origins in the old North Brompton club.

Barmy army

The death of a Fulham supporter outside the ground in 1998 tarnished Gillingham's otherwise clean-living image, which the club continues to deserve. Teams the fans love to hate are Millwall, Swindon Town and the Priestfield's erstwhile ground-sharers Brighton.

In print

There's no Saturday evening paper but the daily ***Kent Today***, weekly ***Kent Messenger*** and more locally orientated ***Medway News*** (also weekly) all devote plenty of column inches to the Gills.

Fanzine ***Brian Moore's Head Looks Uncannily Like London Planetarium*** (29 Onslow Road, Rochester, ME1 2AL) has been going for more than ten years and is as witty as ever.

Roy Triggs' Gillingham book in the ***Images Of England*** series (Tempus, £9.99) tells the story of the club through archive pictures and contemporary press reports.

On air

Now that ***Invicta Supergold*** (1242 AM) no longer has exclusive live commentary, the choice is really between ***BBC Radio Kent*** (96.7 FM) and ***Medway FM*** (107.9 FM).

In the net

Gillingham's **official website** still hadn't seen the light of day in the summer of 1999 despite several rumours to the contrary. Happily, the unofficial ***Gills Online*** is one of the most thorough sites of its kind you'll find in the lower divisions, with a news and video archive, the latest stadium developments, and a (very necessary) search engine. It's all at: home.clara.net/keith.pestell/Gillspage/gills.htm. Also try the ***Donkey's Tale*** webzine at: www.geocities.com/Colosseum/Midfield/5437/index.htm.

Grimsby Town

Formation	1878 as Grimsby Pelham
Stadium	Blundell Park, Cleethorpes, DN35 7PY. ☎01472/697111
Ground capacity	8,870
First-choice colours	Black and white stripes with red trim
Major honours	Second Divsion champions 1901, 1934; Third Division champions 1980; Third Division (North) champions 1926, 1956; Fourth Division champions 1972; Auto Windscreens Shield winners, 1998
Position 1998/99	11th in First Division

'Pound for pound, class for class, the best football team I have seen in England since the war,' was how Bill Shankly recalled them. He went on: 'In the league they were In they played football nobody else could play. Everything was measured, planned and perfected. You could not wish to see more entertaining football.'

Shanks wasn't talking about the Liverpool of the Sixties and Seventies. He was thinking back to his days as a young manager in the dugout at Blundell Park, in charge of a Grimsby Town side striving to escape the old Third Division (North) in 1952, playing against the likes of Barrow, Gateshead and Workington Town.

Shankly wasn't the first footballing visionary to cut his teeth in England's most celebrated fishing port. Herbert Chapman was a player here, at the turn of the last century, as was Graham Taylor much later. And Lawrie McMenemy had his first major success as a manager when he did what Shankly failed to do – lift Grimsby out of the League's bottom drawer – in 1972.

The supporters have paid a high price for this tradition of innovation, enduring endless rides on the rollercoaster of promotion and relegation as the club has endeavoured to find its true level. Grimsby have spent a dozen years in the top flight, but have not appeared in it since 1948. They've applied for re-election twice, and left the League completely at one point. They waited 120 years to reach Wembley, then played there twice in as many months at the end of the 1997/98 season.

Samp to salt cod – Ivano Bonetti signs, 1995

The long and winding road began in 1878, when the club was formed as Grimsby Pelham – the latter the family name of the big local landowners. It became Grimsby Town a year later, rather ironically since the team actually played home games in Cleethorpes, just along the Humber estuary. (They continue to do so today.) A series of impressive FA Cup runs earned Town their berth in the Second Division of the Football League in 1892, and they were champions nine years later.

Grimsby were back down again within two years, however, and by 1922 the team's form had collapsed to the point where the club found itself an unwilling founder member of the Third Division (North). More promotions and relegations followed until, in 1934, a young Welsh striker called Pat Glover ushered in what historians consider to be the club's golden era. It was Glover's 42 goals in 1933/34 that brought Town the Second Division title, and in three seasons of First Division football he scored nearly 100 times. His top-flight haul included five in one game against Sunderland in 1937, while his own favourite came against Liverpool in the same year. 'I hit the ball as though it owed me money,' he later told an interviewer. 'It simply flew into the net.'

A year earlier Grimsby had reached the semi-finals of the FA Cup for the first time, and in 1939 they did so again, drawing nearly 77,000 to Old Trafford for their tie against Wolves – more, Town fans point out, than Manchester United have ever attracted to the ground. But Grimsby lost the match, just as they'd lost the earlier semi. Fifth place in the First Division of 1935 remains the club's highest League finish, and no player has ever surpassed Glover's final tally of 180 goals for the club. Plagued by injury as the Thirties drew to a close, the Welshman retired to run a pub in Devon, and World War II loomed.

After hostilities had ceased, Town never recovered their momentum. They finished 16th in 1947, bottom a year later, and by 1951 they were back in the Third Division (North). Charlie Spencer, who had been team manager since 1937, retired through illness and was replaced by Shankly, a charismatic, straight-talking Scot who was coaxed south from Carlisle United. Double relegation had forced drastic cuts in Grimsby's first-team squad, but Shanks turned this limitation to his advantage, fielding an unchanged side for much of the season as he set about instilling his ethic of 'hard work and entertaining football'.

In early 1952, Shankly's side won 11 games in succession with just one change in personnel. They scored 32 goals, nine of which fell to Billy Cairns, a hulking 39-year-old who his manager reckoned was 'the best header of a ball in the game'. That run remains unmatched in the club's history, but it was not quite enough to earn Town promotion; they were pipped by local rivals Lincoln City, and Shankly was devastated. He bounced back the following season,

Big if not beautiful – Blundell Park in 1975, before the Taylor Report halved its capacity

training alone on Christmas Day to signify the effort he saw as being necessary for promotion. But Shanks' players could do no better than finish fifth in 1953, and in October that year the Scot stunned Grimsby by resigning to manage struggling Workington.

Play-off point – Alan Buckley (right) confronts Keegan, 1998

The elusive promotion finally came in 1956, but the team's stint in the Second Division lasted only three years, and the Swinging Sixties seemed largely to pass South Humberside by. Town were relegated to the Fourth Division by a difference in goal average of 0.008 in 1968, and a year later had to apply for re-election.

It took the efforts of another inspirational team manager, Lawrie McMenemy, to bring the good times back. Different in style from Shankly but no less outspoken or effective, McMenemy encouraged Grimsby's players to trust their own ability, slow down and pass the ball, at a time when English lower-division football was becoming increasingly rough and ready. At the end of his first full season in charge, 1971/72, Town won the Fourth Division championship.

McMenemy left for Southampton in 1973, just as Grimsby were establishing themselves as a force to be reckoned with in the Third Division. They were relegated in 1977, promoted two years running in 1979 and 1980, and enjoyed a period of relative stability in the Second Division before two relegations on the spin in 1987 and 1988.

Time for another great leader to take charge – Alan Buckley. It was the end of the Eighties and while much of the country was contemplating an economic downturn, Grimsby fans were partying, waving their *Harry Haddock* inflatables from Blundell Park's Pontoon terrace as their side embarked on a run that would bring them another two successive promotions, along with some notable cup successes. Like Shanks and Lawrie Mac before him, Buckley told his team to go out and play, ignoring the contemporary orthodoxy, as propagated by Graham Taylor, that the ball should always go forward early.

The Second Division became the First in 1993, and Town contrived to stay in it with style. But that brought its own problems. The club's elevated status meant it had to implement the recommendations of the Taylor Report rapidly and in full. Blundell Park's capacity was halved almost overnight, devastating gate receipts.

Alan Buckley left in 1994, and the reign of his replacement, Brian Laws, was memorable only for the punch-up between manager and the former Sampdoria defender Ivano Bonetti, which left the Italian with a black eye and a desire to board the first plane out. Laws was replaced by Kenny Swain in the middle of the 1996/97 season, but Grimsby went down anyway.

Happily, for the club at least, Buckley had not enjoyed the same success post-Grimsby as his illustrious predecessors. He returned in May 1997 after being sacked by West Brom, and immediately set about performing some more miracles. His first season back ended with the side playing their own brand of *Fantasy Football.* They beat Bournemouth with a Wayne Burnett 'golden goal' to win the Auto Windscreens Shield at Wembley, and were back there five weeks later to edge Northampton 1–0 in the promotion play-off final, having seen off Kevin Keegan's Fulham in the semis. The Northampton game was Grimsby's 68th fixture of the season, and Buckley was as animated on the bench as he had been for the first.

The club's 1998/99 campaign was dogged by a chronic lack of goals – only relegated Bury found the net less often – yet an 11th-place finish did not flatter Grimsby, who at one stage had looked a decent each-way bet for the play-offs.

Buckley admits the current side are not always as attractive as the Grimsby of the mid-Nineties, but they are more solid at the back and, in any case, these are early days for the manager's second spell in charge. He is convinced the club could 'do a Bradford' and clamber up into the Premiership, but living comfortably at such a level would almost certainly depend on Grimsby finding a new, bigger home out of town – a move supported, if recent polls are to be believed, only by a slim majority of fans.

Here we go!

Remember, you should be heading for Cleethorpes, not Grimsby. Coming from the west, **motorists** will find the M180 motorway becomes the A180, the Grimsby Road in Cleethorpes. Stay straight on this road for just under 3miles and you will see Blundell Park on the left, behind the *McDonalds*.

Approaching from the south along the A46, go straight on at the Bradley Crossroads roundabout and straight on at the next one, then get into the right-hand lane for a right turn at the next set of traffic lights, into Weelsby Road. Go through the underpass, straight on at the next two roundabouts, then left at the Isaacs Hill roundabout; this turning is Grimsby Road and the ground will be on your right in about a mile.

There is no car park at the ground but **street parking** is in plentiful supply.

Visiting supporters travelling **by train** as part of a large party may be met at New Clee station by police and escorted to the ground. However, New Clee is normally served only by local services and small groups will probably wind up at Cleethorpes main station, about a mile east of the ground and served by direct trains from Manchester and Sheffield.

From the station, you can get to the ground by **taxi** (£3) or by **bus** (#3F, #9X or #45) from the stop near the *Pier 39* club on the waterfront. Alternatively, take in some North Sea air by walking along the promenade for about half a mile and then crossing the railway bridge, from which Blundell Park is easily visible.

For evening kick-offs, however, note that the last train leaves Cleethorpes at 2116 – only of use if you're content with watching the first hour.

Just the ticket

The club asks **visiting fans** to seat themselves in the Osmond Stand, which has a capacity of less than 2,000. Book in advance through your own club if you think space might be tight. Ticket prices in 1998/99 were adults £13, OAPs £7, juniors £5. Enter through turnstiles #5–14 in Constitutional Avenue. Visiting **families** are welcome in the Appleby Stand but should book in advance through Grimsby on ☎01472/697111.

The Main Stand, built in 1901 and the oldest surviving structure in English first-class football, has facilities for **disabled supporters** – again, book in advance through Grimsby.

Swift half

The club recommends ***The Leaking Boot*** on Grimsby Road (open Sat matchdays 11am–4pm & 7–11pm, midweek all day, ☎01472/691530) to all visiting supporters fancying a swiftie before kick-off. There's often a police presence here on matchdays but don't let that put you off. You'll find three separate bar areas; Wards and Vaux beer on draught; pool, darts and television; and an outdoor play area for kids.

For **food**, try any of the numerous fish-and-chips outlets between the ground and Cleethorpes train station. You'll work hard to find fish that isn't expertly fried, but are the locals sick of the stuff? The drive-thru ***McDonalds*** adjacent to Blundell Park does a roaring trade.

Father figure – Lawrie Mac looks on (top left of picture) as Grimsby lift silverware, 1998

Club merchandise

Grimsby's **club shop** is located at one end of the John Smiths Stand, at the end of Imperial Avenue. Historically, the club has shunned the worst excesses of football fashion, and the red trim on Town's shirts has acquired a symbolic significance (not least because it distinguishes a Mariner from a Magpie). In recent years, some fans have been unhappy that the red has been used gratuitously to highlight sponsors' logos.

Barmy army

At the opposite end of the ground from the Osmond Stand is the **Pontoon**, the scene of much inflatable haddock-waving at the end of the '80s and still lively today, despite the replacement of the creaking timber terracing by plastic seats. The stand was originally built by public subscription, so Grimsby's hardcore support have every right to regard it as their own.

In print

The ***Grimsby Evening Telegraph*** offers authoritative and respected coverage of club affairs, and publishes a separate *Sports Telegraph* edition on Saturdays.

Exiled Town fans produce the wry fanzine ***Sing When We're Fishing***, available from 10 Glen Eldon Road, St Anne's, Lancs, FY8 2AU.

In the book department, Robert Briggs' ***Grimsby Town FC – An A-Z*** (Soccer Books, £5.99) was published in 1997 and is as recent as it gets.

On air

BBC Radio Humberside (95.9 FM) is the fans' choice even though Town have to share airtime with Hull City and the much-derided Scunthorpe United.

In the net

The club's official site is ***MarinersNet***, a really well laid-out effort with just the right amount of graphic content and an approachable style, and with live matchday commentary among its features. Find it at: www.gtfc.co.uk/.

The unofficial ***Electronic Fishcake*** is if anything even more comprehensive than the official site, and has the added bonus of a fans' perspective. Again, restrained graphics and a well-ordered layout are the order of the day, at: www.grimsby.org/.

Halifax Town

Formation	1911
Stadium	The Shay, Halifax, HX1 2YS. ☎01422/353423
Ground capacity	9,300
First-choice colours	All blue with white trim
Major honours	Conference champions 1998
Position 1998/99	Tenth in Third Division

On 11 September 1911, Halifax Town AFC lost their first-ever match, 6–2, to Bradford City reserves. Some would say the club's life has been an uphill struggle ever since. The trophy cabinet is still bare, save for minor oddities such as the West Riding Senior Cup, and the side have got off the bottom rung of the Football League ladder only three times. The last of these journeys was in the wrong direction, down into the Conference in 1993. Halifax remained there for five seasons, longer than any former League side since formal relegation began – just one of several unwanted records held by the club.

Since promotion back to the League in 1998, however, the team appear intent on reversing the long trend of decline. Like so many clubs that have had a brush with insolvency, Halifax want to prove that lower-division football can be practicable, profitable and fun. Bit by bit, the statistics are being turned on their head. In 1998/99, Halifax received more transfer money for a single player than ever before (£300,000 from Fulham for striker Geoff Horsfield), maintained a steady presence in and around the Third Division play-off places, and broke their own record for gate receipts: more than £36,000 for a second-round League Cup tie – against Bradford City, of all people.

Historically, the close proximity of longer-established clubs has hindered the club's progress. Bradford and Huddersfield are both less than ten miles away, while Leeds and Manchester aren't much further afield. Just as seriously, this neck of the woods is often perceived, both locally and elsewhere, as rugby country, with league and union codes both enjoying a sizeable following.

Against this somewhat unpromising backdrop, Halifax Town were formed via the well-trodden Edwardian route of a group of city fathers gathering in a local pub, quaffing a few pints and deciding to start a football club. They had been drawn to the hostelry in question, the Saddle Hotel, by a letter in *The Halifax Evening Chronicle* from somebody who chose to sign himself *Old Sport*. The mystery man turned out to be one A E Jones, who revealed his identity at the meeting but then declined to take on an official role at the new club. Instead, Jock McClelland became club secretary, a job he combined with that of team manager between 1912 and 1930.

McClelland's early sides competed, with no little success, in the Yorkshire and Midland Combinations, playing first at Sandhall Stadium, moving to Exley in 1919, and two years later finding their present home, The Shay, on the site of a former council rubbish dump. At the same time, Halifax became founder members of the Third Division (North), where they played with almost total anonymity for more than three decades.

In 1953, a club record crowd of 36,885 rolled up at the Shay to watch Tottenham knock Halifax out of the fifth round of the FA Cup – the furthest the club has ever gone in either of the two major cup competitions. Five years later, the Shaymen found themselves in the unusual (for them) dilemma of being in the right place at the right time: their seventh-place finish in the League was just good enough to earn them a place in the fledgling Third Division, as

Dark and distant – The Shay before it was regenerated by Football Trust and rugby league cash

opposed to the Fourth. There they remained until the 1962/63 season, when they conceded 106 goals, finished bottom, and were relegated.

They were promoted again in 1969, and two years later, in the first of two spells under George Kirby's management, they came within four points of promotion to the old Second Division, eventually finishing third, behind Preston and Fulham but ahead of Aston Villa. They then beat Manchester United in the pre-season Watney Cup, in front of nearly 20,000 at The Shay. But Kirby left soon after, and without him Halifax struggled, dropping back down into the basement in 1976.

Over the next ten seasons, the club was obliged to make five applications for re-election to the League, all of them successful. The team began the Eighties by knocking Manchester City out of the FA Cup third round, but even this, the club's finest hour in the modern era, was a slightly subdued occasion. More than half The Shay was given over to City fans, and after the match, as the Halifax players popped open the champagne to toast Paul Hendrie's winning goal, the TV cameras were in the visitors' dressing room, spying on City boss Malcolm Allison as he railed against his team of millionaire misfits.

After the scrapping of re-election in 1986, Halifax somehow avoided finishing bottom of the League for six seasons, until a home defeat by Hereford on the last day of 1992/93 condemned them to the Conference. With local interest at an all-time low and the economy in recession, gate receipts plummeted, and after two seasons of struggle outside the League (enlivened only by a 2–1 win over West Brom in the 1994/95 FA Cup), the board formally announced that the club was to fold – Halifax couldn't afford a £70,000 bond required of them by the Conference. Supporters rallied round to raise funds, and the Conference played their part by lowering their demands. Their short-term future thus assured, the team took the bull firmly by the horns – by finishing 15th and 19th in the next two seasons. For a time, further relegation beckoned.

Enter a second white knight: George Mulhall, a former Scottish international

Towering target – striker Dave Hanson

winger whose coaching career had taken him to a series of lower-league clubs via South Africa. Like Kirby before him, Mulhall had left The Shay once, only to be lured back by the chance of producing success against the odds. After a spell as youth coach he resumed first-team duties in February 1997, and in less than 18 months had guided Halifax back to the Football League. On the pitch, a pair of old heads – Brian Kilcline and Kieran O'Regan – kept the ship steady while forwards Horsfield and Jamie Paterson took most of the chances that came their way.

On 18 April 1998, Halifax won 2–0 at Kidderminster Harriers to seal the Conference championship, and nearly 6,500 souls packed into The Shay a week later to watch the team parade the trophy.

That summer, the 62-year-old Mulhall stepped up to a new position as director of football, Kilcline retired, and O'Regan was made player-manager. The Irishman was given a new right-hand man in player-coach Peter Butler, signed from West Brom, and though the loss of Horsfield was a blow, Paterson's goals helped give Halifax their best start to a League season in a decade.

What happened next bewildered fans. With Halifax still in with a shout of a play-off place, O'Regan and his assistant Andy May were sacked after a goalless draw at neighbours Rochdale. The board's decision was unanimous but chairman Jim Brown did nothing to improve his popularity with supporters by admitting he had 'no fixed ideas' about a replacement manager. Dave Worthington stepped into the breach as caretaker boss but could not improve the team's consistentcy and Halifax finished tenth. Mark Lillis was then appointed as manager for 1999/2000.

If progress has slowed on the pitch, the club is still in an expansive mood off it. The arrival of the local rugby league team, Halifax Blue Sox, as ground-sharers in 1998 was not universally welcomed among Town fans, but the injection of cash from Rupert Murdoch's SuperLeague should ensure that development of The Shay continues apace.

Plans are on the drawing board for a new East Stand which will incorporate banqueting and hospitality areas, executive boxes, a physiotherapy and rehabilitation suite, a crêche and a travel agency, the idea being to create what the Council calls 'a seven-day trading situation' at the site.

When built, this development will allow the pitch to be moved nearer to the Skircoat Shed, giving Blue Sox fans some of the 'close to the action' atmosphere they say has been lost since their move to The Shay. Some of the money, however, will have to come from the sale of the rugby league club's old ground at Thrum Hall.

Here we go!

Motorists will almost certainly be unable to avoid the M62 motorway. The exit to head for, assuming the traffic has allowed you to get to it before kick-off, is junction 24, signposted Huddersfield and Halifax. Take the A629 toward Halifax, stay on this road into the town centre, and about a mile from *The Quays* pub (see *Swift Half*, below), get into the right-hand lane to turn right at the traffic lights into Shaw Hill. The ground will be on your left.

The **car park** at the ground is open to all but you need to get there early to be sure of a space. Failing this, the best bet is to double back on yourself and seek **street parking** on the other side of the Huddersfield Road.

Returning hero – George Mulhall, architect of a Conference title

Halifax **station** is on the trans-Pennine line which runs from Leeds and Bradford at one end to Rochdale and Manchester at the other (trains every 30mins). There's also a direct service to and from Burnley, Blackburn, Preston and Blackpool (hourly). Passengers from London should travel to Bradford Interchange (12mins from Halifax) and change trains there. For the latest timings call ☎0345/484950.

From the station it's no more than a ten-minute walk to the ground. Turn left out of the station into Church Street, then bear left into South Parade, turn right up Hunger Hill, and The Shay is on your left.

Fans from Yorkshire or Manchester should get home by train from a midweek game, but Londoners won't be so lucky.

Just the ticket

The Shay has two new terraces at either end of the ground, with the uncovered North Terrace being reserved for **visiting fans** – enter from Hunger Hill. Ticket prices in 1998/99 were adults £8, juniors and OAPs £4, children under-12 £2. Almost 4,000 fans can be housed here, so buying tickets on the day shouldn't be a problem. **Disabled supporters** have just 14 spaces at the front of the Terrace, however; book in advance on ☎01422/353423.

Swift half

Pubs near the ground such as *The Shay*, on the corner of South Parade and Hunger Hill, are strictly home fans only. ***The Quays***, on the Huddersfield Road about a mile from the ground, welcomes away fans, offers a fine choice of real ale on draught, and has particularly good facilities for families.

Those with their own transport also have some good pub options in Elland, between Halifax and the M62, and in Sowerby Bridge, the other side of Halifax along the Calder Valley.

For food, the atmospherically cloistered **Piece Hall** on Westgate in the centre of town has a number of café options dotted among its twee craft shops, all of them a better bet than eating inside the ground.

Club merchandise

The **club shop** (opening hours sporadic, ☎01422/353423) is located in the South (Highway Glass) Terrace and will sell you, among many other things, a home shirt for £34.99 (children's sizes £24.99), a scarf for £6.99, or a fridge magnet for 99p. Best stick with the magnet.

Barmy army

Hardcore support tends to gather in the South Terrace and the Skircoat Shed, and between them these two can make The Shay a surprisingly atmospheric place – the more so since the old speedway track was removed. The surrounding Pennines provide a picturesque backdrop as well as a natural valley for the chanting to echo

The Shay today – new terracing, bright outlook, scenery as lush as ever

around. Trouble is unheard of unless Burnley are in town, which isn't very often.

In print

The ***Evening Courier*** which played such a pivotal (if unwitting) role in the club's formation is still going strong, though its reporting on Halifax Town can be sketchy. The ***Yorkshire Post*** runs the odd story on the club, as does its sister paper the ***Evening Post***, the Saturday 'Pink' edition of which normally gets to Halifax by 6pm.

For a fanzine perspective try ***Shaymen Down South***, available from 175 Peartree Lane, Welwyn Garden City, Herts, AL7 3XL.

Dave Wright's ***Shaymen 'Til We Die*** (HTFC, £6.99) charts the club's ups and downs from falling out of the League in 1993 to the early part of the 1998/99 Third Division season.

On air

Neither ***BBC Radio Leeds*** (92.4 FM) nor ***Huddersfield FM*** (107.9 FM) devotes as much airtime to Halifax Town as the fans would like, but the former did play Queen's *We Are The Champions* to celebrate the club's 1998 Conference title.

In the net

The **official website** is at: www.geocities.com/Colosseum/stadium/3043. It's a fair effort, with few frills but plenty of news, squad information and stats. The club shop publishes a price list here but there's no online shopping as yet.

An unofficial ***Halifax Town Shaysite*** is at: www/ephtl.demon.co.uk/ephtl/. It's even better than the official site for news and match reports, and you can choose between framed and frameless versions, depending on your browser's capabilities.

To get the **Australian** perspective on Halifax (yes, really), head for: www.geocities.com/Colosseum/Midfield/8941/. The site is maintained by Queensland's Under-19 indoor goalkeeper, and as well as offering a refreshing take on lower-league life, the site also blows a cheesy electronic version of *Waltzing Mathilda* down your computer's speakers.

Hartlepool United

Formation	1908 as Hartlepools United
Stadium	Victoria Park, Clarence Road, Hartlepool, TS24 8BZ. ☎01429/272584
Ground capacity	7,200
First-choice colours	Blue-and-white stripes
Major honours	None
Position 1998/99	22nd in Third Division

Does any League club endure as much notoriety as Hartlepool United? A club which, after entering the League in 1921, had to wait 47 years for its first promotion? Which has applied for re-election more times than any other? And which, despite a brief period of prosperity in the early Nineties, continues to languish at the wrong end of the League ladder even now?

As if such a record of failure wasn't enough, Hartlepool fans seldom get the chance to give outsiders any other impression. Their town, steadily re-inventing itself as a north-eastern Heritage-Centre-On-Sea after the decline of its traditional coal, steel and shipbuilding industries, has far more to offer than its reputation suggests. Yet many fans of away teams take one look at their road atlas and decide not to bother. It's a long way and, they reason, if we lose it'll be an embarrassment, while if we win it won't be much cause to celebrate. It's only Hartlepool, after all.

Given all this, the club's very tenacity deserves high praise. For Hartlepool, despite their many travails, have never lost their League status. Unlike Durham City, South Shields or Gateshead, all clubs for whom location allied to poor form ultimately proved their undoing, Hartlepool's applications for re-election were always successful, often very comfortably so. Unlike Darlington, the team down the road whose history has many parallels, Hartlepool have never been relegated to the Conference. In 1998/99, they even managed to pull themselves away from the danger zone (just) before the final day of the season. They might take a lot of flak up at Victoria Park, but they shall not be moved.

This was the pits – Gustavo di Lella and a surviving wheel

Winter chills – the training ground's grand surroundings

Surprisingly, for a club that has never lifted a single piece of major silverware, it was local achievement in national competitions which led to its foundation. The success had come the way of West Hartlepool, an amateur side from what was then a 'new town' of Victorian development being built on the riches of steelmaking, west of the old 'Headland' town which could trace its history back to medieval times. West Hartlepool were founded in 1881, and for most of their existence were content to play friendly matches against other nearby teams of similar outlook such as Bishop Auckland, Middlesbrough and Stockton. In 1904/05, however, they won the FA Amateur Cup, travelling to London to beat the local favourites, Clapton, 3–2 at Shepherd's Bush.

This distant and apparently unlikely triumph inspired the town, and in 1908 a group of founding fathers got together with the intention of forming a professional football club. Their original idea was to bring West Hartlepool together with some of the smaller teams that had started to spring up in the 'Old' town, so they called their club Hartlepools United. Much of West Hartlepool's membership, however, was suspicious of professionalism, so when the new team took over the Victoria Ground from West Hartlepool rugby club (still in existence today, shuttling awkwardly between the top two divisions of the rugby union code), they initially shared with West Hartlepool FC until the latter disbanded in 1910. Meanwhile, Hartlepools United had joined the North-Eastern League and also enjoyed instant glory in the Durham Senior Cup, winning it in their first two seasons. Football League status was harder to acquire, though, the club being consistently rebuffed before World War I. On the morning of 16 December 1914, there were 235 ships in Hartlepool Docks, prompting the first aerial bombardment of England by Germany. The Victoria Ground escaped undamaged, but two years later its Main Stand was destroyed by bombs dropped from a fleet of Zeppelin airships.

After the war, the team gained admittance to the Football League's newly formed Third Division (North) in 1921, joining at the same time as Darlington. United began by finishing fourth in their first season but struggled thereafter, having to make the first of their record 13 applications for re-election after finishing second from bottom in 1924.

The years before and after World War II were uneventful, the decline of the region's shipbuilding industry preventing United from reaping much reward from the postwar surge in interest in the game that swept the rest of the country. With money tight as always, long-serving manager Fred Westgarth kept chickens under the Clarence Road Stand to supplement his income. Eventually, Westgarth's hard work paid off – after a couple of top-five finishes in the Third Division (North), his team, led from the front by prolific scorer Ken Johnson, finished as runners-up in 1956/57, unfortunate that a fine Derby County side was in the division at the same time to finish above them. There was no promotion for second place then, but that season Manchester United's Busby Babes came to the Victoria Ground for an FA Cup third-round tie and were lucky to escape with a 4–3 win. A crowd of more than 17,000, the highest in the club's history, had turned up to watch.

Westgarth retired soon after, and United would not get a manager of similar dedication until a young Brian Clough jacked in his job as youth coach at Sunderland to take charge in 1965. From a historical point of view, Clough and his assistant Peter Taylor were on a hiding to nothing. Yet they were smart enough to realise that, at Hartlepools United, even the slightest success would attract attention and reflect favourably on them. They earned it, too, creating the side which, under their successor Gus McLean, would win the club's first-ever promotion in 1968. Just as important, the need to 'muck in' at the Victoria Ground (Clough helped install corrugated iron roofing over the terraces while Taylor repainted the stands) gave both men a taste for running a club, not just a team – experience that would stand them in good stead when Derby County made them an offer they couldn't refuse in 1967.

That same year, in an attempt to arrest decades of economic decline, the twin boroughs of Old and West Hartlepool merged to form a single town. The football club's name no longer made sense, and by the time McLean's team made it up into the Third Division, they were playing under the simplified title 'Hartlepool'. The new image made little difference to the fortunes of either the town or the team – 'Hartlepool' were relegated after just one season, and would spend the next two decades back in the League's basement, changing their name to 'Hartlepool United' in 1977, the year the last steelworks closed.

With the ice rink that once adjoined the Victoria Ground also closed and not so much as a cinema in the town, the air of depression was almost all-pervading by the time Cyril Knowles was appointed manager in 1989. The former Tottenham full-back had been brought up in the area and had already enjoyed a successful spell in charge of Darlington. Now, together with another veteran north-east campaigner Bryan 'Pop' Robson, he set about building a bold young side that would bring previously unknown glory to the club. With a young Don Hutchison marshalling the defence and the fearless Joe Allon as target man, Hartlepool finished third in 1990/91. Both those players were soon sold – Allon to Chelsea for a club record £300,000 – but the team had enough strength in-depth to keep the momentum going and achieve a top-half finish in the Third Division the following season.

The great tragedy was that Knowles was not around to see the club's finest hour. In 1991 he had stepped down through ill health (leaving Hartlepool's chief

In Cloughie's footsteps – Chris Turner

executive Alan Murray to take charge of team affairs) and died of cancer soon after. Equally tragic, in its own way, was that after the club had staged a testimonial match for Knowles' family, the cheque bounced.

Promotion had brought a fresh sense of purpose to the team, but it had not made it any easier for chairman Garry Gibson to pay people's wages. In 1994, after the inevitable relegation, Gibson made way for Harold Hornsey, a man determined to ensure that Victoria Park, as the ground was now renamed, should reflect the new spirit of confidence that was descending on the town.

But, while their ground was rebuilt with the help of Football Trust and other grants, Hartlepool United were back to their bad, old bottom-of-the-League ways. The appointment of Keith Houchen as player-manager pomised much but delivered little. His successor, Mick Tait, was likewise unsuccessful, despite the arrival of such exotica as the Argentine midfielder Gustavo di Lella and Peter Beardsley on a non-contract basis. Midway through the 1998/99 campaign, with United again in fear of falling into the Conference, Tait made way for the former Sunderland goalkeeper and Leyton Orient co-manager Chris Turner. That Turner eventually managed to steer the team to safety owed much to the efforts of Jan Ove Pedersen, a striker brought over from Brann Bergen, and one of several Norwegians to arrive at United since the club was acquired by *IOR*, an Aberdeen-based oil firm with strong Scandinavian connections.

Alas, in the close season Pedersen returned to Norway to play summer league football with Brann. Would the reborn Hartlepool, with its marina, its superstores, its chic restaurants and its (shock, horror) cinemas, be attractive enough to tempt him back? Or would the club's desperate history weigh against it, as it had so often in the past?

Here we go!

Motorists approaching on either the A1(M) or the A19 should exit onto the A689 toward Hartlepool. Stay on this road as far as the junction

Have a good trip home – Beardsley, Stephenson and Clark salute the faithful, Peterborough, 1999

at the *Middleton Grange Shopping Centre*. Go straight on and then left onto the A179 Clarence Road – the ground is on the left. There should be plentiful **street parking** around Victoria Park but, if not, there are car parks in the nearby marina complex.

Hartlepool **train station** is served only by local trains on the Newcastle-Middlesbrough line. Change at Newcastle for mainline services, and don't expect any useful departures after a midweek game. Call ☎0345/484950 for the latest timings.

Getting to the ground from the train station couldn't be easier. Turn right at the end of the station approach onto the main road, and you'll see the floodlights from here.

Just the ticket

Visiting fans are allocated the whole of the covered, newly seated Rink End – entrance in Clarence Road. Cost in 1998/99 was £11 adults, £8 concessions. **Disabled supporters** have space in the East (Cyril Knowles) Stand, as do **visiting families**. Book in advance for either on ☎01429/272584.

Swift half

The ***Corner Flag*** club, built, owned and run by the Supporters' Club in the north-west corner of the ground, welcomes visiting fans before and after games (guest admission 50p), and is a convivial place in which to sup a cheap pint.

Families and those in search of a slightly quieter atmosphere might be better off at ***Jackson's Wharf***, a new (but old-looking) pub in the marina complex, a 5min walk from the ground.

Club merchandise

After years of mucking about with checks, pinstripes and other abominations, Hartlepool have gone back to their original broad blue-and-white stripes. The **club shop** in the Cyril Knowles Stand will have the latest version.

Barmy army

The acoustics at Victoria Park make it surprisingly easy for the home faithful to raise a roar, despite the chill wind that does nobody any good. Trouble is rare outside of the annual Darlo game.

In print

The local ***Hartlepool Mail*** publishes a Saturday evening edition, and you may also find copies of the Middlesbrough-based ***Evening Gazette***.

The fanzine is ***Monkey Business*** ('Monkey Mansions', 12 Swanage Grove, Hartlepool, TS24 9RR), while Gordon Small's ***Definitive Hartlepool United FC*** (T Brown, £8.99) traces the 'Pool' story as far as 1998.

On air

Play *Spot The Pool Item* amid all the 'Boro talk on ***BBC Radio Cleveland*** (95 FM) and ***Century Radio*** (101.8 FM).

In the net

There's no **official site** as yet, and the most professional of the unofficial offerings is probably ***Pool Online***, run by the *Evening Gazette* at: www.eveninggazette.co.uk/hpl/index.htm.

Also worth a peek are ***Virtual Victoria Park*** at: www.cee.hw.ac.uk/~ceecnw; and ***Ballistic!*** at: www.geocities.com/Colosseum/Midfield/4235.

Huddersfield Town

Formation	1908
Stadium	The Alfred McAlpine Stadium, Leeds Road, Huddersfield, HD1 6PX. ☎01484/484100
Ground capacity	24,000
First-choice colours	Blue-and-white stripes
Major honours	League champions 1924, 1925, 1926; Second Division champions 1970; Fourth Division champions 1980; FA Cup winners 1922
Position 1998/99	Tenth in First Division

From the heights of Kilner Bank, the Alfred McAlpine Stadium makes as bold a statement as it is possible for a football ground to make. A sea of flowing, blue-and-white painted steel against an urban backdrop that is pure West Yorkshire Victoriana, it stands out like an acid house bassline in a Gilbert & Sullivan operetta. And its message is more than aesthetic. For the town, it is a deeply symbolic structure, representing a dramatic departure from the area's industrial past and a tantalising glimpse into a bright new commercial future. For Huddersfield Town FC, it signals a rediscovery of the spirit of innovation for which the club was famous between the wars, but which had lain dormant for decades. Other League clubs may have built new stadia before, and others have done so since – but none made the massive break with convention, both architecturally and spiritually, that is 'the Mac'.

Of course, a new home alone is no guarantee of success on the pitch. Five years after the McAlpine first opened its doors for a football match, it is still awaiting its debut Premiership fixture. Town had a decent season in 1998/99, spending a brief period at the top of the First Division table and enjoying the limelight of an FA Cup run. But their final tenth place, 15 points shy of the play-off zone, was a letdown for club and supporters alike.

Small wonder that Barry Ruberry, the millionaire who acquired a 70% stake in the club during the season, decided to dispense with the services of manager Peter Jackson and lure, in his place, Steve Bruce from Sheffield United. During the close season Bruce was given a transfer budget that was beyond his wildest dreams at Bramall Lane, but like Jackson he is relatively inexperienced as a manager – only time would tell whether Huddersfield, 28 years after they last graced the top flight of the English game, could make the leap their new arena so clearly deserves.

The contrast between Huddersfield's football and its surroundings is apt because, throughout the club's history, it has either been leading the way or been left far behind, with little room for treading water in between. League champions three years in a row during the Twenties, at the forefront of a management revolution in the Fifties, the club has also faced extinction twice and plumbed the depths of the old Fourth Division.

It is also appropriate that the McAlpine Stadium should have been built in conjunction with – and be shared by – Huddersfield's *Superleague* club, for perhaps more than any other Yorkshire town, this one has a rich association with rugby league, the code having been born here in 1895. Indeed, it was the early dominance of rugby which initially presented a barrier to the development of soccer in Huddersfield, with the first moves toward setting up a professional football club in the town not being made until 1906.

The (round) ball was set in motion by members of the Huddersfield & District FA, who convened a meeting at the *Imperial Hotel* to discuss the lack of a local focus for fans of their game. The will was there,

Mission statement – the Alfred McAlpine Stadium, as viewed from Huddersfield's Kilner Bank

but the resources weren't until an obliging benefactor emerged in the form of J Hilton Crowther, a leading light in the town's then thriving woollen industry who pledged £2,000 as the founding capital for a new club. On 26 June 1908, Crowther arranged a meeting at the *Albert Hotel*, bringing the club, Huddersfield Town AFC, together with the holding company that owned a suitable ground at Leeds Road. The latter's board had already arranged for an as yet unnamed representative team from the town to become members of the North-Eastern League – and Crowther's club was only too eager to form that team.

On 8 September, about 1,600 souls turned up at what was then a very rudimentary ground to see Huddersfield Town win their first fixture, a friendly against Bradford Park Avenue, 2–1. However, life in the North-Eastern League proved difficult both on and off the pitch, with the team struggling to adapt to the level of football and travelling costs proving prohibitive – hence a switch to the Midland League for 1909/10.

At the end of that season, and on the back of a long FA Cup run, Huddersfield made an audacious bid for Football League status and, somewhat surprisingly, were elected to the Second Division in place of Grimsby Town. Yet not even League football and massively improved facilities could draw more than a few thousand to Leeds Road on a regular basis, and after just two seasons in the Second Division, the club went into liquidation in 1912. Enough finance was arranged to relaunch Town in time for the 1912/13 season, but soon after, World War I interrupted the club's progress. On 6 November 1919, the local *Examiner* newspaper ran a story suggesting that Huddersfield were to move to Elland Road as the replacement team for Leeds City, thrown out of the League for financial misdemeanours a month earlier.

Out of time – Leeds Road's last season of top-flight football, November 1971

In retrospect, this was the kick up the backside that football in the town had so sorely needed. Hundreds took to the streets in protest, thousands more signed petitions, and the proposed move was hastily abandoned. Not only that, but the team, inspired to new heights of endeavour by the crisis, reached the FA Cup final and won promotion from the Second Division for the first time. Few clubs have engineered a climb from the depths of despair in such a short space of time, but for Huddersfield, the 1919/20 season was only the start.

The following year, Herbert Chapman arrived at Leeds Road as manager and almost singlehandedly changed the destiny of the club. His previous job, ironically, had been at Leeds City. Temporarily suspended by the FA for his alleged role in the pre-war payments scandal which had brought that club to its knees, he was unable to work for City's successor team, Leeds United. He was subsequently cleared of any wrongdoing (which he had always denied), and was only too happy to remain in his native Yorkshire with Huddersfield.

Sensing that the side he was inheriting was already on a roll, Chapman made almost no changes to Huddersfield's personnel. Instead, he instigated a rigorous disciplinary regime, years ahead of its time, that would rid his squad of the mentality of also-rans. Smoking was forbidden, and on the alcohol front, only a glass of sherry was allowed, at bedtime as an aid to sleep. As the players made their way out onto the pitch, they were given a glycerine tablet and a pat on the back from their manager, come rain or shine.

At the end of the 1921/22 season, Chapman's first in charge, Huddersfield reached another FA Cup final, where virtually the same line-up that had lost to Aston Villa two years earlier now overcame Preston with a penalty from the boot of winger Billy Smith – the first time the Cup had been won from the spot. A celebration parade, organised personally by Chapman, saw 40,000 take to the streets and the celebrations carry on well into the night – at long last, Huddersfield was in love with football. The marriage was consumated in spectacular style, with Town winning three League titles on the spin from 1924. Throughout the period there were more attractive sides in the First Division, but none with Huddersfield's supreme confidence, consistency and iron will to win. Arguably their best championship was their last, in 1925/26, driven by the joyous goalscoring of centre-forward George Brown. But by the time it was won, Chapman had been tempted away by the vast salary and unlimited transfer budget dangled in front of him by Arsenal.

After 1926, Huddersfield continued to challenge for honours but, significantly, won nothing. They were League runners-up in 1927, 1928 and 1934, losing Cup finalists in 1928, 1930 and 1939. Popular interest in the team was at an all-time high – a record 67,000 saw Chapman's Arsenal at Leeds Road for an FA Cup tie in 1932 – but there was to be no more dancing in the streets.

After World War II the team drifted aimlessly between the top two divisions. While so many other Yorkshire clubs were revelling in a mini-boom, Huddersfield were down on their luck, and Leeds Road, starved of investment from a club that had clearly failed to capitalise on its unprecedented prewar success, was looking increasingly forlorn.

In 1956, Bill Shankly strode in to spread his own particular footballing gospel through the club, and in the spectacular young inside-forward Denis Law, he appeared to have the perfect pupil. But Shankly left for Liverpool before his preaching had had any discernible effect on the team, and when Law was sold to Manchester City for £55,000 in 1960, the money had to be put toward equipping Leeds Road with floodlights.

There was still time for a brief revival under Ian Greaves, who engineered a Second Division championship in 1970. But both club and ground looked ill-equipped to play anything more than a bit part in the fantasy football of the Fancy Dan era. At a time when other clubs boasted pop stars and models as fans, Town's best-known supporter was the pipe-smoking former Prime Minister, Harold Wilson. Even the team's new nickname, 'the Terriers', sounded old hat. After only two years in the top flight, Huddersfield were relegated.

Further decline was as steep as it was inevitable – by 1975 Huddersfield were in the Fourth Division, and crowds had dipped below five figures. On 30 April 1979, the visit of Torquay United prompted just 1,624 clicks at the turnstiles.

Former coach Mick Buxton was promoted to the manager's role and led Huddersfield to the Fourth Division title in 1980, and three years later the club had been promoted again. But Second Division football lasted only until 1988, and Town would not climb again for another seven years, after a 1995 play off final win over Bristol Rovers.

Even that minor triumph was tarnished when the manager responsible for it, Neil Warnock, decamped to Plymouth after failing to secure money for new signings. While Huddersfield RLFC, the local Kirklees council and the Football Trust had all been willing partners in the scheme, Town had ploughed everything they had – financially and logistically – into their new stadium. Further success on the pitch would have to wait.

Four years on, and the supporters are still waiting. The McAlpine Stadium may be a fine venue for rock concerts, but Huddersfield fans would rather be dancing in the streets, just as their counterparts did in a bygone age...

Here we go!

Motorists coming from the south should exit the M1 at junction 38 and follow the A637 and A642 toward Huddersfield. Just before the town centre, turn right at the *Aspley* pub into St Andrew's Road – Stadium Way is a little way ahead on the right.

From all other directions, take the M62 as far as junction 24 and the A629 Halifax Road into Huddersfield. Follow the Ring Road round and exit onto the A62 Leeds Road, then take the second right-hand turn into Gasworks Street – this becomes Stadium Way after the crossroads.

There are various **car parks** in the vicinity of the McAlpine, which is just as well as the one at the ground itself fills up quickly.

Huddersfield **train station** is on the trans-Penine line between Leeds and Manchester Piccadilly (three trains per hour, journey 25mins from Leeds, 40mins from Piccadilly). Some trains continue on in either direction to Hull, York or Liverpool, and there are also direct trains to and from Sheffield. For the latest timings call ☎0345/484950.

The station is a 15min walk from the ground. Turn left down Railway Street, straight on into Northumberland Street, then across the Ring Road onto the A62 Leeds Road. Take the second right into Gasworks Street, which becomes Stadium Way.

Just the ticket

Visiting fans are allocated the South (Gardner Merchant) Stand at the McAlpine, with seats for up to 4,000. Ticket prices in 1998/99 were adults £12, concessions £6. **Disabled visitors** have spaces at the back of this stand – book in advance on ☎01484/484123.

Swift half

You can get a pie and a pint at the ground, but Huddersfield's town centre offers more interesting options, including ***The Albert***, near the town hall, with its wide range of real ale, and ***The Slubbers*** on the corner of Bradford Road and Halifax Old Road, midway between the train station and the McAlpine. Families arriving by car have an agreeable option in ***The Aspley*** on St Andrew's Road, which has a large menu.

An uphill battle – Marcus Stewart, 1998

Club merchandise

The **club shop** at the ground (☎01484/484144) has the expected range of blue-and-white gear and trinkets, plus some Leeds Road memorabilia.

Barmy army

For a hardcore support that once attacked the visitors' goalkeeper and manager during a visit from Millwall in the early Eighties, the atmosphere at the McAlpine is friendly almost to the point of being laid-back – amazing what a decent stadium will do.

That said, the town centre isn't always as welcoming, so keep colours covered.

In print

The local ***Examiner*** which first broke the news of the proposed move to Leeds in 1919 is still going strong, offering excellent coverage of Town but, alas, no Saturday evening edition.

The fanzine is ***Hanging On The Telephone*** (PO Box 57, Huddersfield, HD8 0XS), while ***The Huddersfield Town Story*** by Ian and Gwen Thomas is available from the club shop and covers the first 90 years of Town's existence.

On air

Fans will reluctantly tune into ***BBC Radio Leeds*** (92.4 FM) in the absence of much footie coverage on the local ***Huddersfield FM*** (107.9 FM).

In the net

Huddersfield's **official website**, developed and maintained by the club itself (hurrah!), is a little slow but has most of the essentials, including a news-feed from the *Examiner* (see *In print* above) but, surprisingly, no e-commerce as yet. Head for: www.huddersfield-town.co.uk.

There are two very complete unofficial sites worth recommending. ***The Huddersfield Net*** is at: www.richmills.cwc.net/thn/index.html; while ***Down At The Mac*** is at: www.geocities.com/Colosseum/Sideline/4016/main.htm. You'll also find an extensive club history online at: www.maxpages.com/huddersfieldt.

Hull City

Year of formation	1904 as Hull Comet
Stadium	Boothferry Park, Kingston upon Hull, HU4 6EU. ☎01482/327200
Ground capacity	13,000
First-choice colours	Amber and black
Major honours	Third Division (North) champions 1933, 1949; Third Division champions 1966
Position 1998/99	21st in Third Division

Hull City AFC began life sharing a ground with one of the city's two rugby league clubs, and the tension between the two games has influenced the club's development ever since. Any anorak will tell you that Kingston upon Hull is the largest English city never to have had a football team in the top division. And every two-bit pundit charged with uncovering the reason why comes back chanting the same mantra: 'Hull is a rugby town in which soccer will always struggle to command popular support.'

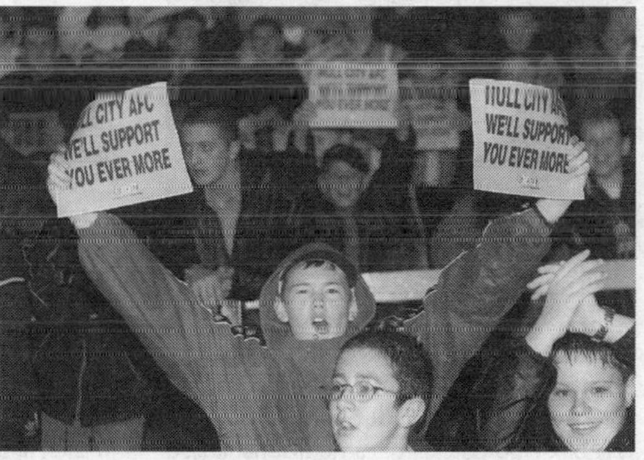

No surrender – fans in the week that City nearly closed, 1998

What neither cliché reveals is the extent to which the two sports once co-operated in the city – or why, in a modern era that has seen football and rugby league embrace one another in towns such as Huddersfield and Halifax, the prospect of such a *rapprochement* gripping Humberside seems so remote.

The latest figure in City's history to fall foul of the soccer-rugby rivalry was a one-time professional sportsman whose background was in neither. When David Lloyd, former British Davis Cup captain and multi-millionaire owner of a chain of tennis and leisure centres, acquired Hull City in 1997, he thought it would be a good idea to buy up Hull FC – one of the aforementioned rugby league teams – at the same time. After an aborted attempt to merge the latter with the city's other rugby league side, Hull Kingston Rovers, in 1995, Hull FC had won promotion to Rupert Murdoch's summer Superleague, in which they would play as Hull Sharks. By merging the Sharks with the 'Tigers' (to use City's nickname), Lloyd reasoned that both clubs would benefit from administrative streamlining. More pertinently, the double acquisition gave him two pieces of city real estate (City's Boothferry Park and the Sharks' Boulevard) to sell. The proceeds would go toward a new super-stadium for the two teams to share, and which would have retail and leisure development attached to it – the means by which Lloyd would recoup his investment.

That investment was substantial. Buying City alone cost Lloyd £3.3million, while Hull FC set him back a further £1million, and both grounds needed money spending on them just to keep them safe, regardless of their long-term future. While

City saviour – player-manager Warren Joyce

appreciating Lloyd's contribution to the team's precarious finances (City might well have gone under without him), fans of the football club quickly became disenchanted with the new regime. Player-manager Mark Hateley was given no new money for reinforcements, and after finishing the 1997/98 season 22nd in the Third Division, the Tigers were occupying bottom place at the start of the following one.

What really bothered City fans, though, was the idea of 'sleeping with the enemy' – rugby league. The pain began when switchboard operators at Boothferry Park started answering the phone with the greeting 'Hull Tiger Sharks'. Before long, there was no switchboard there at all – City's offices had been moved to the Boulevard. After he failed to persuade the *KwikSave* supermarket chain to sell its lease on one end of Boothferry (the shop's land had been sold to stave off an earlier cash crisis in 1982), Lloyd admitted the ground's sale would not realise enough money to finance his 'super stadium' development. The only solution was for the Tigers to move in with the Sharks – to the fans, sacrilege.

Ironically, crowds at Boothferry Park rose at the start of the 1998/99 season, as fans rallied around the football club and its beloved ground. But David Lloyd's patience was wearing thin. Vilified for not spending enough time in Hull, abused when he did turn up for games, in October 1998 he threatened to close City down within a week if nobody came up with £2million to buy the club from him. He eventually backed down, but within a month he had sold City to a consortium led by former Scunthorpe chairman Tom Belton – though he retained Boothferry Park, and also kept his controlling interest in the Sharks.

The new owners immediately set about attending to the team – something Lloyd had overlooked. Hateley was replaced by City's experienced midfielder Warren Joyce, assisted by the former Derby and Forest captain John McGovern. With a string of cheap signings and a switch to a more direct style of play, Joyce and McGovern steered the team to safety and a final 21st placing. Belton also went out of his way to assure City fans he had no interest in the rugby league side of Lloyd's business, pushing a full merger off the agenda.

Perhaps it was the club's previous experience of sharing the Boulevard, almost a century ago, that made the idea of going back there so unpalatable. After starting out in life as Hull Comets and evolving into Hull Association FC, the team assumed the name of a defunct amateur side, Hull City, when they turned professional in 1904, and began playing on Hull FC's ground. It was never a particularly hospitable home. In September 1904, City had to forego home advantage when an FA Cup tie clashed with a rugby fixture, and six months later rugby league's governing body of the time, the Northern Union, banned all ground-sharing between its members and soccer teams.

Having been rejected by rugby, City turned to Hull Cricket Club's ground, the Circle, on Anlaby Road. It was from there that the club launched a successful bid to join the Second Division of the Football League in 1905, and within six months the Tigers were playing on their own proper football pitch laid adjacent to the cricket ground. In 1910 the team missed out on promotion on goal average, after losing 3–0 to the club that went up instead, Oldham, on the last day; this remains the closest City have come to reaching the top flight.

Stability in the Second Division was the order of the day for the next two decades, until Bill McCracken guided City to the semi-finals of the FA Cup, via wins over Newcastle and Manchester City. The Tigers held Arsenal, the eventual winners, 2–2 in the first game before losing the replay 1–0. The result seemed to have a demoralising effect on the team, who were subsequently relegated for the first time.

Three years later City won the Third Division (North) title, in a season which yielded 100 goals – 41 of them coming from centre-forward Bill McNaughton. But within two years they were down again, and after the outbreak of World War II the club ran out of cash and folded. It was reformed in 1944, but with the Anlaby Road ground flattened by Nazi bombing, City moved back to the Boulevard for a season before Boothferry Park – to which the club had been intending to move for 15 years – was made ready in 1946.

That the ground was built at all owed much to local businessman Harold Needler, who took control of the club in January 1946. Needler's vision was that Boothferry would become an 80,000-capacity stadium, and although postwar building restrictions confined him to a more modest ground initially, optimism was high as 25,000 turned up to see City's first match there.

Inside-forwards Raich Carter and Don Revie were the team's stars of the era, and at the end of Carter's first year as player-manager (City were pioneers of the concept) in 1948/49, the team were divisional title winners again. The same season, 55,000 were at Boothferry Park to see Manchester United sneak a 1–0 win in the FA Cup quarter-finals – so much for Hull being a 'rugby town'.

Carter retired as a player in 1951, and Revie was sold to Manchester City the same year. The Tigers' decline was slow but inevitable – they were relegated in 1956, promoted from the Third Divsion three years later, then relegated again. Meanwhile Boothferry Park, though never to be completed to Needler's blueprint, was impressive enough to be used by Hull Kingston Rovers for 'home' derbies against Hull, and for games with touring sides from Australia and New Zealand. These provided City with useful extra income until 1963, when the Football League banned rugby from its members' grounds, a move just as narrow-minded as that of the Northern Union 60 years earlier.

Undeterred, Harold Needler tried to bridge the gap by gifting the club £200,000

Home for now – Boothferry Park, photographed from the *KwikSave* end of the ground

worth of shares and offering manager Cliff Britton a new ten-year contract. Britton repaid his chairman's faith by assembling what older City fans still regard as the club's most attractive side, with Ken Wagstaff, Chris Chilton, Ken Houghton and Ian Butler all hungry for goals and encouraged to go out and get them. All four were in the team that won the Third Division title in 1966, drawing more huge crowds to Boothferry along the way – 40,000 for a top-of-the-table clash against Millwall, 45,000 for an FA Cup quarter-final replay defeat by Chelsea.

Britton moved upstairs to become general manager in 1970, recruiting as his player-manager the former Arsenal centre-half Terry Neill. With Wagstaff, Chilton, Houghton and Butler all still on the playing staff, Neill's side finished fifth in the Second Division in 1971. Then, as the old boys retired one by one, City lost their way. Ken Houghton was persuaded to return as manager in 1978, but could do nothing to prevent relegation.

Houghton's dismissal led to City dropping into the old Fourth Division under Mike Smith in 1981. And although the arrival of Don Robinson as chairman and Colin Appleton as manager sparked a climb back up the League ladder during the Eighties, the club was beset by constant money worries. Meanwhile, Hull and Hull KR dominated British rugby league and attracted the lion's share of both media and public attention.

When Harold Needler's son, Christopher, sold his share of the club to David Lloyd in 1997, it ended more than 50 years of his family's involvement with Hull City. Sadly, it did not end the boardroom turmoil which continued through Lloyd's reign and rumbled on even after his departure. Meanwhile, the local council commissioned a feasibility study into a new out-of-town stadium that could be used by all three of the city's professional clubs, football and rugby alike. But City fans have seen it all before in their dreams. And also, it must be said, in their nightmares.

Here we go!

Unless coming from the south, **motorists** will approach Hull on the M62, which turns into the A63 at its end. Stay on this road until just before the Humber Bridge, then exit onto the A1105 (signposted Hessle, Hull). Stay on this road for three miles until it becomes Boothferry Road – the ground is on your right, behind *Kwik Save*.

Arriving from the south along the Humber Bridge (toll payable), turn right at the roundabout after the bridge onto the A1105 and follow directions above.

There is a **car park** at the ground but this is usually reserved for season-ticket holders and coaches. **Street parking** rarely poses a problem, however.

Direct cross-country **trains** link Hull with Leeds, Huddersfield and Manchester (service hourly, journey time 2hrs from Manchester). Fans coming along the East Coast mainline must change at Doncaster onto the Sheffield–Hull line (hourly, 1hr from Doncaster). Call ☎0345/484950 for the latest timings.

From the station, you can get to the ground by **taxi** (£3.50) or by **bus** (*Stagecoach #2, East Yorkshire #66*) from the bus station which adjoins its rail counterpart. On foot it's quite a hike – turn right into Ferensway, then right again into Anlaby Road and continue along for about two miles, after which you'll see the ground on your left, just beyond the railway bridge.

The last Manchester train leaves at 2153, the last Doncaster one at 2235 – with a connection for the north-east but not for London.

Just the ticket

Only months after David Lloyd spent £150,000 to reopen the East Terrace, City faced another extensive programme of works following a damning report on Boothferry Park by local safety inspectors.

Assuming this work is carried out in the summer of 1999, **visiting fans** will again be housed in the narrow strip of terracing in front of *Kwik Save* – enter through turnstiles #5–7. Those wanting a seat can get one at the north end of the main West Stand (turnstile #8). Ticket prices in 1998/99 were standing £8 (concessions £4), seating £11 (£5.50), with rises of around 25% expected for 1999/2000. There are facilities for

disabled fans in the south-east corner of the ground, again subject to works, as well as commentary for the blind in the West Stand – book either on ☎01482/327200.

Swift half

Favourite spot for home fans – and usually welcoming to visitors – is ***The Three Tuns*** just across the road from the ground. The pub can get very busy on matchdays, however, and the doormen get a bit edgy when there's a big club in town. Families are probably better off at ***Fiveways***, on the last roundabout before the ground if approaching along the A1105 Boothferry Road, with plenty of space and authentic Yorkshire fare on offer before and after the match.

Alternatively, ***The Olde White Hart*** and ***The Black Boy*** are recommended in Hull's old town area (follow the A63 along the Humber estuary).

Club merchandise

The **club shop** (open Mon–Sat 9am–5pm, later on matchdays) is next-door to *KwikSave*. The board asked fans to vote on the club's new kit for 1999/2000, with the result that City are reverting to traditional amber and black stripes, with no hint of white and absolutely no silly 'tiger' markings as worn earlier in the Nineties.

Barmy army

City's players are probably more at risk of being assaulted than visiting fans, after a succession of pitch invasions during 1998/99.

Scunthorpe and Grimsby are ridiculed, but Scarborough's last-gasp relegation in 1999 was a little too close to the bone to inspire much celebrating.

In print

The ***Hull Daily Mail*** has had endless fun with the takeover sagas of the past couple of years, and publishes a Saturday afternoon ***Sports Mail*** edition. City's travails have also inspired a particularly lively fan culture. There are now three fanzines, each with its own website (see below): ***Amber Nectar***, ***TOSS!*** and ***The Three O'Clock At Kempton***.

Book publishers have also been busy, with at least two new tomes about the club due to be published in autumn 1999: ***Hull City Football Club*** by Christopher Hilton (Tempus, £9.99) and David Bond's ***Hull City Saga*** (Breedon, £12.99).

On air

BBC Radio Humberside (95.9 FM) has match reports and a Tuesday evening fans' phone-in, but doesn't seem to have the ear of City's hardcore support.

In the net

Amber, City's once-official website, has been hijacked by the fans, with David Lloyd mickey-taking aplenty at: www.hullcity.demon.co.uk.

Amber Nectar can be found at www.angelfire.com/ok/ambernectar; ***TOSS!*** at www.karoo.net/dallandra/Hull_City/; and ***Three O'Clock At Kempton*** at www.geocities.com/Colosseum/Rink/8800/.

The most comprehensive site of all, though, is Andy Beill's offering at: www.karoo.net/beill/hullcity.html.

Tiger light – Gary Hobson models 'that' kit

Ipswich Town

Formation	1878 as Ipswich AFC
Stadium	Portman Road, Ipswich, IP1 2DA. ☎01473/400500
Ground capacity	22,500
First-choice colours	Blue and white
Major honours	League champions 1962; Second Division champions 1961, 1968, 1992; Third Division (South) champions 1954, 1957; FA Cup winners 1978; UEFA Cup winners 1981
Position 1998/99	Third in First Division (eliminated in play-off semi-finals)

A white Suffolk Punch horse strides out from the Ipswich Town badge, head up, tail flapping, football poised under one hoof. Its symbolism could not be more apt. Animal encyclopedias tend to refer to the Suffolk Punch as a cart-horse, better used for agriculture than for sport. But in the days of royal tournaments and crusades, Suffolk Punches were bred for their speed, stealth and stamina. As for Ipswich Town FC, they too should by rights be an agricultural lot, sole League representatives of a county where the fields of green are used for pasture, not passing. Yet this club has a reputation for stylish and innovative football as proud as any in the postwar English game – and deserves every ounce of it.

Exactly what has made Ipswich into a team capable of sealing domestic and European honours with a swagger is hard to pin down. For all its modest resources, the club is certainly ambitious, current chairman David Sheepshanks being the latest embodiment of the club's spirit of invention. On the other hand, Ipswich have also set great store by the unfashionable qualities of consistency and loyalty. There have been only nine first-team managers here since World War II, and two of those – Alf Ramsey and Bobby Robson – left only because the England job beckoned. The club's first president, in 1878, was T C Cobbold, and there has been a member of his family on the board ever since.

Perhaps the real answer, though, lies in the nature of East Anglia itself. So often dismissed as a soccer backwater, undervalued and overlooked, it has suffered none of the rugby distractions which bug the west, none of the industrial decline which has devastated the great football powers of the Midlands and the north, and none of the arrogance which has been the downfall of so many clubs in the capital.

In short, Ipswich Town have a lot going for them. There are no other senior clubs in the area; they have a modern, compact ground that does not need big numbers to generate an atmosphere; and they boast a proven record of developing young talent. All they need now is an extended spell in the Premiership – to prove they can provide the English game with more than just a potent historical footnote from the white horse with the golden touch.

The long-term stability which has helped fuel the team's development hasn't always been a formula for growth. One of the reasons Ipswich's success in the Sixties, Seventies and Eighties caught people by surprise was that the club was such a latecomer to the party, having turned professional only in 1936 and joined the Football League with just one season to go before World War II.

What took Ipswich so long? Left to its own devices, the club would probably still be amateur today. But the prospect of a professional side setting up shop in Town's backyard was enough to galvanise the board into action in the Thirties. And it had been much the same story back in the 19th century, when the club that would be known as Ipswich Town was founded as a rival attraction to one playing by the name of 'Ipswich FC'. The latter offered no direct threat, since the team played by rugby

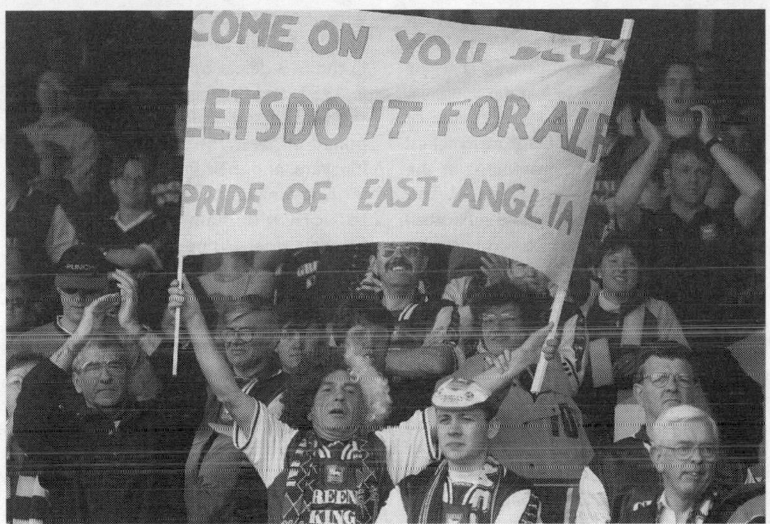

Portman pride – Ipswich are exhorted to make one last effort for promotion after Sir Alf's death

rather than soccer rules. But the locals who gathered at the Town Hall in 1878 to hear T C Cobbold's proposals managed to cloud the issue by calling their club Ipswich AFC. So now the town had two teams, both called Ipswich, playing different games at different venues, with neither able to generate much of a crowd.

Ipswich AFC had played at a number of (very rudimentary) grounds before settling at Portman Road in 1884. With Ipswich FC also laying claim to the venue, the sensible thing was for the two clubs to amalgamate in 1888, with the committed oval-ball brigade within Ipswich FC's membership leaving to form their own club five years later. The name chosen for the amalgamated club was 'Ipswich Town', but aside from this, it was very much business as usual. While the Football League was being established to increase the earning potential of professional clubs, Ipswich remained firmly amateur, not even deigning to enter local league competitions until 1899. Eight years later, the team moved to its current pitch at Portman Road (having previously used what is now the training area) and set up a limited company to build the first, none too impressive, stand.

The army then commandeered Town's home during World War I, and after they'd left in 1920, assorted farmyard animals moved in, courtesy of the groundsman, who kept them in the Main Stand. So it was that while the Southern League was being re-invented as the Third Division (South) of the Football League, Ipswich Town stayed out of both, preferring the company of chickens... No wonder the area was branded a backwater.

In 1935, however, chairman Captain John Cobbold was invited to a match at Highbury by the Arsenal director Samuel Hill-Wood, and left resolving to make Ipswich 'the Arsenal of East Anglia'. Cobbold's conversion to the professional ethos was timely, since Town would soon face the prospect of a newly formed full-time outfit, Ipswich United, opening their doors at the nearby Suffolk Greyhound Stadium. Almost overnight, the club's Supporters' Association raised £13,000 to improve

Portman Road, while Captain Cobbold reorganised his board and appointed Scott Duncan as his secretary-manager, charging him both with applying to join the Southern League and preparing a team capable of holding their own in it. Duncan excelled himself – Ipswich were champions at the end of their first season, 1936/37, and although his first application to the Football League was rejected, the club was admitted a year later, after he had written to every club individually to canvass support.

Ipswich finished that one pre-war League season seventh in the Third Division (South), a remarkable achievement for a club that had only been paying its players wages for three years. Attendances had more than doubled from the average of 8,000 that turned up in the amateur days, proving that Ipswich, for so long the biggest town in England without a professional club, had soccer in its soul, after all.

Perhaps inevitably, the club's rise was accompanied by mounting debts as costs sprinted on ahead of income, and one of Captain Cobbold's last acts before he was killed by a Nazi buzz-bomb in World War II was to plough £14,000 of his own money into Ipswich, so that the team could start again with a clean slate at the end of hostilities. Duncan then continued where he'd left off, attaining top-half placings in the League despite having to build the team again from scratch. In 1953/54 his side won the Third Division (South) title, but inept defending in the Second Division saw them relegated a year later.

The board now took a momentous decision. While Duncan continued as the club's secretary, it was agreed that the team needed a full-time manager if the next step up in status in was not to result in an immediate drop. Yet instead of appointing an experienced figure, Ipswich recruited a man with no track record in management at all – a former England international right-back, Alf Ramsey. As a member of Arthur Rowe's 'push-and-run' Tottenham side, Ramsey had won Second and First Division titles in successive seasons, so knew what it took to build momentum at a club. Equally, he had earned his last England cap in the 6–3 defeat by Hungary at Wembley in 1953, and had been deeply affected by the way he and his fellow defenders were pulled all over the park by the 'Magical Magyars' and their fluid formation.

Knowing that he had limited resources to work with, Ramsey began his job at Ipswich emphasising the togetherness of the team and the importance of tactics. His squad trained seven days a week, and although Duncan's personnel were not all to the new manager's taste, Ipswich were divisional champions again within two years of Ramsey's appointment.

With his club in the Second Division, Ramsey began scouting around for new players, preferring other people's cast-offs to youngsters. In the forward line, wing-half John Elsworthy and inside-forward Ted Phillips remained from Duncan's time, and Ramsey augmented them with Ray Crawford, a gritty centre-forward signed from Portsmouth for £6,000. Behind him, Jimmy Leadbetter, an inside-forward converted to an outside-left by a manager who loved to adapt players to new roles, made the midfield tick, with Roy Stephenson another reborn player on the right-hand side. At the back, Andy Nelson was turned into a towering centre-half, making sure the defence kept its shape.

The team's progress wasn't as quick as it might have been, but Ipswich was the antithesis of a 'pressure' club. Ramsey was left to get on with his job, and he in turn showed huge faith and patience when dealing with his players. Nobody was dropped, bullied, threatened or transfer-listed. When Ramsey was told Ipswich needed a goalscorer to get out of the Second Division, he replied: 'I've got one [Phillips]; but he's injured. I'll wait until he's fit again.'

He didn't have to wait long. In 1960/61 Ipswich won the Second Division title, scoring 100 goals in the process. During the close season before the club's first-ever campaign in the top flight, Ramsey made just one major signing, breaking the club's transfer record to bring inside-forward Dixie Moran from Falkirk for £12,000. Moran completed a three-man forward line (with Phillips and Crawford) at the head of a 4–3–3 formation that Ramsey was convinced would baffle First Division opponents just as it had left those in the Second Division standing. If it was going to work, however, it would have to work fast – before the other teams got the chance to prepare for it. And work fast it did. Ipswich won the 1962 championship by three points from Burnley, the title sealed with a 3–0 mauling of Arsenal on the season's penultimate day.

Though history paints Ramsey's Ipswich with the full glow of romantic nostalgia, they were not universally popular at the time. The 4–3–3 system compressed play, sparking accusations that the team's instincts were essentially defensive. It was also felt that the side lacked international class (only Crawford would ever play for his country), and that Ipswich's title was a triumph for organisation over ability. That was true, up to a point. But Ramsey's side was richly entertaining for all that, the cultured passing of Leadbetter and electric shooting of Phillips particular highlights.

The manager's worst fears about his team's limitations were swiftly realised, however. Their tactical approach soon lost its edge, as did the fitness level of a squad with an average age of 28. Jostled and jaded, Ipswich finished 17th in 1962/63.

Ramsey left to take charge of England, and a gamble by chairman John Cobbold (son of Ipswich's pre-war Captain) to bring in an outsider, Jackie Milburn, as manager backfired badly. Ipswich were relegated in 1964, and the title-winning squad drifted apart, though not before repaying the loyalty Ramsey had shown them – his first-choice 11 of 1962 went on to play nearly 3,000 Ipswich games between them.

Milburn resigned and was replaced by Bill McGarry, who got Ipswich back up into the First Division before leaving for Wolves in 1968. Cyril Lea took over as caretaker-manager for a couple of months, before Bobby Robson parked his car outside the ground for the first time in January 1969.

The club Robson joined was a very different beast from that which had welcomed Ramsey 14 years earlier. The Supporters' Association, whose subscriptions had paid for the building of Portman Road in the face of indifference from the local business community, was kicked off the board after the directors decided they would raise their own funds from now on.

In other respects, though, nothing had changed. John Cobbold assured Robson there was no need for a written contract, and as the young manager struggled to impose himself on the squad and Ipswich hovered around the relegation zone in the early Seventies, his chairman quipped to reporters: 'The manager's name at this club is not written in chalk on his door with a wet sponge nailed by the side.'

Eventually, after strengthening the club's scouting network to boost the intake into

The unlikely lads – celebrating with the FA Cup, Wembley, 1978

Sinking St-Etienne – Muhren and Platini, 1981

the club's youth setup, Robson got the recipe right. Ipswich finished fourth in the League in 1972/73, repeated the feat the following year, and went one place better in 1974/75, missing the title by two points. This was Robson's first great Ipswich side, and it was prodigiously talented, with established full-back Mick Mills joined by a clutch of home-raised players including Brian Talbot, Trevor Whymark, Kevin Beattie and John Wark.

The near miss of 1975 caused a temporary loss of confidence, and Ipswich had been relegation candidates for much of the 1977/78 campaign, before easing their way clear in preparation for an FA Cup final date with Arsenal. The Londoners were clear favourites but Ipswich, with a quick-witted forward line of David Geddis, Paul Mariner and Clive Woods, dominated the match. With 13 minutes remaining, utility man Roger Osborne swung his left boot at a loose ball to score the only goal of the game, then immediately fainted in the heat. Mills lifted the club's first FA Cup, while in the VIP box, Lady Blanche Cobbold, widow of Captain John, was asked if she wanted to meet the Tory leader Margaret Thatcher. She replied that she would rather have a gin and tonic.

The Wembley win provided the cue for another assault on the League, as Robson reinforced his squad with the central defensive duo of Russell Osman and Terry Butcher, striker Alan Brazil (latest in a long line of Scotland-via-Suffolk graduates) and a pair of Dutch international midfielders, Arnold Muhren and Frans Thijssen. In the event, the title would continue to elude Ipswich, who finished third in 1979/80 and second to Aston Villa the following year, when defeat in the East Anglian derby by a relegation-threatened Norwich halted their flow at a crucial stage.

But consolation that season came in the UEFA Cup. Ipswich had become European regulars under Robson, the manager revelling in the chance to sample the football culture of other nations, while his chairman made sure he got home in one piece after away legs by writing the name of his hotel on his cuffs.

In 1980/81 Ipswich beat Aris Salonika, Bohemians Prague and Widzew Lódz before annihilating the great French club Saint-Etienne in the quarter-finals, and sequeezing past Cologne in the semis. In the final they met a little-known Dutch side, AZ 67 Alkmaar. A 3–0 win at Portman Road in the first leg was, perhaps, the finest all-round display of the Robson era. And though AZ won the return 4–2, it was a game Ipswich always seemed to have control of – Thijssen and Muhren were outstanding on their home soil, the former grabbing an away goal early, the latter exerting total mastery over the midfield.

Twelve months later, the bombshell struck. Having rejected the advances of Leeds, Manchester United and Barcelona among others, Bobby Robson succeeded Ron Greenwood as England manager. His former assistant, Bobby Ferguson, took over at Ipswich, and while the UEFA Cup-winning side was gradually broken up, new talent suddenly stopped flowing through the Portman Road youth setup. John Cobbold's more austere (but no less eccentric) brother Patrick succeeded him as chairman, and the club seemed to lose sight of the things that made it special.

Relegation in 1986 was the inevitable consequence, and after a play-off defeat by Charlton the following year, Ferguson's contract was not renewed. His replacement, John Duncan, fared even less well, becoming the first Ipswich manager to be sacked in 1990, with the team still in the Second Division.

Former West Ham manager John Lyall stepped into the breach and the team, with John Wark inspirational in a defensive role after his second return to the club, were promoted to the newly formed Premiership as Second Division champions in 1992. Unlike Ramsey and Robson, however, Lyall had already achieved a great deal in management and, while he continued to live in London and took an increasingly 'hands-off' approach to team affairs, he was in no position to motivate as his predecessors had done. He resigned just before Christmas 1994, and George Burley, a former favourite as a right-back in Robson's teams of the Seventies, could not prevent relegation to the First Division.

Since then the club has reached the promotion play-offs three years in a row, and bowed out at the semi-final stage each time, prompting a feeling among fans that the only way Ipswich will reclaim their Premiership status is by finishing in an automatic promotion place. Meanwhile the Sancerre still flows in the boardroom, the white horse still stands proud on the badge, and manager Burley, secure in his position, preaches the old-fashioned Suffolk virtues of dedication, loyalty and patience. Someday, soon, they will pay off.

Here we go!

Portman Road is an old-fashioned town centre ground with all the problems of access for **motorists** which that implies. Coming from the south, take the A1214 London Road off the A12 toward Ipswich. Signposts will take you as far as a turning on the right, West End Road, along which there are several pay-and-display **car parks** on the right-hand side, while Portman Road is a 5min walk away on the left.

From the north and west, take the A14 eastbound as far as the A12/A1214 intersection, then follow the directions above.

Ipswich **train station** is served by direct trains running between London Liverpool Street and Norwich (fast trains hourly, journey 1hr from Liverpool Street, 45mins from Norwich). Evening kick-offs shouldn't present a problem but best double-check on ☎0345/484950.

The station is a 5min walk from the ground. Head straight out of the main entrance, across the river and down Princes Street – Portman Road is on the left.

Just the ticket

Visiting fans are accommodated at one end of the Cobbold (what else?) Stand in block V – entrance in Portman Road. There are 1,700 seats here, crammed rather tightly together, and no overspill area for big games.

Disabled supporters have 40 spaces in the West (formerly *Pioneer*) Stand – advance booking essential on ☎01473/400555.

Swift half

Ipswich has a thriving pub scene that also happens to welcome visiting fans. The official away fans' pub is the ***Drum And Monkey*** on Princes Street, where the friendly atmosphere is unaffected by a matchday police presence – they may even have videos of your team on the telly.

Rail travellers have the excellent ***Station Hotel*** between the station and the river, while there's a huge range of eating and drinking options in the town centre, a 5min walk along Princes Street in the opposite direction from the station and West End Road car parks.

Club merchandise

Ipswich joined the ranks of clubs offering supporters a say in the design of its latest kit. Opinion was divided, though – fans favoured a predominantly blue shirt with white under-sleeves but didn't like the blue shorts that came with it – so the club compromised and replaced them with white ones from one of the less popular designs.

See the results for yourself at the **club shop** behind the Cobbold Stand, right next-door to the visiting supporters' turnstiles, or at the Tower Ramparts store in the **town centre**.

Barmy army

Even when the hooliganism epidemic was at its most virulent, Portman Road had a reputation as a safe, friendly ground. Trouble is very rare, the town's easygoing atmosphere helping to head off the threat of violence before it starts.

That said, the whole place becomes unrecognisable when Norwich City are in town, and all hell breaks loose.

In print

The local ***Evening Star*** newspaper ublishes a Saturday evening *Green'Un* at around 5.30pm.

Fanzine ***Those Were The Days*** (PO Box 87, Ipswich, IP4 4JQ) isn't as backward-looking as it sounds, but Ipswich aficionados still have plenty of ways to get their nostalgia kick from books such as Tony Moyse's ***Suffolk Punch – Ipswich Town FC 1936–96*** (£9.99) and ***In Quest Of Glory*** (£7.99) which concentrates on the Robson years. Bobby Robson's own autobiography ***An Englishman Abroad*** (£16.99) has some fondly related chapters about Ipswich, while ***The Beat*** (£12.95) is the autobiography of one of Robson's favourite players, Kevin Beattie, whose majestic ability was never quite allowed to flourish after a series of disruptive injuries.

On air

Local commercial option ***SGR*** (91.1 FM) is primarily a 'better music mix'-type station but has some football programming on Saturday afternoons. Otherwise it's back with the Beeb at ***BBC Radio Suffolk*** (103.9 FM).

In the net

Ipswich Town claim to have had the **first football website in the world**, created as a single page of news and statistics at a *BT* research centre near the town in 1990. The site moved to the worldwide web in 1992 and five years later got its own domain name: www.itfc.co.uk.

Many of those responsible for the original site are still involved today, producing a site that's a nice blend of grahpics and hard info, including a complete season-by-season archive of results.

There's nothing among the unofficial sites to match it, although ***Stateside Punch*** is worth a look for the American perspective at: members.xoom.com/itfcusa/.

Déjà view – Matt Holland (left) and Mark Venus contemplate another play-off disaster, May 1999

Leeds United

Formation	1919 (after disbanding of Leeds City, formed 1904)
Stadium	Elland Road, Leeds, LS11 0ES. ☎0113/226 6000
Ground capacity	40,000
First-choice colours	All white
Major honours	League champions 1969, 1974, 1992; Second Division champions 1924, 1964, 1990; FA Cup winners 1972; League Cup winners 1968; Inter-Cities Fairs' Cup winners 1968, 1971
Position 1998/99	Fourth in Premiership

Leeds United are a team that inspire extremes of emotion. In the late Sixties, when they won the League for the first time under their uncompromising manager Don Revie, they were reviled in the wider footballing community for the way they would grind opponents down with a mixture of defensive discipline, intimidation and, at times, outright thuggery. Yet by the early Nineties, when Howard Wilkinson's side beat Manchester United to the title against the odds, they'd become the nation's darlings, a regular David to Old Trafford's Goliath. And in 1998/99, after losing their manager George Graham in mid-season and the accession of his likeable assistant David O'Leary, Leeds became every neutral's Premiership favourites, the only major team prepared to give youth its head, while all around them were locked in a race to buy the most outrageously expensive foreign imports.

When winning was everything – Don Revie, 1974

This change in the outsider's perception of the club is not reflected in Leeds itself, where United are regarded not just as a symbol of the city but of the entire region. In the absence of a major challenge from Sheffield – and with Bradford only just rediscovering top-flight football after decades in the wilderness – Leeds United are Yorkshire's great white hope, a source of mass inspiration and dogged, defiant pride, in a footballing elite that seems increasingly devoid of both. The team's relentless support has helped make Elland Road every bit as forbidding a fortress as Anfield or Old Trafford, perhaps more so. It has also, in the past, overflowed all too easily into violence, giving Leeds one of the

Can't say, won't say – the death of Leeds City

The precarious existence of **Leeds City FC**, founded 1904, never promoted above the Second Division and temporarily placed in liquidation before World War I, was brought to an end at a meeting in London's *Russell Hotel* in **October 1919**. City were alleged to have made illegal payments to players during the war, and after the club refused to co-operate with an FA inquiry, it was forcibly wound-up.

In fact, the illegal payment of so-called 'guest' players (other than legitimate expenses) was widespread during the war. Leeds City's problem was that they were found out. Or were they…?

The club's trauma appeared to begin at the end of hostilities when one of its players, **Charlie Copeland**, asked for his wages to be doubled from £3 to £6 per week. City offered him a rise of ten shillings (50p), so Copeland threatened to report the club to the FA over illegal payments. He was offered a free transfer to Coventry City, but went public with his allegations anyway. Once the story was out in the open, the authorities were forced to act.

Yet the whiff of scandal had been in the air for much longer. After war broke out, City's secretary-manager **Herbert Chapman** left the club to take charge of a munitions factory. The man he appointed to replace him, schoolteacher **George Cripps**, soon found himself embroiled in a personality clash with chairman **Joseph Connor**. Cripps wasn't popular with the players, either – at one point they threatened to go on strike if he continued coaching them.

When Chapman returned to his post in 1918, Cripps was shunted aside. Furious, he demanded a £400 pay-off and, like Copeland, threatened to expose alleged financial irregularities if his demands were not met. In the end he settled for £55, and under the terms of the deal, all the papers relating to his period in charge of the club were sealed in a box and stashed away in the safe of a Leeds solicitor.

A few months later, when Copeland chose to break the silence Cripps had kept, the FA asked City's directors to produce all the club's official documents from the wartime period. The directors refused, claiming they could not break the sealed box as it was being held under a legally binding contract.

Whether this was just subterfuge, a tall tale told in an attempt to head off the inquiry, or whether City were genuinely powerless, nobody has ever discovered. What is fairly certain is that if Charlie Copeland had got the pay rise he wanted, Leeds United would not exist today.

biggest hooliganism headaches in Britain for much of the Seventies and Eighties.

Today the atmosphere has cooled considerably, even if trouble has not been completely eradicated. And if the club is allowed to develop the expanse of suburban wasteland that currently surrounds the stadium as it wants, then Elland Road will, like Stamford Bridge, make the transition from down-at-heel, vandalised relic to ultra-modern sport and leisure complex, with all the benefits for the club – and side-effects for supporters – which such a change implies. Ensuring that the adrenalin levels continue to be pumped up inside the ground shouldn't be too difficult, however. Don Revie may be long gone and today's team may pay no more than lip-service to the doctrine he espoused, but the passion he helped to create remains as a lasting legacy. Revie brought Leeds and football together in marriage, and even now the city is too deeply in love with its team for there to be a risk of separation.

It wasn't always so. Soccer came late to the city of Leeds, where rugby was more popular throughout the late 19th century. In 1877, members of the local FA in Sheffield, where football had already established itself, took two teams, referees and goalposts to the Holbeck Recreation Ground for a demonstration match. The game was apparently well-received, but made no lasting impression on the Leeds public. Holbeck itself was home to one of five Leeds clubs thriving in what was then the Northern Union, later to become the rugby league. And it was the Holbeck rugby club which, in 1897, moved to an empty sports ground on Elland Road and built the first stands there.

Two years later, another of the city's successful rugby clubs, Hunslet, spawned a football-playing section. For a few years 'the Twinklers' played with modest success, winning the West Yorkshire Cup four times and beating the Old Etonians on the way to the quarter-finals of the FA Amateur Cup. But like all the city's soccer-playing teams of the time, Hunslet struggled to find a regular home and, without one, were unable to build a solid fan base. They finally gave up the ghost in 1902, but their directors remained convinced that a niche could be found for football in Leeds. When Holbeck rugby club disbanded following a play-off defeat to St Helens in 1904, the former Hunslet men saw their chance – they took over the lease to Elland Road (at which, curiously, Hunslet AFC had played one of their West Yorkshire Cup finals in 1898), and formed a new club by the name of Leeds City.

Despite City having no track record whatsoever, the club's directors – who included the landlord of the *Old Peacock* inn opposite the ground – decided to apply for membership of the Football League. Leeds was now the biggest city in England without a senior football club, and as luck would have it, the League was just about to enlarge its Second Division to 20 teams. In June 1905, Leeds were duly admitted along with Chelsea, Clapton Orient, Hull City and Stockport County. The team began their League career with a 1–0 defeat at Bradford City, but finished the 1905/06 season a commendable sixth. Average gates were around 10,000 – and, crucially for the future of football in Leeds, attendances at the city's rugby league clubs were all down.

The following season, despite the signing of centre-forward Billy McLeod from Lincoln, Leeds City slumped to tenth in the Second Division, beginning a gradual decline which was to culminate in an application for re-election in 1912. Herbert Chapman, newly arrived as manager from Northampton Town, campaigned successfully for City to be kept in the League, but while his emphasis on teamwork would soon see the club's form revive, off the pitch City were deeply in debt, being run by an official receiver until Joseph Connor, president of the West Riding FA, took over just prior to World War I.

After hostilities, City began the 1919/20 season promisingly, with only two defeats in their first eight games. Then came the bombshell. Former player Charlie Copeland

The Gentle Giant – John Charles outside Elland Road, 1963

told the FA that City had made illegal payments to players during the war (see panel p.260). After the club's board refused to co-operate with an FA inquiry, City were forcibly wound-up, their record for the season being taken over by Burslem Port Vale, who were admitted to the League in their place. Five club directors were banned from football for life, including Connor and Chapman – though the latter would be reprieved when it became clear he was helping the war effort at the time the payments were alleged to have been made.

As for the players, they were sold off at an auction at the *Metropole Hotel* in Leeds, attended by around 30 clubs. Billy McLeod made the top price of £1,250, but many others went for £250 or less. Also sold off were the club's goalposts, netting, shirts, shorts and boots.

For City's supporters, it was a desperate sight. About 1,000 of them went straight from the *Metropole* auction to Leeds' Salem Hall for a meeting aimed at forming another professional club to take City's place. While League chairman John McKenna insisted the club's punishment was justified 'to keep the game absolutely clean', the fans believed he would not allow Leeds to go unrepresented in the League for long.

They decided to call their new club Leeds United, and although Herbert Chapman could not become their first manager (he was still suspended by the FA), one of his former players, Dick Ray, stepped into the breach. It was hoped that Elland Road could be used for the new team, but the wealthy chairman of Huddersfield Town, Hilton Crowther, had other ideas. Frustrated by the lack of local support for his team, Crowther proposed that Town play all their remaining fixtures in the 1919/20 season in Leeds. His plan sparked a furious backlash in Huddersfield, and was soon abandoned – but Crowther himself had become committed to Leeds, and decided to back United to the tune of £35,000.

Secure financially and with a ground they knew they could call home, Leeds United were elected to the Football League Second Division in May 1921. Their first game, ironically, was against the Port Vale side that had replaced City the previous season. United lost 2–0, and poor away

The big man at the back – Jack Charlton is unruffled in Leeds' old blue-and-gold kit

'Like Real Madrid, feared by everyone, challenging for everything' – Revie spells it out, 1968

form (also a trait of City's before World War I) restricted them to 14th place in the final standings. Within three years, however, Crowther's cash had brought in enough talented players for the Second Division title to be won, and although Leeds were to endure two further brief spells outside the top flight, the foundations of a major professional club had been laid. Between 1933 and the outbreak of World War II, Leeds were a solid if unremarkable First Division side, with regular crowds of 20,000 being drawn to an increasingly developed Elland Road.

After the war, however, Leeds made the mistake of trying to resume with too many of the players who'd brought the club stability in the Thirties. The team were relegated at the end of the first postwar season, 1946/47, with just 18 points to their name. The following campaign was little better, with away form again a problem, and a first-ever drop to the Third Division being avoided by just two points. Attendances fell at a time when they were rising across much of the rest of the country, and after making modest profits in the pre-war era the club was now firmly back in the red. Suddenly in need of a lifeline, the board appointed the experienced Major Frank Buckley as new team manager. He immediately put the emphasis on youth, with one player in particular, the towering Welsh centre-forward John Charles, standing out as a potentially world-class talent. Yet while Charles would go on to break United's goalscoring record with 42 in the 1953/54 season, Buckley couldn't eradicate the team's inability to travel.

The Major did, however, lay the groundwork for his successor, Raich Carter, to take Leeds back into the First Division in 1956, with Charles again majestic and a young centre-half called Jack Charlton gaining in confidence at the back. When asked, much later, to pinpoint the difference between his game and that of his younger brother Bobby at Manchester United, Jack replied simply: 'Bobby could play – all I could do was stop other people playing.'

It was a while, however, before the rest of the Leeds side approached Charlton's levels of resilience. The team had gone 34 games unbeaten in their promotion season, but after Charles was sold to Juventus in 1957, Leeds lost their spark. After two changes of manager in quick succession, the side were relegated again in 1960.

By the time Don Revie was appointed player-manager in March 1961, almost all

Hunter and hunted – Norman leaves Keegan trailing

strip (the livery of the borough council) in favour of all white. 'We shall be like Real Madrid, feared by everyone, challenging for everything,' the manager told a sceptical press. With the addition of Irish winger Johnny Giles, snapped up by Revie after falling out with Matt Busby at Old Trafford, Yorkshire's Real Madrid had won their first honour – the Second Division title – within less than a year. The following season, Leeds bridged the gap between the divisions with a contemptuous ease, at one stage challenging for a League and Cup double after going 25 games unbeaten in the First Division and reaching the FA Cup final for the first time in the club's history. But Manchester United ended the title dream by winning at Elland Road in April, and the following month, Liverpool won 2–1 at Wembley, with all the goals coming in extra time.

of Buckley's and Carter's work had been undone. The club was £100,000 in debt at the bank (despite the £65,000 received for Charles from the Italians), and Revie's first full season in charge was a struggle – only a last-day defeat of Newcastle prevented his side from dropping into the Third Division. Fortunately, the board kept faith with Revie, who'd been fascinated by tactics as an inside-forward at Leicester, Hull and Manchester City, and who was already talking a good game at Elland Road, even if his team's actions still left a bit to be desired.

By the start of the 1962/63 season, Revie saw no reason to keep playing. The diminutive Scot Bobby Collins was doing his job in the team, cajoling youngsters such as full-back Paul Reaney and midfielders Billy Bremner and Norman Hunter into playing the way the manager wanted – nice and tight, with no tackle shirked and no lost cause given up. John Charles returned briefly before being tempted back to Italy by Roma, and Leeds finished fifth in the Second Division that season.

On the eve of the 1963/64 campaign, Revie ditched United's old blue-and-gold

With unprecedented glory beckoning, Leeds had seen red at the last minute. But the board were not fooled by the lack of silverware in the cabinet. They gave Revie a new seven-year contract, and the 1965/66 season saw United fighting (in some cases literally) on four fronts, with European competition coming to Elland Road for the first time. By the end they had only a second runners-up spot in the League to show for their efforts, but after more close calls the following year, Leeds began to win things with a vengance in 1967/68.

First the League Cup was secured by Terry Cooper's goal against Arsenal at Wembley, and then, in a two-leg final that was postponed to the start of the following season, the Inter-Cities Fairs' Cup was won with a 1–0 aggregate win over the Hungarian side, Ferencváros. Leeds had been fortunate to draw mainly Scottish opposition en route, but by the time of the final the club had played 16 European ties in three years, and some of Revie's favourite young players – including winger Eddie Gray and forwards Peter Lorimer and Mick Jones – had come through the continental test with flying colours.

Though they didn't know it at the time, the 1968/69 season would begin as it ended – with a trophy being paraded around Elland Road. This time it was the League championship, finally secured after a 28-match unbeaten run, and with a new record points total (under the regime of two points for a win) of 67. Only Burnley and Manchester City had beaten Revie's team all season, while Charlton, Bremner, Reaney, Hunter and 'keeper Gary Sprake had missed only one game between them.

Goals were still thin on the ground, however, and outside Leeds, Revie's team were not popular champions. Not even the addition of Allan Clarke to the menu of attacking options for 1969/70 could pacify the critics. Undaunted, Leeds embarked on a quest for a 'treble' of League title, FA Cup and European Cup. In each event, they fell near the last – Everton pipped them to the championship, Chelsea won the Cup

Paris in the springtime – the end of Revie's dream

After reaching the semi-finals of the competition in 1970, Leeds came one step closer to winning the **European Cup** five years later – only to fail in a blaze of controversy and bad publicity.

Swap shop – Bremner meets Beckenbauer

Jimmy Armfield had taken over as manager following Don Revie's move to the England job and Brian Clough's ill-fated 44-day reign. The trauma had already dealt a fatal blow to the team's chances of retaining their domestic title, but Europe was another matter.

Swiss champions **FC Zürich** were first to the slaughter, losing 5–3 on aggregate, with Allan Clarke scoring three across the two legs. Next up were the Hungarians of **Újpesti Dózsa**, who were beaten home and away, as were Belgium's **Anderlecht** in the quarter-finals.

A 2–1 win at home to **Barcelona** in the semis set up a potentially awkward second leg at the Nou Camp, but **Peter Lorimer** grabbed a vital away goal to settle the nerves, and although Leeds then had **Gordon McQueen** sent off and conceded an equaliser, they hung on for a famous aggregate victory.

The final would be against the holders **Bayern Munich** at the Parc des Princes in Paris. It was a game Leeds dominated for the first 70 minutes, having two good penalty appeals turned down in the first half, then apparently taking the lead through a blistering Lorimer volley from the edge of the box. But as the ball threatened to burst the net behind Sepp Maier's goal, the linesman flagged for offside against **Billy Bremner**. Standing in the six-yard box, he was not obscuring Maier's view yet the French referee ruled that he was interfering with play – an unthinkable decision today.

The decision visibly shook Leeds' confidence, and within ten minutes Bayern had scored twice on the counter through **Franz Roth** and **Gerd Müller**. After the match, Leeds fans rioted inside and outside the ground, leading to a one-year ban from European competition. And while commentators reflected on the ugliness of Bayern's sweeper system, a generation of Leeds players – Lorimer, Bremner, Reaney, Madeley, Hunter and Giles – knew their last chance of European Cup glory had gone. The Revie era was at an end.

after a replay, and in Europe, Celtic beat a clearly tiring side home and away at the semi-final stage.

In 1970/71, Leeds were again runners-up in the League, this time to Arsenal, who were a given a clear path to the double after Revie's men had uncharacteristically come to grief in the FA Cup at Colchester. The pain of losing to a Fourth Division side, however, was nothing compared to Leeds' distress in the title race, which they seemed poised to win before West Brom came to Elland Road and took both points with a clearly offside goal. Referee Ray Tinkler was besieged by Leeds players, Don Revie told the media he had 'never felt so sick', and the pitch invasion that followed would force United to play the first four games of the 1971/72 League season on neutral ground.

Europe was still a profitable battleground, however, and before the campaign was out, Leeds took the Fairs' Cup for a second time after beating Juventus on away goals in the final. With the new UEFA Cup coming in for 1971/72, Leeds were invited to play Barcelona, the first winners, for permanent possession of the Fairs' Cup. They lost 2–1 – another case, perhaps, of the pressure to perform backfiring on the team's morale.

Light in Eighties gloom – Arthur Graham

At Wembley the following season, though, the never-say-die attitude came into its own again, as the FA Cup was finally won for the first time. Two men personified the Leeds ethos against Arsenal – Allan Clarke, who braved a sea of flying footwear to score the only goal of the game with a diving header, and his strike partner, Mick Jones, who played on despite sustaining a broken arm, and somehow managed to inch his way up the famous steps to receive his winner's medal despite appalling pain.

Just two days later, Leeds had the chance to emulate Arsenal's double by drawing with Wolves at Molineux. But they lost 2–1, with Revie claiming his team should have had three penalties, before himself being the subject of allegations – never substantiated – that he had tried to bribe the Wolves players before kick-off. (With Liverpool also failing to win that night, the title went to Brian Clough's Derby County, who were on holiday in Mallorca at the time.)

Far from rejoicing in the club's misfortune, public opinion now sympathised with Leeds. For much of the 1971/72 campaign, Revie's side had played breathtaking possession football, and were scoring goals too – including seven in one game against Southampton. In a further move to bury their old image of 'Revie's Robots', the players began to sport number-tags tied around the tops of their socks, which they would hand to the Elland Road crowd after each home game.

In 1973, after the twin disappointment of losing both the FA Cup final (to Sunderland) and the Cup-Winners' Cup final (to AC Milan) by the only goal, Leeds freshened their appearance further by creating a bold new strip in association with the sportswear manufacturer *Admiral*. With the blue and gold revived as trim colours, a bold new club badge and further embellishments to the sock tags, the outfit became the first replica kit to have mass appeal across the country, confirming the team's transition from local Yorkshire heroes to that of a nationwide cult.

Just to put the icing on the cake, Leeds christened their new kit by romping to another League championship, with three Scots players – goalkeeper David Harvey, stopper Gordon McQueen and striker Joe Jordan – emerging to freshen the legs of an ageing squad. Leeds finished five points clear of Liverpool, and though Revie then left to become manager of England, the board felt they had the perfect replacement in Brian Clough.

How wrong they were. Revie's players were loyal not just to the man but to the gospel he preached, and when Clough attempted to turn the side's tactics on their head, he met with a brick wall of resistance every bit as strong as the defence that had brought Leeds so much success in the preceding decade. After just 44 days he was sacked, and the less abrasive Jimmy Armfield appointed in his place.

Domestically, Armfield's first season was a let-down – a mid-table finish in the League, together with a goalless draw at home to non-League Wimbledon in the FA Cup and defeat by Chester City in the League Cup. Excellent progress in Europe (see panel p.265) provided a welcome distraction, but after Leeds had fallen at the final hurdle abroad, a lethal atmosphere of melancholy was allowed to set in. Armfield won nothing in four years. His successor, Jock Stein, decided there'd be less pressure in the Scotland manager's job, and was soon proved right – the man who replaced him, Jimmy Adamson, was the subject of a hate campaign by fans before being dismissed at the start of the 1980/81 season.

Revie's shadow still loomed large over the club, and in an attempt to go back to the future, Leeds appointed Allan Clarke as manager. Clarke had performed a minor miracle in the lower divisions with Barnsley, but now he was torn between the need

A little local difficulty – Strachan at Rangers

to make attractive, big-name signings and plugging the leaks in the Elland Road defence. His nervous, uncertain team were relegated in 1982, and Clarke himself was replaced by Eddie Gray. A hard-working and occasionally inspiring player-manager, Gray put the focus back on youth but could not get Leeds promoted. By 1983 the club was £2million in debt, and chairman Manny Cousins issued a dire warning that if Leeds' growing hooliganism problem attracted any more FA fines, he would be forced to call in the receivers.

It never quite came to that, but hooligan trouble continued to hit the club hard in both pocket and heart. By the time Gray made way for yet another of Revie's old boys, Billy Bremner, in 1985, all Leeds games (home and away) had been made all-ticket in a bid to stop the troublemakers, with incalculable losses in gate revenue. For Bremner and those fans old enough to remember, the 1986/87 season was a 'so near yet so far' campaign to rival anything from Revie's time, Leeds going out to Coventry 3–2 in the FA Cup semi-finals, then losing a promotion-relegation play-off

A saviour from Sheffield – Howard Wilkinson

to Charlton in extra time of a replay at neutral St Andrew's. After that, it was downhill all the way for Bremner's reign – after being given a new contract in 1987, he was sacked barely a month into the 1988/89 season.

His replacement was Howard Wilkinson, an outsider who represented a break with tradition – in more ways than one. He'd left Sheffield Wednesday in the right half of the First Division table, but was attracted to Leeds by the ambition of club chairman Leslie Silver. Both men wanted to look forward, not back. Wilkinson took down all Revie-era memorabilia from the Elland Road foyer and sacked Norman Hunter from the coaching staff. Yet there were striking parallels between 'Wilko' and Revie. Like Revie, Wilkinson was a thinker who demanded total commitment from his players and repaid them with the benefits of a shrewd tactical mind. He was also, like Revie, a shrewd transfer-market operator with an eye for players whose value was lowered by poor form, but who could be revived with the right motivation.

One such was Gordon Strachan, the Scottish international midfielder Wilkinson plucked out of Alex Ferguson's leftover bin in 1989. Like Johnny Giles before him, Strachan would prove that there was life after Old Trafford, and go on to dominate Leeds' approach play with the same confident energy.

In the summer of 1989, Don Revie died after a long battle against motor neurone disease. Twelve months later, Leeds returned to what he always regarded as their rightful place in the First Division, promotion being sealed – amid yet more violence from the club's travelling support – with a last-day victory at Bournemouth.

To a promotion-winning squad that included inventive right-back Mel Sterland, combative midfielder Chris Kamara and striker Lee Chapman, Wilkinson now added goalkeeper John Lukic and playmaker Gary McAllister. With the homegrown David Batty and Gary Speed operating on either flank, Leeds were compact enough to finish fourth in 1990/91, their first season back in the top flight. Then, with Leeds and Manchester United locked in a two-way battle at the top of the table midway through the following campaign, Wilkinson pulled off another transfer masterstroke. Sheffield Wednesday had brought the nomadic French forward Eric Cantona to England for a trial, but couldn't decide whether to sign him permanently. So Wilko pounced, throwing Cantona straight into the first team and seeing an immediate widening of his team's attacking range.

Yet as the championship loomed closer, both sides were stricken by nerves. It was a case not so much of who would win the title, but of who would lose it. In the end, with one match to go, Leeds won a bizarre game at Sheffield United and, two hours later, Alex Ferguson's side lost 2–0 at Liverpool. Leeds were champions again.

The inevitable comparisons with Revie's side irked Wilkinson, but were pertinent nonetheless. In 1992/93, Leeds' form in the newly created Premiership collapsed, while in Europe, after gaining a reprieve from defeat by VfB Stuttgart when it emerged the Germans had used an ineligible player, Wilkinson's team were beaten home and away by Rangers – depriving the club of a lucrative and morale-boosting ticket to the Champions' League. Shortly afterwards, Cantona was sold to Manchester United, who would get the same vital boost in creativity on their way to the title. Leeds finished 17th.

European football returned to Elland Road after fifth-place Premiership finishes in both 1994 and 1995. Yet it was by now clear that whereas Revie had built a young team capable of serving the club for a decade or more, Wilkinson's side needed constant tinkering to keep it fresh. Some signings, such as the spectacular Ghanaian striker Tony Yeboah, were a success. Many more, including the out-of-shape Swedish forward Tomas Brolin, were calamitous.

The manager was booed by Leeds fans after his side had lost the 1996 League Cup final 3–0 to Aston Villa, and within six months both he and the chairman who had hired him, Leslie Silver, were gone. The club had been taken over by the *Caspian* media group and the new-look boardroom appointed George Graham, returning to the game after his worldwide ban, as the team's new manager. Graham was appalled at the lack of depth in the squad – there were some raw, promising youngsters together with a bunch of old pros nearing the end of their careers, but little in between. Yet the former Arsenal boss would not be panicked into spending huge sums on players, and Leeds' mid-table finish in 1997 was earned by gritty defending and the goalkeeping of Nigel Martyn.

In 1997/98, the arrrival of Dutch striker Jimmy Floyd Hasselbaink from Boavista and the transformation of Australian Harry Kewell from marauding full-back to auxiliary forward turned Leeds almost overnight from a sullen, safety-first team into a thoroughly watchable enterprise. Fourth place in the Premiership meant European football again, and all seemed rosy until Graham was lured back to London by Alan Sugar's Tottenham. After an abortive attempt to poach Martin O'Neill from Leicester, club chairman Peter Ridsdale gave the manager's job to Graham's former assistant, David O'Leary, and Leeds, with youngsters Lee Bowyer, Jon Woodgate and Alan Smith all inspired, equalled their Premiership placing of the previous year.

With record signings Michael Bridges and Michael Duberry arriving in the close season and O'Leary promised further funds, there is no doubting Leeds' ambition. As ever, though, second-guessing the team's future direction is a thankless task; predicting the wider public's reaction to it, harder still.

Here we go!

Elland Road is in the shadow of the M621 motorway. **Motorists** should exit at junction 2 onto the A643 Elland Road – there's parking just past the ground on either side of the road.

Leeds **train station** has its own branch of the East Coast mainline with direct trains from London King's Cross via Peterborough and Doncaster (service hourly, journey time 2hrs 30mins from King's Cross). There are also direct trains to

Dutch of class – Jimmy Floyd Hasselbaink

and from Manchester, Sheffield, Nottingham and a range of other destinations – check the latest timings on ☎0345/484950.

The station is a long and tedious walk from Elland Road – far better to get one of the regular shuttle buses that leave from just outside in Neville Street. Allow 10–15mins for the ride.

Just the ticket

Visiting fans are allocated either the whole of the South Stand or the south-east corner of it, depending on how many are expected. Ticket prices vary according to whether the fixture is 'A' or 'B' category, and note that concessions are only available if booked through the visiting club in advance.

Disabled supporters have superb facilities in the towering East Stand. Book in advance on ☎0113/226 6000. Visiting **families** are also welcome in the lower tier here – again, advance booking essential.

Swift half

The ***Old Peacock*** opposite the ground, whose landlord (not the current one, obviously) helped to found Leeds City at the turn of the century and from which United took their original nickname of 'Peacocks', admits visiting fans at the doorman's discretion. Once inside, the pre-match atmosphere is grand if a little chaotic.

Those arriving and departing by train have an alternative in ***The Scarborough Arms***, next to the station.

Club merchandise

The **club shop** (open Mon–Sat 9.30am–5.30pm, later on matchdays, entrance in Elland Road) at the ground has been supplemented by additional outlets at Burtons Arcade in the city centre and at the *Ridings Centre* in Wakefield. All sell a vast range of merchandise, including Leeds' new Lazio-style away shirt (£44.99, kids' sizes £29.99).

Barmy army

Bournemouth, Birmingham, Paris and tasteless chants about the Munich air crash notwithstanding, the worst of Leeds' many hooligan outbreaks came in 1985/86 when, just days after the club's all-ticket rule had been lifted, a group of 'supporters' sought to re-create the atmosphere of the Valley Parade fire by setting light to a burger van at Bradford City's temporary home of Odsal Stadium.

The days when the stomach turned (and the club's finances shrank) as a result of such acts are gone, but trouble has not been eradicated completely. A pity, as the vast majority of Leeds fans are as calmly well-informed about the game as their club's best-known managers have been.

In print

Look out for the 'pink' ***Yorkshire Sport*** on Saturday evenings, in addition to fanzines ***Square Ball*** (47 Holborn Towers, Leeds, LS6 2QD) and ***We Are Leeds*** (4 Avenue Place, Harrogate, HG2 7PJ) before kick-off.

The Revie era is recounted in detail by Andrew Mourant in ***Leeds United – The Glory Years*** (Bluecoat Press, £8.95), while the Wilko years get more sceptical treatment in ***Made In Leeds – From Bournemouth To Banqueting Suites*** (£5.99), a compilation of the best writing from the *Square Ball* fanzine. Bernard Bale's authorised biography ***Bremner! – The Legend Of Billy Bremner*** (André Deutsch, £14.99) is a worthy tribute to the former Leeds captain and manager who died in 1997 at the age of 54.

On air

BBC Radio Leeds (95.3 FM) offers excellent coverage of United including a well-patronised phone-in on Saturday evenings.

In the net

Leeds' **official site** is run by *Planet Internet* but is definitely one of the company's better offerings, with not too many graphics on the homepage and a thorough (and unusually frank) club history. A proper fans' forum and the usual comprehensive multi-media section complete the picture at: www.lufc.co.uk.

On the unofficial front, ***Jabba's Leeds United Site*** has up-to-the-minute news, a big historical archive and lots of video action, all packaged with a nice friendly attitude at: www.etrigan.demon.co.uk/leeds/index.html.

Finally, ***Square Ball*** fanzine is online at: www.luafc.ndirect.co.uk.

Leicester City

Year of formation	1884 as Leicester Fosse
Stadium	Filbert Street, Leicester, LE2 7FL. ☎0116/291 5000
Ground capacity	22,000
First-choice colours	Blue shirts, white shorts
Major honours	Second Division champions 1925, 1937, 1954, 1957, 1971, 1980; League Cup winners 1964, 1997
Position 1998/99	Tenth in Premiership

The 1999/2000 season may be the last that Leicester City play at Filbert Street, their home for more than a century. Unable to develop the old ground any further than it already has, the club wants to build a new, 40,000-seater arena on the other side of the River Soar, as part of a vast new retail and leisure complex. It could be ready for use in August 2000, but first there are a few hurdles to be jumped. While the City Council performed a spectacular U-turn to grant outline permission for the plan in February 1999, it came with strings attached, not least the possibility that the Government could call a public inquiry.

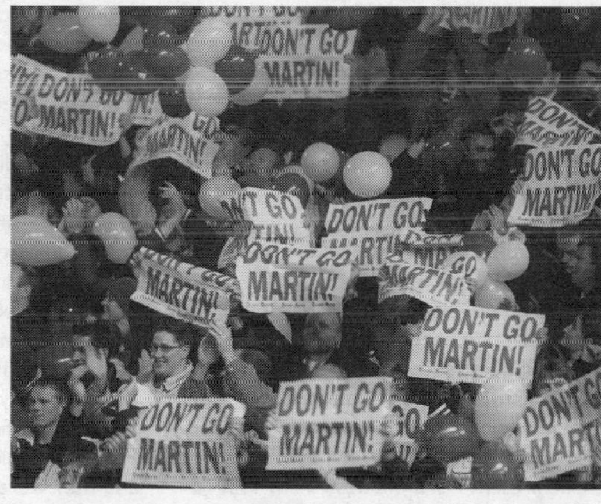

Foxes in ferment – fans plead for manager O'Neill to stay, 1998

All new football grounds are controversial, but City's stirs more emotion than most. It isn't just a question of the club leaving Filbert Street, a ground which, despite obvious limitations, justly inspires huge pride among the Leicester faithful. Setting their nostalgic attachments to one side, some fans doubt whether the team could regularly draw 40,000 to the new ground – the old one's capacity of just over half that wasn't always filled during 1998/99, when crowd levels dipped slightly by comparison with the previous year. And then there is the site itself which, although brownfield (it used to be a timber yard) rather than greenfield, still sets planners' nerves tingling because it is technically just outside the city centre, in an area where new shops are not supposed to be built. The impression is that the Council agreed to the club's ideas not because they were perfect, but because they were the only concrete proposals put forward for the regeneration of the city's Bede Island South district. Given the stadium's £25million budget, it will have a lot to live up to.

Then again, if City do go ahead and make a success of their move, it will be only the latest example of the club proving its point against the odds. Leicester may be big and bustling, but there are plenty of rival football attractions a short drive away, and the city itself supports a successful first-class cricket team (Leicestershire were county champions in 1998) and, unusually for the Midlands, a top-notch rugby union side (Premiership champions in 1999). For much of their history, City have appeared on the fringes of English football's high table, occasionally popping up for a top-half League finish or a Cup final appearance, but usually leaving long before the coffee, brandy and cigars. In the late Nineties, however, both team and club have taken on an air of surprising stability, proving that even in the pay-TV era, you do not need to spend millions on players, ride roughshod over supporters' views, or indulge in crass commercialism to play the big boys at their own game, and still get among the silverware. As well as success on the pitch, there have also been awards for environmental friendliness and, aptly in a city with a rich ethnic mix, City have been at the forefront of attempts to kick racism out of football. Cunning Foxes Leicester may be, but sly? Emphatically not.

For an insight into how tough life has been for Leicester City and to gain a broader perspective on the team's contemporary achievements, the obvious starting point is the club's inaugural meeting, held in Fosse Way in 1884. Most of those present were old boys from Wyggeston School, who wanted to formalise their team outside academic jurisdiction. But the whip-round they held for membership money raised only ninepence, and they had to hold a second one to buy their first ball. They decided to call their team 'Leicester Fosse', after the Roman road in which the meeting house stood, and for years afterwards the side would play under the unpromising nickname 'the Fossils'.

Yet there was plenty of life in the club, despite the name. Leicester turned professional in 1888, became members of the FA in 1890 and were invited to join the Midland League the following year, their election coinciding with the move to Filbert Street. The new ground, though built on a modest scale initially, was the first arena the club had had to itself, having previously hosted matches on a racecourse, a cycle track, a cricket field and a rugby pitch (twice). Suitably inspired, Leicester gained admission to the Football League Second Division in 1894, and Filbert Street was deemed sufficiently grand to stage a promotion/relegation 'test match' (a forerunner of the modern play-off, with which the city has since become wearily familiar) between Derby and Notts County the following year.

At a time when clubs were slipping in and out of the League with almost monotonous regularity, Leicester survived an application for re-election in 1904, and eight years later they were promoted to the First Division for the first time. Twelve months on they were straight back down again, having suffered a string of heavy defeats including a 12–0 hammering at the hands of Nottingham Forest. On the eve of World War I they were again having to apply for re-election, but whereas many clubs lost their momentum during the hostilities, for Leicester they proved a more welcome turning point. In 1919 Leicester Fosse was wound up, to be re-invented as Leicester City. The board hoped the new name – together with a new nickname, 'the Foxes' – would broaden the club's appeal, and they were right.

Under manager Peter Hodge, who'd taken charge in the year Fosse became City, and with Johnny Duncan and Arthur Chandler scoring goals aplenty, Leicester won the Second Division title in 1925. A year later they were top of the League, and although they didn't stay there long, the club's mood was confident. In 1927 Filbert Street was given a bold new double-decker Main Stand, and the following year more than 47,000 packed into the ground for an FA Cup meeting with Tottenham. Chandler scored six in a 10–0 demolition of Portsmouth in the League, and in 1929 City finished only a point behind Sheffield Wednesday in the race for the title.

The same heights would never quite be scaled again. Leicester reached the semi-finals of the FA Cup in 1934, but they lost 4–1 to a vengeful Portsmouth, and a year later they were relegated. Another Second Division title in 1937 proved to be a false dawn, and City finished the last full League

Tickling Filbert Street's fancy – Lenny Glover leaves another full-back grounded, 1972

campaign before World War II bottom of the First Division.

The club remained stuck in the Second Division for another decade after the end of the war, but there were to be a few highlights along the way, not least a fine 1949 FA Cup run under Duncan's management; after scoring ten times to beat Luton over two games in the fifth round, they beat Brentford in the quarter-finals and Portsmouth in the semis to set up the club's first Wembley final, against Wolves. That City lost 3–1 surprised nobody, for they had come up against a higher-ranked team at the peak of their powers – a pattern Leicester fans were to see repeated on more than one occasion.

A year after their Cup final defeat, City signed a burly inside-left, Arthur Rowley, from Fulham. Nicknamed *The Gunner* because of his wartime service in Germany and Palestine, Rowley was too good for Second Division defences and helped himself to 28 goals in his first Filbert Street season. He would go on to net 265 times for the club (second only to Chandler in City's all-time scoring stakes) and play a part in two Second Division title-winning sides, in 1954 and 1957. That manager David Halliday allowed Rowley to sign for Shrewsbury as player-manager in the summer of 1958 bewildered Leicester fans, and rightly so – his trusty left peg enabled him to keep scoring for the Shrews for another six seasons even though his pace faded, and his final career haul of 434 goals made him the most prolific scorer the League has ever known.

Yet Leicester did not miss Rowley's all-action style, as a quiet revolution took place at Filbert Street with the appointment of Matt Gillies as manager in 1959. A commanding centre-half during a three-year spell with City in the early Fifties, Gillies let his players know who was boss with the same cool authority he had exuded on the pitch. He also had an eye for emerging talent, bringing midfielder Frank McLintock, left-back David Nish and a young goalkeeper called Gordon Banks to the club. Banks and McLintock were both in the side that beat Sheffield United after two replays to reach the 1961 FA Cup final, when it was Leicester's misfortune to meet Bill Nicholson's irrepressible Tottenham, on course for the double and in no mood to allow Gillies' compact but limited side to get in the way; City lost 2–0.

Two years later it was a similar story. Leicester were firmly established in the First Division by now, but while their form throughout the 1963 FA Cup campaign had been impressive, in the final they could not match the burgeoning creativity of a Manchester United side just coming to terms with the aftermath of Munich. Another defeat, 3–1. Gillies remained in charge until 1968, having controversially sold Banks – a World Cup-winning hero with England in 1966 – to Stoke City in the belief that another 'keeper coming through the club's youth ranks, Peter Shilton, was a better long-term bet.

Gillies' successor, Frank O'Farrell, inherited a tidy and respected if unambitious side. To make Leicester more attractive, he gave free rein to Nish and the side's young outside-left, Lenny Glover, to join the attack whenever possible. City's football was flowing and Filbert Street lapped it up. Nish, who had got his first-team Leicester call-up while still at school, became the youngest captain in an FA Cup final when he led O'Farrell's side out at Wembley aged 21 in 1969. Yet despite a man-of-the-match performance from young

Fruit market to Filbert fave – the Boy Lineker

When Gary Lineker signed for the Japanese club **Nagoya Grampus Eight** in 1992, he joked that he had chosen them to 'fulfil a boyhood dream'. He had already done that, of course, by signing for his hometown club Leicester City as an apprentice 15 years earlier. Uncertain as to whether he would make the grade as a professional footballer, Lineker initially carried on working a shift at his family's fruit 'n' veg stall in town. But once he'd made his first-team debut against Oldham on **New Year's Day 1979** there was no stopping him – other than his uncertain first touch, his inability to hold play up and his reluctance to head the ball…

It was Leicester manager Jock Wallace who encouraged Lineker to begin **prowling in the penalty box**, rather than hang out wide on the right as had been his habit. With his range of skills steadily broadening, Lineker top-scored for City four years in a row from 1983, single-handedly keeping the club in the top flight before being **sold to Everton** for £800,000. At Goodison he won both England's player of the year awards, and subsequent moves to Barcelona (where he returned to the flanks under Johan Cruyff's eccentric coaching) and Tottenham (where he led the goalscoring charts again under Terry Venables) kept Lineker in the public eye. It was as **England's goalscoring hero** of the 1986 and 1990 World Cups that he will best be remembered, however – his exploits immortalised by the stage play *An Evening With Gary Lineker*, his place in popular culture sealed by TV celebrity and *Salt & Lineker* crisps. Not until Michael Owen would there be another *Boy's Own* footballer like him.

Tight fit – the Eighties' City slicker

striker Allan Clarke, Leicester were beaten 1–0 by Manchester City – their fourth Wembley defeat in a row. Worse was to come, too, as the fixture backlog created by a harsh winter obliged the team to play five games in three weeks after the final, and relegation was the consequence of inevitable fatigue.

The board sold Clarke to Leeds but stuck by O'Farrell, who engineered promotion before leaving for Manchester United and being replaced by Jimmy Bloomfield in 1971. Despite Nish being lured to Derby for a then British record fee of £225,000, Bloomfield set about creating arguably the most inventive side the club had ever seen, with Glover, Jon Sammels, Alan Birchenall and Keith Weller providing the passes for forwards Steve Earle and Chris Garland to knock home. A year later Bloomfield tossed another, even more flamboyant attacker, Frank Worthington, into the mix, and Filbert Street was transformed into an epicentre of mid-Seventies 'Fancy Dan' football culture. Back-heels, reverse passes, overhead kicks and flying headers were all part of the Leicester repertoire, and if it all broke down (as it often did), there was always Shilton in goal to keep the other lot out.

Bloomfield's side won nothing, but Leicester's mid-table stability of the time mirrored Gillies' record in the Sixties, and with a team that took a lot more risks. Eventually, though, the Fancy Dans went their separate ways. Shilton followed in Banks' footsteps to Stoke, while many of the outfield players went to America, where they were given more space to show off their skills, where the money was better, and where groupies brought a whole new dimension to the post-match bath. In September 1977 Worthington was sold to Bolton, and some would say the club has never been the same since. Bloomfield was succeeded by McLintock, whose lack of managerial experience was a factor in City dropping into the Second Division.

What followed was more than a decade of oscillation between the top two levels of the English game, as an array of managers – Jock Wallace, Gordon Milne, Bryan Hamilton and David Pleat – succeeded in making Leicester look top-flight material everywhere but in the top flight itself. There was no shortage of playing talent, particularly upfront where Gary Lineker (see panel p.274), Mark Bright and Alan Smith all learnt their trade as predatory strikers well-suited to the cut and thrust of the English game in the Eighties. But the club itself had lost its sense of purpose.

The supporters' patience was tested to its limits in 1991, when Leicester finished 22nd in the old Second Division, averting what would have been a first-ever drop into the Third only because the top flight was reverting from having 20 teams to 22. Pleat's coach Gordon Lee briefly took charge of first-team affairs while Leicester arranged for Brian Little to be brought over from Darlington as manager for 1991/92.

Little's impact was immediate. Touched by his straightforward enthusiasm, players such as Julian Joachim and Simon Grayson were encouraged to use their pace and vision, and Leicester looked as if they meant business again. There were successive play-off final defeats by Blackburn and Swindon before Little's side made it third time lucky with a 2–1 win over Derby County in 1994.

Alas, Little was poached by Aston Villa and his replacement, Mark McGhee, succeeded only in dragging Leicester back down again before fleeing to Wolves, in a blaze of bad publicity, at the end of 1995. City needed another young messiah, and found one in Martin O'Neill. Like Gillies before him, O'Neill was an intelligent motivator whose outward pragmatism belied an immense inner ambition. His passion for the game breathed new life into old pros such as Steve Walsh, Garry Parker and Steve Claridge, while raw talents like Emile Heskey and Muzzy Izzet were quickly refined. With team spirit soaring, Leicester reached a fourth play-off final in five years and beat Crystal Palace with a last-minute goal from Claridge.

It's in the net – the League Cup winner, 1997

O'Neill had no intention of stopping there, even if the pundits had already installed Leicester as relegation favourites at the start of the 1996/97 Premiership campaign. Occasionally inspired, always tough to break down, his team finished a comfortable ninth in the table, and were back at Wembley again for a League Cup final against Middlesbrough. City had won the trophy under Gillies in 1964, when the competition was in its infancy, the final was played over two legs and few regarded it as a 'major' honour. Now things were different: the 1997 final gave O'Neill the chance to put one over 'Boro's millionaires, and land a place in Europe to boot. City's resilience was tested to the full, as the manager knew it would be. But Emile Heskey's late equaliser earned them a replay, where Claridge stole the only goal in extra time.

Leicester might have earned an FA Cup final clash with the same opposition, but for a controversial penalty award to Chelsea in the fifth round. O'Neill, whose honesty in interviews was as potentially troublesome as it was refreshing, would have more cause to question a referee's judgement when City were knocked out of the following year's UEFA Cup by Atlético Madrid – despite outplaying the Spaniards for much of the tie, and taking the lead in the Calderón.

In 1999, a refereeing decision would again impair Leicester's progress, as they attempted to regain the League Cup. This time, though, it was uncontroversial: the sending-off of Tottenham's Justin Edinburgh in the final at Wembley crucially altered the Londoners' tactics, halting City's momentum just at a time when they were gaining the upper hand. Allan Nielsen's last-minute goal then deprived Leicester of the 30 minutes of extra time in which they might have made their man advantage tell.

Earlier in the season, O'Neill had appeared to waver over the chance to take over as manager of Leeds United, after they had lost George Graham to Spurs. By the time the Premiership campaign was over with Leicester again cosy in mid-table, and with the likes of Robbie Savage, Neil Lennon and Steve Guppy all playing the best football of their careers, there were further rumours linking the manager with Nottingham Forest. His next move, like that of the planners on City's new stadium, may prove very significant.

Here we go!

Like many city-centre grounds, Filbert Street can be a pig to get to by car. **Motorists** coming from the north or west should go into Leicester city centre on the A50 and follow signs for Rugby as far as Almond Road. From here turn right into Aylestone Road and then left into Walnut Street and left again into Filbert Street. The same approach can be used from the A47 to the east, but those coming from the south along the M1 or M69 should exit at junction 21, head toward town along the A46, go under the railway bridge and then turn right into Upperton Road. Follow this over the River Soar, and you will see the ground on your right. There is no official club **car park** but impromptu ones spring up around the ground on matchdays. Street parking is feasible but beware the area's fiendish one-way systems – it may take you a while to get back to where you originally wanted to be!

Leicester **train station** is on the main line between London St Pancras, Derby and Sheffield (hourly, journey time 1hr 15mins from London), with connections for Nottingham, Coventry and Birmingham. There are late-evening departures from midweek games, but bear in mind that the station is about a mile from Filbert Street, with no bus linking the two. For the latest train timings call ☎0345/484950. From the station, walk up Waterloo Way as far as the T-junction with Walford Road, turn right and them immediately left into Aylestone Road (heading in the opposite direction to the one-way traffic), then right into Walnut Street – the ground will soon appear on your left.

Just the ticket

Visiting fans approaching from the other side of the River Soar can't fail to be impressed by Filbert Street's majestic new Carling Stand, built in 1993. Unfortunately, they are then ushered into the south end of the much smaller (and older) East

Twin Towers of longing – Leicester's Wembley jinx

If the rumours are true and the Twin Towers of Wembley stadium are indeed going to be demolished, then Leicester City fans may breathe a sigh of relief. Their team's 1–0 defeat by Tottenham in the 1999 League Cup final was only the latest in a long line of **luckless defeats** at England's national stadium. Discounting play-off finals and a Charity Shield win over Liverpool in 1971, the club has yet to win a trophy there.

City's 1964 League Cup triumph was secured over home-and-away legs against Stoke, while the 1997 edition came in a replay at Hillsborough. Even the club's play-off record is middling – two wins out of four, with many fans never quite coming to terms with the **dubious penalties** with saw them lose the finals of 1992 and 1993.

It's in the FA Cup, however, that City's **worst Wembley nightmares** have been played out. Three days prior to Leicester's first Cup final appearance, against Wolves in 1949, their young playmaker Don Revie suffered a **freak nosebleed** that left him too weak to leave hospital for the match. City lost 3–1.

Against Tottenham 12 years later, Leicester left-back Len Chalmers was floored by a crunching Les Allen tackle after 17 minutes, and hobbled through the rest of the game as a passenger, suffering **chronic knee damage**. No substitutes were allowed; Spurs won 2–0.

None other than goalkeeping hero Gordon Banks chose the 1963 final against Manchester United to have the worst Wembley game of his career, twice **spilling the ball** for David Herd to score in a 3–1 win.

Finally, in 1969, Leicester's Peter Rodrigues had a great chance to equalise Neil Young's opener for Manchester City. But as the ball came to him it bobbled up suddenly and Rodrigues **miscued completely** before falling over backwards onto the sacred Middlesex turf. There would be no clearer opening.

Feels familiar – O'Neill consoles Cottee

Stand, from which the view could be a lot better. Ticket prices here in 1998/99 were adults £15 (concessions £7.50) for Block T, £18 (9) for the slightly superior Block U. The former has 17 spaces for **disabled visitors** – book through your own club, not Leicester.

There are only 2,000 spaces in total for visiting supporters and these are often sold out in advance. Check with your own club or call Leicester's ticket information line on ☎0116/291 5296.

Swift half

The city's rugby-soccer divide is thrown into sharp relief by its pubs, whose matchday clientèle tends to divide along code lines.

The Victory, at 21 Aylestone Road, is suspiciously close to the rugby ground but prides itself on being 'Leicester's Sporting Pub' with a broad appeal. ***Morgan's Sports Café*** in Belvoir Street is built into the ground floor of the *Grand Hotel* and has the expected massed ranks of big-screen TVs, while near the train station, ***The Wyvern*** at 57 Grandby Street has the screens and a wide range of real ales, too.

Club merchandise

City was one of the first clubs to broaden its range of merchandise from replica sportswear into the general clothing arena, through its *Fox Leisure* brand. The city centre ***Fox Leisure*** store in Churchgate (open Mon–Sat 9am–5.30pm) carries the full range, as does the **Filbert Street shop** at the north end of the Carling Stand. Never realised you needed nine different varieties of fleece? You do now.

Barmy army

There is a small but persistently troublesome element within City's hardcore support. Centred mainly in the South Stand (Kop) end of Filbert Street, their current favourite pastime is to hurl coins in the direction of visiting fans sitting at right-angles to them.

That aside, Filbert Street prides itself on being welcoming – providing a wholesome football experience without the anodyne connotations of what masquerades elsewhere as 'family entertainment'. Whether this genuine atmosphere can survive a change of venue remains to be seen.

In print

The back pages of the ***Leicester Mercury*** newspaper offer unbiased comment, with a refreshing amount of space being given over to fans' views. The Saturday morning ***Sporting Blue*** (formerly Green, but don't let that bother you) previews the day's big game while the ***Sports Mercury*** (colour – buff) delivers its verdict on proceedings after the final whistle.

As its name implies, fanzine ***Where's The Money Gone?*** (PO Box 391, LE5 0ZZ) is sharply critical of the current board, and chief executive Barrie Pierpoint in particular. ***The Fox*** (PO Box 2, Cosby, LE9 1ZZ) is more light-hearted but equally worth reading. ***When You're Smiling*** (PO Box 649, LE4 5YQ) is produced by the *Foxes Against Racism* organisation.

The most recently updated history of the club is ***We Love You Leicester!*** by Chris Lynn (CRL Publishing, £9.99), a book that strays far from the trail of statistics and is much the better for it. Frank Worthington's autobiography ***One Hump Or Two?*** (Polar, £9.99) is as idiosyncratic as the man himself.

On air

BBC Radio Leicester (104.9 FM) has the quality reporting; commercial station ***Leicester Sound*** (105.4 FM) has the phone-ins.

In the net

City's **official website** is *Planet*-produced but easy on the graphics compared with some of their offerings. You'll find it at: www.lcfc.co.uk.

The ***Leicester Mercury*** runs a much more objective (and equally informative) site at: www.lcfc.com.

For Fox Sake is maintained by members of the City internet mailing list, and is both thorough and funny at: www.forfoxsake.com.

Leyton Orient

Formation	1888 as Glyn Cricket & Football Club
Stadium	Brisbane Road, Leyton, London, E10 5NE. ☎0181/926 1111
Ground capacity	13,500
First-choice colours	Red and white
Major honours	Third Division champions 1970; Third Division (South) champions 1956
Position 1998/99	Sixth in Third Division (beaten play-off finalists)

When boxing promoter Barry Hearn strolled into Brisbane Road to rescue Leyton Orient from liquidation in 1995, he invited his sportswriter friends to a press conference and told them: 'Hold on to your hats, boys. We're gonna have some fun here.'

It was a prophecy which, thus far, has proved a fair way wide of the mark. Over the last four years, Orient have been relegated to the Third Division, had a series of applications for *National Lottery* cash turned down in their battle to rebuild their stadium, and at the end of the 1998/99 season somehow managed to play 300 minutes of play-off football without scoring a goal – missing out on promotion as a result.

Helping hand – Wim Walschaerts gets a lift from West Ham

There's still cause for optimism, though. With Hearn's business brain working overtime, the club has become financially stable again, crowds at Brisbane Road have risen, and the team under Tommy Taylor have become a compact, attractive unit, liberally reinforced with cheap signings from places like Peterborough, Swansea, Antwerp and Mexico City. Crucially, too, all this has been achieved without damaging Orient's reputation as an honest, likeable club. Far from being seen as local rivals, the O's have traditionally been regarded with affection by London's bigger teams, surviving on cast-offs from the likes of West Ham, Spurs, Palace and QPR, who seemed only too happy to release players for little or no fee, even though they may have had a few good seasons left in them.

One of the reasons Orient inspire such generosity is their sheer longevity. For decades the club has eked out an existence

Defiant in defence – Phil Hoadley, 1972

on the fringes of professional football in the metropolis, yet Orient were only the second London team to gain admission the Football League, and the first from north of the river Thames.

That was in 1905, by which time the club had already been in existence for 17 years, originally forming as the footballing branch of Glyn Cricket Club. One of their players worked for the *Orient Steam Navigation* company, so the team decided to call themselves 'Orient' – particularly apt given that the club's roots were firmly in London's East End, where much of the employment was provided by shipping.

In 1896, however, the team moved to Millfields Road in the more affluent area of Clapton, and within two years they had assumed the name 'Clapton Orient' in an attempt to win the hearts of local fans. It worked, to a degree, and also went down well at the Football League, who were always keen for clubs to have a 'sense of place' in their name, and who, with so many big London clubs at that time in the rival Southern League, were more than happy to welcome this team with a short past and uncertain future into their newly expanded Second Division. Orient finished their first season there, 1905/06, bottom of the table, but gradually got the measure of what was a mucher higher level of football than they'd previously played.

Perhaps because of the team's mediocre results, popular support was still hard to come by, and the club staged a variety of other events at Millfields Road to raise funds, including (ironically, in view of subsequent events) boxing. After World War I, a brief surge in both performances on the pitch and attendances prompted Orient to build two new stands at the ground. But by the mid-Twenties the side were back at the wrong end of the table, and the board reluctantly allowed a greyhound racing syndicate to take over Millfields Road, which became the Clapton Greyhound Stadium.

Now crowds of 30,000 could – and did – watch Orient's bigger games. But the greyhound syndicate took the lion's share of gate receipts, and after relegation to the Third Division (South) in 1929, the club teetered on the edge of extinction. A move to a speedway stadium at Lea Bridge caused more problems than it solved, and Orient were threatened with expulsion from the League because of their debts.

After rejecting a proposed merger from the East End-based Thames Association club, which had played just two seasons of League football and gave up the ghost soon after, Orient accepted an offer from Herbert Chapman's Arsenal to become a 'nursery club' for Highbury – an arrangement which guaranteed the club's financial future until the move to Brisbane Road in 1937.

Brisbane Road had been occupied since 1905 by the Southern League side Leyton FC, and would have remained so had they not fallen behind with their rent. When Leyton's lease expired, Orient moved in. And it was this new home, together with the vision of chairman Harry Zussman and team manager Alec Stock, that finally brought the club the stability it had craved after World War II. Zussman changed the club's name to 'Leyton Orient' (much to the old Leyton club's disgust) and set about rebuilding Brisbane Road into a proper football ground – something the club had never really had. Stock, meanwhile, was assembling a team of passion and purpose that would finish second in the Third Division (South) in 1955, and claim the title a year later.

After Stock left in 1959, his successor Johnny Carey picked up the flag and took the Orient express one station further – to the First Division in 1962. His side had few stars. But had the forward line of David Dunmore (ex-Spurs and West Ham, naturally), Malcolm Graham and Norman Deeley been able to keep up the goalscoring pace they showed in a 9–2 thrashing of Chester City in the 1962/63 League Cup, Orient might not have found the top flight such an inhospitable place. As it was, First Division defences were breached all too rarely, and the team were ten points adrift of anyone else when they were relegated at the end of the season.

By 1966 Orient had slipped further back into the Third Division, and the money was running out again. With liquidators poised to wind the club up, fans got together to raise cash, reaching their target by passing buckets around the ground on matchdays. Once saved, the club opted to drop 'Leyton' from its name and become plain Orient once again. It was a bold move, and before long the team would be reflecting the same courageous spirit, winning the Third Division title in 1970, and going on to spend the next dozen seasons in the Second.

Though the Seventies sides never attained the same League status as the one created by Stock and Carey, they were arguably more attractive, with Nigerian internationals John Chiedozie and Tunji Banjo playing the kind of improvisational football Brisbane Road had only previously dreamt about. Managers Jimmy Bloomfield and George Petchey did their best to encourage it, often in difficult circumstances, and the high point came in 1978 when, under the former's second spell in charge, Orient reached an FA Cup semi-final, losing 3–0 to Arsenal at Stamford Bridge. After that, Stan Bowles and Peter Taylor arrived to play out the last years of their careers but, entertaining as they were, they also distracted Orient from the main business in hand – the team were relegated in 1982.

Enter Frank Clark, who ended the 1981/82 season as manager. Once a marauding full-back who had won European honours with Newcastle and Nottingham Forest, Clark had seen at first hand how one man (in Forest's case Brian Clough) could improve his chances of raising a winning ream by becoming more closely involved with the running of the club. At Brisbane Road Clark became managing director as well as team manager, and while Orient's coffee-merchant chairman Tony Wood provided the money (and also decided to change the club's name back to Leyton Orient), it was Clark who did the

The rescuer from ringside – Barry Hearn

administrating, somehow fitting coaching, transfers and team selection into a busy schedule of inter-departmental meetings and memos.

In truth, Clark's side achieved little on the pitch, being relegated to the Fourth Division in 1985 before crawling back up via the play-offs four years later. His real achievement, meanwhile, lay in bringing stability to a club which had often seemed to be living a hand-to-mouth existence.

That stability, however, would not last long into the Nineties. Clark left in 1991, to be replaced by a more conventional manager, his former assistant Peter Eustace. His side maintained a steady presence in what had now become the Second Division, but after four years of treading water he made way for the partnership of Chris Turner and John Sitton. They were an unlikely partnership – Turner the team's experienced, always mild-mannered goalkeeper, Sitton the abrasive coach who'd maintained a threatening presence in Frank Clark's defence during the Eighties. The dressing-room atmosphere was fraught, but nothing could prepare the club for what happened next.

Tony Wood's coffee empire was based on plantations in Rwanda. When civil war erupted there in 1994, Wood managed to get out alive but his assets had disappeared overnight. When Sitton walked into his office one morning and found his phone had been cut off because Wood couldn't pay the bill, alarm bells began to ring. The PFA stepped in to pay the players' wages, while local businessman Phil Wallace tried and failed to raise enough money to buy Wood out. Of all the crises Orient had faced, this seemed the most dire – which is why there was such a collective sigh of relief when Essex-lad-made-good Barry Hearn felt a tug at the heart-strings from the club he had supported as a boy, and agreed to inherit Orient's debts, Ken Bates-style, in exchange for a fiver. In its history the club had been saved by Gunners and by buckets; now, to borrow from boxing parlance, it was saved by the bell.

Hearn dismissed Turner and Sitton, installing Pat Holland (a West Ham old boy, like Eustace) in the knowledge that a drop down to the Third Division could not now be averted. Meanwhile the new chairman announced a grand stadium rebuilding scheme titled *Orient 2000*, in which the pitch would be rotated by 90 degrees and Brisbane Road would become a facility for the local community – which opened up the possibility of *National Lottery* funding. The latter proved elusive, however, as did success on the pitch. Holland was replaced after 18 months by Tommy Taylor (ex-West Ham, funnily enough), who Hearn poached from Cambridge United – together with his assistant, Paul Clark – in circumstances that can best be described as acrimonious.

The duo have failed to work any miracles just yet, but as the team take the field to the strains of Herb Alpert's *Tijuana Taxi* for another season in 1999/2000, the suspicion is that it could be Orient's year.

Here we go!

From outside London **motorists** will approach as ever on the M25. Exit onto the M11 southbound at junction 27, and bear right at the bottom onto the A406 North Circular Road, westbound. Stay in the left-hand lane and exit onto the A104 toward Whipps Cross, then take the second exit at the next roundabout toward Leyton, then left down Leyton Green Road and left again at the T-junction into Leyton High Road. The ground is on your right at the next junction after about a mile. It's **street parking** for all around Brisbane Road and many of the streets closest to the ground are coned-off on match-days. Arrive early, be prepared for perhaps a 10min walk, and keep valuables hidden.

Leyton **tube station** is on the Central Line – allow 30–40mins from central London termini. As you leave the station, turn right onto Leyton High Road and the ground is on your left after about half a mile. The walk should take no more than 10mins.

Just the ticket

It's all change at Brisbane Road for 1999/2000, with a new South Stand (much smaller than planned with a capacity of around 1,300) scheduled to rise up during the close season and the remaining terracing in the Main (East) Stand being replaced by seats. **Visiting fans** will therefore now have to sit, though their location is as before, in the south wing of the Main Stand – entrance in Brisbane Road. Ticket prices in 1998/99 were adults £12, concessions £8.

Disabled supporters have a small area in front of the North Terrace. Book in advance on ☎0181/556 5973.

Swift half

The **supporters' club** at the ground welcomes away fans (guest admission £1) and comes *CAMRA*-recommended. If it's full, you can't go wrong at ***The Coach & Horses*** between Brisbane Road and Leyton High Road, where fans of all loyalties mix freely and there's yet more good real ale to choose from.

Club merchandise

Orient cut a dash during 1998/99 with their Croatia-style red-and-white chessboard shirts, but this looked set to change during the close season after the club attracted a new sponsor, the suitably laddish and upbeat pay-TV station, *Bravo*. See the latest design for yourself at the **club shop** in the Main (East) Stand.

Barmy army

There were 25,000 O's fans at Wembley for the 1999 play-off defeat by Scunthorpe, and the fact that many of them were really Spurs, Arsenal or West Ham fans in disguise doesn't bother Barry Hearn. No rivalries, no trouble – no worries.

In print

There's no Saturday evening paper and a real shortage of books about the club, but the fanzines make up for it. Choose from ***CheeryO's*** (10b Inglebourne Gardens, Upminster, RM14 1BG) and the long-established ***Leyton Orientear*** (2 Chelmsford Court, Chelmsford Road, London, N14 4JJ).

On air

GLR (94.9 FM) may offer a little more Orient coverage than ***Capital Gold*** (1548 AM).

In the net

Infamous Brisbane Road DJ Andrew Buonocore is the man behind the club's **official site**, still very much under construction at press time but looking quirkily promising at: www.matchroom.com/orient/. Best-established of the unofficials is ***O-Net***, which offers news and match-report archives and plays *Tijuana Taxi* through your PC speakers. Flag it down at: www.onet.clara.net/.

From the south to the Orient – Amara Simba, ex-French national striker, makes himself at home

Lincoln City

Formation	1884
Stadium	Sincil Bank, Lincoln, LN5 8LD. ☎01522/880011
Ground capacity	11,000
First-choice colours	Red-and-white stripes
Major honours	Third Division (North) champions 1932, 1948, 1952; Fourth Division champions 1976; Conference champions 1988
Position 1998/99	23rd in Second Division (relegated)

The headline on the evening newspaper hoardings was unequivocal. 'Disaster For City,' it read. But what did it mean? Was the river Witham about to burst its banks? Or the cathedral poised to collapse onto the town below? A major employer cutting hundreds of jobs, perhaps? It was, as a multiple-choice exam paper might put it, none of these. The headline referred to the fact that Lincoln City FC had lost their last game of the 1986/87 season, and as a result had become the first Football League club to be relegated automatically to the Conference. The sadness, as far as the fans were concerned, was that relatively few of the city's population had known of the mortal peril the team were in, or seemed to care. And now that the local *Echo* newspaper had spelt it out to the absent thousands, it was too late.

Fortunately for Lincoln – the city and its club – Conference football was endured for only a season, and has not returned since. But there was another 'Disaster For City' in 1999, as the team were relegated to the Third Division after spending only a year on the next rung up – their fate confirming the impression that this is still a troubled corner of the English professional game, for all the improvements made to the club's ground at Sincil Bank in recent years, and the modest increase in popular support it has helped to engender.

Like so many of the country's great tourist haunts (Chester, York, Oxford and Cambridge, to name but four), the city of Lincoln has at best an ambivalent attitude to the game. The cathedral dominates life here in more ways than one, providing as it does a small but influential ecclesiastical community that has little time for the travails of Lincoln City, and drawing a larger transient population of visitors that is even less interested. Meanwhile, rival League clubs to the north on Humberside and to the west in Yorkshire and Nottinghamshire, not to mention senior non-League sides elsewhere in Lincolnshire, all present alternative attractions for supporters to whom the idea of a club knocking around the basement of the Football League somehow lacks appeal.

And yet, in contrast to all the towns mentioned above, Lincoln has a long association with the game going back to the earliest days of organised football in Britain, while City themselves can trace their lineage to the Football Alliance, the competition set up as a rival to the Football League toward the end of the 19th century. If today's dispirited fans need grounds for optimism, they'll find them in the game's local heritage.

The city's first formal club, Lincoln FC, was founded in 1861. Players wore a uniform comprising 'red caps, belts and socks, with white jerseys, bearing on the left breast the Lincoln arms' – an outfit that would seem particularly appropriate when, ten years later, the club merged with the Lindum cricket club, after which the team became known as Lincoln Lindum.

The Lincolnshire FA was formed in 1881, and three years later, Lincoln City FC was founded with the objective of giving the city more of a presence in the many local and national competitions then coming into existence. Retaining the old Lincoln club's red-and-white colours – though sadly

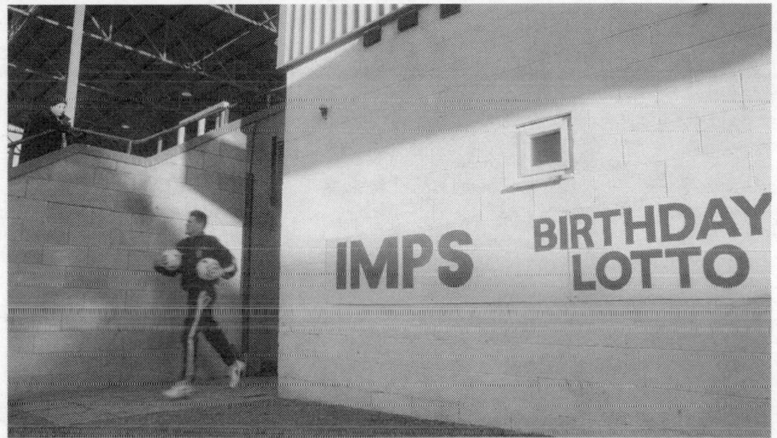

Late arrival – a Lincoln coach makes his way through the rebuilt Sincil Bank after getting lost

ditching the caps and belts – City played their first game against Sleaford on 4 October 1884, on a field known as John O'Gaunt's, opposite the city's Guildhall.

A couple of years later, City reached the Lincolnshire Cup final and the last 16 of the FA Cup, and in 1889 they became founder members of the Midland League, winning the competition in its first season. The team spent one more year in the Midland League before being invited to join the Football Alliance, which was now in its third year. But City's first Alliance season in 1891/92 would be their last, for the following year it was swallowed up by the Football League. Three Alliance teams were elected to the First Division of the League, while the remainder – including City and their near neighbours Grimsby Town – were invited to help create a new Second Division.

City were forced to seek re-election at the end of their first League season, and when their landlord at John O'Gaunt's died, they found themselves seeking a new home, too. They found a suitable site on Sincil Bank, but the ground needed substantial expenditure to be made usable, so in 1895 City turned themselves into a limited company capable of raising capital. On the pitch, the first few seasons at Sincil Bank were a struggle. But by 1900 Lincoln had eased into mid-table, and in 1902 they finished fifth in the Second Division – a performance the club has not bettered since. Another decent few years followed, but by 1908 City were back at the bottom of the League, and this time their application for re-election was turned down. The same fate would befall the club twice more, in 1911 and, after League competition was suspended during World War I, again in 1920. But each time City were re-elected within a year, their last reprieve coinciding with the formation of the Third Division (North) for 1921/22.

The club trod water for much of the next decade, but City felt confident enough to buy the freehold to Sincil Bank in 1929, and three years later, with centre-forward Allan Hall in inspired form, the team won the Third Division (North) title. The side could not, however, sustain football at the higher level and were relegated soon after.

The same pattern was followed in the years immediately after World War II, when Bill Anderson was appointed as the team's first full-time manager and led City

The Alicde test – striker Colin runs rings around Stevenage in the FA Cup, 1998

to promotion in 1948 and relegation a year later. Anderson, however, had more ambition than the secretary-managers of the pre-war era, and in the early Fifties he built a team of greater depth. In 1951/52, his side swept all before them in the Third Division (North), scoring 121 goals (including 11 in one match against Crewe, with Andy Graver grabbing six) and notching up 69 points. Nine solid if unremarkable seasons of Second Division football followed, with Graver returning to the club on two separate occasions to become the top League goalscorer in Lincoln's history.

Eventually, in 1961, Anderson's adventurous approach backfired. City were relegated twice in successive seasons, tasting Fourth Division football for the first time, and finding even that hard going – the club had to make four applications for re-election in five years to 1967, the last after the team had finished bottom of the entire League.

It was time for a fresh start, and while manager Ron Gray gave youth its head, the board set about trying to re-market the club to the local population. Out went the team's old nickname of 'Citizens'. Now City were the 'Red Imps' – the name taken from carvings of imps inside the cathedral – and, inspired by Bill Shankly's Liverpool, they wore all red. Initially the facelift seemed to work. Lincoln raised themselves to mid-table in the Fourth Division and knocked top-flight Newcastle out of the FA Cup third round – a club record 23,000 turned up for the visit of Derby County in the fourth. A couple of top-ten finishes followed, but by 1971 City were back to seeking re-election again.

Enter Graham Taylor, a 28-year-old former Grimsby Town full-back who'd moved to Lincoln just in time to join the 'Red Imp' revolution, and who the board made their new team manager in 1972. Like Anderson before him, Taylor consolidated for a couple of seasons before advocating attack as the best form of defence. In 1975/76, City won the Fourth Division title at a canter, scoring 111 goals and setting a new League points record of 74.

Taylor left for Watford in 1977, but not before instigating a number of innovations off the pitch, including the forging of closer links with the community and the setting up of youth schemes beyond City's normal catchment area. It was the product of the latter that helped Colin Murphy return Lincoln to the Third Division following relegation in 1979, despite the sale of star striker Mick Harford to Newcastle.

Murphy's football was more measured and defence-minded than Taylor's, but if anything it was even more effective. After winning promotion in 1981, City came within a single point of going straight up to the Second Division the following year.

Had they obtained that second promotion, Lincoln might not have fallen prey to the mood of crisis that was to sweep the club during the mid-Eighties. But sustaining Murphy's ambitions was proving expensive, and with losses mounting, City sold Sincil Bank back to the local council in 1983. Murphy was dismissed at the end of the 1984/85 campaign, but the last match of his reign would be remembered for other, much sadder reasons – a visit to Bradford City which would end with the Valley Parade fire.

Lincoln had been struggling in that last season under Murphy, but in his absence the team went into freefall, being relegated to the Fourth Division in 1985/86, and needing to win their last game of 1986/87, at Swansea, to be sure of retaining their League status. After sitting pretty in eighth midway through the season, they won only three of their remaining 22 games and, after losing at Swansea on a day when Burnley, Torquay and Tranmere all avoided defeat, City were down on goal difference.

Since winning the Conference at the first attempt in 1988, Lincoln have never come close to suffering the same demotion again. Long-serving chairman John Reames has spent much of the Nineties concentrating on rebuilding Sincil Bank, with a series of new stands made necessary, ironically, by new safety standards arising from the Bradford fire to which the club had been such an intimate witness, and built with the help of community and business funding made possible, in part, by the crusading spirit of Graham Taylor in the Seventies.

On the playing front, former Cambridge manager John Beck lifted the team to the edge of the play-off zone in 1997, but was then sacked over a contractual dispute midway through the following season. Beck's assistant, Shane Westley, won Lincoln automatic promotion in a caretaker capacity, but within months of the 1998/99 campaign, the club's first at this level for 13 years, he too had been shown the door.

Rather than recruit, to use his own words, 'another young manager with no experience or training for the job,' Reames appointed himself, as Michael Knighton had done at Carlisle and Ron Noades was doing at Brentford. Like those two, Reames surrounded himself with good coaching advice, but no matter how strongly held his conviction, he was powerless to prevent Lincoln from slipping back into the Third Division in 1998/99. Not quite the 'Disaster For City' of a dozen years ago, but a regrettable reverse, all the same.

Here we go!

Sincil Bank is notoriously difficult for **motorists** to find, but fortunately it is now well-signposted

Wearing his manager's hat – John Reames

That empty feeling – queuing up for Lincoln's legendary grub

Street, including the **Golden Eagle** at #21, which comes *CAMRA*-recommended and is the favoured haunt of the *Deranged Ferret!* fanzine.

Club merchandise

The all-red strip didn't last long, and City's home shirt for 1999/2000 is a nice traditional striped affair. The **club shop** at the ground sells both this and the team's fetching violet away shirt (£37.95, kids' sizes £27.95), plus a range of other items.

from the A64 Lincoln bypass. There's a small **car park** behind the Stacey West Stand at the ground, but street parking isn't normally too much of a problem.

Lincoln Central **train station** is on a branch of the East Coast mainline – change at Newark if coming from London King's Cross or Doncaster from the north. There are also direct trains to and from Sheffield and Nottingham. Call ☎0345/484950 for the latest timings.

The station is a 15min walk from the ground, out of town along Lincoln High Street. Turn left when you get to Scorer Street, then right at the T-junction onto Sincil Bank.

Just the ticket

Visiting fans are accommodated in the Stacey West Stand, named after two Lincoln fans who lost their lives in the Bradford fire – Bill Stacey and Jim West. The stand was scheduled to be made all-seater for 1999/2000. Prices are expected to be £12 adults, £8 concessions.

Disabled visitors have spaces in City's excellent Simons Stand – plenty of room so no need to book unless you want to reserve car parking.

Swift half

The **Centre Spot** social club at the ground, under the South Park Stand directly opposite the Stacey West, welcomes visiting fans and serves excellent food as well as decently priced beer. Otherwise there's a range of pubs along the High

Barmy army

The atmosphere in the city centre can get a bit edgy on derby days, but otherwise Lincoln is a safe and welcoming day out. At the ground, some home fans still bemoan the loss of the Stacey West terrace on which they once congregated.

In print

The ***Echo***, sponsor of Sincil Bank's St Andrew's Stand, still publishes the Saturday evening edition that broke the bad news in 1988 – available from around 6pm.

The ***Deranged Ferret!*** (see *Swift half* above) can be contacted at 185 Burton Road, Lincoln, LN1 3LT, while ***Lincoln City FC – The Official History*** (Yore, £16.95) by Ian and Donald Nannstad is available from the club shop.

On air

BBC Radio Lincolnshire (94.9 FM) has the ear of most fans.

In the net

City's **official website** is an excellent effort with news, e-commerce and a fine historical archive. Submit links, too, at: www.redimps.com.

Among a plethora of unofficial sites, ***Impernet*** is promising a revamp for 1999/2000 at: isfa.com/server/web/lincoln/; ***MRM On The Net*** is equally comprehensive at: website.lineone.net/~richmrm/default.htm; and ***Impnet*** has the tongue-in-cheek angle covered with spoof news stories aplenty at: www.impnet.co.uk.

Liverpool

Formation	1892
Stadium	Anfield Road, Liverpool, L4 0TH. ☎0151/263 2361
Ground capacity	45,300
First-choice colours	All red
Major honours	League champions 1901, 1906, 1922, 1923, 1947, 1964, 1966, 1973, 1976, 1977, 1979, 1980, 1982, 1983, 1984, 1986, 1988, 1990; Second Division champions 1894, 1896, 1905, 1962; FA Cup winners 1965, 1974, 1986, 1989, 1992; League Cup winners 1981, 1982, 1983, 1984, 1995; European Cup winners 1977, 1978, 1981, 1984; UEFA Cup winners 1973, 1976; European SuperCup winners 1977
Position 1998/99	Seventh in Premiership

Rogan Taylor, Liverpool fan, former chairman of the Football Supporters' Association and now director of the soccer research unit at Liverpool University, has no difficulty identifying the most influential event of the club's past decade. The Hillsborough disaster, he says, 'softened Liverpool as an institution'.

Prior to the events of 15 April 1989, Liverpool's players had appeared the epitome of relaxation, laughing, joking and singing their way through a period of domination – of both England and Europe – the like of which had never been seen before and will probably never be seen again. Yet their carefree demeanour disguised the precise, carefully controlled inner workings of a club which was, to use Taylor's description, 'like a cross between the KGB headquarters and a nunnery…austere, pure, efficient, a little bit frightening.' The supporters, Taylor says, 'didn't get inside the club – didn't expect to do anything other than walk through the gates on a Saturday afternoon'.

Then, in April 1989, the gates of the once-forbidding citadel of Anfield were flung open and its hallowed turf covered in a sea of flowers. The rivalry with Everton, a sustaining influence on the club ever since its inception, was symbolically reconciled by a string of alternating red and blue scarves stretching across Stanley Park. And the Kop's theme song, *You'll Never Walk Alone*, was turned overnight from a footballing exhortation into a lament for the dead. As the record surged inevitably to the top of the singles charts, hope and

A happy habit – the third European Cup, 1981

charity were in plentiful supply. But what of the faith?

There can be no doubt that the fans still have it. But, at the turn of the millennium, the old order which brought them so much joy has been turned upside down. The players appeared nervous and uncertain, terrified of making mistakes and burdened by the huge weight of history on their shoulders. The club, on the other hand, had lost its mystique and, in the process, its sense of purpose.

Why was Steve McManaman not offered an extended contract the moment the Bosman ruling came in? Why was Roy Evans not released from his post before the arrival of Gerard Houllier, rather than being forced to endure six months of ill-fated 'co-managership'? Why did Liverpool spend more than £20million on foreign players in the summer of 1999, when the club once boasted the best scouting network in the British Isles?

These are the sort of strategic errors Anfield seemed almost incapable of making for 30 years, from the time Bill Shankly hauled the team out of the Second Division in the early Sixties to the resignation of Kenny Dalglish in the aftermath of Hillsborough. Now, sadly, they appear to be the rule rather than the exception. Liverpool's absence from European competition in 1999/2000 was the most tangible consequence, and it will not be the last.

It was a clear, determined vision of the future that Shankly and the men who followed in his footsteps brought so powerfully to bear at Anfield, and it was the same vision that led to the club's foundation in the late 19th century. John Houlding, local businessman and future mayor of Liverpool, had been renting a pitch on Anfield Road from the *Orrell Brothers* brewery and sub-letting it to Everton FC since 1884. But by the time Everton had become founder members of the Football League in 1888, relations between the club and its mentor had cooled, with Houlding being increasingly resented for the amount he was charging in rent and for his insistence on a monopoly on catering at the ground.

The Saint who didn't lose his accent – Ian St John, Anfield, 1968

Listen, hear – the wit and wisdom of Bill Shankly

Breakfast table banter – Shanks and big fork

In the years since his death in 1981, the old chestnut about football being more important than life and death has haunted the memory of **Bill Shankly**, tending to obscure the fact that his obsession with the game was balanced by an idiosyncratic view of life and a generous sense of humour which he maintained throughout his career. Nothing sums this up better than Shanks' enormous legacy of quotes and anecdotes, most of them dating from his time as manager of Liverpool.

Many of the funniest were directed at the players Shankly brought to Anfield to build his first championship-winning side. Fellow Scot **Ian St John**, for instance, was asked to remember two things – 'don't over-eat, and don't lose your accent'. Hard man **Tommy Smith**, meanwhile, was told he 'could start a riot in a graveyard' and warned not to feign injury: 'What do you mean you've hurt your knee? It's Liverpool's knee!'

Other verbal salvos were for the media's consumption. 'If a player is not interfering with play or seeking to gain an advantage,' Shankly once told a journalist when discussing the offside law, 'then he should be'. Keen to stoke up Merseyside's traditional football rivalry, he also claimed that 'if **Everton** were playing at the bottom of my garden, I'd close the curtains'.

Even as retirement approached, Shankly retained his mischievous wit. When *Adidas* phoned to tell Anfield of their plans to give him a Golden Boot as recognition for his achievements, **Bob Paisley** took the call and asked Shanks what size boot he wore. 'If it's gold,' replied the great man, 'then I'm a size 28.'

In January 1892, Everton rejected Houlding's offer of the freehold to Anfield Road and decided to move across Stanley Park to build their own ground, Goodison Park. Houlding was unceremoniously booted from the Everton board, and now faced a dilemma. He could sell his lease on the Anfield land for building, but that would mean destroying the extensive stands and other facilities which he'd had built (at not inconsiderable expense) only a few years earlier. Alternatively, he could form a new team to play at the ground, a path that was also strewn with hazards, not least of which was the fact that Everton already had an established fan base and there was no obvious constituency of support for a rival club less than half a mile away.

Encouraged by a small number of Anfield loyalists, however, Houlding plumped for the latter option. He called his new team 'Liverpool FC', but while such a title might attract support from a broad area of the city, Houlding still needed a team to attract it with. Fortunately his business associate, John McKenna, offered to become club chairman, and began searching for players in his native Ireland and in Scotland – areas that would continue to be a prime source of Liverpool's playing talent for much of the next century.

On 1 September 1892, Liverpool FC played their first match – a friendly against Rotherham Town at Anfield, won 7–1. Two days later came a first competitive fixture in the Lancashire League, an event all too easily coped with by McKenna's organised, tactically aware team. After winning 17 of their 22 games and capturing the title at the first attempt, Liverpool applied to join the Football League. They were duly admitted to the recently formed Second Division in time for the start of the 1893/94 campaign, playing their first League game away at Middlesbrough Ironopolis on 2 September 1893.

Once again, Liverpool were simply too good for most of their opposition, winning the Second Division title at the first attempt after going the entire 28-game season unbeaten. The principle of automatic promotion and relegation had not yet been agreed, however, so Liverpool were obliged to play a 'test match' against second-placed Newton Heath (the team that would become Manchester United) at Blackburn to decide who would go up. Liverpool won 2–0, and one of English football's best-known rivalries was born.

Within a few months, another rivalry was given its first exposure on the field of play, when Everton entertained Liverpool at Goodison for a First Division match on 13 October 1894. The home side won easily, 3–0, and although Liverpool managed to scrape a 2–2 draw in the return fixture, it was clear they still had a lot of catching up to do. Most of the 44,000 at that first game had been Everton supporters, and Liverpool's shortage of local players made it hard for fans to identify with them.

Lack of success in the top flight was also a factor, for 12 months after their first test match, Liverpool were back at Blackburn for another – this time after finishing bottom of the First Division. They lost 1–0 to Bury and were relegated, but McKenna vowed his side would be back within a year and, under new team manager Tom Watson, they won the Second Division title again in 1896. After triumphing in a test-match 'mini-league' featuring West Brom, Small Heath (now Birmingham) and Manchester City, Liverpool were in the top flight again.

This time their First Division stay would be longer. After finishing as runners-up to Aston Villa in 1899, Liverpool won the League for the first time two years later, with a compact, highly organised side in which Scottish international defender Alex Raisbeck was the pivotal figure.

Yet Watson's team, for all their ability to keep possession and wait patiently for openings, were not as consistent as they might have been. The death of John Houlding in 1902 had an effect on Everton as well as Liverpool (at his funeral, pall-bearers were nominated from both clubs), but it was the latter that lost its more immediate inspiration, and within two years, Liverpool fans were watching Second Division football again.

Once more, Liverpool won promotion without hesitating, this time sustaining their momentum to take the League title itself within a year. Raisbeck still ran the show in that 1906 championship-winning side, but he now had England goalkeeper Sam Hardy behind him and a prodigious goalscorer in John Hewitt upfront.

The players were rewarded with a short holiday in France, but the supporters received a more enduring gift – a major rebuilding of Anfield. This included a new Main Stand designed by the *doyen* of British stadium architects, Archibald Leitch. But more attention was focused on a bank of terracing, the biggest in England, which was erected at the same time at the Walton Breck Road end of the ground. This was soon christened the 'Spion Kop' by Ernest Edwards of the *Liverpool Daily Post*. Although this term had earlier been used at Woolwich Arsenal, it had particular poignancy on Merseyside. The original Spion Kop was a hill in Natal (the phrase means 'vantage point' in Afrikaans) from which a vain attempt was launched to lift the siege of Ladysmith during the Boer War in January 1900 – 300 British soldiers died, many of them from Liverpool.

With these additions, Anfield could now hold 50,000 – an indication of how far the club had come in terms of popular support, which now mirrored that of Everton. From the word go, however, the Kop's sheer size made it hard to control, and the gates had to be locked with the terracing well below capacity for its first Merseyside derby on 29 September 1906.

Nor did the Kop witness immediate success on the pitch, Watson's team posting only a single runners-up spot of note in the years prior to World War I. And as if such anonymity weren't bad enough, the club managed to cover itself in notoriety on the eve of the conflict. With Liverpool safely in mid-table before the last match of the 1914/15 season and their opponents, Manchester United, needing a win to avoid relegation, the two teams arranged for United to take the game 2–0. When details of the plot emerged, four players from each side were banned from football for life. Yet neither club was forcibly relegated, as might have been expected, and after the war all the bans were lifted. The official reason for this leniency was that both clubs needed all the help they could get in rebuilding their teams after suffering wartime losses – but the fact that the president of the Football League was now one John McKenna might also have played a part...

After the war, new manager David Ashworth put together a fresh side which combined Liverpool's traditional attributes of finely honed tactics with more modern fitness and training regimes. The effect was devastating – two fourth-place finishes in the first two postwar seasons, followed by back-to-back championships from 1921/22. Again, much of the strength lay in defence, where Irish international 'keeper Elisha Scott and long-serving full-backs Ephraim Longworth and Don McKinlay provided the stability from which the team could counter-attack.

The press were convinced Liverpool would go on to dominate English football in

Pass the parcel – Hall, Lloyd, Smith, Lindsay and Clemence complete a lap of honour, 1973

the Twenties, but both they and the club were unprepared for the whirlwind of Herbert Chapman's Huddersfield Town, who promptly stole Anfield's title away in 1924 and clung on to it for another two seasons. While the team had moved on, much of the club's organisation was still laid along pre-World War I lines, and Liverpool could not match the spirit of innovation encouraged by Chapman at Leeds Road and, subsequently, at Highbury.

In 1928, the Kop was extended to accommodate 30,000, and given the roof that would provide it with its matchless acoustics. But the fans who crowded into it had little to cheer during the Thirties, as Liverpool dropped dangerously close to the bottom of the First Division and Goodison regained Merseyside ascendancy.

Yet Anfield could not have begun the period after World War II in better style. Manager George Kay continued where he'd left off before the conflict, providing vital continuity while the squad itself was dramatically altered. Most influential of the newcomers was Billy Liddell, a lightning-quick winger from Scotland who'd signed for Liverpool just as war was about to break out. On the opposite wing from Liddell was Bob Paisley, a less spectacular but still useful performer who'd signed at the same time from Bishop Auckland. With forwards Bert Stubbins and Jack Balmer both in feverish goalscoring mood, Liverpool won the League in 1946/47 with what was, perhaps, the most exciting of all the club's title-winning teams thus far.

Greece is the word – in the news in Athens

Yet the team's sense of adventure would cost the club dear. As their old defensive solidity deserted them, Liverpool slid down the First Division table in the late Forties, and after Kay retired due to ill health in 1952, the side began to look increasingly directionless. Liddell's ability to take on defenders, cut inside and score goals was preserving the club's top-flight status almost singlehanded, but relegation eventually came in 1954.

The following year, the team finished 11th in the Second Division – the lowest League position in the club's history. Don Welsh became the first Liverpool manager to be sacked, and his successor Phil Taylor strove gamely to revive the club despite having a limited squad. In November 1959 Taylor resigned, and Anfield chairman T V Williams knew who he wanted to appoint in his place – the manager of Huddersfield Town, Bill Shankly. At Huddersfield, Shankly had initially worked as an assistant to his friend Andy Beattie before taking the manager's job for three seasons. But he had also been in charge of Carlisle, Grimsby and Workington Town, and at each club he had pursued his trademark approach – assembling successful teams while also inspiring a surge in local support with his almost evangelical zeal for the game. Now Williams wanted 'Shanks' to do the same at Anfield, but the former Scottish international wing-half came with a list of demands – not least that the Liverpool board give up their long-held influence over team selection, and put the manager in sole charge of transfer policy.

Williams agreed, and Shankly immediately bought two muscular Scots players he'd wanted at Huddersfield but had not been able to afford: Motherwell forward Ian St John and centre-half Ron Yeats from Dundee United. Cleverly, Shankly also sought to ensure that local fans were not alienated by appointing Paisley, an Anfield man, along with a thoroughbred Scouser, Joe Fagan, as his assistants.

Even so, the club's squad was rich on hard-working players and relatively low on natural talent. Over the ensuing first 12 months of his reign, Shankly released half of Liverpool's senior playing staff, trusting instead in younger talents such as outside-right Ian Callaghan and centre-forward Roger Hunt. With left-back Gordon Milne, a cheap buy from Preston, Shankly now had a side capable of winning promotion. Sadly, the old stager Billy Liddell would not be around to share in it, hanging up his boots in 1961 after scoring 216 goals in almost 500 games for the club. Liddell's departure from the scene was poignant because, unlike so many who were at Liverpool in the Fifties, he was very much Shankly's kind of player – not a 'marathon runner' obsessed with fitness, but a ball-player who liked nothing better than to be part of a team.

For this was to be the new Anfield gospel – better to pass the ball back to a red shirt than lose possession by banging it forward. In some ways the philosophy harked back to the club's earliest glory days at the turn of the century. But under Shankly it was to become part of a much wider message. His players would improve together by playing together, until they had formed their own community. And the fans, particularly the seething mass that stood on the Kop, would feel that they, too, were a part of that community. In 1962, Shankly's Liverpool won the Second Division championship, scoring 99 goals and finishing eight points clear of Leyton Orient in second place. The following year the side finished eighth in the First Division – a creditable debut, but not enough to satisfy Shankly, who then strengthened his squad with goalkeeper Tommy Lawrence and wingers Willie Stevenson and Peter Thompson.

In 1963/64 the jigsaw was complete. Liverpool were League champions again, and Shankly's whole footballing philosophy, honed over long years at a succession of impoverished clubs, was finally vindicated at the highest level. Hunt and St John, lavishly supplied from the flanks by a team that used every blade of grass on the Anfield pitch, scored 52 goals between them, while the defence in front of Lawrence was the meanest in the division.

English football was converted to the Shankly religion, and during 1964/65 the continent followed suit, Liverpool progressing to the semi-finals of the European Cup before losing to Inter Milan, in a tie later exposed to have been refereed by an official bribed by the Italian club. Back home, Matt Busby's Manchester United snatched Liverpool's title from them, but there was compensation in the FA Cup. This had never been the club's favourite competition, though Billy Liddell's team had made a solitary Wembley appearance, losing 2–0 to Arsenal in 1950. Shankly's side would present a stiffer barrier, beating Leeds 2–1 in a game that did not come to life until extra time, when Hunt and St John, inevitably, scored Liverpool's goals.

In 1965/66, keen to win his title straight back, Shankly rebuilt his side around Tommy Smith, another defensive hard man and another product of Anfield's now burgeoning youth system. The modest change of tack, with Smith masterminding a more cautious approach than two years earlier, worked a treat, Hunt scoring another 30 title-winning goals. At the end of the season Hunt was also on target at Hampden Park – where Liverpool lost the European Cup-Winners' Cup final to Borussia Dortmund after extra time – before going off to help England win the 1966 World Cup. With the country in euphoric mood and Merseybeat providing the soundtrack to it, the Kop adopted Gerry & The Pacemakers' *You'll Never Walk Alone* as its signature tune – though its blend of optimism and melancholy, perfectly suited to the ups and downs of football, ensured that it was quickly adopted at other clubs.

As it turned out, Anfield would have a fair bit to be melancholy about over the next few years. Shankly made a series of poor signings, and defeat by Arsenal in the 1971 FA Cup final raised questions as to whether his purist approach to the game might be less effective in the face of the work-rate ethic espoused by the Gunners' Bertie Mee and Don Revie at Leeds. Shankly would have none of it, and within two years, his new strikeforce of Kevin Keegan and John Toshack, together with a reinforced backbone containing goalkeeper Ray Clemence, Larry Lloyd and Emlyn Hughes among others, brought the League championship back to Anfield. They also captured the UEFA Cup, the club's first European honour, beating Borussia Mönchengladbach 3–2 on aggregate after taking a three-goal advantage to Germany.

The following year, an effortless Wembley display, with Keegan, winger Steve Heighway and the veteran Callaghan all outstanding, saw the FA Cup regained with a 3–0 mauling of Newcastle. Two months later, Shankly called a press conference to introduce his latest signing, Arsenal striker Ray Kennedy. He then stunned the assembled media by announcing his retirement. It was a typical gesture from a man who loved to have the last laugh, but it left the media muttering darkly about the end of an Anfield era.

Yet the aura of invincibility Shankly had constructed – from the dedicated atmosphere of the boot room to the symbolic 'This Is Anfield' notice above the players' tunnel – was to be not just preserved but enhanced by his appointed successor, Bob Paisley. After a transitional season in 1974/75, Paisley led the club to a second 'double' of League title and UEFA Cup, and in 1977 Liverpool not only retained the domestic championship but attained the holy grail of the European Cup, again beating Mönchengladbach – 3–1 in the final in Rome. Only an unlucky 2–1 defeat by

The finisher from Flint – Ian Rush celebrates sealing a League and Cup double, 1986

Exit from Europe – the horror of Heysel

Inconsolable – Dalglish walks from the pitch

Of all the English clubs regularly involved in European competition during the Seventies and Eighties, **Liverpool** were thought to have one of the less serious hooligan problems – until the events of 29 May 1985 unfolded in all their macabre, monstrous detail.

Joe Fagan's side were due to meet the Italian champions **Juventus** in the European Cup Final – an eagerly awaited climax to the season which would pit the Liverpool of **Hansen, Dalglish** and **Rush** against a Juve line-up containing a string of internationals including **Scirea, Platini** and **Boniek**. Thousands of fans from both clubs had converged on the Belgian capital, **Brussels**, for the game, and during the day local police seemed happy to let Liverpool supporters drink large quantities of strong local lager in the city's *Grand Place*.

Yet the carnival atmosphere of the afternoon would turn ugly once supporters had converged on the **Heysel Stadium**. An element of Liverpool's support, scarred by the brutal treatment they'd received from police in **Rome** after the previous year's final, were determined to exact a twisted revenge on their Italian counterparts. Juve's support contained a violent contingent of its own, but most of them were at the other end of the ground when, in the minutes before kick-off, a group of Liverpool fans attempted to storm a section of the stadium theoretically allocated to neutrals. In the rush of bodies, a concrete wall collapsed, crushing 39 people to death, most of them Italian.

To avert the risk of further deaths in an atmosphere that was becoming increasingly poisonous, the match was played out after a long delay, Juve winning with a single goal from the penalty spot – though it was clear that neither set of players' hearts were in it.

In the aftermath, English clubs were **banned from European football** for five years, with Liverpool serving a further year before being re-admitted in 1991. Fourteen Englishmen were prosecuted for manslaughter by the Belgian courts, some of them turning out to be not Liverpool fans at all but far right-wing troublemakers with no interest in football. Given lengthy prison sentences, they were soon released. Yet the damage, both to the lives of those affected by the tragedy and to the reputation of the club, had already been done.

Manchester United in that season's FA Cup final blotted the copybook.

For Paisley, continuity was the key to everything. Shankly's passing style was sacrosanct, and as each new signing arrived, so the manager made sure they would play the Liverpool way. When Kennedy struggled upfront, Paisley switched him to midfield, where he would become more influential than he'd ever been at Highbury. When Keegan exercised the option he'd requested to leave the club after the European Cup was won, Paisley spent most of the £500,000 transfer fee received from Hamburg SV to bring a tailor-made replacement, Kenny Dalglish, to Anfield from Celtic. Together with two other Scotsmen, central defender Allan Hansen and combative midfielder Graeme Souness, Dalglish led Liverpool to a successful defence of

A docker's dream – Scouse idol Robbie Fowler

their European crown in 1978, Wembley providing the backdrop for a calmly controlled 1–0 win over Belgium's Club Bruges.

Brian Clough's Nottingham Forest won the League that year, and the following season they would put Paisley's side out of Europe before going on to lift the European Cup themselves. But Liverpool were nothing if not resilient. They seized back the domestic title in 1979, retained it the following year, and regained their European crown in 1981, full-back Alan Kennedy stealing forward to grab the only goal of the game against Real Madrid in Paris.

With the Militant Tendency running the city council and putting Merseyside on a collision course with the Thatcher Government, the atmosphere at Anfield had changed from Shankly's day. Then, Liverpool's football seemed to confirm the promise of a brighter world. Now it offered an escape from the grim realities of rioting, rising crime and unemployment. When the man himself died of a heart attack in 1981, the club sought to bridge the gap between the two eras by erecting 'the Shankly Gates' at the main entrance to the ground.

It was a touching gesture (if a little ironic – Liverpool had pointedly declined to offer Shankly a back-room post after his decision to quit) but, in footballing terms at least, hardly necessary. Shankly's spirit was kept alive not by wrought iron but by each new piece of silverware the team lifted as the Eighties went on. Liverpool had never won the League Cup before 1981, yet once they had beaten West Ham in a replayed final that year, they took semi-permanent possession of it, winning it every season for another three years. There were three more championships in a row from 1982, and in 1984 another European Cup – the team's extrovert Zimbabwean goalkeeper, Bruce Grobbelaar, famously wobbling his knees to distract Roma's hapless penalty takers in the shoot-out that would bring Liverpool victory.

By now Joe Fagan, part of Bob Paisley's coaching staff alongside Ronnie Moran and Roy Evans, had taken over as manager. The team he inherited was led by the rampaging Welsh goalscorer Ian Rush, ably prompted by Sammy Lee and Ronnie Whelan in midfield, and with Mark Lawrenson now playing alongside Hansen in the centre of the defence. It was perhaps the best-balanced Liverpool side of all, a team that had turned the axiom of 'pass and move' into something as natural as buttering the toast. In addition to being heroes in their own backyard, the players achieved the rare distinction, for a side so dominant, of being popular among a wider public, inspiring genuine fondness as well as respect.

For all its promise, however, Fagan's reign was always going to be a short one. Its ending was marred by the Heysel tragedy (see panel p.297), and when the club appointed Dalglish as player-manager to replace Fagan, it seemed like a panic move from an institution traumatised by the events of Brussels on that warm May night in 1985. Yet within a year Dalglish had led the team to a League and FA Cup double – an accolade that had eluded all three of his illustrious predecessors.

The deadly dribble – McManaman at Wembley, 1995

Peter Beardsley, John Barnes, Steve McMahon and Ray Houghton, classic Anfield ballplayers all, arrived with minimal fanfare and maximum impact. Ian Rush was sold to Juventus in 1987, by which time Dalglish already had a lookalike replacement John Aldridge. When Rush returned after a nightmare year in Italy, the two of them played side by side, making goals for each other. Liverpool surprisingly lost the 1988 FA Cup final to Wimbledon after Aldridge had missed a penalty, yet even this somehow became a media victory. When Dalglish's team were beaten, football was the loser, too.

Less than 12 months later, however, the Hillsborough disaster (see panel p.300) silenced even the great spin doctors of the Anfield boot room. At first, it seemed that the tidal wave of emotion that began with the replayed Cup semi-final against Forest and Wembley final victory over Everton would sustain the club through its darkest hour. In 1990 Liverpool won the title – business as usual. Or was it? In an FA Cup semi-final that year, Liverpool lost 4–3 to Crystal Palace, a side they had beaten 9–0 earlier in the season. Dalglish, now retired as a player, had neglected to pick any forwards among his substitutes, and when Rush hobbled off injured, his team were toothless. Victory would have set up a Cup final meeting with Alex Ferguson's Manchester United. Later on, the 1990 FA Cup would come to symbolise Old Trafford's rise and Anfield's fall. The house Shankly built was crumbling.

In 1991, out of the blue, Dalglish resigned. Along with his players he had attended the funerals of many Hillsborough victims and the accumulated grief and stress had extracted a heavy toll.

His replacement, Graeme Souness, had worked wonders for Rangers in Scotland, but made the mistake of trying to impose the same strategy that had worked at Ibrox onto Anfield's finely honed traditions. A massive clear-out of playing staff, much of it unwarranted, was followed by a string of new signings who were not – and, crucially, could not be turned into – 'Liverpool material'. And Souness' hard-tackling game, though not quite the betrayal of Shankly's legacy some sections of the media claimed it to be, alienated supporters.

With nothing to show for his efforts but the 1992 FA Cup, Souness departed in January 1994, to be succeeded by Roy Evans – a man Anfield had overlooked ever since Joe Fagan had stepped down nearly a decade earlier. It was an attempt to turn back the clock, and it was always doomed to failure. At the end of the 1993/94 season the Kop was demolished to make way for a new all-seater stand, but the squad rebuilding carried out by Evans was slower and less successful. Despite the emergence of fresh talents such as Steve McManaman and Robbie Fowler, Liverpool's inconsistency remained. If under Souness their play had been too rough, under Evans it was not tough enough.

As the years went on, the management's failings became particularly apparent in Europe, once the club's favourite playground, and in the under-achievement of foreign signings, which had breathed fresh life into so many other Premiership sides, but which at Anfield seemed merely to get in each other's way. Like Souness, Evans won only one major honour – the 1995 League Cup. In the summer of 1998 he was joined by Gerard Houllier, former coach of the French national team, but also an 'honorary Scouser' who had taught in Liverpool and felt a natural affinity with Anfield. Within months Evans had gone, and Houllier, obliged to start from scratch with the exceptions of Fowler, Michael

Mourning unbroken – the legacy of Hillsborough

Silent vigil – the tenth anniversary, April 1999

It spoke volumes for the culture of violence that still pervaded football in 1989 that, when spectators began spilling onto the pitch at the Leppings Lane end of **Hillsborough** at the start of the FA Cup semi-final between **Liverpool** and **Nottingham Forest**, commentators assumed the cause was 'trouble'.

But what sort of trouble, exactly? With the seconds ticking away before kick-off, thousands of Liverpool fans were still queuing to get into the ground. Despite outnumbering their Forest counterparts, they had been allocated a more compact area of the stadium. In the confusion, an exit gate was opened so that fans could pass into the ground more quickly.

Yet this gateway led directly down into a central part of the Leppings Lane terrace that was already full, whereas there was ample space to either side. The pressure of so many people converging on such a small area was unbearable – 96 fans were asphyxiated against the perimeter fences which, as at most grounds then, had been erected to prevent pitch invasions.

While the disaster led directly to the publication of the Taylor Report and the modernisation of football grounds all over the world, discussion of the events that led to the tragedy has always been less frank. The official verdict of 'accidental death' bewildered families of the dead, and over the years new evidence has emerged – of post-mortem blood tests for alcohol levels being carried out on the victims, of paramedic facilities not used until too late, of police files not being released to the coroner – which has turned that bewilderment into anger.

With public interest in the controversy sparked by Jimmy McGovern's 1996 TV drama but appeals for a new public inquiry rejected, the **Hillsborough Family Support Group** felt obliged to bring private prosecutions for manslaughter against two (retired) South Yorkshire police officers who were on duty at the time of the disaster. The families did not claim that these two men alone were responsible for the tragedy, but the prosecution was the only means left open to them in their pursuit of justice and the truth.

'All we want is the truth,' said HFSG chairman Philip Hammond. 'Then we can finally bring an end to our mourning and get on with the rest of our lives.'

Owen, captain Jamie Redknapp and a sprinkling of youngsters, looked to Europe, not Liverpool's traditional hinterland of the Celtic fringe, for a new beginning.

Faced with a scout's dossier on a new prospect landing on his desk, Bill Shankly once quipped: 'Never mind all this – can he play?' In 1999/2000, Liverpool were the only members of the so-called 'G14' of European super-clubs not taking part in continental competition. Houllier's new signings had only a year in which to prove they were up to it, and deliver, at the very least, a return to Europe.

Here we go!

Motorists coming from any direction should make for the M57 motorway, reached either via the M6/M62 (coming from the south or east) or the M6/M58 (from the north). Exit the M57 at junction 4 onto the A580 East Lancashire Road, heading in toward Liverpool. This road becomes Walton Hall Avenue and, after crossing Queen's Drive, Walton Lane.

Following the road round, Goodison Park is on your right and Stanley Park on your left, with Anfield at the other end of it. Either turn left into Priory Road for **car parking** in Stanley Park, or use the car park at Goodison and walk across the park to Liverpool's ground.

Liverpool Lime Street **train station** (see Everton for services) is a good couple of miles from Anfield, so hop on a #14, #F4 or #F5 bus from the gyratory opposite the station to Walton Breck Road.

Just the ticket

Visiting fans are allocated a section of the Anfield Road Stand (size depending on fixture), at the other end of the ground from the Kop – entrance in Anfield Road. Prices in 1998/99 were adults £20, with a combined adult and child ticket £30. There are spaces for only six **disabled visitors** here. Advance booking is therefore essential on ☎0151/261 8680.

Swift half

The Arkles at #77 Anfield Road is big enough to house the masses that give it a cracking matchday atmosphere – there's football on TV and the local *Cains* bitter on draught. A little further along is ***The Sandon***, former property of Liverpool's founder, John Houlding, and once the venue for Everton's changing rooms. It's now been restored with its own sports memorabilia bar.

The best takeaway **food options** are on the other side of the ground along Walton Breck Road, while those seeking a sit-down meal before or after the game are best off in the centre of Liverpool.

Club merchandise

The ***Liverworld*** store built into the new Kop Stand (open Mon–Fri 10am–4.30pm and on matchdays with extended hours, ☎0151/263 1760) has the latest Seventies-inspired red strip, together with a new green-and-black away number. Since green was originally introduced to Liverpool as the corporate colour of manufacturer *Adidas*, it seems strange that it has now been revived by current supplier *Reebok*. Funny old game, this replica shirt business.

Barmy army

Reports of the death of the Kop have been proved premature – Liverpool still seem more inspired whenever they are attacking it, as Manchester United discovered toward the end of the

A doomed marriage – Evans and Houllier, May 1998

Boys' Owen – young Michael in full flight

1998/99 season. Only when United are the visitors does the threat of trouble become serious.

In print

The morning ***Daily Press*** and evening ***Liverpool Echo*** are produced by the same company (see Everton) – look out for the pink ***Football Echo*** on Saturday afternoons after the final whistle.

The *Post & Echo* group don't have the rights to publish Liverpool's official magazine but, despite not having access to the same 'player exclusives', their unofficial publication ***The Kop*** is often a better read than the club-sanctioned ***Liverpool – The Official Magazine***, produced in London by *Northern & Shell*.

The fanzine scene is constantly shifting. Try ***Red All Over The Land*** (PO Box 296, Loughborough, LE11 4ZR), ***Another Vintage Liverpool Performance*** (13 Winwick Lane, Lowton, WA3 1LR) and ***Through The Wind & Rain*** (PO Box 23, Bootle, L30 2SA).

You could set up your own bookstore selling Liverpool tomes alone. Stephen F Kelly's ***Illustrated History Of Liverpool 1892–1998*** (Hamlyn, £17.99) is an obvious starting point, as is David Prole's lighter but very readable ***Unofficial Biography Of Liverpool*** (Pan, £4.99). Among the worthwhile biographies are ***Shanks*** by Dave Bowler (Orion, £5.99) and ***Out Of His Skin (The John Barnes Phenomenon)*** by Dave Hill, published in 1990 but still available in some outlets.

On air

The choice is between ***BBC Radio Merseyside*** (95.8 FM) and ***Radio City*** (96.7 FM).

In the net

Alongside newcomers Bradford City, Liverpool were the only Premiership club with no **official website** as of summer 1999, despite promises dating back two years or more. What this says about the club's ability to communicate effectively to fans is a matter for debate.

Happily, there are plenty of unofficial options. ***Liverpool – The Mighty Reds*** has as much information as you could digest in a lifetime, including an outstanding news archive (with daily updates) which collates stories from right across the web. It's at: anfield.merseyworld.com.

Mersey Reds concentrates on nostalgia (as Barry Norman might say – and why not?) and includes a historical narrative as well as a breakdown of all Robbie Fowler's first 100 goals for Liverpool, at: members.tripod.com/~merseyreds.

The ongoing post-Hillsborough campaign has two sites worth visiting in ***Justice For The 96*** at: freespace.virgin.net/p.harvey/justice; and the ***Hillsborough Family Support Group*** at: www.hfsg.org.

Finally, **Bill Shankly** has a superb site, covering his entire playing and coaching career not just his time at Anfield, dedicated to him at: www.shankly.com.

Luton Town

Formation	1885
Stadium	Kenilworth Road, Luton, Beds, LU4 8AW. ☎01582/411622
Ground capacity	10,000
First-choice colours	White with blue and orange trim
Major honours	Second Division champions 1982; Third Division (South) champions 1937; Fourth Division champions 1968; League Cup winners 1988
Position 1998/99	12th in Second Division

Entering the away end at Luton Town, you pass through a space where somebody's front hall and kitchen ought to be. Once inside the ground, the toilets appear to be in a living room, while along one side of the pitch there is no stand at all, only a row of executive boxes. At Kenilworth Road, space is at a premium, to put it mildly.

Dome alone – Luton supporters want answers, 1998

Luckily, the club owns part of the row of terraced housing which stands between the street and the Oak Road End of the ground, while those boxes have balconies in front of them, so that, weather permitting, the players do actually see some fans along the Ivy Road and Beech Road side. But Luton still want to leave Kenilworth Road – have wanted to do so, in fact, for the best part of three decades. Club chairman David Kohler spent much of the 1998/99 season, as he had the year before that, the year before that and the year before that, pursuing his dream that an oval-shaped, retractable-roofed new stadium, modestly named the Kohlerdome, might be built out of town, on a site close to junction 10 of the M1 motorway. Then a firebomb was hurled through the letterbox of his house, and Kohler put Luton Town, whose debts he had been personally underwriting, into administrative receivership.

With the League threatening to exclude any club still in administration from the 1999/2000 fixture list, the town became a riot of takeover talk. Supporters formed *FLAG*, the *Friends of Luton Action Group*, aimed at turning Luton into a community football club, Bournemouth-style. Alan Sugar was rumoured to be asking the FA to change its rules so that he could turn Luton into a nursery club for Spurs. *General Motors*, one of the town's biggest employers with its *Vauxhall* and *Bedford* plants, was said to be interested in helping out, as was the cut-price airline *easyJet*, which has its headquarters at Luton Airport. And, most bizarrely of all, David Kohler himself was thought to be part of a consortium trying to relaunch the club by reaching a compromise deal with its creditors.

The prospect of Kohler returning to Luton, just months after he'd washed his hands of a club whose board he'd joined at the start of the Nineties, didn't exactly fill supporters' hearts with joy. At one stage

The midfield maestro – Ricky Hill, 1983

the Kohlerdome dream had looked likely to become reality, but a shift in transport policy, begun in the last days of the Conservative Government and accelerated after Labour's election win in 1997, put paid to the widening of the M1 at exactly the point the new stadium was supposed to be built. Without improved road access, the planners said, the development could not go ahead. Luton's appeal went all the way to the Secretary of State, but was rejected in the early part of 1999.

Now that the dream was fading, fans became increasingly restless. Kohler had ploughed thousands into architects' plans, feasibility studies, legal fees and other costs associated with his pet Dome. Now that it wasn't going to be built, supporters wondered, what could the team have achieved if it had been given the same resources? Luton spent most of the 1998/99 campaign scrapping in mid-table in the Second Division, with beleaguered manager Lennie Lawrence fending off criticism from supporters, board members and media alike. But all agreed, when pressed, that he had precious few resources to work with.

The mood in the stands became even darker, however, when Kohler began to investigate possible alternatives to the site rejected by the planners. Among these, the fans discovered, was one at Milton Keynes – only three junctions up the motorway but, with its sleek, modern boulevards, its ranks of prim housing estates, its landscaped roundabouts and its hi-tech trading parks, a world away from good old industrial, multi-cultural, multi-ethnic Luton. Milton Keynes had no historical football culture of its own (unless you counted its infamous legion of living-room Manchester United fans), whereas Luton had supporters so desperately committed, they felt justified in terrorising the chairman's family by setting fire to their home.

Ironically, the fellow property developer with whom David Kohler took over Luton Town in 1990, Peter Nelkin, walked out within two years after receiving death threats from 'fans'. The anger then, as now, was fuelled by the club's failure to relocate. But even before then, when Luton's football was among the most attractive in the country during the Eighties, Kenilworth Road had been the focus of bitter controversy. Indeed, older fans and those with a sense of history might point out, the club's potential has been limited ever since it first moved to the ground, a little over a century ago.

It is another of the rich ironies associated with Luton that, while the town's proximity to London makes it hard for the team to attract more than a small local following, the club's founding fathers were further advanced in their thinking than their counterparts at any other club in the south-east. 'Luton Town Football Club' was founded in the town hall on 11 April 1885, when two existing teams, The Wanderers and The Excelsiors, agreed to a merger. The idea came from the latter, but the new name came from the former, who had become 'Luton Town Wanderers' three months earlier, and entered the FA Cup under that name. Wanderers members were initially sceptical about throwing in their lot with another club, but were talked round when it was pointed out that the new team could make use of The Excelsiors' superior ground at Dallow Lane.

The uncrowned king of Kenilworth Road – David Pleat

Luton Town entered the FA Cup at the first opportunity in 1885/86, and five years later became the first football club in the south of England to turn 'professional' by paying players expenses – a practice still frowned upon in the teams of public-school old boys that were influential locally.

In 1897, Luton applied to join the Football League – then dominated by clubs from the north and Midlands, and only too happy to admit a side based so close to London. Luton became a limited company, moved to a new ground at Dunstable Road, and made their Second Division debut on 4 September, drawing 1–1 at Leicester Fosse. Dressed in striking cochineal pink shirts and navy-blue shorts, Town made quite an impact in their first season, finishing a decent eighth. Yet after only two more years they had sunk to second from bottom and, crippled by travelling costs (only Woolwich Arsenal were within easy range), the club declined to apply for re-election and joined the Southern League whence it had come.

The team would remain there for the next two decades, but progress was made away from the field of play when, in 1905, the club moved to Kenilworth Road. The move did Luton's form little good, however, and by 1912 they had plunged into the Southern League's Second Division. By the end of World War I they were back in the First, which was just as well, as in 1920 most of the clubs within it took the decision to form a new Third Division of the Football League. Twelve months later this became the Third Division (South) after a group of northern non-League sides made a similar switch. Whatever name it went under, Luton would be stuck in it until 1937, when rampant centre-forward Joe Payne led the club to the Third Division (South) championship – in total the team scored 103 goals, with Payne alone netting 55 of them.

Payne left for Chelsea in 1938, but the club had another demon goalscorer to replace him in Hugh Billington, who would net no fewer than four hat-tricks in the first half of the 1938/39 season. Luton were more comfortable in the Second Division than they'd expected, and their consolidation would continue after World War II, despite Billington following in Payne's footsteps to Stamford Bridge. In 1952 they reached the quarter-finals of the FA Cup, and three years later, under the managership of the former Derby County winger Dally Duncan, they were promoted to the top flight for the first time in their history.

Setting the tone for what would become a Luton tradition, Duncan's side was quick-footed and intelligent. Captained by their commanding centre-half Syd Owen, the team included an under-rated goalkeeper in Ron Baynham and two key internationals – Northern Ireland's Billy Bingham on the flanks and Scotsman Allan Brown at inside-right.

The team's high point in the League was an eighth-place finish in 1957/58, but the following season was made more memorable by a first FA Cup final appearance, Luton losing a tight but often absorbing game 2–1 to Nottingham Forest.

After that, Owen retired as a player to succeed Duncan in the manager's job, and Luton lost the plot. By 1965 the club had tumbled all the way to the Fourth Division, a slide halted – but not reversed – by the brief return of pre-war manager George Martin.

Having fallen so far so fast, however, Luton then ascended the League ladder with similar impatience, under a succession of different managers. Allan Brown led them to the Fourth Division title in 1968; Alec Stock got them out of the third (with the help of Malcolm Macdonald's goals) two years later; and Harry Haslam won promotion back up to the First in 1974.

Macdonald and another of Luton's most influential Sixties figures, Bruce Rioch, had moved on by now, and despite the presence of the veteran former Manchester United winger John Aston, the adoption of fluorescent orange shirts (in preference to the club's now traditional white) and the wit of comedian Eric Morecambe on the board, Town were relegated after only one season back in the top flight.

An extended spell of Second Division football followed, to be broken after the arrival of David Pleat as Haslam's replacement in 1978. With no great top-flight tradition to uphold and little pressure from fans, Pleat took his time building a bright, young team that would take the same considered attitude to the game as Dally Duncan's side 30 years earlier. By 1981/82 his line-up was complete, and Luton won the Second Division title, having lost only four games all year.

The contrast between Pleat's Luton and the local rivals who came up with them, Graham Taylor's Watford, could scarcely have been greater. Neither manager set much store by star players, yet while Watford were all belt, braces and bravado, Luton had quiet, unassuming quality in every corner of the pitch, from Northern

Snow on the terraces – but Luton's plastic pitch means the game goes on, March 1986

Come out wherever you are – Phil Gray looks for a team-mate

Ireland international Mal Donaghy at full-back, through to deft playmaker Ricky Hill in midfield and the big but highly skilled Brian Stein upfront.

But as Watford battled their way to a runners-up spot behind Liverpool in their first top-flight season, Luton struggled. Their style won high praise in the media, but it was no substitute for points. As relegation loomed, a banner at Kenilworth Road read: 'The football's right – now show us you can fight.' On the last day of the 1982/83 season, Luton were indeed fighting for their First Division lives. There were barely three minutes remaining of a match they had to win at Maine Road when Yugoslav substitute Raddy Antić (later to find fame and fortune as manager of both Real and Atlético Madrid) half-volleyed a hopeful shot from the edge of the box into the Manchester City net. Luton were safe, City were down, and David Pleat shook his *Farah* slacks onto the pitch in a jig of unbridled joy.

Now the club had a bridgehead from which to expand, and with Pleat somehow keeping his key players from the clutches of bigger clubs while bringing on new talents such as Danny Wilson, Roy Wegerle and Kingsley Black, Luton continued to make progress. In 1985 they reached an FA Cup semi-final against Everton. Two years later, despite Pleat's departure for Tottenham, they finished seventh in the First Division, the club's highest-ever League position. And in 1988 came the crowning glory – a 3–2 victory over Arsenal in the League Cup at Wembley, a first major trophy for the club, a triumph for the team's bright, enterprising approach.

And yet, while their football won more and more friends every year, behind the scenes Luton were also making enemies. An artificial pitch, laid in 1985, might have been good for the players' ball skills and enabled the club to play through (and earn extra money during) harsh winter weather, but, as at QPR, Oldham and Preston, it was also fiendishly difficult for visiting sides to adjust to. The replacement of the old Bobbers Stand by executive boxes enraged traditionalists among the fans, and turned one side of Kenilworth Road into a chant-free zone. Finally, after a riot by Millwall fans had caused thousands of pounds' worth of damage to fixtures and fittings, Luton's chairman, the controversialist future Tory MP David Evans, banned all away fans from the ground.

Other clubs were furious, as were the League, which temporarily banned Luton from the League Cup (a ban which, as luck would have it, was lifted just in time for the 1987/88 victory). But Evans maintained it would make Luton a friendlier club.

It didn't, and by 1991, both the plastic pitch and the away fans ban were lifted. Encouraged by having grass to play on and some of their own fans to cheer them on, visiting teams suddenly found Kenilworth Road an agreeable place to come and play. In 1992, Luton were relegated.

David Pleat, who had returned for a second spell as manager, found his neat, tidy brand of football was now ineffective amid the clamour to get promoted into the newly formed Premiership. After a series of fine Cup runs and the sale of young striker John Hartson to Arsenal for £2.5million in 1995, Pleat departed again, this time for Sheffield Wednesday.

A disastrous start to the 1995/96 campaign saw Lennie Lawrence replace Terry Westley after the latter had had barely six months in charge, and relegation to the Second Division was inevitable. Defeat by Crewe in the 1997 play-off semi-finals was a shock to the system, but in the two seasons since then, fans have simply been thankful that Luton have avoided being dragged into another relegation dogfight.

If there were the prospect of a new stadium just around the corner (or at least, on a nearby motorway junction), then perhaps the team's slide in fortunes could be more easily borne. As things stood in the summer of 1999, however, Luton's supporters had better things to worry about than moving house – they had their club's very existence to worry about.

Here we go!

Whatever direction they come from, **motorists** will find themselves coming into Luton on the A505 (junction 11 off the M1). On entering the town's central one-way system, follow signs for Dunstable until you see the ground on your left.

There's no obvious alternative to **street parking**, which is normally in plentiful supply, but those who fancy a pie and a pint in the town centre will find a variety of car parks within a 10–15min walk from the ground.

Luton **train station** is on the main line between London St Pancras, Leicester and Nottingham (service hourly, journey 25mins from St Pancras, 1hr 30mins from Nottingham) – change at Leicester for Derby, Sheffield, Leeds and a range of other destinations. There are also *Thameslink* services to King's Cross, Gatwick Airport and Brighton. Call ☎0345/484950 for the latest timings.

From the station, buses #31, #37 and #38 run along Dunstable Road. Alternatively, it's a 15–20min walk along Station Road, Mill Street and Telford Way to Dunstable Road.

Just the ticket

Visiting fans have more than 2,000 seats in the Oak Road Stand, contrary to initial appearances. Tickets in 1998/99 were adults £13.50, concessions £7, the latter available only in advance from your own club. **Disabled supporters** have a small area in front of the Main Stand. Advance booking essential on ☎01582/416976.

Swift half

Two roads to remember – Dunstable Road near the ground is fine for **takeaway food**, but the **pubs** are better in the town centre, particularly along High Town Road opposite the station. Luton's large Indian community ensures the local **curry houses** seldom disappoint.

Club merchandise

Orange is confined to away shirts these days, and there's no sign of the cochineal pink making a comeback. Check it out yourself at the **club shop** behind the Kenilworth Stand.

Barmy army

With so much energy being channelled toward saving the club, trouble with rival fans is rare.

In print

The Bedforshire News Group publishes a variety of local papers including ***Luton News*** and the ***Herald & Post*** – but there's no Saturday evening edition of either.

The established fanzine is ***Mad As A Hatter*** (38 Twigden Court, Mount Pleasance Road, Luton, LU3 2RL), while club historian Timothy Collings' ***The Luton Town Story***, published in 1985, is worth searching out.

On air

BBC Three Counties Radio (103.8 FM) is the Luton fans' choice and has been a focus for protests over the Kohlerdome and receivership.

In the net

There's no official site but ***Hatters Online*** is a good first stop with its history, news and areas devoted to Kenilworth Road and the Kohlerdome. It's at: www.btinternet.com/~ben.w.

The ***Fans of Luton Action Group*** has its own site at: www.flag.org.uk.

Macclesfield Town

Year of formation	1874
Stadium	Moss Rose, London Road, Macclesfield, Cheshire, SK11 7SP. ☎01625/264686
Ground capacity	6,000
First-choice colours	Blue shirts, white shorts
Major honours	Conference champions 1995, 1997; FA Trophy winners 1970, 1996
Position 1998/99	24th in Second Division (relegated)

As Macclesfield Town stepped out for their Second Division match at home to Manchester City on 12 September 1998, they provided a timely reaffirmation of the English game's precious fluidity. Eleven years earlier, the two clubs had been six levels of football apart – City up in the old First Division, Macclesfield down in the Northern Premier League. That City were desperate to win the game was obvious from the way they and their fans celebrated the 1–0 victory, secured thanks to a defensive error in the dying minutes. For Macclesfield, a point was proved regardless of the final score. The team had held their own against the most illustrious opposition the Second Division could muster, barely two years after attaining League status for the first time.

That said, the 1998/99 campaign was always going to be tough for Macclesfield. Having taken the team from the Conference to the Second Division of the Football League in successive seasons, manager Sammy McIlroy was given little time or money to improve his squad and, while it was sound enough in most departments, scoring goals at this new level posed problems. Macclesfield didn't need a more productive strikeforce; they needed a strikeforce, full stop.

The signage says it all – the Silkmen are in the League

High scoring hasn't historically presented Macclesfield with such difficulty, certainly not in the mid-19th century, when 'Macclesfield Football Club' played rugby rather than soccer. The club's switch to 'association football' came in 1874, when the code was still strictly amateur and there were no organised competitions for the team to play in. Local derbies against sides from Stoke, Crewe, Stockport and Leek were, however, easy to arrange and began to attract a small following to the club's modest ground at Bowfield Lane.

Macclesfield were quick to enter the Cheshire Senior Cup when it began in 1880, and ten years later they won it for the first time with the help of trainer John Alcock, a local publican whose ideas on physical preparation (strict diet, country walks, Turkish baths and a smoking ban) were about a century ahead of their time. Macclesfield retained the Cup a year later, when they also became founder members of a 12-team local combination league that also included Northwich Victoria, Wrexham and a club from the Derby area.

In September 1891 the club moved to its present home, the Moss Rose Ground, after shrugging off criticism that it was dangerously close to the nearest pub. It became a limited company in 1895 but within two years was declared bankrupt. An amateur club, Hallifield, moved into Moss Rose and joined the Manchester District League, adopting the name Macclesfield in 1902. After experimenting with both amateur and professional structures, the club did a 'double' of Manchester League and Cheshire Senior Cup in 1911.

By the time the club was re-formed after World War II, however, the local football scene was undergoing radical change. The Manchester League had folded and, rather than seek entry to the Football League, Macclesfield opted to play in the Cheshire League, where competition was less fierce and clubs were mainly amateur.

Throughout the Twenties and Thirties, Macclesfield built on their reputation as a force in their own chosen arena, with cultured players like Leonard Butt and Albert Valentine bringing crowds of 6,000 and more into Moss Rose. The town as a whole, though, remained indifferent to the idea of a having a senior football club – Macclesfield only just managed to raise enough cash to avoid another bankruptcy in 1936 – and for two decades after World War II the team continued to play in the relative obscurity of the Cheshire League, occasionally breaking into the national consciousness with an appearance in the first round of the FA Cup.

In 1968 Macclesfield beat Stockport County to advance to the second round for the first time, then accounted for Spennymoor United in front of a record Moss Rose crowd of 7,002. Around 10,000 fans then made the journey to Fulham for a third-round tie against a team then in the First Division of the Football League. Macclesfield went in at half-time 2–1 up thanks to goals from Fred Taberner and Brian Fidler, and only a disputed penalty allowed the home side back into the game; Fulham finally won 4–2.

The 1967/68 season was also significant because it was Macclesfield's last in the Cheshire League. The club was to become a founder member of the Northern Premier League, a new competition for semi-professional sides. The team said

Home for more than a century – the quaint, quirky and above all friendly Moss Rose

farewell to the Cheshire League in style, sealing a sixth title with a Good Friday win at Altrincham in front of 9,000 fans.

With the guidance of manager Frank Beaumont and the goals of Dick Young, Macclesfield won the new League at the first time of asking, finishing 12 points of clear second-placed Wigan Athletic. In 1969/70 things got even better: the team retained the NPL title, reached the first round of the FA Cup (where they were beaten by Scunthorpe and Kevin Keegan), and became the first winners of the FA Trophy, which had replaced the Amateur Cup.

There were 28,000 at Wembley to see Macclesfield beat Telford United 2–0 in that FA Trophy Final, but in the Northern Premier League the club's average gate was less than a tenth of that. By the mid-Seventies, most of the professional staff at Moss Rose had been released to cut the wage bill to manageable proportions. After going through nine managers in six years, Macclesfield ended the Seventies at the bottom of the Northern Premier League – from which, luckily, there was no relegation at the time.

The team finished eighth in 1979/80 but even this was a somewhat false position, since the best NPL teams had now graduated to the Alliance Premier League, the long-awaited 'top layer' of the non-League pyramid which England's leading semi-pro clubs hoped would one day act as a gateway to the Football League.

Finishing top of the Northern Premier would gain Macclesfield promotion to the Alliance, but that wasn't achieved until 1986/87, under Peter Wragg. Four of Wragg's first-choice players were seriously injured in a car crash a week before the season began, but the squad was still strong enough to win not just the NPL but two minor Cup competitions as well – no wonder Macclesfield fans danced on the plastic pitch at Hyde United on the last day of the campaign.

By this time the Alliance had become the Conference and Macclesfield quickly

Bandana, nose-clip, bottle – Efe Sodje

made themselves at home in it. Carlisle became the club's first League victims in the FA Cup for 20 years, and after crowd trouble in that first-round match, Peter Wragg had to climb a floodlight pylon to calm the Moss Rose faithful prior to the second-round game with Rotherham; it didn't calm his players, who won 4–0. Macclesfield lost 1–0 at Port Vale in the third round but the town was back on the football map with a vengeance. The team finished their first Conference season a decent 11th.

Wragg left for Halifax in 1992, taking several players with him, and the following year the club only secured its Conference status on the last day of the season. The tide turned again with the appointment of Sammy McIlroy as manager. McIlroy, once a forward with Manchester United and Northern Ireland, brought big-club organisation and ambition to the club. Under his guidance Macclesfield won the Conference title in 1995, but were refused entry to the League because the Moss Rose was deemed unsuitable.

Quite apart from the resentment any club would feel at being denied the proper reward for a successful season, there was a bitter irony here. Between 1990 and 1992, Chester City had played League matches at Moss Rose after the sale of their old Sealand Road ground, and the League had seen nothing wrong with Macclesfield's facilities then. True, more stringent standards applied by 1995, but when Macclesfield asked the League's permission to share Chester's newly built Deva Stadium while the necessary improvements were being made to Moss Rose, they were rebuffed.

Undeterred, though, McIlroy kept his team together, won the FA Trophy with Macclesfield in 1996, and guided the team to another Conference title a year later. A hat-trick from Chris Byrne and a goal from veteran striker Peter Davenport gave 'Macc' a 4–1 win at Kettering on the final day, and results elsewhere contrived to make them champions.

There was no argument now about the suitability of the improved Moss Rose, and after a season in which Macclesfield found Third Division life easier than their fans had dared hope, there was a kind of poetic justice in the way the team assured themselves of a second successive promotion with a 3–2 home win over their former tenants, Chester City, in April 1998. Given the ill feeling their club's two years in Macclesfield had generated among Chester fans, the goodwill shown by the visiting contingent – who boasted former chairman Ray Crofts among their ranks on the Moss Lane terrace – was a joy to see.

Macclesfield's rise couldn't, and didn't, last. Despite some cultured football from the likes of Efe Sodje and Steve Hitchen, the team's inability to break down Second Division defences cast them adrift at the bottom of the table, and that was where they finished, eight points from safety.

Here we go!

Thanks to the M6, the former silk-producing town of Macclesfield is pretty easily accessible; Moss Rose is to the south of the town centre along the A523 London Road. Coming from the north, **motorists** should exit the M6 at junction 19. Follow the A556 toward Northwich for around half a mile, then turn left onto the A5033. Follow this into Knutsford, then follow signs for the A537 Macclesfield. On entering the town, go straight on at the Broken Cross roundabout, then turn left at the next roundabout. Proceed down Cumberland Street and Hibel Road to another roundabout and turn right onto Silk Road, signposted Leek; this is the A523 and becomes London Road. The ground will be on your right after a mile and a half.

From the south, exit the M6 at junction 17, signposted Sandbach. Follow the A534 to Congleton, then the A536 toward Macclesfield. Go past the *Rising Sun* pub on the outskirts of town, then turn right into Moss Lane immediately after the *Texaco* garage. The road turns back on itself behind the garage and leads directly to the visitors' end of the ground.

There is no car park at the ground and **street parking** can be problematical – the surrounding housing estate is a maze and car crime is not unknown there. Parking on London Road itself is likewise not recommended, so the best bet is to park up at the Lyme Green retail development, about a quarter of a mile south of the ground along London Road.

Macclesfield is also well served **by train** with services running direct to and from London Euston (hourly) and also Manchester, Stockport, Stoke-on-Trent, Wolverhampton and Birmingham (every 30mins). For the latest timings call ☎0345/484950.

From the station, you can get to the ground by **taxi** (£3) or by **bus** (#9), though beware that the latter is much less frequent in the evening than during the day. The bus station is almost adjacent to the train one.

You *can* walk it from the station, but it's a good half-hour's hike along Sunderland Street (turn left out of the station), Mill Lane and London Road – and that's always assuming you don't stop off at one of the pubs along the way (see *Swift Half* below).

London-based fans have the common problem of there being no feasible onward train connection after the final whistle.

Just the ticket

The Silkman Terrace houses **visiting fans** in a currently uncovered stand holding just under 2,000 – entrance in Moss Lane. Ticket prices here in 1998/99 were adults £10, juniors/OAPs £6. There are facilities for just nine **disabled supporters** in front of the London Road Stand but the club says there's no need to book in advance.

Swift half

Home and away fans mix freely before kick-off at ***The Silkman*** right next to the ground at 159 London Road. Families are welcome here but, because of the sheer number of customers on matchdays, may be better off at ***The Flower Pot***, a spacious pub with its own beer garden and kids' play area at the side; go to the top of Moss Lane and turn right.

Those travelling to or from the train station have a range of alternative pubs to choose from. ***The Sun Inn***, at 45 Mill Lane, is a good halfway house between station and ground and is renowned locally for its range of strong, hand-pulled ales.

For **food**, it's the usual story of trying to avoid what's served at the ground. Sunderland Street boasts a range of takeaway options, while on Waters Green, opposite the train station, you'll find ***The Millstone***, which reputedly serves the best pub grub in town, albeit at a price.

Club merchandise

The club has only recently taken over the running of its **shop** (open before and after matches, plus weekdays 9am–5pm by arrangement) from the Supporters' Club. You'll find it outside the ground between the Commercial Office and the *Silkman*.

Barmy army

The trouble that surfaced at Moss Rose in Conference days is a thing of the past, and today's big noise in the Star Lane End terrace (above the seats, unusually) is as likely to come from children as anyone else. You want family atmosphere? You got it.

In print

Local fans have to rely on the ***Manchester Evening News*** for newspaper coverage of the club, and there isn't much of that. The paper's Saturday afternoon ***Pink*** rarely makes it this far south at a decent hour, if at all.

For more concentrated Town news, fanzine ***Hang 'em High*** is available from 62 Coare Street, Macclesfield, Cheshire, SK10 1DW.

Against All Odds by Paul Atherton and Neil Howarth (self-published, £19.95) tells the story of Macclesfield's first season of League football with the help of moody monochrome photography. If all else fails you can get it from the club shop, or from *Sportspages*.

On air

The BBC's ***Greater Manchester Radio*** (GMR, 95.1 FM) generally has the edge over independent ***Silk*** (106.9 FM), even though the latter has more local bias.

In the net

The club's official site, ***Silkmen Online***, is at: www.mtfc.co.uk/. It's extremely well-organised and very comprehensive for a Second (sorry, Third) Division club, with daily news, a detailed club history and a proper site map, too.

Macc one – Sammy McIlroy milks the applause

Manchester City

Formation	1887 as Ardwick FC
Stadium	Maine Road, Moss Side, Manchester, M14 7WN. ☎0161/224 5000
Ground capacity	31,500
First-choice colours	Sky-blue shirts, white shorts
Major honours	League champions 1937, 1968; Second Division champions 1899, 1903, 1910, 1928, 1947, 1966; FA Cup winners 1904, 1934, 1956, 1969; League Cup winners 1970, 1976; European Cup-Winners' Cup winners 1970
Position 1998/99	3rd in Second Division (promoted via play-offs)

'We want to win on Saturday, but we also want to win the European trophy. So it won't be a case of holding back... Our programme is a full one, but I've always felt there is only one way to go into a season, and that's to try to win every game, going flat out.'

They might have been the words of Alex Ferguson prior to the 1999 FA Cup final. They were, in fact, spoken by the Manchester City manager, Joe Mercer, as his team homed in on a unique 'double' of the League Cup and the Cup-Winners' Cup during the 1969/70 season. FA Cup winners a year earlier, champions of England a year before that, City were the talk of the nation, indicating that while United's European Cup triumph had been a glorious finale to the Busby era, it was the city's other club that faced a rosier future.

How City fans today must hope that history will repeat itself. While Mercer and his assistant Malcolm Allison were able to lord it over United during the early Seventies, there have been few triumphs since then. Old Trafford's fortunes revived quickly, and after a period in which there was little to choose between the Manchester sides, in the Nineties the two clubs have seemed further apart than ever. The higher United's star has risen in the sky (or should that be *Sky*?), the further City's has dropped. No wonder the Maine Road signature tune is *Blue Moon*...

On the other hand, it is not really in the nature of the club or its supporters for City to be seeking United-style domination. Quite the reverse, in fact. Old Trafford's relentless pursuit of perfection inspires as much mockery as envy among the Maine Road faithful, for whom the imperative has always been that their team go out and have a good time – and hang the consequences. City may stagger while United swagger, but the blue half of Manchester would rather have Mark & Lard than Zoë Ball, any day.

If City draw a perverse pleasure from being unpredictable, then it is by no means a new phenomenon. In its formative years the club went under four different names, moved home five times, toyed briefly with the idea of sharing Old Trafford with United, and at one point went out of business altogether.

Prior to 1923, the club's roots were planted firmly in the east side of Manchester. Most historians chart City's ancestry back to the cricket team of St Mark's Church, West Gorton, whose members decided to form a football section in 1880. The team played their first game in November that year, on a field next to the church in Clowes Street. This was too cramped, however, and within a year the team had taken up the offer of a winter residency at Kirkmanshulme cricket club nearby. This time the field was too good for the team – the cricketers didn't like what winter football was doing to their carefully manicured turf, and in 1882 the West Gorton team were evicted. With green spaces being at a premium and another season of fixtures

The Maine men – City line up for the cameras before the start of the 1969/70 season

looming, the club teetered on the brink of extinction. At the last minute, however, a pitch was found at Clemington Park and West Gorton were saved, their matches beginning to attract four-figure crowds for the first time.

Two years later, the club loosened its links with the church by merging with another local side, Gorton Athletic, to form Gorton FC. The team moved home again, to a patch of disused land discovered by one of their players on Pink Bank Lane. In 1887 they rented a pitch from the *Bull's Head* pub on Reddish Lane, before at last finding a more permanent resting place at Hyde Road, again on the recommendation of a player. After this last move the team became Ardwick FC, after the district surrounding Hyde Road, and the identity under which the club would be elected to the Football League in 1892, after a year in the rival Football Alliance.

Their city neighbours Newton Heath had finished runners-up in the last season of Alliance football, while Ardwick had come seventh – hence the former were admitted directly into the First Division of the League, while Ardwick became founder members of the Second. But within two years Ardwick had been wound-up, and the new limited company formed in their place was christened Manchester City, in an attempt to gather support from a wider area; in contrast, Newton Heath did not become Manchester United until 1902.

It was as City that the team entered the FA Cup for the first time in 1897, and won the Second Division title two years later. They were relegated after just three seasons but then immediately promoted, before tasting real success for the first time by winning the FA Cup in 1904. Their 1–0 victory over Bolton Wanderers in the final was something of an upset, and aroused suspicion among the powers-that-be. Amid accusations of illegal payments, the FA suspended a former City chairman, the club secretary, two directors and 17 players – including the Cup-winning goalscorer, Welsh international winger Billy Meredith, who was forced to miss nine months of football. Each individual involved was also fined heavily.

The conventional wisdom is that these suspensions gifted the local initiative to United at a crucial time in the two clubs' development. Yet there is little evidence to support this. Despite having to field weakened teams, City had no trouble retaining their top-flight status. And although Meredith signed for United in 1906 and went on to win League and Cup honours with them, support for City remained high, with overcrowding a constant problem at Hyde Road. To attribute United's rise to City's punishment is to under-sell both clubs.

The period after World War I signalled something of a trough for both City and United. Meredith returned to City in 1921, and two years later, with the lease on Hyde Road due to expire, the club built a new home for itself at Maine Road. The venue, in the Moss Side area of new council estates to the south of the city centre, moved City closer to Old Trafford and away from their traditional home. But the club had grand plans and needed space in which to hatch them. Maine Road was to be a 'Wembley of the North', built at a cost of more than £100,000 and capable of housing up to 90,000 fans. (The crowd of 84,569 which watched an FA Cup tie between City and Stoke in March 1934 is a British record for any game outside London or Glasgow.)

As so often happens, being in elaborate new surroundings at first impeded the team's progress on the pitch. City were relegated in 1926, despite reaching their first Wembley Cup final – lost 1–0 to Bolton. They then missed out on promotion by 0.002 of a goal, after their rivals Portsmouth scored five in the second half of their last game of the season. But there were to be no problems with goal average in 1927/28, when target man Tommy Johnson led a rampaging City to a season total of 100 goals and the Second Division title.

In the close season City signed a young wing-half by the name of Matt Busby, who would turn out to be every bit as influential as a player at Maine Road as he would in a managerial role across town. With Busby leading the way, City homed in on another FA Cup triumph. They reached the semi-finals in 1932, the final the following year (lost 3–0 to Everton) and then, with a side including incomparable goalkeeper Frank Swift, wing-half Eric Brook, inside-forward Alec Herd and centre-forward Sam Tilson, beat Portsmouth 2–1 at Wembley, in a game some fans would maintain was the best one-off display mounted by any City team.

Within three years – and despite Busby's departure to Liverpool – City were League champions for the first time, their instinctive attacking football, inspired by manager Wilf Wild and his new signing, the tall, elegant Ulster-born inside-forward Peter Doherty, drawing huge crowds to Maine Road. What happened the following season, 1937/38, says more about City than any other year in the club's history. Despite continuing to play the same brand of football that had won them the title 12 months earlier, reaching the quarter-finals of the FA Cup and scoring more goals than any other team in the First Division, Wild's team were relegated. Even more painfully, United were promoted at the same time. World War II then intervened, and while it was Old Trafford that bore the brunt of

Sticking his neck out – Trautmann saves against Newcastle

Nazi bomb damage, City too teetered on the brink of extinction, with manager Wild, who'd been at the club since becoming assistant secretary in 1920, pulling every string he could to keep the football going.

After the war Wild stepped up to become general manager, appointing one of his former players, Sam Cowan, in his place. Cowan immediately guided City back up to the top flight, then promptly resigned after the board insisted he move back to Manchester from his home in Brighton.

In the aftermath of war, City shared Maine Road with United while Old Trafford was being rebuilt. Financially this suited City, who bagged £5,000 a year in rent plus a share of United's gate money. But as the team struggled to make headway in the First Division under Jock Thomson, the board blamed the poor state of the Maine Road pitch, and asked United to leave at the end of the 1948/49 season. Except at the bank, it made no difference – Thomson resigned midway through the following season, City were relegated and, just to make life a little more bitter, Matt Busby built his first great United side.

Enter Les McDowall, a City captain before the war, who took over as manager with the side already doomed to drop. McDowall reversed Thomson's safety-first strategy, encouraging City to play expansive football again. On gaining promotion in 1951, the team were a free-scoring force once more. Comparisons with the pre-war City were obvious, but if Wilf Wild's teams had been built around talented individuals doing their own thing, McDowall was more tactically minded. The first British manager to react positively to Hungary's double humiliation of England in 1953/54, McDowall evolved the so-called 'Revie plan' whereby Don Revie, signed from Hull City two years earlier, would play as a deep-lying centre-forward, pulling markers out of position just as Nandor Hidegkuti had done to England.

The tactic was scoffed at by the coaching establishment, but City reached two successive FA Cup finals with it. The first, against Newcastle in 1955, saw City play most of the game with ten men after their England full-back Jimmy Meadows had suffered a career-ending knee injury – they lost 3–1. The second, against Birmingham, was won by the same scoreline, thanks to the courage of City's German goalkeeper Bert Trautmann, who played on without realising he'd broken his neck, and the genius of Revie, whose increasingly fraught relationship with McDowall would have led to his omission, had the would-be replacement, Bill Spurdle, not been stricken with an attack of boils.

McDowall shed no tears over losing Revie to Sunderland in 1956, but City lacked a forward of the same vision and flexibility until they broke the British transfer record to sign Denis Law from Huddersfield for £55,000 in 1960. The club had been flirting with relegation again in the preceding couple of seasons, yet Law's arrival seemed likely to usher in a bold new era when the Italian club Torino offered £110,000 for him in 1961. This was an offer even a club of City's stature could not refuse, and Law's sale – and subsequent return to Manchester with United – led to relegation in 1963.

McDowall resigned after 13 years at the helm, and his successor George Poyser failed to get City promoted in two seasons before making way for Joe Mercer in the summer of 1965. Mercer had a reputation for being able to lift mediocre sides, but had suffered a stroke while in his last job at Aston Villa, and wanted a strong assistant to share the workload at City. He found one in Malcolm Allison, a young coach who'd just been sacked by Plymouth Argyle. The two were a perfect match – Mercer the genial old joker who'd seen it all as captain of Arsenal and England, Allison the aggressive motivator, brimming with confidence and fresh ideas.

Between them they set about not just the rebuilding of the team but the revival of the whole club, which was in danger of wilting under United's shadow. While Mercer sought out new players with the help of

Tommy guns for Tottenham – Hutchison (submerged) gives City the lead at Wembley, 1981

chief scout Harry Godwin, Allison raised fitness levels and instilled a new will to win.

In their first season City reached the quarter-finals of the FA Cup and won the Second Division title with five points to spare. The following year, with winger Mike Summerbee signing from Swindon, midfield ball-winner Colin Bell arriving from Bury and 32-year-old defender Tony Book being reunited with Allison from Plymouth, City avoided relegation and established a reputation for stylishly unpredictable football.

In October 1967, Mercer went to Bolton and told their leading goalscorer, Francis Lee, that he was the one player City needed to become a truly great team. Lee signed, and by the following May, City were champions. The title was sealed with a 4–3 win at Newcastle on the final day, but the campaign's pivotal match had been played in March at Old Trafford, where reigning champions United had been beaten 3–1. After months of being told their team would never match United's achievements, it was a sweet moment for Mercer and Allison. Most United staff refused to comment, with the exception of George Best, who admitted he'd been stunned by City's power and athleticism. 'That night at Old Trafford,' he said after the title was lost, 'we never saw which way they went.'

There would be no more League championships, but plenty more medals. City beat Leicester 1–0 to win the FA Cup for the fourth time in 1969, and were back at Wembley the following year to claim the club's first League Cup, beating West Brom 2–1. The real goal for Mercer and Allison in 1969/70, however, was the Cup-Winners' Cup. A year earlier, Allison had boasted that City's championship-winning team would 'scare Europe to death' and that Continental coaches were 'cowards'. Yet City's 1968/69 European Cup campaign was finished before it had started, with defeat at Fenerbahçe, a Turkish side who Allison conceded he had under-estimated.

City approached the following year's adventure with more humility, and were richly rewarded. First they beat Ronnie Allen's Athletic Bilbao 6–3 on aggregate, then trounced the Belgian part-timers Lierse and (rather nervously) edged out Académica Coimbra of Portugal. In the semi-finals City were beaten 1–0 by Schalke in Gelsenkirchen, but swamped the Germans 5–1 at Maine Road, in a game which saw Joe Corrigan – in his first full season as City's goalkeeper – play throughout despite a broken nose. City's opponents in the final were Górnik Zabrze, who'd beaten AS

Roma in the semi-finals on the toss of a coin. They included Polish internationals Gorgon, Latocha and Lubanski in their line-up but, on a wet and wild night in Vienna, they had no answer to Allison's power-play tactics. The final score of 2–1 didn't begin to suggest City's superiority.

Though nobody on Moss Side knew it at the time, Vienna was to be Mercer's swansong. In October 1971 he moved 'upstairs' to become general manager, with Allison taking the manager's seat. This suited neither, and by March 1973 both were gone. Deprived of their inspiration, the team drifted into mid-table, with little to show for their entertaining football until a second League Cup, won by Dennis Tueart's awesome overhead kick against Newcastle at Wembley, arrived on the mantelpiece in 1976.

By now Tony Book had become manager after serving Johnny Hart and then Ron Saunders as coach. With money to spend from a boardroom now led by the ambitious Peter Swales, Book brought Asa Hartford, Brian Kidd and Joe Royle to Maine Road, and they took City to within a point of the title in 1977. None was exactly in the first flush of youth, however, and when Swales moved Book into the general manager's post to accommodate a returning Allison in early 1979, it was with the intention of totally regenerating the team. In the 20 months that followed, Allison sold most of the club's established stars, attempted to blend £1million signings Steve Daley and Kevin Reeves with untried juniors – and failed utterly. At the time of Allison's sacking in October 1980, City had gone 12 League games without a win. Swales' mistake – and it was to be the first of many – was to give Allison control over transfers as well as team selection and tactics, a level of responsibility he had never carried in the Mercer years.

Allison's replacement, John Bond, steered City to safety and even took them to an FA Cup final against Tottenham, where veteran Tommy Hutchison scored for both sides in a 1–1 draw, and Steve Mackenzie's majestic volleyed goal for City in the replay was eclipsed by Ricky Villa's solo winner for Spurs. Bond's team had everything Allison's lacked: spirit, discipline and organisation. But he was found unable to augment those qualities with any invention, and City were already on the way down when he made way for his assistant John Benson toward the end of 1982/83.

Billy McNeill got City up again in 1985, but within two years, after the manager had defected to Villa Park and left his assistant Jimmy Frizzell holding the baby, there was another relegation. On the bright side, City had won the FA Youth Cup in 1986, and Frizzell's successor, Mel Machin, managed to blend some of the stars of that team – Paul Lake, Andy Hinchcliffe and Ian Brightwell among them – with signings of his own, including Ian Bishop, Trevor Morley and Clive Allen. Machin's side won promotion in 1989, and marked the club's return to the top flight with a 5–1 thrashing of United. Alas, Swales' patience was tested by some poor results shortly afterwards, and Machin had made way for

Numb Nineties – Pallister outjumps Quinn

Howard Kendall before the year was out. Kendall broke up Machin's young team and brought in a string of players from his former club Everton. Just 12 months after his arrival, however, he stunned City by walking out to rejoin…Everton. Fortunately, one of Kendall's acolytes, Peter Reid, then took over as player-manager and ushered in a period of rare stability. Under Reid, City finished fifth in the League in 1991 and 1992. An FA Cup quarter-final defeat at home to Tottenham in 1993, however, sparked a pitch invasion by fans for whom the ousting of Swales had become an obsession. When Swales replaced Reid with Brian Horton one month into the 1993/94 season, it was the last, desperate act of a corrupt and inept regime.

Finally, in February 1994, Swales sold out to a consortium led by Francis Lee, the former idol of the Kippax terrace who'd been building a multi-million pound business from toilet rolls even before he'd joined City as a player. Lee was the fans' choice to move the club forward, but his extravagant promises of progress soon foundered on the financial mess left by Swales, who had sold off the rights to the club badge and agreed a flat fee for the franchise to run the club shop – no matter how many replica shirts City sold, the income they received was the same.

With new stands at Maine Road to be financed and extravagant player contracts to be honoured, Lee was re-negotiating City's overdraft, rather than pumping fresh money in. The appointment of his old chum Alan Ball as manager in 1995 then led to accusations of cronyism, precisely the trait for which Swales had been despised. It also led – despite the presence of the single most talented player in the Premiership, Georgi Kinkladze – to relegation in 1996.

Two years and another four managers later, City dropped down to the third tier of English football for the first time in their history, their squad decimated first by Ball's wage bill-cutting, then by Frank Clark's eccentric transfers. By the time Joe Royle set about trying to lift the club out of the Second Division, Lee had himself bailed out, making way for *French Connection* chairman David Bernstein in 1998.

Incredibly, attendances in the Second Division during 1998/99 were actually higher than they'd been in the Premiership.The fans' loyalty knew no bounds, and nor did their elation when, in the last five minutes of the 1999 play-off final at Wembley, City clawed back two goals before beating Gillingham on penalties. The comparisons with United's display in the Nou Camp a few days earlier were obvious, but Bernstein and Royle wisely declined the offer of a United-style parade through the streets of Manchester. The desire to outshine Old Trafford has already cost Maine Road quite enough and, in any event, City fans would rather their club was not considered the same as United. Equal, maybe, but not the same.

Here we go!

Coming from the north, east or west, **motorists** should exit the M63 at Junction 9 and follow signs to the A5103 Manchester. Turn right at the crossroads after just under 3miles into Claremont Road, then right into Maine Road.

From the south, exit the M56 at Junction 3 and follow the A5103 as above.

Street parking around the ground is possible but police warn against it because of car crime. A better bet is one of the many impromptu **car parks** that spring up around the ground on matchdays, many at local schools.

From Manchester Piccadilly **train station** follow signs for Piccadilly Gardens bus station and take a #41, #42 #43, #44 or #46 bus to Platt Lane, which is a 5min walk from the ground.

Manchester Piccadilly is a major rail hub with direct services to Liverpool, Leeds, Newcastle, Sheffield, Birmingham and London among others. There are late departures after midweek games for most destinations except London. Check the latest timings on ☎0345/484950.

Just the ticket

Visiting fans are accommodated in blocks S, T and U of the North Stand, where there are 2,300 seats. A further 1,000 are made available for big games in block UU – the infamous 'Windy Corner' overspill stand. Ticket prices in 1998/99 were adults £12, concessions £7, with £1 off for Windy Corner. There is limited space for **disabled visitors** in the North Stand – advance booking essential on ☎0161/226 2224.

Swift half

Most of the pubs around Maine Road are 'home only', but fans arriving by car can stop off at ***The Princess*** on the corner of the A5103 Princess Parkway and Mauldeth Road West. Alternatively, you can normally get a pint inside the ground, or at the club's **training centre** on the corner of Platt Lane and Yew Tree Road – where families are welcome, too.

Club merchandise

Far more than United, City have always emphasised looking the part. The team won the 1956 FA Cup wearing dazzling claret shirts with white pinstripes, and 13 years later won the same trophy wearing a Milan-style red-and-black kit inspired by Malcolm Allison.

Two years ago the club abandoned its traditional sky blue in favour of cyan (known officially as 'Lazer'), but the future of this was uncertain in 1999 as City delayed the unveiling of a new kit after the withdrawal of 12-year sponsors *Brother*.

Discover the latest model for yourself at the ***City Store*** (open Mon–Sat 9.30am–5.30pm, later on matchdays, ☎0161/232 1111) next to the supporters' club entrance in Maine Road.

Barmy army

The historic Kippax Terrace was replaced by a new three-tier stand in 1995 and much of City's hooligan problem went with it – though there was a (perhaps inevitable) surge of violence when Millwall visited Maine Road in 1998/99.

On a brighter note, it was City fans who pioneered the inflatables craze with their giant bananas in the late Eighties, and the *Forward With Franny* and *Free The Manchester 30,000* campaigns, mounted to oust Swales and Lee respectively, were for the most part peacefully constructive.

In print

The ***Manchester Evening News*** has been a dispassionate chronicler of events at Maine Road for longer than most fans care to remember. Its Saturday evening ***Pink*** is required reading after the final whistle.

The *MEN*'s great local media rival, the *Guardian* group, produces the monthly magazine ***City*** – not a bad read for an official publication.

Fanzines include ***King Of The Kippax*** (25 Holdenbrook Close, Leigh, WN7 2HL), ***Bert Trautmann's Helmet*** (217 Dumers Lane, Radcliffe, M26 2GE) and ***Chips 'n' Gravy*** (PO Box 140, Manchester M14 6AA).

Talking With Wolves (Breedon, £16.99) contains vivid recollections of the club's Fifties heyday and later, from many of the players involved, courtesy of the *Express* and *Star* archives.

The most comprehensive of the recent City history books is ***Manchester – The Greatest City*** by Gary James (Polar, £24.95), lavishly illustrated as well as movingly written.

On air

BBC station ***GMR*** (95.1 FM) has phone-ins before and after games, well-patronised by City fans pouring their hearts out. The local commercial offering is ***Piccadilly Radio*** (103 FM).

In the net

City's **official site** is *Planet*-run but one of the company's better efforts, at: www.mcfc.co.uk.

The best way to navigate around the bewildering array of unofficial sites is to consult ***Wookie's Man City Links*** at: www.wookie.u-net.com/citylow.htm.

Wembley, 1999 – Edghill kisses the badge

Manchester United

Formation	1878 as Newton Heath LYR
Stadium	Old Trafford, Sir Matt Busby Way, Manchester, M16 0RA. ☎0161/872 1661
Ground capacity	56,500
First-choice colours	Red shirts, white shorts
Major honours	League champions 1908, 1911, 1952, 1956, 1957, 1965, 1967, 1993, 1994, 1996, 1997, 1999; Second Division champions 1936, 1975; FA Cup winners 1909, 1948, 1963, 1977, 1983, 1985, 1990, 1994, 1996, 1999; League Cup winners 1992; European Cup winners 1968, 1999; European Cup-Winners' Cup winners 1991; European SuperCup winners 1991
Position 1998/99	Premiership champions

In his book *Left Foot Forward,* the journeyman striker Garry Nelson describes Old Trafford as 'that perfectly focused ground where all you can do is play football'. Nelson had come to the ground with Charlton Athletic for an FA Cup tie and, though his team's 3–1 defeat has long since been buried in the archives, it remains vivid in his mind as 'the biggest, most important game of my career'.

It is not just the players who view Old Trafford as special. Geoff Mann, the architect behind Coventry City's Arena 2000 stadium project, puts it this way: 'At Blackburn and Sheffield Wednesday you can look up and see Auntie Gladys hanging out her washing in her back garden. There are gaps everywhere. When you are inside Old Trafford you really start to believe it all – because all you can see is football.'

It was the football, above all else, that brought the Premiership title, the FA Cup and the European Cup to Old Trafford in 1999. Yet the truly remarkable thing was not that all three honours were won on the pitch (though heaven knows, it took some doing), but that the players, their manager and coaching staff managed to stay 'perfectly focused' throughout.

In the course of United's treble-chasing, epoch-making 1998/99 season, the club occupied as much space on the front pages as it did on the back ones. Whether it was the *BSkyB* takeover or Becks' and Posh's baby, an accountant's report claiming they were the richest team in the world or their part in a European Superleague, United were an issue to be bitten into, chewed over and spat out, from the opening grin of *The Big Breakfast* to the final soundbite of *Newsnight.* When a miniature tabloid camera lens poked through the barbed-wire fencing of the club's private car park to snap five Ferraris, three Porsches and a Bentley, the club had been elevated to the status of public property number one. And why not? Now that the Royal Family have been re-invented as 'ordinary people' and there are no true popstars any more, what better to plaster over the papers than Manchester United's Motors? If sex sells, then sport sells more, soccer sells more than that, and Manchester United now sells the most of all.

Through it all, the players had to remain as if permanently cocooned by the stands at Old Trafford, the 'Theatre Of Dreams' in which the outside world can go hang, and the football can do all the talking. Short of playing every match there, they would have to be totally single-minded in their approach. And it spoke volumes for the club's internal discipline that they managed it with scarcely a flicker of dissent, from the first whistle at home to Leicester City in August 1998, to that last, lofted corner-kick into the Bayern Munich box in Barcelona, nine months later.

Just can't keep my hands off it – Sir Alex, the European Cup and an open-top bus, May 1999

There is nothing new under the sun, and United had, of course, been here before. Just as the team's progress through the Nineties under Alex Ferguson culminated in a crescendo of media attention as the treble came into view, so Matt Busby's rebuilding of the team in the aftermath of the Munich air crash reached its natural pinnacle with the 1968 European Cup final at Wembley – and, if anything, an even louder ballyhoo on the part of the press.

In between those two highs, United's history proffers many instances of what can happen to England's most celebrated club when the football is accorded secondary importance, no matter how fleetingly. And the pre-Busby era, when United were the epitome of mediocrity, yo-yoing between the top two divisions, offers a more distant but perhaps also more potent reminder. For between the wars the club descended rapidly from a position of prominence that had seemed there for the taking just prior to World War I – United's first golden age.

Even that was a good while coming. United had officially come into being in 1902, and spent the first four years of their existence as a Second Division side. But the club could trace its roots back much earlier, to the formation of the Newton Heath Cricket & Football Club in 1878. The club was founded by the dining-room committee of the carriage and wagon works of the *Lancashire & Yorkshire Railway Company*, and the football team began playing at a modest ground on North Road in Newton Heath. Despite the pitch often being covered by clouds of steam from the adjacent railway line and the fact that the players had to get changed in the *Three Crowns* pub, a quarter of a mile away on Oldham Road, Newton Heath were immediately successful, cutting a dash in green-and-yellow halved shirts and black shorts, and comfortably beating a variety of other local works teams.

In 1885 members decided to sever links with the railway line and formed the club into a limited company under the name

Newton Heath FC. A year later the team won their first trophy, the Manchester Cup.

The Football League was formed in 1888, but while clubs from nearby Bolton and Accrington were invited to join its inaugural season, Newton Heath were ignored. Undaunted, the club became a founding member of the rival Football Alliance, alongside the likes of Sheffield Wednesday, Nottingham Forest and Small Heath – today's Birmingham City. The team finished their first Alliance season, 1889/90, in eighth place out of 12, and came ninth the following year. In 1891/92, Newton Heath were joined in the Alliance by a rival club from just across town, Ardwick. Whether they were inspired by the new competition or had merely got the hang of Alliance football by now, the team finished in second place that season, two points behind Forest.

The runners-up placing had far-reaching consequences. When the League agreed to restructure and the Alliance was dissolved for 1892/93, Newton Heath were given a place in the expanded First Division, whereas Ardwick – who'd finished seventh in the Alliance – were sent to the new Second Division.

Not that being in the First Division did Newton Heath any favours. They lost their first League game 4–3 at Blackburn, and went downhill from there, finishing bottom of the table after winning only six out of 30 matches. Only a 5–2 win over Small Heath in a 'test match' replay at Bramall Lane kept them in the First Division.

A year later, after finishing bottom again, Newton Heath weren't so lucky – they were beaten 2–0 by Liverpool in their test match at Blackburn, and relegated. Twice more in the next three seasons, the team were involved in test matches after finishing in the top three of the Second Division, but each time they failed to win promotion. When the test-match phase of the League programme was finally abandoned after 1898, no team were happier than the 'Heathens'. While the ordeal of playing-off for divisional status was over, the club's problems were in other ways only just beginning. Failure to win promotion had been costly, and while the board agreed that new players were needed if the club was to rejoin the First Division, the bank account was empty.

In 1902, with the club on the edge of bankruptcy, local brewer John H Davies took control and decided on a change of image. The team had left the neighbourhood of Newton Heath nine years earlier, to a new ground at Bank Street, after complaints about the state of the North Road pitch. Meanwhile the team's neighbours, Ardwick, had already changed their name to Manchester City. Davies argued that Newton Heath, too, should give the impression of being a big-city club, and after the names Manchester Central and Manchester Celtic were rejected, another board member, Louis Rocca, threw 'Manchester United' into the barrel. The name was formally adopted on 26 April 1902, and registered for the 1902/03 season.

As well as a new name, the club would soon have a new manager, Ernest Magnall, who had once cycled from Land's End to John O'Groats, and received a similar dedication to fitness from his players. In 1904, he also received a stroke of good fortune. Manchester City had won the FA Cup that year, but their success brought allegations of illegal payments. Virtually the entire City squad was suspended from football, and when they were eligible to play again, a group of them, led by gifted Welsh international winger Billy Meredith, decided to sign for United. They had already won promotion from the Second Division in 1906. Within two years, with Meredith and company onboard, they would be crowned League champions, setting a new record of 82 goals scored in a season, and playing a quick, exciting brand of football that was the talk of Manchester and beyond.

A year later, though the title was lost to Newcastle, Magnall's side lifted the FA Cup for the first time, Meredith making the difference in a poor final against Bristol City at Crystal Palace, won by a single goal from

Sandy Turnbull. If the game itself was nothing special, the reception that awaited United when they returned home was spectacular. Some 300,000 lined the streets, with a further 30,000 waiting at Bank Street where United, a little worse for wear after drinking champagne from out of the Cup, lost a League game to Arsenal.

The huge local acclaim bestowed on the team was welcome news for John Davies, who had already signed up to move the club from Bank Street (which was also criticised for its poor pitch, not to mention the noxious odours pouring forth from an adjacent chemical works) to a new ground at Trafford Park, five miles away. Davies now believed his club commanded support from across the Manchester area, and felt justified in planning for a fabulous new arena capable of holding 80,000.

Despite having cover on only one side, 'Old Trafford', as United's home became known, represented a quantum leap ahead in stadium design, with its massage rooms,

When time stood still – the meaning of Munich

You could see it on the faces of the United players gathered in one corner of the aircraft for a game of poker. The *BEA* Elizabethan plane had already made two aborted attempts at take-off from Munich's snowbound Riem airport, and as the wheels churned up the slush on the runway for a third time, **Johnny Berry** turned to **Liam Whelan** and said: 'We're all going to die.'

In fact Berry was to survive, but Whelan, along with Roger Byrne, Geoffrey Bent, Eddie Colman, Mark Jones, Dave Pegg and Tommy Taylor, would all perish as the plane failed to take off, overshot the runway and crashed into a house. **Duncan Edwards**, the youngest player ever to be capped by England and arguably the most gifted of the lot, died in hospital after a 15-day struggle against horrific internal injuries.

Glass apart – Duncan Edwards immortalised

Also killed were three members of United's back-room staff, the co-pilot, three passengers unconnected with the club and eight journalists, including former England goalkeeper **Frank Swift** and **Tom Jackson** – ironically, the man who had first coined the phrase 'Busby Babes'.

'There was no screaming, no crying, no moaning,' recalled **Harry Gregg**, United's 'keeper. 'Just darkness and sparks and the stench of aircraft fuel.' Like all those who survived the events of 6 February 1958, Gregg felt a peculiar guilt in their aftermath.

Yet in time the disaster became a source of energy and hope. Manager **Matt Busby**, who recovered after twice being read the last rites in hospital, emerged more determined than ever to capture the European Cup he'd been convinced his 'Babes' would win. **Bobby Charlton** went on to win the 1966 World Cup with England and become, in the process, the country's best-loved sporting personality. And all the while, the **stopped clock** outside Old Trafford remained as a reminder of the crash, and of its long-lasting, perhaps permanent effect on the world's most famous football institution...

gymnasium, plunge pools and other exotic facilities. It was also, even then, a ground that encouraged good football – in their first full season there, United recaptured the title, with Meredith and club captain Charlie Roberts continuing their inspired vein of form.

As so many clubs had discovered before and since, however, good football cuts no ice with the bank manager. Building Old Trafford had placed a huge financial burden around United's neck and, while crowds were high, the ground had never been filled to capacity. Sensing that all was not well, Ernest Magnall left for Manchester City at the end of the 1911/12 season. A year later, United had no choice but to accept Oldham Athletic's offer of £1,500 for Roberts. The team had now lost its two most important figureheads, but the books still wouldn't balance, and the last thing United needed was to be relegated on the eve of World War I. So it was that on Good Friday 1915, Liverpool came to Old Trafford and were beaten 2–0 – a result that enabled United to avoid the drop. The referee reported that he thought Liverpool's attitude 'strange', and it was soon revealed that four players on each side had fixed the result from the start. The United players clearly wanted to protect their careers and, had they left it at that, they might have got away with it. But they had also placed bets on the 2–0 scoreline, arousing suspicions at a local bookmaker who, in turn, alerted the authorities. All those involved were banned for life, but the bans were lifted after the war, as both clubs sought to rebuild squads decimated by four years of bloody conflict.

United resumed competitive football in 1919 looking a shadow of their former selves. Key players had been sold, while the club's finances were such that only a handful of youngsters could be bought in, mainly from non-League clubs. Attendance levels briefly soared in the postwar euphoria – to a high of more than 70,000 for the visit of Aston Villa in 1920 – but the team's football wasn't much to look at, and in 1922 United were relegated.

They were back up again within three years, but there were only a couple of good FA Cup runs to write home about in the latter half of the Twenties, and by 1931, amid further FA inquiries into misconduct, the mass boycotting of matches by fans and the appointment of former referee Herbert Bamlett as manager, United had been relegated again. This time the decline was more fundamental. The Great Depression was biting deep into Manchester's industrial wealth, and with the board refusing to accede to fans' requests for a greater say in the running of the club, many supporters voted with their feet – gates in the Second Division averaged less than 4,000. Before long, United were £30,000 in debt, and would surely have gone to the wall had they not been saved by businessman James Gibson, who promised to write off the debt in exchange for a seat on a reconstituted board. But while they were now financially secure, United needed a last-day victory at Millwall, to avoid dropping down to the Third Division (North) in 1934, and even promotion to the First two years later was followed by immediate relegation. In 1938, United came

At home in the Theatre – Sir Matt at Old Trafford

back up to stay – but World War II still stood between the club and its dramatic rebirth…

Matt Busby signed up as manager of United on 19 February 1945. In a brief press statement, club secretary Walter Crickmer said Busby would 'build up the team and put it where it belongs, at the top.' Busby had first made an impact locally as a stylish half-back with Manchester City, before moving to Liverpool and being capped by Scotland. He was keen to return to Manchester, and while at Sandhurst military academy at the end of the war, he received a letter from Louis Rocca – now an Old Trafford scout – informing him of the vacancy at United, and immediately set up a meeting with Crickmer.

Although Busby is usually credited with creating the first of his great United sides in the aftermath of the war, much of that Forties team was already at the club when he arrived – including goalkeeper Jack Crompton, skipper Johnny Carey at full-back, centre-half Allenby Chilton, Charlie Mitten on the left flank and the incomparable Jack Rowley at centre-forward. Busby knew how talented his players were and treated them with respect, eschewing indi vidual coaching in favour of group therapy – United would go out as a team, play as a team, enjoy themselves as a team, so long as they concentrated on the job in hand.

This wasn't as easy as it sounded. Old Trafford had been badly damaged by Nazi bombing and United were playing home games at City's Maine Road ground. Even so, they managed a runners-up spot behind Liverpool in the first postwar League season. And the following year, 1948, they beat Blackpool 4–2 in the FA Cup final at Wembley, in a match so beautifully balanced between ebb and flow that contemporary reports described it as the greatest final ever.

In 1949 Old Trafford re-opened its doors, Charlie Mitten becoming the first player to score a goal at the ground for eight years, in a 3–0 win over Bolton. The following year, however, Mitten led a rebel group of professional players to an unofficial league in Colombia, where they were promised undreamt of salaries (£2,500 per year, as opposed to a maximum £600 in England). In his one season with the Bogota Santa Fe club, Mitten helped a Colombian select side to a historic win over the World Cup holders Uruguay. He then returned to England, officially still a United player – but Busby made it clear there was no future for such a rebel at Old Trafford.

On 24 November 1951, United gave a debut to two rising young stars, centre-half Jackie Blanchflower and full-back Roger Byrne, at Anfield. 'United's "Babes" were cool and confident,' wrote Tom Jackson in the *Manchester Evening News* – the first time the phrase 'Babe' had been used in relation to the club. That same season, after several near misses in both League and Cup, Busby finally brought the title back to Old Trafford. While the 'Babes' played their part, this was not their title, but a last hurrah for the likes of Carey and Rowley – just reward for a team that had kept United in the top four for the entire postwar period, and in style, too.

As the Fifties went on and the old faces faded from the scene, Busby gradually replaced them with more 'Babes' – many of them originally members of a junior setup that won the FA Youth Cup five times in a row from 1953. They included stopper Billy Foulkes, Irish inside forward Liam Whelan, outside left Dave Pegg, centre-forward Dennis Viollet and an immensely skilful giant of a man who seemingly could play almost anywhere, Duncan Edwards.

By the time the 1955/56 season came around, the Babes were being touted as title contenders, but only as an outside bet – most pundits agreed the team were too young to reach the very top. They were soon made to eat their words. United were top by Christmas and never looked back, finishing 11 points clear of second-placed Blackpool. No team had dominated the League so comprehensively since before the war – and the average age of Busby's team was just 22.

Sex object in a sombrero – simply the Best

George Best was the first British soccer superstar. Dozens of other players had enjoyed celebrity status in the game's boom period after World War II, but none had the trappings of fame that would beckon Best at the end of the Sixties. At the peak of his fortune he had a white E-type Jaguar, three boutiques, a nightclub and a house with curtains activated by sunlight. He was seen with a succession of spectacular girlfriends and journalists tracked his every move.

Heads I win – a superstar in training

Yet he was first and foremost a uniquely gifted footballer and – though this is often forgotten – a dedicated athlete who scored 178 goals in 466 games for Manchester United. He was discovered by assistant manager **Jimmy Murphy** and, after returning home to the back-streets of Belfast at the age of 15 because he was homesick, Best was coaxed back to Old Trafford by **Matt Busby**, who offered to act as a father figure. With his effortless change of pace, outstanding vision and tireless running, Best was the perfect playmaker for the third and last of Busby's great United sides. He played a key role in the title wins of 1965 and 1967, and was dubbed **'El Beatle'**, the perfect synthesis of sporting hero and pop icon, after returning from a victory over **Benfica** wearing an outsized sombrero. It was also against Benfica that he delivered his single most memorable football moment – a brilliant solo goal in United's European Cup triumph at **Wembley** in 1968.

From there it was mostly downhill. The greater his fame became, the less capable Best was of dealing with it, and Busby's instinctive shield of protection, for once, was punctured. Increasingly overweight and underwhelmed by what English football could do for him, Best finally **left for America** in 1974.

The critics continue to claim that the finest years of his career were laid to waste by his lifestyle, but Best himself has no regrets. As he says: 'I spent a lot money on birds, booze and gambling – the rest I just frittered away.'

A repeat performance the following year, with young hot-shot Bobby Charlton added to an already formidable line-up, seemed almost inevitable. Much less easy to predict was United's debut in the European Cup – an innovation bitterly opposed by the English authorities, who'd already prevented Chelsea from participating the previous year, but which United were keen to enter. Matt Busby was convinced his young side would have the measure of Europe and, after risking the wrath of the Football League, in 1956 he got his answer. Despite again playing at Maine Road (Old Trafford had no floodlights at the time), United demolished the Belgian champions Anderlecht 10–0 in the preliminary round, with Viollet scoring four alone. They went on to reach the semi-finals, where the great Real Madrid of the era edged them out.

A controversial 1957 FA Cup final defeat by Aston Villa then deprived Busby's side of a League and Cup double, but by now Old Trafford's sights were set firmly on Europe. In 1957/58 the progress continued, with United knowing they were in the semi-finals again as their plane left Yugoslavia after a 3–3 draw with Red Star Belgrade. A routine refuelling stop at Munich, and the squad would soon be home. But then the snow started to fall, and Busby's Babes were fated to play no further part in the development of the game, either at home or abroad...

Yet the Munich air crash (see panel p.325) did not stop the football. With Busby gravely ill in hospital, his assistant Jimmy Murphy led a makeshift side to a gallant European Cup semi-final defeat by AC Milan, and to another controversial Cup final loss, this time at the hands of Bolton. A year earlier, United 'keeper Ray Wood had been clattered out of the game by Villa's Peter McParland; now it was Harry Gregg's turn to be assaulted, bundled over the line by Bolton's Nat Lofthouse. Again, United's protests were to no avail.

After a protracted rehabilitation, Busby returned to his job, and faced a dilemma. He had thrown so many juniors into the United first team that the club's youth setup was bereft of promise. His instinct was to wait for new talent to come through the ranks, but both manager and club were impatient to rebuild after Munich, so he went shopping. With an apparently limitless chequebook provided by United's meat-merchant chairman Louis Edwards, Busby outbid other clubs for the services of Noel Cantwell, Maurice Setters, David Herd, Pat Crerand and, once it became clear he was desperate to leave Torino, the former Manchester City inside-forward Denis Law.

The new team's first success came in the 1963 FA Cup, with a 3–1 win over Leicester at Wembley. Two years later, with George Best (see panel p.328) and Nobby Stiles added to the armoury, the title was won, and with it the chance to enter the European Cup for the first time since Munich – United again got as far as the semi-finals, before losing narrowly to Partizan Belgrade. After another League championship in 1967, United did what they'd failed to do ten years earlier – beat

The Doc's finest hour – United have won the FA Cup and stopped Liverpool doing the treble, 1977

Real Madrid in the semis. Their opponents in the final, pre-arranged by UEFA for Wembley, would be the Portuguese club Benfica, who United had beaten with something to spare in the quarter-finals two years earlier. The visitors had the great Eusébio in their ranks but, after shocking United with a late equaliser to cancel out Bobby Charlton's opener, they were brushed aside in extra time as Best, with a solo special, Brian Kidd, with a nod-in on his 19th birthday, and Charlton again sealed the victory.

For Matt Busby, it was the culmination of more than 30 years' work at Old Trafford – he was knighted for his services to football, and seldom was the awarding of such an honour so popular in the anti-establishment atmosphere of the Sixties. Yet the triumph was also the cue for complacency. Nobody knew it at the time, but United would have to wait 23 years for another European trophy, and even longer for another League title.

The great man became general manager in 1969, with Munich survivor Wilf McGuinness appointed head coach. With the European Cup-winning side ageing and another paucity of fresh faces, United lost their shape, the team constantly tinkered with while results gradually piled up against them. At the tail-end of 1970 McGuinness was dismissed, and Busby returned for a brief rekindling of the magic. His permanent replacement, the former Leicester manager Frank O'Farrell, lasted barely 18 months before being sacked following a 5–0 defeat at Crystal Palace.

The 'new Best' – Norman Whiteside

Into O'Farrell's shoes thundered Tommy Docherty – in theory a visionary similar to his fellow Scot, Sir Matt, but in practice a man whose management philosophy could not have been more different. Keen to try out new tactical schemes, possessed of a sparkling wit and at his happiest when there was a media audience in tow, 'the Doc' severed almost all links with the Busby era – only for the rejected Denis Law to back-heel a goal for Manchester City and send United down to the Second Division in 1974.

To their credit, the board stuck by Docherty and he repaid them by winning the Second Division title at the first attempt. An average crowd of more than 48,000, a record for the division, watched the Doc's lively young side destroy just about everything that moved. With Martin Buchan and Brian Greenhoff in the centre of defence, Gordon Hill and Steve Coppell on the flanks, and Stuart Pearson and Lou Macari upfront, United were looking like a team again. They finished third in 1975/76, their first season back in the top flight, and also reached the FA Cup final. The inevitable comparisons with the Busby Babes were, however, beginning to burden Docherty's prodigies and, in a flood of tears and unfulfilled potential, United were beaten 1–0 at Wembley by Second Division Southampton.

Yet they returned a year later to beat Liverpool 2–1, with the winner rebounding off the chest of Brian Greenhoff's elder brother, Jimmy. United had ruined their great rivals' chances of a unique treble, and Docherty, dancing around Wembley in his red polyester shirt and white kipper tie, was the Seventies football-manager hero *par excellence*. The image was complete when, a few months later, news broke of the Doc's affair with Mary Brown, wife of United physio Laurie. The tabloids had a field day and the board, terrified by the whiff of scandal, felt they had no option but to sack their manager, just as he appeared to have created a side capable of challenging for the title.

Dave Sexton was hastily appointed in Docherty's place, and again, the players had to get used to a change of style. Studious to the point of solemnity, Sexton always talked a good game and, at times, his team played it, too. There was another trip to Wembley for the 'five-minute final' defeat by Arsenal in 1979, and a runners-up spot in the League the following year.

But the team were stagnating and, in a complete U-turn of policy from four years earlier, United's board went for a more colourful presence in the dugout when they dispensed with Sexton's services at the end of the 1980/81 season. They certainly got it. Ron Atkinson, who was to jewellery what Docherty had been to ties, walked into Old Trafford as if he owned the place, and quickly created an energetic, extrovert team in his own image. With Bryan Robson following his manager from West Brom to become United's new captain, Dutch midfielder Arnold Muhren arriving from Ipswich and Norman Whiteside, a lanky midfielder who had the misfortune to be dubbed 'the new Best' because of his Belfast roots, Big Ron's side were never less than good value for the admission money. Yet despite Cup final victories over Brighton in 1983 and Everton two years later, not to mention the odd swagger across Europe, the team were only peripheral figures in each year's title race.

Just as the European Cup had been Old Trafford's goal for more than a decade under Matt Busby, so the championship became an obsession now – not least because Liverpool were beginning to monopolise it with such easy arrogance.

Barça beaten – Hughes and Cup-Winners' Cup

With another challenge clearly heading for the sand midway through the 1986/67 season, Atkinson was shown the door.

Was his replacement, Alex Ferguson, the 'new Busby' United had been seeking since the early Seventies? Initially, it seemed not. A journeyman striker in the Scottish League who'd begun his managerial career as player-boss at East Stirlingshire, Ferguson had won huge acclaim after taking Aberdeen to both domestic and European glory in the early Eighties. In his background, demeanour and attitude to the game, he showed many similarities to Sir Matt. Yet it took him longer to make his mark on United than either Atkinson or Docherty.

Some members of Big Ron's team, such as 'Captain Marvel' Robson and big Welsh striker Mark Hughes, were retained. But others, like defender Paul McGrath and midfielder Gordon Strachan, were released, only to revive their careers elsewhere – much to the chagrin of United's fans. Inconsistency was the norm in the League, Europe was out of bounds after the Heysel

Race for honours – Beckham and Cantona get off to a flying start, 1997

ban, and even Wembley was not reached until, after surviving what appeared to be a fresh crisis of confidence with every round, Ferguson led his team out for the 1990 FA Cup final against Crystal Palace. The match was drawn 3–3, but United won the replay 1–0 with a goal from Lee Martin – a now forgotten player whose five-second contribution to the club's development in the Nineties cannot be under-estimated.

So began the incredible decade, a period of success which, in terms of sheer silverware alone, was unprecedented in the history of the club, indeed of any club. After the Cup-Winners' Cup had been lifted in the year English clubs returned to continental competition, two key foreign signings strengthened Ferguson's hand for 1991/92 – Ukrainian winger Andrei Kanchelskis, who matched acceleration with massive upper-body strength, and Danish international 'keeper Peter Schmeichel, by common consent the most formidable player in his position Old Trafford had ever set eyes on. United's nerves got the better of them in the 1992 title run-in, but the following season, with a third import, the enigmatic Eric Cantona, arriving from Leeds, there was no mistake.

The following year, the first League and Cup 'double' in the club's history arrived (it would have been a treble but for defeat in the League Cup final by Aston Villa), with the imports at the peak of their power, young Ryan Giggs on the opposite flank from Kanchelskis, Roy Keane and Paul Ince never less than competitive in midfield, and a solid back four of Parker, Bruce, Pallister and Irwin.

By now, a combination of Premiership TV cash, a massive expansion of the club's merchandising network and a public flotation masterminded by Louis Edwards' son, Martin, had given Ferguson a critical advantage in the transfer market. Yet, aside from the arrival of Andy Cole and David May, he chose not to use it, preferring to put his faith in emerging youngsters such as Nicky Butt and David Beckham. The result was the 'double double' of 1996, sealed with a kiss by Cantona's goal in the FA Cup final against Liverpool.

Uniquely among Premiership managers, Ferguson acted early after the passing of the Bosman ruling, offering lengthy new contracts to Giggs, Beckham, Butt, Paul Scholes and the Neville brothers. 'Fergie's Fledglings' would be safe with United, and United would be safe with them. As their talents blossomed, Old Trafford came closer to its European goal – a semi-final in the Champions' League of 1996/97, a quarter-final the year after.

It was ironic, then, that the holy grail of the European Cup would finally be attained in 1998/99, when United entered the competition for the first time as League runners-up – an innovation Ferguson had opposed. The £22million close-season signing of Jaap Stam and Dwight Yorke went against the grain somewhat, yet their arrival gave United's squad the depth it needed to compete effectively on three fronts.

Significantly, after the club's effortless title run-in, after Giggs' wonder-goal in the FA Cup semi-final, after the stirring wins over Inter and Juve, the killer blows against Bayern Munich were delivered by unheralded squad men – Teddy Sheringham and Ole Gunnar Solskjær. It was also fitting that the drama was played out at Barcelona's Nou Camp, another venue that effectively cuts you off from the rest of the world, where all you can see is the football.

In the dressing room before the 1958 FA Cup final, United's captain and Munich survivor Bill Foulkes told his team-mates to forget the media hype surrounding the side's comeback from the disaster, and concentrate on their football. The football. Always the football…

Here we go!

From most directions, the easiest option for **motorists** is to take the M60 motorway as far as junction 7, then exit onto the A56 toward Stretford. Stay on this as it becomes Chester Road, over the roundabout and across the lights, and you'll see Old Trafford on your left.

There's **car parking** both off Chester Road itself and off to the right next to Talbot Road, by the Old Trafford cricket ground.

Old Trafford has its own **train and *Metrolink* stations**, the former right next to the ground, the latter a 5min walk straight down Warwick Road and Sir Matt Busby Way. Both receive frequent services from Manchester Piccadilly (see Manchester City for connections).

Just the ticket

With practically every game all-ticket for United supporters, **visiting fans** often have a better chance of getting in to Old Trafford than the home brigade. That said, the south corner of the East (Scoreboard) End allocated to visitors for Premiership fixtures (more space is available for Cup games), holds only 3,000 and demand is often high. Check the situation with your own club before travelling. Tickets in 1998/99 were very reasonable, all things considered, at £20 for adults, £10 concessions.

Disabled visitors have a small area in the same corner of the ground – advance booking essential on ☎0161/872 1661.

Swift half

The pubs nearest the ground tend to be 'home only' and are so packed, you could wait an hour to be served. But a little further down Chester Road is ***The Gorse Hill Hotel***, a large, traditional and welcoming pub with big-screen TV. Alternatively, get off the *Metrolink* tram a stop earlier at Trafford Bar for ***The Tollgate Inn***, opposite the station, which does hot food if you get there early enough and welcomes families.

When it comes to **food,** the canalside area of Salford Quays, the other side of the ground from Chester Road, has some smart options, though again note that some of the pubs around here are 'home only'.

Club merchandise

At the last count, there were three separate shops at Old Trafford – the ***Superstore*** on Sir Matt Busby Way, the ***Megastore*** behind the Stretford End (West Stand) and the ***Matchday Store*** on the corner of the North and East Stands – the last is, as its name implies, open on matchdays only.

The range of goods on offer is every bit as wild as you've been led to expect, and while the stalls that set up around the ground before a game are cheaper, the quality of the official merchandise is beyond reproach.

Barmy army

It's a fact of Old Trafford life that the Stretford End no longer roars as it once did, and the arena as a whole can have an eerie, echoing quality to it when the idols are still finding their feet (much like the Nou Camp, in fact).

That said, the vast new North Stand found its voice during the 1998/99 European campaign, and United fans deserve praise for their willingness to sing out despite the forbidding nature of the bowl. Also worthy of note were the passionately well-organised campaigns to bring standing areas back to Old Trafford and, more recently, the (successful) fan-led protest against the proposed Murdoch buyout. Trouble of a more violent kind is very rare these days.

In print

The ***Manchester Evening News*** publishes its excellent 'Pink' after the final whistle on Saturdays, but the mass of **official and unofficial magazines** offer little to interest the neutral.

A clutch of lively fanzines proves there's more to United fan culture than shopping and eating – try ***United We Stand*** (PO Box 45, Manchester, M41 1GQ) and ***Red News*** (PO Box 384, London, WC1N 3RJ).

On the book front, the ***Illustrated History 1878–1998*** (Hamlyn, £17.99) by Tom Tyrrell and David Meek is a good starting point, while ***Always In The Running*** (Mainstream, £7.99) is Jim White's run-through of a post-Busby dream team, far better than the run of the mill.

Two more off-the-wall books are ***For Love Or Money*** (Andre Deutsch, £6.99), a peek into the financial dealings surrounding both United and the England team during the 1997/98 season by Alex Fynn and Lynton Guest; and ***Bogota Bandit*** (Mainstream, £14.99) Richard Adamson's tribute to Colombian rebel Charlie Mitten.

Due in the autumn of 1999 was ***Managing My Life*** (Hodder & Stoughton, £17.99) a new Alex Ferguson autobiography, co-written with Hugh McIlvanney.

On air

For the impartial view you can tune into ***GMR*** (95.1 FM) or ***Piccadilly Radio*** (1152 AM). Alternatively, there's matchday broadcasting on the club's own ***Manchester United Radio*** (1413 AM) within a fair radius of the ground.

Despite having its own studio at Old Trafford, ***MUTV*** is disappointingly lightweight, its re-runs of reserve-team fixtures and interviews with micro-celebrities failing to make up for the lack of first-team action. Subscribing costs around £5 per month, and the channel is available only as part of a *Sky Digital* satellite package.

In the net

United's **official website** has come a long way since it was run as an area of the *Sky Sports* site two years ago. Now it's a fully fledged, slickly designed and highly commercial operation, with (as you'd expect) a comprehensive e-commerce section. By comparison with some big official sites, however (notably Arsenal and Chelsea), it still lacks depth. But judge for yourself at: www.manutd.com. Among the unofficials, ***Theatre Of Dreams*** has the historical context the official site lacks, plus lots of fan input and plenty of multi-media bits and bobs, at: mufc.simplenet.com. There were more than 100 United sites on the web at the last count, so the ***Ultimate Manchester United Links*** page has to be worth a couple of minutes at: www.ozemail.com.au/~rdurie/manutd.htm.

The generation gap – Ryan and Bobby exchange glances

Mansfield Town

Formation	1897 as Mansfield Wesleyans
Stadium	Field Mill Ground, Quarry Lane, Mansfield, NG18 5DA. ☎01623/623567
Ground capacity	7,000 (before rebuilding scheduled for 1999/2000)
First-choice colours	Yellow and blue
Major honours	Third Division Champions 1977; Fourth Division Champions 1975; Freight Rover Trophy winners 1987
Position 1998/99	Eighth in Third Division

English lower-division football is afflicted by many ailments, and Mansfield Town seem to be suffering from almost all of them. The team have their small band of loyal supporters in this former centre of the East Midlands coal industry, but beyond, the closeness of Derby and the two Nottingham clubs makes it hard for Town to broaden their fan base. The club's ground, Field Mill, is in an advanced state of disrepair, its condition not helped by indecision as to whether Mansfield should refurbish it, or start all over again with a new stadium out of town. The chairman, Keith Haslam (son of former Sheffield United manager Harry Haslam), was hailed as a saviour when he bought the club in 1993, but more recently has been subjected to terrace cries of 'Haslam Out!' The manager, Steve Parkin, just failed to get Mansfield into the Third Division play-offs in 1998/99 and, frustrated by Haslam's insistence on paying outside debts before making cash available for players, resigned in June 1999.

When Mansfield celebrated their centenary two years ago, work was expected to begin on the total rebuilding of Field Mill – in conjunction with a wider development of surrounding land – into a 10,000-seat stadium. But during the 1998/99 season, despite an increased grant from the Football Trust, the club was too busy fending off winding-up orders and paying back taxes to put the plans in motion. The bulldozers were finally expected in over the close season, but nobody in the town was holding their breath.

Close and a cigar – erstwhile boss Andy King

Romantics, at least, should be grateful that the beautiful game, or at least a version of it, will continue to be played at Field Mill, one of the oldest football grounds in the world. It was in 1840 that the Greenhalgh family founded a cricket club to play matches here – they ran a nearby cotton mill and named the ground after it. In 1861 four Greenhalgh brothers decided to start a football team, Greenhalgh FC, also using Field Mill as a base. (One of the brothers

Not another brick in the wall – Tony Ford (far left) broke the League appearance record in 1999

went on to play for England in the first-ever international against Scotland in 1872.)

In 1894, Greenhalgh FC merged with a club calling itself Mansfield Town, to form Mansfield FC. The new club moved away from Field Mill, leaving the ground to become the home of Mansfield Amateurs and then Mansfield Mechanics before World War I intervened. After the war, the Mechanics considered a merger with another club now playing under the name Mansfield Town. The forerunner of the current club, this 'Town' had begun life as a branch of the local Wesleyan Boys' Brigade, playing under the name Mansfield Wesleyan from 1897. Eight years later, the team had turned professional – much to the horror of their founding fathers, who insisted the side change their name to Mansfield Wesley. After the club had entered the Notts & District League, the name was changed again, this time to Mansfield Town in 1910 – a year after the team had entered the FA Cup for the first time. A postwar merger between Mechanics and Town made a lot of sense – the former had the right ground, the latter superior playing resources. But while the talks were going on, Town were secretly negotatiating with Field Mill's owner, the Duke of Portland, to go it alone as the exclusive tenants of Field Mill. Thus snubbed, the Mechanics continued to play as a separate team until folding in 1923 – by which time Town had become members of the Midland League, Field Mill had been sold to a local consortium (with the proviso, laid down by the Duke, that it should always be used for sporting activities) and the ground had been used for the last time as a cricketing venue.

Thus established as the main footballing force in Mansfield, the team were nicknamed the Stags and set about trying to join the Football League. The club had been involved in talks which led to the formation of the Third Division in 1920, only to be refused entry to it. When the Division was regionalised a year later, Mansfield applied to join the northern section, but were rebuffed no fewer than five times. In 1928/29, the team embarked on a famous FA Cup run, beating Football League sides Barrow and Wolves before finally losing to Arsenal in the fourth round. The good publicity encouraged Mansfield to change tack in their negotiations with the League. In 1931 they applied to join the Third Division (South) and were immediately successful, replacing Newport County for the 1931/32 season.

Without gaining promotion, Mansfield then found themselves swapping divisions regularly, as the club's location prompted the League to boot the Stags from southern to northern sections of the Third Division and back again, whenever geographical make-up dictated. It was in the Third Division (North) that goalscoring legends Harry Johnson and Ted Harston did their most profitable business, Johnson scoring more than 100 League goals and Harston setting a Third Division record (unlikely ever to be beaten) of 55 goals in a season in 1936/37.

While individual achievements were easy to come by in the Thirties, however, it wasn't until after World War II that the town really had a team worth shouting about. The postwar era began inauspiciously – Mansfield had to apply for re-election for the first and only time after finishing bottom of the Third Division (South) in 1947.

Yet the club would soon reap the rewards of Britain's postwar football boom, with crowds flocking to Field Mill in unprecedented numbers and the team regularly attaining a top-half placing in the League. In 1950/51, Town finished runners-up in the Third Division (North) and reached the fifth round of the FA Cup. Two years later, a record crowd just shy of 25,000 packed into Field Mill to watch the Stags lose to Forest in the third round.

When the Fourth Division came into being in 1958, Mansfield easily made the cut to stay in the Third. Within two years, however, they'd been relegated to the Fourth, and in 1961, after two of the club's players had gone to prison for their involvement in the Peter Swan-Tony Kay match-rigging syndicate, Town narrowly escaped having to apply for re-election for a second time. The team's star player, young outside-left Mike Stringfellow, was sold to Leicester to balance the books, and Mansfield didn't escape the basement until 1963, when the finishing of centre-forward Ken Wagstaff helped them to a haul of 108 goals – enough for them to win promotion ahead of Gillingham on goal average.

Wagstaff left for Hull City soon after but the Stags managed to consolidate their position in the Third Division, missing another promotion only because their goal average was inferior to Bristol City's in 1965. After that it was a case of plodding on in mid-table for the remainder of the Sixties and the early part of the Seventies – though the arrival of striker Dudley Roberts from Coventry in 1968 did inspire Mansfield to their best ever performance in the FA Cup, the West Ham side of Moore, Hurst and Peters being among the victims as the Stags galloped all the way to the quarter-finals in 1968/69.

Together with Malcolm Partridge, Roberts formed a confident strikeforce which seemed capable of lifting Mansfield higher up the League ladder. Instead, both were sold and the team were back in the Fourth Division by 1972. Dave Smith, one of the few managers to have left a lasting impression on the club in the postwar era, pulled Town back up to the Third as champions in 1975, his team sealing the title with a 7–0 pasting of Scunthorpe in front of 11,000 at Field Mill.

The stars of Smith's side – goalkeeper Rod Arnold, veteran right-back Sandy Pate, playmaker Gordon Hodgson and uncompromising striker Trevor Eccles – stayed together to play under his successor, Peter Morris, an inventive midfielder at Mansfield during the Sixties who now returned to the club as player-manager. In 1976/77,

Morris' team shrugged off better-resourced challenges from Brighton and Crystal Palace to take the Third Division title.

For the first time in the club's history, Mansfield Town had reached the second tier of the English game. They were to stay there for only a season, but there would be some memorable games along the way, notably a 3–3 draw at home to Tottenham in which Glenn Hoddle lobbed Spurs an equaliser in the fifth minute of stoppage time. By that time Morris had been replaced as manager by Billy Bingham – a panic appointment by the board and a man who, despite a sharp footballing brain, could not inspire the same dedication and teamwork as his predecessor.

Mansfield were seven points from safety when they were relegated at the end of the 1977/78 season, and by the turn of the Eighties, despite Bingham signing his fellow Ulsterman John McClelland to shore up the Stags' defence, they had tumbled all the way down to the Fourth Division.

The following two decades have seen the club shifting uneasily between the bottom two rungs of the league ladder, its uncertain progress illuminated by the odd cup success. Ian Greaves led Mansfield to glory in the Associate Members' Cup (in its Freight Rover Trophy incarnation) with a Wembley win over Bristol City in 1987, in the first game beneath the Twin Towers to be decided by a penalty shoot-out.

Seven years later, an equally charismatic manager, the former Everton forward Andy King, inspired the Stags to a 1–0 aggregate victory over Leeds in the League Cup; after winning at Elland Road, they kept their advantage with surprising ease in the return.

Unable to drag Mansfield out of the bottom flight, however, King was relieved of his duties in 1996, to be replaced by Steve Parkin as player-manager. Despite modest resources and rarely playing in front of home crowds of more than 3,500, Parkin's side should arguably have clinched a play-off place in 1998/99, and probably would have done so but for their unconvincing away form. With young striker Lee Peacock always likely to score goals and veteran winger Tony Ford breaking Terry Paine's long-standing League appearance record during the season, Town seemed to have just the right blend of talents.

Just who will be guiding them, in what sort of stadium, and under what kind of boardroom regime, Mansfield's supporters were still waiting to know as the countdown to the 1999/2000 campaign began.

Here we go!

From just about any direction, **motorists** will probably approach Mansfield on the M1 motorway. Exit at junction 28, the A38 signposted Mansfield, and stay on this road for 4miles, passing through the adjacent town of Sutton in Ashfield. Go straight across the King's Mill roundabout, turn right at the next major crossroads, then second left into Quarry Lane – the ground is about a mile ahead on the left.

Field Mill has a large **car park** (£2) but space here may be restricted if and when the rebuilding work ever gets going. Street parking is not too problematical, however.

Mansfield **train station** is on the quaintly named but not particularly useful Robin Hood Line, which links Nottingham with Worksop (service hourly, journey time 35mins). Nottingham itself has direct connections for London St Pancras, Birmingham, Sheffield, Manchester and Liverpool. There are only limited connections after an evening kick-off, however, and no service at all on the Robin Hood Line on Sundays. For the latest timings call ☎0345/484950.

From the station, it's a 10min walk to Field Mill, the ground being visible as you exit. Follow the signs to Stockwell Gate and the bus station, go down the steps, turn left along the dual carriageway and continue straight on at the first set of lights along Portland Street. Then turn right at the next lights into Quarry Lane.

Just the ticket

If all goes according to plan, the north and south ends of Field Mill will be the first to be rebuilt during the 1999/2000 season, with the Main (West) Stand also being improved at a later date – though its distinctive art-deco exterior will be kept intact. Meanwhile, **visiting fans** will be asked to use the Bishop Street Stand, where an allocation of around 500 seats and a similar number of standing spaces will be available. Ticket prices are expected to be £11 seating, £9 standing, concessions half-price.

There should be some space for **disabled supporters** in a covered section of the Bishop Street Stand, but check with the club beforehand on ☎01623/623567.

Swift half

The ***Early Doors***, next to the ground at the junction of Quarry Lane and Nottingham Road, presents a modern, football-friendly face to the world, but is also the site of Field Mill House, home of the Greenhalgh family who did so much to shape sport in the town in the late 19th century. Reflect on history as you sip your choice of real ale or tuck into a Tex-Mex meal. The food is served all day and families are welcome, too.

Club merchandise

The **club shop** (open Mon–Sat 9.30am–5.30pm, later on matchdays) is set to be considerably expanded as part of the Main Stand modernisation plans. Whether this will allow the club to sell any more of its distinctive but not always tasteful yellow and blue replica shirts remains to be seen.

Barmy army

Mansfield fans bear their burden with dignity and good humour. Trouble won't kick off here unless visiting fans bring it with them, as the locals are too busy channelling their energies into more constructive projects, such as the *SOS* unofficial supporters' club.

In print

The only Saturday evening paper is published by ***The Nottingham Evening Post***, which finds little favour among Mansfield fans (for obvious reasons) who prefer the local ***Chad***. Fanzine ***Follow The Yellow Brick Road*** (10 Co-operative Street, Staunton Hill, Sutton in Ashfield, NG17 3HB) is more than 40 issues old and scarcely has an edition gone by without the future of Field Mill being debated – more fun than it sounds.

The essential Stags book is ***Mansfield Town – The First 100 Years*** (Glen, £18.95), co-written by Paul Taylor and the late Jack Retter.

On air

The town finally got its own radio station, ***Mansfield FM*** (103.2 FM), in 1998. As well as giving Town fans programming that doesn't treat the club as an afterthought to Forest and County, station manager Tony Delahunty has supported a local consortium intent on buying out club chairman Keith Haslam.

In the net

The club's **official site** is neat, clean and original, if currently quite limited in scope. It's at: www.geocities.com/Colosseum/Field/7145.

Rather more ambitious is the unofficial ***StagsNet***, which offers still images and video footage of classic Mansfield games among many other features, and acts as a focus for various supporters' groups including *SOS* and *Follow The Yellow Brick Road* fanzine. A first-rate site, meticulously maintained and worthy of its awards, at: www.stagsnet.co.uk.

Depth of feeling – Field Mill, oldest ground in the Football League

Middlesbrough

Formation	1876
Stadium	Riverside Stadium, Middlesbrough, Cleveland, TS3 6RS. ☎01642/877700
Ground capacity	35,000
First-choice colours	Red and white
Major honours	First Division champions 1995; Second Division champions 1927, 1929, 1974; FA Amateur Cup winners 1895, 1898; Anglo-Scottish Cup winners 1976
Position 1998/99	Ninth in Premiership

Over the past 100 years, the footballing fraternity on Teesside have schemed many schemes and dreamed many dreams. Their club, Middlesbrough FC, has built two grand new grounds in absurdly short spaces of time, has nurtured some of the most extravagantly talented players the English game has ever seen, has attracted some of the most colourfully exotic imports, and has inspired a level of support bordering on the hysterical. And for what? Three appearances in major Cup finals (all lost), a total of eight promotions (and nine relegations), and victory in the Anglo-Scottish Cup of 1976.

Middlesbrough's consistent failure to join the game's elite is one of English football's great unsolved mysteries. At various intervals along the way – not least when the liquidators moved in and the club nearly ceased to exist in the mid-Eighties – the fans have lost their faith. Today, though, the fire of self-belief burns like never before. 'Boro now have the stadium, the infrastructure, the management, the players and, perhaps most important, the vision finally to shake off their tag as noble also-rans. We *will* get there, the supporters say. It's only a matter of time.

Exactly how much time is a matter for conjecture. Approaching Middlesbrough's great, gleaming Riverside Stadium, it's hard to be unimpressed. But it's equally hard to ignore the arena's splendid isolation. After being conceived as a centrepiece for the rejuvenation of Teesside's old industrial heart, the Riverside continues to stick out like a sore thumb, four years after it was built. Middlesbrough is an ambitious, dynamic town but, as things stand, it needs a good few years' development before it can be called the new Barcelona. Bryan Robson, if pushed, would probably say the same about his football team.

When all the dreaming started more than a century ago, Middlesbrough was a very different place. Cargo ships plied the Tees estuary, in front of where the Riverside now stands, carrying coal, iron ore and steel to all corners of the globe. The port had been thriving ever since the *Stockton & Darlington Railway* pulled into town during the 1830s, and Middlesbrough FC seemed perfectly placed to capitalise on the football boom that was sweeping the north-east of England when they were formed in 1876.

As in so many English towns, it was the game of cricket that got the soccer ball rolling, with members of Middlesbrough CC deciding they needed an alternative pursuit to keep them fit in the long, winter months. Initially their team played on a purely amateur basis, even though the watching public were charged admission money as early as 1879. By 1887, 8,000 people were turning up at Middlesbrough's Archery Ground in Linthorpe Road to see an FA Cup derby clash with Sunderland. The game finished 2–2, and although 'Boro lost the replay, they progressed to the next round after Sunderland were disqualified for fielding three professionals.

The Football League was founded the following year, and it wasn't long before

The ship that came in – Middlesbrough's Riverside Stadium (right) graces the Tees estuary

the debate over whether to turn professional gripped the club. When the board opted to remain amateur, a group of disaffected players left to form their own professional team, which they named Middlesbrough Ironopolis, in celebration of the town's working roots. Over the next few years there were several attempts at reconciliation between the original team (then nicknamed the Scabs) and the breakaway side (the Washers), all of them unsuccessful. Both were founder members of the Northern League, but in 1893 Middlesbrough Ironopolis joined the Football League, and their rivals declined to follow them. Perhaps it was the original club that had got its sums right – after only a single season in the Second Division, Middlesbrough Ironopolis crumbled under a mountain of debt.

If the Washers were all wrung out, the Scabs had been given a new lease of life. They won the Northern League title in 1894, 1895 and 1897, and the FA Amateur Cup in 1895 and 1898. A year later, 'Boro themselves decided to take the plunge into professionalism, and were elected to the Football League Second Division.

Their first season there was uneventful, but in 1901 Middlesbrough finished sixth, and a year later, with goalkeeper Reg Williamson making his debut, they conceded just 24 goals all season, came second and were promoted. Williamson would go on to play 603 games in a 'Boro career spanning more than two decades, but the club was also planning to build a new ground that would serve for much longer.

In December 1902, 'Boro were told that their lease on the Archery Ground would not be renewed, giving them barely nine months in which to build themselves a new home. That home would be Ayresome Park, built on land next to that once occupied, ironically, by Middlesbrough Ironopolis' Paradise Ground, and capable of holding 33,000 when it opened, bang on schedule, in September 1903. It was as good a ground as then existed anywhere in the Football League, and 'Boro were resolved to ensure they had a side of similar grandeur, becoming the first English team to buy a player for £1,000 when they signed centre-forward Alf Common from Sunderland in 1905. The transfer fee was so controversial that questions were asked about it, appropriately enough perhaps, in the House of Commons. The feeling was that 'Boro were attempting to 'buy' their way out of relegation, an idea that many clearly found distasteful at the time. Distasteful or not, it worked – Common scored four goals in the team's last ten games and the drop was duly dodged.

The following season, Common netted 24 League and Cup goals as 'Boro finished 11th, and 12 more in 1907/08, when the team came sixth. He was then stripped of the club's captaincy after being accused of drunken violence, but Middlesbrough still finished a decent ninth in 1909.

The team's form dipped over the next couple of seasons, prompting the arrival of Tom McIntosh as manager in 1911. It was McIntosh whose calm, disciplined approach inspired what remains the club's best-ever League season – the 1913/14 campaign, when 'Boro finished third, only a point behind Aston Villa but eight shy of champions Blackburn. Whether that side, with George Elliott now the chief goalscorer in place of Common, would have gone on to challenge for top honours will never be known. World War I intervened, and although McIntosh resumed his managerial duties after the war, precious continuity had been lost and Middlesbrough drifted back into mid-table.

McIntosh departed in 1919, and five years later 'Boro were relegated under Herbert Bamlett. In October 1925, Bamlett signed a 22-year-old centre-forward, George Camsell, from Durham City for £600. An instinctive goalscorer who was capable of shooting from anywhere and with either foot, Camsell got his first run in the side at the start of the 1926/27 campaign and never really looked back – he went on to net 59 League goals during the season (with nine hat-tricks among them), out of a club total of 122. (The latter is still a record, but Camsell's personal haul would be surpassed by Everton's Dixie Dean within a year.) Middlesbrough ran away with the Second Division title, and although Camsell was subdued the following year as the team went straight back down, he inspired 'Boro to another promotion in 1929.

This time the club would retain its top-drawer status with confidence, a series of mid-table placings during the Thirties being topped off by a fourth-place finish in 1939 – just in time for war to halt the team's progress once again. The stars of the immediate prewar era were Wilf Mannion and Mickey Fenton. Both were local lads who'd cut their footballing teeth in the South Bank area of Middlesbrough. Both received expert guidance from the club's manager of the time, Wilf Gillow. But there the similarity ended. While Fenton was a big centre-forward who successfully prised the #9 shirt from the ageing Camsell, Mannion was a short, stocky inside-forward whose quick feet and low centre of gravity made him both creative and, to opposing defenders, elusive.

Together with another former South Bank player, left-back George Hardwick, Fenton and Mannion resumed playing for 'Boro after World War II – though their mentor, Gillow, had died in the hostilities. All three players were capped by England, and local interest in the club had reached new levels; a record Ayresome Park crowd of more than 53,000 watched 'Boro entertain Newcastle in December 1949.

While Fenton and Hardwick would later serve the club as coach and manager respectively, it was Mannion who made all the postwar headlines. He missed the first half of the 1948/49 season after 'Boro blocked an intended transfer to Oldham by putting a ludicrous price on his head, and in 1955 he was suspended by the League for making newspaper allegations about players receiving illegal payments. By then, he had left Middlesbrough after the team were relegated at the end of the

1953/54 season. Fenton and Hardwick had both departed at the turn of the Fifties, and new manager Bob Dennison had his work cut out trying to rebuild the squad.

Dennison had no shortage of gifted players on his books. Forwards Brian Clough (see panel) and Alan Peacock were kept well-supplied from the flanks by the hard-working Billy Day and Edwin Holliday. Yet while the goals flowed at one end, they were also conceded at the other, and throughout the remainder of the Fifties, Middlesbrough's defensive frailty undermined their chances of promotion. Most of the club's stars, Clough included, had moved on by the time Dennison, after nine years of trying to teach 'Boro how to sit on a lead, finally called it a day in 1963.

The new manager, Raich Carter, was even less successful at plugging the leaks. By

Too bold, too bright – Brian Clough at 'Boro

Slightly built, fearless in the challenge, quick in both thought and movement, **Brian Howard Clough** spent most of his playing career as a centre-forward with Middlesbrough in the Second Division, and was in a league of his own.

Poised to score – a classic Clough pose

Born in the town in 1935, Clough left school to work as a **clerk for ICI**. He played football for what was effectively the works team, Northern League side Billingham Synthonia, but then stepped down a rung or two, to Great Broughton of the Teesside League, before Middlesbrough signed him **as an amateur** in 1951. He made his first-team debut in September 1955, and scored his first 'Boro goal the following week.

Clough initially struggled to get regular first-team football, but by the start of the 1956/57 season, Middlesbrough manager **Bob Dennison** had made him first-choice striker. Over the next four campaigns Clough would score 38, 40, 43 and 39 League goals, in a side to whom attacking came naturally. But 'Boro failed to win promotion and Clough, increasingly ambitious, vented his frustrations on his team-mates.

Dennison hoped that by making him **club captain** in the summer of 1958, the player's abrasive personality would be given a productive outlet. Clough responded by scoring five times in a 9–0 win over Brighton, but while he had become a terrace hero at Ayresome Park, the other players had had enough of their skipper's sniping. In November, all except goalkeeper **Peter Taylor** signed a letter demanding that Clough be stripped of the captaincy, and Dennison agreed.

In the summer of 1961, the club finally agreed to what had become an annual transfer request, and Clough was **sold to Sunderland** for £45,000. There his playing career would be cut short by a knee injury, sustained when he slipped on the Roker Park turf while chasing a lost cause. But he remained in the north-east to become **manager of Hartlepool** in 1965, with his old Middlesbrough buddy Taylor as his assistant – a winning partnership was born.

A good first 'tache – Graeme Souness, 1974

the time Ayresome Park was being prepared to host three matches of the 1966 World Cup, 'Boro were on the brink of a first-ever relegation to the Third Division – a fate that could not be averted by the last-gasp sacking of Carter and the appointment of Stan Anderson in his place.

With several new signings including the attack-minded full-back John Hickton and centre-forward John O'Rourke, Anderson's 'Boro escaped the Third Division at the first attempt, 40,000 watching the 4–1 home win over Oxford that clinched the runners-up spot. Anderson then consolidated Middlesbrough's position with the help of an enviable home record – 'Boro went unbeaten at Ayresome Park for more than a year between 1968 and 1969. After that there were consistent top-half finishes but no real threat of a return to the First Division.

What 'Boro needed for that was discipline in defence – something that had never been a club strong point. It finally came, though, when Jack Charlton replaced Anderson as manager in 1973. Having just retired as an uncompromising centre-back, 'Big Jack' felt his predecessor had built a fine squad whose talents were being misdirected. Prior to the 1973/74 season he made only one signing – midfielder Bobby Murdoch on a free transfer from Celtic – yet Middlesbrough's transformation was as dramatic as it was rapid. Well-drilled and strongly motivated, 'Boro won the Second Division title with seven games to spare, and finished 15 points clear of Luton Town in second place. Most crucially of all, they'd conceded just 30 goals in 42 games.

Inevitably, the stars of Big Jack's side were grafters rather than dazzlers. Goalkeeper Jim Platt was a model of reliability; centre-backs Willie Maddren and Stuart Boam were masters of their craft, just as the manager had been; and the midfield was dominated by a pair of workaholic anchormen, David Armstrong and Graeme Souness. The latter arrived after failing to make the first team at Spurs, Anderson picking him up for a modest £32,000, while Armstrong had been with Middlesbrough since he was nine, and would go on to make 356 appearances for the club without missing a game.

Charlton's side finished seventh in their debut First Division season and also reached the quarter-finals of the FA Cup. Their dour, disciplined football ('Boro conceded nine fewer goals than Brian Clough's title-winning Derby County that year) won them few friends outside Middlesbrough, but the manager insisted his tactics were the only means by which a club of relatively limited resources could thrive at the top level. Within two years, however, even Charlton himself was becoming frustrated by what he saw. He told the 'Boro board he needed two new players to mount a bid for major honours, but was informed no money was available. Just before the end of the 1976/77 season, Jack walked out.

The manager who replaced him, John Neal, could not have been more different in outlook. Forced to sell Souness to Liverpool, Neal built a new midfield around two more players who would subsequently head for Anfield, Craig Johnston and David Hodgson, and an astonishingly quick, tricky Irish winger, Terry Cochrane. The Ayresome Park crowd loved it, not least because it allowed them to shake off the 'Boring, Boring, 'Boro' tag which the club had been shackled with under Charlton. Neal, though, had cause to reflect that his team were playing in front of 'not great quantity, but quality' support. Unemployment was starting to hit Middlesbrough hard, and fewer fans could afford tickets, no matter how attractive the event.

In an attempt to create a new source of income away from the turnstiles, the board decided to build a new community sports hall adjacent to Ayresome Park. It took years to complete, by which time Neal had quit and 'Boro had slipped into the Second Division. Average attendances dropped to four figures, and a succession of managers (former players Murdoch and Maddren, along with a clearly past-his-prime Malcolm Allison) struggled to bring consistency to the team while working under crushing financial constraints.

In May 1986, 'Boro lost their last game of the season at Shrewsbury and were relegated to the Third Division. Within two months the club was in the hands of liquidators with debts of £1.8million, and padlocks were fitted to the gates of Ayresome Park. A consortium including *ICI*, *Scottish & Newcastle Breweries* and the cargo company *Bulkhaul* got together to found a new club, Middlesbrough Football & Athletic Co (1986) Ltd. But new manager Bruce Rioch, who'd stepped up from the coach's position toward the end of the 1985/86 season and worked through the summer without wages, had to take his team to play home games at Hartlepool at the start of the 1986/87 campaign, as the 'new' club fought a legal battle over the right to use Ayresome Park.

Rioch had no option but to build a new team from local youngsters, among them the central defensive pairing of Tony Mowbray and Gary Pallister, and another rapid winger in what was now something of a Middlesbrough tradition, Stuart Ripley. They ran rings around the Third Division, winning promotion with seven points to spare. A year later they completed one of the most dramatic comebacks in recent English football history, beating Chelsea over a two-leg play-off to clamber back into the top flight in 1988.

It was a classic case of too much, too young. 'Boro were relegated immediately, Pallister was sold to Manchester United for £2.3million, and the following year the team came within a whisker of sliding all the way back down to the Third Division. Inevitably, Rioch was sacked and replaced by his assistant, Colin Todd, who lasted barely a year before a play-off failure prompted the arrival of Lennie Lawrence. Under Lawrence there was another tilt at promotion, this time successful, and another instant relegation.

Middlesbrough were becoming an archetypal 'yo-yo' club, and Steve Gibson, the multi-millionaire owner of *Bulkhaul* and the most passionate 'Boro fan on the board, felt something had to be done. Together with the Teesside Development Corporation, the quango charged with rebuilding the area for the post-industrial world, Gibson hatched a plan to build a new stadium on the site of disused docks. Some of the more conservative board members opposed the move, so in early 1994 Gibson bought them out, leaving *ICI* as the only other shareholder.

Less than 18 months later, the Riverside Stadium had risen from the wasteground where Margaret Thatcher had once embarked on a famous photo opportunity. After her 1987 General Election victory, she talked of the need to rejuvenate Britain's crumbling inner cities; eight years later, it was football, one of her least favourite industries, that was actually doing something about it in Middlesbrough.

Of course, a major-league arena needed a major-league team, and new manager Bryan Robson delivered precisely that to Gibson with a First Division title win and promotion to the Premiership in 1995.

With a long-term sponsorship deal from *Cellnet* in the can, the money from record season-ticket sales in the bank and the inspired signing of the Brazilian footballer of the year Juninho, 'Boro coasted through the 1995/96 season on a wave of optimism, and finished 12th.

The following season saw two more Brazilians, Emerson and Branco, arrive at the Riverside, along with Italian international striker Fabrizio Ravanelli (see panel p.347). 'Boro again began confidently. But while the imports earned the club a fortune in sales of replica shirts and other merchandise, and were undeniably good for the big occasion, they were less well-equipped to deal with Tuesday night matches in the league.

The stars were all miraculously fit to play in Middlesbrough's two Wembley Cup finals – a League Cup tussle with Leicester, in which 'Boro conceded a late Emile Heskey equaliser before losing the replay, and an FA Cup game with Chelsea, effectively lost in the first 30 seconds to Roberto di Matteo's speculative shot. But when a mystery virus swept through the locker room and 'Boro unilaterally cancelled a Premiership visit to Blackburn, the club was deducted three points by the FA – three points which, it transpired, would have saved Middlesbrough from the relegation that subsquently befell them on the last day of the season.

None of the big names would stomach First Division football, so Robson was obliged to start again from scratch in 1997/98. Once bitten by a nasty foreign bug, the manager now opted to spend his transfer booty on some old Premiership pros. The likes of Paul Merson and Paul Gascoigne were good enough to get 'Boro back up at the first attempt, and into another League Cup final (again lost, to Chelsea of all people).

But although the team looked solid enough in retaining top-flight status in 1998/99, Merse's and Gazza's alcohol problems provided the Riverside with yet another unwanted sub-plot – no sooner was the former sold to Aston Villa, than the latter was entering a rehab clinic.

A change of tack is surely necessary for the millennium, and no doubt Gibson and Robson will dream something up. If not, the fans will dream it up for them.

Here we go!

The Riverside is one of the easiest grounds in England to get to. It's also one of the hardest to park next to, since there are spaces for coaches next to the arena, but precious few for cars. **Motorists** will almost certainly approach the ground along the A66 Northern Route, which is well-signposted from the main north-south A19. The best bet is to ignore signs for Riverside Park and leave the A66 at the third exit after the A19, following signs for Long Stay Parking. Leave your car in one of the car parks here, then follow the 'Boro fans through the tunnel that runs under Cargo Fleet Road.

Middlesbrough **train station** is not as well-served as it might be. Travelling along the East Coast main line, you need to change trains at Darlington for the local shuttle service (half-hourly, journey time 20mins). There are no onward connections to London suitable for evening games, but you can get to Leeds and Manchester. For the latest timings call ☎0345/484950.

Once at the train station, leave by the north exit onto Bridge Street West. This becomes Bridge Street East, which you should follow for about a quarter of a mile, then turn right into Windward Way. This in turn becomes Dockside Road, from which the visiting supporters' turnstiles are easily accessed on the left.

Just the ticket

Visiting fans are accommodated in one end of the South Stand, with around 3,500 seats now available since the corners of the Riverside were filled in during the summer of 1998. Check with your own club regarding availability (it's still an all-season ticket scenario for home fans), or call 'Boro themselves on ☎01642/877809. Ticket prices in 1998/99 were adults £18, concessions £10. There are spaces for 12 **disabled visitors** in the South Stand – book in advance on ☎01642/877745.

Swift half

Bitter, lager, red and white wine are all available in the **concourse bars** of the Riverside, though this can be a chilly way to sink a swift one before kick-off.

With no other bars in the immediate vicinity of the stadium, the best bet is to head for the town centre, around a 10min walk from the car parks mentioned above and 2mins from the train station. Linthorpe Road, where 'Boro played in their amateur days, has a pub in the ***Hog's Head*** chain; the building was once the *Empire Hotel*, which used to overlook the ground.

For more obvious nostalgia, try the ***Ayresome Park*** on Albert Road, which runs parallel to Linthorpe Road; it contains a number of items salvaged from the old ground and is popular with 'Boro fans, though it is not exclusively a 'home' pub, unlike some in the same street. For families, ***Dr Brown's*** on Marton Road is the place.

Club merchandise

The Riverside **stadium shop** (open Mon–Sat 9am–5pm, later on matchdays, ☎01642/877720) is behind the West Stand and every bit as bright and bustling as you'd expect.

It will pale into insignificance, however, next to the **new town-centre store** that's set to open in Middlesbrough's Captain Cook Square retail development in autumn 1999. Twelve times the size of the former Cleveland Centre outlet which it replaces, the new shop will sell 'more

Light as a Feather – Fabrizio Ravanelli

It's the summer of 1996, and Fabrizio Ravanelli has just won the **European Cup with Juventus**. He is on a family holiday in Sardinia when his agent phones to tell him that the Turin club has agreed to **sell him to Middlesbrough** for £7million. Ravanelli, an elegant striker whose journeyman's career finally looks to be coming to fruition and who Italian fans have nicknamed 'the White Feather' because of his prematurely grey locks, doesn't even know where Middlesbrough is. Surely his agent has made a mistake?

Dream debut – Rava hails a hat-trick

Apparently not. All the player has to do is agree personal terms with the Teessiders. Panic-stricken, Ravanelli hopes to scare 'Boro off by demanding **£42,000 per week** in wages. The club agrees. Off you go then, son…

Initially all went well. Ravanelli scored a hat-trick on his debut at home to Liverpool, **wowing the Riverside** with his shirt-over-the-head celebrations. He continued scoring at the rate of a goal every other game, but off-field things were far from well. Accustomed to state-of-the-art facilities at Juve, Ravanelli was exasperated by having to **get changed at home** after training because the 'Boro ground had no showers. Bewildered by the English players' taste for fish, chips and lager, he seldom socialised with them and, unlike the club's Brazilian contingent, made little attempt to **learn the language**.

Even before relegation at the end of 1996/97, Ravanelli had made it clear he wanted out. Finding a club willing to match Middlesbrough's original purchase price (not to mention the player's wages) was never going to be easy, though, and it wasn't until the end of September that **Marseille stepped in**. 'Boro lost £1.5million on the deal, while the player took a £17,000 weekly pay cut. The Feather fluttered away, and few on Teesside were sorry to see him fly.

Pinch and I'll squeal – Robbo welcomes Gazza

than just a range of 'Boro products', according to the club. Captain Cook Square is being built on the site of the former town baths, next to the bus station and a stone's throw from Linthorpe Road.

Barmy army

Looking round at a full Riverside now, it's hard to believe John Neal ever had cause to bemoan Middlesbrough's scant support. Town and football club are prospering together, and the new ground, for all its modernity, buzzes with old-fashioned north-east passion.

Trouble is practically unheard of at the ground itself, but beware 'home only' pubs (see *Swift Half* above) in the centre of town.

In print

The local ***Evening Gazette*** is the paper to turn to for well-balanced reporting on 'Boro. There's a pink ***Sports Gazette*** after the Saturday final whistle, and the paper also covers Darlington and Hartlepool from the same dispassionate perspective.

The official club magazine, ***Riverside Roar!***, is published quarterly but has little to engage the interest of non-'Boro fans.

Currently the only fanzine is ***Fly Me To The Moon*** (Unit 7, Brentnall Centre, Middlesbrough, TS1 5AP), which laughs at the expense of the club as well as the expected Geordie and Mackem targets.

Two 'Boro books can be heartily recommended. ***Doom To Boom*** by Dave Allan and Adrian Bevington (Mainstream, £14.99) is a compelling chronicle of the club's progress from the crisis of the mid-Eighties to the arrival of Ravanelli and company in 1996.

Even more poignant, though, is Willie Maddren's autobiography ***Extra Time***. Maddren is terminally ill with Motor Neurone Disease and his book starkly juxtaposes football memories with reflections on the nature of life and death. All profits in the £9.99 purchase price go to MND research. Order from the *Willie Maddren MND Fund* at 30 Silver St, Stockton on Tees, TS18 1HT.

On air

Commercial station ***Century Radio*** (100.7 FM) may just have the edge over ***BBC Radio Cleveland*** (95 FM) when it comes to 'Boro coverage, thanks to lively commentary and a fans' phone-in every weekday evening. The club's ***Boro TV*** cable station features an old Ayresome Park favourite, Bernie Slaven, as its main presenter.

In the net

Middlesbrough's **official website** is the standard *Planet* fare, with precious little real news, although the *Boro TV* multi-media section is handy for those without cable television. Find it at: www.mfc.co.uk.

For a more authentic feel of the club, try ***Boro Onine***, run by the *Evening Gazette* at www.boro.co.uk; or the fan-run ***Riverside Reds***, which features a fine player archive, at: www.riversidereds.ac.psiweb.com.

Finally, ***Middlesbrough Ironopolis*** get a posthumous site of their own thanks to Nigel Gibb at: members.aol.com/ironopolis/index.htm.

Millwall

Formation	1885 as Millwall Rovers
Stadium	The Den, Zampa Road, London, SE16 3LN. ☎0171/232 1222
Ground capacity	20,150
First-choice colours	Blue and white
Major honours	Second Division champions 1988; Third Division (South) champions 1938, 1948; Fourth Division champions 1962
Position 1998/99	Tenth in Second Division

How did the Lions lose their roar? Just over a decade since Tony Cascarino and Teddy Sheringham fired Millwall into the top flight and sent one of London's most fiercely devoted bands of football supporters into unprecedented ecstacy, the club has faded into the background, more unloved than ever. In the early Nineties. the more things Millwall tried to do right, the less well they turned out. They built a fine new arena just down the road from their old ground, The Den, but whereas most clubs that have moved to new stadia saw crowds rise, Millwall's actually fell. The team's football, inspired by young talents like Jimmy Carter, Ben Thatcher and Mark Kennedy, was better to watch than it had ever been in Cas' and Sherry's time – yet rather than climb back into the top drawer, Millwall got relegated again. In the spring of 1999, the club took a huge, vociferously vocal following to Wembley for the Auto Windscreens final, only for the less well-supported Wigan to nick it with a goal in the dying seconds.

A physical presence – new Den, old problems

With an ambitious young manager and a buoyant spirit in the squad, the team's fortunes have actually revived since 1997/98, when a stumble down into the basement looked a distinct possibility. But while the Lions may be learning how to prowl menacingly again, they are still a long way from becoming a Premiership pride.

The twisted ironies of the past ten years have been difficult for Millwall's hard-core support to swallow, but they are nothing new. The club is 'South London' and proud of it, but derives its name from an area north of the Thames, where matches were played for the first 25 years of its existence. Millwall have a fine tradition of cultivating young players, yet prior to 1988 they were the only senior London side never to have played top-flight football. And while the club has won awards for its community spirit and its ground-breaking liaison with its local council, the violent elements within its fan base have been blazing a trail for would-be hooligans everywhere – something they continue to do today.

Above all, Millwall suffer from there being too many other teams nearby. No matter how much noise they make – both audibly and metaphorically – the fans just

Lewisham's Lions – Cascarino and Sheringham, 1988

don't have the numbers to put the club on the fast track back to stardom. It's a problem Millwall have suffered for most of their history and, indeed, was the reason why the team moved across the water in the first place.

The club was formed in 1885 by workers at the *J T Morton* jam and marmalade factory in West Ferry Road, on the Isle of Dogs. The company had recruited extensively in Scotland and most of the team's early members were from north of the border – hence the adoption of the Scottish flag's rampant lion as the club's motif. At a meeting in *The Islanders* pub on Tooke Street, it was decided to call the new team Millwall Rovers. A pitch (of sorts) was found on Glengall Road, and it was here, on 3 October 1885, that the Rovers played their first fixture against Fillebrook, and were thrashed 5–0.

A year later the team moved to a field behind the *Lord Nelson* pub and launched their first competitive campaign in the newly organised East End Senior Cup. Millwall made it all the way to the final against another Scottish-influenced side, London Caledonians, and after the match finished 2–2, the two clubs were given possession of the trophy for six months each.

The following year Millwall entered the FA Cup for the first time, then took full possession of the East End Cup, winning it three years in a row and being allowed to keep the trophy permanently as a mark of their achievement. The club moved to a third home at East Ferry Road, where cycling, athletics and tennis events also took place, and turned professional in 1893. Now playing under the name of Millwall Athletic to reflect the superior facilities of their new home, the team helped form the Southern League and appeared to be going from strength to strength. But then the owners of the East Ferry Road athletic ground decided to turn it into a timber yard, and Millwall were on the lookout for a home once again. They found one at North Greenwich, close to where Island Gardens light railway station now stands, but crowds were poor despite a couple of runs to the semi-finals of the FA Cup, and if the club moved any further south, it would be in the Thames.

In fact, south was the logical direction to take – across the river to the suburbs of Bermondsey and New Cross, which were more densely populated than the Isle of Dogs, and which enjoyed easier links to neighbouring communities. Anxious not to lose their identity, the team retained the name 'Millwall', but it soon became clear that their new home at Cold Blow Lane would be a permanent one. The ground was easily reached by train and crowds rose steadily despite the interruption of World War I.

In 1920, Millwall joined the exodus from the Southern League to the new Third Division of the Football League, which in turn became the Third Division (South) a year later. The team won the divisional title in 1928, and spent six moderately successful seasons in the Second Division before slipping down again.

To counter the effects of economic depression, the board appointed Charlie Hewitt as manager in 1936. Hewitt had already led Chester City into the League, and his evangelical spirit would soon find its niche at The Den, where executive seats, PA music and a 'ladies' lounge' were all installed to boost the club's public image. Millwall's bright new outlook was reflected on the pitch, too, where Hewitt's side won promotion back to the Second Division – only for World War II to halt their progress at a critical time.

Hewitt returned to his post in 1948, but by now the team had been relegated again and the developments he had put in place before the war had lost their novelty value. Millwall bought the freehold to The Den from their railway landlords in 1951, but no great progress was made in the League – when the Fourth Division began in 1958, the club's 23rd-place finish in the Third Division (South) the previous season made it a reluctant but inevitable founder member.

Millwall spent the early part of the Sixties moping miserably between the lower divisions, but two successive promotions from 1965 put them back in the limelight. With a defence containing the indomitable left-back Harry Cripps and commanding centre-half Barry Kitchener, and an expansive midfield in which Derek Possee, Eamonn Dunphy and Keith Weller always seemed game for a run, the team established themselves as a battling Second Division side, and The Den became an intimidating venue once more. In 1972, wearing a Leeds-style all-white strip and roaring every bit as ferociously as Don Revie's team, the Lions came within a point of promotion to the First Division.

After that, with the best players either sold or approaching retirement, Millwall slumped. They spent a year in the Third Division in the mid-Seventies, then another five years becalmed there in the first half of the Eighties.

Fresh inspiration was needed from somewhere, and Millwall got it in the shape of two forward-thinking managers. First, George Graham lifted the team back into the Second Division in 1985. Then, after Graham had been lured away by Arsenal, John Docherty arrived and took his predecessor's work in progress to fruition. Graham's side had always been well-drilled – now Docherty gave the formation the spearhead it had lacked, with the signing of Tony Cascarino to partner Teddy Sheringham upfront. Amply supplied by the big boots of Alan McLeary, Keith Stevens and

Sporting occasion – Lisbon come to Bermondsey to inaugurate the new Den, 1993

Terry Hurlock, the two strikers were a perfect match, Cascarino the willing, powerful target man, Sheringham the stealthy penalty-box stalker, prowling for any scraps his fellow Lion might leave behind.

In the Second Division of 1987/88, Millwall were simply irresistible, leaving the likes of Aston Villa, Middlesbrough, Leeds and Manchester City trailing in their wake, and sealing the championship with an emotional victory at Hull City on the season's final day. The fairytale continued the following year, when the team finished tenth in what was the club's first-ever season in the top division. Sheringham and Cascarino became national figures, and crowds of 15,000 and more made The Den a more forbidding home than ever. Chairman Reg Burr announced plans for a public flotation, and began negotiating with the club's sponsors, Lewisham borough council, for a parcel of land on which Millwall could build a new stadium.

Across the river from New Cross, the club's spiritual home of the Isle of Dogs was being transformed by the giant Canary Wharf office development. In contrast, the area around The Den was a wasteland of inner-city blight, and it seemed only natural that an upwardly mobile team like Millwall should want some gleaming new surroundings of their own.

But then, as work at Canary Wharf was halted by the London property crash, so Millwall's world began to fall about their ears. Cascarino was sold to Villa in March 1990, by which time the team were already doomed to drop, their long-ball style now rumbled by better-equipped opponents. Docherty was replaced by Bob Pearson, who lasted only a matter of months before making way for Bruce Rioch.

Having briefly been the most focused of all South London's clubs, Millwall now lost all sense of direction. Their parent company diversified into other aspects of the leisure industry, with disastrous results. Building of the new Den proceeded apace, but many fans resented the move, and there were angry protests against Burr (who deserved better) when the team played their last match at Cold Blow Lane at the end of the 1992/93 season. Smart, spacious and well-equipped while the new Den was, it failed to attract the kind of non-footballing events that were part of its *raison d'être*, and when only half-full – as it was much of the time – it lacked the atmosphere of the old place.

When Mick McCarthy's Millwall lost 3–1 at home to Derby in a First Division play-off semi-final in 1994, visiting players and officials were attacked, proving that, in this corner of London at least, a new stadium would not necessarily cure old problems of hooliganism. And if the silent majority of fans thought that was bad, they got a nasty jolt two seasons later, when Millwall were relegated again, on goal difference from Portsmouth.

Former West Ham manager Billy Bonds nearly presided over yet another fall, but the slide has since been arrested by two old boys from the late Eighties era, Keith Stevens and Alan McLeary. Along with chairman Theo Paphitis, Stevens has a knack of appearing optimistic despite Millwall's continuing problems. But then, these Lions always have had a taste for irony.

Here we go!

Motorists wishing to avoid London as much as possible should approach along the A2 (junction 2 off the M25). Follow this road across Blackheath, through Deptford and the New Cross one-way system until it becomes the Old Kent Road. Turn right almost immediately into Ilderton Road, and the ground is about half a mile ahead on the right. There's no **car park** any more but the side streets are more promising than they used to be around the old Den – be prepared for perhaps a 5–10min walk.

South Bermondsey overground **train station** is almost in front of the ground and gets trains leaving at least half-hourly from London Bridge, which is served by the Bank branch of the Northern Line tube. Allow 5mins for the journey from London Bridge, but up to 30mins to reach the latter from other London termini. Alternatively, Surrey Quays **tube station**, on the East London Line (change at Whitechapel for other lines), is a 20min walk from the ground along Rotherhithe New Road, Ilderton Road and Zampa Road.

Just the ticket

Visiting fans are allocated the North Stand behind one goal. Ticket prices for 1999/200 were expected to be adults £13, concessions £7.

Disabled supporters have a large area in the West Stand – booking not necessary.

Swift half

No pubs can be recommended in the vicinity of the ground, leaving two choices – either sink a swiftie at the bar at London Bridge station while waiting for your train, or wait until you get to the new Den, where the above par catering facilities extend to pies, burgers, chips and...beer.

Club merchandise

Millwall's ***Corner Shop***, so-called because it's at the corner of the West and North Stands, stocks the full range of memorabilia. Fans have former manager Gordon Jago to thank for bringing blue back to the club after the all-white experiments of the Sixties and Seventies.

Barmy army

From throwing seats onto the pitch at Luton in 1985 to attacking Derby players nine years later and organising pre-meditated violence at Manchester City in 1998/99, Millwall's lunatic fringe have a long history behind them and, it would appear, quite a future. An increased security presence has lessened the likelihood of trouble inside the Den itself, but keep colours covered outside.

In print

The ***South London Press*** covers Millwall (as well as Charlton and Palace) in some detail but, in common with all local London papers, does not publish on a Saturday evening.

Luckily, the fanzines bridge the gap with good humour and the minimum of hype. Try ***No-one Likes Us*** (30 Wendover Road, Bromley, BR2 9JX), ***Tales From Senegal Fields*** (85 Lower Road, Maidstone, ME15 7RH) and ***The Lion Roars*** (157-159 Boundfield Road, London, SE6 1PE).

Chin up – one-club man Keith Stevens

The last-mentioned has also published a compilation book of its best writing, ***The Trouble With Millwall*** (£8.99). Eamonn Dunphy's ***Only A Game – The Diary Of A Professional Footballer***, first published in 1979 before he turned to penning U2 biographies and critiques of Jack Charlton's Ireland, has recently been reprinted (Penguin, £6.99).

On air

It's the usual London choice of ***GLR*** (94.9 FM) and ***Capital Gold*** (1548 AM).

In the net

Millwall's **official site** was reorganised and relaunched in the summer of 1999, with some areas not yet complete but news, squad information and multi-media sections up and running. Go to: www.millwallfc.co.uk.

The unofficial ***Out Of The Blue*** is neat, complete and well-organised at: wkweb4.cableinet.co.uk/mgeorge.lions. And ***House Of Fun*** offers the authentic Den experience with its fresh design, 'virtual cinema' and irreverent humour at: www.hof.org.uk.

Newcastle United

Formation	1881 as Stanley FC
Stadium	St James' Park, Newcastle-upon-Tyne, NE1 4ST. ☎0191/201 8400
Ground capacity	37,000 (before stand extensions)
First-choice colours	Black-and-white stripes
Major honours	League champions 1905, 1907, 1909, 1927; First Division champions 1993; Second Division champions 1965; FA Cup winners 1910, 1924, 1932, 1951, 1955; Inter-Cities Fairs' Cup winners 1969
Position 1998/99	13th in Premiership

If the north-west is the cradle of English football, then the north-east is the game's kindergarten, the place where young talent is traditionally spotted, encouraged and matured. From Veitch to Milburn, from Gallacher to Waddle, Beardsley and Gascoigne, the region's reputation for nurturing players of skill, vision and bravery is second to none. And nowhere does this tradition loom larger than over its biggest club, Newcastle United – its very name a byword for the gestation of talented players, as much as for the unrivalled passion of its popular support.

Whether the tradition will be sustained for much longer is a moot point. The Newcastle team that lost the 1999 FA Cup final to Manchester United contained players from France, Germany, Greece, Peru, Georgia and Croatia. The club reacted to the defeat by making further foreign signings, and releasing eight youngsters.

St James' Park, where local teams have played the game since 1880, is being extensively rebuilt to give it a capacity of more than 50,000. When complete, the Milburn and Sir John Hall Stands will tower over Newcastle, a monument to the men in black-and-white that will be visible from miles around. The club will symbolise the city as never before, but what about the players?

The media are in no doubt. After the Cup final defeat, they railed against Ruud Gullit for his apparently indifferent attitude to Newcastle, and on the foreign stars for their 'lack of commitment' to the cause. They may be talented, the argument went, they may be accomplished internationals and heroes in their homelands – but they do not have St James' Park in their souls.

Yet all this sounded suspiciously like a pre-written obituary. And the Toon Army knows better (as does anyone who actually watched the game). Newcastle lost to Manchester United not because they weren't trying but because, if anything, they tried too hard. Roared on by what was comfortably the more vocal of the two sets of fans (and knowing, also, that a million and more Geordies were at Wembley in spirit via their TV sets), Gullit's side ran and chased, harried and tackled – and forgot that they were there to play football. By the time they remembered, it was too late. That's the problem with tradition. Inspiring as it can be to a modern generation, it can also be the least bearable of burdens.

Had their team beaten Manchester United and lifted their first piece of serious silverware for 30 years, Newcastle fans wouldn't have given a damn where the team's players had come from. And for as long as the current side plays the game as it should be played, artfully, deftly and courageously, the people of Newcastle will fill all those extra seats, week in, week out, making St James' Park – now that all Old Trafford's ambitions have been fulfilled – football's authentic theatre of dreams.

From a historical point of view, too, the Toon Army are right not to be fussy about the origin of their players. Heretical as it may sound to some, Newcastle actually have a long tradition of failing to sign the players who are on their doorstep, leaving rich pickings such as the Charlton brothers to clubs outside the area. And while there has always been a strong undercurrent of English nationalism beating at the heart of Geordie pride, the city of Newcastle would not be what it is today had it not been for a strong Scottish influence. In the late 19th century, when the economy of the north-east was booming, tens of thousands of Scots came flooding across the border to fill the vacancies in the pits, the factories and the dockyards. The region came late to the idea of professional football, but once it had arrived it was able to take a vital lead in the development of the game, thanks to the input of the Scots players who were queueing up for a run-out.

The first team to play at St James' Park (then known more commonly as Gallowgate, the area in which the ground stands deriving its name from being the former site of public hangings) went by the name of Newcastle Rangers. The pitch had an 18ft slope from the adjacent Leazes Park to the opposite Gallowgate End, and was used only sporadically, for practice matches.

Rangers moved out in 1882, to be replaced four years later by Newcastle West End, the footballing section of a local cricket club. Under their secretary-manager Tom Watson, West End had acquired a number of well-known players including two Scots internationals, Bob Kelso and Ralph Aitken. But in the summer of 1888 Watson was lured away to a rival club, Newcastle East End. This team too had begun life as part of a cricket club, playing in the Byker area under the name of Stanley FC. They had since moved to the Heaton district and had gradually grown in strength – a position cemented by Watson. When East End turned professional in 1889 they were given a further boost, not least because professional football was still barred in Scotland and Watson now had the perfect lever with which to lure talent southward.

By 1890 East End had formed itself into a limited company and the team were in danger of eclipsing West End, whose fortunes had dipped while their rivals had risen. During the 1891/92 season, in which East End beat West End five times, the directors of the latter club threw in the

Symbol of tradition – Jackie Milburn's statue outside St James'

The last trophy – Bobby Moncur takes the Fairs' (now UEFA) Cup through the streets, 1969

towel. They offered to wind West End up and merge with East End, who would then gain a number of players and back-room staff and, crucially, the chance to take over the lease at St James' Park.

East End duly began the 1892/93 campaign in their new home, but found they were playing to disappointing crowds. West End loyalists refused to patronise the new team, while East Enders felt their club had betrayed its roots by moving across town. The board decided a higher standard of football was needed to bring in the crowds (East End were in the Northern League at the time), so applied to the Football League for membership. They were offered a place in the Second Division but turned it down, on the grounds that any additional income would be lost through the expense of travelling to away games. The League wasn't going to admit a new club directly to its First Division, so at the end of 1892 East End tried another tack – they changed their name to Newcastle United, in the hope of attracting support from across the area.

In the summer of 1893 they were again offered membership of the Football League's Second Division, and this time they accepted, playing their first game at fellow newcomers Woolwich Arsenal in September that year. On the face of it, the club was doing everything right. It had a new name, it was in a more demanding competition, and it even had a new image – East End's old red-and-white striped shirts having been ditched in favour of a more distinctive black-and-white. Yet still the turnstiles refused to turn, prompting the club to release an official statement that: 'The Newcastle public do not deserve to be catered for as far as professional football is concerned.'

Then, just as it looked as though the club would cease to exist, the crowds began to arrive. By New Year's Day 1896 there were 14,000 at St James' to see an FA Cup tie against Bury, and by May 1898, under the guidance of an ambitious new secretary, Frank Watt, Newcastle had won promotion to the First Division.

Once in the top flight, the team went 11 games before managing a win. After that initial adjustment, however, Newcastle rose to become a leading light in the English game, dominating the Edwardian era. The key influence, once again, was Scottish. Whereas English players still saw football as an essentially individual game, the Scots philosophy was based on being able to pass the ball around the team. In the Football League, Aston Villa had deployed this tactic successfully in the late 19th century, but Newcastle now took it one stage further – at St James' Park, possession was to be kept at all costs, even if it meant the ball going sideways or backwards, rather than towards the opposition goal.

The men who made this possible were all expert controllers and passers of the ball in their day – the versatile Colin Veitch, who initially appeared for Newcastle under the assumed name 'Hamilton' to avoid detection by his college; Jackie Rutherford, whose dashing runs down the right touchline earned him the nickname 'Newcastle Flier'; full-back Bill McCracken, who would go on to pioneer the offside trap and force a change in the laws during the Twenties; and left-half Peter 'the Great' McWilliam, who arrived at St James' only after being hijacked by United officials while on his way from Inverness to play for Sunderland.

The team won their first League title in 1905, and would have done the double

The lonely soul of St James' – Hughie Gallacher

Standing only five-foot-five and looking as though he could do with trimming some inches from his waistline, **Hughie Gallacher** overcame his awkward build to become one of the most complete centre-forwards British football has ever known. Having played alongside his future Scottish international team-mate **Alex James** while at school, Gallacher made his name at **Queen of the South** and **Airdrieonians**. His £6,500 transfer from the latter to **Newcastle** in 1925 led to street demonstrations by supporters who believed it signalled the end of the Scottish League.

Gallacher made an immediate impact at Newcastle, scoring 25 goals in the 22 games left of the 1925/26 campaign. The following season he captained the team to the League championship, scoring all the while with fearless headers (he possessed a prodigious leap) and shots from either foot. In 1928 he was reunited with James in the Scottish **'Wembley Wizards'** team that annihilated England 5–1 – a result which did nothing to diminish his celebrity status on Tyneside, where Gallacher pursued his taste for the high life, womanising his way from pub to pub in sharply cut suits, accompanied by matching white spats, umbrella and fedora hat.

He was such a gifted player that his Newcastle team-mates were often incapable of anticipating him, and Gallacher was as quick to condemn them as he was the opposing defenders who cut his shins to shreds. His quick temper also got him into trouble with authority – he was arrested after brawling with his future brother-in-law on Newcastle's High Level Bridge; suspended by the FA for pushing a referee into the post-match bath at **Huddersfield**; and accused of 'smelling heavily of whisky' when yelling obscenities at the crowd after being sent-off during a tour of Hungary.

After falling out with Newcastle's manager Andy Cunningham in 1930, Gallacher was sold – against his will – to **Chelsea** for £10,000. But he never settled in London, nor at any of his subsequent professional clubs. He ended his playing career at **Gateshead**, having scored 387 goals in 541 League games.

A brief spell as a sportswriter ended with his being banned from St James' Park, and Gallacher had become a lost and lonely factory worker when, on 11 June 1957 – the day before he was due to appear in court charged with assaulting his son – he threw himself in front of the London-to-Edinburgh express, just south of the Tyne. The headline in the *Newcastle Journal* read: 'Hughie Of The Magic Feet Is Dead'.

had they not lost the FA Cup final to Aston Villa at Crystal Palace – where, in front of 101,000 (the biggest crowd ever to watch Newcastle, then and now), they were beaten 2–0 after conceding a goal in the first minute. Another Cup final defeat (to Everton) followed a year later, but in 1907 Newcastle were champions again.

And so the pattern continued – the team were almost invincible in the League, winning a third title in 1909 despite losing 9–1 to Sunderland at St James' Park, but seemingly incapable of winning the Cup, their 1908 final defeat by Wolves in South London prompting local papers to brand Newcastle as suffering from 'Palaceitis'. The club finally broke its FA Cup duck in 1910 – but not, significantly, at Crystal Palace, where the final was drawn 1–1 with Barnsley. The replay, at Goodison Park, was won 2–0 with both goals coming from the boot of Albert Shepherd.

The Palace jinx continued to haunt Newcastle the following year, when they were held 0–0 in the Cup final by Bradford City. This time, however, they lost the replay (at Old Trafford) amid the first real signs that the most golden of eras was drawing to a close. The team's League form was already in steep decline before the onset of World War I, and although some of the title-winning side such as Veitch, McCracken and veteran goalkeeper Jimmy Lawrence returned to the team after hostilities, their influence was waning. Newcastle's compact, close-passing game was no longer a novelty and the club initially struggled to find new players capable of injecting fresh ideas into the side.

By the early Twenties, however, that generation was beginning to emerge. It was directed from the left flank of the pitch by two key figures. One was full-back Frank Hudspeth, McCracken's partner-in-crime in the St James' Park offside trap and an expert user of the ball from deep positions, who now became captain of the side. The other was winger Stan Seymour, whose pace and ability to score goals were complemented by a natural understanding with forward Tom McDonald.

In 1924, Newcastle won what was only the second FA Cup final to be played at Wembley, beating Aston Villa 2–0 with

Supermac surrounded – Malcolm Macdonald slips past future Arsenal team-mates, 1972

goals from Seymour and Neil Harris. That might have been the extent of the side's achievements, had the club not then spent six months watching a short, stocky centre-forward from Airdrieonians called Hughie Gallacher (see panel p.357). When he finally signed for Newcastle at the end of 1925, Gallacher immediately added a new dimension to the team's football, turning smart but otherwise ineffectual passing movements into goals. In 1926/27, with Gallacher scoring 36 goals, Seymour 18 and McDonald 17, Newcastle broke Huddersfield Town's title monopoly, clinching the League with five points to spare on the Yorkshire side (and, poignantly, scoring 96 goals compared with Huddersfield's 76).

There should have been plenty more where that came from. But Gallacher's invention was carrying an ageing side, and when he was suspended for ten games at a crucial stage of the 1927/28 season, Newcastle lost their way. In 1929, the board appointed Andy Cunningham as the club's first modern team manager. Out went Hudspeth and Seymour (with the latter complaining bitterly about unpaid benefits), and within a year Gallacher was also on his way, despite saving Newcastle from relegation almost singlehanded.

Over the next couple of seasons Cunningham chopped and changed the first-team line-up as it had never been chopped and changed before. A 2–1 win over Arsenal – secured controversially as the ball appeared to go out of play immediately before Newcastle equalised – brought the FA Cup back to Tyneside in 1932, but the victory served only to disguise the team's steady decline. By 1934 Newcastle were relegated, entering the Second Division for the first time since 1899, and looking increasingly like a team of the past.

Yet they would stay out of the top flight for only two seasons after World War II, a conflict that did so much to disrupt football around the country, but which at Newcastle allowed precious pause for reflection. Just before the war, Stan Seymour had been unexpectedly recalled to the board to act as 'honorary manager' after the failure of Cunningham's replacement, Tom Mather. It was a role Seymour would occupy for nearly two decades, sometimes with the assistance of full-time managers, but always with a sense of purpose that derived from his single-minded vision of the club.

Worshipped under a blue star – King Kev

It was this vision that brought Jackie Milburn to St James' Park. If Gallacher had been 'Wor Hughie' then Milburn was always 'Wor Jackie', a former pit apprentice and champion sprinter who arrived at Newcastle as a youth player during the war, and who would go on to become the most worshipped of all the Geordie public's footballing idols. In playing terms, Milburn had a lot in common with Gallacher – he could shoot powerfully with either boot, had instinctive close control, and was at his most dangerous when pushed into a tight corner. In terms of character, however,

Jackie could not have been more different – polite, reserved and modest, he seemed at times almost unaware of why he had brought so much pleasure to so many fans.

Yet pleasure Milburn most certainly did bring. After promotion in 1948, Newcastle established themselves as top-five regulars in the League, before turning the FA Cup into something resembling a private tournament. In 1951, captained by inspirational right-half Joe Harvey and featuring the white-gloved Jack Fairbrother in goal, Newcastle met Blackpool in the final and won 2–0, with both goals coming from Milburn. Twelve months later they were back to retain the trophy, beating Arsenal 1–0 in a much tighter game, thanks to a late goal from George Robledo, one of a pair of Chilean brothers on the St James' Park books at the time. As the team's train steamed into Newcastle station after the game, a huge banner declared: 'Well done, lads – it's still Wors!'

If the old Crystal Palace venue had been cursed, then Wembley was surely now blessed for Newcastle. In 1955, they made it three Cup final wins in five years, beating Manchester City 3–1 after Milburn – dropped by manager Duggie Livingstone but re-instated by the board – had scored the opening goal in the first minute. It was to be Wor Jackie's last hurrah. Though his side were comfortable in the League, they never came close to winning it, and in 1957 Stan Seymour, one of Milburn's staunchest allies, let him become player-manager of Linfield in Belfast. He had scored 239 goals in nearly 500 games for the club, and there would never be another Newcastle player quite like him.

Joe Harvey, too, had departed the scene, having acted as coach to the 1955 Cup-winning side. By the time he returned to become Newcastle manager in 1962, the club had entered another of its bleak phases. Relegation the previous year had been the culmination of a long-running boardroom feud between Seymour and chairman William McKeag, and the club seemed ill-equipped for the modern era of player power and mass media exposure that was to come. Harvey would prove that theory wrong. His side, a mixture of bargain buys and local kids, didn't escape the Second Division until 1965, after which Harvey made some important signings including goalkeeper Willie McFaul and courageous target man Wyn Davies. While the former would go on to play more than 300 games between the sticks, the latter forged a productive partnership with Bryan 'Pop' Robson in attack. Now Newcastle were going places – further, in fact, than they could possibly have imagined.

In 1968 the club appeared to be consolidating nicely by finishing tenth in the League. But the rules then governing entry to the Inter-Cities Fairs' Cup (forerunner of the modern UEFA Cup) barred entry to more than one team from any given city, and this, combined with Manchester United's victory in the Champions' Cup and West Brom's admission to the Cup-Winners' Cup, unexpectedly catapulted Newcastle into Europe.

The club had no experience of continenal competition, but Harvey was determined to turn the players' innocence into a virtue. And why not? Utterly fearless and roared on by a St James' Park crowd starved of Cup drama, Newcastle began by knocking four past Feyenoord and never really looked back, accounting for Sporting Lisbon, Real Zaragoza, Vitória Setúbal and Rangers before facing Újpesti Dózsa, the team of the Hungarian secret police, in a two-legged final. They walked the home leg, 3–0, but were two down at half-time in Budapest when Harvey, knowing that an away goal would still seal the tie, told his players to 'just get one from somewhere'. They did, within a minute of the restart, through captain Bobby Moncur – and went on to win 3–2 on the night, 6–2 on aggregate. The trophy was paraded through the streets of Newcastle in an atmosphere of euphoria the city had not seen since Milburn's time. Harvey's team lacked star quality, yet had pulled off the most unlikely victory in the club's history.

But while romance would etch the manager's name into Newcastle's roll of honour, it would also prove his undoing. Harvey used the club's European money to build another promising team for the early Seventies, with men such as John Tudor, Irving Nattrass, Terry Hibbitt and Stewart Barrowclough providing the platform on which a big, bruising and rather bright young striker called Malcolm Macdonald could display his talents. In January 1972, 'Supermac' and his acolytes made the long journey down to non-League Hereford for an FA Cup tie – and lost 2–1.

Yet the side recovered from the ignominy sufficiently to reach a Cup final against Liverpool two years later. Joe Harvey was keen to protect his record of never having lost a final as player or manager, while the press hyped up Newcastle's excellent record at Wembley. On the day, though, they were simply outplayed, Kevin Keegan stealing the show for Liverpool with two goals in a 3–0 win. Jackie Milburn, watching from the stands, said of Macdonald's performance: 'The only thing he did today was tie his bootlaces.'

Back on Tyneside, the Toon Army greeted the players as if they had won the trophy, never imagining they would have to wait 24 years for another FA Cup final appearance. Harvey stayed on for another year before resigning, under pressure from the board, at the end of the 1974/75 season. His successor, the dour Gordon Lee, took Newcastle to the 1976 League Cup final, where they were beaten by Dennis Tueart's overhead kick for Manchester City. Within months 'Supermac' had been sold to Arsenal as Lee declared there would be 'no more stars' at St James' Park. Actually, before long there would be no more Lee – he was tempted away by Everton in January 1977, and a player revolt led to the rash appointment of his assistant, PE teacher Richard Dinnis, in his place. Dinnis lasted only a matter of months before making way for Bill McGarry, but the damage was done – Newcastle were relegated in 1978.

They had gone down before, of course, but this time things were different. The economy of the north-east was grinding to a halt, and relegation was the excuse many fans needed to keep their admission money in their pockets. McGarry, the self-styled 'most unpopular man in football', lived up to his own billing and was replaced by Arthur Cox in 1982. Cox's team were easier on the eye but pushed no harder for promotion until the manager pulled off a masterstroke by bringing Kevin Keegan to St James' Park for the 1982/83 season. The man who had tormented Newcastle at Wembley eight years earlier now inspired Tyneside, doubling crowds

A Magpie mismatch – Mirandinha (left) and Gascoigne, 1988

Wor Alan – Shearer and the Gallowgate salute

overnight and, with the help of two emerging Geordie talents, Chris Waddle and Peter Beardsley, leading the team to promotion in 1984.

His objective achieved, Keegan retired, while Cox also left to take over at Derby. Jack Charlton – alerted to the vacancy by his uncle, Jackie Milburn – succeeded Cox, but his negative tactics and controversial selling of Waddle to Tottenham enraged fans and Big Jack was gone within a year. Willie McFaul, initially just a caretaker boss, could not refuse Liverpool's £2million offer for Beardsley, then pinned his faith in the unlikely creative combination of Brazilian midfielder Mirandinha and the club's latest local discovery, Paul Gascoigne. Despite their obvious individual talents, the two never hit it off, and by the time Newcastle were relegated again under Jim Smith in 1989, both were gone – the Brazilian back to São Paulo, Gascoigne to Spurs.

In 1990, after a play-off semi-final defeat by Sunderland had consigned the club to another season of Second Division football, the Toon Army's patience snapped. Thousands of fans swarmed onto the St James' Park pitch to demand boardroom resignations. Chairman Gordon McKeag and his fellow director Stan Seymour junior had patched up their families' differences and had been running the club for years – now the supporters held them accountable for the lack of ambition which had seen the brightest young Eighties stars sold.

Yet the directors clung defiantly on, attempting to quell the revolt by appointing an exotic new manager, Ossie Ardiles. By January 1992, Newcastle were bottom of the Second Division and facing the possibility of life at the third level for the first time in their history. Two men stopped the drop – Sir John Hall, who'd taken control of the club a month earlier, and Kevin Keegan, who Hall coaxed out of retirement to replace Ardiles and get the black-and-white show back on the road.

Hall, a former pit surveyor who'd proved there was life in the local economy by building the *MetroCentre* retail palace in Gateshead, had spent millions of his own personal fortune in a fight for Newcastle shares with McKeag. Once on the board, he launched a public share flotation that went down in the Toon like a lead balloon, forcing him to make up the shortfall for a majority stake he seemed not to want. Now, however, in the club's hour of need, Hall acted positively. 'This isn't going to be pretty,' Keegan warned the media after his appointment. But his rough-and-ready approach did the trick. Newcastle avoided relegation and, after Keegan and his assistant Terry McDermott accepted Hall's offer of long-term contracts, there was just no holding them.

The following season, after winning all their opening 11 games, Keegan's side won the Second Division title with two matches to spare. Promotion couldn't have come at a more opportune time, taking the club as it did into the newly formed Premiership. Once there, the squad would need to be reinforced. But season-ticket sales were soaring as the faithful sought the chance to pay homage to King Kev, while Hall's commercial director Freddie Fletcher was overseeing a 15-fold rise in income from merchandising. Symbolically, Peter Beardsley came back to cement the revival.

A third-place finish in 1994 meant a return to European football, and while Keegan was forced to defend the sale of striker Andy Cole to Manchester United on the steps of St James' Park, his subsequent purchase of David Ginola and Les Ferdinand had given Newcastle a 12-point lead at the top of the Premiership table in January 1996. That the lead quickly evaporated was not unconnected with the signing of Colombian forward Tino Asprilla, whose arrival, far from strengthening the team, seemed to tip it off-balance.

Yet when Alan Shearer, the all-action Geordie goalscoring hero, was signed from Blackburn for £15million in the summer of 1996, Keegan and Newcastle still looked to have a great future together. The manager was six months into a new ten-year contract when, in January 1997, he walked out, apparently unable to cope with the stress of life at the top of an empire he himself had helped to construct. To replace him, the board turned to Kenny Dalglish, a manager who had himself walked out on his club (Liverpool) citing stress as the cause at the start of the decade.

Dalglish would soon have plenty of reasons to be stressed out, but didn't know it at the time. His side finished second in the Premiership in 1997, opening the door to a first-ever Champions' League campaign. This began brilliantly, with the Georgian Temuri Ketsbaia grabbing a dramatic last-minute winner in Zagreb to secure Newcastle's passage to the group stage, and Asprilla and Keith Gillespie (the makeweight in the Andy Cole deal) tearing Barcelona apart at St James' three weeks later.

Then Dalglish's Newcastle fell apart. Shearer was struggling with injuries, Asprilla was looking for a way back to Parma, and since Ferdinand and Ginola had been sold to Spurs in the summer to cut the wage bill (shades of the Eighties?), St James' Park had no strikeforce worthy of the name. The team bowed out of Europe, slipped to mid-table in the Premiership, and fired blanks at Arsenal in the 1998 FA Cup final.

Two weeks into the 1998/99 season, Dalglish was dismissed and replaced by Ruud Gullit. 'I thought someone was winding me up,' Dalglish reflected on the fateful phone call. Not a bit of it. The Newcastle board, to which executive directors Shepherd and Douglas Hall (Sir John's son) had inexorably returned after insulting the local female and football-loving populations on tape, were flexing their muscles again. Gullit was given money Dalglish had dared not dream about, but the end result – FA Cup final defeat – was the same.

Here we go!

Unless coming from Carlisle United or Berwick Rangers, **motorists** will likely approach Newcastle from the A1(M). At Junction 65, take the A1 toward Newcastle, then the A68 and the A6127 across the river Tyne. At the next roundabout, take the first exit into Moseley Street. Turn right into Neville Street, then right at the T-junction into Clayton Street and left into Newgate Street. The ground is on the left off Leazes Park Road.

There are plenty of council-run **car parks** around the ground and street parking is also an option if you're patient before the game and impatient after it.

Newcastle **train station** is on the East Coast main line with fast trains to York, Doncaster, Peterborough and London King's Cross. Change at Doncaster for Yorkshire, the north-west, the Midlands and the west country. There are no trains to London after evening games but Leeds should be within reach. Check the latest timings on ☎0345/484950.

To get from the station to the ground, jump on the **Tyne & Wear Metro** to St James' station. Come out of the station and the stadium is right behind you.

Just the ticket

Having ditched the idea of building a completely new stadium, Newcastle are stuck with having to extend St James' Park. This is good news for the home fans, who were suspicious of the proposed move, but bad news for **visitors** who are unlikely to see an increase in their allocation of 1,800 seats just yet. That said, if you do get in the view from the north-east corner of the Sir John Hall Stand. Prices in 1998/99 were adults £21, concessions £13. **Neutrals** should note that, pending the completion of the stand extensions, every fixture is all-ticket in the home sections. **Disabled visitors** have a dozen or so spaces in the Sir John Hall Stand – booking essential on ☎0191/261 1571.

Swift half

You can get a beer at the ground, but if you've come all this way you might as well sample a fraction of the many and varied bars central Newcastle has to offer.

The Bigg Market area, between St James' Park and Newcastle train station, is where Tyneside's pretty young things hang out, trip up and fall over – normally safe enough although you may want to take the precaution of covering colours on a Saturday night.

For those over the age of 25, the Quayside area south of Bigg Market is more refined (and more expensive), though not necessarily any less busy. Families have a good option not far from here in ***The Bridge Hotel***, at the north end of the High Level Bridge.

Club merchandise

The club operates shop franchises right across Tyneside, with branches inside most local *Asda* stores (courtesy of Newcastle's link with the chain's clothing designer George Davies) and further shops in Eldon Square and – inevitably – the *MetroCentre*. The main shop at **St James' Park** (open Mon–Sat 9.30am–5.30pm, later on matchdays, ☎0191/201 8426) is at the corner of the Gallowgate and Milburn Stands, just across from the Metro station.

Newcastle gave a debut to their Seventies-influenced millennium home kit at the 1999 FA Cup final – the shirts are £40 (kids' sizes £30) with an extra £10 for personalisation. Alternatively, most outlets stock vintage replicas from Gateshead-based company *TOFFS*, including a very fetching round-collared Sixties variant.

Barmy army

Aside from the protests that followed play-off defeat by Sunderland in 1990 (see main text), the most significant outbreak of hooliganism at St James' came in 1974, when a pitch invasion midway through an FA Cup quarter-final against Nottingham Forest caused play to be suspended for 20 minutes. Forest were leading at the time, but the game was ruled void and Newcastle went through after two replays at neutral Goodison.

Today the atmosphere at St James' Park has lost all the sinister overtones of the Seventies and Eighties – though not all of the frustrations – and non-football fans in the city centre are more likely to cause trouble than anyone at the match.

In print

St James' Park must have more **fanzines** per ticket-holder than any ground in the country. Choose from, among others, ***Talk Of The Tyne*** (49 Valley View, Sacriston, DH7 6NX), ***The Giant Awakes*** (82 Greenlands Road, Redcar, TS10 2DH), ***The Mag*** (Unit 12, 25 Low Friar Street, Newcastle-upon-Tyne, NE1 5UE) and ***Half Mag, Half Biscuit*** (14 Hertford Close, Whitley Bay, NE25 9XH).

At least three books about the club can be recommended. ***United: The First Hundred Years And More*** (Polar, £24.95) is the best of Paul Joannou's many Newcastle books; ***The Toon*** (Mainstream, £7.99) by Roger Hutchinson is a less detailed but more evocative history; and for the fan's perspective there's ***The Magpies*** (Mainstream, £9.99) by Michael Bolam.

On air

BBC Radio Newcastle (104.4 FM) has phone-ins before the match, while ***Metro Radio*** (97.1 FM) has them afterward. Listen out also for ***Magpie Radio*** (1413 AM) on matchdays.

In the net

Newcastle's **official website** is run by *Planet Internet* and suffers from the usual ailments. There is, however, a fascinating range of vintage player profiles and a complete stats database of every footballer who's ever pulled on the black-and-white jersey. Find it at: www.newcastle-utd.co.uk/.

Best of the **unofficial homepages** is at: www.nufc.com/. No frills, but it has many unusual features, including a list of pubs around the world where you can see Newcastle play on the box. The news service promises (and delivers) 'a daily mix of tittle-tattle, innuendo and crap'.

Northampton Town

Formation	1897
Stadium	Sixfields Stadium, Upton Way, Northampton, NN5 5QA. ☎01604/757773
Ground capacity	7,600
First-choice colours	Claret and white
Major honours	Third Division champions 1963; Fourth Division champions 1987
Position 1998/99	22nd in Second Division (relegated)

Driving past Northampton on one of the trunk roads that surround the town, you pass row after row of industrial estates, haulage warehouses and retail parks. Everything that's noteworthy about the scenery is manmade, yet nothing stands out as unique. You feel you could be anywhere and, in a sense, you are. For Northampton is to Britain's road network what Crewe is to the railways – a place millions of people pass through on their way somewhere else, but few stop to visit for long.

Pre-Sixfields hero – big Frank Larges it for the Cobblers

As it is with travel, so it is with Northampton Town FC. Dozens of top-drawer professional players have either begun or ended their careers at the club, but few have spent their best seasons here. The result is a typically chequered lower-division history, brilliantly illuminated in the Sixties when Dave Bowen's side climbed all the way from the Fourth to the First Division in five breathless seasons. Northampton tumbled back down again with even greater speed and have never played in the top half of the League since – though they came within a play-off final of doing so at the end of 1997/98.

Legend has it that in the club's heyday, manager Bowen would take the idea of 'just passing' to extremes, finalising incoming transfers in a motorway service area on the M1, rather than risk exposing new players to Northampton's facilities. Apocryphal or not, the story serves to illustrate the inadequacy of the team's home at the time, the County Ground. Town have often played in the shadow of successful local rugby union and cricket teams, and the County Ground was a permanent reminder of this, being shared with Northamptonshire CCC. There was no stand on one side of the pitch, and part of the playing surface was ruined each summer by being used as a car park by the cricket club. For all its lovable eccentricities, it was no place for a forward-looking football team.

Today things could hardly be more different. Northampton moved to the new, council-owned Sixfields Stadium in 1994, and, far from feeling embarrassed by its surroundings, the club now reckons they help to swing wavering transfers in its favour. Attendances have soared since the move, and while relegation in 1999 put an unforeseen brake on Town's rise, the mood is still, on balance, optimistic. And since

Don't try this away from home – local bicycle gangs get a free view of the action at Sixfields

Sixfields is located on a major trunk-road junction, visiting fans with cars can now do as the rest of the country does, and avoid the town completely.

Cricket is still played at the County Ground (it was a World Cup venue in 1999), and it will always have a place in Northampton's history as the scene of the club's formation in 1897. The men responsible were teachers belonging to the *Northampton & District Elementary Schools' Association*, who despite modest origins and even more modest means (the club was £675 in the red at the end of its first year) persuaded the Midland League to grant them admission in 1898. Within three years Town had progressed to the professional Southern League, and in 1906 the team entered the FA Cup for the first time.

Northampton acquired the nickname 'Cobblers' after the town's then-dominant shoe industry, and continued to step forward with purpose, thanks to the appointment of Herbert Chapman as a young player-manager in 1907. Six years earlier, Town had been the first club to offer Chapman a professional contract, enabling him to give up his day job as a mining engineer. Now, after spells with Notts County and Tottenham, he returned to begin what would be one of the most important managerial careers in the history of English football.

Though yet to develop his most advanced tactical ideas, Chapman set an example to Town's players with his disciplined approach to the game, and also displayed a knack for PR with the signing of Fanny Walden, an outstanding young outside-right who wowed the crowds despite measuring only five-foot-two – his pace and close control helped the team to the Southern League title in 1909.

Chapman left for Leeds City in 1912, but not before signing a gifted, elegant wing-half, Walter Tull, from his former club Tottenham. Tull had been the first black outfield player in the Football League, and joined Northampton after suffering racial abuse at Spurs. The County Ground took him to its heart, and he made 110 appearances for Town before the onset of World War I – in which, tragically, he would lose his life after rising to the rank of officer, a technical impossibility for a black soldier at the time.

For all its horrific consequences, the war did not halt Northampton Town's progress. In 1921, they and most of the rest of the Southern League became founder members of the Football League's new Third Division (South). Walden returned from a spell at Spurs in 1926, and two years later, with the goals of centre-forward Ralph Hoten, Northampton finished second to runaway winners Millwall in their division.

That was the closest the Cobblers came to promotion before World War II, however, and it wasn't until the arrival of goalscoring wingers Jack English and Tommy Fowler that the club's spirit revived at the end of the Forties. Enterprising though they were, they also couldn't win Town promotion, and when the League was reorganised in 1958, the club missed the cut by a single place and ended up in the Fourth Division.

The man who got them out of it was Bowen, who'd served the club as a left-half before going on to captain Arsenal, and who returned to the County Ground to succeed Dave Smith as manager in 1959. Though not always as pretty to look at as some of Northampton's earlier postwar teams, Bowen's sides were never less than immaculately organised in defence. In 1960/61 Town lacked the goalscoring power of Peterborough and Crystal Palace yet still finished comfortably inside the promotion places behind them. After that, Bowen set a pattern for progress. With each rise in status he would further reinforce his defence; after each promotion, Town would consolidate for a year before mounting another challenge for the top.

Centre-half Terry Branston was the iron behind the Fourth Division promotion, and Irish full-back Theo Foley arrived from Exeter to keep Third Division forwards at bay as Town won the title at a canter in 1962/63 – this despite losing star striker Cliff Holton to Palace, just 15 months (and 50 goals) after his arrival. Bowen replaced Holton with target man Frank Large for what would be the first of three colourful spells at the club, then signed the versatile Joe Kiernan from Sunderland. In 1965 Northampton's climb was complete – the team finished only a point behind Second Division winners Newcastle, and six points clear of Bolton in third.

While the rest of the country was looking forward to the 1966 World Cup, the County Ground had more parochial pre-occupations, fans standing on boards along the unbuilt side of the pitch as crowds approached 25,000 for the visits of Leeds, Liverpool and Manchester United, as Town tried desperately to maintain their First Division status. It was always an unequal struggle, yet if the team had enjoyed better luck with injuries and the run of the green in a couple of key games, they might have done it. As it was, Northampton finished second from bottom, two points clear of safety, and the downward spiral had begun. An identical finish to 1966/67 resulted in a second successive relegation, Foley and

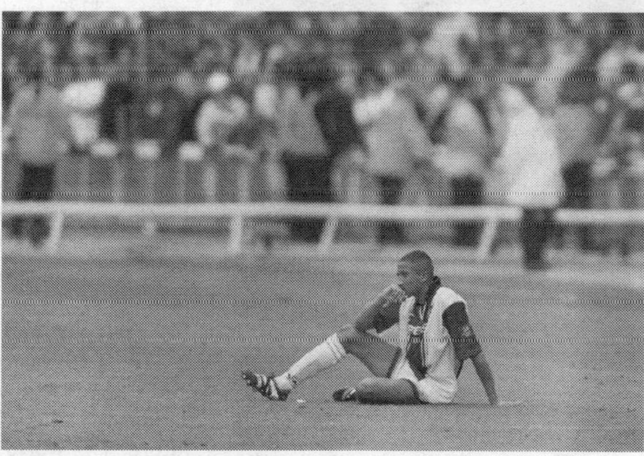

Claret cloud – Chris Freestone contemplates defeat, Wembley, 1998

Kiernan were sold, and before long Bowen himself had thrown in the towel.

Northampton ended the Sixties as they'd begun them – in the Fourth Division. And though Bowen returned to become general manager and secretary of the club during the Seventies, he was no more than a helpless board member when post-Bradford safety regulations rendered the County Ground barely usable for football in 1986. With their ground capacity slashed, Town could not capitalise on the Fourth Division title won by affable manager Graham Carr the following year, and relegation in 1990 prompted a full-blown boardroom crisis, with successive chairmen unable to stem the club's tide of debt.

Just when it seemed the Cobblers had stitched their last, the sort of luck that had deserted them at their Sixties peak now came their way in spades. The accountant appointed to act as an administrator, Barry Ward, turned out to be a fan who became chairman of a reconstituted board, with the backing of a recently formed Supporters' Trust. Secondly, the local council met almost the entire cost of building Sixfields, and agreed to let Town move to the new stadium on the understanding that it would be shared with other local sports clubs (but not, crucially, rugby union or cricket). Thirdly, just as Town were poised to be relegated from the League in 1994, the team earmarked to replace them, Conference winners Kidderminster Harriers, were refused admission because (a rich irony, this) their ground did not come up to scratch.

Worthy Cup win – Wilko outjumps Rio, 1998

So Northampton moved into Sixfields as a confident, financially solvent Football League club – something that seemed inconceivable at the turn of the Nineties. And with former Cambridge and Colchester boss Ian Atkins in charge of the team from January 1995, the team's form began to reflect that of the supporters.

A play-off final win over Swansea City pulled Northampton up into what was now the Second Division in 1997, and a year later, after matching the previous season's achievement by finishing fourth, only a 1–0 defeat by Grimsby at Wembley denied them a second successive promotion.

The optimism continued into the start of the 1998/99 campaign, with West Ham beaten over two legs in the League Cup and eventual winners Tottenham getting a scare at Sixfields in the following round. But while Atkins had succeeded in keeping his squad together, the long season gradually took its toll on experienced professionals such as Kevin Wilson, Colin Hill and Paul Wilkinson. The board found money for Atkins to strengthen, the club breaking its transfer record of £90,000 to bring striker Steve Howard in from Hartlepool, but results elsewhere contrived to make the game against Burnley on the last day irrelevant, and Town were down.

The 1,500 season tickets the club sold in the month following this disaster showed the degree of confidence fans have in the future. The world may be passing by, but for once Northampton Town aren't standing still, either.

Here we go!

Sixfields really couldn't be easier to find for **motorists**, located as it is right on the junction of the A45 and A4500 trunk routes, between the M1 and the town centre. If you take a wrong turn on one of the area's many roundabouts, the signposts to follow are those marked 'Sixfields Leisure'. **Car parking** isn't as easy as it should be now that the surrounding area has become an all-shopping, all-eating leisure complex. Arrive early to find a space in the designated South Car Park at the ground.

Northampton Castle **train station** is on the London Euston to Birmingham New Street line (fast trains hourly, journey 1hr 20mins from Euston, 1hr from New Street). There are late departures in both directions for evening games, but check the latest timings on ☎0345/484950.

The station is a long, dull walk from Sixfields but fortunately most **buses** departing the stop just over the road from the station go to Sixfields – check with the driver first.

Just the ticket

Visiting fans are housed in the South Stand – those attempting to sit anywhere else will be ejected. Pay your money at the Portakabin first, then show this at the turnstiles. Ticket prices for 1999/2000 are adults £11, concessions £8.

Disabled facilities at Sixfields are outstanding, with spaces in all four stands. There's plenty of room but the club asks you to book in advance on ☎01604/588338.

Swift half

This is where the fun starts. There are a couple of pubs on the Sixfields site but neither is keen on visiting fans wearing colours and, even if they let you in, the crush can be unbearable.

Fans arriving by train should check out ***The Mail Coach*** in Derngate in the town centre, frequented by fans of all persuasions, while the club suggests motorists stop off at a country pub on the outskirts of town. Alternatively, have a drink with some food at the ***Pasadena*** or ***Bella Pasta*** at Sixfields – both welcome families.

Club merchandise

Northampton asked fans to choose from four new styles of shirt for the millennium and (surprise, surprise) the winner was a simple design redolent of the club's Sixties style, with a claret body and white sleeves. The refurbished **club shop** (open Mon–Sat 10am–4pm) has adult sizes at £37.99, children's at £27.99, and if that seems a bit steep for a souvenir, there are always bars of fudge and nougat for 99p.

Barmy army

Sixfields is the epitome of the spacious, all-seated, hooligan-free arena. All very cosy and Nineties, but the real test will come if either of the county's big Conference sides, Kettering and Rushden & Diamonds, gain promotion to the League. Rushden, thanks to the antics of their millionaire *Dr Marten's* chairman (and former Northampton board member) Max Griggs, are particularly unpopular.

In print

The local ***Chronicle & Echo*** was gushing in its praise of Northampton's two play-off campaigns but was scathing for much of 1998/99. There's no Saturday evening edition.

Fanzine ***What A Load Of Cobblers*** or ***WALOC*** (123 Draycott Road, Sawley, NG10 3BX) has a tough job providing an alternative angle, given the presence of the Supporters' Trust on the board, but manages it with humour.

The ultimate Town book is ***The Official Centenary History*** (Yore, £18.95) by Frank Grande, while Brian Barron's ***Fanny, Phil And Others*** (Byline, £17.99) provides a fitting epitaph for the old County Ground.

On air

BBC Radio Northampton (104.2 FM) devotes much airtime to the local rugby union club but is worth a listen.

In the net

Northampton's **official site** is nothing special to look at but has all the essentials at: www.ntfc.co.uk. The club is also set to become an internet service provider with its ***Cobblers Connect*** operation, offering free web access and e-mail.

The most thorough of the **unofficial sites** is at: www.cobblers.free-online.co.uk. For something more off the wall, try ***Planet Cobblers*** at: www.angelfire.com/co/bblers/.

Norwich City

Formation	1902
Stadium	Carrow Road, Norwich, NR1 1JE. ☎01603/760760
Ground capacity	22,000
First-choice colours	Yellow shirts, green shorts
Major honours	Second Division champions 1972, 1986; Third Division (South) champions 1934; League Cup winners 1962, 1985
Position 1998/99	Ninth in First Division

Norwich is the kind of place that lives on its stomach. Strolling through the city centre, it's hard not no notice the sheer number of pubs, cafés, tea-rooms, restaurants and other eateries that line the historic streets. In the vast market square, farmers and traders from all over Norfolk come to sell their produce to a large, eager and obviously rather hungry audience. Meanwhile, the *Colman's* mustard factory provides local employment for thousands. How appropriate, then, that the board of Norwich City FC should have, as its most public face, the purveyor of the perfect omelette, Delia Smith. A Norwich fan since childhood, the TV presenter with the champagne touch in the kitchen joined the club's board in 1997, just as City were bidding farewell to their hero-turned-villain chairman, Robert Chase.

Like their East Anglian neighbours and fierce rivals Ipswich Town, Norwich have often looked across the North Sea for inspiration, and the restaurants and executive lounges of Carrow Road are reminiscent of those at football grounds in Belgium and Holland. But while they may prefer a glass or two of the strong stuff in the Ipswich boardroom, at Norwich they're tucking in, before, during and after the match – and, since *Colman's* became the club sponsor, presumably with relish.

Not that the action on the pitch has done much to whet the appetite in recent years. With an admirable reputation for producing high-quality football on low revenues, and having flown the flag for East Anglia in Europe as recently as 1993, Norwich City have fallen on hard times. The team have spent the past four seasons scratching a living out of the middle of the First Division, and with money still tight, the chances of an early escape depend on the board cooking up a fresh, tasty recipe from modest ingredients.

Norwich are latecomers to the table of top-class football in England, not having made their debut in the old First Division until 1972. But football had been played in the city for more than a century before that, with a club called Norwich City being formed as early as December 1868. The club had around 60 members and players wore violet-and-black jerseys, white shorts, and yellow-and-black tasselled caps. They played to either the Cambridge University or Football Association rules, depending on the opposition, but the matches were all friendlies and the code strictly amateur.

The modern-day Norwich City club can trace its origins back to a meeting organised by two local schoolmasters in the *Criterion Café* on 17 June 1902. Bemoaning the lack of a senior team playing competitive football in the city, they decided to form their own side and approached the Norfolk County FA for permission to use their ground on Newmarket Road. One of the first competitions entered by the new 'Norwich City' was the Amateur Cup, but in 1904 an FA Commission judged that the club was professional because players were being paid travelling expenses, and threw City out.

So a decision had to be taken. Should City seek to retain their amateur status, or turn professional? Unlike Ipswich, who would remain amateur until the Thirties, Norwich decided to take the plunge into

San Siro salute – Mike Walker pays his dues to City's travelling support at Inter Milan, 1993

professionalism, forming themselves into a limited company and joining the Southern League. This appears not have gone down too well with the Norfolk FA, which then did everything it could to get City out of Newmarket Road. In 1908 they succeeded, and the team moved to a disused chalk pit in Rosary Road which would become known as The Nest. The obvious explanation for this was the shape of the ground, which had a sheer cliff at one end. But by this time the team had acquired the nickname of 'Canaries' after the city's trade in breeding and exporting pet birds. And if the Canaries were to have a new home, then it might as well be called The Nest.

For the inaugural match at the ground, a friendly against Fulham on 1 September 1908, City's players took to the field wearing yellow and green in order to live up to their nickname – a colour combination that would remain, more or less without interruption, throughout the club's progress up the ladder of professional football.

This progress was, in truth, rather slow. Norwich seemed content to stay in the Southern League, where they played with some success, until after World War I. Then, in 1919/20, they reached the FA Cup quarter-finals, and a year later joined most of the rest of the Southern League in helping to form the new Third Division – later the Third Division (South) – of the Football League. There they played all too anonymously until 1933, when new manager Tom Parker led them to a third-place finish and, the following year, to the championship and promotion to the Second Division.

Yet success came at an awkward time for City. While it had its own eccentric charm, The Nest was never an ideal venue for first-class football. Quite apart from the fact that the ball kept bouncing back off the cliff into play whenever a player shot wide at that end of the ground, the old chalk workings under the pitch were prone to subsidence, causing patches of turf to give way at awkward moments. Then there was the safety issue. After barriers on top of the cliff gave way in 1922, some 60 fans fell onto the pitch below – although, miraculously, only one was seriously injured.

Better to wait – Paddon holds it up, 1977

Even so, when a crowd of more than 25,000 was drawn to a Cup tie against Sheffield Wednesday in February 1935, the FA decided to act. On 15 May they wrote to the Norwich board advising them that The Nest would no longer be considered suitable for large crowds.

Club chairman Billy Hurrell was horrified but, like City's founding fathers a generation earlier, he reasoned that arguing with the FA would be pointless. So an agreement was hastily made for the club to take over a ground near Thorpe train station, previously used by the sports club of the *Boulton & Paul* engineering works and owned – surprise, surprise – by the *Colman* mustard company. The paperwork was signed on 1 June 1935, and by 17 August most of the work needed to equip the ground with terraces and a small stand had been completed. It had been the biggest construction project Norwich had seen since the building of the city's castle, and nearly 30,000 justifiably proud supporters gathered on 31 August for the opening game of the 1935/36 season. Club president Russell Colman cut the ceremonial ribbon under the Main Stand roof which, as luck would have it, carried a huge advertisement for his firm's mustard. A 4–3 victory over West Ham ensued, and everyone went home happy.

The euphoria was short-lived. On the eve of World War II Norwich were relegated, and it was to be another 20 years before Second Division football returned to Carrow Road, as the new ground was called. Just before it arrived, Norwich reached the semi-finals of the FA Cup as a Third Division side in 1959. The team, starring Terry Bly and Terry Allcock upfront and long-serving defender Ron Ashman marshalling the backline, beat Manchester United and Spurs to set up a semi-final against Luton Town. Thousands of fans made the trip for the match, the streets of North London being filled with the surreal sight of grown men dressed as canaries stomping about in search of White Hart Lane. City came from behind to draw the game, 1–1, but lost the replay at St Andrew's to a Billy Bingham goal against the run of play.

Fortunately, manager Archie Macaulay kept the team together, and the following year Norwich won promotion. They then opened their Second Division account by finishing fourth in 1961, four points behind Bill Shankly's Liverpool, and the following year they won the fledgling League Cup competition in its second year, beating Rochdale 4–0 on aggregate in a two-legged final. The club then consolidated for the remainder of the Sixties, with Ashman, who'd captained the League Cup-winning side, taking over as manager for a spell.

In 1969, Ron Saunders moved into the hot seat and Norwich began to make further strides toward the footballing elite. While the club was negotiating to buy the freehold to Carrow Road, Saunders was turning an already talented group of young players into a cohesive, disciplined unit. With Kevin Keelan ultra-reliable in goal,

Dave Stringer bossing the defence, Graham Paddon a creative force in midfield and Ken Foggo a free-scoring spirit on the right side of attack, Saunders' side won the Second Division title in 1972. The following year they again reached the League Cup final, by now a major Wembley event, and were unlucky to lose 1–0 to Tottenham.

By the time City returned for a repeat performance against Aston Villa in the same competition two years later, they'd been relegated and, extraordinarily, were on their way back up again – beginning a sequence of three instant promotions mounted each time the club went down during the Seventies and Eighties. Ron Saunders was now manager of Villa, but City had another charismatic boss of their own in John Bond, whose purchase of his former Bournemouth strike partnership of Phil Boyer and Ted MacDougall was proving inspired. Yet the result was the same – a 1–0 Wembley defeat, and more coachloads of man-sized canaries heading back up the A11 proud but disappointed.

As the Seventies went on, chairman Arthur South – who'd helped galvanise public support when City had faced a cash crisis in the mid-Fifties – seemed intent on improving Carrow Road rather than boosting the team, and after Bond was called away to rescue Manchester City from the drop in 1980, the club he left was relegated instead. With playmaker Kevin Reeves already sold to Maine Road for £1million and striker Justin Fashanu going for the same money, new manager Ken Brown somehow engineered an immediate promotion, then attempted to achieve First Division stability by emphasising experience. When Norwich reached yet another League Cup final in 1985, the team's attacking stars were Mick Channon and Asa Hartford, who had a combined age of 70. Yet on the day, against a Sunderland side which, like City, were destined to be relegated at the end of the season, Norwich's most influential players were young defenders – goalkeeper Chris Woods and stoppers Dave Watson and Steve Bruce. An own-goal by Sunderland's Gordon Chisholm settled a tight game, and at the third time of asking, the Canaries were dancing down Wembley Way.

Despite the looming shadow of relegation, the club began to plan confidently for Europe – only for the Heysel tragedy at the end of the season to end those ambitions before they had begun. UEFA's

A golden boy in goal – Chris Woods, League Cup winner

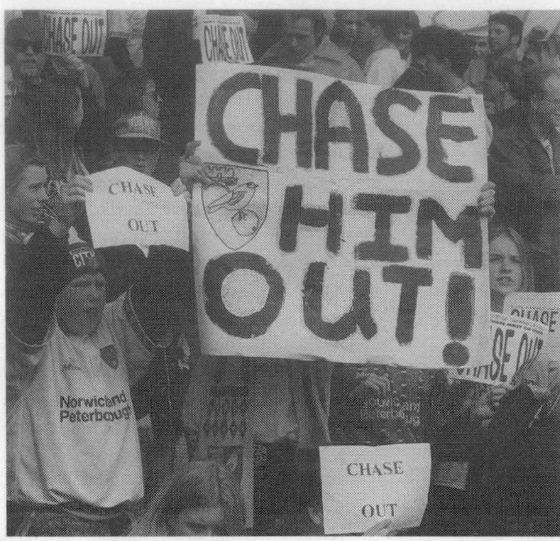

A message for the chairman – protests after relegation, 1995

blanket ban on English clubs was a travesty of justice for City's easygoing fans, who for obvious reasons were utterly blameless in connection with Heysel, or indeed any of the other instances of hooliganism involving English clubs abroad. But if Europe was a closed door for now, at least the faithful at Carrow Road's Barclay End had something to celebrate with the Second Division title in 1986.

With Dave Stringer succeeding Brown a year later, another quick-thinking, fast-moving team were created. Watson and Bruce had moved on to Everton and Manchester United respectively, but with Andy Townsend as playmaker and Robert Fleck and Robert Rosario upfront, there was enough talent around for Norwich to reach an FA Cup semi-final against Everton – played and lost on the same day as the Hillsborough disaster – in 1989.

Three years later, Mike Walker succeeded Stringer and got City to another FA Cup semi, this one surprisingly lost to Second Division Sunderland. This was to prove only a minor setback, however. Of all the club's free-flowing sides of the period, Walker's was the best balanced. Solid at the back, with Bryan Gunn in goal and the likes of Mark Bowen, Ian Culverhouse and John Polston in front of him, the team had a quick enough engine to counter-attack from almost any situation – despite the sale of Tim Sherwood to Blackburn. Chris Sutton provided the goalscoring power, assisted by Mark Robins and the whippet-like Ruel Fox. Thus Norwich third in the first Premiership season of 1992/93 – the highest final placing in the club's history. The following season, with Sutton now irresistible upfront and Efan Ekoku and Jeremy Goss blossoming into new creative talents, Norwich made the most of their belated introduction to Europe. Vitesse Arnhem were brushed aside in the UEFA Cup first round, then Bayern Munich were beaten in Germany, and only a couple of lucky 1–0 wins saw a Dennis Bergkamp-influenced Inter Milan past City in the third round.

It would prove to be an all too brief spell in the glare of the continent's lights. In January 1994 Walker left for Everton, and the following summer Sutton followed Sherwood to Blackburn for £5million. New manager John Deehan didn't make it to the end of the following season, and neither did his replacement, Martin O'Neill, who walked out after only months in charge, complaining bitterly about the lack of money available for players. Gary Megson stepped into the breach but could not halt City's dramatic slide down the Premiership table. They were five points from safety when their relegation was confirmed in April 1995, and the only consolation was that Ipswich were also down, and had finished beneath Norwich, too.

It would have been easy to blame the players, not to mention any or all of the managers. But Norwich fans had identified their enemy. Like Arthur South before him, chairman Robert Chase had once helped the club stave off insolvency (in 1984, after Norwich's Main Stand burned down), but had now made the mistake of ploughing transfer receipts into the development of Carrow Road and adjacent plots of land, rather than strengthening the squad. The supporters wanted him out, but Chase was proving hard to shift, hedging against a takeover by pursuing City's small shareholders and making them offers they couldn't refuse.

Finally, after more than two years of campaigning, Chase caved in. But the damage had been done. After a brief and ill-advised return by Mike Walker, City now had a nice, tidy ground and plenty of scope to develop it in the future but, like several other mid-table First Division sides, a team that were going nowhere fast. As they like to say in these parts – food for thought.

Here we go!

For **motorists**, the A47 leads to Norwich from the west and then acts as a bypass around the southern edge of the city. Stay on the bypass, rather than go into the city centre, then exit onto the A146 toward Norwich – the ground is well-signposted from here. If coming from the south along the A11, follow signs for Norwich (East) onto the A47 then use the directions above. There's no **car park** at the ground itself but the one in front of County Hall has plenty of space on Saturdays. To reach it from the ground, continue along Carrow Road, turn left into King Street and left again into Bracondale, then right at the roundabout – the car park is on the right. Allow 15mins to walk back to the ground.

Norwich Thorpe **train station** is served by direct trains running from London Liverpool Street (fast trains hourly, journey 1hr 45mins). There are also cross-country connections to the East Coast mainline at Peterborough, 1hr 30mins away. Evening kick-offs shouldn't pose a problem, at least not for London-based fans, but double-check on ☎0345/484950.

The ground is a 10min walk away – go straight across the car park, turn left along the riverside and the ground will be on your left at the junction with Carrow Road.

Just the ticket

Visiting fans are accommodated at one end of the South Stand – enter through turnstiles #1–3. The amount of space allocated depends on the fixture, as do ticket prices.

Disabled supporters have 115 spaces, shared by home and away fans, in the corner between the South Stand and the River End. Book through your own club.

Swift half

No shortage of choices here. Close to the ground, at #81 Carrow Road, the ***Clarence Harbour*** offers both home and away fans a warm welcome with real ale and an extensive menu. For those coming by train, the ***Complete Angler*** is right outside the station – though beware this may not be open for a post-match pint. For those with a bit more time, the city centre is a 15min walk from the ground and offers more food and drink options than you could sample in a life-

A change to the published recipe – Delia Smith mulls it over

time. Turn right onto King Street at the junction with Carrow Road and keep going.

Club merchandise

Delia Smith was on shaky ground when she invited Bruce Oldfield to redesign City's kit two years ago – the subsequent all-yellow outfit went down like a lead balloon with fans. Happily the traditional green shorts have returned for 1999/2000, while the *Colman's* name remains proudly in red.

See for yourself at the **club shop** in the corner of the River End and the City Stand, entrance in Carrow Road.

Barmy army

There's never much trouble here unless visiting teams bring it with them, which is not unheard of. The increased police presence for the annual arrival of Ipswich is much-needed and normally does the job.

In print

The *Eastern Counties Newspapers* group, former hosts of the club's official website (see *In the net* below), publishes a ***Pink'Un*** after final whistle on a Saturday evening – normally on sale in Norwich at around 5.30pm.

Of the fanzines, try ***Man United Are On The Tele Again!*** (Pennyroyal, Old Catton, NR6 6JH) or ***Cheep Shot*** (17 Southerwood, Catton, NR6 6JN).

On the book front, the club has published ***Glorious Canaries*** (£14.99), Mike Davage's who's who of the club covering the period to 1994, while ***The Second Coming*** by *This Supporting Life* author Kevin Baldwin (Yellow Bird, £8.99) is a fan's-eye view of the 1996/97 season which saw the return of Mike Walker and the arrival of Delia Smith.

On air

BBC Radio Norfolk (104.4 FM) has the best City coverage among the local stations.

In the net

City's **official website** was due to be relaunched with a new service provider for 1999/2000, but is expected to remain at: www.canaries.co.uk.

Among the unofficial sites, the most complete is ***Canary.net***, a regularly updated, smartly designed offering at: canary.fsn.net.

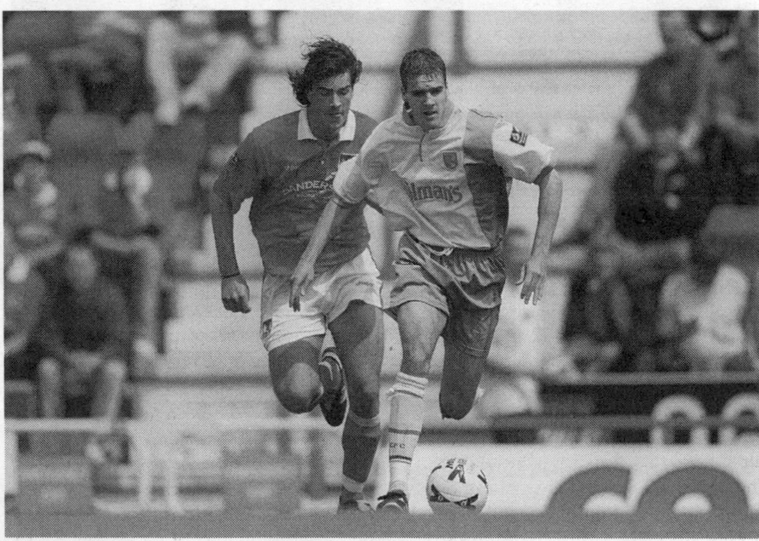

Birds dressed to fly again – return of the Canaries' green shorts, 1999

Nottingham Forest

Formation	1865 as Forest FC
Stadium	City Ground, Nottingham, NG2 5FJ. ☎0115/982 4444
Ground capacity	30,600
First-choice colours	Red shirts, white shorts
Major honours	League champions 1978; First Division champions 1998; Second Division champions 1907, 1922; Third Division (South) champions 1951; FA Cup winners 1898, 1959; League Cup winners 1978, 1979, 1989, 1990; European Cup winners 1979, 1980; European SuperCup winners 1980
Position 1998/99	20th in Premiership (relegated)

Records and historical landmarks stick to Nottingham Forest like glue. Forest were the first team to use such innovations as a referee's whistle, shinpads for players, and goalnets and a crossbar. Their derby fixture with neighbours Notts County is the oldest of its kind in the world. In more recent times, they made the first £1million transfer deal between British clubs, were involved in the first League game to be broadcast live on television, and set a record for the longest unbeaten run in the old First Division. But amid this trend for trend-setting, one fact stands out – when Forest won the European Cup in 1979 and 1980, Nottingham became the smallest city ever to produce the victorious team. It's a record that still stands today and, with the Champions' League becoming ever more greedy and overweight, it's unlikely ever to be beaten.

Psycho thriller – Stuart Pearce, captain and manager, 1997

Forest's European triumphs under Brian Clough were a source of immense pride on the banks of the Trent. Even some County fans felt the heart-strings tug a little. They were victories against all the odds, but they were also, from a historical point of view, just reward for a city whose spirit of innovation brought it to the very forefront of football's development as a serious, competitive sport with huge social and commercial implications. Nottingham had helped give the idea of senior football to the world – now the world was coming back to Nottingham to pay homage.

Sounds like a good idea – Forest's early inventions

Nottingham is the spiritual home of English competitive football, and Forest's sense of adventure, coupled with a discipline rare in the game in the late 19th century, saw them instigate a series of key developments. For instance, in one of their earliest games a Forest player had the idea of giving the referee a whistle so that he could stop the game – for obvious reasons, this quickly replaced the previous method of the official **waving a white flag**.

As football developed it became an increasingly tough game to play, and in 1874 Forest's **Sam Widdowson** hit upon the idea of protecting his shins with pads, which he wrapped around the outside of his socks. Of course Widdowson looked an idiot, and he was mocked by team-mates – but they soon saw the method in his madness. Before long shinpads, now worn inside socks, became standard issue.

As well as caring about his own physical protection, Widdowson was also interested in soccer strategy, and it was at his instigation in 1884 that Forest became the first club to adopt the formation of **two full-backs, three half-backs and five forwards** – a tactic that would prove popular in England until Herbert Chapman's 'W–M' formation of the Thirties, and which continued to be used in many countries for years after World War II.

Sartorially, while Notts County's black-and-white stripes were to prove the inspiration for clubs as diverse as Newcastle United and Juventus, Forest's **preference for red** found much wider favour. To help spread the gospel, in 1886 the club sent a complete set of red shirts to two former Forest players who were setting up a new club in the south-east London suburb of Woolwich – the club would later become known as Arsenal.

Meanwhile, at a representative match between teams from the North and South at **Forest's Town Ground** in 1891, a crossbar was bolted to the goalposts for the first time, and netting tacked to the frame to stop the ball running away whenever a goal was scored. After moving to the City Ground, Forest added a further refinement in 1921, becoming the first club to use oval- rather than square-section goalposts. So now you know how to blame the next time your team hits a shot that bounces off both posts before being cleared…

The question today is whether Forest are likely to come close to such a pinnacle again. Three times since those victories in Munich and Madrid the club has restructured its finances in an attempt to keep pace with the evolving football world, to little avail. Clough's influence on the team waned as he himself aged, fading to the point of irrelevance by the time he quit after seeing his side relegated at the end of the first Premiership season.

Since then it's been a case of shuttling between the top two divisions, trying to find the right niche. Managers have come and gone with a frequency that would have shocked Forest's old establishment, and players have done likewise. Yet aside from a brief return to Europe in the UEFA Cup under Frank Clark in 1995, Forest have been on the outside looking in. The train toward a European Superleague has left the station, and the club hasn't even reached the ticket hall. The only thing Forest are likely to be at the forefront of now is a promotion race. So much for the spirit of innovation.

Even if David Platt were to win instant elevation back to the Premiership in time for the new millennium, Forest would still face a fundamental problem. That record of being the smallest populated European Cup-winning town, proud as it was at the time, now haunts the red half of Nottingham. The City Ground holds a tad over 30,000 – modest by Premiership standards, tiny by European ones. All grand schemes aimed at housing Forest and County under the roof of a new super-stadium have been rejected by both clubs. And the old rivalry itself, while burning less fiercely than before as the team in black-and-white have slid down the League ladder, continues to work against Forest, syphoning off a small but important segment of the fan base. No other English city of this size has the burden of trying to support two senior football clubs. But then, no comparable city has this kind of football heritage, either.

Forest's early history is densely intertwined with that of County. The latter club was founded first, before any other current League side, perhaps as early as 1862. But the team's membership was drawn squarely from Nottingham's professional class, and County quickly attracted a reputation for snobbery. This attitude got up the noses of the craftsmen and artisans of the Forest shinney team (shinney was a form of hockey popular in Victorian England), who were keen to try this new game of football, but felt excluded. They were called Forest because they played at the Forest Recreation Ground, a series of pitches laid out within a racecourse on the outskirts of town.

At a meeting in the *Clinton Arms* pub in December 1865, members decided to form their own soccer-playing side, to be known as Forest Football Club. The captain of the shinney team, Walter Roe Lymbery, offered to perform the same role on the football field, and before long the club was dedicated solely to the new game.

On 22 March 1866, Forest were ready for their first fixture – a home game against County. Conflicting contemporary reports suggest either a 1–0 win for Forest or a goalless draw – though the latter result, reported by the *Nottingham Daily Guardian*, is thought to have come from information supplied to the paper by a County official, who also claimed that whereas his team had the regulation 11 players, Forest had fielded 17. A return fixture, played three weeks later, finished 0–0.

Right from the outset, Forest were well-organised, dressing in smart red shirts and matching caps, and drawing up a strict

Before the Forest fire – early August 1968, with Storey-Moore and Hennessey in the line-up

code of conduct. The problem was the lack of meaningful opposition, other than from County. The local Cup competitions which were instigated as the years went by failed to present a serious test of the team's mettle, and Forest had nothing to get their teeth into until they were invited to enter the FA Cup for the first time in 1879. They then shocked the public-school establishment of the day by reaching the semi-finals, losing to the Old Etonians at Kennington Oval. The following year they reached the same stage of the competition, going down to Oxford University at the same venue.

In between these two Cup runs, Forest had moved grounds twice, first to the Meadows (now Queen's Walk) and then to Trent Bridge cricket ground, home of Nottinghamshire CCC. But in 1882 the cricket club's secretary, Edwin Browne, assumed a similar role at Notts County, and Forest lost their winter tenancy at Trent Bridge to their rivals. This served only to increase the tension between the two teams, which had earlier been inflamed when County dropped Forest from their regular fixture list, apparently incensed by the latter's adoption of the revolutionary nickname 'Garibaldis'.

For the next eight years Forest would play in the suburb of Lenton, first at a ground called Parkside on Derby Road, then at the Gregory Ground, which was almost next-door. Back in town, meanwhile, County had turned professional in 1885, and when the Football League's founders were scouting the area for a Nottingham representative, it was County, not Forest, that drew their attention. So it was that while County began the first Football League season of 1888/89, drawing crowds as high as 4,000 to Trent Bridge, for Forest, out in the sticks was out of mind. Having been overlooked by the League, they signed up for the rival Football Alliance in 1889. The following year their search for a more central home ended with a move to Woodward's Field, provocatively just across the river from Trent Bridge, and soon to be renamed the Town Ground, to drive home the point that Forest were now back in Nottingham.

In 1891 the club signed its first professional players, and their introduction had a spectacular effect. Whereas Forest had spent their first two years of Alliance football in mid-table, now they were champions, winning 14 of their 22 matches. A trip to Clapton Orient in the first round of the FA Cup ended with a 14–0 victory – to this day Forest's biggest in a competitive fixture.

By the summer of 1892, the Alliance was no more. The Football League had agreed to expand and form a Second Division, but Forest's title win in the Alliance's last year would be a passport direct to the First Division. Unlike the team that came straight up with them, Newton Heath (today's Manchester United), Forest were instantly at ease at their new elevated level, settling comfortably into mid-table. They continued to perform well in the FA Cup as well, reaching the quarter-finals on three occasions before getting to the final for the first time in 1898. Forest's opponents at Crystal Palace would be their East Midlands neighbours Derby County, complete with their rampant goalscorer Steve Bloomer. But while

Chewing it over – Clough and Taylor at their peak

Far post flurry – Trevor Francis stoops to conquer Malmö and win the European Cup, 1979

Bloomer would indeed score for Derby, for the most part Forest's defence, marshalled by Frank Forman, held firm, and they ran out 3–1 winners.

Coinciding with the club's first chunk of real silverware was its last move – across the river to a site a stone's throw from Trent Bridge cricket ground, and which, even though it was technically in West Bridgford rather than the city of Nottingham, became known as the City Ground. Rather than raise funds to develop the ground by transforming themselves into a limited company, as so many other clubs were doing at the time, Forest issued bonds to a mixture of local businessmen and fans. The campaign realised only limited funds, resulting in the City Ground being a fairly modest arena for the first 60 years of its existence.

Twelve months after the Cup triumph, Frank Forman and his brother Fred played alongside each other for England, and a year later Forest reached the FA Cup semi-finals again. In 1904, Frank Forman was appointed to the committee that ran Forest, and a year later he helped to organise a tour of summer tour of South America. It took the party of 13 players and two officials more than three weeks to reach Montevideo by boat, but it was worth it – Forest won all their eight matches on the tour, scoring 56 goals and conceding only three.

The club returned to English football with something of a bump, however, suffering relegation for the first time after finishing 19th in 1906. The goalscoring of the Welsh 'Prince of the Inside Forwards', Grenville Morris, pulled Forest straight back up as Second Division champions, but by 1911 they were down again. As World War I approached, Morris hung up his boots after scoring 217 goals in 458 matches – a club record that has yet to be beaten. Without him, Forest stayed in the Second Division until becoming its champions in 1922, then lasted only three seasons in the top flight before being relegated once again.

The club stayed becalmed in the second tier for the remainder of the inter-war period, despite appointing its first full-time manager, Harry Wightman, in 1936. The

'He'll earn us 15 points a season' – Peter Shilton lives up to Cloughie's billing, 1979

innovation was hardly a success, with Wightman's first season in charge ending with Forest escaping a further relegation by 0.002 of a goal. In 1939 Wightman was replaced by Billy Walker, whose work was disrupted almost immediately by World War II.

The City Ground escaped Nazi bombing almost intact, but the progress of the Forest team did not – they were relegated to the Third Division (South) for the first time in 1949. In a move typical of the club's 'steady as she goes' outlook at the time, Forest's committee kept faith with Walker. He in turn signed centre-forward Wally Ardron, whose outstanding aerial ability enabled him to score 25 goals in his first season at the City Ground, and a club record-breaking 36 in his second, at the end of which Forest won the divisional title.

Ardron retired from the game in 1955 but Walker was not finished just yet. In 1957, as new stands were being built at the City Ground to take the venue into the modern era, Forest won promotion back to the top flight. Two years after that, with a side driven by the formidable half-back line of captain Jack Burkitt, Scots centre-half Bobby McKinlay and former Busby Babe Jeff Whitefoot, Forest beat Birmingham, Bolton and Aston Villa to reach the FA Cup final for the first time since 1898.

Their opponents at Wembley would be Luton Town, and with both sides plodding in mid-table in the First Division, critics predicted a dull game. Yet it turned out to be a minor classic, Forest taking an early two-goal lead through Roy Dwight and Tommy Wilson, and hanging on to win 2–1, despite playing the last hour with only ten men after Dwight had broken his leg. (Roy Dwight's nephew, Reg, would enjoy a less painful outing on the Wembley turf before the 1984 final as the chairman of Watford – Elton John.)

In 1960, Walker retired as manager and was appointed to the Forest committee, to be replaced by Andy Beattie, whose own undistinguished reign lasted three years before the arrival of the former Manchester United captain Johnny Carey. With ambitious new club secretary Ken Smales in charge of the committee, Carey was given money to spend in the transfer market, and by and large used it well, buying central defender Terry Hennessey from Birmingham, left-winger Alan Hinton from Wolves and striker Joe Baker from Arsenal. With the homegrown Ian Storey-Moore offering balance on the right side of midfield, by 1966/67 Carey's side were in contention for a League and Cup double. But Forest's smart football lacked a killer instinct, and after being knocked out of the FA Cup semi-finals by Spurs, they finished runners-up in the League to Carey's former employers, United.

After that, former Rangers midfielder Jim Baxter arrived from Sunderland for £100,000, and when nearly 50,000 packed into the City Ground for a 3–1 defeat of United in October 1967, glory seemed to be beckoning. But Forest were to finish disappointingly in mid-table, and during the first game of the 1968/69 season against Leeds, the club's Main Stand was gutted by fire. Fans escaped onto the pitch and there were few serious injuries, but almost all the club's records dating back to 1865 were destroyed. Forest were forced to play six 'home' games across the river at County's Meadow Lane ground, and won none of them. When they returned to the City Ground, with the Main Stand still closed, the arena had taken on a melancholy air. It was the end of an era. At the turn of the year Carey was sacked, and his successor Matt Gillies presided over relegation in 1972.

By the time Brian Clough strode into the City Ground on 8 January 1975, Forest were in danger of being relegated to the Third Division. The team had just lost a Christmas derby 2–0 at home to Notts County, and club chairman Stuart Dryden lured Clough out of temporary retirement to replace Allan Brown as Forest boss. Since taking Derby to the League championship in 1972, Clough had hit something of a low point. Frustrated by a lack of resources at Brighton, he'd walked out to succeed Don Revie at Leeds, only to be ousted by a player revolt after just 44 days. Yet Forest seemed right up his street – rich enough to indulge his whim in the transfer market, but with a squad unaccustomed to success and open to new ideas.

Crucially, too, in July 1976 Clough was rejoined by his old sparring partner from the Baseball Ground days, Peter Taylor. Between them they fashioned a side capable of winning promotion back to the First Division within a year – although Forest's distant third-place finish, behind Chelsea and Wolves, gave little indication of the glories to come.

Yet within a year Forest had won the League for the first time in their history. The side had few stars. Goalkeeper Peter Shilton, who Clough had promised would 'earn us 15 points every season' when he'd signed him from Stoke at the start of the campaign, lived up to his billing. Kenny Burns, Larry Lloyd, Viv Anderson and Frank Clark were an intimidating back four. Former Derby stalwarts John McGovern and Archie Gemmill ran a compact midfield show, with John Robertson and Martin O'Neill providing the flair. And upfront there were the complementary skill-sets of target man Peter Withe and the deeper-lying Tony Woodcock.

However, Clough's achievement lay not in his players' individual performances but in the team's overall outlook. As at Derby, he had brought a hard-working group of players up from the Second Division and, through the sheer force of his own personality and his squad's lack of any fear or pre-conceptions, had then taken the top flight by storm. Just to put the icing on the cake, Forest also won the League Cup that year, beating Liverpool 1–0 in a replay at Old Trafford.

Next came the European Cup, where two new arrivals from vastly differing backgrounds would each play a key role. Garry Birtles, a rookie striker signed from Long Eaton United, helped put out holders Liverpool in the first round. Then, after more Birtles goals had eliminated AEK Athens, Grasshopper Zürich and Cologne, Trevor Francis, the £1million man from Birmingham City, stole in at the far post to head home the only goal of the final against Malmö FF of Sweden in Munich's Olympic Stadium.

And still there was more. The League Cup was retained and so, in 1980, was the European Cup, Robertson scoring a trademark goal from the left flank to beat Kevin Keegan's Hamburg 1–0 in the Bernabéu.

Keen to expand on the team's success, Forest finally gave up their mutual status in 1982, and became the last League club to evolve into a limited company. Yet the change did not bring in the fresh capital the club was expecting, and with Peter Taylor retiring on health grounds, Clough's side lost their way. Francis was sold to Manchester City, Woodcock to Cologne. Clough in turn looked to Europe to buy players, years before foreign imports gained mass acceptance in England, signing among others Swiss international Raimondo Ponte and, to replace Shilton in goal, the giant Dutchman Hans van Breukelen.

On the eve of the 1983/84 season Taylor, who had recovered and returned to

Bavarian blues – back into Europe, 1996

management at Derby, agreed to buy John Robertson from Forest in a deal over which Clough was not consulted. Furious, he vowed never to speak to Taylor again. (He did, however, attend Taylor's funeral in November 1990.)

The Robertson affair was typical of the muddle that was to plague Forest in the mid-Eighties. Yet by the end of the decade Clough had somehow assembled a bright new team capable of lifting silverware again. With England defenders Des Walker and Stuart Pearce, Steve Hodge and Neil Webb in midfield and Clough's son Nigel alongside Lee Chapman in attack, Forest beat Luton to regain the League Cup in 1989, then retained it against Oldham the following year.

In 1991 Forest reached the final of the FA Cup – the one trophy that had eluded Clough throughout his career. Yet once Walker's own-goal had put Spurs 2–1 in front on the day, the Forest manager cut a forlorn figure, silent, lost and alone on the Wembley touchline, when in earlier years he would have been barking instructions until his voice was hoarse. Within two years, his reign at the City Ground was at an end, his team bottom of the table and relegated, his face long and bloated by what he later admitted was 'a glass of wine too many from time to time'.

Since Clough's departure from the scene, Forest's story has descended into farce, as the club has struggled to come to terms with the glitzy new world of the Premiership. Frank Clark returned to the club as manager and succeeded in getting Forest promoted and back into Europe. But his team were sliding back down again by the time Stuart Pearce took over as a reluctant player-manager at the end of the 1996/97 season.

Promotion specialist Dave Bassett then arrived to work his magic, and Forest surprised many by winning the 1997/98 First Division title by keeping the ball on the floor. Alas, one of the players most responsible for putting it there, Dutchman Pierre van Hooijdonk, went on strike for the first half of the 1998/99 campaign in protest at the club's lack of close-season investment on new players. Having sacked the promotion specialist, the board then appointed the original Premiership Houdini, Ron Atkinson, to steer the team from relegation. But it was too late – by the time van Hooijdonk was back in action, Forest were effectively back down.

Two years earlier, an acrimonious takeover saga had seen property developer Julian Markham, former Spurs chairman Irving Scholar and football historian and author Phil Soar arrive at the City Ground to float Forest on the Alternative Investment Market. But by the time of the 1999 relegation money was tight again, and venture capitalist Nigel Doughty was trying to take control. The outcome of Doughty's bid, which had to be approved by a majority of Forest's shareholders, would have far-reaching implications for the man charged with putting the team back among the record-breakers, new manager David Platt.

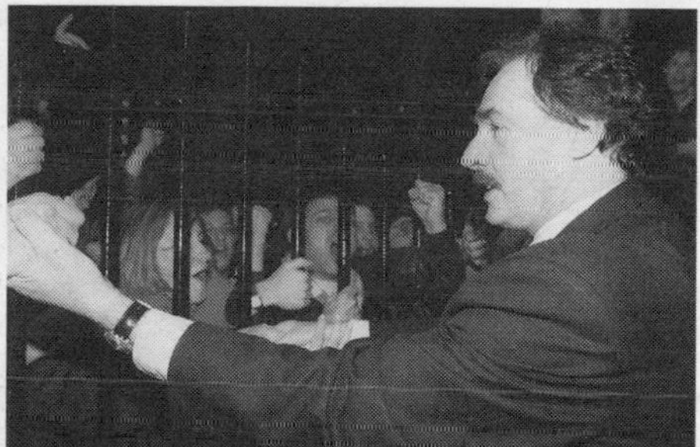

Takeover tour – Phil Soar presses the flesh

Here we go!

Police efforts to ensure that Nottingham's plethora of organised sporting events all run smoothly mean that routes into the city for football traffic are carefully planned and meticulously well-signposted. **Motorists** should simply follow the signs along the A6011 approach road – both Forest's and County's grounds are indicated, along with Trent Bridge for the cricket.

You'll need to arrive early for a **street parking** space close to the ground. If you've no joy, try crossing the Trent Bridge and parking on the other side of the river, which is quiet on Forest (as opposed to County) matchdays.

Nottingham **train station** gets regular fast trains from London St Pancras (service hourly, journey up to 2hrs). There also direct trains from Birmingham, Sheffield, Manchester and Liverpool. The last evening departures can be a bit hairy for midweek games – check the latest timings on ☎0345/484950. From the station, catch one of the regular shuttle buses which leave from the Broadmarsh Centre, in Canal Street to the right of the main station entrance.

Just the ticket

Visiting fans are allocated the lower section of the Bridgford End – the furthest end away from the river. Ticket prices vary according to the fixture, and concessions are available only if your club also offers them to visiting supporters.

Disabled visitors have space in front of the Bridgford Stand. Book through the club on ☎0115/982 4444.

Swift half

Two choices here. For those coming from the train station, ***The Vat And Fiddle*** on Queen's Bridge Road is a solid, no-nonsense place that's next-door to the *Castle Rock* brewery and serves a number of its beers, as well as many others. Fans are welcome so long as they're quiet, and there's good food on offer.

Closer to the ground, try the ***Trent Bridge Inn*** on Radcliffe Road between the cricket ground and the City Ground, a cavernous pub with a traditional feel that also makes families feel welcome, though it can be very busy on Forest matchdays.

Club merchandise

The **club shop** between the ground and the Trent Bridge itself stocks the expected range of items. Some Forest fans expressed disquiet about black being introduced onto their shiny red shirts and hope that it will be dispensed with as soon as possible.

The lone celebrator – Pierre van Hooijdonk beats the crush after scoring in 1998/99

Barmy army

The City Ground continues to be plagued by a small thug element, but most supporters' energies have been devoted to keeping pace with the various takeover battles that have proved such a distraction in recent seasons. When it comes to atmosphere, the new(ish) Trent End may look striking from the river but doesn't quite pack the audible punch of the old one.

In print

The Nottingham Evening Post is an excellent read and also produces a Saturday evening ***Football Post***. For a fanzine perspective try ***The Tricky Tree*** (149 Blake Road, West Bridgford, NG2 5LA), while for the complete lowdown on the club's story, chief executive Phil Soar's ***Official History Of Nottingham Forest*** (£19.99) is hard to fault.

On air

BBC Radio Nottingham (95.5 FM) vies with commercial stations ***Trent*** (999 AM) and ***Century*** (106 FM) for sports fans' attention.

In the net

Forest's **official website** is good-looking and on the ball, with online shopping and a superb 'Pressroom' area which offers rolling news from a number of different web sources, including the club's own press office. You'll find it all at: www.nottinghamforest.co.uk.

Among the unofficials, ***Garibaldi Reds*** has a very complete historical archive at: www.ccc.nottingham.ac.uk/~ccznffc/NFFC.html. And ***Nottingham Forest Gazette*** is one of those annoyingly well-run Scandinavian sites with plenty of English content at: hem1.passagen.se/pearce/Indexgb.htm.

Notts County

Formation	1864 as Notts FC
Stadium	The County Ground, Meadow Lane, Nottingham, NG2 3HJ. ☎0115/952 9000
Ground capacity	20,300
First-choice colours	Black and white stripes
Major honours	Second Division champions 1897, 1914, 1923; Third Division champions 1998; Third Division (South) champions 1931, 1950; Fourth Division champions 1971; FA Cup winners 1894; Anglo-Italian Cup winners 1995
Position 1998/99	16th in Second Division

The world's oldest senior football club has spent too much of its life in the lower divisions, devoted too much energy to a bitter rivalry with its city neighbours, and been too pre-occupied with rebuilding its ground to improve its footballing lot. If that was true 20 years ago, it's even more so today, with Notts County approaching the millennium as a modest Second Division side whose first instinct is to survive, rather than lift silverware.

Man in black (and white) – County boss Sam Allardyce

The burden of expectation that descends on County at the start of every season is similar to that felt by a string of other English clubs whose past seems infinitely more glorious than their present – Blackpool, Burnley, Huddersfield and Sunderland to name but four. By comparison with all the above, however, the Meadow Lane trophy cabinet looks bare. Notts have never won the League, and their only FA Cup triumph came in the 19th century.

It is County's sheer antiquity, rather than any on-the-pitch achievements, which gives fans and critics alike cause to expect better things. The club is older than the League, older than the FA Cup – older, even, than the FA itself. It was formalised as 'Notts FC' in 1864, but the team had been playing on an *ad hoc* basis for at least two years before that (one reason why County celebrated their centenary in 1962). Most of the players were professionals from Nottingham's banks, law firms and lacemaking companies, and their first matches were played out on the city's desirable Park Estate. Notts' first serious opposition came from the Sheffield club founded in 1865 (no relation to either of the modern-day professional sides in that city), but a year later they were given rivals closer to home: Forest FC.

Even before the two sides met for the first time on 22 March 1866 (in the first cross-city football derby to be played anywhere), there was tension between them. Both had adopted provocative nicknames, County calling themselves the 'Lambs' after an infamous gang of Nottingham thugs, while Forest went for the revolutionary connotations of 'Garibaldis'. After the match, even the result was disputed, Forest claiming a 1–0 win while the *Nottingham*

Keeping fit on the banks of the Trent – County in training, 1935

of their upper-class pretensions, ditching their cricket-inspired, chocolate and blue shirts in favour of black-and-white stripes, changing their nickname to 'Magpies', and turning professional in 1885. It was a transformation that couldn't have been better timed. Rivals Forest were still amateur, so when the embryonic Football League sought a founding member in the Nottingham area, the obvious choice was County. After a couple of middling seasons, the team finished third in 1891, and also reached their first FA Cup final, losing 3–1 to Blackburn at The Oval.

Daily Guardian reported a goalless draw, its information supplied by a County official. The game was played at the Forest Recreation Ground which had given County's rivals their name. A return match three weeks later, at County's ground in the Meadows area of town, ended goalless.

If the two clubs could agree on that much, they could find precious little else in common. They fought tooth and nail over the city's prime sporting venues, Forest at one stage moving into the Meadows ground, while both sides also had spells at Trent Bridge, home of Nottinghamshire County Cricket Club.

In 1877 County cemented their reputation for snobbery by dropping Forest from their fixture list – apparently because the latter's humble, artisans' background was viewed in a poor light by the club's other regular opponents. The two sides were forced to meet each other within a year, though, when they were paired in the FA Cup – and Forest won 3–1 in front of 5,000. The local press used the result as an excuse to round on County, who in addition to trying to exclude Forest from their social circle had also turned their backs on the city, moving three miles out to the 'Gentlemen of Notts Cricket Club' at Beeston. Suitably chastened, the team returned and started to shed themselves

Two years later County made an unwanted piece of history, becoming, together with Accrington, the first club to be relegated via a 'test match' or play-off. While Accrington folded, County kept their heads above water in the Second Division, twice finishing in the top three but failing to win promotion after test-match defeats at the hands of Preston and Derby. There was success of another kind, though, in 1894, when County beat Bolton 4–1 at Goodison Park to become the first Second Division side to win the FA Cup – with the team's centre-forward, Jimmy Logan, becoming the first man to net a Cup final hat-trick.

Promotion was finally won in 1897 after County finished top of a test-match 'mini league'. Top-flight status was then retained, albeit mostly in mid-table, until 1913, the team often looking to their eccentric giant of a goalkeeper, Albert Iremonger, for salvation. (He would go on to play more than 600 times for County; Iremonger Road near the club's ground is named after him.)

The League, meanwhile, was getting restless about County's use of Trent Bridge, which was reserved for cricket in May and September, forcing Notts to ground-share with Forest in those months. So in 1910 the club moved to the County Ground in Meadow Lane, just across the river Trent from Forest's City Ground. It was inaugurated on 3 September 1910, with a 1–1 draw against Forest watched by 27,000.

After a couple more relegations and promotions, County dropped out of the top flight with a thud in 1926, finishing bottom despite more heroics from Iremonger in his last full season for the club. By 1930 the team were in the Third Division (South), and although they climbed straight back up again, another relegation in 1935 prompted a huge drop-off in support and the first, dark mutterings that County should consider a merger with Forest. Supporters' pride (on both sides) soon put a stop to that, but there was no disguising the club's decline, which continued after World War II.

Imagine the sense of shock in the game, then, when England centre-forward Tommy Lawton, at the peak of his powers, decided to leave top-flight Chelsea and join County in November 1947. Even as unlikely transfers go, this one seemed incredible. Yet Lawton had walked out on a big club before (Everton), and had turned out for County as a guest during the war. He was so desperate to escape the pressure-cooker of the First Division that he was happy to sacrifice his international career, while County, for their part, gambled that the £20,000 Lawton cost them would soon be recouped at the turnstiles.

They were right, too. On 22 April 1950, County needed to beat Forest to clinch promotion to the Second Division. Watched by an all-ticket crowd of 46,000 at Meadow Lane, Lawton and Jackie Sewell grabbed a headed goal each, and the match was in the bag.

Lawton went on to score 90 League goals for County, but once he had left to become player-manager of Brentford in 1952, the Meadow Lane revival began to run out of steam. There were a couple of close things before the Magpies dropped back down to the Third Division, and this time they kept falling – despite a brief return by Lawton as manager – all the way to the Fourth in 1959.

In the Sixties, slum clearance in the Meadows area displaced much of County's natural support, attendances slumped to four figures, and the club was again thinking the unthinkable – merger with Forest. If County's saviour in the early postwar era had been the magnetic personality of a player, now it would be the turn of a chairman, local MP Jack Dunnett (later to become president of the League), and a manager, Jimmy Sirrel. Both men thrived on adversity and saw County's plight as an irresistible challenge. Under Sirrel, whose bluff exterior belied an intense appreciation of the game, the team won the Fourth Division in 1971 and the Third two years later. Sirrel left in 1975 but was persuaded back by Dunnett three years later, and in 1981, County had risen to the top flight for the first time in 55 years.

Sirrel's Second Division promotion side was an odd mix. Big Yugoslav Raddy Avaramović kept Albert Iremonger's spirit

Staying alive – Avramović and Kilcline, 1982

alive with some bizarrely effective goalkeeping; local lad Brian Kilcline was an immovable object in defence; and Rachid Harkouk, a Londoner of Algerian descent, always had an eye for goal. Keeping it all moving, meanwhile, was Irish international playmaker Don Masson, now in his second spell at County and nearing the end of his career, but going out on a high all the same.

Against all the odds, Sirrel's team survived for three First Division seasons. And, as before, when the drop came it was severe – by 1986 County were in the Third Division and in need of another chairman-and-manager double act to pull them out of the mire. They found the former in Derek Pavis, a self-made millionaire and a former director of Forest who'd left the City Ground under a cloud after a row with Brian Clough in 1984. Pavis was happy to put money into County but needed a manager he could trust. In 1989 he appointed Neil Warnock, an ambitious man whose long career as a journeyman professional had taken him to all the League's brightest spots (Hartlepool, Aldershot, York) and who knew what it took to lift a team through the flotsam of the lower divisions.

In contrast to Sirrel's teams, Warnock's County thrived on guts and raw energy, terrifying defences with their all-action style. With a youthful backbone of central defender Dean Yates, midfielder Mark Draper and striker Tommy Johnson, they scrapped their way to two play-off finals in a row in 1990 and 1991, and won both.

Suddenly Notts County were back in the top flight again but, in a sense, success had come too soon. Those quick promotions had forced the club to comply with the requirements of the Taylor Report, and though Pavis managed to negotiate the dramatic rebuilding of Meadow Lane at a bargain-basement price, there still wasn't enough money in the kitty to sustain anything like top-flight football. County fell almost as quickly as they'd risen, hitting rock-bottom with relegation to the basement in 1997.

Under another bold, young manager, Sam Allardyce, a rejuvenated team won the Third Division title with 17 points to spare in 1998, becoming only the second League club ever to assure itself of promotion in March. A 16th-place finish in the Second Division of 1998/99 wasn't quite as good as some pundits had predicted, but with Allardyce's ability to breathe new life into disenchanted players and Pavis enjoying running a football club again after the tribulations of the Nineties, Meadow Lane's future looks bright. There's life in the oldest dog yet.

Here we go!

Motorists see Nottingham Forest – Meadow Lane is across the Trent from Forest's City Ground, but if there's a big game on at County, it may make sense to park on the 'Forest' side of the river and walk across. Otherwise, there are plentiful car parks around the ground.

Nottingham **train station** (see Forest for services) is closer to Meadow Lane than to the City Ground. Turn left and left again out of the station onto Queen's Road, then right onto London Road and first left into Cattle Market Road – the away turnstiles are a little way ahead on the right. The whole walk takes around 10mins.

Just the ticket

Visiting fans are housed at the Kop end, one of three stands totally rebuilt by the club after both County and Forest had turned down the chance to move to a jointly owned stadium at the turn of the Nineties. There are more than 5,000 seats in the Kop and, if need be, the club provides further space for visitors at one end of the Jimmy Sirrel Stand. Ticket prices in 1998/99 were between £11 and £13, with concessions available on a reciprocal basis only.

There's plenty of room for **disabled visitors** in front of the Family Stand, behind the opposite goal from the Kop. Book through the club on ☎0115/952 9000.

Swift half

Two choices here. For those coming from the train station, ***The Vat And Fiddle*** on Queen's Bridge Road is a solid, no-nonsense place that's next-door to the *Castle Rock* brewery and serves a number of its beers, as well as many others.

Fans are welcome so long as they're quiet, and there's good food on offer.

For those who've parked their car on the opposite side of the Trent, the pubs most frequented by Forest fans are blissfully quiet on County matchdays. Try the ***Trent Bridge Inn*** on Radcliffe Road in front of the cricket ground, a cavernous pub with a traditional feel that also makes families feel welcome.

Club merchandise

County's modern **club shop** (open Mon–Sat 9.30am–5.30pm, later on matchdays) is built into the Family Stand. The club's black-and-white striped shirt inspired Juventus to start wearing a similar strip at the turn of the century, but today fans are divided as to whether it should incorporate amber trim (a throwback to the club's earliest days that was revived in the Warnock era) or remain unadorned.

Barmy army

If there's going to be trouble in Nottingham, it'll be at the City Ground, not Meadow Lane. On the other hand, the hatred County fans reserve for Forest is rarely reciprocated with the same vigour – witness the number of red shirts that turned out at Wembley to cheer the Magpies on at the play-off finals of 1990 and 1991.

In print

Fans are grateful that ***The Nottingham Evening Post*** – and its Saturday evening ***Football Post*** – continues to be even-handed in its coverage of County and Forest. Always a worthwhile read.

Meadow Lane is a haven for fanzine-sellers. Try ***The Pie*** (9 Yew Tree Close, Radcliffe on Trent, NG12 2AY); ***No More Pie In The Sky*** (39 Dunvegan Drive, Rise Park, NG5 5DX); or ***Flickin 'n' Kickin*** (7 Loughborough Road, Burton on the Wolds, LE12 5AF).

For the complete story of the world's oldest club, pick up Tony Brown's ***Notts County – The Official History 1862–1995*** (Yore, £16.95).

On air

See Nottingham Forest; County fans seem to favour ***BBC Radio Nottingham***.

In the net

There's no official site and many of the unofficial ones are either poorly updated or have fallen off the web completely.

The notable exception is ***Notts County Supporters On The Internet***, who've been online since 1995 and offer a broad range of features including a good news-and-reports archive covering the last decade. Tilt your browser at: www.nottscounty.net/.

The last top-flight derby – Richard Dryden (right) equalises for County, January 1992

Oldham Athletic

Formation	1895 as Pine Villa
Stadium	Boundary Park, Furtherwood Road, Oldham, OL1 2PA. ☎0161/624 4972
Ground capacity	13,700
First-choice colours	All blue with red trim
Major honours	Second Division champions 1991; Third Division champions 1974; Third Division (North) champions 1953
Position 1998/99	20th in Second Division

Never mind the rise of the Foreign Legion, satellite television, multi-million pound merchandising and the European Superleague – English football can still be a stubbornly conservative beast. And nowhere more so than on the touchy subject of co-operation between clubs which have historically been bitter rivals. In Europe, when football teams merge to ensure their survival – and, indeed, to increase the likelihood of future success – the public accepts the idea with a detached, logical shrug of the shoulders. In England, where only two professional clubs share a ground, let alone a board of directors, the concept of merger has acquired the status of sacrilege. Thames Valley Royals? Fulham Park Rangers? They never had a chance.

The hapless chairman of Oldham Athletic, Ian Stott, must have known the fate that awaited him when, in early 1999, he publicly mooted the idea of a merger between his club and two of its near neighbours. Stott claimed his words had been taken out of context. Asked by the *Manchester Evening News* whether he had ever considered merging Oldham with another in the area, he made the mistake of mentioning a brief chat he'd had with the chairmen of Bury and Rochdale while the three found themselves travelling on the same train together, bemoaning soaring costs. That was about a year earlier – and none of them had pursued the idea any further. Yet within days the national media had worked itself up into a lather about an unprecedented 'three-way merger' that was 'in the process of being completed'.

Stott resigned, feeling that he had 'inadvertently embarrassed the club'. But he retained his seat on the board, merely swapping places in the pecking order with his former vice-chairman, David Brierley. A pitifully small price to pay, some fans would argue, not so much for thinking the unthinkable, but for daring to talk about it. Step down as chairman? Off with his head, more like.

If football nationally was quick to try and condemn Stott as a traitor, Oldham fans themselves were more circumspect. They had – and have – bigger fish to fry. They knew all along that, even if Stott had been deliberately floating the idea of a merger to gauge public reaction, he was in no position to carry it through. For Oldham Athletic are almost unique in the English game in that the club's major shareholders, the local *J W Lees* brewery, have no representation on the board. The directors, meanwhile, own no more than about 10% of the shares between them. So Stott (who as chairman since 1982 presided over a golden era on the pitch, and who continues to command the respect of many fans) can ruminate on the subject of mergers all he wants – he is powerless to act without the consent of *J W Lees*.

The passive role played by the brewery in the club's affairs would be all well and good if Oldham were on a firm financial footing. Yet the team are crying out for an injection of funds after being relegated twice in the past five years, and *J W Lees* – despite earning huge profits from the broader leisure industry as well as from beer – have failed to invest a penny, while

'The goal that broke the heart of the club' – Mark Hughes beats the Latics' offside trap, 1994

simultaneously treating all suggestions of a takeover or share flotation with silent disdain. In 1998 supporters launched a *Stop The Rot* campaign to draw attention to Oldham's plight, and to persuade the brewery to change its attitude to the club. In the former objective the campaign has achieved some success; in the latter, no progress has been made whatsoever.

The frustration of the fans is understandable, given that Oldham have thrived against the odds for much of their existence. Despite the close proximity of the big Manchester clubs, the 'Latics' have carved out a distinctive identity and catchment area of their own. They have also fought bravely against the rival attraction of rugby league, which has always enjoyed a strong following in the town. Above all, Oldham have proved that footballing success doesn't have to be bought – all it needs is a modicum of financial stability, the right spirit, attitude and personnel, and the odd stroke of luck here and there.

All of those played a part in the club's early progress from obscurity to the Second Division of the Football League at the turn of the century. Ironically, given Athletic's present problems with brewers, the club was actually founded, in 1895, by a pub landlord – John Garland, owner of *The Featherstone And Junction Hotel.* His was a modest team at first, deriving their name, Pine Villa, from the Pine Cotton Mill in whose shadow they played, and starting out in the Oldham Junior League. The town's big soccer cheeses at the time were Oldham County, but when they went to the wall in 1899, the liquidators persuaded Pine Villa to take over their Athletic Ground in Sheepfoot Lane. In keeping with their new, more grandiose surroundings, Villa changed their name to Oldham Athletic, and turned professional. Yet within a year Athletic had fallen out with the ground's landlords (the *J W Lees* brewery – who else?) and moved to a pitch at nearby Hudson Fold.

By 1906, however, the side's progress through the Manchester League and Lancashire Combination had prompted a move back to Boundary Park, as the Athletic Ground was now called, and the club had formed itself into a limited company. A year later Oldham entered the FA Cup for the first time, and in 1908 they were admitted to the Second Division of the Football League.

Unlike many clubs, Oldham needed no period of adjustment to League football. They finished third at the end of their first season, and won promotion to the First

Flying high – Ritchie ahead of Pearce, 1990

Division as runners-up in 1910. In 1913 they reached the semi-finals of the FA Cup, where they were unlucky to lose 1–0 to the eventual winners, Aston Villa.

Dave Ashworth, the manager whose ambition had taken Athletic up from the Lancashire Combination, stepped down in 1914. His successor Herbert Bamlett made one key signing, centre-half Charlie Roberts from Manchester United, then led the club to the brink of a League championship on the eve of World War I. With one match of the 1914/15 season remaining, Oldham were level on points with Everton at the top of the table. But the Latics were beaten at home by Liverpool, while Everton managed to hold Chelsea at Goodison.

Oldham would never come so close to the title again. Although a postwar boom in the town's cotton industry ushered big crowds through the Boundary Park turnstiles, the conflict had torn the heart out of Bamlett's side. They clung on grimly to top-flight status for three postwar seasons before being relegated in 1923.

After 13 years of respectable Second Division football, Oldham went down again, to the Third Division (North), and stayed there until well after World War II. Former Middlesbrough full-back George Hardwick joined the club as player-manager in 1950 and led Athletic to the divisional title, but their stay in the Second Division lasted only a year. And when the League was reorganised in 1958, the team's 15th-place finish saw them drop automatically into the newly formed Fourth Division.

The early Sixties saw another still-born revival. With canny Scots midfielders Bobby Johnstone, Jimmy Frizzell and Johnny Colquhoun feeding goal-hungry centre-forward Bert Lister, Oldham won promotion to the Third Division in 1963. Two years later a young Ken Bates bought the club from local businessman Freddie Pye, made himself chairman, and dressed the players in orange shirts to set them apart from the crowd in the north-west of England. But Bates soon got fed up with commuting from his home in London, while there were many at Boundary Park who felt he was trying to push the club too far, too fast. He resigned in 1968, selling his majority shareholding to John Lowe.

In 1969 Oldham were relegated back down to the Fourth Division, but the appointment of Frizzell as manager the following year, after the team had finished five places from the bottom of the League, was a significant turning point. Frizzell had been at Boundary Park for a decade and knew how to get the best out of his former team-mates. He also had a crucial insight into the dynamics of the club – asked to condemn fans for not fully backing the team, Frizzell replied that paying admission money entitled them to criticise.

Not that they had much to complain about. Frizzell's side won promotion in 1971, and three years later were crowned Third Division champions. The team's rapid reversal in fortune detracted attention from events in the boardroom, where John Lowe sold his stake in the club to *J W Lees*, who installed one of their own directors, Harry Wilde, as chairman. The brewers' commanding position among Athletic's shareholders, and their continued ownership of the freehold to Boundary Park, were felt at the time to be a good thing. They would remain so until 1982, when economic recession bit hard into local industry, and the team's attractive take on Second Division football proved insuffficent to stem dwindling crowds. Oldham were deeply in debt, and had to be bailed out by J W Lees to the tune of £70,000.

None of this seemed to bother Joe Royle, the former Everton and Manchester City striker who took over from Frizzell the same year. At first the players struggled to play Royle's favoured counter-attacking game on Boundary Park's frozen mud-cake of a pitch. So in 1986 Oldham replaced the surface with an *Omniturf* one and, just as at Loftus Road, Deepdale and Kenilworth Road, it immediately raised individual skill levels. It also proved a nightmare for visiting teams, Arsenal and Everton both being humiliated on it before Royle's side embarked on their amazing double Cup run of 1989/90.

Oldham's line-up that season was expertly balanced. Jon Hallworth was as assured a 'keeper as the Second Division could boast; young defenders Denis Irwin and Earl Barrett were accomplished way beyond their years; Mike Milligan won the ball and Rick Holden flew down the flanks with it in midfield; and when it came to goalscoring there were three cool, professional heads in Roger Palmer, who'd been with the club for a decade, Andy Ritchie and Frankie Bunn.

Ritchie got two goals to beat one of his former clubs, Leeds, in the second round of the League Cup, and Bunn scored six out of the seven Scarborough conceded at Boundary Park in the third. Arsenal and Southampton were next to succumb on the plastic, and West Ham were hit for six on it in the semi-final first leg, rendering Oldham's 3–0 defeat in the second game meaningless.

With the club's first Wembley appearance in the bag, Royle's side were also making steady progress in the FA Cup, beating Everton in a second replay at Boundary Park to book their place in the quarter-finals, where title contenders Aston Villa were brushed aside, 3–0.

In the League Cup final at Wembley, the bigger pitch, hot sunshine and stifling tactics of Nottingham Forest snuffed out Oldham's front-running, and they lost 1–0. But there was still the FA Cup and a semi-final against Manchester United to look forward to. In a game every bit as enthralling as the Liverpool-Crystal Palace semi that had preceded it, Athletic held United 3–3 at Maine Road, and if anything played even better in the replay, which looked to be heading for another draw before Mark Robins' coolly taken winner for United deep into extra time.

Oldham's Cup exploits had given them celebrity status across the country, and their football, arguably, was the most watchable anywhere that season. Yet the team's enormous fixture backlog ultimately cost them promotion, for which the fans had to wait another year.

I have the touch – Joe Royle reaches out

From 1991, Boundary Park saw three difficult but often entertaining seasons of top-flight football, with Oldham winning the last four games of the 1992/93 campaign to stay up, before bowing out gracefully at Carrow Road in 1994. In parallel with that year's relegation dogfight, Royle's side had somehow managed to mount another assault on the FA Cup. They were a goal up in the semi-final against Manchester United at Wembley when, in the last minute of extra time, Mark Hughes evaded the Oldham offside trap and scored with a spectacular volley. Royle has since described Hughes' strike as 'the goal that broke Oldham's heart', and its effects went far beyond the 4–1 mauling Athletic suffered in the semi-final replay at Maine Road. With relegation came not only Royle's departure to Everton but also the loss of several key players, and the predictable drop in Boundary Park crowds.

Royle's successor was another former Everton target man, Graeme Sharp, who'd joined the club as a player in 1991. With an ever-diminishing squad and no money available with which to expand it, he could achieve no more than mid-table finishes in 1995 and 1996, and Oldham's fall from grace was seemingly complete when they were relegated to the Second Division in 1997. Sharp resigned, despite having earned some sympathy among the fans, and his successor Neil Warnock, not normally one to quake before an uphill struggle, followed him out a year later, bemoaning the same bitter equation: no cash plus no ambition equals no prospects.

Andy Ritchie's first season in charge in 1998/99 would almost certainly have ended in yet another relegation, had it not been for the hard work of veteran midfielders Lee Duxbury and John Sheridan – and for Joe Royle's Manchester City, of all people, doing Boundary Park a favour by beating York City 4–0 on the final day…

Grey day – Boundary Park under a cloud

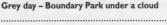

Here we go!

Coming from the north, west or east along the A627(M) (junction 20 off the M62), **motorists** should take the left-hand slip road at the end of the motorway. Take the first exit off the roundabout into Broadway, go straight on at the lights, then turn first right into Hilbre Avenue, at the end of which is the **club car park** – usually a better bet than street parking as many of the roads adjacent to Boundary Park are coned off after about 1.30pm.

Travellers from the south who want to avoid the M62 can take the M6 until junction 19, then the A556 toward Manchester, followed by the M56, the M60 ring road, the M67 and the A6017. Follow this road until just before the start of the motorway, then follow the directions above.

Oldham Werneth **train station** is served by local trains between Manchester and Rochdale, though beware that not all services run via Oldham. There are late departures to Manchester after evening games – see Manchester City for onward connections. For the latest timings, call ☎0345/484950.

The station is a good mile or so from the ground but, in the absence of usable buses or taxis, there's no other option but to walk it, through the town centre onto Featherstall Road North, then left into Maygate and right into

Westhulme Avenue – Boundary Park is at the T-junction with Sheepfoot Lane

Just the ticket

Conveniently, **visiting fans** are accommodated in the Ellen Group Stand – next-door to the car park and right in front of the junction of Westhulme Avenue and Sheepfoot Lane. Ticket prices in 1998/99 were adults £12, concessions £5. There's normally plenty of room here (accompanied, alas, by probably the coldest wind in English football), and also excellent facilities for **disabled fans** who should book in advance on ☎0161/624 4972.

Swift half

There are more pubs per square mile in Oldham than anywhere else in England, so there's plenty of choice – which is just as well, since Athletic fans would rather you didn't drink at any of the many hostelries run by the dreaded *J W Lees*.

The Old Grey Mare, on the Oldham Road just where it becomes Rochdale Road, lies behind the club car park and welcomes both home and away fans. It serves good **bar meals** before and after kick-off, and also welcomes families.

Inside Boundary Park, the only beer available is brewed by...you know who.

Club merchandise

Athletic's **club shop** is between the Ellen Group Stand and the George Hill Stand. The club has its own *Latique* brand of leisurewear as well as conventional replica kit. Boundary Park also has a *Trophy Centre* selling silverware, glassware, medals and the like – the closest the club will come to a cup for a while, cynics would say.

Barmy army

The *Stop The Rot* campaign began in earnest with a post-match sit-in at Boundary Park on Easter Monday, 1998. It has dominated the fans' agenda ever since, with little vocal criticism being hurled at Andy Ritchie's under-achievers in 1998/99.

In print

As befits a town where time sometimes seems to stand still, the local ***Evening Chronicle*** is a traditional, family-run paper that has had just eight editors since 1854. It offers detailed reporting

Keeping Latics in the Second – John Sheridan

of Boundary Park matters but doesn't publish on Saturdays – when the *Pink* edition of the ***Manchester Evening News*** is normally available in Oldham before 6pm.

Fanzine ***Beyond The Boundary*** (17 Saville Street, St Catherine's, Lincoln, LN5 8NH) has been an important focus for *Stop The Rot* action.

Best among the books is Stewart Beckett's ***Pine Villa & Oldham Athletic – A 100-Year Journey*** (Comprehensive Art Services, £17.95).

On air

Choose between the BBC's ***GMR*** (95.1 FM) and the commercial ***Piccadilly Radio*** (1152 AM); both have phone-ins after the match.

In the net

Oldham's **official site** is minimal to the point of frustration, but is at least reliably maintained at: www.oldhamathletic.co.uk. Matt Kilcast's unofficial site, ***Don't Look Down***, is very smartly designed, witty and to the point. It includes a terrific *Hall Of Shame* rundown on the current squad, at: freeweb.digiweb.com/pages/kil/index.html. ***Beyond The Boundary*** is online at: www.homeusers.prestel.co.uk/oasia/mainpage.htm.

Oxford United

Formation	1893 as Headington FC
Stadium	The Manor Ground, Headington, Oxford, OX3 7RS. ☎01865/761503
Ground capacity	9,500
First-choice colours	Yellow shirts, black shorts
Major honours	Second Division champions 1985; Third Division champions 1968, 1984; League Cup winners 1986
Position 1998/99	23rd in First Division (relegated)

When the McAlpine Stadium was only a pipe dream, when the Reebok hadn't been thought of and when even the Bescot hadn't yet reached the drawing-board stage, Oxford United were planning to move to a new home, out of town. Today they've got one. But while ten or more British clubs have built a new ground (or had one built for them) over the past decade, Oxford's has remained unfinished, a brooding hulk of concrete and rusting metalwork in the middle of a derelict farm next to the city's Blackbird Leys estate. It was supposed to be ready for August 1997, but work didn't start until the summer of 1996, and shortly after it did, the sub-contractor appointed by the builders, *Taylor Woodrow*, went out of business. Before long the club, too, was struggling financially, and what had been billed as 'a slight delay' in building Minchery Farm became a permanent one.

The impasse reached crisis point three months into the 1998/99 season, when the Oxford board admitted the club was more than £13million in debt. Much of the money had gone into planning for Minchery Farm, and without the additional income from retail, conference and leisure facilities which the new ground was scheduled to generate, the club's cashflow position had gone into freefall. Chairman Robin Herd, a Formula 1 racing car designer who had fallen in love with Oxford United during his days in the city as an undergraduate and stayed loyal ever since, had drifted from the scene, though he still owned a majority stake in the club. His managing director Keith Cox, the man who had dragged the club from the ashes of Robert Maxwell's collapsed business empire in the early Nineties, was still at the helm and leading the hunt for a buyer to come in and rescue Oxford all over again. But in February 1999 he resigned following newspaper reports that he was wanted for questioning in Florida about fraudulent land deals. (All charges against him were dropped, but Cox felt it would be better PR for him to leave anyway.)

Meanwhile, supporters formed *FOUL* (*Fighting for Oxford United's Life*), a campaign group aimed at raising the club's profile and ensuring that no stone would be unturned in the search for salvation. While the PFA paid players' wages and manager Malcolm Shotton trimmed his staff, a number of groups emerged as possible buyers. One was a consortium led by sports TV presenter (and Oxford fan) Jim Rosenthal. But they were outmanoeuvred by Firoz Kassam, a London hotelier who pledged to pump £1million into the club to enable Oxford to complete the season. At the end of March, Herd sold out to Kassam, and a new dawn could begin. The worry for Oxford fans was that they had seen such new dawns before, and been let down by what followed them.

Historically, part of the club's problem has been the antipathy of city institutions, not to mention the university, towards its plight. The scenario is mirrored at Cambridge United, a club which has a lot in common with Oxford. Both have struggled for decades to garner more support from their cities' student populations (Robin

No site for sore eyes – the main stand at Minchery Farm as it looked in January 1999

Herd being the exception that proved the rule at Oxford). Both have been desperate to escape their tight, old-fashioned grounds – although while Oxford were theoretically ready to leave the Manor Ground, Cambridge appear to have given up in their search for a replacement for the Abbey 'Stadium'. And both came late to the Football League, having first won a war for supremacy with rival local sides (both called City) previously more closely identified with the centre of town.

But it was Oxford that entered the League first, and while Cambridge have never played football at the highest level, top-flight action did come to the Manor during the heady days of the mid-Eighties, when the team won two promotions and the League Cup in three seasons.

Assuming Oxford do finally complete Minchery Farm, it will be the first time the club has moved away from its roots in the suburb of Headington. While Cambridge began life as Abbey United, so Oxford were known as Headington United from the year after their inception until as recently as 1960.

They began life as plain 'Headington FC' in 1893, the brainchild of a Dr Hitchings and his friend, the local vicar, who between them arranged the club's first meeting at the *Britannia Arms* off London Road. In those days Headington was a village community in its own right, quite separate from Oxford – hence the club's name. Within a year the team were playing under the name Headington United, but then, as now, finding a suitable home posed problems. They began playing on the recreation ground of a local quarry, but by the time the club had entered the Southern League in 1896 they had moved on to Wootten's Field, before moving again two years later to a pitch roughly on the site of today's Manor Ground. However, they were forced to leave this after the club's lease ran out in 1902, and endured five more changes of venue before moving back, for keeps this time, in 1925. The 'Manor Ground' had changed beyond all recognition, with facilities for cricket, tennis and bowls as well as football. But spectator accommodation remained rudimentary until after World War II, when the cricket club moved out and Headington United were given permission to develop the ground.

The building work, much of it paid for by the supporters' club, coincided with United turning professional in 1949. Having been in the lower reaches of the Southern

Hero against Chelsea – striker Dean Windass

League during the inter-war period, the club had missed the chance to join the Third Division (South) when the Football League expanded in the Twenties. But then again, so had Oxford City, the area's established club. And, crucially, as United embarked on the road to professionalism after World War II, City stayed amateur – the stage was set for a shift in the balance of local football power.

Headington first enquired about the possibility of joining the League prior to the reorganisation of 1950, when the regional Third Divisions were expanded by two clubs each. But their claims were ignored in favour of Colchester and Gillingham, and it would be another four years before the name Headington United finally sank into the national consciousness, with a run to the fourth round of the FA Cup.

Was this name a problem, though? Arthur Turner, who took over from Harry Thompson as manager in 1959, certainly thought so. After months of patient lobbying, he persuaded the board to adopt the name Oxford United. The objective was twofold – to make it easier for fans, particularly those who worked at the giant *Morris* car plant in Cowley on the southern edge of Oxford, to identify with the team; and to persuade the Football League that the city could not be ignored next time it was looking for new members.

It worked. Turner's team enjoyed three more FA Cup runs and won the Southern League championship twice. With crowds rising, the Football League admitted the club in 1962, after the collapse of Accrington Stanley had created a vacancy in the recently formed Fourth Division.

The momentum didn't stop there. In 1964 Oxford reached the quarter-finals of the FA Cup, the first team from the Fourth Division ever to do so, after knocking out League leaders Blackburn – they eventually fell 2–1 at home to Preston, in front of a record 22,750 at the Manor. A year later they earned promotion from the Fourth Division, and in 1968 they won the Third Division title, putting the better-established League sides around them in the shade.

There was no denying Turner's inspirational qualities as a manager, but in his captain, wing-half Ron Atkinson, he also had a remarkable leader of men. Atkinson's Oxford career had begun in the Southern League, yet with his instinctive vision and strong running he made the transition to League football effortlessly. With Ron's younger brother Graham, who proved a lethal finisher upfront, flexible left-back John Shuker and assured centre-half Maurice Kyle, Turner's side had a backbone that was as creative as it was consistent.

Their odyssey came to an end in 1969, when Turner moved upstairs into the general manager's role and Ron Saunders briefly took over team affairs. Saunders' reign lasted only a matter of months, and both his successor, George Summers, and Turner himself had been sacked by the time Oxford were relegated in 1976.

A period of mediocrity in the middle of the Third Division followed, but the club revived after the arrival of Ian Greaves as manager in 1980. Though constantly bemoaning the city's indifference to its professional football club, Greaves brought ambition and confidence back to the Manor Ground, laying the groundwork for the revolution that was to come in 1982.

This had two main protagonists, as diametrically opposed in personality as town and gown could ever be. First there was Robert Maxwell, who had used Oxford as a base for his publishing empire and maintained a home close to United at Headington Hall. When the club teetered on the edge of insolvency after expensively pursuing plans to relocate (no wonder fans feel a sense of *déjà vu*) in the early Eighties, Maxwell stepped in to become Lord of the Manor as well as Master of the Hall.

After dropping controversial plans to merge Oxford with Reading to form a new club called Thames Valley Royals, Maxwell gave his manager whatever funds he needed to strengthen the squad and push for promotion. Not that said manager, Jim Smith, would necessarily ask for much. Smith was an arch spotter of bargains who wisely refused to change his ways just because Maxwell's chequebook was in his suit pocket. So in came striker John Aldridge from cash-starved Newport County, Chelsea's cast-off winger Peter Rhoades-Brown, target man Billy Hamilton from Burnley and playmaker Trevor Hebberd from Southampton. Creative players all, but not averse to knuckling down, either. In 1984 they repeated the feat of Turner's team by winning the Third Divsion title, and the following year surpassed it by scooping the Second Division championship at the first attempt, taking a series of top-flight scalps in Cup upsets as they went. Leafy, languid Headington had never seen anything like it.

Yet just as Oxford were set to consolidate in the top division of the League for the first time in their history, Jim Smith surprised everyone by leaving for Queen's Park Rangers. His coach, Maurice Evans, took over and soon made Smith feel he'd made the wrong decision – Evans' side beat QPR, 3–0, in the 1986 League Cup final at Wembley, with goals from Hebberd, Jeremy Charles and emerging midfielder Ray Houghton.

Had the Heysel ban not been in force and Oxford been given a passport to Europe after their win, perhaps Robert Maxwell's interest might have been retained a little longer. But by now he had sunk his hungry teeth into bigger fish at Derby County, leaving his son, Kevin, in charge at the Manor Ground. After three seasons of struggle at the wrong end of the First Division table, and despite the arrival of deadly young striker Dean Saunders to replace the Anfield-bound Aldridge, Oxford were relegated. Mark Lawrenson replaced Evans but left within months, leaving Brian Horton to somehow prevent the club from falling further after Robert Maxwell had himself fallen from the deck of his boat into the Mediterranean.

Oxford were eventually relegated again in 1994, but came back up with a young side under Denis Smith, and appeared to have settled into mid-table in what was now the First Division until the latest cash crisis took a grip. New manager Malcolm Shotton, an unsung hero at the heart of the Oxford defence in the mid-Eighties, did his best to keep spirits up, and the city (already well-used to TV cameras, what

Smile, please – pay-per-view telly comes to the Manor Ground

with all those tourist videos and episodes of *Inspector Morse*) now became the centre of sports media attention. Wherever the Oxford tale went, the film crews followed – to the half-built shell of Minchery Farm, to the town-hall lobbying of *FOUL*, to the team's diabolically unlucky FA Cup draw with Chelsea's millionaires, to the first pay-per-view match in English history, at home to Sunderland. They were even there when Oxford, needing to score four to have a chance of staying up on the final day, beat Stockport 5–0 – and went down anyway.

While the club appeared financially secure during the summer, there were still questions to be answered. Would the council allow the club to build the multiplex cinema that Firoz Kassam now insisted was essential for the completion of Minchery Farm? Would Shotton get his promised money for transfers? Would the club's creditors sign up to an agreement that would give them no more than about 7p for every £1 that United were in debt? It was a tall order for *University Challenge*, let alone *Inspector Morse*.

Here we go!

Motorists approaching from junction 8 of the M40 have a simple life. Just follow the A40 towards the city centre as far as the Headington Roundabout, then take the A420 London Road exit. The ground is on the right. From other directions, simply join the A34/A40 ring road, follow this round to the Headington Roundabout, and proceed as above. Once in Headington, it's **street parking** – try the New High Street or Windmill Road areas.

Oxford **train station** is on the line between London Paddington and Birmingham New Street (service hourly, journey 1hr from Paddington, 45mins from New Street). There are also onward connections for Manchester, and at Reading for links to the West Country and Wales. For the latest timings call ☎0345/484950.

The station is not walkable from the ground, so take a taxi or any bus heading for the centre, from which you can take a #2 or #7 bus out to Headington. Alternatively, London-based fans have the option of *Oxford Tube* and *CityLink* coaches, which run every 30mins from Victoria and stop right outside the ground on their way into Oxford city centre.

Just the ticket

Visiting fans are allocated standing space in the Cuckoo Lane terrace and a flexible amount of seating in the adjacent Osler Stand. Prices in 1998/99 were adults £14 (concessions £9.50) for a seat and £11 (£6.50) to sit. **Disabled visitors** are located in front of the Main Stand – book in advance on ☎01865/761503.

Swift half

The Britannia, where the good Dr Hitchings and his vicar first proposed the formation of Headington FC in 1893, is still a favourite haunt of fans and is opposite the main entrance. It can get very crowded, so families and anyone wanting a tad more peace and quiet should head along to ***The White Horse*** at #1 London Road.

Club merchandise

The **club shop** is behind the 'home' London Road terrace.

Barmy army

Oxford fans are unexpectedly venomous when it comes to their rivalry with Swindon and Reading, but trouble at the Manor is practically unheard of.

In print

The ***Oxford Mail*** has covered the club's problems in detail and is good for match previews, but doesn't publish on a Saturday evening.

The fanzine is ***Rage On*** (17 Foster Road, Abingdon, OX14 1YN), while ***The Boys From Up The Hill*** (£9.99) by Geron Swann and Andrew Ward is the last history to be published.

On air

BBC Thames Valley (95.2 FM) is most fans' choice locally.

In the net

Oxford's **official website** is a bit basic but getting there at: www.OUFC.co.uk. Alternatively try ***OxTales*** at: www.oxtales.com; or the official ***FOUL*** site at: olympia.fortunecity.com/bischoff/404/.

Peterborough United

Formation	1934
Stadium	London Road Ground, Peterborough, PE2 8AL. ☎01733/563947
Ground capacity	15,300
First-choice colours	Blue and white
Major honours	Fourth Division champions 1961, 1974
Position 1998/99	Ninth in Third Division

Somehow, the words 'Posh' and 'Barry Fry' don't quite go together. Yet in a curious way, Peterborough United – 'the Posh' to their fans – are the perfect team for English football's least predictable management personality. The club's image seems to suit the man down to the ground – bold, ambitious, a little bit cocky, contemptuous of authority and determined to have a laugh. A bit like Fry's former club Barnet, but with the crucial advantage of a bigger catchment area and, as a result, greater long-term potential.

From Fourth to First – victory in the play-offs, 1992

Potential is not, however, a particularly concrete asset, as fans have discovered to their cost since the Posh were relegated to the basement in 1997. Two years on and the club is still there, showing glimpses of automatic promotion form, but ultimately failing even to make the play-offs. With Fry having to curb his instincts to enter the transfer market with all guns blazing, the club's recently established youth academy – one of the few in the lower half of the League – is the most likely source of any future improvement. But again, it's a case of potential needing time to reach maturity.

Peterborough supporters, however, are grateful that their club now has that time in which to consolidate and plan for the new millennium. The man who bought it for them was Peter Boizot, former chorister at Peterborough Cathedral, noted jazz lover and millionaire owner of the *Pizza Express* restaurant chain. With previously unknown historical debt preventing Fry from taking over the club in January 1997 and the Posh looking in danger of going to the wall, Boizot stepped in to balance the books and allowed Fry to get on with what he's best at – running a football team, rather than a limited company. The new regime, however, has refused to wave a magic wand over the team, and with crowds at Peterborough's London Road ground still not as high as they might be, the club is talking a good game, rather than playing one. It's all about potential, y'see.

The debt is this big – Barry Fry in front of London Road's new Freemans Stand, January 1997

Strangely, it's not the first time that Peter Boizot's family has had a close association with football in the town. Back in the Thirties his uncle, Vic Leverett, was wowing the crowds on the left wing for what was then the town's major club, Peterborough & Fletton FC. Founded in 1923, this was a semi-professional side that played in the Midland League until it was suspended by the FA for financial irregularities and disbanded 11 years later.

Furious supporters, determined to maintain senior football in what was now a rapidly expanding town on the main rail and road artery between London and the north, convened a public meeting in May 1934 to form a new club. At the meeting, the local worthies nominated to the board promised fans 'a posh team' – hence the club's nickname. The name Peterborough United was adopted, a limited company formed, and it was agreed that the team should be professional from the start.

United successfully applied to join the Midland League, and beat Gainsborough Trinity 4–1 in their opening game in August 1934. But no great progress was made until well after World War II, when the club began to prosper under the influence of a succession of young managers with wide Football League experience. First former Newcastle 'keeper Jack Fairbrother led Peterborough to a first-ever berth in the third round of the FA Cup in 1953/54. His work was continued by another well-known former goalkeeper, Arsenal's George Swindin, whose side won the first of a string of Midlands League titles in 1956. Swindin left to become Highbury manager two years later, but the old Sheffield United favourite Jimmy Hagan kept the momentum going, and the club's dominance of the Midland League was a key factor in its successful application for Football League status – the Posh were admitted in 1960, replacing Gateshead.

Hagan, a free-scoring inside-forward as a player, preached an all-out attacking game and, in their first season of League football, Peterborough did not disappoint. The team romped to the Fourth Division title, scoring a record 134 goals, 52 of them from Terry Bly, a smart close-season signing from Norwich City.

Midway through the following season, the team looked in with a chance of a second successive promotion when Hagan fell out with the board over transfer policy.

He was dismissed and replaced by the returning Fairbrother, and Peterborough finished fifth. Bly was sold to Coventry, and after that the team slid into a mid-table niche in the Third Division.

Still, it wasn't bad going for a club that was only just celebrating its 30th birthday, and in 1964/65 the Posh poked further fun at the establishment, drawing crowds of 30,000-plus to London Road for FA Cup wins over Arsenal and Swansea, and more than twice that to Stamford Bridge for their eventual quarter-final defeat by Chelsea.

The fall, when it came, arrived out of the blue. In 1967, a joint FA and League inquiry was launched into alleged financial impropriety at London Road. It emerged that the club had been so desperate for promotion the previous season, it had offered illegal bonuses to players. For the establishment, this was one mickey-take too many – at the end of the 1967/68 campaign, Peterborough were docked 19 points, precisely the number needed to put them bottom of the Third Division table.

The club's stay in the Fourth was longer than anticipated, but Noel Cantwell got them back up in 1974, and four years later his successor John Barnwell came within a fraction of a goal of getting Peterborough into the Second Division. On the last day of the 1977/78 season, his side were held 0–0 at Wrexham while Preston were winning – that put the two clubs level on points, with North End ahead on goal average and into the promotion zone at the Posh's expense. And as so often happens, a narrow failure quickly became a much broader one. Barnwell resigned, and Peterborough were relegated 12 months later.

This was to condemn the club to 13 years of Fourth Division football, most of it uneventful – a couple of chases for promotion here, the odd mood-swing toward the bottom of the League there. But while the team's football was steady, the club's finances were anything but. In 1988 the Football League appointed administrators to run the club as Peterborough's debts began to spiral out of control. Faced with oblivion, the club was saved – first time around – by Oxford-based property developer John Devaney, who brought in Mark Lawrenson as manager (from Oxford) and provided fresh funds for team rebuilding for the first time in years.

Lawrenson was no more successful as a manager at London Road than he'd been at the Manor Ground, but his replacement Chris Turner (a Posh centre-half from the Seventies, not the former Sunderland goalkeeper of the same name) used his knowledge of the club to get Peterborough promoted in 1991, and into the play-offs the following year. Though it boasted long-serving Mick Halsall in midfield, Worrell Sterling on the flanks and the lively Ken Charlery upfront, Turner's side lacked star quality. Yet the players had no shortage of verve. They won a memorable semi-final second leg 2–1 at Huddersfield, then beat Stockport County by the same scoreline at Wembley to secure their second promotion in a row.

Posh hat – goalkeeper Mark Tyler in command

Extreme sports – this isn't normally necessary at London Road

On paper it was even better – the advent of the Premiership meant that the Posh had leapt from the Fourth to the First Division in just two years. The reality was that Peterborough had a team in the top half of the League for the first time, and that was good enough for the fans.

Alas, it wasn't good enough for the bank manager. Despite all its successes, the club was still losing money, and midway through the 1992/93 season, Turner and club director Alf Hand bought John Devaney out. Now the emphasis was to shift away from the team towards developing the club's commercial activities, reducing dependency on income from the turnstiles.

The consequences were typical of lower-division clubs in the mid-Nineties. Facilities at London Road were improved, with a superb new 4,700-seat stand built in 1996, after Turner had led a march by fans to the town hall to get the plans approved in the face of opposition from local residents. Yet the more comfortable the supporters, the less able the team were to entertain them. After a decent First Division season in 1992/93, Peterborough were relegated the following year, and the decline continued until after Fry's arrival, with the drop to the basement in 1997.

Here we go!

Motorists should be mightily relieved that the roadworks which have disfigured the A1 around Peterborough finally appear to be over. The result is a stunning eight-lane motorway which makes access to the town a breeze for those driving south-north. From the A1, exit onto the A1139 Fletton Parkway towards the town, then take the third exit onto Nene Parkway, and the first exit from this into Shrewsbury Avenue (turn right at the junction off the Parkway). Turn right at the lights into Oundle Road, and you'll see the ground on your right, just across the roundabout. There's a **car park** on the left just before this roundabout, which is a good bet as the one at the ground fills up quickly.

Peterborough **train station** is on a major rail junction and receives direct trains from a range of cross-country destinations as well as on the East Coast mainline. You'll get back to King's Cross no problem after an evening game, but other places may not be so easily reached. Check the latest timings on ☎0345/484950.

From the main station entrance, turn right and follow the road round left past the *Great Northern Railway Hotel*, cross over the footbridge and head down to the bus station, which is underneath the *Queensgate* shopping mall. From here, buses #13, #14 and #53 run along London Road, stopping just outside the ground.

Just the ticket

Visiting fans can either stand on the Moy's End Terrace or sit at that end of the Main Stand. Prices for 1999/2000 are £9 to stand (no concessions), £10 to sit (concessions £4).

Disabled supporters have areas allocated to them in the Freemans Stand and the London End. Booking essential on ☎01733/563947.

Swift half

The designated away fans' pub is ***The Bridge*** which is (ahem) on the bridge just along London Road from the ground. For more substantial food there's ***The Cherry Tree*** next to the car park on Oundle Road.

Those arriving by train can stop off for a (perhaps slightly costly) drink at the bar of the ***Great Northern Railway Hotel***, prop. P Boizot.

Club merchandise

'Pay for blue shirts and we'll wear blue shirts,' the board told the supporters' club back in 1937, after fans complained that Peterborough's green kit was bringing the team bad luck. The fans duly stumped up, and the Posh have been in blue ever since.

The **club shop** next to the *Posh* pub behind the main stand has the latest model, plus a wide range of leisurewear including a 'Baby Blue' collection – fine if you've had a boy. If Peter Boizot gets his way, a new megastore will soon be built along London Road.

Barmy army

Trouble is rare but not unknown at London Road, particularly when local rivals such as Cambridge are in town. The latter's promotion in 1998/99 should calm things down a bit.

In print

The ***Evening Telegraph*** is the paper to look for when it comes to reports and previews on the Posh, but doesn't publish on Saturday evenings.

On air

BBC Radio Cambridgeshire (1026 AM) has its own studio in Peterborough and provides decent coverage of the club.

In the net

The **official site** is a bit like the club itself – lively and laddish, with slightly OTT graphics but great content underneath it all. There are good pages on history and community, and extensive areas dedicated to Peterborough's thriving youth and reserve teams. Find it at: come.to/pufc.

Two **unofficial offerings** worth a surf are **www.posh.net** and ***World Of Posh*** at: www.geocities.com/Colosseum/Loge/4439/.

Plymouth Argyle

Formation	1886 as Argyle Athletic
Stadium	Home Park, Plymouth, PL2 3DQ. ☎01752/562561
Ground capacity	19,600
First-choice colours	Green, white and black
Major honours	Third Division champions 1959; Third Division (South) champions 1930, 1952
Position 1998/99	13th in Third Division

Plymouth Argyle live life on the edge. It's not just a question of geography – although that must come into the equation when you consider that this is comfortably the most westerly senior club in England. With the possible exception of Carlisle, away travel is a bigger part of the annual budget here than at any other League club. Argyle don't so much travel to away games, as mount expeditions to them. It cuts both ways, too – few sides relish the prospect of travelling to Home Park, fewer still that of returning home again after a defeat. Had Plymouth been hovering at the wrong end of the League at the time of re-elections in the Fifties, Sixties and Seventies, they'd surely have followed such geographical undesirables as Workington Town, Barrow and Gateshead into the drawer marked 'Application Failed'.

In addition to location – and stemming from it – is the issue of culture. The city of Plymouth is Devonshire to its core, yet just across the Taimar estuary lies Cornwall, where no League football has ever been played and, in all likelihood, never will be. On both sides of the river, rugby union has traditionally exerted a strong influence over sporting development and continues to do so today.

Against this backdrop, you could argue that Argyle have to be different in order to survive. And different they surely are, playing as they do in the middle of a huge suburban park, under a unique name of which nobody has ever quite ascertained the origin, and in a one-off colour scheme.

Plymouth have defied the odds to continue playing League football here for 80 years, and can be forgiven, perhaps, for being suspicious of change. They do not want to leave the city's Central Park, in which their Home Park ground is situated, although they are warming to the idea of joining the city council's proposed new stadium complex there (the controversial 'Tradium') rather than developing Home Park on their own.

They are not going to change their name, either – even if the Football League were to follow the example of cricket and rugby and adopt American-style team names, it's hard to imagine 'Plymouth' being suffixed by anything other than 'Argyle'.

As for the strip, well, all the other League clubs that once wore green have long since succumbed to the theory that it is an 'unlucky' colour for football, and changed to something more conventional. Argyle, on the other hand, have generally done all right by green, and the club is now inextricably associated with it. Why sacrifice your identity for the sake of paranoid superstition?

The sad thing, given all these admirable qualities of longevity and eccentricity, is that at the turn of the millennium, the team are struggling as never before. Intrepid away-game adventurers Argyle may be, but the basement level of the Football League had been uncharted territory up until 1995, when they were relegated to what is now the Third Division.

With so much of the club's attention and resources being devoted to the design of its new home, and with crowd levels inevitably down on what they were at the turn of the Nineties, when Argyle were solid survivors in the old Second Division,

Premier payday – Derby County come calling in the third round of the Cup, 1999

the signpost to promotion seems to point uphill. But that should not deter the Plymouth faithful, whose club has faced moments much more uncertain than this, and emerged the better for it.

The first of these obstacles was the struggle to get the club established in the first place. Football had already been played in Plymouth, mainly by former public schoolboys, for some years when the Argyle Athletic Club was formed in 1886. Soccer was to be a part of its activities from the start, but there were also sections dedicated to rugby, cricket and, as the name suggests, athletics.

Today's fans should be thankful that, at the club's inaugural meeting in the *Borough Arms* coffee house, the name 'Pickwick' was among those rejected. But precisely why members plumped for 'Argyle' is unclear. Was it a tribute to the Argyll & Sutherland Highlanders, who were stationed in Plymouth at the time, and whose football team had just won the Army Cup, playing a brand of swift passing football which the club's founders admired? Was it the name of a street in Plymouth in which the club's committee used to meet? (The *Argyle Hotel*, now owned by the club's Youth Development Trust, is situated where this road was said to be, and points straight at Home Park.) Or was it merely that 'Argyll' and 'Argyle' were names to savour at the time, made fashionable by Queen Victoria's love of all things Scottish? The further away we go from the original event, the less likely we are to unearth the answer.

What is certain is that in 1898, local rugby club Devonport Albion moved out of Home Park, the ground that had been laid for them, after a row with their landlord. In came Argyle AC and their enterprising chairman, local department store-owner Clarence Spooner. Seeing that the football section of the club was the most successful, and that cities like Portsmouth and Southampton had professional football clubs while Devon had none, Spooner arranged a series of pioneering friendly matches at the ground, the first seeing Aston Villa trounce Argyle 7–0 in front of 16,000. Attendances at subsequent

Goals in green – Tommy Tynan, 1985

games rose even higher, and Spooner became convinced that the city of Plymouth could learn to love the game of football after all. He signed up for a new lease, built a new stand with an advertisement for his shop painted on the roof, and in 1903 successfully applied for membership of the Southern League, who encouraged him to change the team's name to Plymouth Argyle to give a stronger sense of identity.

A year later Spooner's side entered the FA Cup for the first time, and in 1905 Bob Jack was appointed secretary-manager, a post he would hold until long after Plymouth, in common with many of their Southern League contemporaries, defected to help form the new Third Division (South) of the Football League in 1920.

Under Jack and his trusted Welsh international captain Moses Russell, and with centre-forward Sammy Black scoring consistently, Argyle acquitted themselves well in the League, finishing as runners-up in the Third Division (South) for six seasons in a row from 1921/22. Promotion went only to the divisional champions then, and Argyle would not get their hands on the title until 1930.

Bob Jack remained at the helm as Argyle consolidated their Second Division status, and his replacement Jack Tresadern, who took over in 1938, was weighing up the likelihood of an assault on the top flight when World War II put all future planning on hold. The proximity of the Devonport naval base led to Home Park being bombed to pieces by Nazi warplanes, and although the ground was rebuilt in time for the resumption of peacetime football in 1946, the bombs had struck a savage blow at the team's ambitious heart. Instead of challenging for promotion, Argyle were relegated by 1950.

The remainder of the Fifties would be spent idling between divisions, but after the combination of wing-half Johnny Williams and goalscorer Wilf Carter had made Argyle the first winners of the newly unified Third Division in 1959, the team were set fair for another decent spell in the Second Division.

Forceful managers Andy Beattie and Malcolm Allison both had a year in charge during the Sixties, with Allison quitting in 1965 after a row with directors who kept overruling his team selections. When Allison got the job as coach at Manchester City, his captain, the experienced full-back Tony Book, soon followed him out of Home Park, and the side never really recovered from the loss of his leadership – Plymouth were relegated again in 1968.

Almost the whole of the Seventies would be spent in the Third Division, with future England striker Paul Mariner playing as target man for three years before being sold to Ipswich in 1976, and Tony Waiters, the former Blackpool goalkeeper who would go on to coach Canada at the 1986 World Cup, providing steady, sanguine leadership from the bench until his departure the following year.

Allison returned for a cameo appearance at the end of the decade, and there would be uneventful spells in charge for Bobby Saxton and Bobby Moncur before John Hore, who'd played more than 400 games for Argyle before taking the well-trodden path to their local rivals Exeter in 1976, took over as manager. Hore would have only one season in charge, 1983/84, but what a season – Plymouth escaped relegation to the Fourth Division by only two places but, as an aside, also happened to reach the semi-finals of the FA Cup. No Third Division side had ever reached the final but Argyle came as close as any, losing 1–0 to Graham Taylor's Watford at Villa Park in a tight and evenly contested game.

Plymouth's goalscoring hero in that campaign, the much-travelled Tommy Tynan, left for Rotherham in 1985, but would return on loan within months to help Argyle win promotion from the Third Division. Manager Dave Smith re-signed Tynan permanently in the summer of 1986, and his goals lifted the side to a seventh-place finish in the Second Division a year later – the closest the club has come to the top flight in the modern era.

Smith left in 1988, and when Tynan was sold to Torquay two years later, the rot began to set in. Another of the club's favourite strikers, David Kemp, sowed the seeds of relegation as manager before leaving in 1992. His successor was ex-England goalkeeper Peter Shilton, who initially found his player-manager's role very much to his liking, taking Plymouth into the Second Division play-offs in 1994. His own battle to stave off personal bankruptcy, however, coincided with the club record signing of defender Peter Swan from Port Vale for £300,000. The Home Park locker room wasn't big enough for the both of them, and 'Shilts' left three months before Argyle's first-ever relegation to the League's bottom drawer in May 1995.

Finger of blame – Shilton identifies the guilty party, 1994

Neil Warnock, an old hand at pulling clubs up the League ladder by their bootstraps, nursed Plymouth through the play-offs in 1996, with a team in which striker Mickey Evans was outstanding. Argyle got a club record £600,000 for Evans from Southampton but they also lost Warnock in the process. On the last day of the 1997/98 season, a 2–1 defeat by Burnley (the team that had beaten Plymouth in the 1994 play-offs) resulted in relegation and an end to the managerial career of Warnock's assistant Mike Jones.

His replacement, Kevin Hodges, played more than 500 games for Argyle in the Eighties but, regardless of his affinity with the club, could achieve no more than a mid-table finish in the Third Division in 1999. Hodges' side ended their season, oddly enough, with a mammoth round-trip to Carlisle that will be remembered long after their part in it is forgotten. There is a certain comfort to be drawn from that – Plymouth may be on the edge, but they're not as close to it as their opponents were on that eventful day in May.

Here we go!

Home Park is very well-signposted from the A38 approach road and **motorists** should follow these signs. Take the second exit off the Mandon roundabout on to the A386 Outland Road. The ground is on the left after about 2miles, with a huge free **car park** in front.

Plymouth **train station** is just under a mile away. Turn right past the taxi rank, go down the hill under the bridge to the *Pennycomequick* roundabout, then up Alma Road ahead – you'll see Home Park from the top of the hill. Plymouth gets regular trains from London Paddington (shortest journey time 3hrs) and from Bristol (2hrs). For the latest timings call ☎0345/484950.

Just the ticket

Visiting fans are accommodated either in the Barn Park terrace or in a portion of seating at that end of the Mayflower Stand. Plymouth have held ticket prices for three years in a row: £8.50 (no concessions) for the terrace, £13 (concessions £11) for the seats. The latter are usually preferable in winter when the uncovered Barn Park end can get extremely cold.

Disabled visitors can make use of spaces in front of the 'home' Devonport End – book in advance on ☎01752/562561.

Swift half

The pubs around the ground tend to be 'home only', so drive into the centre of Plymouth and sample the local ales and pasties there.

Fans arriving by train can stop off at the excellent ***Pennycomequick*** at the roundabout of the same name (see *Here we go!* above).

Club merchandise

The ***Pilgrim Leisure Shop*** (☎01752/558292), tucked behind the corner of the Mayflower and Devonport Stands, will sell you a replica shirt for £34.99 or a children's size for £26.99.

The club admits it has had quality problems with previous suppliers but says these have now been ironed out.

Barmy army

Argyle's small but stubborn hooligan tendency comes to the fore when Exeter are in town, and fitfully at other times of the season. The silent majority, meanwhile, are becoming increasingly exasperated at the antics of Dan McCauley, Plymouth chairman since 1991, whose claims at having found 'mystery' backers to level the club's mountain of debt have become almost a monthly occurrence.

McCauley's plan to sell Home Park for retail development and build a new ground next-door have been thrown out by planners, leaving Argyle with little choice but to become a partner in the multi-sports 'Tradium' development, which will need *National Lottery* cash before it sees the light of day.

In print

The evening ***Plymouth Herald*** enjoys a strong relationship with the club, having been the main sponsor in 1998/99. The ***Western Morning News*** is also worth keeping an eye on – it also covers Exeter and Torquay. Neither paper publishes on Saturday evenings.

Fanzine ***Rub Of The Greens*** (14 Craven Way, Bristol, BS15 5DR) offers the terrace-level view while Gordon Sparks' Plymouth book in the ***Images Of England*** series shows Home Park as it was before the wartime bombing.

On air

BBC Radio Devon (103.4 FM) has the ear of Argyle fans despite shared coverage with Exeter and Torquay.

In the net

Argyle have only just launched an **official website** and much of it was under construction at press time. Expect online shopping and audio interviews when it's complete at: pafc.co.uk.

Two unofficial sites are worth a peek. ***Green Army*** is the website of *PASOTI (Plymouth Argyle Supporters On The Internet)*, and has a neat, established feel at: www.argyle.org.uk. Meanwhile ***Greens On Screen*** has the latest on the proposed Tradium development and a small multi-media section among its features at: www.btinternet.com/~greenscreen/.

Portsmouth

Formation	1898
Stadium	Fratton Park, Frogmore Road, Portsmouth, PO4 8RA. ☎01705/731204
Ground capacity	19,000
First-choice colours	Blue shirts, white shorts, red socks
Major honours	League champions 1949, 1950; Third Division champions 1962, 1983; Third Division (South) champions 1924; FA Cup winners 1939
Position 1998/99	19th in First Division

Long before Southampton had ever appeared in the top flight, the spiritual home of senior football on England's south coast was at Fratton Park. The famous Chimes – 'Play up Pompey, Pompey play up!' – were sung by crowds of 50,000 as Portsmouth went from being a modest Southern League side to FA Cup winners between the wars, and went on to win two successive League titles after World War II. The club remained in the First Division for the rest of the Fifties, only for decline to set in just as its deadly rival from along the coast was beginning to move in the opposite direction.

Bent over backwards for Pompey – Jimmy Dickinson

Since those heady days – and aside from a brief and disastrous flirtation with the top division in 1987/88 – 'Pompey' have staggered from one calamity to another, the team often as short on inspiration as the club has been short of cash. A succession of managers and boardroom personnel have tried to move Portsmouth forward, only for the shadow of the past to keep calling them back. As soon as a glimmmer of light has appeared, key players have departed, or the manager's received a better offer, or the club itself has been put up for sale. Up in Lancashire, it's a common phenomenon. But down south, Portsmouth are pretty much unique in suffering from the malaise.

The question at the turn of the millennium is whether a Serb-born entrepeneur, an ex-Arsenal full-back, and the son of a former chairman can finally turn back the tide of history and give Portsmouth, home of the Royal Navy, a football club worth showing to the world again. The club spent much of the 1998/99 season in administration. As the creditors sought to extract what cash they could from a debt-ridden Fratton Park, manager Alan Ball had his Mercedes repossessed by a local garage, and players were told to take their used jock-straps home and wash them because the club couldn't afford new ones.

Enter, from across the water, Milan Mandarić, a 60-year-old Serbian businessman based in America who had made his money from the electronics industry, and who now wanted to realise a long-held ambition to own an English football club. Mandarić was not the only US-based business figure trying to take over an English team, but whereas Chester's Terry Smith had a background in gridiron, Portsmouth's white knight had been heavily involved with the development of 'soccer' Stateside. He had ten years at the helm of the San José Earthquakes on his CV, plus an administrative role with the United States Soccer Federation during the 1994 World Cup.

To add further to his credibility, Mandarić put together a consortium that also included Bob McNab, left-back in Arsenal's 1970/71 double-winning side, and David Deacon, son of Portsmouth's chairman during that last top-flight season in the Eighties, John Deacon. The club's creditors accepted the consortium's compromise offer (the usual 6p or so in the pound routine), and the final hurdle was cleared when Portsmouth's former ruling Gregory family failed in a bid to stop the takeover on a technicality. Meanwhile, events on the pitch mirrored those in the boardroom, as Ball's side avoided relegation to the Second Division on goals scored, despite losing at home to Bolton in their final fixture.

So Pompey lived to fight another day, and no football supporter with an ounce of sentimentality would begrudge them their escape act. For this is a club with a history every bit as romantic as an old mariner's tale, with hope and loss, tragedy and comedy served up in equal measure.

The evolution of the current club began in 1898, when local brewer John Brickwood called a group of like-minded professionals and business people to a meeting at the offices of his solicitor, Alderman J E Pink. The men decided to pool their resources and buy a plot of land in Fratton on which to build a football ground. The land cost them £4,950, and the football ground, which would become Fratton Park,

Casting a shadow of tradition – Edwardian splendour at the entrance to Fratton Park

Shaggy's smash and grab – Darren Anderton puts Pompey ahead against Liverpool, 1992

was built in less than 18 months. The impetus for all this derived from the fact that Royal Artillery, the town's leading club at the time, had been suspended by the FA for making illegal payments. The 'RA' club was supposed to be amateur, but the men who met in Alderman Pink's offices resolved that their new club would be professional from the start. The name they chose for it, Portsmouth FC, had its origins in another amateur side, formed some 15 years earlier by local architect Arthur Cogswell. Legend has it that this team's first goalkeeper, entered in the records as A C Smith, was none other than Arthur Conan Doyle, creator of the fictional detective *Sherlock Holmes*.

There was nothing fictional, though, about the way the new team at Fratton Park went about their business. Dressed in salmon-pink shirts with claret collar and cuffs, they inaugurated their ground on 5 September 1899 with a 'friendly' against Southampton. After entering the Southern League that year, they remained unbeaten at home until 1902, having been crowned champions of the League for the first time the previous year. A series of FA Cup victories against Football League opposition began with a 2–0 win over Small Heath (now Birmingham City) in 1905.

Yet the first of Portsmouth's many cash crises was not far away. Having declined the chance to join the Football League, they were relegated to the Second Division of the Southern League in 1911, and as crowds fell on the eve of World War I, a new Portsmouth Football Company had to be formed to clear the debts.

By the end of the war the club had recovered, and Portsmouth were the last champions of the Southern League First Division before it was swallowed up to become the new Third Division of the Football League in 1920. Four years later they earned promotion after winning the Third Division (South) title, having conceded only 30 goals all season. In 1926/27 they were promoted to the First Division on goal average from Manchester City, with their defence – together with the goalscoring of Billy Haines – again the telling factor.

The Twenties were roaring and Portsmouth were making plenty of noise of their own. Fratton Park was modernised and extended to give it a capacity of 40,000, and after the team's confident, charismatic manager Jack Tinn had steered his charges to safety from a couple of close shaves with relegation, Pompey reached the FA Cup final of 1929. They were beaten 2–0 by Bolton, but their Wembley appearance had given them a taste for the high life, and in the ensuing years the club gradually ascended the First Division table.

In 1934 Portsmouth reached another FA Cup final, and after this was lost 2–1 to Manchester City, the club stunned fans by selling star player Jimmy Allen to Aston Villa for £10,000. Yet while some of this money would be spent on another new stand at Fratton Park, a portion of it went to the wily Tinn, who rebuilt his team around young defenders Jimmy Guthrie and Bill Rochford. In 1939, his efforts were finally rewarded when Portsmouth made it third time lucky at Wembley, thrashing a much-fancied Wolves side 4–1 with two goals from outside-left Cliff Parker.

World War II prevented Portsmouth from defending the FA Cup, but in a town where every seaborne loss of the conflict was felt as if it were family, that was the least of anybody's worries. And yet, despite the area's enormous human suffering – indeed, perhaps partly because of it – the Pompey Chimes were sounding louder than ever as competitive football resumed.

Jack Tinn remained as manager only for the first postwar season of 1946/47, yet four players who arrived at Fratton Park under his auspices would form the foundation for new boss Bob Jackson to build the club's greatest line-up. Half-back Jimmy Scoular and outside-right Peter Harris came from Gosport Borough, just across the bay. Jack Froggatt was signed from the RAF to give width on the left. And then there was Jimmy Dickinson – another local lad from nearby Alton, whose understanding with Scoular would help turn Portsmouth into a team the League feared.

The side won their first championship in 1948/49, with Harris scoring more goals than any other player in the League, and Matt Busby's first Manchester United team trailing in their wake. The following year they retained the title, finishing above Wolves on goal average. Dickinson was capped by England, and more than 51,000 went through the turnstiles at Fratton Park to see an FA Cup sixth-round tie against Derby County. There would be no more honours after that, yet with the exception of Scoular, who went to Newcastle, the core of the team stayed together, bound by a sense of loyalty to a club that had let them play football the way they wanted to play it, and had been successful with it, too.

At the end of the Fifties came rapid decline. An ageing Pompey side, its tactics and outlook suddenly looking like hangovers from the pre-war era, finished bottom of the First Division in 1959, then 21st in the Second two years later. In 1962 they won the Third Division title, but only a vintage display by Dickinson, at the age of 40, in the final game of the 1964/65 season averted another relegation. It would be the last of his 834 games for the club, and while 20,000 turned up for his testimonial match the following year, the irony was that Portsmouth had scrapped the youth system that had nurtured him, as part of a

Easy Ball – manager Alan relaxes now that the club is safe

Family appeal – 'Blue Nose Day' in the midst of a crisis, 1999

cost-cutting exercise, a few months earlier.

The club spent the next ten years mired in the middle of the Second Division, and the longer its exile from the top flight continued, the more perilous the financial situation became. In 1976, Pompey finally dropped down to the Third Division. Manager Ian St John was forced to field teams made up almost entirely of teenagers, and with the club on the edge of bankruptcy, chairman John Deacon launched an *SOS Pompey* campaign to raise funds. At the end of the 1976/77 season St John was replaced as manager by Jimmy Dickinson, but within a year Portsmouth had been relegated to the Fourth Division for the first time.

In March 1979, with the team struggling to get into the promotion places, Dickinson suffered a heart attack after a match against Barnsley – he stood down at the end of the season, and would suffer a second, fatal attack in 1982, prompting a popular legend that his devotion to Portsmouth had cost him his life.

Ironically, it was Dickinson's replacement, Frank Burrows, who began the club's revival in the Eighties. For the second time, Pompey sold their star player – this time defender Steve Foster – to raise cash for team rebuilding. Portsmouth escaped the Fourth Division at the first attempt in 1980; Bobby Campbell took them to the Third Division title in 1983; and in 1987 Alan Ball completed the comeback by leading the club into the First Division, on the back of Mick Quinn's prodigious goalscoring.

Alas, despite some brave displays from the likes of stopper Billy Gilbert and goalkeeper Alan Knight, Pompey failed to 'play up' in the top division, and were relegated after only a season. Deacon sold out to former QPR chairman Jim Gregory, Ball's side was broken up, and by 1989 the manager himself had gone.

While the club spent much of the early Nineties trying to find a way of leaving Fratton Park that was acceptable to local planners, Portsmouth's players battled without much conviction to win promotion to the newly formed Premiership. In 1992 Jim Smith led a Darren Anderton-inspired side to the semi-finals of the FA Cup, where they were two minutes from Wembley against Liverpool before eventually losing on penalties. Inevitably, Anderton was sold, and in 1995 Smith jumped at the chance to join Derby County.

Jim Gregory's son, Martin, was now running the club, while maintaining that Portsmouth needed outside investment to grow again. In August 1996 he invited former England manager Terry Venables to Fratton Park in an attempt to attract that investment, but the only man who seemed interested in taking control was Venables himself. 'El Tel' appeared to negotiate a majority stake in the club for £1, while simultaneously becoming national-team coach of Australia and signing several Aussie players for Portsmouth – players who kept being called away because of international commitments.

Whenever Venables was away with the Aussies, day-to-day team management fell to the inexperienced Terry Fenwick, who failed to inspire the players. When Venables returned, he became embroiled in a dispute with the Gregory clan.

By the summer of 1998, Fenwick had made way for Ball, Venables had departed to work his financial magic at Crystal Palace, and the Gregorys had taken a back seat. Portsmouth were as rudderless as they were penniless, a proud old ship, sailing on with a crew but no captain. But, after the Mandarić takeover, they at least approached 1999/2000 confident of acquiring some new jock-straps.

Here we go!

Motorists face a straightforward task – the ground is actually in an area of Southsea, away from the town centre, which always helps. Simply follow the A3(M) onto the A27, then exit onto the A2030 toward Southsea. You'll see the ground up ahead where the road meets the A288 Milton Road. Your best bet is **street parking** – follow the A2030 Goldsmith Avenue past the ground, and with Fratton station on your right, a network of streets off to the left usually offers up some spaces.

Fratton **train station** is served by most – but not all – trains running from London Waterloo to Portsmouth. Check that your train is calling there on the departure board at Waterloo. For the latest timings call ☎0345/484950.

From Fratton station, it's a 10min walk to the ground along Goldsmith Avenue – turn left when you hit the main road, then left again into Apsley Road for Fratton Park.

Just the ticket

Visiting fans are allocated seats in the uncovered Milton End. Prices in 1999/2000 are adults £13, concessions £5.

Disabled visitors are accommodated in the opposite Fratton End (the KJC Stand) – advance booking essential on ☎01705/731204.

Swift half

Milton Road is a good bet for pubs, with a great pre-match atmosphere guaranteed at ***Mr Pickwicks*** and the ***Brewers Arms*** almost next-door. Families and those in search of hot food are recommended the ***Good Companion*** on Eastern Road in Milton – you'll see it from the A2030 before the junction with Milton Road.

Club merchandise

The splendid Edwardian ***Pompey Shop*** next to the main entrance stocks the full range of gear in blue, white and red – the colours the club adopted just prior to World War I in response to the local military influence.

Barmy army

Hatred of the 'Scummers' of Southampton tends to dominate life at Fratton Park, although the two teams haven't met in a competitive game for years. There's a small hooligan element, but this shouldn't detract from the rightly prized passion of the majority, which at Portsmouth are anything but silent.

The club's travelling support is likewise legendary, with 15,000 making the trip to Liverpool for a Cup tie in 1981 and singing throughout, despite their side losing 4–1.

In print

The local ***Sports Echo*** publishes a Saturday evening edition, but sadly the pioneering fanzine ***Frattonise*** is no more (but see *In the net* below). You'll see a variety of newer fanzines sold at the ground.

The essential Pompey book is ***Portsmouth FC 1898–1998*** (£30), by Peter Jeffs and Colin Farmery and available from the club shop. Jeffs has also penned ***Pompey's 'Gentleman Jim'*** (Breedon, £9.95), a biography of Jimmy Dickinson.

On air

BBC Radio Solent (999 AM) has a Saturday sports show between 1pm and 6pm.

In the net

The **official site** is run by *Planet Internet* but was still in its early stages at press time. It's at: www.portsmouthfc.co.uk

Wot's The Story – Pompey Glory is a fine historical site at: www.btinternet.com/~PGlory/start.htm. And ***PompeyWeb*** is a good all-rounder with a link to *Getting Off At Fratton*, the online continuation of *Frattonise*. Find it all at: www.mech.port.ac.uk/StaffP/pb/pfc.html.

Port Vale

Formation	1876 as Burslem Port Vale
Stadium	Vale Park, Burslem, ST6 1AW. ☎01782/814134
Ground capacity	22,350
First-choice colours	White and black with yellow trim
Major honours	Third Division (North) champions 1930, 1954; Fourth Division champions 1958; Autoglass Trophy winners, 1993
Position 1998/99	21st in First Division

Few professional football clubs in England have had their recent history dominated by the belief and determination of one man. But such a club is Port Vale, and such a man is John Rudge.

When Rudge took over as first-team manager in December 1983, he'd already been on the coaching staff at Vale Park for nearly four years. When he was dismissed in January 1999, he'd become the second longest-serving manager among the 92 clubs. Vale offered him a post 'upstairs' as director of football, but Rudge declined, preferring to watch the team's struggle against relegation from the Second Division at a distance.

Defiant in defeat – John Rudge, manager for a generation

Vale fans, furious at what they saw as the betrayal of a club legend, demonstrated as part of campaign to 're-instate Rudgie', while simultaneously supporting new boss Brian Horton and his beleaguered squad. Looking at Rudge's record, it's not hard to understand the esteem in which he is still held. Three visits to Wembley, stirring Cup wins over the likes of Spurs and Everton, and no fewer than eight seasons of football in the English game's second tier – all were achieved under his reign. To fully grasp the magnitude of Rudge's legacy, though, you need to go back to the club's early history and discover what Port Vale had done – or not done – before his arrival in 1980.

Every record book lists Vale's year of foundation as 1876 but, technically, the club formed in that year no longer exists. The men who founded it reputedly met at a house in the Potteries town of Longport called 'Port Vale' – hence their choice of name for the club. By 1882 Vale had become the leading club in the north of the Stoke-on-Trent conurbation, and after playing at several locations in the area the team settled in Cobridge. Confusingly, the club was now known as Burslem Port Vale, after an adjacent town in which the side had earlier played. It was under this name that the club was elected to the Football League in 1892, but after some 15 years of struggle the cash ran out, and Burslem Port Vale was wound up.

In 1906, an amateur club called Cobridge Church took over the ground and decided to play under the name Port Vale. Fear of subsidence prompted another move, in 1912, to the Old Recreation Ground in Hanley, and it was from here

Never the twain – Vale (left) and Stoke run out for a Potteries derby at Vale Park, 1998

that the team launched a successful drive to regain Football League status – Port Vale replaced Leeds City in the Second Division in 1919.

Vale made little impact on the League during the Twenties but were beginning to acquire a reputation as Cup fighters. In 1927/28, the goals of Wilf Kirkham powered the side into the fifth round of the FA Cup, where Vale came within a minute of beating Arsenal. Only a year later, the team were relegated to the newly formed Third Division (North) and Kirkham was sold to Vale's hated local rivals, Stoke City. Yet the team bounced back instantly, becoming the first Champions of the new Division, and ending the 1930/31 Second Division campaign in fifth place – to this day the club's highest-ever League finish.

There was another relegation in 1936 and, like several other Midlands clubs, Vale found themselves being moved between the two regional Third Divisions as their geographical composition shifted. World War II saw Vale again crippled by debt, being obliged to sell their ground to the local council and then lease it back from them to stave off bankruptcy. After the war, though, the club bought a patch of waste ground in Burslem, sold part of it to a mining company, and used the spare cash to finance the construction of what is now Vale Park. The ground was originally conceived as an elaborate 'Wembley of the North' holding 70,000, but there was room for less than half that when it was finally inaugurated in 1950, and the rest of the grand scheme was never realised.

The main reason was lack of cash. Vale were still living very much in Stoke's shadow, and not even the 1953/54 *Iron Curtain* season, when the team conceded just 21 League goals, won the Third Division (North) title and reached an FA Cup semi-final against West Brom, did much to improve the club's financial position.

In 1965, several ups and downs later, Vale appointed Stanley Matthews, once a Stoke City hero, as general manager with a brief to overhaul the club's flagging youth system. It didn't work – local youngsters, it seemed, would rather play for Stoke. Vale were relegated to the Fourth Division, then expelled from the League for making illegal bonus payments to players. They were immediately re-elected and fined £4,000 instead, but club morale had sustained another body blow.

Matthews was replaced by Gordon Lee in 1968, and Lee at least managed to guide Vale back into the Third Division two years later. After Lee departed in 1974, Roy Sproson took over as manager – a popular choice since he had been with the club since 1950 and made a record 761 appearances as a player in that time. Sproson's side managed a sixth-place finish in 1975, but after that it was downhill all the way, and Vale ended the Seventies back in the basement, having appointed four more managers in as many years.

John McGrath took the team back up in 1983, but Vale had gone 15 Third Division games without a win at the start of the 1983/84 season when the board decided to sack McGrath and appoint his assistant, John Rudge, as first-team boss. This put Rudge in an invidious position (he owed his post at the club to McGrath), but after initially accepting the role as caretaker, he was sufficiently encouraged by the team's potential to take the job on a permanent basis. He could not prevent relegation in 1984, but his instinctive pragmatism would soon pay rich dividends.

As a young player at Huddersfield, Rudge had moved into digs vacated by Denis Law, and found a pair of the great man's boots at the bottom of a cupboard. They fitted perfectly but, rather than wear them himself, he gave them to his dad – reasoning that he already had a decent pair of his own. Two decades later, he and John McGrath nurtured the talents of Mark and Neville Chamberlain at Port Vale, only to see them sold to Stoke because Vale could not afford to offer them a long-term contract. It was time to revive that old 'make do and mend' philosophy.

Once in sole charge, Rudge shifted the emphasis from youth development to the lower end of the transfer market, instructing his scouts to look out for bargains. If Vale could buy them and then keep them, all well and good; if not, they could probably sell them on at a profit. Having been forced to sell Mark Bright to Leicester for a paltry £66,000 in 1984, Rudge then spent just £5,000 of that to bring young Welsh striker Andy Jones from Rhyl. Two years and a promotion later, Jones was sold to Charlton for £350,000 – 'it was like winning

Crush hour – Vale's Anglo-Italian Cup final pulls in the punters, Wembley, 1996

the pools', Rudge said. Fans were worried but they needn't have been. Rudge had earlier asked them to club together to buy a replacement striker, Darren Beckford, from Manchester City for £15,000, and had poached another promising young forward, Robbie Earle, from Stoke; Vale fans sensed the tide of history was turning their way.

They were right, too. Vale knocked Spurs out of the FA Cup in 1988, and earned promotion to the Second Division via the play-offs a year later. In 1990, Stoke were relegated to the Third; it was only the second time in history that Vale had played football at a higher level than their wealthier neighbours.

Beckford and Earle were out of contract by 1991 but, in those pre-Bosman days, their transfer fees netted Vale a tidy £1.7million. The club needed it – implementing the Taylor Report was going to be expensive and Vale were breaking even, at best. There was a certain inevitability about relegation in 1992, but the board and the supporters stayed loyal to Rudge and he repaid them in kind. Vale won the Autoglass Trophy at Wembley a year later, and although they lost the play-off final to West Brom the following month, it was only a temporary blip and they were promoted to the First Division, as it now was, in 1994.

Vale made one more trip to Wembley, losing the Anglo-Italian Cup final 5–2 to Genoa in 1996, but the real progress was being made in the League, where the team finished 12th that year and eighth the following season. By now, Rudge's skills in acquiring cut-price talent were becoming legendary. Alex Ferguson has recalled that 'every manager dreaded getting a call from John; he'd come on saying he had no money and asking what you had, bit by bit you gave in, and eventually he'd get a cheap player and turn them into a better player'.

In this way Ian Taylor, Jon McCarthy, Robin van der Laan and Lee Mills were all bought and sold at a profit, but the club was now losing £30,000 a month. At the end of the 1997/98 season, Vale stayed up with a 4–0 last-day win at Huddersfield, but with the team back in the drop zone come January 1999, chairman Bill Bell's patience snapped and Rudge was sacked.

The fans were up in arms, players openly admitted they were 'devastated', but the board were not for turning. Rudge's replacement, Brian Horton, lacked his predecessor's charisma but the squad seemed to respond to him, and Vale guaranteed First Division survival for at least another year when they beat QPR one week from the end of the 1998/99 campaign.

Even so, the supporters will not forget Rudge – or forgive the board.

Here we go!

Burslem turns out to be a much more attractive destination than many visiting fans think but, from whichever direction, **motorists** face an awkward journey to get to it.

From the north, leave the M6 motorway at junction 16, take the A500 south toward Stoke-on-Trent, then the A527 toward Tunstall. Follow the Tunstall road left off the next roundabout, then turn right at the following mini-roundabout onto the B501 which is Newcastle Street. Continue straight on into Moorland Road, take the second left into Hamil Road and Vale Park is on your left.

Coming from the west, you should already be on the A500 and can follow the route as above. From the south, exit the M6 at Junction 15 and follow the A500 north into Stoke, then take the A527 toward Tunstall and proceed as above.

From the east, take the A52 toward Stoke-on-Trent, follow the road through Ash Bank and Werrington, then get into the right-hand lane to go straight over at the Limekiln Bank crossroads. Stay in this lane and turn right into Keelings Road, then right again at the next roundabout. Go straight over three mini-roundabouts into High Lane, then take the fourth left which is Hamil Road. Vale Park is on the right.

The club will charge you £4 to use its **car park** and you may be better off seeking street parking off Hamil Road. Beware of congestion both before and after the match, particularly on Saturdays when the centre of Burslem can be a frenzy of shopping traffic.

Pain in vain – Lee Mills helps Vale into a 4–1 lead over QPR in 1997, but the game finished 4–4

The nearest **train station** is Longport, about a mile from the ground, but this is served only by local trains and most visiting fans will arrive at Stoke, which can be reached direct from London Euston, Birmingham, Manchester, Nottingham and Derby. Change at Stafford or Crewe for local services if coming from elsewhere. For the latest timings call ☎0345/484950.

Stoke station is a good four miles from Vale Park. A **taxi** will set you back at least £6, a PMT **bus** #24 or #25 to Burslem will be substantially cheaper; to catch one, turn left out of the station toward Stoke Road, then left again, and the bus stop is across the road, opposite Signal Radio. Once in Burslem, cross Waterloo Road into Moorland Road, then turn immediately left into Hamil Road – Vale Park is up ahead on your left.

Note that there are no trains from Stoke back to London after a midweek match.

Just the ticket

Their club having turned down the chance to ground-share with Stoke, Vale fans are now furious that the local council has ploughed £6million into City's new Britannia Stadium, while donating precisely nothing to improvements at Vale Park. In fact, the council's closure of Vale's profitable Sunday market has deprived the club of a vital source of revenue. Despite these grievances, the club remains committed to developing Vale Park, and an impressive new Lorne Street Stand is due to open during the 1999/2000 season. **Disabled supporters** will be accommodated here; book in advance on ☎01782/814134.

Visiting fans are asked to use the all-seated Hamil Road Stand, where prices in 1998/99 were adults £15, juniors and OAPs £11. This end of the ground can hold 4,500 fans and is rarely full; seasoned anoraks will note that its roof once covered the Main Stand at Chester City's old Sealand Road ground.

Swift half

Most pubs in the vicinity of Vale Park have doormen on matchdays, but few are religiously 'home only'. Decent-looking away fans can normally get a pint at ***The Vine Inn***, on Hamil Road just by the visiting supporters' entrance to the ground, although there can be a bit of a crush inside in the hour before kick-off.

Two more spacious, family-orientated pubs, ***The Pack Horse*** and ***The Duke of Bridgewater***, lie along the access road from Longport station. Both serve food prior to afternoon games.

Club merchandise

The **club shop** (☎01782/814134) is due to move into the Lorne Street Stand and has home shirts for £36.99 (children's sizes £26.99), a rather fetching range of *Mizuno* leisurewear with prices from £24.99, and a set of *Valiants* dart flights at 70p for a set of three – why not pick up two while you're passing?

Barmy army

The most vocal support gathers at the Bycars end of the ground, but low average attendances, coupled with the distance between the stands and the edge of the pitch (a hangover from the 'Wembley of the North' blueprint) and the expanses of parkland around can make Vale Park eerily quiet. The fans' two biggest enemies are the local council and Stoke City, neither of whom turn up very often.

In print

Potteries paper ***The Evening Sentinel*** boasts Martin Spinks, who's been reporting on Vale for a decade, and publishes a Saturday *Green'Un*, normally available from around 6pm. Aware that it has a delicate balancing act to perform, the *Sentinel* sponsors a stand at both Vale Park and Stoke's Britannia Stadium.

The self-mocking irreverence of fanzine ***The Vale Park Beano*** was sorely tested by the Rudge sacking, about which the editorial staff were particularly scathing. Order a copy from: PO Box 485, Kidsgrove, Stoke-on-Trent, Staffs, ST7 3BZ. The seminal book on the club is Jeff Kent's ***The Port Vale Record, 1879-1993*** (Witan Books, £12.75); the same author has also penned ***The Potteries Derbies*** (Witan, £12.75) covering 180 matches played between Vale and Stoke in all competitions.

A more anecdotal read is ***Port Vale Grass Roots*** (Chell Publications, £5.95), a collection of wittily told tales by Denis Dawson, the club's groundsman since 1966.

On air

Vale fans generally seem to prefer ***BBC Radio Stoke*** (94.6 FM) to its independent rival ***Signal Radio*** (102.6 FM). The former used its clout to get the first interview with Vale chairman Bill Bell after the sacking of John Rudge.

In the net

The club's **official website** is at: www.port–vale.co.uk. Meticulously maintained and updated, it manages to combine the resources of an official site with the frankness of a fan-run affair. You'll find a match-report archive, a lively multi-media section and an electronic version of Vale's merchandising catalogue for secure online ordering.

Standing tall among the unofficial sites is ***ValeWeb*** at: adelaide.dcs.hull.ac.uk/people/pip/PortVale/PortVale.html. Statistics and links are its great strength.

A lively, efficiently updated online version of the ***Vale Park Beano*** fanzine is at: ourworld.compuserve.com/homepages/rfielding/frame.htm.

Preston North End

Formation	1881
Stadium	Deepdale, Preston, PR1 6RU. ☎01772/902020
Ground capacity	21,400
First-choice colours	White shirts, navy-blue shorts
Major honours	League champions 1889, 1890; Second Division champions 1904, 1912, 1951; Third Division champions 1971, 1996; FA Cup winners 1889, 1938
Position 1998/99	Fifth in Second Division (eliminated in play-off semi-finals)

When the Football Museum opens its doors at Deepdale in the early part of the new millennium, it will provide a unique repository for artefacts from throughout the game's long and colourful history. Old boots and shirts, rattles and scarves, magazines and programmes – every aspect of the heritage of the game will be showcased. And not just the English game, either. The Museum has been chosen as the new home for the FIFA Collection, probably the biggest assemblage of football memorabilia in the world.

Face in the crowd – Tom Finney immortalised at Deepdale

The choice of Deepdale is an apt one. Preston North End have been playing here since their formation in 1881, the longest residency at a single ground of any club in the League. They were the first-ever winners of the world's first league competition, and since they also won the FA Cup that year (1889), they were England's first double-winners, too.

But today's Deepdale is not all about history, and the reasons for locating the Football Museum there are not entirely sentimental. Preston's current owners, *Baxi*, have already built two entirely new stands at the ground (named after two of the club's playing legends, Tom Finney and Bill Shankly), and the Museum will occupy space in both of them. When the whole ground has been rebuilt, the idea is that the Museum will run all the way round. The two entities – football club and historical archive – will be run independently, with the new Deepdale an inspiring home for both.

And Preston North End is a club inspired right now. After decades of mediocrity in the wrong half of the League, the team have revived as their surroundings have been reconstructed – leading to the

'The Invincibles' – the Preston North End team that won the League and Cup double in 1888/89

Third Division title in 1996, and a place in the Second Division play-offs at the end of season 1998/99. They're a long way off getting into the Premiership, but they are fortunate that the club's golden era is so long ago, the pressure to perform from fans is less insistent than at Burnley, say. Of the other local rivals, the recent achievements of Blackburn are envied, but also held up as an example of what could come Deepdale's way, given a bit of luck and a following wind.

Oddly, it was Blackburn that provided Preston with a yardstick when the latter club first took up senior football. The team had their origins in the North End Cricket and Rugby Club, which was formed in 1863 and moved to Deepdale 12 years later. Members played a variety of different sports, and began playing football in 1879. By 1881 they'd decided the game should be their sole pursuit, and they invited Blackburn Rovers, the first team from the north-west to challenge southern supremacy in the FA Cup, to a friendly match at Deepdale. Blackburn won 16–0.

The man most responsible for ensuring there would be no repeat of that disaster was Major William Sudell. As chairman of the club's sports committee, Sudell was as close as North End came at the time to having a team manager in the modern sense. One of the first men in England to view football in terms of team tactics, rather than as a glorified individual pursuit, Sudell used a blackboard and chalk to illustrate his ideas to players – a revolutionary idea at the time.

Sudell also realised that the club would need to widen its horizons if it was to progress. It was at his instigation that North End turned openly professional in 1885 – one of the first clubs to do so – and with money available to lure migrant workers to Preston, he set about signing players from Scotland who would fit more comfortably into his tactical schemes. Among the imports was big defender Nick Ross and his younger brother, Jimmy, a goalscoring outside-right; a tough-tackling centre-half, David Russell; and wing-half Geordie Drummond. Other key players were centre-forward Johnny Goodall, who contributed most to Sudell's pre-match discussions, and Arthur Wharton, Britain's first black professional footballer, in goal.

On 15 October 1887, 'the Invincibles', as Sudell's side were becoming known, beat Hyde 26–0 in the first round of the FA Cup. So much time was spent bringing the ball back to the centre-spot for restarts (there were no goalnets in those days) that the referee added five minutes to the regulation 90 – as if Hyde's agony were not already bad enough. The match, the result of which still stands today as the biggest victory in an English first-class game, was part of an incredible 42-match winning streak which had begun the previous August. Yet the run had ended by the time Preston reached the 1888 FA Cup final, the club's first, against West Bromwich Albion. The team played poorly on the day, and lost 2–1.

The players were despondent, but they had done enough during the season to earn their club founder membership of the Football League, which was due to kick-off that autumn. Now the Invincibles would truly live up to their name, going that entire first 22-game campaign, 1888/89, without losing a match, and winning the title by 11 points from second-placed Aston Villa. They also returned to the Oval for a second FA Cup final, and this time beat Wolves 3–0. The first 'double' was won.

The team returned to Preston by train and were met by a crowd of 20,000, some of whom went on to the town's Public Hall to hear a rousing victory speech from Major Sudell.

The following year, Preston retained their title despite losing four matches. They then finished runners-up in the League in three successive seasons. But in 1893, the club was formed into a limited company and control was wrested away from Sudell. Two years later he was found guilty of embezzling £5,000 from his employers and received a three-year prison sentence.

Without Sudell's influence, 'the Invincibles' lost their mystique. Preston were relegated for the first time in 1901, and for long periods both before and after World War I, the club yo-yo'd between the top two divisions.

But if League form was inconsistent, North End were still tough Cup opposition. In 1922, only a controversial penalty for Huddersfield stood between them and victory in the FA Cup final. Fifteen years later, led by two influential Scotsmen, Bill Shankly and Jimmy Milne, they reached the final again, only to be outplayed by Sunderland, 3–1. They made up for it a year later by gaining revenge on Huddersfield, who they beat to take the Cup with a last-minute penalty – but Milne, who had broken his collarbone earlier in the season, could only watch from the stands.

The undrinkable – fans sprayed with champagne after promotion, 1996

Milne's involvement with Preston's trips to Wembley was far from over, but when a bold new side emerged at Deepdale after World War II, all eyes were on a much younger man – Tom Finney. A local plumber who signed for North End as a part-timer in the early part of the war, Finney was arguably the most complete footballer of his generation, a man able to shoot powerfully with either foot, and to play almost anywhere in the forward line. Outside-left, inside-right or centre-forward – Finney was comfortable there.

Bill Shankly, who played briefly alongside Finney in the years immediately after the war, reckoned he was the best teammate he'd ever had – as selfless a provider as he was individually skilful. Yet Finney, who remained loyal to Preston throughout his career, would have little to show for his endeavours save for two footballer of the year awards and his haul of 76 England caps. In 1953, his team missed out on the title on goal average to Arsenal. Twelve months later, a side captained by Finney and trained by Milne were unlucky to lose a fine FA Cup final 3–2 to West Brom. And four years after that, Preston were title runners-up again, this time to Wolves.

In 1960, Finney retired to concentrate on his plumbing business, and somehow the club was never the same without him. Relegated in 1961, Preston did conjure one more FA Cup final appearance, with Milne now in the manager's seat, in 1964. Yet once again he was to be on the losing side, West Ham winning 3–2 in stoppage time after a 17-year-old Howard Kendall had helped Preston take the lead twice.

How to describe the club's career since then? Like so many of Lancashire's once influential hotbeds of football, Preston were sent reeling by the abolition of the minimum wage which had enabled them to keep hold of talents like Tom Finney. The club tasted Third Division football for the first time in 1970, two years after Milne had retired, then again in 1974, during Bobby Charlton's ill-fated managerial career. By 1985 the club had sunk into the Fourth Division, and a year later Preston finished second from bottom of the entire League.

The club was hauled back up to something like respectability by a combination of down-to-earth manager John McGrath and the installation of an artificial pitch at Deepdale, which theoretically raised skill levels but which visiting teams struggled to get to grips with. With target men John Thomas and Gary Brazil in irrepressible form, Preston escaped the basement in 1987, and two years later McGrath's team reached the Third Division play-offs, going down to Port Vale over two legs.

After that, depression set in again. McGrath departed in 1990, while the plastic pitch lasted for another four years before it was ripped up at the League's insistence. Yet within a few months *Baxi*, a local boiler-making firm, had acquired a controlling interest in North End, and announced plans to rebuild Deepdale into a modern arena – one capable of housing a unique monument to the past, but also one fit for what looks a bright future.

Here we go!

From junction 31 of the M6, **motorists** should take the A59 toward Preston and follow signs for the football ground along the A583 and A5085 Blackpool Road. Turn left at the lights onto the A6063 Sir Tom Finney Way (formerly Deepdale Road) and the ground is on the left as you turn. There's no problem with **street parking** around Deepdale but don't ignore police cones or you risk being towed away.

Preston **train station** is on the West Coast mainline with services from London Euston, Rugby and Crewe (hourly, journey 3hrs from Euston, 50mins from Crewe). A range of cross-country trains also serve Manchester and Liverpool. Call ☎0345/484950 for the latest timings. From the train station, it's a 10min walk to Preston bus station – turn right along Fishergate and head for the Guildhall. Bus #19 runs along Sir Tom Finney Way.

Just the ticket

Visiting fans are allocated a section of the Bill Shankly Kop at one end of the ground (adults

£13, concessions £8), built to replace Deepdale's old Kop terrace in 1997.

Disabled supporters are accommodated in the Tom Finney Stand, where the old West Stand once stood. Advance booking advisable on ☎01772/902020.

Blue day – David Eyres sees red against Arsenal, 1999

Swift half

The ***Legends*** bar/nightclub at the rear of the Tom Finney Stand welcomes home and away supporters, including families before daytime games.

Other eating and drinking options are some way away – the best is the ***Sumners Hotel***, recently refurbished and with a full menu, further up Sir Tom Finney Way going away from the town centre, across the junction with the Blackpool Road. Try and look smart for the benefit of the doorman.

Note that many town centre pubs will refuse to serve away fans.

Club merchandise

The **club shop** is just along from *Legends* and has the latest example of Preston's classic white shirt (£39.99, kids' sizes £32.99).

Barmy army

Trouble is rare outside of derby games with Blackpool and Burnley, though the town centre is not as welcoming as it might be (see *Swift half* above).

In print

The ***Lancashire Evening Post*** is the best local source for Preston news, but after Saturday games the only choice is Manchester's ***Pink***.

John Booth's biography of ***Tom Finney*** (£14.99) was published by the club in 1998 and rivals Paul Agnew's earlier ***Finney – A Football Legend***, now sadly out of print. The original ***Preston Piemuncher*** fanzine has mutated into the club-sponsored ***Raising The Coffin***, with some fans less than enamoured of the re-incarnation.

On air

Plenty of North End coverage on both ***BBC Radio Lancashire*** (103.9 FM) and the commercial ***Red Rose Radio*** (999 AM).

In the net

Preston's new **official *NorthEnder* site** was a bit basic as of summer 1999 but boasts a refreshingly clean design at: www.prestonnorthend.co.uk.

There are plenty of unofficial sites, the most complete being ***PNEWeb*** at: freespace.virgin.net/paul.billington/PNEWeb_HomePage.htm. Try also ***Who's That Jumping Off The Pier?*** – an exceptionally well-designed online fanzine at: www.defused.com/whosthat/html/welcome.html.

Queen's Park Rangers

Formation	1885 as St Jude's Institute
Stadium	Rangers Stadium, South Africa Road, London, W12 7PA. ☎0181/743 0262
Ground capacity	19,000
First-choice colours	Blue and white hoops
Major honours	Second Division champions 1983; Third Division champions 1967; Third Division (South) champions 1948; League Cup winners 1967
Position 1998/99	20th in First Division

Whatever has happened to QPR? It's a question many non-Rangers fans were asking themselves even before the last match of 1998/99, which saw the team needing to beat Crystal Palace at home to ensure First Division status. The fact that QPR duly walked the game 6–0 may have calmed a few tempers in west London, but only temporarily so. When the euphoria died down, the full horror of the rest of the season rose up again to challenge the supporters' faith. Two managers, one caretaker manager, three assistant managers and enough coaches to fill Shepherd's Bush Green twice over – none of them could arrest the team's slide until it was almost too late.

As if performances on the pitch weren't bad enough, away from it Rangers had been resembling a corporate soap opera. Shares in the club's holding company, Loftus Road plc, plunged in value from a high of £1.20 to just 13p, forcing chairman Chris Wright to halt incoming transfers until players were sold. The chief scout, Steve Burtenshaw, was ordered to pay £10,000 for receiving transfer bung payments during his time at Arsenal. And Vinnie Jones, the man who was apparently being groomed to become a future manager, seemed more interested in pursuing a career in Hollywood. All we needed was for a body to be uncovered under the Ellerslie Road Stand, and this bumper omnibus edition of *WestEnders* would be complete.

All this, at a club which not so long ago came within 13 minutes of winning the League, which reached the FA Cup final in 1982, which flew the flag in Europe with pride and rare elegance and which could call upon a home support more feverish than almost any in London – and certainly more intimate than in the wide open spaces of nearby Stamford Bridge...

The advances made at Chelsea in recent years have been hard for QPR fans to take. For much of the Seventies and Eighties, Rangers were the west London team to follow. Yet while Chelsea have now turned their sizeable chunk of prime real estate to their advantage, what was once one of QPR's strongest assets – the tightly and loudly packed Loftus Road – has become a liability. The club can't move forward until it sells the ground, yet the site is too small to attract anything but a modest residential scheme. Wasps rugby union club (the other component of Loftus Road plc) could also sell its former home at Sudbury, but this is subject to planning restrictions. And in the meantime, the board still haven't found a location for a new stadium.

Chris Wright says Rangers and Wasps will be playing in a new arena 'within five years'. But QPR, at least, have rarely performed well when there has been uncertainty about their home. And there has been no shortage of that since the club was first formed back in 1885.

Rangers deserve their reputation as English football's rootless nomads. No other club has moved house so often – 18 times in 78 years – although the club has generally stayed within an area of suburban north-west London encompassing

Kilburn, Kensal Rise, Park Royal and Shepherd's Bush.

The long journey began when members of the St Jude's Institute football team decided to merge with another local side, Christchurch Rangers. Most of the players came from Queen's Park – hence the new name the club would adopt within a year. (Oddly, despite all the moving and shaking, the club has never been based in Queen's Park itself.) Their first pitch was an area of wasteground near Kensal Rise Athletic Ground.

In 1888 QPR rented the London Scottish rugby ground at Brondesbury (a move not as controversial then as co-habitation with Wasps is now), but within a year the pitch had become unplayable, and over the next three seasons Rangers could be found at no fewer than four different grounds, including one on Wormwood Scrubs. The club entered various local league and cup competitions, and began playing in hooped shirts for the first time – though at this stage these were green and white. By 1898, though, QPR were worried about losing players to rival clubs, so they turned professional and joined the Southern League.

In 1907, another five homes after they'd left the Scrubs, Rangers moved to a new ground at Park Royal, capable of holding 60,000. They never got near filling it, but they did win the Southern League in their first season there.

QPR expected to be admitted to the Second Division of the Football League, as other Southern League winners had been, and resigned from the latter. But they were passed over in favour of Tottenham, who'd finished eighth, and had to be re-admitted to the Southern League at the last minute – all their games in season 1908/09 were played in midweek because the fixture list had already been drawn up by the time Rangers were let back in.

In 1912 QPR won the Southern League for the second time, but they had to wait until after World War I before the Football League would finally have them, the club entering the newly formed Third Division in 1920. During the war, the Park Royal ground was commandeered by the military and the team took over the home of the defunct Shepherd's Bush amateur club – a former refuse tip, Loftus Road.

Salvation – Kiwomya hits a hat-trick, May 1999

Rangers finished their first League campaign in third place, but by 1924 they were having to apply for re-election, and two years later they had to do so again, having set a record low points total of 21. The 1926/27 season would be a significant one,

Man who made the difference – Rodney Marsh

though. First, QPR swapped their 'unlucky' green hoops for blue ones. And second, they signed George Goddard, who solved the team's goalscoring problems at a stroke. Over the next seven seasons Goddard would score 186 goals for QPR, a record that remains unbroken today. (In all the excitement, Rangers inexplicably forgot to enter the FA Cup in 1927.)

Local interest in the team rose steadily as they consolidated their position in what was now the Third Division (South). To make the most of this popularity, in 1931 the Rangers board decided to move matches from Loftus Road to White City, a vast arena just up the road which had been built for the 1908 Olympic Games, and which was now mainly used for greyhound racing and speedway. At first the move was a success – more than 40,000 saw QPR entertain Leeds United there in the third round of the FA Cup in January 1932. But after two seasons the club was £7,000 down on the White City deal, and the players were complaining about the lack of atmosphere inside the bowl. So back to Loftus Road they went.

The return to more intimate surroundings was welcomed by fans but produced little in the way of results – QPR were still struggling to get into the Second Division when World War II broke out. During the war, midfielder Dave Mangnall was appointed player-manager and it was he who inspired the team to the Third Division (South) title in 1949. The club bought the freehold to Loftus Road and Mangnall, having initially stuck by the team who'd won promotion, was given money to buy reinforcements. There were signs that the club was over-reaching itself, however, and in 1952 QPR slipped back into the Third Division (South).

Mangnall's replacement, Jack Taylor, achieved almost nothing in seven years' tenure of the job, and the arrival of Alec Stock, a former Rangers player who'd proved a successful manager at non-League level, was greeted with relief. Stock's first signing was striker Brian Bedford, who scored 27 goals in his first QPR season. Once Stock had found Mark Lazarus and Bernard Evans to partner Bedford in attack, the team began to play the kind of football with which Rangers would be associated over the coming decades – cool, calm and intricate, and above all never dull.

It would be a while before QPR's League status matched their style. A brief stint back at White City in 1962/63 proved disastrous, and the club appeared to be merely treading water when Jim Gregory became chairman in March 1965. The archetypal East End barrow boy made good, Gregory had left school aged 14 unable to read or write, yet had made enough money out of the motor trade to retire by the time he was 37. He gave Stock *carte blanche* to expand Rangers' half-baked coaching and youth structures, and also handed the manager enough money to make QPR serious players in the transfer market. Among Stock's purchases during the 1965/66 season was Rodney Marsh, who arrived from Fulham for £15,000 and immediately inspired the team to a 6–1 thrashing of Millwall. Rangers ended the season playing the best football in the Third Division and, although too far behind to catch the leaders, they would continue in similar vein the following year.

The 1966/67 season marked the end of the club's honest mediocrity. With Lazarus, Les Allen and Roger Morgan all profiting from Marsh's knack for attacking improvisation, QPR strolled to the Third Division title, scoring 103 goals. They also won the first League Cup final to be played at Wembley, coming back from two down at half-time (during which Stock later admitted he 'tore a strip' off his nerves-stricken players) to beat West Brom 3–2, with Marsh revelling on the grand stage.

There was more to come the following year, Stock's side adjusting comfortably to life in the Second Division and finishing the season as runners-up, just a point behind Ipswich, to secure a place in the top flight for the first time. Gregory sanctioned the building of a new South Africa Road Stand, and the club seemed only one more step from achieving true greatness.

Actually, it was more of a leap, and QPR couldn't take it just yet. After Marsh broke his ankle in a pre-season friendly, Gregory

There's a Wasp in my soup – rugby at Rangers

When Richard Thompson sold QPR to the **Chrysalis media millionaire** Chris Wright in 1996, Rangers fans couldn't have been happier. At last they were free of the old board's penny-pinching and, with Wright promising to float Rangers on the **Alternative Investment Market**, the fans would have the chance to own a slice of the club themselves.

Temporary sign – QPR badges covered up for rugger

What they didn't realise was that Wright was about to add **Wasps rugby union club** to his portfolio, and that it would be a new holding company responsible for both clubs, **Loftus Road plc**, floated on AIM. Even so, the share issue was substantially over-subscribed, with investors drawn by the prospect of a **rugby boom** fuelled by pay TV cash, and a parallel pay-per-view revolution sweeping soccer.

Neither predictions have come true. And while QPR could yet boost their finances by climbing back into the Premiership, Wasps are **struggling to make ends meet**, despite some success on the field. Crowds for rugby at Loftus Road have been pitifully low, the local populace less interested in the oval-ball code than the residents of **more genteel Sudbury**, Wasps' former home.

Initially ambivalent about the idea of rugby being played on 'their' ground, QPR fans have become **increasingly restless**. They were unhappy when the playing surface was dug up and replaced by a 5% plastic version (shades of the Omniturf experiment) **better-suited to rugby**. More pertinently, they wonder how the estimated £1million a year Wasps are currently costing Loftus Road plc could be spent – by Rangers…

eased Stock out of the way, first making him general manager while Bill Dodgin took charge of the team, then releasing him on 'health grounds'. Stock's successor, Tommy Docherty, walked out after only 28 days, leaving Les Allen to take over as player-manager – the fourth boss QPR had employed in less than a year. The team finished bottom of the First Division, having won only four games.

It was Allen who signed Terry Venables from Spurs as part of Rangers' bid to get straight back into the First Division, but the former's lack of managerial experience cost the club dear – there were mid-table finishes in 1970 and 1971, before Gordon Jago replaced Allen. In March 1972 Jago sold the wantaway Marsh to Manchester City for £200,000. The team's form actually improved without him but promotion would not be achieved until the following year, after Jago had signed a proper replacement for Marsh, Stan Bowles. In tandem with another new arrival, Don Givens, Bowles out-smarted most Second Division defences, and within a year he was getting the better of First Division ones, too – QPR finished the 1973/74 season a confident eighth.

Jago was then lured to America but his replacement, Dave Sexton, was similarly positive in outlook. In 1975/76, the team were bolstered by the experienced Frank McLintock and John Hollins but also refreshed by the blossoming of a QPR youth product, Gerry Francis, in midfield. The side took 27 out of a possible 30 points at the end of the campaign, and finished their season top of the League – only for Liverpool, fulfilling their last fixture ten days later, to pip them by beating Wolves with three goals in the last 13 minutes.

Although the title had eluded them, Rangers had captured the imagination of the country with their romantic, almost impudent attitude to football. The Sixties may have been swinging down Chelsea way, but over at Shepherd's Bush, the Seventies had a sublime swagger. The Europeans weren't immune to it, either. In 1976/77, though inconsistent in the League, Rangers beat Brann Bergen, Slovan Bratislava and Cologne to reach the quarter-finals of the UEFA Cup, where an injury backlog, a wild Greek crowd and a penalty shoot-out prevented them from beating AEK Athens.

The bubble burst when Sexton left for Manchester United in 1977. Two former coaches, Frank Sibley and Steve Burtenshaw, proved unable to make the step up into management and Rangers slid down into the Second Division in 1979. Tommy Docherty then patched up his differences with Gregory and returned to Loftus Road, staying just long enough to give young forwards Paul Goddard and Clive Allen regular first-team football, and to sign another great playmaker in the Rangers tradition, Tony Currie.

By October 1980, though, the Doc was gone again, to be supplanted by Venables, whose transition from player to coach and thence to manager had been successfully made at Crystal Palace. Having just left Palace, Venables signed several of their players and led QPR to an FA Cup final against Tottenham in 1982 – a game Rangers won tactically but could only draw 1–1. They lost the replay to a Glenn Hoddle penalty.

The sense of disappointment was short-lived, as a year later Venables led QPR back into the First Division, after a season in which they'd lost only twice at home. The club had controversially installed an Omniturf plastic pitch a year earlier; Venables insisted the surface encouraged a passing game, which was true – but it also upset visitors unaccustomed to the bounce of the ball, which was most of them.

So began a 13-year spell in England's top division which, for all that it lacked the romance of QPR's Seventies stay, brought a mood of defiant stability to the club. In 1984 Rangers finished fifth and qualified for Europe again. Venables took over the PA system on the last day of the season to publicly commit his future to QPR; within a month he was at Barcelona.

While Venables' relationship with Gregory (the manager coached the team while the chairman bought the players) would stand him in good stead on the continent, the latter never really got over losing his favoured son. Venables' successor, Alan Mullery, couldn't establish the same rapport with the players and was axed after less than a year. His replacement, Jim Smith, was a better motivator, but the football his team played lacked sparkle – a point well made in the 1985 League Cup final, when QPR never got into gear and were beaten 3–0 by unfancied Oxford United.

Wembley wonder – Bob Hazell (dark shirt) stretches Spurs, 1982

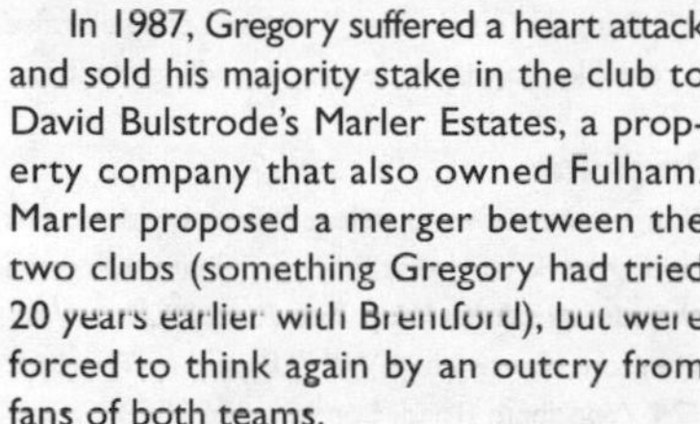

In 1987, Gregory suffered a heart attack and sold his majority stake in the club to David Bulstrode's Marler Estates, a property company that also owned Fulham. Marler proposed a merger between the two clubs (something Gregory had tried 20 years earlier with Brentford), but were forced to think again by an outcry from fans of both teams.

Bulstrode's death in 1988 resulted in 24-year-old entrepeneur Richard Thompson becoming chairman. Having ripped up the Omniturf pitch and replaced it with grass, he appointed Trevor Francis as player-manager. The QPR side of the time boasted David Seaman, Paul Parker and Ray Wilkins, but Francis' reign was characterised by disharmony, and in 1990 his coach Don Howe took over for a year before making way for Gerry Francis.

On New Year's Day 1992, QPR beat Manchester United 4–1 at Old Trafford with the help of a Dennis Bailey hat-trick, and another era of battling for major honours appeared to beckon. Thompson, however, had neither Gregory's vision nor his passion for the club. Rangers managed four consecutive top-ten League finishes in the mid-Nineties despite the loss of Francis to Tottenham in 1994 (Ray Wilkins was a popular successor), yet little of the £10million raised through the sale of talents such as Andy Sinton and Les Ferdinand was re-invested in players.

In May 1996 QPR dropped out of the Premiership and Thompson sold up to Chris Wright (see panel p.433). Nobody doubted that the new owner, a Rangers fan since childhood, had his heart in the right place. But he was a poor judge of managers – his first appointees, Stewart Houston and Bruce Rioch, had given way to Ray Harford within 18 months – and they in turn committed a series of catastrophic errors in the transfer market. Trevor Sinclair, Andy Impey and Nigel Quashie were all allowed to leave, to be replaced by a long line of de-motivated journeyman pros.

By the time Gerry Francis had arrived for a fourth spell at the club in September 1998, the club was a laughing stock. The fans were laughing on the other side of their faces after the last-day destruction of Palace – but for how long...?

Here we go!

Motorists from the north and west should avoid the centre of London and approach the ground from the A40 Westway, itself an extension of the M40. Exit at signs for the A40 White City, turn right into Wood Lane, go under the flyover and past the BBC office block (on the site of Rangers' former White City home), then right at the lights into South Africa Road – the ground is a little way up on the left.

From the south, approach from Hammersmith via Shepherd's Bush Road and the A40 Wood Lane, go past the BBC Television Centre on the left and White City tube on the right, and turn left into South Africa Road.

The club has no **car park**, and **street parking** is both limited and, given the level of car crime, ill-advised. Instead stay on Wood Lane and use either the Ariel Way industrial estate car park, or the one at the BBC – both are usually open to non-permit holders on Saturday matchdays, but you'll pay £5 for the privilege.

Coming into London by **train**, choose between Hammersmith & City and Central Line tube services. Shepherd's Bush station is the one to use on the former (with direct links to Paddington, Euston, St Pancras and King's Cross). Emerging on Uxbridge Road, turn right out of the station then right again into Loftus Road – the ground is on the left. On the Central Line (best from Liverpool Street and southern termini), White City is the closest stop but, if you want a beer or butty first, it makes more sense to get out one stop earlier at Shepherd's Bush – confusingly, this is a different station from that mentioned above. Turn right out of the station, walk along Uxbridge Road, go past the Hammersmith & City Line station on your right and follow directions above.

Just the ticket

Visiting fans are accommodated in the School End – entrance in Bloemfontein Road. The view from the upper tier is restricted and, in any case, it is often closed. Lower-tier prices in 1998/99 were £16–18, depending on the match, concessions 50% reduction.

Disabled visitors have a few spaces in the Ellerslie Road Stand – booking essential on ☎0181/740 2575.

Swift half

Just as there are two tube stations called Shepherd's Bush, so there are two watering holes called ***The Springbok***. The **pub** of that name close to the ground on South Africa Road is not popular with Rangers fans but, despite this, can get impossibly busy on matchdays. The ***Springbok Sports Bar***, downstairs in the Shepherd's Bush Green shopping complex, is less of a crush and does a nice line in South African sausages.

There's a bewildering array of ethnic **food options** on the other side of the Green.

Club merchandise

The **club shop** (open Mon–Sat 9am–5pm, later on matchdays) is in the South Africa Road Stand. The range of goods is wide, but prices are high for a non-Premiership club.

Barmy army

Like Chelsea, QPR was a regular trouble blackspot during the late Sixties and Seventies. Things have calmed down a lot since then, and violence is rare now unless visiting fans bring it with them – as Portsmouth did a couple of years ago.

Rangers' celebrated 'Loft' end can still raise a roar like no other, despite dwindling numbers.

In print

Rangers have two excellent fanzines with origins dating back to the still-born Fulham merger a decade ago: ***A Kick Up The R's*** (Hillcrest, Walgherton, Nantwich, CW5 7LB) and ***In The Loft*** (24 Woodham Road, London, SE6 2SD).

The club plans to publish a new **official history** to celebrate the millennium. Further details on ☎0181/749 6862.

On air

It's the usual London choice of ***GLR*** (94.9 FM) and ***Capital Gold*** (1548 AM) – the latter's phone-ins are well-patronised by Rangers fans.

In the net

Rangers' **official website** is not one of the *Planet* operation's better efforts, heavy-handed on the graphics and with a particularly uninformative 'news' section. Browse if you have to at: www.qpr.co.uk. ***The Unofficial QPR Website*** is in a different league altogether – funny, informative and offering a proper perspective on the club. The site also hosts an online version of *A Kick Up The R's*, at: www.qpr.org. Not to be outdone, *In The Loft* is also on the web, as part of ***The Alternative QPR Website*** at: www.altqpr.freeserve.co.uk/itloft/.

Reading

Formation	1871
Stadium	Madejski Stadium, Royal Way, Reading, Berks, RG2 0FL. ☎0118/968 1100
Ground capacity	24,000
First-choice colours	Blue and white hoops
Major honours	Second Division champions 1994; Third Division champions 1986; Third Division (South) champions 1926; Full Members' Cup winners 1988
Position 1998/99	11th in Second Division

Multi-millionaire backer, state-of-the-art stadium, dedicated Youth Academy… mid-table Second Division team. That's Reading FC at the turn of the Millennium. Nobody who sees the club's new facilities, rising like a hi-tech phoenix from the site of a former refuse tip just off the M4 motorway, can fail to come away impressed. It all looks extraordinary, and the beauty is far from skin deep. Those silver posts around the ground are methane gas vents, ensuring there is no build-up of gas from within the decades' worth of industrial rubbish that still lurks under the stadium. The pitch has been sunk below ground level and is watered automatically, using rainwater run-off from the stand roofs which is cleaned before it is allowed into the soil. And not a single square yard has been wasted – from the impressive Royal Berkshire Conference Centre adjoining the West Stand to the plethora of concourse bars, from *Shooters* themed sports café to the fully stocked *Megastore*, the club is doing all it can to ensure the Madejski site pays its way.

Road to somewhere – but best leave the car somewhere else

You could say that all this is just another example of the English game's creeping, crass commercialism. But again, this is a Second Division club, not a Premiership giant. And that, really, is Reading's dilemma. For as long as the team are stuck in the third tier, the stadium will remain half-full at best, the restaurant cash tills will be quiet, and those natty RFC carpet slippers will stay stubbornly on the shelves.

The stadium has already achieved part of its objective – turning the town's nondescript image on its head. Now it must act as the catalyst for a renaissance on the pitch, or risk becoming a white elephant.

The contrast between the Madejski complex and Reading's former home, Elm Park, couldn't be more stark. The team played there for more than a century, yet the place had little of the charm so often associated with long-lived, lower-division grounds. But at least it was better than some of the venues used by the club in its early years, which included two grounds shared with local cricket clubs, and another, King's Meadow, which was so close to the River Thames that it was prone to flooding.

In the late 19th century the town played a leading role in football's development in the south of England, and Reading FC was a relative latecomer to the party. By the time the club had been formed after a meeting at the Bridge Street Rooms in 1871, it already had competition from the likes of Earley FC and the Reading Hornets. The latter merged with Reading in 1877, the year the club entered the FA Cup for the first time, and Earley were tempted into the fold 12 years later.

While they may have been in the game's spiritual home in the south-east, Reading FC were still no match for the best the north had to offer – they were demolished 18–0 by Preston in the first round of the Cup in 1894. Undeterred, Reading became founder members of the Southern League the same year, and turned professional in 1895. The move to Elm Park came the following year, and when *Huntley & Palmer* took over the Berkshire County Cricket ground opposite, the team became known as the 'Biscuitmen' – a nickname that would last officially until *H&P* left in 1974, and which fans still refer to, despite the club's subsequent adoption of the tag 'Royals'.

Reading won the Southern League's Second Division title in 1911, but it wasn't until after World War I and the formation of the Third Division (South) of the Football League that the club really found its feet. In 1925/26, Reading won the divisional title, assuring themselves of promotion with a 7–1 thrashing of Brentford. The following season, Brentford were again the victims in Reading's best-ever FA Cup run, an Elm Park record crowd of 33,000 showing up to see the West Londoners beaten 1–0 in the fifth round. Reading were finally accounted for in the semis by Cardiff City, the eventual winners, 3–0.

In 1931, Cardiff accompanied Reading in relegation back to the Third Division (South). Reading then managed a top-six finish every year between 1932 and 1939, without ever quite gaining promotion, and were leading the table when the 1939/40 campaign was abandoned with the onset of World War II.

Reading resumed football postwar with a bang, thrashing Crystal Palace 10–2 in September 1946, and finishing runners-up in the Third Division (South) in 1949 and 1952, the latter being notable for its haul of 112 League goals, of which 39 were scored by Ron Blackman. The big centre-forward would go on to score 158 goals in 218 games for the club, a tribute not just to his own finishing but to the adventurous style of football encouraged by Reading's manager of the time, Ted Drake. He and Blackman left together in 1953, and the

Hi-tech and handsome – the Madejski stadium has room for further expansion, someday

team were still stuck at the same level when the non-regional Third Division was founded in 1958. They were to remain there until the club's centenary season of 1970/71. Whatever celebrations were planned for that campaign, they took a back seat to the team's problems on the field, which culminated in a painful relegation to the Fourth Division on goal average.

Reading were promoted back up in third place in 1975/76, but slipped down again – on goal difference this time – the following season. If that was a false dawn, the next glimpse of daylight was slightly more substantial. Under the managership of Maurice Evans, and with 'keeper Steve Death going 1,074 minutes without conceding a goal, Reading were crowned champions of the Fourth Division in 1979.

The following year, Evans signed young striker Kerry Dixon from non-League Dunstable. Having been rejected by Tottenham two years earlier, Dixon was anxious to prove himself as a professional and made an immediate impact at Elm Park, averaging a goal every other game as Reading finished tenth in the Third Division.

The decline that followed was brisk and very nearly terminal. In 1982 goalkeeper Death hung up his gloves, after 536 games for the club, and a year later Reading were relegated. Dixon was sold to Chelsea for £300,000, but that made only a minor dent in the club's mounting debts. Manager Evans was tempted up the road to Oxford United, where the chairman was one Robert Maxwell. Seeing Reading's plight, Maxwell proposed to merge the clubs and form a new team, Thames Valley Royals. Whether the proposal was serious or not, Reading fans weren't taking any chances. They launched a bitter anti-Maxwell campaign, and soon found their saviour in entrepreneur Roger Smee, whose boardroom coup in 1983 consigned the Thames Valley Royals to the dustbin of history.

With his background in the property business, Smee was keen to move the club and sell Elm Park for development as quickly as possible. But his first priority

Senior citizen – Trevor in his second spell

was the team, and in Ian Branfoot he made an inspired choice of new manager. Branfoot in turn signed striker Trevor Senior from Portsmouth, and with his goals the team made an immediate return to the Third Division. Two years later they were promoted again as Third Division champions, after winning all their first 13 games.

Reading's stay in the Second Division lasted only two seasons, but it did contain a memorable trip to Wembley for a Full Members' (Simod) Cup Final against Luton Town, won 4–1 in front of more than 61,000, the largest crowd ever to watch a Reading match.

Senior was sold to Watford for £325,000 in 1987 (only to return little more than a year later), while Branfoot left in 1989, by which time Reading were back in the Third Division. The property crash of 1990 took its toll on Roger Smee, who was forced to quit as chairman. His successor, the *AutoTrader* publisher John Madejski, was seeing his fortune multiply during the recession as more people bought secondhand cars. Madejski was more a fan of the town than of the club, and refused to lavish money on players. The Taylor Report did, however, persuade him to revive Reading's plans for a new stadium, on the same refuse-tip site first identified by Smee a decade earlier.

While Madejski was using his business acumen to plot the construction of the arena that would bear his name, Reading were performing wonders on the pitch under the stewardship of Mark McGhee. Returning to the club's adventurous style of old, McGhee's side were strong in all departments: Shaka Hislop an oustanding young talent in goal, Adrian Williams a pillar of strength at the back, Mick Gooding a smart operator in midfield, Jimmy Quinn an expert goal-poacher in attack. They won the Second Division title in 1994, and a year later finished runners-up in the First Division – despite the mid-term departure of McGhee to Leicester and the bizarre appointment of Gooding and Quinn as joint player-managers.

In any other year, Reading's League position would have been good enough for promotion to the Premiership. But 1995 was the year the top drawer thinned its membership from 22 to 20, and there was only one guaranteed promotion spot. So Reading entered the play-offs, beat Tranmere 3–1 on aggregate in the semi-finals, then took a 2–0 lead against Bolton in the Final at Wembley. That they evetnually lost 4–3 after extra time was heartbreaking for the fans, but it may have been a blessing in disguise. At the time, the Madejski Stadium was still two years from completion, and Elm Park was not fit to host Premiership football. So where, exactly, would Reading have played…?

As it was, 'keeper Hislop was sold to Newcastle for £1.5 million, to be replaced by Bulgarian international Bobby 'Wiggy' Mihaylov, who then missed much of the following season through injury. Quinn and Gooding kept the team in the First Division with a 3–0 win over Wolves (now managed by McGhee) on the last day of the 1995/96 season, Adrian Williams then joined McGhee at Wolves, and after another year at the wrong end of the table, the joint managers resigned.

Reading's last season at Elm Park, under Terry Bullivant in 1997/98, ended in relegation, and his successor, Tommy Burns, had too much rebuilding to do for the club to make an immediate return to the First Division in 1998/99.

On the subject of building, the stands at Reading's new home are made from precast concrete which was simply bolted together on-site. All Reading have to do is order some more concrete, and the capacity can be expanded by 5,000. That, however, will have to wait for Premiership football. In the meantime, the paperwork stays in John Madejski's 'pending' tray.

Here we go!

You can see the Madejski from the M4 motorway and most **motorists** will approach it from this road. Exit at Junction 11, take the A33 Basingstoke Road towards Reading, following the new relief road round to the left – the ground should be well signposted from here.

If by chance you do happen to find yourself in Reading town centre, beware that well after the Madejski opened there were still some signs showing 'Reading FC' but leading, in fact, to Elm Park.

The **parking** situation could be better. Between them, the stadium's own car park and that of the adjacent speedway track have only 2,000 spaces, and these fill up well before kick-off on most matchdays. The club has reduced parking charges from £5 to £3 after an outcry from fans, and set up park-and-ride schemes at nearby schools (also well-signposted).

However, given the shortage of eating and drinking venues near the stadium, it might be better to drive into the centre of Reading and park at one of several multi-storeys near the train station (see below), and take the shuttle bus #79 from there.

For a town of its size, Reading is exceptionally well served **by train,** with services running direct to and from London Paddington about every 15mins (journey time 40mins). These trains originate from the West Country or Wales. There are also direct cross-country links to Oxford, Coventry, Birmingham and Manchester. For the latest timings call ☎0345/484950.

Emerging through the main station exit, you'll see the *Three Guineas* pub – the #79 'Football Special' bus departs from opposite the pub's roadside entrance (every 15mins).

Just the ticket

Visiting fans are housed behind one goal in the South Stand – enter through gates #9 and #10, pay your money at a window, then show your ticket at the turnstile. Ticket prices in 1998/99 were on the high side: adults £14, juniors/OAPs £8. But you get a seat, the view is fine, the roof will keep the rain off, and away fans are allocated up to 4,000 spaces, so turning up on the day isn't a problem.

Facilities for **disabled fans** are also excellent, with 28 spaces in the South Stand – no need to book. There are also 12 places with commentary for blind supporters (home and away) in the West Stand.

Swift half

There are no decent pubs even remotely close to the stadium, so why not have a beer inside it? All 13 of the Madejski's **concourse bars** are licensed and will normally serve alcohol up to the usual 15mins before kick-off. Expect to pay about £2 a pint.

At the station, ***The Firkin*** is preferable to the ***Three Guineas***, but neither pub is keen on fans wearing team colours.

For **food**, there are various outlets inside the station – ***The Lemon Tree*** will show you just how far railway sandwiches have come in the last few years.

Club merchandise

The Reading ***Megastore*** is at the north end of the West Stand, offering a vast range of goods. Home shirts are £39.99 (kids' sizes £26.99), a mouse mat £4.50 (we're in Silicon Valley, after all), and a pair of slippers £8.99. Lovely.

Barmy army

The most noise at the Madejski comes from the North Stand, but lack of numbers in 1998/99 caused a lot of it to echo uncomfortably around the arena. Trouble is rare, though, and unless Robert Maxwell is found to be alive and well and living in Swindon, things are likely to stay that way.

In print

The fanzine ***Junction 11*** has now transferred publication from paper to the internet, at: www.pulfer.freeserve.co.uk.

The Greatest Footballer You Never Saw, by Paul McGuigan and Paolo Hewitt (Mainstream, £7.99), catalogues the life, loves and untimely death of striker Robin Friday, who was on the club's books during the Seventies – a grittily original read.

The ***Thames Valley Auto Trader*** is widely available at newsagents around town.

On air

The locals' favourite is ***Classic Gold*** (1435 AM), which replaces its tired music formula with lively football commentary and phone-ins on Saturday afternoons.

In the net

The **official website** is at: www.readingfc. co.uk. And very slick it is, too, with lots of info on the Madejski Stadium and (hurrah!) a proper site index.

Online fanzine ***Hob Nob Anyone?*** is light in every sense – not much here, but what there is will raise a smile. Take a bite at: www.royals.cx.

Cock-a-hoop – Reading take a 2–0 lead at Wembley, 1995

Rochdale

Formation	1907
Stadium	Spotland, Sandy Lane, Rochdale, OL11 5DS. ☎01706/644648
Ground capacity	9,200
First-choice colours	Blue shirts, white shorts
Major honours	None
Position 1998/99	19th in Third Division

Spotland is the sort of place that isn't supposed to exist any more. Technically, in fact, it doesn't – the local council having officially renamed it the Denehurst Park Stadium a few years back. But Spotland it has always been and Spotland it shall remain, modest, unassuming, almost impossibly friendly, and serving a mean pie. Fans of Premiership clubs disenchanted with the way football matches have been turned into 'events' and in need of an antidote should spend a couple of hours at Spotland, where the view is clear, the legroom is fine, and it only takes a minute to get into the ground. No wonder it was voted the best football venue in the League in a recent poll.

Then again, it's just as well visiting supporters derive so much pleasure from their trip, since fans of the home side, Rochdale AFC, don't exactly get a lot of bang for their buck. Since joining the Football League in 1921, Rochdale have put together one of the most abject records of any of the current 92 clubs. Never out of the bottom half of the League, at times lucky to get four-figure attendances through the gate, the club has somehow managed to avoid either having its applications for re-election refused or being demoted automatically to the Conference. A cynic would say that it's only a matter of time.

And warm though the reception at Spotland may be, there is just no disguising the struggle that is bound to afflict any football club in this neck of the woods, with the Manchester clubs just up the road and rugby league commanding a loyal, long-established following. On the other hand, Oldham Athletic made it into the top flight not so long ago, and Bury have had a brief dalliance with the First Division, so why not 'Dale? It's not just the pies that bring the faithful to Spotland – the fans genuinely believe their club has the potential to move forward, and they're not going to miss it when it happens.

For a time, at the turn of the century, it looked as though football in Rochdale wouldn't get moving at all. The first local club, also playing under the name Rochdale AFC, was founded in 1896. The team played at the town's Athletic Grounds until Harvey Rigg, former secretary of a defunct rugby club, offered them the St Clements Playing Fields which that club had been using – and which were later to evolve into today's Spotland. The footballers duly moved in around 1900, but poor crowds forced them to disband within a year.

Meanwhile, another soccer club called Rochdale Town had been formed in 1900, playing at nearby Dane Street. When the first Rochdale AFC collapsed, Harvey Rigg invited Town to his ground in 1902 – but, again, their stay lasted barely more than a year. Like many sports enthusiasts in the area, Rigg was a rugby fan first and foremost. But he needed an attraction of some sort to pay the rent at St Clements, and with Rochdale Hornets now established as the main rugby event in town, he was determined to make a go of soccer. So in 1907 he called a meeting of fans of the round-ball game and proposed reviving the Rochdale AFC name for a new club.

For Rigg – and for football in the town – it was third time lucky. The new club won immediate membership of the Manchester League, outgrew that competition after only a season, and graduated to the Lancashire Combination in 1908. By 1910

Hitting the Spotland – for football and rugby, pies and pints, nowhere else comes close

Rochdale AFC was a limited company, and after moving another rung up the competitive ladder by joining the Central League, on the eve of World War I the club purchased the freehold to the ground for the princely sum of £1,700.

Suitably equipped, Rochdale entered the FA Cup for the first time, and also applied for membership of the Football League Second Division. They were rejected, resulting in the club becoming one of the leading lights in the bid to get the League extended after the war. Rochdale soon got what they wanted, as the two regional Third Divisions were added and the club gained admittance to the northern section in 1921.

Once in the League, the team made decent progress there, finishing only a point behind promoted Wolves in 1924, coming third two years later, and making runners-up spot again in 1927. But as competition strengthened with the influx of more former Second Division sides, Rochdale's influence on proceedings faded. By 1931 they were having to make an application for re-election – the first of many – after finishing 21st. The following year they were bottom, after conceding 135 goals, and might have faced oblivion then had it not been for the withdrawal of Wigan Borough midway through the season.

The period immediately after World War II saw a brief revival, with Ted Goodier's side finishing third behind Doncaster and Gateshead in 1950. Eight years later, 'Dale managed to make the cut into the new national Third Division when the old regionalisation came to an end, thanks to the determined management of a young Harry Catterick. But they remained there for just one season after Catterick had left for Sheffield Wednesday, and spent the next ten years in the Fourth Division.

Rochdale did, however, get their name in the record books when, in 1962, the team reached the League Cup final. The competition was in only its second year and had not yet attracted the wholehearted support of the bigger clubs, while the final – a two-leg affair that was effectively over when 'Dale's opponents, Norwich City,

Rare event – an away goal at Southend, 1998

came to Spotland for the first game and won 3–0 – was something of a let-down. But even so, Rochdale had become the first Fourth Division team to reach a major Cup final, a distinction they still hold today.

In 1968/69, Len Richley finally engineered what many fans had come to consider the impossible – promotion back to the Third Division. Richley's team was blessed with a resolute defence and an excellent record at Spotland, assets that would continue to serve Rochdale well as they enjoyed four years of respectability in mid-table of the Third. In 1974, however, they finished bottom and were relegated – never to return, alas, for the remainder the 20th century.

The next ten years were grim indeed. In the mid-Seventies Rochdale had the lowest crowds in the League after Southport and Workington, and both of them would be voted out before the decade was over. With debts mounting, the club was forced to sell Spotland in 1980, and though they were able to re-purchase it with local council help three years later, the team's form had, if anything, worsened. In the ten seasons from 1977/78, 'Dale never managed to finish higher than 18th in the Fourth Division.

A renaissance, of sorts, began in 1988/89. The club's finances had been boosted by Rochdale Hornets moving in to share Spotland as tenants, and on the pitch, the influence of manager Terry Dolan was breathing confidence into a young but enthusiastic side. At last 'Dale managed to haul themselves – just – into the upper half of the Fourth Division. And in 1989/90, they were desperately unlucky not to progress beyond the fifth round of the FA Cup (still the club's furthest marker in the competition) when losing 1–0 at the home of eventual finalists Crystal Palace, despite an inspired performance from Keith Welch between the sticks.

The Cup run coincided with a new agreement over the future of Spotland, which saw Rochdale AFC, Rochdale Hornets RLFC and the local metropolitan borough council become joint owners of the ground. The Hornets, with money to spare after selling their home to developers, brought £500,000 to the party, while the council wrote off money it had previously loaned to both clubs. The atmosphere at Spotland had always been welcoming – now the ground would get some modern facilities to match, including a new Main Stand, designed by council architects in 1992.

Thus far, Rochdale's football hasn't quite lived up to the progress that's been made off the pitch. After three years of mediocrity and a desperate finale to the 1998/99 season, manager Graham Barrow was dismissed and the board seized on the chance to sign up Steve Parkin, who'd walked out on Mansfield Town only a few days earlier. With early signs indicating a shift to a more considered style of football under Parkin, 'Dale could yet mount another of those oh-so rare promotion bids in the not too distant future. In which case, the hope must be that a step up in status doesn't usher in a change in the menu at Spotland. The pies are just fine as they are.

Here we go!

Approaching on the M62, **motorists** should exit at Junction 20 onto the A627(M) toward Rochdale. Take the first exit off the roundabout at the end, then move into the middle lane to take the second exit from the next roundabout into Roch Valley Way. Go straight on at the lights at the top of the hill and you'll be in Sandy Lane – Spotland is about half a mile ahead on the right.

There's a large **car park** behind the new WMG (Pearl Street) Stand which is rarely full.

Rochdale **train station** is on the trans-Pennine line between Leeds and Manchester Victoria (half-hourly, journey 1hr 15mins from Leeds, 25mins from Manchester). You'll have few problems getting back in either direction from an evening game, but onward connections could be trickier. For the latest timings call ☎0345/484950.

From the bus station in the town centre, catch a #444 bus to Spotland Road.

Just the ticket

Visiting fans can either stand in the terrace along the Willbutts Lane side of the ground, or sit at the Pearl Street end of the Main Stand. Ticket prices in 1998/99 were adults £8 to stand, £10 to sit, no concessions for visitors.

Visiting families are welcome to use the Family Stand (adults £8, maximum two children £1 each, OAPs £4), but advance booking is essential on ☎01706/644648. **Disabled visitors** should likewise book on the same number for spaces in the Main Stand.

Swift half

The ground itself has two options – ***Studds*** social club, within the WMG Stand, which serves hot food and welcomes families, and the ***Ratcliffe Arms*** at the other end of the ground on Sandy Lane, which has a more traditional pub atmosphere. If you want to avoid *J W Lees* beer (see

Open space – plenty of room for fans, plenty of room for improvement from the team

Oldham Athletic), ***The Cemetery*** at the top of Sandy Lane on the corner of Bury Road is a free house with a range of real ales, and decent food as well.

Club merchandise

The **club shop** (☎01706/47521) is behind the Main Stand, but is still eagerly awaiting a revival of the white shirt with blue and yellow diagonal sash with which 'Dale graced the old Third Division in the early Seventies.

Barmy army

Spotland welcomes all except Burnley fans, although as with all the smaller clubs in the area, anyone wearing a Manchester United shirt can expect to have the mickey taken out of them.

Trouble is unheard of unless the refreshments kiosks run out of pies.

In print

There's no Saturday evening paper dedicated to Rochdale but Manchester's ***Pink*** normally carries a 'Dale match report – in town from about 6.15pm.

The fanzine scene was quiet in the summer of 1999 but there are two 'Dale books worth recommending. Steven Phillipp's ***Definitive Rochdale AFC*** (T Brown, £7.99) tracks the club's statistical history as far as 1995, while ***Kicking In The Wind – The Real Life Drama Of A Small-Town Football Club*** (Headline, £6.99) is Derek Allsop's atmospheric, bluebottle-on-the-wall account of the 1996/97 season at Spotland, also available in hardback at £14.99.

On air

Local BBC station ***GMR*** (95.1 FM) is best for Rochdale coverage, with previews and reports each Saturday.

In the net

Rochdale's **official website** disappeared during 1998/99 but may have returned by the time you read this. Give it a go at: www.rochdale-football-club.co.uk.

The unofficial arena is lively. The ***Alternative Dale Website*** features a daily news archive and a good links area at: member.aol.com/upthedale/index.html; while ***DIAZ***, the *Dale Independent Audio Zone*, also has news as well as Spotland chants and songs for you to download at: website.lineone.net/~diazone/.

Finally there's the online fanzine ***Live From The Sandy*** at: www.lftsrochdale.freeserve.co.uk/index.html.

Rotherham United

Formation	1877 as Thornhill United
Stadium	Millmoor, Rotherham, S60 1HR. ☎01709/512434
Ground capacity	11,500
First-choice colours	Red and white
Major honours	Third Division champions 1981; Third Division (North) champions 1971; Fourth Division champions 1989; Auto Windscreens Shield winners 1996
Position 1998/99	Fifth in Third Division (eliminated in play-off semi-finals)

Rotherham fans, who had travelled down to London in their thousands, could only watch in horror. Who would have thought that a season in which their side had beaten all the leading teams in the Third Division, and had played some of its most exciting football, could end with defeat in a penalty shoot-out after 210 minutes of goalless play-off action? Had manager Ronnie Moore, probably the most important figure in the club's postwar history, not taken his players through some penalty practice prior to the game? And if so, why were Rotherham so bad at taking them, and their opponents, Leyton Orient, so good? Why was football – like life – so unfair?

Dis-Orientated – Danny Hudson (white shirt) gets a kick

Not that it did Orient much good. They lost the 1999 Third Division play-off final to Scunthorpe United, and would now be resuming their acquaintance with Rotherham in 1999/2000. But that was cold comfort to supporters of the South Yorkshire club, who had approached the play-offs with a bullish confidence on the back of their side's latter-day League form. A confidence which, in the end, proved misplaced.

Such has been Rotherham's lot for much of their history. Never in the top flight, the club has moved up and down the remaining three divisions with alarming frequency. Stability and security have rarely been on the agenda at Millmoor. And while this has made life eventful for the fans, it has also frustrated them, testing loyalty to breaking point in a part of the world where the draw of Sheffield's two big clubs is never far from the imagination of the uncommitted supporter.

On the other hand, at least the club's solid off-the-pitch foundations have kept hopes high, at a time when neighbouring

The main man – Ronnie Moore, former scourge of Second Division defences, spells it out

Doncaster Rovers have been asset-stripped and arson-attacked out of the League.

The club's origins are typically convoluted. The first football club in the town, Rotherham FC, was formed as early as 1870. Occupying a winter tenancy at the Clifton Lane cricket ground, the team changed their name to Rotherham Town in 1882. Nine years later they moved to their own ground at Clifton Grove, and from here successfully applied to join the Second Division of the Football League in 1893. But in three seasons they never finished better than 12th in what was then a 16-team competition, and with local interest falling away, Town folded in 1896.

Meanwhile, in 1877 another club, known as Thornhill United, had formed and soon began playing at the Red House ground, just north of today's Millmoor, where the pitch was so narrow the club was banned from hosting FA Cup ties there. The club appeared to have Rotherham's footballing interest to itself when Town folded, only for another Rotherham Town club to appear at Clifton Lane in 1905. As a response, in 1907 Thornhill changed their name to Rotherham County, and crucially moved to Millmoor, where facilities were far superior to those at any of the other venues which had hosted football in Rotherham – and where the pitch was wide enough to meet with the authorities' approval.

County joined the Midland League and played in it with some style, before successfully applying to join the Football League Second Division – just as the old Town club had done – in 1919. With League football pulling in the crowds and a new main stand to house them in, County now had an insuperable advantage over the upstart Rotherham Town club. In 1925, Town agreed to merge with County to form a new club, under the title of Rotherham United.

By this time, though, County had been relegated to the Third Division (North), and when the new United club was born, it struggled both on and off the pitch for almost all of the period prior to World War II.

The outlook brightened after the war. In 1949, on the back of rising attendances, United bought the freehold to Millmoor and added new terracing which allowed spectator accommodation on all four sides. Two years later, the team won the Third Division (North) championship. In 1952, identical record crowds of 25,170 turned up to watch first Sheffield United, then Wednesday, in Second Division action.

Then Rotherham came desperately close to a further promotion which, had it been achieved in tandem with their growing popularity, might just have enabled them to expand further. In 1954/55 they finished third in the Second Division, level on points with Birmingham and Luton above them, but with an inferior goal average. The two other clubs were promoted to the top flight – while Rotherham were destined never to come so close again.

Still, United remained a respectable Second Division side for the remainder of the Fifties and for much of the Sixties. In 1961, they reached the final of the first-ever League Cup competition, beating Aston Villa 2–0 in the first leg at Millmoor with goals from Barry Webster and Alan Kirkman. But Villa drew level in the return, then won the new Cup with a goal in extra time.

In 1967, the club pulled off something of a coup in coaxing former Chelsea manager Tommy Docherty to Millmoor. But within a year he had been lured away by QPR, leaving United's team midway through a makeover. The result was relegation, and the start of a decline that would see Fourth Division football come to Rotherham for the first time by 1973.

The team were back up within two years, though, and in 1981 Rotherham won the Third Division title. The 1981/82 season, with former Liverpool and England captain Emlyn Hughes as player-manager, Tony Towner providing the crosses and target man Ronnie Moore knocking them in, was spectacular. Struggling at the wrong end of the table in the new year, United won 13 games on the spin to come within touching distance of the promotion places. They eventually finished seventh, but not before thrashing Chelsea 6–0 at Millmoor, in a game that had the faithful dancing on the terraces.

The music stopped abruptly a year later, when Hughes resigned and Rotherham were relegated. Club chairman Anton Johnson lost interest, leaving the club with debts of £250,000. With post-industrial gloom descending on South Yorkshire and attendances falling, Millmoor's finances reached such a state that bailiffs were arriving to take furniture away. But in 1987, Ken Booth stepped in to clear the club's debts (now up to around £800,000) and become United's new chairman.

Supporters feared that Booth, whose scrap metal business surrounded Millmoor on three sides, might run the club down so that he could take over the site or, at best, that he would move Rotherham to a new stadium out of town. Both fears proved groundless. Though unable to prevent relegation to the Fourth Division in

The beauty from Bermuda – Shaun Goater

Mine all mine – Jemson holds the Auto Windscreens Shield

1988, Booth was first and foremost in love with the club, and he remains at the helm today, 12 years after he wrote out that six-figure cheque to save United from extinction.

Since the Booth takeover there have been two promotions and two relegations, under management personalities as diverse as Archie Gemmill and Danny Bergara. There has also been glory at Wembley in the 1996 Auto Windscreens Shield final, United's 2–1 win over Shrewsbury being the reward for a bold, attacking team in which Nigel Jemson and Shaun Goater always looked capable of scoring goals.

The appointment of Ronnie Moore as Bergara's successor at the end of the last relegation season, 1996/97, has so far delivered only gradual progress, and Millmoor itself, the subject of much-needed improvements during the summer of 1999, can still be on the grim side. Supporters, on the other hand, would probably swap a new main stand for some better penalty-taking in the play-offs.

Here we go!

Motorists are best off approaching Rotherham from junction 33 of the M1 – take the A631 and M18 to the M1 if coming from the A1(M). After exiting the M1, take the A630 toward Rotherham. Go left at the first roundabout, right at the next, and straight on at the next. You'll now see the Millmoor floodlights on the left, but visiting fans are asked to continue straight on and then double back down the dual carriageway at the roundabout, for specially allocated **free car parking** at the *Zone* nightclub. Rotherham Central **train station** is served by trains running between Sheffield and Hull via Doncaster (service hourly, journey 15mins from Sheffield, 30mins from Doncaster). Change at Doncaster for the East Coast mainline, or see Sheffield United for onward connections from Sheffield. And, as always, check the latest timings on ☎0345/484950. The station is a 5min walk from Millmoor. Go left over the bridge toward the floodlights, under the dual carriageway via the subway, and up Masbrough Street – the ground is on the left.

Just the ticket

Visiting fans can either stand on the Railway Terrace or sit in the adjacent Millmoor Lane Stand. Ticket prices in 1998/99 were £7.50 to stand and £10 to sit, with concessions only available if your club also offers them to visitors.

Visiting families are welcome in the Family Stand, while **disabled supporters** have a small area in front of the Millmoor Lane Stand. Advance booking essential on ☎01709/512434.

Swift half

The ***Tivoli Club*** at the Masbrough Street end of the ground welcomes visiting fans but may be closed for refurbishment in the early part of the 1999/2000 season.

Train travellers have a good option in ***The Phoenix*** in College Road, while families should head for ***The Effingham Arms*** opposite the bus station, a very traditional pub with a full menu and wide range of real ales.

Club merchandise

The ***Millersports* shop** at the corner of Millmoor Lane and Masbrough Street (open Mon–Fri 9am–5pm, Sat 10am–12 noon, later on matchdays, ☎01709/512760) stocks the expected range of red-and-white items, including replica shirts at £38 (kids' sizes £25). Fans seem to prefer it when United wear an Arsenal-style red shirt with white sleeves, the combination worn whenever Rotherham have been doing well – ie. in the mid-Fifties and early Eighties.

Barmy army

Fans have a bit of a chip on their shoulder about locals who support either of the Sheffield teams, but the rivalry is never bitter or violent. Millmoor is an exceptionally friendly ground.

In print

Local newspapers the ***Rotherham Star*** and ***Rotherham Advertiser*** are both good for news and previews, but on Saturday afternoons the only offering is the Sheffield-based ***Green'Un***.

The fanzine is ***Moulin Rouge*** (178 Greatwood Avenue, Skipton, BD23 2SQ), while Wayne Houghton's book ***Windmills Of My Mind*** (Juma, £7.95) describes a life supporting Rotherham United – not as grim as it might sound.

On air

Again, Steeltown dominates, but ***BBC Radio Sheffield*** (88.6 FM) usually finds airtime for Millmoor news and reports.

In the net

The club has relaunched its **official site** with a pleasing new design at: www.themillers.co.uk/rufc. In content terms, however, it still has some catching up to do on some of the unoffiicial offerings, notably ***Millers On-Line***, which has good basic club info, some history and an excellent rolling news service and archive – all at: www2.krisalis.co.uk/wwwneil/index.html. The ***Moulin Rouge*** fanzine (see *In print* above) is online at: www.geocities.com/Colosseum/Midfield/6316.

Scunthorpe United

Formation	1910 as Scunthorpe & Lindsey United
Stadium	Glanford Park, Scunthorpe, DN15 8TD. ☎01724/848077
Ground capacity	9,000
First-choice colours	Claret and sky-blue
Major honours	Third Division (North) champions 1958
Position 1998/99	4th in Third Division (promoted via play-offs)

Keegan, Botham and jokes about the name aside, you could be forgiven for thinking there wasn't much worth knowing about Scunthorpe United. The town is nobody's idea of a bustling metropolis, dominated by steel mills which gives the club its nickname 'the Iron'. Its setting is somehow not quite Humberside and not quite rural Lincolnshire, either. As for the team, United have come close to winning little and actually won even less. There haven't even been any brushes with relegation from the League – unless you count a couple of applications for re-election – to spice things up a little.

Look again, though. No League club had built itself a new ground since the Fifties when Scunthorpe sold the Old Show Ground and moved into purpose-built Glanford Park in 1988. This was before Hillsborough, remember, and there was no Football Trust to distribute pools levies as construction grants. Neither were there any of the specialist consultants, planners and architects who have since smoothed the way for clubs the length and breadth of the country to up sticks.

Glanford Park is not much to look at, but the fans have made it home. And in 1999, the team responded in kind. Eleven years since the Old Show Ground's last act saw Scunthorpe miss out on promotion from the old Fourth Division, the team worked their way through the play-offs (after finishing fourth – ironically the same position as in 1988) before assuring themselves of a step up in class by beating Leyton Orient 1–0 at Wembley.

A bargain-basement building Glanford Park may be, but it deserves better than bargain-basement football. Now, at the dawn of a new millennium, it will get it.

It wasn't just the lack of precedent that made it tough for Scunthorpe to move home. The Old Show Ground had been used for football for nearly a century, and by clubs to which United could trace their early roots. Precisely *which* clubs, however, remains a subject for debate.

Some say that in 1895, a football team called Brumby Hall took up residence, under the chairmanship of a W T Lockwood. They spent four years playing friendlies in front of modest crowds at the Old Show Ground, before deciding to increase their pulling power by merging with a number of other local clubs to form Scunthorpe United. This club in turn merged with North Lindsey United in 1910.

Version two has North Lindsey United as the side playing at the Old Show Ground until 1910, under the aegis of local solicitor R A C Symes (whose firm still exists today). They then merged with Scunthorpe Town, a church team founded by the Vicar of Frodingham around 1885.

What everyone agrees is that the club formed in 1910, Scunthorpe & Lindsey United, is the forerunner of the current one. (In fact, the team continued to play under this name until 1958, when the '& Lindsey' bit was finally dropped.) Even after all these mergers, United played at a moderate level initially. They agreed a rent of £10 a year with the Old Show Ground's owners, the Parkinson family, and faced the likes of Scunthorpe Midgets, Barton Terriers and Ashby Rising Stars (a misnomer if ever there was one) in the local Lindsey League, before forming a limited company, turning professional and entering the Midland League in 1912.

Their first game in the Midland League was away to Leeds United, and Scunthorpe lost 1–0. They went on to lose another four matches before beating Mexborough 5–3 to chalk up their first professional victory at the Old Show Ground.

World War I brought the inevitably halt to proceedings, but by 1920 United were confident enough to apply for membership of the Third Division (North) of the Football League. With neighbours Grimsby Town finishing bottom of the Second Division the previous year and Lincoln City having left the League altogether, there was a decent case for Scunthorpe. But Grimsby were assured of their place, Lincoln returned to the fold – and United's application was rejected out of hand.

The Old Show Ground, 1968 – with Keegan in the Iron line-up

Failure to achieve League status hit Scunthorpe hard at the turnstiles, and there were further money worries in 1924, when the club bought the Old Show Ground outright for £2,700, only for the Main Stand to burn down months later. Unable to pay players, the board contemplated leaving the Midland League and returning to the amateur game. Salvation came in the form of a series of fund-raising events, including the raffling of a pig, which broke loose and ran onto the pitch just as the draw was being made.

Their bacon saved, United bounced back, building a new Main Stand that would survive until the bulldozers arrived in 1988, and winning the Midland League title in 1927. Depression in the early Thirties caused only a temporary blip, and by the end of the decade, with centre-forward Harry Johnson rampant, the Midland League was looking too small for them. In 1938/39 United scored 133 goals, with Johnson's personal haul of 51 including three hat-tricks, a four, a five and a six.

Football League status continued to elude Scunthorpe, however, and during World War II Grimsby Town rubbed their noses in it by playing First Division fixtures at the Old Show Ground, their own Blundell Park home being considered a target for Nazi bombing. United were again turned down for a place in the League at the end of the war, but on 3 June 1950, after a meeting a London's *Café Royal*, they were finally elected (on a third ballot) as a member of the newly expanded Third Division (North).

More than 11,000 turned up at the Old Show Ground to see United draw 0–0 with Shrewsbury in their first League game on 19 August 1950, with a young full-back called Jackie Brownsword, rejected by Hull City two years earlier, instantly making his mark as a player of League stature. That

The trend-setter – when built, Glanford Park was the first all-new League ground for 30 years

couldn't be said of many of his team-mates, though, and Scunthorpe laboured in mid-table for three seasons before finishing third in 1954 and 1955.

The less unwieldy name 'Scunthorpe United' was finally adopted three years later, when manager Ron Stuart, harnessing the prolific goalscoring of Jack Haigh and Ron Waldock, guided the team to the Third Division (North) title. The last game of the season, a 3–1 win over Carlisle, was watched by 12,500, and followed by the presentation of the championship shield by the vice-president of the Football League, Harold Shentall – for a club that had toiled so long to gain admittance to the League, this was a poignant moment.

The celebrations were soon cut short, however, when the Old Show Ground was again the scene of a fire, this one destroying the East Stand. The local steel industry, seeing an opportunity to showcase its expertise, built a replacement – the first cantilevered stand in Britain – in just three-and-a-half months. (United wanted to take this piece of footballing history with them when they moved house in 1988, but the cost proved prohibitive.)

On the pitch, the side took a while to adjust to the step up in class, particularly in attack where Second Division defences were proving hard to crack open. Enter Barrie Thomas, a former England youth international whose career was at a cross-roads when he arrived at Scunthorpe from Mansfield Town in September 1959. Assuming the mantle of the veteran Haigh as United's first-choice centre-forward, Thomas had all the pace, vision and strength the club's earlier frontline had lacked. By 1961/62 he was scoring goals for fun, with 31 already to his name for the season before Newcastle snapped him up in January 1962. Older United fans maintain to this day that, had Thomas not been sold when he was, the team would have been promoted to the First Division as runners-up to Liverpool. As it was they finished fourth, five points behind second-placed Leyton Orient.

After that, manager Dick Duckworth kept Scunthorpe in the Second Division for two more seasons before resigning after relegation in 1964. The more fickle element within United's support deserted them, and as the club became increasingly reliant on young playing talent (including a raw Ray Clemence in goal), another relegation brought Fourth Division football to Scunthorpe for the first time in 1968. Undeterred, manager Ron Ashman dispensed with the club's traditional claret and blue strip and dressed his players in all red, in mimicry of Liverpool. He also signed a young forward by the name of Kevin Keegan on apprentice forms, and gave him his first-team debut in December 1968. Keegan made an immediate impact, becoming an ever-present in Ashman's team, building an easy rapport with striker Nigel Cassidy and scoring 17 goals himself.

Keegan's quick feet and quick thinking couldn't get Scunthorpe promoted on their own, however, and at the end of a 1970/71 season in which the team had finished 17th in the Fourth Division, Liverpool offered £35,000 for him – a deal later described by Anfield boss Bill Shankly as 'robbery with violence'. Low as it might have been, United couldn't afford to turn it down.

So began nearly two decades of obscurity at the Old Show Ground, illuminated only by the prodigious goalscoring of Steve Cammack in the early Eighties, and by the cameo appearance as a non-contract player of England cricketer Ian Botham at the same time. Botham's employers were terrified he would get injured as a central defender braving X-rated challenges on muddy Fourth Division pitches. But he insisted the football was keeping him in shape during cricket's off-season, and went on to play 11 games.

Diversions aside, by the mid-Eighties United were deeply in debt and unable to afford the rebuilding of the Old Show Ground required after the 1985 Bradford fire. Club secretary Don Rowing hit upon a novel solution to the problems – sell the site for development, and use the £2.5million proceeds to build a new stadium out of town. Eyebrows were raised in footballing circles, but after the *Safeway* supermarket chain declared itself interested in the Old Show Ground's location and Glanford borough council had offered a suitable building plot, the planners waved the whole thing through without so much as a cough. The move came as a shock to the faithful but the idea of Glanford Park appealed to some of United's fairweather fans – attendances soared after it opened at the start of the 1988/89 season. Sadly, the team's football failed to rise in tandem, although Scunthorpe did come within a penalty shoot-out of promotion when they lost a play-off final to Blackpool in 1992.

The turning point was the arrival of former Grimsby manager Brian Laws in February 1997. As bold and committed as Glanford Park itself had been, Laws shook up the squad, signing two key forwards in Jamie Forrester from Grimsby to partner Alex Calvo-Garcia, a Spanish forward who'd arrived the previous year to improve his English, and stayed.

In 1997/98, Scunthorpe would have made the play-offs had it not been for a run of eight consecutive defeats in mid-season. The following year, though, there was no mistake. A semi-final win over Swansea set United on the road to Wembley again, and once there Calvo-Garcia's smartly taken goal was enough to lift the Iron out of the basement.

Here we go!

One of the reasons Glanford Park got planning permission so quickly was its ease of access for **motorists**. Simply leave the M180 at junction 3 onto the M181 and follow this motorway to its end. Take the third exit at the roundabout and

From Grimsby with vision – popular manager Brian Laws

the ground is immediately on your right – there's usually plenty of room in the **car park** if you get here in plenty of time.

Despite the fact that the railway line runs behind the stadium, arriving by train is frustrating. Scunthorpe **train station** is 2miles away, and the best option here is probably a taxi (£3).

The Scunthorpe line connects to the East Coast main line at Doncaster (service hourly, journey time 30mins), but there are also direct trains from Manchester, Sheffield and Nottingham. No trains after the final whistle in the evenings, though. For the latest timings call ☎0345/484950.

Just the ticket

Visiting fans are accommodated in the South Stand – enter through turnstiles #6 and #7. Admission in 1998/99 was £10, no concessions.

Disabled visitors have spaces alongside their home counterparts in front of the GMB Stand – book in advance on ☎01724/848077.

Swift half

The pub opposite the ground, ***Tom Cobleigh's Old Farmhouse*** has a wide range of real ales, does good food and is very family-friendly – the downside of this is that large groups of visiting fans wearing colours may be refused admission.

Alternatively try ***The Queensway***, easily accessible if you have wheels. Take the third exit off the Berkeley roundabout, drive to the top of the hill to another roundabout and take the third exit – the pub car park is on the left.

The Scunny Spaniard – Calvo-Garcia at Wembley, 1999

Club merchandise

United reverted to claret and blue in the mid-Eighties and the ***Iron Village*** (open Mon–Fri 9am–5pm and on matchdays, ☎01724/848077) in the Main Stand has a surprisingly wide range of suitably coloured items.

Barmy army

Very little trouble here, even on Humberside derby days with Hull City. Glanford Park's enclosed look may not be easy on the eye but it does mean that 3,000 fans can sound more like 13,000. The hardcore Iron fans are on the *British Steel* Terrace – wouldn't you just know it?

In print

The local ***Evening Telegraph*** once employed Tom Taylor, father of Graham, as its United reporter. The paper's Saturday evening ***Sports Telegraph*** normally gets to Scunthorpe within an hour of the final whistle, and will also have news of Grimsby for those who are interested.

Fanzine **Fe** (19 Old Lincoln Road, Caythorpe, Grantham, Lincs) gets its name from the chemical abbreviation for iron and began publishing in the summer of 1998.

A new ***Official Centenary History*** (Yore, £19.95) of the club was due for publication in August 1999.

On air

BBC Radio Humberside (95.9 FM) is the local station most likely to have match commentary.

In the net

The **official *IronWorld* website** has the kind of irreverent tone more often found on unofficial pages, and has an innovative layout at: freespace.virgin.net/su.fc/. Two unofficial sites are worth a look. ***Iron.Net*** is very smartly designed and has good sections on United's old and new grounds, at: www.iron-net.demon.co.uk. Meanwhile the ***Unofficial Scunthorpe United Homepage*** includes a database of every player to have pulled on a Scunthorpe shirt – including Keegan and Botham. Go to: www-personal.ksu.edu/~njh/sufc/index.html.

Sheffield United

Formation	1889
Stadium	Bramall Lane, Sheffield, S2 4SU. ☎0114/221 5757
Ground capacity	30,300
First-choice colours	Red-and-white stripes
Major honours	League champions 1898; Second Division champions 1953; Fourth Division champions 1982; FA Cup winners 1899, 1902, 1915, 1925
Position 1998/99	Eighth in First Division

If any Yorkshire town can claim to be obsessed with football, then Sheffield is that town. Rugby has never managed to get much of a foothold here, while local cricket – for all that it played a key role in football's development, as it did in many other parts of the country – has its spiritual home in Leeds. Sheffield is home to the oldest football club in the world, and boasts two grounds that have regularly been used as venues for internationals, Cup semi-finals and other big games.

Reflecting this passion for the game perfectly is the rivalry between the city's two professional clubs, United and Wednesday. The fault-line between the two runs as deep as any in England, fans becoming either red or blue, 'Unitedite' or 'Wednesdayite' at an early age, seldom being swayed by the pull of teams from outside the area, and never, ever switching sides during a lifetime.

Yet the rivalry brings its own problems. Sheffield is arguably too small to sustain two ambitious clubs, each with its own proud history of achievement dating back to the 19th century, and keen to rekindle that spirit for the dawn of the 21st. The other towns of the South Yorkshire conurbation have their own teams, tightening the catchment area still further. And while those grounds may be impressive in both size and tradition, they take a lot of maintaining, and are rarely full. No wonder so many of the great Sheffield derbies have been played out in the Second Division…

Inevitably, supporters of the two clubs dearly love to score points off one another. But there is one indubitable fact with which

Blade for life – Sheffield loyalties are set in steel

Wednesday's fans can always taunt United's – it was Wednesday who were founded first, and it was Wednesday, indirectly, that were responsible for creating United.

The Wednesday team, formed as the footballing arm of the Wednesday Cricket Club in 1867, soon began to use the cricket ground at Bramall Lane (see panel) for their most important fixtures. These drew huge crowds to the ground, which became increasingly dependent on football for its income. So when Wednesday announced their intention to lease their own venue in

Just not cricket – the Bramall Lane story

Road to ruin – the view from Cherry Street

For years before it was known as a football ground, **Bramall Lane** played host to cricket. The venue was the brainchild of **Michael Ellison**, a member of the Sheffield Cricket Club who in 1854 agreed to lease eight acres of land on the southern edge of the city from the **Duke of Norfolk**, with the aim of providing a home for more than one club. Thus the ground initially was capable of hosting six cricket matches at the same time.

It wasn't long, though, before football started to make its presence felt. On 29 December 1862, the first football match took place between the original **Sheffield** club (founded in 1857 and still in existence today, recognised as the oldest surviving football club in the world) and another local side, Hallam. The match lasted three hours and finished goalless.

Despite this apparent lack of excitement, football gradually rose to become the most popular sport at Bramall Lane, providing the lion's share of income. **Sheffield Wednesday** played important games there for 20 years from their formation in 1867, and once they had left, the ground's management committee resolved to keep football at the Lane by forming their own team, **Sheffield United**, in 1889. Flush with their League championship success nine years later, United bought the freehold to Bramall Lane from the Duke for £10,000 – though the loan that enabled them to do it would not be repaid until 1947.

The last cricket match was played in 1973, Yorkshire hosting Lancashire for a Roses fixture on 7 August. At last Bramall Lane could finally be given a stand on its fourth 'empty' side, facing Cherry Street. Alas, the 8,000-seater **South Stand** went way over its £1million budget and came close to bankrupting the club.

A decade later, United chairman **Reg Brealey**'s plans to turn the Lane into a multi-sports stadium, the **'Bramall Centre'**, were rejected by Government planners. Instead, the ground has been developed stage by stage since then, with a new **John Street Stand** opening in 1996, and further expansion planned for the future.

nearby Olive Grove in 1887, alarm bells rang among Bramall Lane's managing committee. They grew even louder in March 1889, when an FA Cup semi-final between Preston and West Brom drew more than 22,000 souls to the ground. Watching the fans pouring through the turnstiles, a junior member of the committee, Charles Stokes suggested to his superior Sir Charles Clegg that a new football club should be formed specifically to play at Bramall Lane. At the time Clegg was president not just of the Sheffield FA but also of a cricket club called Sheffield United, and he decided to use this club as the basis for the new team.

At a meeting on 22 March 1889, Clegg proposed pooling players from the existing Sheffield, Heeley and Owlerton clubs. But Sheffield proved reluctant to relinquish their treasured amateur status and withdrew, closely followed by the other two. Now Sheffield United had a football team, but no footballers to play in it.

Undeterred, Clegg placed advertisements in the local press asking for players to come forward, and by 29 May the club was able to announce that it now had a full squad. United played their first game in August 1889, beating the old Sheffield club 3–1. Armed with the proof that it was his team, not those stick-in-the-mud amateurs, that were the future of football in the city, Clegg applied to enter the 1889/90 FA Cup. His side won four preliminary-round ties and then beat Burnley in the first round, before being hammered 13–0 by Bolton Wanderers – to this day, the worst defeat in the club's history.

In 1890/91 United joined the Midland League but failed to play as well as Clegg and his secretary-manager, John Wostinholm, had hoped. Down at Olive Grove, meanwhile, Wednesday were finishing bottom of the Football Alliance, and the main focus of attention in Sheffield was not the performance of the two teams, but the ever-increasing rivalry between them. (Fans of both clubs might reflect that, more than a century later, little had changed in this respect.)

For the 1891/92 season United swapped horses and joined the Northern League, and found this more to their liking, finishing third. Still the board weren't satisfied, however, and determined to join the First Division of the Football League. Inevitably, Wednesday had similar aspirations, and both clubs applied for First Division membership in the summer of 1892. Much to United's chagrin, Wednesday were admitted to the top flight because they had finished fourth in the Alliance that year. United's achievements in the Northern League were not considered of equal standing, and they had to settle for a place in the newly formed Second Division.

The feeling of disappointment would not linger long. United won their first League game 4–2 at home to Lincoln City, and two months later hit ten past Burslem Port Vale. They finishing runners-up to Small Heath in the Second Division table, and were promoted after beating First Division Accrington in a 'test match' at Trent Bridge. Thus began a spell of top-flight football that would not be broken until 1934.

After a couple of seasons in mid-table, United finished second to Aston Villa in 1896/97, and a year later they had won the League, after leading the table for most of the season and finishing five points clear of runners-up Sunderland. By this time Wostinholm had assembled a squad full of internationals, but the team's strengths were primarily defensive and there was no doubting who the stars were: 22-stone goalkeeper Bill 'Fatty' Foulke; wing-half Ernest Needham, whose willingness to track back and tackle earned him the nickname 'Nudger'.

Hotter than a vindaloo – Tony Currie, 1972

The team stayed together for 1898/99 and, while a collapse in League form saw them avoid relegation – a fate suffered by Wednesday that year – by only four points, United embarked on a classic FA Cup run, beating Liverpool after three replays (the second had been abandoned because of a pitch invasion and 'oncoming darkness') in the semi-finals, and coming back from a goal down to beat Derby County 4–1 in the final, in front of nearly 79,000 at the Crystal Palace ground.

United began the 20th century by recovering in the League to finish second to champions Aston Villa, and in 1901, after the shock of FA Cup final defeat at the hands of non-League Tottenham Hotspur, Wostinholm's successor John Nicholson bought the Sunderland centre-forward Alf Common for £325. Now the team's gritty, compact football was given the added dimension of a man capable of conjuring a goal from nothing – United duly returned to Crystal Palace in 1902 to regain the FA Cup, beating Southampton after a replay.

This was to be the last great victory for the team which had, essentially, taken Sheffield United from the status of non-League pretenders to a major force in the land within the space of ten years. Needham retired, Foulke was sold to Chelsea, and Common surprisingly returned to his native Sunderland.

Their match-winners gone, United settled into mid-table for the remainder of the period up to World War I – though they did win the so-called 'Khaki Cup final' in 1915, beating a lacklustre Chelsea 3–0 in front of an Old Trafford crowd comprising mainly soldiers and the odd Unitedite who had made the trip to Manchester despite wartime restrictions.

After the war, Robinson remained in his post and set about building a new United team around the talents of Irish international inside-forward Billy Gillespie (who'd signed from Leeds in 1912) and target man Harry Johnson. Neither could help the club to achieve greater consistency in the League, but both were in the side that reached the 1925 FA Cup final at Wembley, where United beat Cardiff City 1–0.

Ted Davison replaced Nicholson in 1932, and the solidity which had characterised the

It takes all sorts – Harry Bassett at the ground that was his second home for seven years

club's football almost since its inception suddenly evaporated – United finished bottom of the First Division in 1934, after conceding 101 goals. A run to the 1935/36 Cup final (lost 1–0 to a goal by Ted Drake for Arsenal) briefly brightened Second Division life. And on the eve of World War II, inspired by their new signing from Derby, Jimmy Hagan, the team won promotion, pipping Wednesday to second spot behind Blackburn by a single point.

Culture clash – Waddle and Whitehouse at Wembley

The early postwar era at Bramall Lane belonged to Hagan, a former Durham pitman whose instinctive creativity would see him score more than 100 League goals in 360 games for United, before his retirement in 1957. Fans were astounded that Hagan won only one full England cap (despite playing several unofficial wartime internationals), yet the club he was playing for was now less than fashionable, and skilful though he was, he couldn't carry the team singlehanded. This much was made crystal-clear in 1949, when United were relegated once again. The following year, Wednesday gained their revenge by denying United promotion on goal average, and the latter would have to wait another three years for the arrival of the Second Division title in 1953. Another relegation swiftly followed, and it wasn't until John Harris replaced the inventive but thus far unsuccessful Joe Mercer as manager in 1959 that the club was re-acquainted with stability.

The 1960/61 season was the turning point. United finished behind Alf Ramsey's Ipswich in the Second Division table but still comfortably achieved promotion, while there was also a run to the semi-finals of the FA Cup, where top-flight Leicester City were held to a second replay. Harris' side was initially workmanlike, built around the unflappable goalkeeping of Alan Hodgkinson and masterful marking of (unrelated) defenders Joe and Graham Shaw. But after a fifth-place finish in the First Division in 1962, topped off with a celebratory tour of the USA and Canada, Harris became bolder, bringing on younger, more attack-minded players such as playmaker Alan Birchenall and striker Mick Jones.

United's problem, as always, was having to invest in new players while trying to balance the books at the same time. By 1967 the debts were piling up, and both Birchenall and Jones were reluctantly sold. Relegation followed a year later, prompting Harris to move into a general manager's role while Arthur Rowley, fresh from a pioneering career at Shrewsbury, came in as first-team boss. Like most job-shares in professional football, it didn't work – Rowley was dismissed within a year, and Harris took charge of the team once more. A ninth-place finish in the Second Division was all he could manage in 1969, but two years later United were back up again.

This time Harris wasted no time in encouraging his players to express themselves in the top division. And what players they were. With stalwart right-back Len Badger, elegant winger Alan Woodward and playmakers Trevor Hockey and Tony Currie, United went 22 games unbeaten between March and October 1971 – a tenth-place finish in the First Division seemed almost an anti-climax, but there was every reason to think it was only the beginning. In 1973, Bramall Lane bid farewell to county cricket and fans looked forward to the time when their ground would at last have stands on all four sides. Ken Furphy became manager but Harris remained at the club as a senior executive, keeping a watchful eye as ever.

Two years later, United's new South Stand was proudly unveiled for the first game of the 1975/76 season against Derby. The previous season, Derby had won the title while United had finished sixth – their best League finish for 13 years. From now on, however, the only way was down. The South Stand had gone way over-budget, leaving the club strapped for cash and the team's star players seeking employment elsewhere. Furphy was sacked in October with the team bottom of the table, but caretaker boss Cec Coldwell and his permanent successor Jimmy Sirrel couldn't avoid the drop – United finished bottom of the table, having managed only six wins all season. A vertiginously steep descent had begun.

In early 1978 Harry Haslam replaced Sirrel as manager, only to oversee another relegation 18 months later. Haslam's motivational skills were not in doubt but the quality of his squad certainly was. The club had debts of £1million, and Bramall Lane, an arena which could now hold nearly 50,000, was usually less than a third-full. In October 1980 Haslam recruited Martin Peters as manager while remaining as a consultant to the team himself. Another job-share, another disaster – in 1981 United were relegated to the Fourth Division, after missing a penalty in the last minute of the last game that would have kept them up. Peters resigned on 29 May, to be followed a day later by Haslam.

Bramall Lane was now the archetypal haunted house of Eighties football, sulking amid a post-industrial wasteland, increasingly dilapidated and infested with a restless, resentful hooliganism. Reg Brealey arrived as chairman and briefly set supporters dreaming of a new super-stadium, and while that turned out to be a mirage, there was nothing unreal about the £2.5million he pumped into the club, helping new manager Ian Porterfield to lift United out of the Fourth Division as champions in 1982. Two years later there was another promotion, after Porterfield's side ended the season with a goal difference one higher than that of Hull City – what had gone around, came around.

Porterfield was controversially sacked in 1986, and Billy McEwan guided the team to Second Division stability before resigning early in 1988. United were struggling now and Brealey, seeking a radical answer, decided to rescue Dave 'Harry' Bassett from his nightmare at Watford. Bassett couldn't prevent relegation after a play-off defeat by Bristol City, but his no-nonsense, get-the-ball-forward-early style paid instant dividends in the Third Division, and United went straight back up.

This, though, was only the start. With the manic but perpetually mobile strikeforce of Brian Deane and Tony Agana making joyful use of the long-ball service given them by the rest of the team, United made it two promotions in a row in 1990, finishing second behind Leeds United only on goal difference.

Once in the top flight, 'Harry's Game' proved surprisingly effective, the side settling nicely into a mid-table stride as Bramall Lane became one of the grounds the bigger clubs least liked to travel to. The crowning glory of the Bassett era, however, came not in the League but in the FA Cup of 1992/93. After the mercurial Glyn Hodges had inspired the team to an upset win over Manchester United in the fifth round, Bassett's team marched on to a semi-final date with...Sheffield Wednesday. With demand for tickets likely to exceed the capacity of any league venue, Wembley Stadium hosted the game (as it would the other semi between Arsenal and Spurs), which would be a clash not just of old rivals but of footballing philosophies. In the end – and after extra time – Wednesday's brains triumphed over United's bravery. But if the mood in the red half of the stadium was disconsolate, few fans showed it. Both Sheffield clubs were in the Premiership now, while the city itself was stirring with new life after years of economic decline. The big day out at Wembley was a cause for celebration – whether you were on the winning side or not.

A little more than 12 months later, however, United fans were driving home from London with altogether grimmer faces. Needing only a draw to assure themselves of Premiership survival, Bassett's side had been 2–1 up at Chelsea with five minutes remaining, only to concede two goals – the second with the last touch of the game – to lose 3–2. Yet even now the mood at Bramall Lane was optimistic. Only a freak combination of events had sent the team down. Bassett's tactics had got United up before; now they would do so again.

It didn't quite work out that way. Good as Harry's Game had been at keeping the team out of trouble in the Premiership, back in the First Division the team needed more. In December 1995, with United lying 23rd in the table, Bassett left by mutual consent. His successor, Howard Kendall, made few tactical alterations, yet managed to turn what was starting to look like a dangerous tide of self-pity. Off the pitch, meanwhile, a long-running battle for boardroom control between Brealey and entrepeneur Mike McDonald was finally resolved when the latter acquired Brealey's shares.

While McDonald was busy floating the club on the stock-market, Kendall took an experienced but otherwise uninspired side to Wembley for the 1997 play-off final, lost in the last minute to Crystal Palace. Any momentum the team had built up was lost when Kendall returned to his former club Everton a few weeks later, leaving Nigel Spackman in charge at Bramall Lane. Spackman certainly talked a good game, but disagreements over funding led to both his resignation and that of chairman McDonald, and 1997/98 was another season of nearly-but-not-quite, caretaker manager Steve Thompson taking United to the semi-finals of both the FA Cup and the play-offs, but losing both.

The appointment of Steve Bruce as manager in the summer of 1998 should have instilled the winning spirit into a team that already contained its fair share of individual talents, including the Brazilian Marcello and Belarussian striker Petr Katchuro. Yet apart from their infamous FA Cup tie against Arsenal, Bruce's side seldom made the news, their knack for leaking goals at inopportune moments stopping them short of the play-off zone.

At the end of the season Bruce, like Spackman before him, resigned over the great funding issue, opting for the more positive (yet also more pressured) atmosphere of Huddersfield. His successor,

Play it again, ref – Steve Bruce makes it plain, Highbury, 1999

Adrian Heath, faces problems that have been familiar to Bramall Lane not just in the late Nineties, but for generations.

Here we go!

Bramall Lane is actually the A621 Bakewell Road, and **motorists** approaching from the M1 along the A630 are advised to follow signs for 'A621 Bakewell' as they negotiate Sheffield's tortuous one-way system.

It's **street parking** for all around the ground – arrive early and, as ever, beware car crime.

Sheffield **train station** is a 10–15 min walk from the ground, straight down Shoreham Street – take the left-hand exit at the roundabout in front of the station. Sheffield gets regular fast trains from London St Pancras, via either Nottingham or Leicester and Derby (service hourly, journey 2hrs 20mins from St Pancras). There also direct trains for Birmingham, Manchester, Leeds and Newcastle. There are a number of late connections via Doncaster for evening games, but check the latest timings on ☎0345/484950.

Just the ticket

Visiting fans are allocated the lower section of the Bramall Lane end, with the upper section unreserved and available if a big away following is expected. Ticket prices in 1998/99 were adults £11, concessions £7.

Disabled supporters have limited space in the family enclosure of the John Street Stand. Booking essential on ☎0114/221 5757.

Swift half

There's no shortage of football-friendly pubs both in the immediate vicinity of the ground and in the city centre nearby.

Try ***The Royal Hotel*** on London Road, ***The Red Lion*** between Arundel Gate and Arundel Street, or the ***Champs*** sports bar on Ecclesall Road, unusual for its type in offering both a wide range of real ales and a welcome to families.

Club merchandise

United want to build a new *Megastore* and club museum but in the meantime the **club shop** (open Mon–Sat 9.30am–5.30pm, later on matchdays) behind the South Stand has the expected riot of red-and-white items, including a wide range of glasswear and porcelain. Well this is, er, Steeltown after all.

Barmy army

The trouble that disfigured Bramall Lane in the late Seventies and early Eighties – all the more so when Wednesday were the visitors – has all but died out. Be discreet about colours in the city centre, however.

In print

Local paper the ***Sheffield Star*** publishes a *Green'Un* on Saturday evenings, while the range of fanzines includes the long-established ***Flashing Blade*** (4 Cross Myrtle Road, Sheffield, S2 3EL) and ***The Red & White Wizaaaard*** (PO Box 111, Sheffield, S8 7YU), the journal of the Blades Independent Fans Association.

The Hallamshire Press has published an excellent two-volume history of ***Sheffield Football*** (available at £32 for both books), while those who only want the United side of things should head for Denis Clarebrough's ***Sheffield United Football Club*** (£9.99).

Local anthropologist Gary Armstrong has penned ***Football Hooligans – Knowing The Score*** (Berg, £14.99), with observations based on the United-Wednesday rivalry, as well as ***Blade Runners – Lives In Football*** (Hallamshire, £16.95), which features interviews with United personalities (players, managers, chairmen, you name it) of the last 50 years.

On air

BBC Radio Sheffield (88.6 FM) and commercial ***Hallam FM*** (97.4 FM) both offer excellent post-match phone-ins on a Saturday.

In the net

United's **official site** is fairly standard *Planet*-run fare, but does have some interesting historical bits and is at least up-to-date, which is more than can be said of the unofficial offerings. Find it at: www.sheffutd.co.uk.

Sheffield Wednesday

Formation	1867 as The Wednesday
Stadium	Hillsborough, Sheffield, S6 1Sw. ☎0114/221 2121
Ground capacity	40,000
First-choice colours	Blue-and-white stripes
Major honours	League champions 1903, 1904, 1929, 1930; Second Division champions 1900, 1926, 1952, 1956, 1959; FA Cup winners 1896, 1907, 1935; League Cup winners 1991
Position 1998/99	12th in Premiership

After Sheffield Wednesday lost their top-flight status in 1990, manager Ron Atkinson promised fans he would not resort to the long-ball game, then very much in vogue. 'I've never believed you have to kick your way out of trouble and I'm not going to start believing it now,' he stormed. It was exactly what the supporters wanted to hear. Wednesday's players had done a lap of honour after their 3–0 home defeat by Nottingham Forest on the season's final day, having been told they were safe after Luton Town were held 3–3 at Derby. But there had been no Derby equaliser. Luton had won 3–2, and Wednesday were down on goal difference. Devastated fans made their way slowly home, their desolation made all the deeper by the news that Sheffield United had been promoted on the same day. Yet there was no desire among the Wednesdayite faithful to emulate United's tactics. On the contrary, they wanted the ball kept on the floor, and backed Big Ron all the way.

Symbol of tradition – but is time ticking away for Wednesday?

Their faith was swiftly vindicated. Atkinson's team won promotion at the first attempt, while victory over Manchester United in the League Cup final at Wembley put the first major trophy on the club's mantelpiece in 56 years. Tradition had triumphed, and nobody bore a broader smile than the manager who had stuck to his high-risk guns and won. Since those heady days in the spring of 1991, Wednesday have continued to pin their faith in adventurous football. A succession of managers have preached the virtues of the beautiful game, while the club has spent millions on 'flair' players, many of them from abroad. Yet the teams have never quite added up to the sum of their parts. After Trevor Francis had led the club to two Cup finals in 1993, Wednesday seemed content to bob along in mid-table. So what if no more honours are won and Europe becomes a no-go area? It's the style, not the content, that counts.

Likewise, while so many of the club's peers in the middle ground of the Premiership – the Derbys, Leicesters and Coventrys of this world – have either moved to new stadia or are planning to, Wednesday remain committed to hemmed-in Hillsborough, the vast arena which has a special place in the history of the English game, which has survived the trauma of the disaster on its Leppings Lane terrace

A Hillsborough legend – Derek Dooley

in 1989 and which has been substantially rebuilt since. Yet no amount of new restaurants, retail outlets, conference rooms and shiny new seats and can disguise the age of Hillsborough's design. And while the ground is awe-inspiring when full, sadly that hasn't been very often over the last couple of seasons.

This is the crux of Sheffield Wednesday's problem. Romantic as the club's adherence to tradition might be, for the current generation of fans, it is simply not enough. Too many Nineties seasons have ended with the club looking nervously over its shoulder at the relegation places. Too many of those over-hyped foreign signings have under-achieved. Too many other Premiership clubs are re-inventing themselves for the millennium. And too many supporters are staying at home, or going shopping at Meadowhall...

If the fans feel they deserve better, then so does Wednesday's history, as long and proud as any in the League. The city of Sheffield had already spawned a number of football clubs (including Sheffield FC, the oldest surviving team in the world) when the Wednesday Cricket Club decided to get in on the act in 1867. The club, which took its name from the day of the week when its craftsman players would take the afternoon off work to practise, needed a way of keeping its membership together during the winter, and the emerging game of football seemed the obvious choice. At a meeting at the *Adelphi* pub on 4 September 1867 (a Wednesday, naturally), the proposed football section was formally given the go-ahead. (The *Adelphi*, incidentally, was demolished a century later to make way for Sheffield's *Crucible Theatre*, now the world's favourite snooker venue.)

'The Wednesday FC' played their first game on 31 December against Dronfield, winning 1–0. At this stage the rules of the game varied from club to club and from fixture to fixture, and this first match saw two sets of posts being used at each end. Dronfield reportedly scored four 'rouges' by getting the ball between the outer posts, but these only counted if no 'goals' were scored between the inner ones.

After winning the Cromwell Cup (a trophy the club still holds in its possession) by beating the Garrick Club 1–0 at Bramall Lane in 1868, Wednesday rose to become the leading side in the area. The team played major games at Bramall Lane, then an all-purpose sports field (see panel p.458), while using various venues as their home base. But after entering the FA Cup for the first time in 1881 and losing a long-fought battle against professionalism six years later, the board decided they needed a permanent home of their own. They found one at Olive Grove, just down the road from Bramall Lane, and from now on resolved to play all their matches there.

Yet while Wednesday's decision to turn professional had been taken after leading players threatened to form a rival club (Sheffield Rovers), the club's ground move now had exactly the same effect, as the company that ran Bramall Lane formed

Sheffield United to protect their income. Anxious to stay one step ahead of the upstart club, Wednesday president John Holmes applied for membership of the Football League at the end of its first season in 1889. The League saw now reason to expand its membership from its original 12 clubs, and Wednesday's application, together with those of a number of other teams, was rejected out of hand. Holmes, however, was determined to bring more organised football to Olive Grove. He called all the other unsuccessful applicants together and proposed the formation of a rival competition, the Football Alliance. This duly began in 1889/90, with Newton Heath (later Manchester United), Nottingham Forest and Grimsby Town among the other founder members.

Given that the whole competition was Wednesday's idea, it was perhaps not surprising that they won the Alliance title in its first year. Much more unexpected was the team's progress in the FA Cup, in which Wednesday exacted revenge on three Football League clubs – Accrington, Notts County and Bolton – before losing 6–1 to Blackburn Rovers in the final at the Oval.

At the end of the 1891/92 season, the League finally accepted the desirability of a unified club competition and agreed to expand to two divisions. The Alliance was swallowed up, with Wednesday, despite having finished only fourth in its last season, being one of three Alliance clubs elected directly to the Football League First Division. (United, meanwhile, were elected to the Second.)

Wednesday found First Division life tough at first, but continued to do well in the FA Cup. After reaching the semi-finals in 1894 and 1895, they beat Sunderland, Everton and Bolton on the way to their second final, this time to be played against Wolves at Crystal Palace. In front of nearly 50,000, Wednesday won 2–1, with both their goals scored by winger Fred Spiksley. Thousands lined the streets of Sheffield to welcome the team home, but this outpouring of public support counted for nothing when, just two years later, the club's lease on Olive Grove expired and they were told to leave by April 1899. By that time the team had been relegated, and

A short sharp shock – Lee Chapman takes a deep breath in 1984 football fashions

for a few months of uncertainty, the club's very future appeared to be in jeopardy.

Wednesday eventually acquired a site in the Owlerton area, four miles from Olive Grove and beyond Sheffield's district limits. Moving a few bits of the Olive Grove stands with them made the club feel a tad more at home, but even so, the move was seen as a gamble – the team were some way from their traditional support, and playing Second Division football to boot.

Nobody need have worried. Wednesday's first season at Owlerton saw the team unbeaten at home in the League, their only defeat at the new ground coming in the FA Cup – against Sheffield United. The Second Division title was won in style, and the club soon became synonymous with its new location, to the extent that the team's nickname was altered to 'Owls'. (This, in turn, left United free to adopt Wednesday's previous, steel industry-inspired nickname of 'Blades.')

In 1903, three years after regaining their top-flight status, Wednesday won the title for the first time, finishing a point clear of Sunderland and Aston Villa. Yet the team didn't get the chance to parade the trophy around Owlerton, for Wednesday had already completed their fixtures when Sunderland surprisingly lost at Newcastle to gift them the championship, the Sheffield side being told the news while on a tour to promote football in the West Country.

The following season, 1903/04, the title was retained, and three years later Wednesday upset the odds by beating Everton 2–1 in the FA Cup final – a sweet end to the career of their 34-year-old captain and centre-half Tommy Crawshaw, the only survivor from the side that had first lifted the Cup 11 years earlier, and a key player in both the club's title wins.

In 1912 Owlerton staged its first FA Cup semi-final, and a year later, with the surrounding area now very much a part of Sheffield and a new parliamentary constituency being created for it called Hillsborough, the ground's name was changed accordingly.

There appeared to be progress on all fronts, but World War I came at a particularly bad time for the club, just as the side was being rebuilt after the successes of the Edwardian era. In 1919/20, the first season after hostilities, Wednesday were relegated after a campaign in which they'd used 41 players and won only seven games. Veteran club secretary Arthur Dickinson stood down from team-selection duties and Wednesday appointed their first full-time manager, Bob Brown. Having made a number of signings in the early part of the Twenties, Brown finally got the balance right and the club was back in the First Division by 1926. He wasn't finished there, either. With inside-forwards Jack Allen and Jimmy Seed arriving from Brentford and Tottenham respectively, and after

On the Wembley wing – Nilsson stops Sharpe, 1991

surviving relegation with a great late run in 1928, Brown's side won back-to-back League championships in 1929 and 1930, the latter season yielding 105 goals and a ten-point winning margin over second-placed Derby County, not to mention a run to the semi-finals of the FA Cup.

Although Herbert Chapman's Arsenal would go on to dominate the League in the early Thirties, Wednesday continued to play attacking football and remained a solid top-three side until ill health forced Brown to quit in 1933. His successor, Billy Walker, led Wednesday to another FA Cup triumph in 1935, Ellis Rimmer's two late goals securing a 4–2 victory over West Brom at Wembley. Yet within two years the club had been relegated, and with Wednesday lying bottom of the Second Division in November 1937, Walker resigned. The team recovered under Jimmy McMullan and avoided relegation to the Third Division (North), but the club would never again challenge for League honours with quite the same conviction.

Police escort – Big Ron returns to Hillsborough with Villa

After World War II, Wednesday acquired a reputation as a 'yo-yo' team, comfortable at the top of the Second Division one year, battling relegation from the First the next. They spent almost the whole of the Fifties in this footballing equivalent of the *Twilight Zone*, while the club's board seemed more interested in developing Hillsborough as an international venue.

The man who shook the tree was Harry Catterick, who arrived from Rochdale to become manager in 1958. After selling the fans' favourite Albert Quixall to Manchester United within weeks of his appointment, Catterick built a young, strong-willed and always hard-working side around the talents of John Fantham, Don Megson, Tony Kay and Peter Swan. The team won promotion to the First Division in 1959, reached an FA Cup semi-final a year later, and a year after that finished second to Tottenham's double-winning side in the League.

Catterick's team might have gone on to yet greater things, had the manager not departed for Everton in 1961. His successor, the easy-going Vic Buckingham, was moderately successful but never inspired the same devotion from either players or supporters. His replacement by the harder personality of Alan Brown in 1964 had an air of inevitability about it, but Brown had only been in the job a matter of hours when Hillsborough found itself immersed in a sea of scandal. Three Wednesday players – Kay, who'd since followed Catterick to Everton, Swan and centre-forward 'Bronco' Layne – were alleged by the *Sunday People* newspaper to have 'thrown' a game to further a betting coup. Seven other players were also implicated in the scheme, and after an FA inquiry, all were jailed and banned from football for life.

Brown led Wednesday to the 1966 FA Cup final, but while the match was lost 3–2 to Catterick's Everton, it's doubtful whether even a victory would have lifted the gloom over Hillsborough. The betting scandal had struck deep at the heart of a club which had proudly upheld the values of a noble game for exactly 100 years, and it would take the rest of the Sixties, all of the Seventies and the early part of the

Eighties to mount a full recovery. Brown departed the scene in 1968, and Wednesday began a long exile outside the First Division after they were relegated under former South Yorkshire miner Danny Williams in 1970.

The following year, the board thought they'd pulled off a masterstroke when they appointed Derek Dooley as Williams' replacement. A big centre-forward whose goals had often got Wednesday out of trouble during the yo-yo years of the Fifties, Dooley had become a Hillsborough folk hero after having a leg amputated following a collision with an opposing goalkeeper. Yet his past achievements cut no ice in the dressing room, and with a mystery virus sweeping the team and Wednesday hovering close to the Second Division relegation zone in late 1973, Dooley was dismissed following a boardroom coup.

Two years later, the further relegation that had been threatened duly arrived, after Wednesday won just five games in the entire 1974/75 season. A year later, despite the arrival of new chairman Bert McGee, they needed a last-day win over Southend to avoid dropping into the Fourth Division.

With Hillsborough now echoing eerily to the sound of four-figure crowds and the club losing money hand over fist, a change of direction was needed. What actually occurred was a complete U-turn – the appointment of Jack Charlton as manager in 1977. The defensive tactics of the former Middlesbrough boss went entirely against the Hillsborough grain, but desperate measures were needed and, after a quiet first couple of seasons, a 4–0 thrashing of Sheffield United on Boxing Day 1979 provided the impetus for Wednesday's escape from the Third Division.

In 1982, Charlton's side came within a point of promotion to the top flight. But 'Big Jack' had always said he would quit the job after five years, and once Wednesday had lost an FA Cup semi-final to Brighton in 1983, he fulfilled his promise and resigned.

Jack's replacement, Howard Wilkinson, would prove to be in a similar mould – outwardly severe, but a brilliant motivator capable of drawing towering performances from players of only modest ability. Within a year he had led Wednesday back into the First Division, and in 1986 the team finished fifth in the League, as well as reaching another FA Cup semi-final – this one lost to Everton. With Martin Hodge in goal, Paul Hart at the centre of defence, Brian Marwood providing flair on the flanks and Lee Chapman an intelligent target man, Wilkinson's side looked set for an extended spell at the top of the tree. Yet one by one the talents drifted away, and after a mediocre start to the 1988/89 season, Wilkinson fled, his decision to drop down a division with Leeds United saying much about the atmosphere at Hillsborough at the time.

Wilkinson's assistant Peter Eustace, a member of Wednesday's 1966 Cup final side, lasted barely four months before being replaced by Ron Atkinson, brought in specifically to steer Wednesday away from relegation. This he achieved, and his reward was an extended contract that gave him the confidence to enter the transfer market with a vengeance.

So it was that although Wednesday were ultimately relegated on that day of high drama and emotion in May 1990, the side Atkinson had put together would not only come straight back up but go on to far greater things – providing the foundation for the club's revival in the Nineties. Peter Shirtliff, John Sheridan, Phil King, Roland Nilsson, Trevor Francis – all arrived during that relegation season, and all remained with their manager to help turn the tide. Together with young striker David Hirst and further new arrivals including Danny Wilson and the American defender John Harkes, the team made light work of the Second Division in 1990/91, and if their third-place finish was not as good as it might have been, then the side's spectacular run in the League Cup was an excuse Wednesday fans were happy to accept.

The final at Wembley against Alex Ferguson's Manchester United was not a classic, but then, Atkinson had never intended it to be. Once Sheridan had given Wednesday the lead, club captain Nigel Pearson kept Mark Hughes in his pocket while Nilsson and Harkes 'doubled up' on Lee Sharpe to keep the score at 1–0.

Yet by the time Wednesday were parading the trophy on 31 May 1991, Big Ron had already received an offer to become manager of Aston Villa, the team he had always dreamt of running. Fans were furious when he appeared to decline Villa's offer only to leave Hillsborough days later, and they got the perfect opportunity to make their feelings known when Wednesday were at home to Villa on the first day of the 1991/92 season.

Happily, the board had ensured continuity by making Trevor Francis, whose career had enjoyed an Indian summer under Atkinson, Wednesday's new player-manager. The team's playing style remained unchanged, and Francis appeared to have acquired Big Ron's knack of playing the transfer market to maximum effect. A third-place League finish in 1992 was no less than his side deserved, and the events of the following season, with European football returning to Hillsborough after an absence of nearly three decades and the team reaching the finals of both the League Cup and FA Cup, seemed only to confirm the club's upward trend.

In retrospect, neither the team nor their manager really recovered from losing both those finals to Arsenal. Wednesday had played 63 games in that 1992/93 campaign, and the following year, long-term injuries to Sheridan, Hirst and the talismanic Chris Waddle, plus an uncertain start by new signings Des Walker and Andy Sinton, stopped the renaissance in its tracks. Within a year Francis was gone, yet his successor David Pleat found life at Hillsborough no easier. Always bedevilled by injuries to key players, he had a close shave with relegation in 1996, managed a mid-table finish the following year, and was then sacked 13 games into the 1997/98 campaign, with Wednesday bottom of the Premiership.

That club chairman Dave Richards should then turn to Ron Atkinson for salvation seemed incredible, given the ill feeling that existed between Wednesday and their former manager at the time of the Villa saga. The fans were likewise sceptical, but were won over almost as soon as the team began to climb away from the drop zone. It seemed a classic case of kiss and make-up – until Richards dismissed Atkinson at the end of the season, claiming he'd only ever been seen as a stopgap measure. Big Ron's successor, Danny Wilson, had won many admirers for his work at Barnsley, but his first season in charge, disfigured by the tantrums of Italian fowards Paolo di Canio and Benito Carbone, left fans with another bittersweet taste in their mouths over the summer of 1999.

Here we go!

With Hillsborough a good two miles from the centre of Sheffield, the best advice for **motorists** is to avoid the inner-city area and approach via the M1 and A61 – even if this seems like a long way round on the map. Exit the M1 at junction 36 onto the A61 toward Sheffield, and continue

Bosman bounty – Donnelly, Wilson and O'Donnell, 1999

along this road for about eight miles. You'll see Hillsborough on the right, shortly after the Leppings Lane roundabout. Various impromptu **car parks** spring up around Hillsborough on matchdays and some are signposted from the A61 Penistone Road.

Sheffield **train station** (see Sheffield United for services) is about two miles from the ground. Either catch a matchday shuttle bus from Flat Street (a minute's walk from the station – just follow the signs), or take the *South Yorkshire Supertram* Middlewood Road service as far as the Leppings Lane stop.

Just the ticket

Visiting fans are allocated the upper section of the West Stand, above the former Leppings Lane terrace. Ticket prices vary according to the match category, with concessions roughly two-thirds of the adult price.

Disabled visitors have very limited space in the lower part of the West Stand. Booking essential on ☎0114/221 2121.

Swift half

Pubs around Hillsborough tend to be 'home only', which means heading for the city centre if you've arrived by train or finding somewhere on the A61 by car. For the former, try ***The Red Lion*** between Arundel Gate and Arundel Street, or the excellent ***Champs*** sports bar on Ecclesall Road, near Bramall Lane. For the latter, another ***Red Lion*** on Penistone Road offers a full restaurant menu and a warm welcome to families.

Club merchandise

There are two **club shops** at Hillsborough – one on Penistone Road at the corner of the North Stand and the Kop, the other on the first floor of the refurbished South Stand, and not a red pen in sight at either. Wednesday's 'millennium' home shirts are £39.99, kids' sizes £29.99.

Barmy army

Like Bramall Lane, Hillsborough was once a haven for hooligans, particularly on Sheffield derby days. Now things couldn't be more different, although the hardcore support on the Kop complain that the rebuilt stadium is harder to fill with noise than the old one – despite said Kop having been given a roof in 1986. More fans would, of course, also make a difference.

In print

Local paper the ***Sheffield Star*** publishes a *Green'Un* on Saturday evenings, while the fanzines include ***Spitting Feathers*** (PO Box 97, Sheffield, S10 1YD) and ***War Of The Monster Trucks*** (79 Beechwood Road, Sheffield, S6 4LQ).

The Hallamshire Press has published an excellent two-volume history of ***Sheffield Football*** (£32 for both United and Wednesday books), while redoubtable club author Keith Farnsworth is the man behind ***Wednesday – Every Day Of The Week*** (Breedon, £16.99), a collection of interviews with players, back-room staff and fans covering the period 1933–1998, and produced in conjunction with the *Sheffield Star*.

On air

BBC Radio Sheffield (88.6 FM) and commercial ***Hallam FM*** (97.4 FM) both offer excellent post-match phone-ins on a Saturday.

In the net

Wednesday's **official site** is the only thing they have in common with United – it's run by the same company, the ubiquitous *Planet Internet*, and has the usual audio, video and e-commerce. However, the Wednesdayite version seems slightly superior, with some good background features and not too many in-yer-face graphics at: www.swfc.co.uk.

Among the unofficials, ***Anzowls*** is a comprehensive, frequently updated site, with an outstanding news service, at: www.allsports.com/fapremiership/sheffieldwednesday.

OwlsNet keeps things sleek and simple at: www.sheffwed.net.au. And there's a good historical archive at: www.crg.cs.nott.ac.uk/Users/anb/Football/index.html.

Wednesday's famous Kop Band are online at: members.wbs.net/homepages/k/o/p/kopband.html.

Shrewsbury Town

Formation	1886
Stadium	Gay Meadow, Shrewsbury, SY2 6AB. ☎01743/360111
Ground capacity	8,000
First-choice colours	Blue, yellow and white
Major honours	Third Division champions 1979, 1994; Welsh Cup winners 1891, 1938, 1977, 1979, 1984, 1985
Position 1998/99	15th in Third Division

Shrewsbury Town are a riot of contradictions. They didn't join the Football League until 1950, yet had been playing semi-professionally for more than 60 years before then. Though hailing from a staunchly English town, they have often played – rather successfully too – in Welsh competitions. Often regarded as remote and isolated from the game's developments, they can in fact trace their roots back to the very earliest days of organised football, not just in Britain but anywhere in the world.

A tumble in the Meadow – Paul Evans is sent flying, 1998

The apparent paradoxes continue with the ground. Gay Meadow is one of the most idylically situated venues in the League, surrounded by avenues of trees, overlooked by the spire of St Mary's Church, and so close to the winding river Severn that, over the years, hundreds of over-hit passes and miscued clearances have ended up in the water, to be fished out with a net on a long pole kept specially for the purpose. Look a little closer, though, and it becomes clear that Gay Meadow's condition does not match its location. It's well-kept, but poor facilities and ancient terracing have burdened the club with an estimate of £3.5million simply to comply with the recommendations of the Taylor Report. And, like most lower-division teams, Shrewsbury don't have £3.5million kicking around in their change.

Which is why, in the summer of 1999, the club announced plans to leave its picturesque old ground and move to a 'New Meadow' out of town. The new stadium will have a 10,000 all-seated capacity and become home not just to Town's first team but also to the club's Centre of Excellence and Football in the Community schemes,

A clearing in the trees – but Shrewsbury could soon be moving out of their historic home

and to the Shropshire FA. It will have all-weather facilities for hockey as well as football. And it will not, the club insists, have a 'DIY shed' design. There are even plans to plant trees along one side to shield the ground from the adjacent Meole Brace retail park – and to make fans feel at home, of course.

Before Town can move, several things need to happen. The club needs to find a supermarket chain willing to buy the Gay Meadow site. The new stadium requires planning permission (which was refused when the club attempted something similar in the early Nineties, ironically where the *Currys, Do It All, Sainsbury* and *McDonalds* of Meole Brace now stand). And, most fundamentally, the local council must agree to remove an ancient covenant over Gay Meadow which restricts its use to purely sporting activities.

Frustrating though that covenant may yet prove, it does act as a poignant reminder not just of Shrewsbury's place in footballing history, but of local traditions in general. For old as Town are, the Gay Meadow is far older, having been used for outdoor plays, parties and other events since the late 16th century. Football, though, didn't come to the Meadow until 1910, after the local council had bought the freehold and invited Town to become permanent tenants. This the team were more than happy to do, since they had played at four different venues around Shrewsbury (including two at the old racecourse and another at the local barracks) in the preceding 25 years, and found none of them much use.

It was Gay Meadow that gave the local game a focus – something it had always lacked despite having taken a foothold in Shrewsbury in the early part of the 19th century. The first to play the game here were pupils at Shrewsbury public school, who formed a team to play matches against their counterparts at Eton, Harrow, Rugby, Winchester and elsewhere. Because each school tended to have its own rules (the first official set of laws would not be drawn up by Cambridge University until 1846), the players would agree beforehand on a compromise – sometimes holding and kicking an opponent would be allowed; on other occasions the game would be played on an almost totally non-contact basis.

Important as they were in helping to develop the game, however, the Shrewsbury School team did little to inspire the rest of the town. That would have to wait until 1876, when a club known as 'Shrewsbury Town' was formed by old boys who wanted to keep playing soccer after finishing their education. Their side was instantly successful, winning the Birmingham Senior Cup in 1879. But there was still little enthusiasm for the club, and it was long gone by the time a group of townsfolk got together to form a new club in 1886 – also using the name Shrewsbury Town. (Shrewsbury School old boys continue to play today under the name Old Salopians.)

Like their predecessors, the new Town were essentially an amateur side. Unlike the earlier team, they initially turned their back on competitions in the West Midlands and looked instead to Wales, entering both the Welsh League and the Welsh Cup, and winning the latter for the first time in 1891, thrashing Wrexham 5–2 in the final at Oswestry. The club continued to enter the Welsh Cup for some years, and after a long absence resumed doing so in 1973, notching up the last of five wins in 1985 before English teams were barred from entry at UEFA's insistence. Shrewsbury's league future, however, would inevitably lie in England once the club had turned professional in 1896.

Progress through the league pyramid was, to put it gently, gradual. After playing in the Birmingham League either side of World War I, Shrewsbury joined the Midland League, a competition they would make little impact on before winning their first title in 1938. Ten years later they celebrated the end of World War II by being crowned champions again, and in 1950 they were admitted to the Football League. It had been the club's tenth application, the previous nine having all been rejected on the (unofficial) grounds that Shrewsbury was too isolated to be worthy of consideration. Even the tenth attempt might not have been successful had the League not been expanding that year from 88 clubs to 92, with the two regional Third Divisions gaining two teams each.

Town were initially thrown into the Third Division (North), where they finished 20th at the end of their first season. They were then transferred to the southern section, where they remained in virtual anonymity until 1958 – when they became involuntary founder members of the new Fourth Division. There they may well have stayed, too, had Leicester City not allowed their inside-forward Arthur 'Gunner' Rowley to become player-manager at Gay Meadow. In addition to scoring 38 goals in his first season, Rowley galvanised the entire team with his determination – the result was a fourth-place finish and instant promotion to the Third Division in 1959.

Eighties hero – former boss Graham Turner

Rowley continued playing for Shrewsbury until 1965, and remained manager for another three years after that. By the time he left he'd scored 152 goals, making him the most prolific goalscorer in League history, and Town had just finished third, missing out on promotion to the Second Division by just two points. Rowley's departure, though, prevented the club from maintaining its upward trend. Managers Harry Gregg and Maurice Evans presided over five years of mediocrity before Town were relegated under Alan Durban in 1974.

Durban remained in his job and pulled the club straight back out of the Fourth Division, and the following year signed a young central defender, Colin Griffin, to plug Town's leaky defence. Griffin had been rejected as an apprentice by high-flying Derby but found the lower-pressure atmosphere of Gay Meadow more to his liking – he would be at the heart of the team which, under the guidance of Graham Turner, finally got Shrewsbury into the top half of the League for the first time in 1979. That year Town won the Third Division title and also reached the FA Cup quarter-finals for the first time.

Unlike the promotion side of 20 years earlier, which was based very much around Rowley's individual flair, Turner's had few stars and a knack of grinding out victories, making Gay Meadow, for all its charms, a notoriously hard place for opponents to come and play. With Ian Atkins making the midfield a battleground and Chic Bates and Steve Biggins despatching scoring chances with gleeful efficiency, Shrewsbury made a surprisingly comfortable home for themselves in the Second Division, and also reached the Cup quarter-finals again in 1982. The team's distinctive yellow-and-blue striped shirts – actually a departure from Town's traditional blue-and-white – became a regular fixture on television and for a time it even a tilt at the top flight seemed possible.

The decline began when Turner left for Aston Villa in 1984. Chic Bates took over, initially as player-manager, and enjoyed one more good season before Shrewsbury began to settle in the wrong half of the Second Division table. They were finally relegated under Ian McNeill in 1989, and three years later, during John Bond's typically unpredictable stint in the dugout, they went down again.

Bond's assistant, Fred Davies, took over as manager at the end of the 1992/93 season and led Shrewsbury to the Third Division title within a year. In 1996 Town reached Wembley for the first time, losing 2–1 to Rotherham in the Auto Windscreens Trophy final. Progress in the Second Division had been limited, though, and when Town were relegated in 1997, Davies paid with his job. His successor, Jake King, was a right-back in Graham Turner's side, but has so far been unable to emulate his mentor's success despite putting the emphasis on hard work and team spirit. Over the past two seasons, Shrewsbury have faced yet another paradox – gazing hopefully up at the play-offs, but knowing that any gamble could also plunge them into a battle for League survival.

Here we go!

From most corners of the country it's a fair old drive to Shrewsbury, but the picturesque town is worth the hike, and at least the roads themselves are good. **Motorists** will approach on the M54 which becomes the A5 just before Shrewsbury. Take the first exit, then the fourth exit at the next junction (signposted Town Centre) and follow this to another junction, where the third exit will take you into Abbey Foregate. Follow this road to the Abbey and you'll see a **car park** on the left – Gay Meadow is across the road under the railway bridge.

Shrewsbury **train station** is served by trains linking Birmingham with Wales and Chester (service hourly, journey time 1hr from New Street). There are also less frequent trains from Liverpool and Manchester via Crewe. Feasible evening departures exist for Crewe and Birmingham but not for London via the latter. Call ☎0345/484950 for the latest timings.

As you leave the station, turn left as if you were heading back in and follow the path past the disused platform to the ground, which is visible from the platform.

Just the ticket

Visiting fans can choose between terracing at the Station End or seating in the Station Stand, just around the corner away from the river. Shrewsbury have frozen their ticket prices three years in a row – standing £7, seating £10 – but there are no concessions.

Disabled visitors have a small area in the Station Stand corner. Book in advance on ☎01743/356316.

Swift half

The nearest pub to the ground is ***The Crown*** on Abbey Foregate, where home and away fans mix freely, real ale flows from the pumps and excellent bar meals are served (so long as they're not too busy). Families are also welcome here but may have more room for manoeuvre in the town centre at ***The Nag's Head*** on Wyle Cop.

Club merchandise

The **club shop** is behind the Centre Stand, just along from the Station Stand entrance. Fans were waiting with baited breath during summer 1999 for the rumoured return of Eighties-style yellow-and-blue striped shirts.

Barmy army

The anti-Welsh sentiment common in English border towns occasionally boils to the surface, but if there's going to be any trouble it'll be in town, not at Gay Meadow.

In print

The ***Shropshire Star*** newspaper belongs to the same group as the *Wolverhampton Express & Star* and so has more resources than you might think of a small-town paper – local football coverage is first-class. There are plenty of fanzines to choose from, including ***Three Lions*** (2 Pinewood Road, Quedgeley, Gloucester) and ***The Mighty Shrews*** (17 Priory Ridge, Shrewsbury, SY3 9EH), along with the new ***Meadow Mouthpiece*** (10 Clifford Road, Market Drayton, TF9 1NA), the journal of the official supporters' club.

The seminal book about Shrewsbury is Mike Jones' heavyweight ***Breathe On 'Em Salop***, available from the club shop at £14.95 plus £3.50 postage and packing.

Good to talk – Bond (left) and Davies, 1993

On air

Local commercial station ***Beacon Radio*** (103.1 FM) fights it out with the BBC's ***Radio Shropshire*** (95.0 FM), the former offering a post-match football phone-in..

In the net

There's no official site but ***ShrewsWeb***, which has been flying the Shrewsbury Town flag on the net since January 1997, does receive some assistance from the club, while also acting as an umbrella site for various supporters' groups, fund-raising activities and the like. All in all a complete online resource for the club, at: www.shrewsburytown.co.uk/.

The local ***Shropshire Star*** newspaper has its own site at www.shropshire-online.com.

Southampton

Formation	1885 as Southampton St Mary's
Stadium	The Dell, Milton Road, Southampton, SO15 2XH. ☎01703/220505
Ground capacity	15,000
First-choice colours	Red-and-white stripes
Major honours	Third Division champions 1960; Third Division (South) champions 1922; FA Cup winners 1976
Position 1998/99	17th in Premiership

You don't have to be paranoid to support Southampton, but it probably helps. The evidence for the prosecution is more than merely circumstantial – there is definitely somebody, somewhere, out to get the Saints. Why else would it have taken the club more than a decade to get planning permission for a new stadium? Why else would the team have such a capacity for self-destruction? And why else would their best player, one of the most gifted playmakers of his generation and the best penalty-taker in the country, be sitting at home while England were going out of the 1998 World Cup after yet another shoot-out failure?

Southampton are used to beginning every season as everyone's favourites to be relegated, used to having to make ends meet because their tiny ground prevents them from capitalising on their Premiership status, used to surviving by the skin of their teeth on the last day of the campaign. But, one of these days, it would be nice if they could have a little bit of luck, rather than having to make their own.

They've been making it steadily down at the Dell since 1978, when Southampton won promotion from the Second Division. The 21 years of top-flight football that have followed haven't all been a struggle, but since the Premiership came into being in 1992, the Dell's limited capacity and the club's relatively small catchment area have made it increasingly hard for Southampton to stay with the pace.

Of course, when you're fighting against all the odds, it helps to have God on your side. Matt Le Tissier, a living deity among the latter-day Saints, may not always be of the same mind as the management, may not always be fully fit, may not always deliver the goods as consistently as he once did, but there is no doubt that he has almost single-handedly kept Premiership football at the Dell – his refusal to move to a bigger club as perplexing to his suitors as it has been refreshing to Southampton's fans. England's loss has been their gain.

The last time the team were doing anything other than surviving was at the start of the Nineties, when a lean, confident teenager by the name of Alan Shearer kept getting on the end of Le Tissier's repertoire of chips, lobs, through balls and crosses. But, unlike Le Tiss, Shearer had no wish to spend the rest of his career playing in front of 15,000 fans, no matter how adoring their worship. Seven seasons of Premiership football later, the £3.3million Southampton received for Shearer from Blackburn in July 1992 seems absurdly paltry. Yet at the time it was a British record fee, and Southampton would probably have been happy with half of it. The club was well-used to selling its brightest young stars, Shearer being only the latest in a long line.

Whether Southampton can break out of that cycle will depend on how quickly they can leave the Dell. For the great irony, now that planning permission has finally been granted for a new stadium on the site of a former gasworks in the St Mary's area of town, is that the club now has to find the money before it can proceed. Another two or three like Alan Shearer – or a Kevin Davies, even – would come in handy.

Assuming the move does go ahead, it will be very much a case of Southampton going back to their roots. For the club was formed by members of the St Mary's Church YMCA in 1885. Many of the founders had already played football together as Deanery FC, formed five years earlier. But now they wanted to give their new club broader appeal, so they settled on the name Southampton St Mary's.

Links with the church remained strong for some time – the club's first president was the Rev A B Sole, curate of St Mary's, and the team quickly acquired their nickname of the 'Saints'. Yet within a few months of the team's formation, their official title had been shortened to plain 'Southampton'. In the early days the team used a variety of different grounds, including one that had a public footpath running right the way down the middle. In 1886 they moved to the Antelope Ground, former home of Hampshire County Cricket Club, and so-called because Hants had formed at the *Antelope Inn*. It was while here, in 1894, that the club turned professional and joined the Southern League, having outgrown all the local league competitions. A year later, Southampton entered the FA Cup for the first time.

Confusingly, having played at Hampshire's former home, in 1896 Southampton moved to the cricket club's new one, the County Ground on Northlands Road. This was a more sophisticated ground, and cost correspondingly more to rent. But the team's form on the pitch soon made it worthwhile – the Saints ended their first season there by lifting the Southern League championship for the first time, retained it a year later, and became the first non-League side to reach an FA Cup semi-final for a decade.

The town may not have been a footballing hotbed to match those in Nottinghamshire, south Yorkshire or Lancashire, but its very isolation, coupled with the club's total domination of the local landscape, gave Southampton a strength few opponents seemed capable of recognising until it was too late.

Once again, the club was in danger of outgrowing its home. But in 1898 Southampton enjoyed one huge, and hugely significant, stroke of luck. Local fish merchant and Saints

Sun of God – Matt Le Tissier, saviour of the Saints

Staying fit for the fight – winger Terry Paine, midway through his 808 appearances, 1965

supporter George Thomas ploughed £10,000 into buying and developing the site of a new ground, to be used by Southampton and Southampton alone. Whereas one of the club's early pitches had a path running through the middle, this one had a babbling brook – hence, perhaps, its romantic name, the Dell. Thomas paid for the stream to be covered over and, once the first stands and other luxurious facilities had been built, he charged Southampton only £250 a year in rent.

Suitably inspired, the club rose to new heights, winning a third successive Southern League title, and reaching a first FA Cup final in 1900. The game, played in front of nearly 70,000 at Crystal Palace, was lost 4–0 to Bury, but within two years Southampton were back for another, this time against the Sheffield United side of Foulkes and Common. In between times, Tottenham Hotspur had set a fabulous precedent by becoming the first Southern League team to beat a Football League side in the final. Like Southampton, they had faced Sheffield United. Like Southampton, they forced a replay. But there, alas, the similarity ended, for while Spurs won their replay at Burnden Park, Southampton lost theirs, complaining of a lack of atmosphere as only 33,000 turned up at Crystal Palace, compared with more than twice that for the first match.

Still, Southampton had proved their point. The Southern League was a force to be reckoned with and, as its most successful side at the time, so were they. Two more championships followed in 1903 and 1904, and the future looked rosy. Yet the team soon faced a dilemma. Geographical isolation on the south coast made them unlikely candidates for Football League membership, while Southern League football was becoming too predictable to draw big crowds. By 1906 the club was heavily overdrawn at the bank, and a relentless rise in stature came to a temporary halt.

In fact, there were would be no more significant progress until after World War I, when the top division of the Southern League was more or less absorbed into the new Third Division of the Football

League in 1920. This became the Third Division (South) a year later, and Southampton were its first champions, finishing ahead of Plymouth on goal average.

Promotion to the Second Division gave the team a chance to flex their muscles in more exalted company, and Southampton were far from disgraced at the new level. Yet rather than enhance the side with new signings, the club's board concentrated their energies – and their cash – on improving the Dell. They bought the freehold from George Thomas' widow in 1926, built a new stand, and enlarged an existing one. Then, shortly after Southampton's last home game of the 1928/29 season, the older of the two stands was destroyed by fire, probably caused by a discarded cigarette butt.

Now the club's strategy lay in tatters. Rebuilding the burnt out stand put Southampton a further £10,000 in debt and, just at the point where the team looked capable of mounting a bid for promotion to the First Division, a freeze was imposed on incoming transfers. Locally, the initiative had been gifted to Portsmouth, for while Southampton were to spend the Thirties languishing in mid-table of the Second Division, their rivals along the coast would be serving up top-flight football to vast crowds at Fratton Park and reaching three FA Cup finals into the bargain.

As if to emphasise the point, during World War II Nazi bombers targeting the nearby dockyards blew an 18-foot crater in the Dell's pitch, causing a culvert underneath to burst and the waters of the former babbling brook to flood the turf. Just as Manchester United were temporarily forced to play at Maine Road and Nottingham Forest took up a brief residence at Meadow Lane, so Southampton resumed peacetime football at Fratton.

Happily, the damage was soon repaired and the Saints were free to capitalise on the post war attendance boom at the Dell. The famous 'chocolate box' elevated terraces were built over the Milton Road end to add a few hundred more spaces, as crowds of 25,000-plus became the norm. Yet the team's popularity was not mirrored

The Saints who stole the FA Cup – Steele, Blyth and Rodrigues, Wembley, 1976

by achievements on the pitch. Despite the prolific goalscoring of Charlie Wayman, Southampton failed to gain promotion to the First Division by a point in 1949, and on goal average a year later. But by 1953 the team had moved in the other direction, back down to the Third Division (South), where they were to remain anchored until the dawn of the Sixties.

Again, Southampton's failure was only compounded by Portsmouth's success in the same period. But then, just as Pompey were dropping out of the First Division, the Saints began to climb. In 1960 they were crowned champions of the newly nationalised Third Division, with Derek Reeves netting 39 of their 106 goals. Three years later, 68,000 were at Villa Park to see Southampton edged out of an FA Cup semi-final 1–0 by Matt Busby's Manchester United. Finally, in 1966, Saints entered the top flight for the first time after finishing runners-up to Manchester City in the Second Division.

The man at the heart of the transformation was Southampton's manager, Ted Bates. A Norolk-born inside-forward who'd been rejected by his local club Norwich City, he'd gone on to play more than 200 League games for Southampton either side of World War II, before being offered the manager's job in 1955. Knowing the club so well, he built an instant rapport with the players but, unlike some of his predecessors, was not content for Southampton to drift. The adventurous football Bates advocated made his team top-scorers for most of their Second Division life, and while the attitude would occasionally get the Saints into trouble, it paid dividends.

There was to be no let-up, either, once promotion to the First Division had been achieved. With Welsh striker Ron Davies arriving from Norwich to partner Martin Chivers upfront, Jimmy Gabriel signed from Everton to provide width on the opposite flank from the evergreen Terry Paine, and a young forward by the name of Mick Channon coming through the apprentice ranks, Southampton in the late Sixties were a sight for sore eyes. In 1969, a seventh-place finish and complex Fairs' Cup eligibility rules saw European football come to the Dell for the first time, with Davies, Paine and Channon looking as though they'd been playing against continental opposition all their lives – it took eventual winners Newcastle to silence them in the third round.

Bates finally stepped down in 1973 to make way for the respected young manager Lawrie McMenemy. Softly spoken and always genial in public, the new man seemed an unlikely motivator, and his first task was to get Southampton back into the top flight after relegation in 1973/74. McMenemy had inherited an ageing squad but, rather than wait for new players to come through the Dell's limited youth system, he brought in a number of experienced players such as centre-half Mel Blyth from Crystal Palace, the former Wolves and Manchester United midfielder Jim McCalliog and former Chelsea striker Peter Osgood. If anything, McMenemy overdid it – promotion would not be achieved until many of the old guard had departed in 1979. But before

Decisive influence – Lawrie McMenemy, deep in thought

then, his side gave football in Southampton its finest hour. For once, the Saints enjoyed the rub of the green on their way to the 1976 FA Cup final, the club's first in 74 years. In the quarter-finals they went to Bradford City, then a Fourth Division side, and won with a controversial free-kick. In the semi-finals, while the newspapers joked that top-flight Derby and Manchester United should borrow Wembley's Twin Towers for their game at Hillsborough, Southampton were beating Third Division Crystal Palace 2–0 at

The original Dell boy – Mick Channon in action, 1980

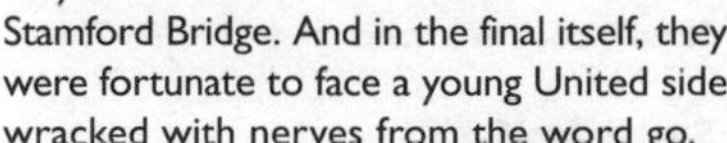

Stamford Bridge. And in the final itself, they were fortunate to face a young United side wracked with nerves from the word go.

Nothing, however, could detract from McMenemy's achievement. His team played a masterful counter-attacking game for 83 minutes before full-back Bobby Stokes deceived United 'keeper Alex Stepney with a long-range shot and won the Cup for Southampton.

The triumph provided the impetus the club needed to win back a place in the First Division, and to reach Wembley again for a League Cup final defeat by Nottingham Forest in 1979, with Chris Nicholl and Ivan Golac outstanding. Yet McMenemy believed he could go further. At a press conference on the eve of the 1980/81 season, he unveiled his latest signing – Kevin Keegan, twice European footballer of the year, and anxious to make a mark on the English game once more after a spell in the *Bundesliga* with Hamburg. With Keegan's help, Southampton became regulars in the upper half of the First Division and European football returned to the Dell. And although Keegan had left for Newcastle by 1982, another key England international, goalkeeper Peter Shilton, arrived to steer the Saints to within three points of League champions Liverpool in 1983/84.

After McMenemy stepped down in 1985, a succession of managers kept Southampton in the top flight without ever quite wielding the same hypnotic influence. Chris Nicholl's side reached a League Cup semi-final in 1987, and with the advent of Le Tissier and the three Wallace brothers – Danny, Rod and Ray – gained a reputation as one of the most entertaining teams in the country. Nicholl's successor, Ian Branfoot, made little impact save for the nurturing and subsequent sale of both Shearer and goalkeeper Tim Flowers, and his dismissal in 1994 paved the way for a return to the Dell by former club captain Alan Ball as manager, and by McMenemy as director of football. The partnership seemed to be working well until Ball left for Manchester City – his replacement, the club's former youth-team coach Dave Merrington, never got to grips with the job.

Another new dawn appeared to break when Graeme Souness saved the club from what appeared imminent relegation in 1996/97, but he left for Torino at the end of the season and McMenemy resigned soon after.

Teenage kicks – Alan Shearer, 1992

After that, it fell to the former Stockport County manager Dave Jones to keep Southampton's ship afloat. He managed it for two seasons, but on the eve of the 1999/2000 campaign, the bookies made him favourite to become the first Premiership manager to lose his job. Another great confidence-booster, from a world that seems to have it in for Southampton.

Here we go!

Motorists will almost certainly approach along the M3, which divides into two branches of the M27 as it reaches Southampton. Both carriageways lead to the A33, which should be followed across one roundabout. At the next one, take the second exit, bearing right, along Winchester Road. Take the first exit at the next roundabout, then straight over a mini-roundabout down Hill Lane. Go straight across at the first set of lights and you'll see the Dell to the left at the next junction, where Hill Lane meets Archers Road and Howard Road. There are some informal **car parks** off these roads, but arrive early to be sure of a space.

Southampton Central **train station** gets direct trains from London Waterloo (three trains per hour, minimum journey time 1hr 15mins), as well as local services to Reading, Bournemouth, Portsmouth and Brighton. For evening games, the last departure for Waterloo is at 2250, but for the latest timings call ☎0345/484950.

From the station, it's about a 20min walk – just follow the red-and-white shirts.

Just the ticket

For as long as Southampton remain at the Dell, all Premiership fixtures will be all-ticket. For **visiting fans** there are just 1,500 seats at the Archers Road end of the East Stand – check with your own club regarding availability, and book well in advance to be on the safe side. Ticket prices in 1999/2000 were expected to be £23 for an upper-tier seat, £21 for the lower tier, with no concessions for visitors. There are spaces for 16 **disabled visitors** in the lower tier of the West Stand – book in advance on ☎01703/667547.

Swift half

The pubs around the Dell all tend to welcome visiting fans, although ***The Winston*** has the greatest concentration of them, since it's opposite the Archers Road end of the ground. It's a large pub, but with the pre-matchday crush, it needs to be. Real ale, bar meals and a welcome for families are all on the menu.

Alternatively try ***The Golden Lion*** on Northlands Road or ***The Cowherds*** on The Avenue, the main route in to the centre of town.

Club merchandise

After a spell of being run by a third-party company, Southampton's merchandising operation has now been brought back in-house as the club saves hard for its stadium move. Alas, the new regime didn't get off to the best of starts when the **club shop** on Hill Lane was broken into during summer 1999 and hundreds of pounds' worth of material was stolen, including the away kit the players were due to wear on a pre-season tour of Norway.

The shop should be properly stocked again by the time you read this, with *Great Escape* T-shirts celebrating Premiership survival at £9.99 (kids' sizes £7.99) and Southampton's bold new home shirt, more white-and-red than red-and-white, at £40 (kids' sizes £30).

Barmy army

The 'Skates' of Portsmouth still excite the most ridicule at the Dell despite the continuing gap in status between the two clubs – one reason why trouble has been so rare at Southampton in recent seasons.

In print

The locally published ***Echo*** produces a Saturday evening 'pink', normally available from around 5.30pm in town.

The official club magazine, ***Saints***, has had a makeover and gone monthly, but has little to interest non-Saints fans other than a column by the irrepressible Mick Channon.

The fanzines are ***Red Stripe*** (PO Box 72, Salisbury, SP2 8RD) and ***The Ugly Inside*** (PO Box 67, Hedge End, SO30 4ZF).

David Bull's new book, ***Dell Diamond*** (£18.99), tells the story of Ted Bates' 'first 60 seasons with the Saints', from promising young inside-forward before World War II to club president in the Nineties.

On air

BBC Radio Solent (999 AM) offers extensive coverage of all matters Southampton, with a pre-match phone-in on Saturdays only.

In the net

Southampton's **official website** is nothing fancy but has everything you need to see – news, club info and history, plus an expanding e-commerce area. Best of all, it has the feel of being a fan-run site. Find it at: www.saintsfc.co.uk.

Most complete of the unofficial offerings is ***Marching In***, with no heavy graphics but, again, lashings of content, regularly updated and delivered with an admirable sense of humour at: www.saintsfans.com/marchingin.

Matt Le Tissier has a page dedicated to him at: www.cpcomp.force9.co.uk/tissfiles/index.html. And from Russia comes a unique joint unofficial homepage for Southampton and **Spartak Moscow** at: www.lgg.ru/~RedWhiteClub.

Southend United

Formation	1906
Stadium	Roots Hall, Victoria Avenue, Southend-on-Sea, SS2 6NQ. ☎01702/304050
Ground capacity	12,300
First-choice colours	Blue and yellow
Major honours	Fourth Division champions 1981
Position 1998/99	18th in Third Division

The turn of the millennium sees Southend United not quite in the best of health. Having enjoyed the most enthralling period of their entire history at the beginning of the Nineties, by the end of the decade the team were looking over their shoulder at the Conference, escaping the drop only after changing their manager within months of the end of the 1998/99 season. Off the pitch, meanwhile, the sale and leaseback of the club's Roots Hall stadium and training ground saw Vic Jobson's majority shareholding transferred to a new holding company, and a new chairman, John Main, taking over the reins. But no sooner had the leaseback deal allowed United to pay off their commercial debts, than the club was hit with a barrage of litigation, including court actions from two former managers, Ronnie Whelan and Colin Murphy, who were both claiming compensation. Once these and other claims had been settled, Main had no choice but to bring forward a new share offer to fill the club's empty coffers...

For a seaside town as brash, breezy and in-yer-face as Southend, United is a modest club that has got where it is today through hard graft and the dedication of its supporters. The town loves its football, but the proximity of London, less than an hour away by train or car, means many fans look toward Upton Park rather than Roots Hall as their Mecca of the beautiful game.

Yet, like Brighton & Hove Albion, Southend United inspire tremendous devotion from the small band of supporters they do have. How else was the club able to build its ground from scratch in the Fifties, and how else did it sustain its brief but boisterous stint in the upper half of the League between 1991 and 1997?

Both achievements were remarkable, and not just because Southend are a small-town team with a limited catchment area and consequently restricted potential for future growth. Historically the town was a latecomer to senior football, and for many, many years after United had been formed and admitted to the Football League, the team's participation in it seemed almost token, so limited was the scale of their successes.

More than most, the club has a genuine reason for calling itself 'United'. For at the turn of the century, when competitive football first began to take a grip on the town, there were many clubs competing for the attention of the Southend public, the vast majority of them amateur in the best south-east tradition. The most successful of these clubs was Southend Athletic, who played in the grounds of an 18th century house, Roots Hall, in the suburb of Prittlewell, just inland from the seafront. But since neither Athletic nor any of the other clubs had the resources to develop further, they joined forces in 1906 to form a professional team, Southend United.

The board then made an inspired appointment in recruiting Bob Jack as the new club's first secretary-manager. As ambitious for the club as he was inspiring to the players, Jack obtained immediate membership of the Second Division of the Southern League even though United had no track record, and three seasons later his side was admitted into the FA Cup for the first time.

Essex boys – training in the countryside inland from Southend-on-Sea, 1998

By the eve of World War I, Southend were in the top division of the Southern League – a handy place to be once hostilities were over, since it effectively became the Third Division of the Football League in 1920, and the Third Division (South) 12 months after that.

During the conflict, however, United's ground had been turned into allotments to aid the war effort, so to go with their new League status, the team also needed a new home. This was to be at the Kursaal, Southend's famous seafront amusement park, where a new pitch was laid especially for the club in 1919. The facilities were nothing special, but the proximity of funfair rides and the other trappings of a Twenties seaside resort made the Kursaal popular with both home and away fans. There were few ups and downs on the field of play, however, as United spent their entire 14-year tenure of the ground stuck in the League's third tier, their best campaign being 1931/32, when they finished third behind Fulham and Reading.

In 1934 the club moved again, this time to a newly built arena called the Southend Stadium. This was a serious multi-sports facility, with a greyhound track lain around the pitch. The stands were bigger than at the Kursaal, but fans complained – as they always do – that they were too far from the action, so after another five seasons of soft-pedalling in the Third Division (South), the United board were looking to move house yet again after World War II.

Remarkably, they found themselves back at Roots Hall, where the site of United's first ground had been excavated for sandstone, leaving a large hollow just the right size for a football pitch. With much of the money – not to mention the hard labour – coming from members of the Supporters' Club, Southend were ready to play their first match at the new ground on 20 August 1955, against Norwich City. It would be some years before Roots Hall MkII had spectator accommodation on all four sides, but the club felt immediately at home there (even though the land was owned by the council) and so, funnily enough, did the players – despite a rather troublesome pitch which, at one stage, had to be reinforced with cockleshells from the beach to improve drainage.

With long-serving stars such as Scots full-back Sandy Anderson, Northern Ireland international Sammy McCrory and

Shrimper Stan – Collymore in full flow, March 1993

As the team bobbed along aimlessly, so the paucity of United's supporter base became more worrying. A record 31,000 were drawn to an FA Cup third-round tie at home to Liverpool in January 1979, but many of them were either 'Essex Reds' or curious locals of no fixed footballing loyalty. By 1984, after the latest of many relegations to the Fourth Division, average gates in the League had fallen to under 3,000. Perhaps unfortunately for the club's long-term future, this did not deter local entrepreneur Anton Johnson from sinking his claws into United – in little more than 12 months he ran up debts of more than £1million, before his labyrinthine network of share dealings involving several other clubs led to his being banned by the League. Control of the club then passed to Vic Jobson, a property developer who first attempted to sell Roots Hall to a supermarket chain, but who ultimately settled for the sale of a patch of land behind the ground's South Bank end for housing. There was then further talk of relocating the club to a new stadium out-of-town, or possibly even to Basildon, midway between Southend and London.

goal-hungry centre-forward Roy Hollis, Southend became one of the most attractive sides in the Third Division (South) in the late Fifties. Their smart football got them precisely nowhere, but the club comfortably made the cut into the new national Third Division in 1958, and remained there until relegation eight years later.

At the time this seemed only a temporary blip. But Southend's squad had been allowed to age together, and that drop to the Fourth Division in 1966 was to be followed by an extended period of shuttling between the bottom two sections of the League, lasting throughout the Seventies and for most of the Eighties.

Ironically, however, just as the chairman was contemplating wrenching the club away from its Roots, as it were, the team rose from their slumbers and became, perhaps for the first time, a focus around which the whole of Southend could rally. After relegation to the Fourth Division in 1989, former Chelsea defender Dave Webb led a young but cultured side straight back up at the first attempt. Dean Austin, Justin Edinburgh and Spencer Prior formed an inexperienced yet confident defensive unit, while upfront, the more mature instincts of David Crown proved too hot for Fourth Division markers to handle.

Twelve months later, despite the loss of Edinburgh to Tottenham (Austin would follow in his footsteps the following year) and the blooding of a new strikeforce of Andy Ansah and Brett Angell, Webb worked his magic again, and Southend attained a second straight promotion. For the first time in its history, the town had a team in the top half of the League.

Remarkably, Southend would have as many managers as they had seasons in the Second (later First) Division, as Webb, Colin Murphy, Barry Fry, Peter Taylor, Steve Thompson and Ronnie Whelan all enjoyed – or endured – a spell in the Roots Hall dugout. Fry's whirlwind stint lasted only a matter of months, but did wonders both for the club's finances and its goals-scored column, with Stan Collymore arriving from Crystal Palace for £750,000 in November 1992, and then, after averaging a goal every other game, being sold to Nottingham Forest in July the following year for £3.5million – a remarkable piece of transfer business, even by Fry's standards.

The decline began when former Liverpool midfielder Whelan sustained a knee injury which ended his playing career in 1996. Unable to wield the same influence from the sidelines, he was dismissed following Southend's relegation to the Second Division at the end of the 1996/97 season. His successor, Alvin Martin, could do no better, overseeing a second relegation in 1998, and departing two-thirds of the way through the 1998/99 season as United contemplated the possibility of a three-year freefall from the First Division into the Conference.

Happily, former York City manager Alan Little arrived to steer the troubled craft to safety, and with all debts apparently cleared, the new boardroom regime was pinning its hopes on its share issue as a means of re-floating Southend's ambitions. If the same spirit among the fans that helped build Roots Hall 45 years ago can be harnessed as effectively again, then the issue should be a success. Whether those same fans will be as closely involved with the building of a new stadium remains to be seen, though.

Jobson's legacy – Eighties flats overlook the south end of Roots Hall, where the Kop once stood

Here we go!

Finding Roots Hall couldn't be simpler for **motorists**. Simply exit the M25 at junction 29 onto the A127, signposted Southend. Stay on this road until it becomes Victoria Avenue in Prittlewell, and you'll see Roots Hall on the right. (Note – if you hit the seafront, you've come too far, so double back the way you've just come and the ground will be on your left.) There's no car park but **street parking** is easy enough in the residential streets around Roots Hall.

Southend is served by two separate train lines from London. Services from Fenchurch Street are quicker, but terminate at Southend Central in the town centre, a fair way from the ground. You'll actually save time by taking a slower **Southend Victoria train** from London Liverpool Street. The nearest station to Roots Hall is **Prittlewell**, one stop before Victoria – check that your train is calling there on the departure board at Liverpool Street.

There are late departures for evening games on both lines, but call ☎0345/484950 to check the latest timings. From Prittlewell station, turn right onto East Street and right again onto Victoria Avenue – the ground is across the road.

Just the ticket

Visiting fans are accommodated at the north end of the ground, in the Universal Cycles Stand, where there are nearly 4,000 seats, some with rather poor views. Ticket prices in 1999/2000 are expected to be £10 adults, £4 concessions if your club offers them to away fans.

Disabled visitors have spaces in the West Stand – book in advance on ☎01702/304090.

Swift half

Visiting fans tend to go for one (or both) of two options – a pint near the ground before kick-off at the ***Golden Lion*** on Victoria Avenue or the ***Nelson*** on North Road, both less than a 5min walk from Roots Hall; or a jaunt along the seafront afterwards, where there are plenty of eating and drinking venues – respect signs discouraging football colours.

Club merchandise

Introducing amber or yellow trim to Southend's traditional royal-blue shirts was one of Vic Jobson's innovations and has gone down well with fans. See the latest design at the **club shop** (☎01702/601351) behind the East Stand.

Barmy army

Forget all the stories about Essex being rough – Southend, at least, is generally welcoming despite the influx of daytrippers and stag-partygoers at weekends.

In print

The ***Evening Echo*** is the paper local fans turn to for news from Roots Hall, but it doesn't publish on Saturday evenings.

The only fanzine at the time of writing was ***What's The Story, Southend Glory*** (PO Box 1930, Leigh-on-Sea, SS9 1TN).

On air

BBC Radio Essex (95.3 FM) offers decent coverage of Southend with previews and reports on matchdays.

In the net

There's no **official website** but Southend fans have managed to create a sizeable internet community of their own. Pick of the bunch is probably ***SUFC Online*** at: www.angelfire.com/on2/SUFC.

There are two online fanzines. ***Pier Pressure*** is at: www.angelfire.com/id/pierpressure; while ***What's The Story, Southend Glory*** (see *In print* above) is at: welcome.to/WTS.Online.

Stockport County

Formation	1883 as Heaton Norris Rovers
Stadium	Edgeley Park, Hardcastle Road, Stockport, SK3 9DD. ☎0161/286 8888
Ground capacity	11,500
First-choice colours	Blue and white
Major honours	Third Division (North) champions 1922, 1937; Fourth Division champions 1967
Position 1998/99	16th in First Division

After decades of gimmickry aimed at trying to drag support away from the big Manchester clubs, Stockport County have been enjoying their brightest period for decades as a result of keeping things simple. The team play a no-nonsense style, the ground is small and welcoming, and the name of the local brewer is plastered across the fronts of the shirts. Yet there they are, entering the new millennium as a First Division side, playing alongside the likes of Birmingham, Wolves, Bolton and, of course, Manchester City, a club traditionally well-supported in Stockport.

Never mind the ball – Kevin Francis (right) causes havoc

Fans of City and United often used to say people were mad to follow County, even if they came from Stockport. For many years, it seemed the board were mad to be attempting to run the club, stuck as it was in the shadow of two footballing giants. Even the team's nickname, 'Hatters', suggested being a few sandwiches short of a picnic. Hence the proliferation of schemes to try to boost the team's profile – from dancing girls and club songs in the Sixties, to dressing the players in replica Argentina shirts after the 1978 World Cup. You name it, County tried it. None of it worked.

Part of the mistake, perhaps, was to see the club only in terms of its rivals, rather than as a focus for local interest in its own right. For one of the things that has helped Stockport raise their sights during the Nineties has been their single-mindedness. Never mind what's going on at Old Trafford or Maine Road – we'll do our own thing, and live with the consequences. At the end of the decade, fans

Descent into dissent – County's Paul Cook gets his marching orders in the FA Cup, 1999

were justifiably proud, not just of their team but also of their town – which, for all that it is tempting to compare it with the likes of Bury, Oldham and Rochdale, has always had its own, distinctly Cheshire character. The 'County' part of the club's name celebrates this distinction, having been introduced after Stockport was accorded the status of a county borough, back in 1889. Prior to that, the club had been known as Heaton Norris Rovers, after the district of the town in which it was first formed.

The story began in 1883, when members of the Wycliffe Congregational Chapel (which still stands today on the A6 near the town centre) decided to form a football team. Under the name Heaton Norris Rovers they began playing at a recreation ground close to the chapel, although the earliest recorded result is of a friendly against Stalybridge on 11 October 1884, won 1–0, and played as a 'home' fixture at a cricket ground at Brinksway. A year later, a rival team playing under the title Heaton Norris were formed but, after playing a couple of derby matches, the two clubs decided to merge during the 1885/86 season. Initially the merged team played as Heaton Norris Rovers, but in 1888 the 'Rovers' bit was dropped. Two years later the team became known as Stockport County, and in 1891 they joined the Football Combination to play competitive league games for the first time. They progressed to the Lancashire League in 1894, having entered the FA Cup for the first time a year earlier.

Victories over Newton Heath (later Manchester United), Ardwick (City) and the great Bury side of the day encouraged County to apply for membership of the Football League in 1899, but this was declined, and Loughborough, Chesterfield and Middlesbrough were admitted instead. Undaunted, the team won the Lancashire League title for the first time in 1900 and then, 12 months after their original application, they were admitted to the Football League along with Barnsley and Blackpool.

Life in the League, however, was not exactly a bed of roses. After four seasons of finishing in the bottom three of the Second Division, and with money always a worry, County had their fourth successive application for re-election rejected.

Part of the club's problem had been the lack of a permanent home, the team having played on at least six different grounds since 1883. This nomadic existence was brought to an end in 1902, when County moved in with the local rugby club at Edgeley Park. Even this did nothing to improve the team's form initially, but after the rugby club folded a couple of years later, things began to look up. Stockport were re-elected to the League after only a season away in 1905, and 12 months later the team had posted a tenth-place finish in the Second Division – a club record high that would remain unsurpassed until 1998.

In the years before and after World War I, County's board concentrated on improving facilities at Edgeley Park, while the team began to struggle once more. Relegation to the new Third Division (North) in 1921 was followed by immediate promotion, and England goalkeeper Harry Hardy managed to keep Stockport up in the Second before departing for Everton – without him, the team went down again in 1926.

Aside from one all too brief visit to the Second Division just prior to World War II, County would now remain in Third Division obscurity all the way through to 1959 – when they were relegated to the Fourth. By 1964, the club's finances had deteriorated to such an extent that Edgeley Park had to be sold to the local council, who then leased it back to County. It was in this era that the emphasis shifted to PR, the board taking a leaf out of Jimmy Hill's book at Coventry by instigating spurious pre-match 'entertainment', specially written club songs and an extensive advertising campaign in the local media. Quite what Harry Hardy, who continued to pay to get into Edgeley Park as a spectator until his death in 1969, made of it all is a matter for conjecture. But at least he was spared the trauma of 1974, when local government reorganisation saw Stockport moved out of Cheshire and into the new metropolitan area of Greater Manchester. In an attempt to move with the times, the board floated the idea of renaming County 'Manchester South FC' – a move which, had it gone ahead, might just have sounded the death-knell for a club that needed all the local pride it could get, as crowds dipped below the 3,000 mark and applications for re-election became the norm.

The 'Manchester South' plan was soon consigned to the dustbin of history, where it belonged. But County's problems were only just beginning. New safety regulations after the Bradford fire of 1985 resulted in much of Edgeley Park being either closed off or demolished altogether, and the cost of this work helped to tip the club to the edge of liquidation. This was averted when, in 1988, property developer Brendan Elwood acquired a controlling interest in the club. Initially his plan was to sell what remained of Edgeley Park as building land,

Megson gets mad – then the club gets even

but by the early Nineties, a renaissance on the pitch had persuaded him that County should get closer to their roots, rather than move away from them.

The origins of the man who engineered the transformation were about as far from Cheshire as it was possible to imagine. Team manager Danny Bergara, born in Uruguay, arrived in 1989 and immediately turned his inexperience of English lower-division football to his – and Stockport's – advantage. Whereas so many of his predecessors had approached the job with a pre-conceived notion of County as stugglers, Bergara took one look at the squad and decided it was capable of more than merely surviving in the Fourth Division.

The response from the players was dramatic. The goalscoring of Brett Angell powered Stockport into the play-offs in 1990, and though they were beaten in the semi-finals by Chesterfield, the following year they finished runners-up in the Fourth Division and went up automatically. Angell departed for Southend, but in giant target man Kevin Francis, County had a more than adequate replacement. In each of the three seasons from 1991/92, Bergara's side made the play-offs, only to lose each time.

The Uruguayan finally departed in 1995, but his replacement, Dave Jones, kept the ball rolling – in 1996/97 Stockport finished as runners-up in what was now the Second Division to earn a place in the upper half of the English professional game for the first time since 1938. The team also reached the semi-finals of the League Cup, the club's best-ever performance in either of the two major Cup competitions, but one which would have far-reaching consequences, since Southampton, one of the teams County beat en route to the semis, would soon snatch Jones away from Edgeley Park.

In the summer of 1997, Stockport poached Gary Megson from Blackpool to be their new manager, and his first season in charge couldn't have turned out better – an eighth-place finish in the First Division, a placing that finally broke that record set back in 1906, and which confirmed County as a club that meant business, regardless of the level.

Megson's second year at the helm, 1998/99, ended with his acrimonious dismissal by Elwood, even though Stockport were still sitting pretty in mid-table. But with drawings at the planning office for a new Railway Stand (and accompanying hotel) to match the superb Cheadle End opposite, the prospect of a change in management style from Andy Kilner, and a band of supporters whose conviction is growing steadily along with their numbers, County's unlikely journey may yet have a few miles to run. And there's not a dancing girl in sight.

Here we go!

If you've time on your side – and it isn't the middle of winter – you can approach Stockport via the scenic route over the Peak District. However, most **motorists** will arrive via the M60 motorway (junction 19 off the M6 via A556 and M56, junction 18 off the M62) which runs close to Edgeley Park. Exit the M60 at junction 1 onto the A560 and follow the signs onto the B5465 Edgeley Road – the ground is on the right, just off Dale Street.

Street parking is getting trickier by the season, and with no car park at the ground, the best bet might be to leave your car in the town centre and walk from there. The local cinema, just behind the train station, has a large car park (60p) that rarely fills up. From it, walk back under the station, up the slip road and turn left into Station Road. At the roundabout ahead, go straight on and follow the road around to the right – you'll see the ground on the left as you come around the corner along Mercian Way. Allow 15mins.

Stockport **train station** has direct trains between Birmingham New Street and Manchester Piccadilly via Stoke (hourly, journey 1hr 30mins from Birmingham, 15mins from Manchester). There are also direct services from Sheffield, but fans coming from London Euston should change at Crewe. Check the latest timings on ☎0345/484950. From the station, follow the directions above.

Just the ticket
Until County's bold new plans for the Railway End are accepted, **visiting fans** will find a windswept open terrace there – all very nostalgic, but warm, weatherproof clothing is a must. Ticket prices in 1998/99 were adults £13, concessions £6 on a reciprocal basis only.

Disabled visitors have a small area in front of the Hardcastle Road Stand – again, exposed to the elements. Book in advance on ☎0161/286 8888.

Swift half
County's sponsors *Robinson's* have a brewery in the town and it's worth seeking out a pub that sells their beer. The ***Red Bull*** is opposite the brewery on Middle Hillgate, while Castle Street, the right-hand exit off the roundabout if coming from the station, has a variety of options, though some of these could be friendlier. Try the ***Grapes Hotel*** at #1.

Club merchandise
County used to have their own *Adidas*-branded store but, like many non-Premiership clubs, they had to look elsewhere for a kit supplier for 1999/2000, eventually settling for *Patrick*. Replica shirts are on sale at the shop on the corner of the Railway End and the Vernon Building Society Stand, price £39.99, kids' sizes £29.99.

Barmy army
It's the Cheshire factor again. County fans seem marginally less bothered by the success of Manchester United than supporters of the smaller Lancashire teams, while City fans, prior to the 1999 play-offs, had come to be regarded almost with sympathy. Trouble is rare.

In print
The Saturday ***Pink*** edition of the *Manchester Evening News* normally reaches Stockport by 6pm.

County's long-running fanzine is ***The Tea Party*** (PO Box 10, Stockport, SK2 5FB), and its editor, Dave Espley, is the man responsible for the book ***Saturday Night And Thursday Morning*** (£9.99), a fan's diary of the 1996/97 promotion season, available from the fanzine address above.

On air
There's no Stockport-specific radio station but ***GMR*** (95.1 FM) and ***Piccadilly Radio*** (1152 AM) do their best from Manchester.

In the net
The club's **official site** is very thorough at: www.stockportmbc.gov.uk/county. But check out also Martin White's **unofficial offering**, which offers better updating and a lively sense of humour at: www.mawhite.dircon.co.uk.

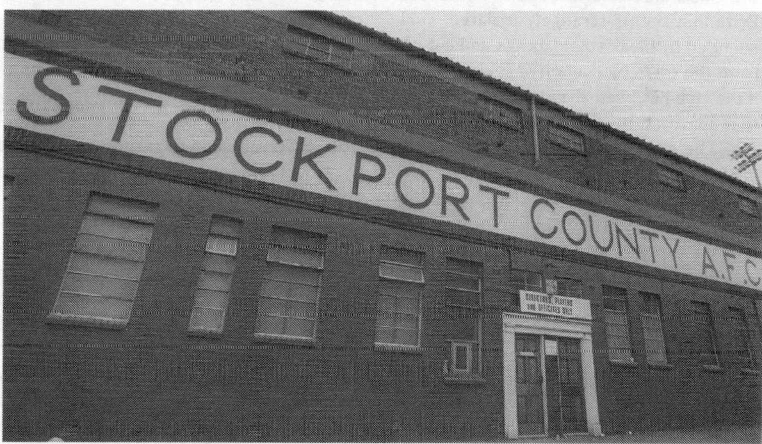

Back to basics – Edgeley Park, birthplace of an unlikely Nineties revival

Stoke City

Formation	1868 as Stoke Ramblers
Stadium	Britannia Stadium, Stoke-on-Trent, ST4 4EG. ☎01782/592222
Ground capacity	24,000
First-choice colours	Red-and-white stripes
Major honours	Second Division champions 1933, 1963, 1993; Third Division (North) champions 1927; League Cup winners 1972; Autoglass Trophy winners 1992
Position 1998/99	Eighth in Second Division

Stoke City are (just about) living proof that a bold new arena, fast-track marketing and TV cash do not necessarily turn a moribund club into a dynamic one. They enter the new millennium heavily in debt, playing Second Division football in front of crowds that barely half-fill their shiny new Britannia Stadium, under their sixth first-team manager in two years. The fans have lost all confidence in the board, and at times the feeling appears to be mutual.

In theory the club could 'do a Middlesbrough' and re-invent itself as a modern, family leisure product. The infrastructure is there, as are the catchment area and intense passion for the game. Yet although it is less than a mile away from the club's old Victoria Ground home, the Britannia seems strangely isolated, surrounded by bleak roundabouts and cut off from the town by dual carriageways. It's as if the club has been abandoned by the area that spawned it – which, to an extent, it has. The new arena's design and facilities are admirable but, as Reading have also found in the Second Division, they're the optional extras. The standard equipment is what happens on the pitch, and if that isn't up to scratch, the punters won't come through the door.

Unlike Reading, Stoke have the additional complication of a long history of top-flight football, having been founder members of the Football League in 1888. Latterly, the ghosts of earlier eras that haunted the Victoria Ground had come to be seen by some as a burden. But if the idea was to make a clean break with the past, then the new stadium has failed. Stoke fans are proud of where their club has come from, and believe that if the players and back-room staff shared that pride, the club would have a clearer vision of its own future. As things stand, it's going to take a very special influence – probably from outside – to improve Stoke's position radically. Top-flight football hasn't been seen since 1985, and the longer the absence lasts, the harder it will be for the club to return. In this context, the shame of Port Vale defying the odds to remain one division higher almost pales into insignificance.

The supporters have every right to be proud. There's enough Stoke City history to fill this entire book, although, it has to be said, much of it is less than glorious. Football came early to the Potteries, and the club's origins are a rare mix of public-school organisation and working-class enthusiasm. While serving an apprenticeship at the *North Staffordshire Railway Company*, two former pupils of Charterhouse School got together with some members of the local workforce to form a team called Stoke Ramblers in 1868.

Initially the Ramblers played friendly matches on a strip of land called Sweeting's Field. But after changing their name to plain Stoke FC, in 1878 they merged with the Stoke Victoria Athletic Club, and moved to their ground on Lonsdale Street. Five years later, Stoke laid out a new ground in an adjacent field – this was to become the Victoria Ground. Two years after their move Stoke turned professional and, with the Football League's founders keen for involvement from the Potteries,

As safe as Banks – goalkeeper Gordon at the Victoria Ground, April 1971

the club was admitted for the competition's inaugural season in 1888/89. The team finished bottom at the end of both the first two seasons, winning only seven out of 44 games. In 1890 they were voted out, to be replaced by Sunderland.

Stoke's absence from the League lasted only a year, as they were re-admitted after the expansion from 12 to 14 clubs in 1891. But the team continued to struggle, and after a season of Second Division football following relegation in 1907, the club resigned from the League altogether, crippled by debts.

A new Stoke club was formed to take the place of the old, bankrupt one, but League football would not return until after World War I – the only consolation being that Port Vale were also forced to play non-League football during this period.

Like Vale, Stoke were re-admitted to the Second Division in 1919. Yet they spent the next decade uncertain as to their true level, winning promotion to the First Division in 1922, being relegated the following year, and dropping down into the Third Division (North) in 1926. A year later, with the club's name changed to Stoke City to reflect its home town's newly conferred status, the team bounced straight back into the Second Division, where they would remain for six seasons before winning the divisional title in 1933.

Seven decades after it was founded, the club now had its first great side. Managed by the stern-faced Scot Bob McGrory, the team rose to a fourth-place finish in the First Division of 1935/36. In centre-half Neil Franklin, centre-forward Freddie Steele and a young Hanley-born outside-right by the name of Stanley Matthews, the team had a confidence and cohesion the like of which the Victoria Ground had only previously seen in the opposition. Word quickly spread of City's abilities, and more than 50,000 showed up at the club's newly expanded ground for the League visit of Arsenal in March 1937.

McGrory's work, however, was only just beginning. In the years immediately

A cake in point – Matthews is 50, 1965

preceding World War II he signed a string of promising youngsters, so that once hostilities had ceased, unlike many sides Stoke were not seriously disrupted. The versatile Frank Mountford, stalwart full-back John McCue and striker Frank Bowyer were all players whose Victoria Ground careers spanned both pre-war and post-war football. As the first League season after the war drew to a close, McGrory's side needed only to win their final game at Sheffield United to clinch the title. But they lost 2–1, and the championship went to Liverpool.

Stoke would not come as close to title honours again, but although Matthews was controversially sold to Blackpool (at the age of 32) for £11,500, the side was strong enough to remain a credible First Division force until McGrory stepped down through ill health in 1952. Relegation followed a year after McGrory's departure, and for the remainder of the Fifties, despite new manager Frank Taylor bringing tracksuit tactics and training methods to the club, Stoke remained a mid-table Second Division side, promising little, delivering less.

Two men helped reverse the slump at the start of the Sixties – new chairman Albert Henshall and the manager he appointed, Tony Waddington. With ambitious plans to modernise the crumbling Victoria Ground, the club needed to regain First Division status quickly. Waddington's approach was the opposite of McGrory's, and his re-signing of Stanley Matthews from Blackpool in 1961 was the first of many seemingly eccentric bids for players who were supposed to be past their sell-by date.

Matthews was 46 when Waddington paid £2,500 for him, yet his return signalled the start of the most successful period in Stoke's history. Though the years had slowed Matthews' bursts of acceleration, they'd done nothing to dim the unpredictability of that 'Twinkle Toes' movement – 30 years after he'd made his League debut for Stoke, opposing full-backs still hadn't sussed him out. In his second full season back at the club, Stoke won the Second Division title. With a succession of other 'mature' signings including Dennis Viollet from Manchester United and Burnley's Jimmy McIlroy, Waddington's team then reached the 1964 League Cup final, losing 4–3 over two legs.

In 1965, five days after his 50th birthday and after playing 701 League games, Stanley Matthews retired from competitive football – though he would subsequently claim he should have gone on for another couple of years. As the Sixties progressed and Stoke consolidated their First Division status, the side began to shake off its *Dad's Army* reputation, and younger players were attracted to the Victoria Ground. George Eastham, a mere stripling at only 30, arrived from Arsenal, while England goalkeeper Gordon Banks signed from Leicester after winning the World Cup in 1966.

With Jackie Marsh and Mike Pejic in defence and the threatening combination of Terry Conroy, Jimmy Greenhoff and John

Ritchie upfront, Waddington had a side capable of carving out its own legend by the turn of the Seventies. In 1971 Stoke reached the FA Cup semi-finals, losing to Arsenal in a replay. The following year they reached the same stage, and lost to the same opponents, in the same way. But, also in 1972, they reached the League Cup final, with Conroy and Eastham getting the goals that beat Chelsea 2–1. It was a sight many fans thought they'd never see – Stoke at Wembley, parading a major trophy, and earning the plaudits of a nation in the process. Goalkeeper Banks was made footballer of the year and sports personality of the year, before a head-on car crash later in 1972 caused him to lose the sight in one eye, and he was forced to retire from top-class football.

The arrival of former Chelsea playmaker Alan Hudson heralded the creation of another great side in the mid-Seventies, when Stoke twice managed a top-five finish in the League. But his departure, in 1976, heralded a decline which ended with relegation and Waddington's resignation, after 17 years as manager, the following year. Eastham stepped briefly into his shoes, but it was his successor Alan Durban who got City promoted again in 1979. Durban's team was more workaday than Waddington's classic sides, but for six seasons in the early Eighties Stoke held their own in the First Division, their status often saved by the gallant goalkeeping of Peter Fox, while young stars Paul Bracewell and Adrian Heath providing the odd flash of flair.

The end, when it came, could hardly have been more emphatic. In 1984/85 a cash-starved side under Bill Asprey's management finished bottom of the First Division with just 17 points, after winning only three matches all season. Both were unwanted records, as well as being an almost fatal blow to the confidence of the man running Stoke's defence at the time, Steve Bould.

The appointment of Mick Mills as the team's player-manager seemed like a bold move, but falling crowds and the increasing cost of maintaining the Victoria Ground left him even shorter of resources than Asprey had been, and by the time he'd been replaced by Alan Ball in 1989, Stoke City were heading for the Third Division for the first time since the Twenties.

A trophy at last – Stoke's players celebrate their League Cup final victory over Chelsea, 1972

A revival, of sorts, began with the appointment of Lou Macari as manager in 1991. He took Stoke to a play-off defeat by Stockport and victory over the same opposition in the Autoglass Trophy final in his first season, then to promotion in 1993. After being tempted away by Celtic, he returned to lead Stoke into the 1996 First Division play-offs, where they were beaten in the semi-finals by Leicester.

That proved as far as the club could go, however. Macari left to pursue a compensation case against Celtic, and since his departure Chic Bates, Chris Kamara, Alan Durban and Brian Little have all played King Canute against the rising tide of mediocrity. More than 100 years of football at the Victoria Ground came to an end on 4 May 1997, and a year later, Stoke's stay in the First Division came to an end, too.

The summer of 1999 saw a new management team of Gary Megson and the former icon of Vale Park, John Rudge, take charge of the first team. But there are no funds for fresh signings (a situation with which both men are at least familiar), no new ideas in the boardroom, and no new hope in the stands of the Britannia – a showcase stadium, with nothing in particular to show.

Pint-sized passion – Inchy Heath returns, 1992

Here we go!

For **motorists**, the Britannia is easily found at the junction of the A500 (junction 15 off the M6) and the A50 Derby Road. However, it is impossible for visiting motorists to park at, so the best bet is to head for the *Booker* cash-and-carry car park, a short walk from the stadium. As you approach the Sideway roundabout on the A500, take the far left of the five lanes and follow signs for *Michelin*. Turn left at the top, then second left at the mini-roundabout, and the car park is on the right. From the cash-and-carry, follow the footpath along the bridge over the A500 to the incinerator access road, then on to another bridge over the canal and railway line to the stadium. Allow 15–20mins.

Stoke-on-Trent **train station** is served by trains running between London Euston and Manchester Piccadilly via Nuneaton (hourly, journey 2hrs from Euston, 45mins from Manchester). There are also cross-country trains for Nottingham, Derby and Crewe. For the latest timings call ☎0345/484950.

The station is an hour's bleak walk from the Britannia, so turn right as you exit, then right again onto Glebe Street, from where **shuttle buses** run to the stadium on matchdays.

Just the ticket

Visiting fans are allocated some or all of the Signal Radio (South) Stand, depending on the fixture. Ticket prices in 1999/2000 are adults £15, concessions £9 on a reciprocal basis only. **Disabled visitors** are also housed here – book in advance on ☎01782/592200.

Swift half

Bitter and lager are available in the **concourse bars** of the Britannia, as are hot snacks. This is just as well, as there isn't a pub for miles around, and the ones in the centre of Stoke village tend to be 'home only.' If you want something more substantial to eat, we're talking motorway service areas or station buffets – at least until the area around the stadium is developed.

Making an entrance – Brian Little fails to impress the press at the Britannia, 1998

Club merchandise

The Britannia's **club shop** (open Mon–Fri 9am–5.30pm, Sat 9am–12 moon, later on matchdays, ☎01782/592222) is in the corner of the Signal Radio and McEwans (West) Stands. There's also a shop in Hanley – the area Stoke fans mean when they refer to the town centre.

Both outlets are positively brimming with stocks of City's latest shirt (£39.99, kids' sizes £32.99), which probably has a bit too much red to please the traditionalists.

Barmy army

The camaraderie of the Victoria Ground's old Boothen End was legendary, but since the first anti-boardroom protests of the late Eighties, the atmosphere at Stoke games has become increasingly threatening – and building the Britannia hasn't rid the club of its hooligan menace. Keep colours discreet, and avoid the pubs in Stoke village (see *Swift half* above).

In print

The local ***Sentinel*** publishes its excellent *Green'Un* at about 5.30pm on Saturdays, while fanzine ***The Oatcake*** (PO Box 276, Stoke-on-Trent, ST4 7SQ) is still going strong after 11 years' continuous publication.

The main Stoke history books seem to be out of print, but Jeff Kent's ***Potteries Derbies*** (Witan, £12.75) offers an insight into the rivalry between City and Port Vale, while you may pick up one of Wade Martin's ***Master Potters*** series of player-orientated books – there are five in all, each covering Stoke's history from a different position on the pitch.

On air

Despite sponsoring the South Stand at the Britannia, ***Signal Radio*** (102.6 FM) has its work cut out fighting ***BBC Radio Stoke*** (94.6 FM) when it comes to football coverage.

In the net

Stoke's **official website** was 'coming soon' during the 1999 close season. You may or may not find something at: www.stoke-city-fc.com.

Alternatively, the *Sentinel* has a dedicated Stoke City site in addition to the general newspaper one. You'll find an excellent historical archive as well as the latest (impartial) news at: www.stokecity.co.uk.

For the fans' view, try ***RAW Stoke City***, which offers a fine match-report service as well as many links at: members.tripod.co.uk/raw_stokecity/index.htm.

Finally, ***The Oatcake*** (see *In print* above) has one of the better fanzine-run websites, with some sample features and a back-issues service among other things, at: www.oatcake.co.uk.

Sunderland

Formation	1879 as Sunderland & District Teachers' AFC
Stadium	Sunderland Stadium of Light, Sunderland, SR5 1SU. ☎0191/551 5000
Ground capacity	41,500
First-choice colours	Red-and-white stripes
Major honours	League champions 1892, 1893, 1895, 1902, 1913, 1936; First Division champions 1996, 1999; Second Division champions 1976; Third Division champions 1988; FA Cup winners 1937, 1973
Position 1998/99	Promoted as First Division champions

When the Sunderland board decided to move the club away from Roker Park, its home for almost a century, and into a purpose-built new arena, they knew they were taking a risk. The atmosphere at the old ground, emphatically embodied by the 'Roker Roar' which echoed around inside, borne by the breezes of the North Sea and increasing in volume with every faintest hint of a goal, would be nigh impossible to replicate. Before World War II, crowds of up to 75,000 had packed into the place. More recently, in the mid-Eighties, as Sunderland tasted Third Division football for the first time and supporters' wallets thinned with the closure of the local mining and shipping industries, the Roar was still there – a little more impatient, perhaps, but worth a goal start all the same.

The board fretted for nothing. The Sunderland Stadium of Light, to which the club moved in July 1997, is one of the most aesthetically pleasing of all the new grounds built in England this past decade. Named after the transparent, local glass industry-inspired columns through which red and white lights are shone at night (and not, as some have suggested, after its namesake on the outskirts of Lisbon), the stadium is beautifully built, perfectly located and much admired, not just in footballing circles. But form must follow function, and the Stadium Of Light, totally enclosed, with immaculate sight lines and even better acoustics, works brilliantly. Whether the players are dancing out onto the pitch to the strains of Prokofiev or the faithful are singing a chorus of *Cheer Up Peter Reid*, the ambience fair takes the breath away.

In addition to the everyday fans whose pride and passion rival anything anywhere else in England, the club itself must take an enormous amount of credit. After the Taylor Report was published at the turn of the Nineties, Sunderland spent four fruitless years trying to get planning permission for a new stadium development on the A19 near Washington, only for the Japanese carmaker *Nissan*, employer of so many Sunderland fans, and whose factory was nearby, to object to the club's scheme – ironically because of concerns about traffic.

Undeterred, the board switched their attentions to the former site of Wearmouth colliery, which closed in 1993. In many respects, this looked a better bet. Whereas the A19 site would have pushed the club out of town, away from the seed beds of its natural support, Wearmouth was next to the town centre, with a symbolic waterfront location to boot. Like Middlesbrough's Riverside, the project would attract European as well as Football Trust funding. Even so, club chairman Bob Murray – a man every bit as determined as Newcastle's Sir John Hall, for all his much lower public profile – still had to underwrite a gap of around £2million.

And now that the stadium is open, the work continues. Unlike Newcastle and 'Boro, Sunderland's two great north-east rivals, the club has capped season-ticket sales to ensure that around 6,000 seats are available on a match-to-match basis. This has implications for cashflow, but enables a wider range of fans to see games. And if the allocation proves insufficient, there are plans to raise the Stadium of Light's capacity to 48,000, the stands having already been designed with such an expansion in mind.

Whether the enlargement is necessary will, as ever, depend on how the team performs. And if the verdict on Sunderland's new home has already been delivered, the jury is still very much out on the football.

A Roar no more – counting down to the end of Roker Park

Peter Reid's team may have crushed all before them in their march to the First Division title in 1999, and the club may have smashed its transfer record to acquire new players during the close season...but Sunderland have been down this road before, and not liked what they found at the end of it. As recently as 1996, in fact, Reid was leading a team into the Premiership on the back of a divisional title, and the talk locally was of a new era for football in the north-east, with all three of the region's top teams enjoying an extended spell among the elite. Yet within a year both 'Boro and Sunderland were down, the latter after failing to beat Wimbledon on the season's final day. Reid's side had notched up victories against the likes of Arsenal and Manchester United, but a lack of goalscoring power had prevented them from ever winning two games in a row. Surviving beyond the year 2000 would depend on breaking that duck.

There was a time, of course, when winning two top-drawer matches in succession was meat and drink to Sunderland – although few of the regulars at the Stadium of Light are able to recall it. Mackem fans are immensely proud of their club's haul of six English League titles, but none of them was won after World War II, and only one came between the wars. Of course there have been glorious times since then, but to trace the grassroots of Sunderland's enormous following, the original source of the Roker Roar and the Stadium Style, you have to go back a very, very long way.

The club was formed in October 1879, at a meeting of schoolteachers called by Jimmy Allan. At first membership was confined to the teaching profession and the team played under the name Sunderland

Light and shade – Sunderland's stadium is large and perfectly formed, and could get larger still

& District Teachers' AFC. Within a year, however, non-teachers were invited to join and the name was changed to plain Sunderland AFC.

A variety of grounds were used, the first two south of the river Wear. In 1883, the club moved across the water to a ground in Roker, then to another at Fulwell and then, in 1886, to its best-equipped home yet, on Newcastle Road, where 15,000 spectators could be housed. The new surroundings, however, could not conceal a growing mood of tension within the club. After professionalism had been legalised by the FA in 1885, Sunderland had begun importing more and more players from Scotland, where playing for money was still taboo. The lack of opportunity for local players to shine angered Jimmy Allan, who left the club, took most of its best English players with him, and formed a rival team called Sunderland Albion.

Allan's club quickly obtained membership of the Football Alliance, the league competition established as a rival to the Football League in 1889. His team performed well, too, finishing third in the Alliance's inaugural season. Acutely aware that the town was not big enough to support two senior clubs, the directors of Sunderland AFC dug deep into their pockets, appointing the ambitious Tom Watson as secretary-manager and bringing yet more Scottish talent into their team. It was Watson who arranged a series of friendlies against Football League opposition, and one of these, a 7–2 thrashing of Aston Villa in 1889, prompted the Villa president (and League founder) William McGregor to comment that Sunderland had 'a talented player in every position'.

In 1890, after Stoke were voted out of the League, Sunderland AFC's 'Team Of All Talents' were elected in their place. The club's election was controversial, as League membership had until now been confined to the Midlands and the north-west, and not all the clubs were keen on travelling to Sunderland for matches. But a notice outside Newcastle Road read: 'We have arrived, and we are staying here.'

So it was that the 1890/91 season began with Sunderland in the League, and Sunderland Albion in the Alliance. In fact the former had only a middling first League season, their plight exacerbated by having two points deducted for fielding an ineligible player. But the higher quality of their opposition drew crowds away from Albion, and at the end of the season, the latter club withdrew from the Alliance. By 1892, Allan's Albion had been wound-up, and the way was clear for Sunderland AFC to fly the town's flag alone.

They certainly did that. Between 1892 and 1895 Watson's team were crowned champions three times, finishing runners-up to Villa in the one year (1894) that they didn't come top. From goalkeeper Teddy Doig, who wore a cap to conceal his bald head rather than shield his eyes from the sun, to centre-forward Johnny Campbell, who top-scored in all three of the club's title-winning seasons, there was scarcely a chink in Sunderland's armour. Above all the famous 'Talents', however, their real strength lay in their understanding as a team – the level of which no team in the League could match.

Even a side as talented as this was not immortal, however, and the turn of the century saw Sunderland rebuilding, both on and off the pitch. By the time the title was won again in 1902, the club had moved in to Roker Park, having outgrown Newcastle Road some years previously. This time, however, the club could not keep its championship side together. The board needed funds to buy the freehold to Roker, and this resulted in the sale of several stars, including Alf Common, whose transfer to Middlesbrough was the first to break the £1,000 barrier.

The middle of the Edwardian era saw Sunderland in the middle of the First Division, but by 1913, long-serving manager Bob Kyle had assembled another great side – greater than the Team Of All Talents, some said. With inside-forward Charles Buchan a majestic maker and a taker of goals, Sunderland strode confidently to the title that year, and were favourites to become the first double-winning team of the 20th century, only for uncertainty in front of goal to deny them in the FA Cup final against Aston Villa – a record crowd of 120,000 at Crystal Palace witnessed their attack of nerves.

World War I broke up Kyle's team before they'd had a chance to make amends, and Sunderland spent the Twenties and the early Thirties challenging for many honours but winning none of them. In 1932, a young forward called Raich Carter made his Roker Park debut. Born in the district of Hendon, where Jimmy Allan and his schoolteacher friends had held their first meeting, Carter was an elegant inside-forward whose understanding with Bobby Gurney would lead the club to its sixth and last championship in 1936. The two grabbed 31 goals each out of Sunderland's total 109, but celebrations were muted in respect for the memory of 22-year-old goalkeeper Jimmy Thorpe, a diabetic who'd died two days after being kicked by an opponent midway through the season.

Twelve months after their title win, Sunderland qualified for their first Wembley

Family values – Sunderland is famous for them

Second Division, not second best – 5 May 1973

Joking aside – it's Sunderland's Cup

Brian Clough, a former Roker player no less, spoke for the nation. 'There is no way Sunderland can beat Leeds,' he told the *ITV* audience before the 1973 FA Cup final. For once, nobody was inclined to disagree with him. Except, perhaps, the 20,000 Wearsiders who journeyed south to watch their team, struggling at the wrong end of the Second Division six months earlier, take on the might of the Cup holders, studded with internationals and managed by the incomparable **Don Revie**.

Sunderland had a charismatic boss of their own, **Bob Stokoe**, and the contrast between the two men – and their teams – couldn't have been greater prior to kick-off. Revie was as tight-lipped as ever, and so were his players. Sunderland, in contrast, laughed and joked with the media in the best underdog tradition, encouraged by Stokoe, whose easygoing north-east charm ensured the Roker Roar would have an extra 60,000 'neutral' voices on the day.

If the pre-match exchanges were a battle of wits, the game itself was a test of physical strength for both sides. Sunderland took the lead midway through the first half when **Ian Porterfield** reacted quickly to a loose ball in the Leeds penalty area and volleyed it home. This stirred Revie's team into action, and in the second half, only a stunning double save from veteran goalkeeper **Jim Montgomery** denied **Trevor Cherry** and **Peter Lorimer** at close range.

As the final whistle blew, Stokoe dashed across the Wembley tuff to hug Montgomery, whose saves had kept Sunderland in the Cup since the third round. The outsiders had won, but there was more to Stokoe's team than giant-killers' bravado. The core of the side had won the **1969 FA Youth Cup** for Sunderland. Many of them would go on to play top-flight football for bigger clubs, and two – stopper **Dave Watson** and forward **Dennis Tueart** – would win England caps.

Still, it was the biggest Cup final upset of the modern era. Just ask Brian Clough.

FA Cup final and comfortably beat Preston 3–1, with Carter taking the captain's armband because of injury to the club's regular skipper Alex Hastings. Gurney and Carter got a goal each.

At the time, few of the Sunderland fans who made the trip to Middlesex can have imagined that their club would not be back at Wembley for another 36 years – and with a Second Division side, to boot. But World War II deprived Carter's team of their best years, and by the time competitive football resumed, the side had broken up.

After the war, Sunderland signed Len Shackleton from Newcastle for a then record fee of £20,050. A series of other expensive signings followed, as Roker became known as home to the 'Bank of England' club. Yet aside from a couple of FA Cup semi-final appearances, the Fifties were a barren decade. The team were entertaining but essentially peripheral figures in the League, and the money was already running out when Sunderland were relegated for the first time in their history in 1958.

The early Sixties saw manager Alan Brown rebuild with Charlie Hurley as captain, young goalkeeper Jim Montgomery and a prolific Brian Clough upfront. Clough sustained a career-ending injury at Roker in 1962, after scoring 53 goals in 58 games for the club. But the momentum was undiminished and Sunderland regained their top-flight status in 1964.

Yet while Roker Park staged four matches in the 1966 World Cup, the club was being left behind by football's modern era. For six years Sunderland toiled to no real purpose in the First Division, never escaping the lower half of the table before being relegated again in 1970. By the time former Newcastle defender Bob Stokoe arrived as manager in 1972, the club was in danger of slipping into the Third Division. Yet with a combination of a relaxed demeanour and homespun north-east charm, Stokoe lifted the players' spirits. Sunderland climbed steadily to finish sixth in the Second Division, then stunned the footballing world by beating Leeds United in the FA Cup final at Wembley (see panel).

While several key members of the Cup-winning side soon departed, sufficient quality remained for Stokoe to lead Sunderland to the Second Division title in 1976. The squad, however, was a small one and when a series of injuries resulted in a poor start to the 1976/77 season, Stokoe resigned. The team were instantly relegated (in controversial circumstances – see Coventry City) under his successor Jimmy Adamson, promoted again under Ken Knighton in 1980, and relegated again under Len Ashurst in 1985, the year the club also reached the League Cup final – lost 1–0 to Norwich City, who also went down.

After that, a disastrous two-year spell under the former Southampton manager Lawrie McMenemy ended with Sunderland dropping down to the Third Division via the newly created play-offs in 1987 – his depleted, demoralised team beaten on away goals by Gillingham in front of a disbelieving Roker, itself now hacked to pieces by post-Bradford safety regulations.

The Roar could still be heard, though, as Denis Smith led Sunderland back to respectability with the Third Division title at the first attempt. Two years later his side, sparked by the goalscoring of striker Marco Gabbiadini, reached the Second Division play-offs, and famously beat Newcastle at St James' Park in the semi-finals. They were then well-beaten by Ossie Ardiles' free-passing Swindon Town at Wembley, but within weeks Swindon had been demoted for making illegal payments, and Sunderland went up in their place.

It was a stroke of good fortune that seemed heaven-sent, yet it was one the club could have done without – the team weren't ready for the step up, and were down within a year. A spell of so-so form in what became the First Division followed. When Malcolm Crosby's team reached an FA Cup final against Liverpool in 1992, the atmosphere on Wearside was strangely

No repeat performance – Ball is tricked by McManaman, 1992

Hitting the spot – Kevin Phillips makes sure of promotion

muted by comparison with 19 years earlier. Clearly Crosby, Sunderland's former reserve-team coach, was no Bob Stokoe but, equally clearly, the gap in class between the top two divisions had widened since Stokoe's day. After a by no means humiliating 2–0 defeat, journeyman striker John Byrne summed it all up: 'We've been given a lesson in football today.'

The man who bridged the gap was Peter Reid, whose arrival in March 1995 prompted a Stokoesque revival – from potential relegation fodder to divisional title winners in just over a year. But the team's strengths were primarily defensive (they set a new club record by going 18 games unbeaten in 1995/96) and their inability to unlock Premiership defences resulted in the club's seventh relegation in less than 40 years. Just as in 1977, Coventry had an inglorious part to play on the final day. While 20,000 Mackems managed to find the notoriously elusive Selhurst Park in time for Sunderland's game away to Wimbledon, a third of the number of Coventry fans, travelling a third of the distance, somehow got stuck in traffic on the way to White Hart Lane, necessitating a delayed kick-off against Tottenham. As news came through of Sunderland's defeat south of the Thames, the Coventry players took their foot off the gas – they had done enough. Unlike in 1977, however, Sunderland fans were philosophical, realising that victory at Selhurst would have made them safe, and the Coventry result immaterial. Much harder to bear were the events of 12 months later, when Reid's side, having finished third in the First Division, allowed Charlton Athletic to come from behind three times at Wembley, draw 4–4 after extra time, then win promotion on a penalty shoot-out. This despite 45,000 Sunderland fans turning genteel Middlesex into a timely reincarnation of Roker, the old ground having been demolished to make way for housing earlier in the year.

Sunderland's irrepressible form in the Stadium of Light ensured there would be no need for a return visit to the Twin Towers in 1998/99, and supporters, players, management, even the bookmakers came to a consensus that, this time, the club was too well-resourced to go down after only a year. The club, and its dramatic new home, deserved for them to be right.

Here we go!

Finding the Stadium of Light is straightforward but, as with so many of the new breed of grounds, parking at it is not. Happily, there's a very usable park-and-ride scheme. **Motorists** approaching along the A19 should cross the river Wear, then take the A1231 toward the town, following signs for Sunderland North. The park-and-ride **car parks** are well-signposted from the second roundabout.

Sunderland **train station** is on the local line that runs between Newcastle and Middlesbrough (hourly, journey 20mins from Newcastle, 1hr from Middlesbrough). Change at Newcastle from and to the East Coast mainline. You'll get back to Newcastle after an evening game, but that's about it. For the latest timings call ☎0345/484950.

The train station is a 15min walk from the stadium on the other side of the Wear. Turn left and then left again as you come out, then keep going straight until you come to Wearmouth Bridge – the stadium is on the left once you're over the river.

Just the ticket

Visiting fans are allocated a section of the South (Metro FM) Stand, size and prices depending on the fixture. Concessions are available on a reciprocal basis only and must be booked in advance through your own club. There are spaces for **disabled visitors** in the South Stand – book in advance on ☎0191/551 5151.

Swift half

You can get a pie and a pint in the lavishly equipped **concourse areas** of the Stadium of Light, where the quality is as smart as the surroundings.

The area around the old Roker ground is full of pubs still well-patronised by Sunderland fans, but many of these are 'home only'.

The town centre is a good alternative, especially for those arriving by train. The ***Brewery Tap*** may be worth a visit for posterity value alone – it's next-door to (and sells the products of) the local *Vaux* brewery which is threatened with closure, much to the dismay of Sunderland fans.

Club merchandise

The **club shop** (☎0191/551 5050) is built into the back of the Main (West) Stand, and sells a surprisingly large number – given the rivalry with Newcastle – of black items. In fact, it was Bob Stokoe who re-introduced the traditional black shorts to Sunderland's red-and-white striped kit, and after some more mucking about in the early Eighties, they now appear to be back for good.

Barmy army

Sunderland prides itself on being a 'family club' but that doesn't mean trouble is unheard of. These days it's more likely to occur outside the stadium – keep colours discreet in the area around the former Roker Park as well as in the centre of town.

In print

The local ***Evening Echo*** produces an excellent Saturday evening *Pink*, and is also good for pre-views, news and gossip. Long-established fanzine ***A Love Supreme*** (1 Hodgson's Buildings, Stadium Way, Monkwearmouth, SR5 1BT) has now spawned a sister publication, ***Sex & Chocolate Aren't As Good As Football*** (same postal address). Also on sale at the ground is ***It's The Hope I Can't Stand*** (PO Box 16335, London, SW1A 1ZG).

Sunderland fans reckon they have their own answer to *Fever Pitch* in ***And Up Steps Michael Gray*** (£9.95), an anonymously told tale of the 1997/98 season that ended so horribly at Wembley. Due for publication in the autumn of 1999 was a new history of the club, ***Into The Light***, by Roger Hutchinson (£14.99).

On air

On the radio waves, local station ***Sun FM*** (103.4 FM) slugs it out with the Newcastle-based ***Metro FM*** (97.1 FM) and ***BBC Radio Newcastle*** (1458 AM).

Sunderland helped to make history when they agreed for their 1999 game at Oxford United to become Britain's first **pay-per-view** televised fixture, courtesy of *BSkyB*. With its regular season-ticket sellouts and large diaspora of exiled fans scattered across the country, Sunderland is exactly the kind of club that could tap into a vital source of extra revenue this way – but the real money won't come until the TV contracts are re-negotiated in 2001.

In the net

Sunderland's award-winning **official website** shows what can be done when a well resourced club creates its own web presence, rather than relying on an outside company. In addition to a novel graphic presentation, there's a stats database covering every game since Sunderland entered the League in 1890, plus online shopping, a news service from the *Echo* and a fans' area called *The Roker Roar*. All this and more at: www.sunderland-afc.com

The ***Love Supreme*** fanzine group has a very smart site, making good use of the *Shockwave Flash* plug-in, at: www.als.sunderland.com. And ***It's The Hope I Can't Stand*** is also online at: dialspace.dial.pipex.com/town/street/ya56.

For a non-fanzine unofficial site try ***Ready To Go*** at: www.readytogo.net.

Swansea City

Formation	1912 as Swansea Town
Stadium	The Vetch Field, Swansea, SA1 3SU. ☎01792/474114
Ground capacity	11,500
First-choice colours	All white with black and maroon trim
Major honours	Third Division (South) champions 1925, 1949; Autoglass Trophy winners 1994; Welsh Cup winners ten times
Position 1998/99	Seventh in Third Division (eliminated in play-off semi-finals)

Cyril the Swan did not, all in all, have a very good year of it in 1998/99. At the end of the season, Swansea City's nine-foot tall official mascot was summoned to an FA of Wales hearing, accused of bringing the game into disrepute by running onto the pitch to celebrate a goal. Cyril already had a record of past misdemeanours, having been found guilty of barging the manager of a rival team and of throwing a pork pie onto the pitch. And despite pleas of leniency from Millwall's Lennie the Lion and the Cardiff Bluebird, he wasn't going to get off scot-free this time. He was fined £2,000, but took his defeat with good grace, posing for photographers on the steps outside the FA's Cardiff headquarters in full costume.

Oddly, the worse things got for Cyril, the better they got for the team. (Not altogether surprising, say fans, an increasing number of whom resent his antics.) Swansea beat Cardiff in the League – always a welcome result in these parts; knocked West Ham out of the FA Cup; and put together an impressive run to qualify for the Third Division promotion play-offs. That they fell in the semi-finals to Scunthorpe probably said more about the club's modest squad than it did about the management team of John Hollins and Alan Curtis, whose combination of cockney up-and-at-'em attitude and cultured Welsh soccer philosophy seemed to be creating an unlikely but successful chemistry.

It was Swansea's second play-off failure in three seasons, after defeat by Northampton at Wembley in 1997. But the club will not be deterred from pursuing a rise in status, and nor is its ambition confined to activities on the pitch. After the 1998/99 season was over, Swansea confirmed their intention to build a new 25,000-seater stadium at Morfa, a couple of miles out of town. The development, funded partly by the local council, which owns the land, will be part of a wide-ranging leisure complex and, as well as being home to City, it will also host matches for a historically more successful team of Whites – the city's rugby union club.

The stadium could be completed as early as the summer of 2000 and, when built, it will be a landmark in the history of spectator sport in Swansea, traditionally a hotbed of rugby, and where the non-handling code of soccer was once so little-known that, in 1894, a local paper felt obliged to publish an outline of the rules and a sketch of standard pitch markings.

Morfa will also mark the end of the line for the Vetch Field, City's home for 86 years. One of the most eccentric grounds in the Football League, it is dominated by the East Stand, built at the turn of the Eighties and a monument not only to the most exciting period in the club's history, but also to the extravagant over-ambition which almost wiped Swansea from the map of senior football barely five years later. The events of two decades ago are open to two opposing schools of interpretation. Either the club's rise from the Fourth Division of 1978 to the top of the League four years later was proof that Swansea deserved a better class of football. Or its subsequent fall back to the basement by 1986 revealed soccer's success in the area to be an unsustainable fantasy.

The move to Morfa, if successful, will provide evidence for the former viewpoint, particularly if it heralds a permanent reconciliation between the oft-warring codes of football and rugby. But a glance through the history of soccer in Swansea would tend to support the latter perspective, no matter how unpalatable to fans.

Nasty one, Cyril – when will the club make him a dying Swan?

The game had been played in the town for some years before the turn of the century (presumably after enough local people had familiarised themselves with the rules), but none of Swansea's teams had managed to summon enough interest to broaden their horizons beyond amateur competitions before Swansea Town was formed at a public meeting in June 1912. The obvious place for their team to play was the Vetch Field, so-called because it had once been used to grow 'vetch', a form of cabbage cultivated for cattle feed. When the farmer moved out, the field became a dirt ground on which local boys would play football rather than rugby. The game's future on the site was then thrown into doubt but, when its owners, the *Swansea Gas Light Company*, failed to get parliamentary permission to build a gasworks there, the Vetch was up for grabs again. There were no stands at first, and not even any grass. Yet the Southern League, keen to continue its expansion into Wales, admitted Swansea Town without hesitation, and the first game played at the Vetch was a local derby against Cardiff on 7 September 1912.

After playing their entire first season on a clinker surface (and winning the Welsh Cup at the first attempt, beating Pontypridd in a replay), Swansea got around to laying some turf in time for the 1913/14 season, and continued to progress despite the interruption of World War I. In 1919 they won promotion to the Southern League's First Division, and the following year joined that division's transformation into the Third Division – later the Third Division (South) – of the Football League.

By 1925 Swansea had won the Third Division (South) title, and the following year they beat Arsenal en route to an appearance in the FA Cup semi-finals, where they were beaten by the eventual winners, Bolton.

Swansea maintainted their Second Division status all the way through to World War II, but lost it after the first full peacetime season. Manager Billy McCandlass pulled the club back up again in 1949, and the Fifties would prove an entertaining if ultimately frustrating period. Playmaker Ivor Allchurch and his brother Len on the flanks, other speedy wingers such as Cliff Jones and Terry Medwin, centre-half Tommy Kiley and utility player Mel Charles were all groomed for stardom at the Vetch – but, with the exception of Kiley, all would be sold to bigger clubs before they had reached their prime.

First game in the First – Alan Curtis, 1981

Another run to the FA Cup semi-finals ended with defeat by another Lancashire side, Preston North End, in 1964, and served only to distract attention from growing inconsistency in the League. The following year Town were down, and by 1968 they'd hit the Fourth Division.

Swansea's attainment of city status saw the club change its name to Swansea City in 1970, and to celebrate, the team won promotion to the Third Division. But they were back down again within three years, and it wasn't until the appointment of John Toshack as player-manager in March 1978 that the club began to recover some of its former confidence. While Toshack's immediate predecessors, Malcolm Struel and Harry Griffiths, deserved credit for rebuilding the team with young talent, it was Toshack who crucially altered the club's outlook, introducing the discipline and professionalism which he had seen work so dazzlingly at Liverpool, and which had been so obviously lacking at the Vetch.

Promotion to the Third Division was won within three months of Toshack's arrival, and a second successive rise took Swansea back into the upper half of the League. After a brief pause for breath, in 1981 the team won promotion to the First Division, while victory in the Welsh Cup brought European football back to the Vetch after a 15-year absence. The team went out of the Cup-Winners' Cup early but their real progress continued to be reserved for the League, where the name of Swansea City sat proudly at the top of the First Division table on three separate occasions, and never left the top six for the whole of the 1981/82 season.

The new East Stand was packed all the way up to its oddly angled roof as the likes of Leeds and Liverpool were humbled, and Toshack led his line majestically, rolling back the years to recall his days as a teenage goalscoring idol at Ninian Park.

Not that he ploughed a lone furrow. Swansea's ambitious board gave their manager money to spend. Ray Kennedy and Colin Irwin arrived from Anfield, while other experienced pros such as Bob Latchford, Leighton James and goalkeeper Dai Davies gave younger men like Alan Curtis, Jeremy Charles and Robbie James the solid foundation on which their talents could flourish. It was a triumph not just for Swansea but for the swift-passing tradition of the game in South Wales – although quite what the squad's influential Yugoslav contingent, Dzemal Hadziabdić and Ante Rajković, made of it all is anybody's guess.

Within a year, the party was over. The building work at the Vetch had run hopelessly over-budget, and local residents whose view had been blocked by the new East Stand were suing the club for compensation. A run to the quarter-finals of the Cup-Winners' Cup in 1982/83, coupled with pursuit of a third successive Welsh Cup, meant the club was fighting on five competitive fronts, aggravating an existing injury crisis. Swansea were relegated at the end of the season, and Toshack resigned at the start of the next one to take charge of Wales, only to return a month later – the upheaval doing nothing to restore already fragile club morale. As another relegation loomed at the end of the campaign, Toshack finally did leave for good, for Sporting Lisbon, and in December 1985, with the team at the wrong end of the Third Division, Swansea City AFC was officially wound-up.

The club's survival was assured only when a rescue package mounted by new chairman Doug Sharpe was accepted by creditors, six months and several visits to the High Court later. By now Swansea had been relegated again, and the rollercoaster ride was complete.

Since then, the club has been on a more or less even keel despite much bluster in the boardroom, and there has been the odd murmuring of a revival on the pitch. Terry Yorath had two spells in charge, the first leading to promotion via the play-offs in 1988, the second almost ending in relegation in 1990. Swansea's last European adventure (the door to the Cup-Winners' Cup having since been closed to Welsh Cup winners who are also members of the English league structure) ended with an 8–0 defeat at Monaco in 1992, but the following year Frank Burrows' side made the Second Division play-offs, where they were beaten by West Brom. A year later there was victory in the Autoglass Trophy final against Huddersfield at Wembley, in front of more than 47,000.

A chaotic 1995/96 campaign witnessed a failed takeover bid and no fewer than five different faces in the dugout, including PE teacher Kevin Cullis who lasted just seven days. The last of the five, former Danish international Jan Molby, arrived too late to prevent relegation.

Following in Toshack's footsteps from Anfield to the Vetch, Molby did what he could to turn Swansea around, but a controversial, twice-taken free-kick for Northampton ended his play-off dream at Wembley in 1997, and he departed soon after, to be followed by Micky Adams, Alan Cork and John Hollins in quick succession.

In 1999, the club at last had a management team it felt it could trust. The mood was upbeat, and the feeling was that, with a little luck, the Swans really could fly again. But first, they must move to Morfa. And they've got to do something about Cyril.

Back to reality – Jan Molby (#10) can't believe his team have let in a last-minute free-kick, 1997

Here we go!

From pretty much any direction, **motorists** should approach on the M4 and exit at junction 42 onto the A483 toward Swansea. Once in the city centre, follow the signs for Mumbles along the A4067 Oystermouth Road and the Vetch Field is on your right, behind Swansea Prison. Just prior to this point there's a choice of public **car parks** on the left, which are a good bet as there's no parking at the ground itself.

Swansea **train station** gets fast trains from London Paddington via Reading, Swindon, Bristol and Cardiff (hourly, journey 3hrs from Paddington, 1hr 30mins from Bristol). Change at Bristol Parkway for connections to the Midlands and north. Call ☎0345/484950 for the latest timings.

The station is a 10min stroll from the ground. Simply walk down the High Street, turn right into the pedestrianised Oxford Street, walk round to the end and you'll see the ground on your left after passing the Grand Theatre.

Just the ticket

Visiting fans can stand at the West End of the ground allocated to them or sit anywhere they like. Ticket prices for 1999/2000 are £8 in the West End (no concessions). or £12 in the adjacent Centre Stand (ditto), with families welcome in the family section of the latter at £16.50 for an adult and one child – book in advance for this scheme on ☎01792/474114.

Disabled visitors have a handful of spaces in front of the Centre Stand – booking essential on the number above.

Popular chap – John Hollins milks the acclaim, 1999

Swift half

The ***Builders Arms*** at the end of Oxford Street, near the theatre, is popular with home fans but also welcomes visitors with real ale on draught and excellent bar meals. Otherwise there's an enormous range of pubs in the Mumbles area which are likely to be quieter.

Club merchandise

Swansea are the original all-whites and you can take a peek at the latest version of the shirt at the **club shop** (Mon–Fri 9am–4.45pm, Sat 9am–3pm, ☎01792/474114) run by lifelong fan Myra Powles from the terraced house at #33 William Street, behind the East Stand. The shirts are £38.99 (kids' sizes £28.99) and if that's too steep there's always the tax disc holder or comb set at £1 each.

Barmy army

Swansea do still have a significant hooligan following and trouble is not, alas, confined to games against Cardiff City, with a number of city-centre incidents during 1999/2000.

In print

The ***South Wales Evening Post*** publishes a Saturday evening edition which strikes a fair balance between football and egg-chasing. There are at least two fanzines – ***Jackanory*** (PO Box 372, Swansea, SA1 6YY) and ***Mag Rag*** (176 Abbotswood Road, Brockworth, GL3 4PF).

On air

Swansea Sound (1170 AM) is the choice for local sport.

In the net

If Swansea's football were as good as the club's web presence, there'd be Premiership football at the Morfa in three years. The **official website** is fresh-looking and is being gradually upgraded at: swansfc.inetc.net/swans2000/homepage.htm. But have a look also at Gary Martin's superb effort at: www2.prestel.co.uk/gmartin/index.html; and at the online fanzine ***Mouthful Of Lead*** at: website.lineone.net/~as_thomas/MOL.htm.

Swindon Town

Formation	1881 as Spartans
Stadium	County Ground, Swindon, Wilts, SN1 2ED. ☎01793/430430
Ground capacity	15,700
First-choice colours	Red and white
Major honours	Second Division champions 1996; Fourth Division champions 1986; League Cup winners 1969; Anglo-Italian Cup winners 1970
Position 1998/99	17th in First Division

For a quiet, unassuming town in the middle of Wiltshire, famous for ts railway industry and (latterly) as the home of a *Honda* car factory, Swindon has endured the full range of footballing emotions. The history of the local team, Swindon Town, is littered with incident, from improbable giant-killing to financial scandal, and embraces a series of record-breaking feats, some of them desirable, others much less so.

The triumph that never was – McLoughlin and Ardiles, 1990

Yet the turn of the millennium finds the County Ground remarkably tranquil. The team are becalmed in the wrong half of the First Division, too impoverished to make any kind of assault on the Premiership, too canny to get dragged down into a relegation dogfight. It sounds like a spell of much-needed stability for a club with a narrow catchment area and restricted resources, yet somehow it just isn't Swindon – you feel they ought to be going somewhere, anywhere, just to keep the plot moving along.

As befits a club that seems to specialise in the indecipherable and the unpredictable, Swindon Town's very formation is shrouded in mist. It's generally assumed that the Rev William Pitt, captain of the Spartans cricket club, decided to form a football section of said club in 1881. It's also assumed that his team initially played under the name of Spartans, although nobody can be sure. At some point before 1883, when the team amalgamated with the footballing wing of the St Mark's Young Men's Friendly Society, the Rev Pitt changed the name to Swindon Town FC. Probably.

Part of the reason for the mystery is that the club moved from one ground to another with distressing frequency in its

Gunners silenced – Roger Smart (centre) celebrates giving Swindon the lead at Wembley, 1969

early years. In 1894, after Swindon's application to join the Southern League had been accepted, the club had to find an enclosed arena in which to play, and located one at the County Ground. But, this being Swindon, nothing is ever that simple – this was not the County Ground as fans know it today, but a field adjacent to the current ground, where the only action that takes place now is cricket.

In 1896, the club moved to its present home, and there the early interest in the tale would have ended, had Swindon not run into a series of cash crises which threatened not just the County Ground but the team's very existence. The club had borrowed £300 to finance its first stand but, when the board defaulted on the loan, it was almost chopped up for firewood. Swindon's first secretary-manager, Sam Allen, organised a long line of fund-raising events to keep the club afloat, and by 1905 he felt sufficiently confident to enter his charges into the FA Cup for the first time.

The Cup was to prove a happy hunting ground for Allen's side, who reached the semi-finals in 1910, the quarter-finals a year later and the semi-finals again a year after that – not bad going for a Southern League team playing in a competition that had been dominated by Football League clubs since the turn of the century.

The end of World War I saw Swindon in the First Division of the Southern League, perfectly placed to graduate to the new Third Division of the Football League – later the Third Division (South) – in 1920. At first they were comfortable at this level but, like several other teams from the same background, they found the going got tougher as the years went by, and more former Second Division clubs were relegated, toughening up the fixture list. When Sam Allen finally stood down in 1933, the club he loved had just finished bottom of the Third Division (South), having lost more than half their games and conceded 105 goals. Luckily, Swindon's application for re-election sailed through.

The team's confidence improved under new manager Ted Vizard, and there was the odd whiff of promotion in the years immediately preceding and following World War II. But after that Swindon fell to the wrong end of the Third Division (South) again, and further re-election applications ensued – the town's easy accessibility by rail undoubtedly helping the club's cause when it came to the crunch.

In 1956, Bert Head took over as manager and didn't like what he saw at the County Ground. A self-confessed admirer of Matt Busby's work at Manchester United, Head wanted to rebuild Swindon by introducing players from the youth setup, and the club's board were happy to give him time for any raw gems he might unearth to be polished up. It was a long process, but by 1963 Head's team, dressed in a carbon copy of United's red-and-white kit and featuring the likes of full-back John Trollope and Mike Summerbee and Don Rogers on the flanks, won promotion as runners-up in the Third Division.

Before long Swindon would become victims of their own success. Bigger clubs swooped for the most accomplished talents, Head himself departed for Bury, and the club was back in the Third Division again by 1965.

This was only a temporary blip, however. Enough of Head's players remained to win promotion again in 1969, and before that was achieved, the club attained nationwide fame by beating First Division Arsenal 3–1 in the League Cup final at Wembley. Roger Smart, another of Bert Head's youth products, opened the scoring after a mix-up in the favourites' rearguard early on, and although Swindon's 'keeper Peter Downsborough gifted Arsenal a freak late equaliser when his clearance bounced back into the net off Bobby Gould, the underdogs kept the initiative as the game went into extra time. Rogers put them back in front at the end of the first period, then jubilantly ran the length of a quagmire of a pitch in the dying moments to seal a famous victory.

Swindon remained a composed and creative force in the Second Division for five seasons at the start of the Seventies, but the club's inability to turn down big transfer offers remained a limiting factor. One by one the stars drifted away, with Rogers, the most grievous loss, rejoining his old mentor Head at Crystal Palace. Relegation followed in 1974, crowds that had averaged 20,000 fell to half that, and after the fans' favourite Trollope hung up his boots in 1980 after two decades of loyal service, he began a spell as team manager that was little short of calamitous. In 1982, Swindon were relegated to the Fourth Division.

The economic crisis of the early Eighties and decline of railway freight business had brought a mood of tension to a formerly relaxed and affluent town. Yet Swindon, handily placed along the M4 corridor, would recover from recession quicker than many parts of England, and as gleaming new hi-tech industries made their home in Britain's answer to Silicon Valley, so the football team revived under the

Admired then maligned – Lou Macari

guidance of a new visionary, Lou Macari. An eager if not totally converted disciple of the long-ball gospel, Macari gave Swindon an energy their lower-division opponents found hard to resist. His team won the Fourth Division title in 1986 with a new record of 102 points, then finished third in the Third Division to clinch a second successive promotion.

Macari left in 1989 but his successor, Ossie Ardiles, inherited a well-equipped and coherent unit, capable of responding quickly to new ideas. Those ideas were certainly revolutionary – a combination of the pass-and-move ethos favoured at Ardiles' former club Tottenham, and the slick counter-attacking game with which the manager had grown up in his native Argentina. Of course, it couldn't possibly function at the feet of a workaday side in the English Second Division, could it? Well, this was Swindon Town, arch purveyors of unlikely footballing stories, so yes, it could work alright. So well, in fact, that within a year Ardiles was leading his team out at Wembley for a promotion play-off final against Sunderland. Swindon won 1–0, with a display of controlled, passing football that had the Wearside supporters, heavily outnumbering their Wiltshire counterparts, sighing with envy from the stands.

Working wonders on the wing – Mark Walters

With Colin Calderwood keeping the backline in shape, the cultured Paul Bodin and Alan McLoughlin running the midfield and a selfless strikeforce of Steve White and Duncan Shearer, Ardiles' side looked all set to make the club's first-ever season of top-flight football one to remember. Then came the bombshell. Within days of Swindon's Wembley triumph, a long-running inquiry into alleged irregular payments at the County Ground found the club guilty of breaching League regulations during the Macari era. While the former manager denied any knowing involvement in under-the-counter deals and his chairman at the time was subsequently jailed for tax fraud, Swindon were forcibly demoted to the Third Division. On appeal, the punishment was halved. But Ardiles' team were deprived of their year in the limelight, while Sunderland were promoted instead.

It took a while for the club to recover. Ardiles left to manage West Brom, but fortunately another former member of the White Hart Lane academy, Glenn Hoddle, took over the reins as player-manager. Leading by example, Hoddle kept the passing game going and, after another play-off victory at Wembley in 1993, this time over Leicester, Swindon's fans finally got the top-division spot they thought their club had earned three years previously.

The next twist in the tale came when Hoddle was lured away from the County Ground by Ken Bates to run Chelsea, leaving his assistant, John Gorman, holding the Premiership baby. Gorman was an inexperienced parent, and his charges were not exactly brimming with top-level expertise themselves. The result was painfully predictable – a bottom-place finish in 1993/94, with only five games won all season and 100 goals conceded, a record for the Premiership which still, alas, stands today.

Gorman stood down at the end of the season, but his successor Steve McMahon inherited a demoralised squad, and Swindon suffered a second successive relegation in 1995. The club's board kept faith with McMahon, and were rewarded when, a year later, powered by the attacking energies of Wayne Allison and Kevin Horlock, the team won the Second Division title at the first attempt.

Three average-to-poor seasons of First Division football have followed since, with McMahon being replaced by Jimmy Quinn during 1998/99, and chairman Rikki Hunt seemingly less than convinced by his latest appointment as the 1999/2000 season dawned. But then, this is Swindon, and there's nothing like a bit of uncertainty to set the imagination whirring.

Here we go!

Modern Swindon's mass of confusing road junctions finds its ultimate expression in the 'Magic Roundabout', a Government-sponsored traffic-flow experiment down the road from the County Ground and comprising five mini-roundabouts where one large one used to be. Luckily, **motorists** will find the ground well-signposted from any approach into town, and by the time you reach the Magic Roundabout, you can actually see the floodlights. There's limited **street parking** but several impromptu car parks spring up on matchdays, also well-signposted.

Swindon **train station** is on the mainline between London Paddington and Wales and the West Country (fast trains hourly, journey 1hr from Paddington). Change at Reading for cross-country services to and from Birmingham, Manchester and elsewhere. For the latest timings call ☎0345/484950.

From the station, turn left down Station Road, across Corporation Street, then right at the roundabout into County Road – the ground is a little way ahead on the left. Allow 15mins.

Just the ticket

With Swindon still unable to win permission to develop the Stratton Bank, visiting fans have been moved to the covered Town End – entrance in County Road. Ticket prices vary according to the fixture, but concessions must be booked in advance through the club on ☎01793/529000.

Disabled supporters have just four spaces in front of the Arkell's Family Stand. Advance booking essential on the number above.

Swift half

The best all-round bet near the ground is a pub in the ***Hungry Horse*** chain on Queen's Drive – turn left at the Magic Roundabout if leaving the County Ground, and it's on the next, er, roundabout. There's a separate restaurant area and families are especially welcome.

Club merchandise

Swindon no longer attempt to look like Manchester United as they did in the Sixties and Seventies, and the introduction of green trim to the team's shirts earlier in the Nineties helped to give the club its own identity. The ***Superstore*** (☎01793/423030) at the corner of the Town End and South Stand has the latest design at £34.99 (kids' sizes £28.99), a wide range of *Mizuno* leisurewear and 'deluxe pens' for £2.99.

Barmy army

Log off, chill out and relax – Swindon is an almost totally hooligan-free zone, and while some complain of a lack of atmosphere inside the County Ground, visitors can expect a warm welcome.

In print

There's no Saturday evening sports paper and no fanzines either, while all the Swindon-specific books were out of print in the summer of 1999.

On air

GWR (97.2 FM or 1161 AM), the club's sponsor during the Ardiles era, is still the best for club news, previews and reports.

In the net

The Swindon web community seems a little too relaxed for its own good, with many sites in dire need of an update as of summer 1999. This was certainly true of the **official site**, which is still busy enough to merit a look at: www.swindon-fc.demon.co.uk. For something more up-to-date, try Graham Reeves' excellent offering at: www.users.globalnet.co.uk/~gterry.

Torquay United

Formation	1899
Stadium	Plainmoor, Torquay, Devon, TQ1 3PS. ☎01803/328666
Ground capacity	6,000
First-choice colours	Yellow, blue and white
Major honours	None
Position 1998/99	20th in Third Division

Of all the towns, cities and suburbs of cities that host senior football in England, Torquay seems the most unlikely. One of three resorts that make up the self-styled 'English Riviera' around Torbay, it's a riot of guest houses, retirement bungalows, palm trees and well-kept lawns. Nobody seems to be in a hurry to do anything – except relax. But then, that's what resorts are for. As Basil Fawlty, fictional proprietor of one of the town's less well-organised hotels, once put it to a disagreeable guest: 'What did you expect, herds of wildebeest galloping across the Serengeti...?'

Add to this the West Country's notoriously indifferent attitude to the round-ball game and the enormous distances any team in a national competition must travel just to fulfil a season's fixture list, and you've got all the ingredients for abject failure. Yet still Torquay United hang on in there, a professional football club set not just against the ambivalence of its local community, but against the harsh realities of the wider world. Happily, that world does bring something back to Torquay, in the shape of thousands of visiting supporters who make the long journey to the Devon coast every year, in anticipation of sun, sea and a six-goal victory...or at least the sea.

For the home fans, life isn't necessarily as tame as the local ambience might suggest. In 1998/99 alone there were a few cameo appearances from Chris Waddle, not to mention the arrival of Neville Southall, who arrived as a stand-in goalkeeper midway through the season, inspired a fine run of form that looked briefly as though it might lead to the play-offs, and ended up with the #1 shirt for 1999/2000. Torquay did not, in fact, make the play-offs, but they did at least assure themselves of their own safety with two games to spare – a notable achievement in itself, for a club that has been looking anxiously over its shoulder almost ever since relegation to the Conference was introduced in 1987.

There have certainly been closer shaves. In that first season, 1986/87, Torquay avoided finishing bottom for what would have been the third successive year in bziarre circumstances. With the team losing 2–1 at home to Crewe on the final day, a police dog ran onto the pitch and bit one of the United players. In the stoppage time that ensued, and with Torquay knowing that results elsewhere meant they had to score, they duly did so – and sent Lincoln City down.

In 1996 they actually did finish bottom, only for the League to rule that Conference winners Stevenage Borough could not be promoted because their ground was not up to scratch.

Not, all in all, the sort of thing the club's founders were likely to have had in mind when they hit upon the idea of forming a football club in the town in 1899. The backdrop to the club's birth had Torquay written all over it. A group of old boys from two local schools, Torquay College and Torbay College, were sitting in Princess Gardens listening to the band when the conversation turned to football, and the fact that none of the existing teams seemed to be organised along serious lines. At a subsequent meeting at the more conventional venue of the *Tor Abbey Hotel* on 1 May, the club was christened Torquay United, and a board of officers was elected.

The club successfully applied for membership of the Eastern League (later known as the East Devon League) and found a ground on Teignmouth Road. Within a year, however, United had moved on to the Recreation Ground, between the town's train station and the seafront. This was a better-established venue but was also prone to flooding, and the club moved back to Teignmouth Road in 1905, when the local council took over the Recreation Ground and rented it out to Torquay Athletic rugby club, then a bigger draw than any of the local football teams. Two years later United moved to Torquay Cricket Ground, where they played until 1910 before moving to their present ground at Plainmoor – ironically, a former home of the rugby club that had ousted them from the Recreation Ground.

Plainmoor was reckoned to be the ideal venue for United because it was closer to the working-class areas of Torquay, and likely to open up a promising catchment area of new support. The problem was that two other football clubs had already had the same idea. One of these, Ellacombe FC, agreed to merge with United in 1910 to form a new club called Torquay Town. But the other, Babbacombe, remained independent until 1921, when they and Town decided to amalgamate and play, somewhat confusingly, under the name Torquay United. The new title was intended to impress the Southern League, which had just lost its entire top division to the Football League and was on the lookout for new members. The newly amalgamated side duly gained admission to the Southern League, yet within six seasons they, too, had joined the Football League, being elected to the Third Division (South) in place of Aberdare Athletic.

Torquay kicked-off their League career, conveniently enough, with a Devon derby against Exeter City on 27 August 1927, drawing 1–1 at Plainmoor. But much of the rest of the campaign was harder work, and

The hardcore support – one man and his wooden seagull against the world

they finished bottom of the table and having to apply for re-election. Helped by the fact that the League's third tier was still organised along regional lines, Torquay were well-supported by the other clubs and their application was waved through without trouble.

Suitably encouraged, the club had no further need of their friends for the remainder of the period preceding World War II, and remained respectably in mid-table for most of the early postwar years, too. Local interest, however, was still not all it could be, and in 1954 the United board decided on a change of image. Since the merger with Babbacombe in 1921, the team had worn a black-and-white kit and been nicknamed (with stunning originality) the 'Magpies'. Now all this was swept aside, as the players were given yellow-and-blue shirts to reflect the golden sand and azure skies of the English Riviera, along with a new nickname of 'Gulls'.

Unlike most such facelifts imposed from above, this one seemed to work. United finished eighth in 1955, fifth a year later, and the season after that would have won promotion to the Second Division had their goal average not been inferior to that of Alf Ramsey's Ipswich Town. Nearly 22,000 rolled up to Plainmoor for a fourth-round FA Cup tie against Huddersfield, and the club's future seemed every bit as bright as the sunshine in the tourist office's brochures.

Yet in 1958 Torquay finished 21st in the Third Division (South), easily bad enough for the club to be thrown into the Fourth Division which was to be created the following season. The Sixties and early Seventies saw United drifting between the bottom two divisions of the League, the club's most complete team being assembled during the managership of Frank O'Farrell toward the end of the Sixties. With young midfielder Ian Twitchin supplying the ammunition for main goalscorer Robin Stubbs, Torquay again flirted briefly with the possibility of Second Division football, without ever consumating the affair.

Relegation back to the Fourth in 1972 signalled the dawn of a particularly grey period, with the club teetering on the edge of extinction after a fire at Plainmoor in

Life on the edge – Garry Monk tries to play the ball out of defence, pursued by the opposition

From record signee to record signer – manager Wes Saunders

1985 (just weeks after the Valley Parade blaze) and the trauma of nearly falling out of the League two years later.

But in 1988, the sale of youth product Lee Sharpe to Manchester United for £125,000, after he had played barely a dozen games for the club, brought some sanity to Torquay's finances. A takeover by local double-glazing millionaire Mike Bateson improved things even further, and in 1991, Torquay made the play-offs after finishing seventh in the Fourth Division. Underdogs throughout, they beat Burnley in the semi-finals and then Blackpool at Wembley on penalties, after the game had finished 2–2. The final had a surreal quality – having kicked-off at 8pm on a Friday evening, after extra time and the shoot-out had been completed, it was nearly 11pm when it finished. As Torquay fans stayed behind to congratulate their hero Wes Saunders, the club's record signing from Dundee who had scored in both normal time and in the shoot-out, they faced an overnight journey back that would not see them home until, at best, dawn the next day.

Eight years on, and Saunders had become the manager. Torquay's play-off promotion had resulted in no more than a season of football at the higher level, and a return to the (now Third Division) play-offs in 1994 had ended in semi-final defeat by Preston.

In 1998/99, the arrival of Waddle (an old mate of Saunders' from Newcastle days), Southall and record signing Eifion Williams from Barry Town kept interest levels high, even if the final League position was low. And that, in Torquay at least, can be considered a victory in itself.

Here we go!

Unless coming from deeper into Devon or Cornwall, **motorists** will appraoch Torquay along the M5, A38 and A380. Follow the A380 through Kingskerswell, then take the first exit at the roundabout after about a mile onto the A3022, signposted Torquay. After a further mile turn left in the direction of Babbacombe. Turn left after about three quarters of a mile into Westhill Road. This becomes Warbro Road – the ground is on the right. It's **street parking** for all.

Torquay **train station** is on a local line between Exeter and Paignton, with some direct services to and from Bristol Temple Meads and London Paddington. If no through train is available, change at Newton Abbot – and if you want to get back from an evening game, stay overnight in a B&B. Call ☎0345/484950 for latest timings.

The station is a long old hike from the ground, and with bus connections on the slow side, the best bet is probably a **taxi** (about £4).

Just the ticket

Visiting fans are accommodated in the open Babbacombe End terrace, entrance in Warbro Road. Prices for 1999/2000 are adults £8, concessions £5. For an extra £1 you can get a seat in the (covered) Homelands Lane Stand. **Disabled visitors** have spaces in front of the Ellacombe End Family Stand – advance booking advisable on ☎01803/328666.

Swift half

The club has its own pub, the ***Boots & Laces***, inconveniently located for visitors between the

Pretty as a picture – blue skies, pastel-coloured houses and freshly trimmed grass on the Riviera

Ellacombe End and the Marnham Road Stand (Popular Side). Definitely worth walking round for, with big-screen TV and facilities for families and the disabled. Otherwise try the ***Sports Bar*** on St Marychurch Road – turn left from the away turnstiles onto Warbro Road, left again at the lights and it's on the left, the first of several welcoming bars in this road.

There are plenty more pubs – not to mention better **food options** – along Torquay harbour front, close to the station. As ever with seaside towns, respect signs discouraging football fans and take your custom elsewhere.

Club merchandise

For 1999/2000 United have reverted to the white-and-yellow striped shirt with blue trim in which they won the Wembley play-off final in 1991 – or at least a version of it. The **club shop** at the Ellacombe End of the ground can prove that it looks better in viscose than it sounds on the printed page.

Barmy army

Aside from derby days, you can expect a holiday atmosphere here.

In print

The local ***Herald Express*** is best for United news and previews, but doesn't publish on Saturday evenings.

The fanzine is ***Bamber's Right Foot*** (PO Box 77, Torquay, TQ2 5YR).

Garry Nelson's ***Left Foot In The Grave – A View From The Bottom Of The League*** (Collins Willow, £6.99) is the sequel to the best-selling *Left Foot Forward* and describes his solitary season as player-coach of Torquay. If anything, even more compelling than the original, and a worthy award-winner.

On air

BBC Radio Devon (103.4 FM) is the spot on the dial for United previews and reports.

In the net

Torquay's **official website** is really no more than a glorified bulletin board, run from Canada(!) at: www.mervo.com/torquay-united.

Easily the pick of the unofficials is ***TUFC Online***, with an up-to-date news service, current squad info, a picture gallery and more, at: torquayunited-online.webjump.com.

Tottenham Hotspur

Formation	1882 as Hotspur FC
Stadium	White Hart Lane, 748 High Road, Tottenham, N17 0AP. ☎0181/365 5000
Ground capacity	36,200
First-choice colours	White shirts, navy-blue shorts
Major honours	League champions 1951, 1961; Second Division champions 1920, 1950; FA Cup winners 1901, 1921, 1961, 1967, 1981, 1982, 1991; League Cup winners 1971, 1973, 1999; European Cup-Winners' Cup winners 1963; UEFA Cup winners 1972, 1984
Position 1998/99	11th in Premiership

The Tottenham Hotspur plc shareholder rose to his feet, straightened his tie, cleared his throat, and read from a prepared statement. 'There is a company in another part of North London,' he began, 'that treats its customers with respect and behaves with decorum. There is another company which treats its customers with contempt, offers an inferior product, invests unwisely and squanders its assets. It also demotivates its employees, exploits its customers and insults their intelligence.' There was a brief pause, then: 'I have to say Tottenham is in that latter category.'

A murmur of agreement spread through some parts of the company's 1998 AGM. The shareholder had spoken alone, but he had spoken for many. Tottenham fans, and not just those with shares in the club, were not happy. Their team were under-performing, no silverware had been won in eight years, and White Hart Lane was a half-rebuilt shadow of its former self (or should that be Shelf?).

A gentleman at his club – Bill Nicholson, 1974

Spurs supporters have high standards, as high as any in the English game, and they expect the people who run their club to adopt the same approach. In this respect, the board led by Alan Sugar was making a lot of big, important mistakes – as Sugar himself would later acknowledge. After all the misjudged managerial appointments, the PR own-goals, the political in-fighting and the sheer bad taste of

The enemy within – George Graham drives past the Red House

the past few seasons, somebody had to be called to account. Which is why that shareholder had found it necessary to stand up, say his piece, and set the record straight.

Part of the reason for Tottenham's obsession with dignity and elegance is that the club's golden age is in the relatively recent past, still vivid in the memories of many of the club's most affluent fans – exactly the kind of people who are likely to be shareholders. The crass commercialism, public acrimony and double-dealing that had bedevilled the club since well before Sugar's arrival in 1991 would never have done in the good old days, the *Glory, Glory Days*, when 'push-and-run' was a football term, not an instruction to staff to sell more replica shirts before the new design comes out.

But another, equally important influence, acknowledged in that shareholder's speech, is the club's long-standing and often self-defeating obsession with Arsenal, the North London rivals who are publicly ridiculed, but whose cool, confident way of conducting business is much envied among the regular visitors to the Red House at 748 High Road, N17. To make matters worse, at the time of that AGM, Arsenal were just about to do the double.

A third of the way through the 1998/99 season, Alan Sugar took the biggest gamble of his Tottenham career by appointing George Graham as manager. On paper, Graham symbolised everything Tottenham's hardcore support loathed – dour, defensive football, coupled with a devotion to Highbury which, had it not been for the transfer bung scandal of the mid-Nineties (a decidedly un-Arsenal affair, all in all), would probably still be intact after 30 years. It was like inviting the Pope to Ian Paisley's birthday party. Still, Tottenham's need was dire. Graham's hapless predecessor, the Swiss-born Christian Gross, was the subject of almost daily ridicule in the media. Goals were being conceded at an almost indecent rate. Star players looked disillusioned, and so did the supporters. Sugar's gamble was that if Graham could restore the team's self-respect, bring some confidence back to White Hart Lane and – who knows? – maybe win a trophy of some sort, then the fans' many reservations and grievances would be forgotten.

On Sunday 21 March 1999, Sugar's prayers were answered. George Graham's Tottenham beat Leicester in the League Cup final, giving the club its first serious trophy since the FA Cup of 1991. The match was not a classic, and seldom can there have been a chant sung at Wembley with richer irony than *One-Nil To The Tottenham*. But the point was made. The manager was accepted. A vital corner, perhaps, was turned.

Precisely what lay around that corner could not be foreseen. But, if a return to the *Glory, Glory Days* was still a little way off, then *Glory, Glory Nights* would suffice. George Graham was quick to point out the importance of Tottenham's return to Europe, an arena historically well-suited both to the club and its current first-team boss. Deep down, though, he and his players knew they would never silence the nostalgia merchants entirely. And why should they, when there is so much in the past to be admired? While many fans hark back to Tottenham's golden periods of the Fifties and Sixties, the club's tradition of pursuing noble causes, of sticking up for the decency of sport in the face of big business, goes back much further.

The story of the club's formation has an apposite innocence. Around August 1882, a couple of boys who were members of the Hotspur Cricket Club decided to form a football team to keep themselves fit during the winter months. Their club had been named after Harry Hotspur, the Shakespearean character and member of the Northumberland family, which owned the land on which the cricket matches were played. Legend has it that a subsequent meeting was held involving about a dozen boys, under a street light on the corner of Park Lane and Tottenham High Road where the club's headquarters now stands, at which it was decided to call the new team Hotspur FC.

The club's date of foundation is normally given as 5 September 1882, the day the first subscriptions were collected from members. But the team had played at least one game prior to that, on 30 August, losing 2–0 to a side calling themselves the Radicals. The following autumn, the club was re-formed under the auspices of the local church.

At first, matches were played on Tottenham Marshes, but after adding the prefix 'Tottenham' to their name, the team moved to their first enclosed ground at Northumberland Park in 1888. This coincided with the inauguration of the Football League, but it would be four years before Spurs themselves entered any kind of league competition, and even then, it was on a strictly amateur basis. Then, in 1895, the club loaned one of its players, Ernie Payne, some money to replace his lost boots. News of the loan reached the FA, who suspended Tottenham for two weeks for breaching rules regarding professionalism. Furious at what they saw as a betrayal of the amateur ethos, Spurs resolved to turn fully professional and joined the Southern League. The team played their first fixture in the event in September 1896, and three years later moved to their present home of White Hart Lane, taking the old main stand from Northumberland Park with them.

The new ground was inaugurated with a friendly against Notts County, one of the founder members of the Football League, a match Tottenham won 4–1 in front of 5,000. More than double that number then turned up for the first competitive fixture at the ground, against QPR – the start of an 1899/1900 Southern League campaign that would see Spurs crowned champions for the first time by its end.

The following year, the club's legendary reputation for mastering Cup competition was initiated in earnest. Prior to the 1901 FA Cup final at Crystal Palace, Spurs were reckoned to be lambs to the slaughter against First Division Sheffield United, who'd already won the trophy in 1899 and been League champions the year before that. Yet in front of more than 110,000

A tragic figure – the late, great John White

people, the biggest-ever attendance for a football match at the time, Tottenham held on for a 1–1 draw, before winning a replay at Burnden Park, Bolton, 3–1.

Never since the foundation of the Football League had a club from outside the competition won the FA Cup, and the result sent shock-waves through the English football community, particularly in the north where southern teams had been dismissed as dilettantes. When the players returned home for a celebratory dinner, the local mayoress draped white and blue ribbons around the Cup – instigating a tradition that has been followed ever since.

Spurs had struck a blow for the Southern League and for the London game in general, and the club would remain loyal to its roots for a few years afterwards. By 1908, however, the likes of Chelsea, Woolwich Arsenal, Fulham and Clapton Orient were all established in the Football League and Tottenham, envious of the bigger crowds these teams were drawing, applied for membership themselves. They were initially rejected, but enjoyed a stroke of luck when Stoke went into receivership and withdrew, allowing Spurs to go in as late replacements.

Speculating to accumulate – Jimmy Greaves

The team put their good fortune to immediate use, winning the Second Division title at the first attempt in 1909. The same year, White Hart Lane was given a new west stand, and in 1910 this was topped with a cockerel sitting astride a ball – apparently because fighting cocks wore spurs, as Harry Hotspur was said to have done when riding into battle.

Symbolism aside, however, the step up in class, which saw Tottenham pitted against the might of Aston Villa, Blackburn and Sunderland among others, proved steep, and after five mid-table seasons, the side finished bottom of the First Division in the last season before World War I.

After hostilities came arguably the club's darkest hour. The League decided to expand both its divisions from 20 to 22 clubs. This meant a reprieve for Chelsea, the team who'd finished just above Spurs in 1915, since their position had come about as the result of the notorious fixed match between Liverpool and Manchester United. Yet no comparable case was made for Tottenham, and when it was agreed that they should be relegated, the Arsenal president Henry Norris argued that his side should be promoted in their place, even though they had finished only fifth in the Second Division. The League agreed, and Tottenham were incensed. They had never liked the idea of Norris moving his team to North London in the first place – now there was real animosity between the two clubs, a poison which some would say has never lost its potentially lethal quality since.

Spurs, however, decided that their most eloquent response could be mounted on the field of play, and duly won the Second Division championship at a canter in 1920, before going on to beat Wolves 1–0 in the FA Cup final at Stamford Bridge a year later. The latter match, played on a rain-soaked pitch that made a mockery of players'

The hero who went to Arsenal – goalkeeper Pat Jennings

attempts to control the ball, was to prove the high point in the life of Tottenham's first great line-up – featuring the improvisational skills of Jimmy Seed, Jimmy Dimmock and Jimmy Cantrell, driven forward from left-half by captain Arthur Grimsdell, and coached by long-serving secretary-manager Peter McWilliam.

The team stayed together the following season but, with a possible League and Cup double beckoning, they were surprisingly beaten by Preston in the FA Cup semi-finals, and finished runners-up in the First Division to Liverpool.

McWilliam's side never recovered from that disappointment, and for five seasons Spurs plodded along in mid-table, with not even a decent Cup run to brighten the gloom. In 1928, new manager Billy Minter took his players on a post-season tour of Holland. They returned to find they'd been relegated, having completed their fixtures early and allowed no fewer than six clubs to leapfrog them to safety.

It took five years and two more changes of manager for Tottenham to regain top-flight status, and even then, their return was brief – after a third-place finish in 1931, Spurs were back down within a year, following an injury-plagued season in which the first team had used 36 players.

The next spell of Second Division football would last into the postwar period, but it had its compensations, not least the emergence of Arthur Rowe, a Tottenham-born centre-half who'd joined the club as a schoolboy in 1921. Injury forced Rowe to quit playing in 1939, but he moved on to a coaching job in Hungary – sadly curtailed by the war – before becoming a physical training instructor in the Army. After the war he moved into management at Southern League club Chelmsford City, and was so successful there that he seemed the obvious choice to take charge of Tottenham after Joe Hulme was sacked in 1949.

While Hulme had the makings of a good squad, it was Rowe who introduced the 'push-and-run' style that would become Tottenham's passport to unprecedented success within a matter of months. In 1950 Spurs won the Second Division title, after winning 27 of their 42 games and finishing nine points clear of runners-up Sheffield Wednesday. A year later they'd brought the League championship to White Hart Lane for the first time, putting Busby's Manchester United, Matthews' Blackpool and Milburn's Newcastle in the shade.

Rowe's tactics were breathtakingly simple. 'Push and run' meant exactly that – pass the ball forward, then run into position ready to receive it back. Goalscoring was spread evenly throughout the team as players moved effortlessly forward from midfield, the precision of Tottenham's off-the-ball movement knocking opponents, in some cases quite literally, sideways. But the system needed talented individuals to work, and in full-backs Alf Ramsey and Ron Burgess, and inside-forwards Eddie Baily and Les Bennett, Spurs had such talent in abundance.

If Rowe's methods had a fault, it was that they also required pace – and his squad was not in the first flush of youth. Rowe

'Still Ricky Villa' – the Argentinian turns after scoring one of the finest goals in Wembley history

himself resigned after a nervous breakdown in 1955 (though he would later to recover to help take Crystal Palace out of lower-division obscurity), and his successor Jimmy Anderson would also leave the job prematurely for health reasons – though not before laying the groundwork for the greatest team in Tottenham's history. With the creative energies of Tommy Harmer and Danny Blanchflower buzzing behind the goalscoring of Bobby Smith, Anderson's side finished second in the League in 1957 and third the following year.

When Anderson stepped down, Bill Nicholson, a lively wing-half in Rowe's title-winning side, stepped up to replace him. Nicholson's line-up was to be more combative than the one he himself had served in (no team with Maurice Norman in defence and Dave Mackay in midfield could be anything else), but it was also patient and dignified – this, after all, was a club that hadn't had a player sent-off since 1928. With Blanchflower now an articulate captain, Cliff Jones and Terry Dyson flying down the flanks and the arch improviser John White providing for Smith upfront, Nicholson's side finished third in the League in 1960, then won the title the following year. A few days later they met Leicester City in the 1961 FA Cup final at Wembley. Tottenham's performance on the day was workmanlike, and Nicholson, ever the perfectionist, was frustrated by it – but a 2–0 win was enough to put his 'Super Spurs' in the history books, as the first team to do the double in the 20th century. A string of other records had also fallen – Tottenham's title had been won with the greatest number of points, the longest run of victories from the start of the season, and with the greatest number of goals scored, an astonishing 115 in 42 games.

The following year, with a young Jimmy Greaves added to the attacking options from AC Milan, Spurs retained the Cup by beating Burnley, after losing their title to Alf Ramsey's Ipswich. In 1963 they became the first British team to win a European trophy, thrashing Atlético Madrid 5–1 in Rotterdam, with Greaves and White both outstanding. Sadly, John White was to die tragically after being struck by lighting while playing golf a year later.

White's death signalled the end of an era, but Nicholson was to build a second side of equal class, even if the same consistency in the League would be beyond them. Goalkeeper Pat Jennings, new captain Alan Mullery, Mike England, Terry

Venables and Alan Gilzean were among the fresh faces as Tottenham returned to their Cup-winning ways with a comfortable win over Chelsea at Wembley in 1967. After that, Jimmy Greaves went to West Ham in a part-exchange deal for Martin Peters, and a new target man, Martin Chivers, arrived – though despite his many qualities, he would always play with the shadow of Greaves hanging over him.

Tottenham's next triumph was in the League Cup final against Third Division Aston Villa in 1971, an insignificant victory had it not led directly to another European honour the following year, Chivers and Mullery scoring the goals that beat Wolves in a two-leg, all-English UEFA Cup final. With the League Cup regained against Norwich in 1973, Spurs wanted history to repeat itself in the UEFA Cup final against Feyenoord a year later. But after drawing 2–2 in the home leg, Tottenham were well-beaten, 2–0, in Rotterdam.

After a poor start to the following League campaign, 1974/75, Bill Nicholson stunned White Hart Lane by resigning. An increasingly quiet and aloof figure, he had been sickened by the crowd trouble that had erupted after Spurs' defeat in Holland and clearly felt that the modern game was running away from him – which, in a sense, it was. His departure, however, created a power vacuum which, arguably, Spurs have not yet filled, 25 years after the event.

The man chosen to replace Nicholson, Terry Neill, spent three almost totally forgettable years in the job – almost, but not quite, for his departure to Arsenal in 1976 was quickly followed by that of terrace hero Jennings and big central defender Willie Young, the backbone of an increasingly fragile Tottenham team. In the meantime, Neill's coach Keith Burkinshaw stepped into his shoes but was unable to prevent relegation at the end of the 1976/77 season.

The players who remained after Neill's swoop, however, gave Burkinshaw a vote of confidence and the board respected their wishes. In 1977/78, captain Steve Perryman, striker Colin Lee, winger Peter Taylor and a young playmaker called Glenn Hoddle all kept their feet on the ground as Spurs bounced straight back up into the top flight. Burkinshaw had the nucleus of a fine side, but in the close season he stunned the football world by signing two members of Argentina's 1978 World Cup-winning squad, Ossie Ardiles and Ricky Villa. Imported players had a poor record in the English game, but Ardiles struck up an immediate rapport with Hoddle, while both players' individual skill and personal modesty suited Spurs' self-image perfectly.

With Steve Archibald and Garth Crooks turning Tottenham's admirable approach play into goals, Burkinshaw's side was ready for great things by the time of the 1981 FA Cup final against Manchester

Gazza's last glory – knocking Arsenal out of the FA Cup, 1991

City. After the first match had ended 1–1, an improbable solo goal by Villa sealed a 3–2 victory in a Thursday night replay – the first Wembley had seen.

The following year, the Falklands war forced Ardiles and Villa to leave English football and Tottenham retained the FA Cup with a second replay victory, over Terry Venables' QPR, without them. But while Villa would not return, Ardiles was back at White Hart Lane as Spurs added to their list of European honours by beating Anderlecht in the 1984 UEFA Cup final on penalties.

Before that match, however, Burkinshaw had already announced his intention to resign. The club had by now been taken over by property developers Irving Scholar and Paul Bobroff, who inherited debts of £5.5million – largely accrued in the building of a new West Stand at White Hart Lane – and were resolved to wiping them out by floating Tottenham on the stock exchange. The move horrified Burkinshaw, who walked out of the gates for the last time uttering the now famous words: 'There used to be a football club in there.'

Yet for a time, there still was. David Pleat was appointed as manager in 1986 and created a side almost as attractive as Burkinshaw's had been, with Hoddle, Ardiles and Chris Waddle the creative force in a five-man midfield, and Clive Allen in a lone striker's role. Pleat admitted he'd adapted the formation from that used by the Belgian national team at the 1986 World Cup, and even signed a Belgian international, Nico Claesen, for a little added authenticity. Yet his team's sole achievement was reaching the 1987 FA Cup final (lost 3–2 to Coventry after an own-goal by Gary Mabbutt), as within a matter of months he was forced to resign after newspaper allegations of kerb-crawling.

Enter Terry Venables, brimming with ideas from his stay at Barcelona, and keen to break Tottenham's title drought, just as he had done at the Nou Camp. He came close, but not close enough. His cultured, quick-passing side, revolving around the playmaking of Paul Gascoigne and the sharp-shooting of Gary Lineker, was no more consistent in the League than any of its immediate predecessors. There was, as ever, glory to be had at Wembley, as Nottingham Forest were beaten 2–1 in the 1991 FA Cup final. That match, however, would forever be remembered for the knee injury sustained by Gascoigne after barely three minutes – an injury which, had it ended the player's career, would have threatened Tottenham's very existence.

For by now the club was once again crippled by debt. Far from providing a stable framework for the future, Sugar and Bobroff had made many of the same mistakes as the previous regime, over-spending on the East Stand, and simultaneously incurring the wrath of fans who resented the transformation of the famous Shelf terrace into an executive area, and protested vociferously. The sale of Waddle to Marseille and of the club's training ground should have been enough to stem those losses, but while the football side was in profit, other areas of the parent company's business, including the *Hummel* leisurewear concern, had lost millions. Now the sale of another player abroad – Gascoigne to Lazio – was

Hand on heart – Sugar has owned up to many mistakes

A popular German – the Klinsmann phenomenon

The two men met for the first time on a yacht moored in **Monte Carlo harbour** in the summer of 1994. **Alan Sugar**, the boat's owner and chairman of Tottenham Hotspur, had invited **Jürgen Klinsmann**, the German international striker then employed by the local club AS Monaco, onboard to discuss a transfer to Spurs.

Klinsmann revealed he had always wanted to play in England and, after making surprisingly reasonable salary demands, duly signed a two-year contract. From the word go, the player turned out to have all the instincts for good football PR that his chairman so patently lacked. His reputation for diving to earn free-kicks and penalties was defused in his first match, as he spreadeagled himself theatrically in celebration of scoring at Sheffield Wednesday. His insistence on wearing his 'lucky' #18 shirt turned out to be a marketing masterstroke, as replicas became the football fashion accessory of the season. And his ability to keep scoring goals, despite the change of manager from **Ardiles** to **Francis**, kept Spurs' spirits high.

The magic number – Jürgen's back

Yet within days of the end of the 1994/95 season, the Lane's heart would be broken. In his long career Klinsmann had never won a League champion's medal and, sensing that Spurs was not the place to break his duck, he signed for **Bayern Munich**. Sugar was furious, seeing the player's failure to fulfil his contract as a personal betrayal. When Klinsmann asked for a #18 shirt as a memento, he was told to pay for it in full, while his chairman quipped: 'I wouldn't wash my car with Klinsmann's shirt now.'

Less than three years later, however, the two men were arm-in-arm on the White Hart Lane pitch once more, as Klinsmann, having won his title with Bayern, returned to help **Christian Gross' Tottenham** escape relegation. Again, a doubting public was won over within days. Forced to wear the #33 shirt as #18 was already taken, Klinsmann unwittingly spawned another runaway retail success, while simultaneously fulfilling his promise to get Spurs out of trouble – his four goals in a 6–2 thrashing of **Wimbledon** providing a fitting finale. *Auf wiedersehen, Pet.*

needed to balance the books again. The famous knee eventually recovered, but not before a takeover battle had broken out between Robert Maxwell and Alan Sugar. Maxwell was distrusted by fans throughout the country after the shenanigans at Oxford and Derby, making Sugar the popular choice. But the *Amstrad* electronics tycoon, who had made his millions by studying the feature lists of rival products, sourcing his own goods in huge bulk and undercutting the competition by a tenner, seemed the antithesis of White Hart Lane's whole philosophy.

Sugar's business skills were not in doubt, and in a short space of time, with the help of the Gazza sale, Spurs were back in the black once more. But his football instincts were open to more searching questions. In addition to the dismissive and insensitive way in which he tended to deal with fans' objections, his managerial

He's Ginola and he's worth it – the League Cup is won against Leicester, March 1999

appointments consistently landed Tottenham with the wrong man, in the wrong place, at the wrong time.

The ill-starred elevation of Venables to chief executive status almost ended Sugar's involvement before it had begun, with the chairman finally sacking both his former manager and his infamous associate, Eddie Ashby, after Venables had refused to dismiss the latter himself. In the meantime, the appointment of Ray Clemence and Doug Livermore as joint managers served only to underline the power vacuum at squad level.

The return of Ossie Ardiles in 1993 promised great things, but while his free-form approach to the game carried echoes of the Burkinshaw era – especially once the likes of Jürgen Klinsmann and Ilie Dumitrescu had arrived in the summer of 1994 – it was hopelessly naïve for the no-nonsense, businesslike world of the Premiership. Gerry Francis, who took over from Ardiles with Spurs bottom of the table, restored some semblance of shape to proceedings, but his teams, for all their solidity, always looked inhibited – terrified of failure in a way that Tottenham had never been, and never wanted to be.

Christian Gross, who replaced Francis in the autumn of 1997, would have been the perfect man to take over a club already doing well, making the odd signing here, fine-tuning the fitness programme there. As it was, fitness was about the only positive contribution he made to a side still desperately lacking in confidence.

As for George Graham, his appointment in October 1998 seemed the most bizarre of all. How could a man so closely identified with Arsenal hope to win over the Tottenham faithful? How was he going to adapt the club's roster of primadonna stars, not least the preening, pouting David Ginola, to his vision of how the game should be played? Above all, how was he going to get Spurs winning things again?

The fact that all these questions were answered within six months says much about Tottenham's current manager. Alas, he will have no influence over the club's corporate culture, about which so much more still needs to be put right.

Here we go!

For **motorists** the good news is that the North Circular Road widening is over and traffic is now merely appalling, rather than impossible. Leave the North Circular (the A406, best-accessed from junction 27 of the M25 via the M11) onto the A1055 and follow this round, back under the A406, then turn right at the lights into Leeside Road. Go straight across the roundabout into Brantwood Road, and left at the T-junction into Tottenham High Road – the ground is on the left.

There's usually some **street parking** in the roads off the A1055, but if not, turn right at the junction with the High Road and head back across the North Circular for some alternative streets – allow for a 20min walk back to the ground from here.

Seven Sisters **tube station** is on the Victoria Line but a fair hike from the ground, so switch to the overground service and take this as far as White Hart Lane.

Just the ticket

Visiting fans are allocated a section of the South Stand (size and ticket prices vary according to fixture) – entrance in Park Lane. There are no concessions for visiting fans and only seven **disabled visitors** can be accommodated here; book through your own club.

Swift half

Many of the appealing-looking bars on the High Road itself are members-only or operate a strict non-away fans door policy. If you've parked around the A1055 then ***The Park*** next to Northumberland Park station and the ***Milford Tavern***, where Spurs players used to get changed for matches before White Hart Lane had proper facilities, both welcome visitors without colours.

The High Road has some excellent takeaway **food options** which are preferable to the lack-lustre fare on offer at the ground.

Club merchandise

The club was due to open a new ***Megastore*** next to the ground in time for the start of the 1999/2000 season. Like many teams, Tottenham gave a debut to their latest kit (supplied by *Adidas*) at the back end of the previous campaign in order to stimulate orders during the summer. All very clever – but does it make any difference to the total numbers sold?

Barmy army

With the Paxton Road (North) Stand now rising high as a two-tier structure housing 10,000, the Lane has a little of its old atmosphere back, though as expected, precious little noise emanates from the former Shelf. Trouble is rare now – a far cry from the street battles of the late Seventies and early Eighties.

In print

As ever with London there's no Saturday evening paper but the ***Evening Standard*** previews all the big games in its Friday edition.

Tottenham's original fanzine ***The Spur*** lost both influence and credibility when it became semi-affiliated to the club. For the current fan's-eye view try ***Cock-A-Dodle-Doo*** (PO Box 6979, London, N5 1JQ).

Phil Soar's ***Official History Of Tottenham Hotspur 1882–1998*** (Hamlyn, £17.99) makes an excellent starting point, but another seminal book is Hunter Davies' ***The Glory Game*** (Mainstream, £7.99), now in its umpteenth reprint after breaking new ground as an inside view of a football club a generation ago, and deservedly so.

On air

The standard London radio choice is between the BBC's ***GLR*** (94.9 FM) and ***Capital Gold*** (1548 AM).

In the net

Tottenham's **official website** says a lot about the club's attitude to its supporters. There are dozens of ways to part with your cash, but precious little in the way of feature material on what makes Spurs (either yesterday or today) special. It's all very slick to look at, but it's not really a website at all, just an electronic shop. Find out if it's improved at: www.spurs.co.uk.

For a historical perspective, look no further than ***Hotspur Hotspot*** which offers one of the best archives (not just stats) in the Premiership at: www.fotball.net/spurs.

For more regular fan sites, try the smartly designed ***SpursWeb*** at: members.aol.com/neilv1/index.htm; or ***Hot Spurs*** at: www.geocities.com/Colosseum/Midfield/8155.

Tranmere Rovers

Formation	1884 as Belmont FC
Stadium	Prenton Park, Prenton Road West, Birkenhead, Wirral, L4 9PN. ☎0151/608 4194
Ground capacity	16,700
First-choice colours	White with blue trim
Major honours	Third Division (North) champions 1938; Associate Members' Cup winners 1990; Welsh Cup winners 1935
Position 1998/99	15th in First Division

The Tranmere manager, John Aldridge, ended the 1998/99 campaign with an appeal to local businesses to sponsor players. This wasn't just a question of a few quid down in return for a mention in the matchday programme – Aldo wanted volunteers to pay people's wages. With a whole string of players set to leave Prenton Park because the club couldn't afford to renew their contracts, it seemed Rovers were almost back where they started in 1982, when chairman Gerry Gould announced the club would close within three weeks as he was 'flogging a dead horse'.

That Tranmere not only survived that scare 17 years ago, but also went on to prosper two levels of football higher than the bottom rung they then occupied, is one of the great fairytales of English football's recent history. What saved them, initially, was the generosity of more glamorous clubs, who arranged a series of fund-raising friendly matches. Yet the very proximity of such wealth, just across the Mersey at Everton and Liverpool, continues to eat away at Tranmere's potential fan base, making it as hard as ever for the Birkenhead club to make ends meet.

Not that Tranmere's founding fathers ever intended their club to play at such an exalted level as the First Division of the Football League. A local dignitary, James Hannay McGaul, was vice-president of the Tranmere Rovers Cricket Club when it decided to launch an 'association football' section in 1881. The team played just one season before deciding to change their name to plain 'Tranmere', under which they played for a further six seasons until disbanding in 1888. Three years prior to that, however, the Rovers name was revived by another team who had played their first season as Belmont. This side, comprising mainly teenage members of the Wesleyan Chapel in Whitfield Street, were soon to have a new benefactor – a certain Mr McGaul. Prior to the start of the 1885/86 season, McGaul chaired a meeting at *Sainty's Cocoa Rooms* (an alcohol-free bar at the back of Birkenhead Market), at which the decision was taken to turn Belmont into Tranmere Rovers.

The team's first home game under this name was a 10–0 romp over Liverpool North End, and it wasn't long before the new Rovers expanded their horizons beyond friendly matches to local cup and league competitions. In the 1887 Liverpool Challenge Cup, they played Everton at Anfield, and lost 9–1 – but the crowd of more than 2,000 helped pay for a move to Ravenshaw's Field, where the club could take gate money for the first time. This ground became Prenton Park in 1895, and would remain Rovers' home until 1912.

The club turned semi-professional at the end of the 19th century, and made its way through no fewer than six regional leagues before joining the Lancashire Combination in 1912. By this time the original Prenton Park had been built over, and Rovers had moved to a new ground just over the road, even going as far as to take their old grandstand with them.

Tranmere won the Lancashire Combination in 1914, and after World War I took the place of Leeds City's reserves in the

Prince of the play-offs – veteran striker Ian Muir ruptures the Leicester rearguard, 1994

Central League. Two years after that, the club was accepted as a founder member of the new Third Division (North) of the Football League. James Hannay McGaul, who'd remained as president until 1911, lived just long enough to see the club enter the League – he died in December 1921.

Rovers' early League progress was nothing to write home about, but the mood at Prenton Park was lightened with the signing of Dixie Dean in 1924. A local lad, Dean had been spotted by Tranmere coach Jack Lee playing for a Birkenhead league side. He played less than a full season for Rovers, scoring 27 goals in as many games, before moving to Everton, the club he supported as a boy. Still, the £3,000 transfer fee was the fattest Tranmere had ever received.

That record didn't last long. In 1928 Rovers sold another big centre-forward, Tom 'Pongo' Waring, to Aston Villa for £4,700. As a boy, Waring had sold chocolate and cigarettes on the Prenton Park terraces, before signing as an apprentice player. He went on to score six goals in one game against Durham City, shortly before his move to Villa, and he would return to Tranmere eight years later – though not before Robert 'Bunny' Bell had surpassed his Durham feat by scoring nine against Oldham Athletic (he also missed a penalty, apparently) in 1935.

Bell was sold to Everton, to be replaced by the returning Waring. 'Pongo' had lost a yard, but his finishing was as reliable as ever, and with new team manager Jim Knowles at the tiller, Rovers finally won promotion as Third Division (North) Champions in 1938.

They needn't have bothered. Waring was sold to Accrington Stanley, and the lack of suitable reinforcements resulted in Tranmere being immediately relegated, having won just six of their 42 games. Perhaps only World War II prevented the club from dropping out of the League altogether, for by the time peacetime football resumed in 1946, Prenton Park had a completely new team – young, adventurous and ambitious.

Life in the Third Division (North) was still tough, however, and after more than a decade of struggle, Rovers needed a last-day victory over Wrexham to squeeze into

The quality of Mersey – Aldridge thumbs a lift

the new national Third Division in 1958. By the time Walter Galbraith took charge of the team in 1961, Tranmere already had one boot in the Fourth Division – and the manager's attempts to buy his way out of trouble ended in failure.

Galbraith quit after less than a year in the job, and his replacement, Dave Russell, was to prove Rovers' first inspirational manager in the modern sense. Despite the prewar discovery of Dean and Waring, it had never occurred to anyone at Prenton Park that Tranmere had a huge well of young talent to tap into on their side of the Mersey. Russell set up a serious youth policy for the first time, and also decided to change Rovers' blue playing strip, famously proclaiming: 'Liverpool are red, Everton are blue, now Tranmere are all-white.'

Russell's early teams included several promising youngsters, but the manager was also adept at making use of other people's cast-offs – Dave Hickson and Barry Dyson both came on free transfers from Russell's former club, Bury, and while the former was probably past his prime, Dyson would go on to score 100 goals for Tranmere.

Russell's team finished fourth behind Stockport, Southport and Barrow in 1967, and won promotion to the Third Division. The following year they reached the fifth round of the FA Cup, beating top-flight Huddersfield and Coventry before losing 2–0 to Everton in front of nearly 62,000 at Goodison.

In 1969, after Tranmere had finished seventh in the Third Division, Russell became general manager, allowing coach Jackie Wright to step into his shoes. Two years later Wright brought big defender Ron Yeats over from Liverpool to become his assistant and 'eyes and ears' on the pitch. But within four months the club's new chairman, radio journalist Bill Bothwell, had sacked Wright and appointed Yeats as manager. Yeats, in turn, brought in a string of his old Anfield cronies, including Ian St John and Tommy Lawrence on the playing staff, and even Bill Shankly in a 'consultancy' role behind the scenes.

While Yeats' side memorably won 1–0 at Arsenal in the League Cup in 1973, their League form was slipping as the former Liverpool contingent aged. The manager hung up his boots a year later and was sacked with Rovers on the brink of relegation in 1975. Yeats was replaced by his coach, John King, whose association with Tranmere dated back to his signing as a player by Walter Galbraith in 1961. King could do nothing to prevent relegation but, with a line-up including Dave Philpotts and Ray Mathias at the back, Bobby Tynan in midfield and strikers John James and Ronnie Moore, he steered the club back into the Third Division at the first attempt.

Before long, Tranmere's old bugbear of poor crowds undermined King's handiwork. Tynan and Moore were sold without being replaced, and King was dismissed after relegation in 1979. Rovers survived an application for re-election under Bryan Hamilton in 1981, but the following year, a takeover by US-based businessman Billy McAteer fell through, and only the launch of a *Save The Rovers* fighting fund, together with an interest-free loan from Wirral Council (who continue to sponsor the club today) prevented Tranmere's extinction.

Another American, San Francisco lawyer Bruce Osterman, took over the club in 1985, and replaced Hamilton with Frank Worthington as player-manager. With the goalscoring of new signing Ian Muir, Worthington's side were attractive to watch. But they weren't making any progress up the table, and Osterman's patience and cash were limited – the club was in the hands of administrators when the *Park Foods* hamper millionaire Peter Johnson bought it in 1987. His first move was to bring John King back to Prenton Park, and Rovers avoided relegation to the Conference with a last-day win over Exeter.

Now, for perhaps the first time since the end of the 19th century, Tranmere had money in the bank. King spent it on a squad of players rather than a couple of individuals and, riding a wave of optimism and rising attendances, Rovers were promoted to the Third Division in 1989.

For Johnson and King, this was only the start. Over the next two years Rovers would appear at Wembley four times. In 1990 they won the Leyland Daf Cup, then lost the play-off final to Notts County. Twelve months on, the roles were reversed – defeat by Birmingham in the Cup, but victory over Bolton in the play-offs to bring Second Division football to Birkenhead for the first time since 1938.

With Ian Muir stricken by injury in 1991, King persuaded former Liverpool striker John Aldridge to join Tranmere from Real Sociedad. The Spanish club's coach, John Toshack, sensed the player's homesickness for Merseyside and put his job on the line to insist that the £250,000 deal went through. Along with other seasoned internationals such as Pat Nevin and Tommy Coyne, Aldridge got Rovers into the play-offs for a place in the Premiership three seasons in a row – though they fell at the semi-finals on each occasion.

The second of these defeats, by Leicester in 1994, came hot on the heels of a League Cup semi-final loss to Aston Villa on penalties – after Tranmere had been leading with only a minute of normal time

It's okay, I've got his favourite blanket – FA Cup scorer Andy Parkinson gets the treatment, 1998

to go. Not long after, Peter Johnson launched a successful takeover bid for Everton, and Rovers were in limbo again: Johnson retained 89% of the shares, but all his resources were now being directed across the Mersey.

Rovers drastically scaled down plans to rebuild their ground and, 12 months after a third play-off semi-final defeat, John King was made 'director of football' and replaced as manager by Aldridge. With loyal club servants Mathias and Philpotts among the backroom staff, 'Aldo' led by example on the pitch, coming within 11 goals of Ian Muir's all-time club scoring record before retiring as a player in 1998.

Consolidation of the club's position, in mid-table of what is now the First Division, was as much as fans could have asked for in 1998/99. Aldridge's knack of selling players at the right time (including goalkeeper Steve Simonsen to Johnson's Everton) has brought around £8million into the club, but with attendance levels faltering again, he has not seen a penny of it to plough back into Rovers' thinning squad. All of which has left supporters considering the unthinkable – the return of Johnson from Everton – as preferable to the sale of his shareholding to an outsider; Rovers have had quite enough of them, thank you very much.

Here we go!

From Liverpool city centre, **motorists** should take the Birkenhead Tunnel (Queensway, toll £1) under the Mersey – the ground is well-signposted to the right, immediately after the tollbooths.

From the south and east, take the M6 and M56, exiting the latter at Junction 15. Then take the M53 as far as Junction 4. Take the fourth exit off the roundabout, the B551 Mount Road toward Bebington, and follow this until it becomes Storeton Road. Turn right into Prenton Road West; the ground will be on your right.

The club's **car park**, just off Prenton Road West, is small and expensive (£3.50). **Street parking** is possible but beware residents' schemes, which are ruthlessly enforced by traffic wardens.

Travelling by **train** involves transferring to the Wirral Line low-level station at Liverpool Lime Street, then taking a Chester or Ellesmere Port service (every 15mins) as far as Birkenhead

Cheap is beautiful – Tranmere's imposing new Kop looms large over Prenton Park

Central (journey time 5mins). From the exit, cross Argyle Street and proceed along Borough Road, parallel with the flyover. Prenton Park is about a 20min walk along Borough Road. Alternatively, hop on a #42, #64 or #177 bus.

There's a choice of late departures from Birkenhead back to Lime Street for evening games, but onward connections from there could be better (see Everton chapter). For the latest timings call ☎0345/484950.

Just the ticket

Visiting fans are given some or all of the Bebington Kop, the only part of Tranmere's ground reconstruction to survive the post-Johnson cost-cutting; enter through turnstiles #22–27. Ticket prices vary according to the fixture, from £10 to £14 in 1998/99, with concessions £7 only if your club offers them to visitors.

Disabled fans have 28 spaces at the front of the Main Stand – book in advance on ☎0151/609 0137.

Swift half

The advice couldn't be simpler: head for ***The Mersey Clipper***, behind the Main Stand on Prenton Road West, where you'll find a big-screen TV, separate family and dining rooms and a tempting menu. Get here early if you want to eat on a Saturday, as the kitchen stops taking orders well before kick-off. Happily, it starts taking them again after the final whistle.

Club merchandise

The **club shop** (open Mon–Sat 9am–5pm, later on matchdays, ☎0151/608 0438) is behind the Borough Road Stand. Recently Tranmere have moved away from the large amounts of green and blue trim that adorned the players' shirts in the early Nineties, toward a more conventional all-white shirt – old Dave Russell would certainly approve.

Barmy army

The novelty having long since worn off for Liverpool and Everton fans, Tranmere are again reduced to the Birkenhead hardcore that has been following them through thick and plenty of thin for years. The problem is that there aren't enough of them to turn Prenton Park into the crackling cauldron it was in the early Nineties – surely that grand new Kop was originally intended for the home fans...?

In print

The Wirral has no daily newspaper of its own, leaving Tranmere fans to wade through the pages of Everton and Liverpool news in the ***Post*** (mornings) and ***Echo*** (evenings). The Saturday ***Football Echo*** can be relied upon for a Rovers match report, but little else.

Dave Goat's ***Give Us An R*** fanzine will tell you more about life as a Tranmere supporter than the papers ever can. Order a copy from: 6 Rockybank Road, Birkenhead, L42 7LB.

Not so long ago there wasn't a Tranmere book on the shelves, now there are...well, several of them. ***Tranmere Rovers – A Complete Record 1921-1997*** by Gilbert Upton and Steve Wilson (self-published, £10) is the standard stats work and is normally updated for each season. Peter Bishop's Tranmere book in the ***Images Of England*** series (Tempus, £9.95) makes excellent use of the picture archive at the ***Post***.

John Aldridge's autobiography ***My Story***, co-written with Hyder Jawad (Hodder & Stoughton, £16.99) takes us all the way from his early days at Newport County to today's administrative angst at Prenton Park – detailed and disarmingly frank.

On air

Rovers fans don't spend much time listening to the radio, since neither ***BBC Radio Merseyside*** (95.8 FM) nor ***Radio City*** (96.7 FM) devotes much airtime to the club. Their phone-ins, likewise, are hogged by Everton and Liverpool fans. The less said about the Wirral's own station, ***MFM*** (97.1 FM), the better.

In the net

Rovers' official website, ***Whites On-Line***, is elegantly laid out and features a personal intro from Aldo, as well as daily news updates. Head for: www.merseyworld.com/rovers/.

There's a fine **unofficial Rovers site** at: www.hilynn.demon.co.uk/trfc/trfcmain.htm. It includes Peter Bishop's fascinating history of the club among its many pages.

Walsall

Formation	1888 as Walsall Town Swifts
Stadium	Bescot Stadium, Bescot Crescent, Walsall, WS1 4SA. ☎01922/622791
Ground capacity	9,000
First-choice colours	Red and black
Major honours	Fourth Division champions 1960
Position 1998/99	2nd in Second Division (promoted)

Walsall, a small town in a big conurbation, knows it is never going to be the epicentre of the footballing universe. Like Brentford in London, Stockport County in Manchester, Halifax in West Yorkshire or Hartlepool in the north-east, Walsall FC seem destined always to play a bit-part role in the greater scheme of things in the West Midlands. There may be a big catchment area to tap, but Black Country neighbours Wolves and West Brom are both better-established (albeit only marginally so), while just down the road, Aston Villa and Birmingham City are two further major attractions.

At one – fairly recent – point in its history, it actually looked as though Walsall FC might be merged with Birmingham. The plan, hatched in the Eighties when shotgun weddings were all the rage in corporate Britain, was quickly scuppered by considerations of logic, feasibility and, above all, supporter antagonism. You can muck up the buses, the trains, the electricity and the gas, it seems – but you mess with Walsall Football Club at your peril.

Nor is the club's fighting spirit confined to the boardroom or the terracing. Exactly 100 years after the team achieved their best-ever League finish of sixth in the old Second Division, Walsall spent the 1998/99 season striving to climb back up to that level, playing an admirable brand of football and drawing enthusiastic crowds to their new(ish) Bescot Stadium. They eventually made it with a bit to spare – and their reward, of course, will be long sought-after competitive games against Wolves, West Brom...and Birmingham.

In fact, the club owes its present-day status in the English game to a merger. Walsall Swifts (founded 1877) and Walsall Town (1879) once played next-door to each other in the town. Both harboured an ambition to join the Football League, but reasoned that they were unlikely to be admitted while there was a strong rival candidate from the same town. So they got together to form Walsall Town Swifts in 1888, and four years later their ambition was realised when the club was allowed to join the newly formed Second Division. (The swift has been the symbol of the club ever since, and in 1995 Walsall broke with a century of tradition when the club badge was altered so that the bird pointed up, rather than down.)

The club was renamed plain Walsall in 1895, but lost its League status the same year. Re-election followed 12 months later, but after that record-breaking season in 1898/99, the team's form plunged again and after finishing third from bottom of the Second Division in 1901, on the same number of points as 15th-placed Barnsley, they were kicked out of the League again.

This time things were more serious. Walsall didn't get back into the League for another two decades, and only then because the competition was expanding with the setting-up of the two regional Third Divisions. Walsall became founder members of the North section, but in years to come would find themselves being booted from North to South and back again on a regular basis, depending on which teams had been relegated from the Second Division – a high price to pay for the town's accessibility. Fans reckoned the

Brightening up the Bescot – Saddlers fans take to the pitch after the team seal promotion, 1999

team always did better in the North, while successive Walsall managers were given the unenviable task of checking up on a whole new set of opponents every few years.

Perhaps not surprisingly, Walsall didn't manage to climb off this rung of the ladder until the Sixties. The club holds the record for the number of applications for re-election from the old regional Third Division, and in 1958 the team slipped briefly into the Fourth.

Walsall did, however, enjoy a golden moment in the limelight when they knocked Herbert Chapman's Arsenal out of the FA Cup in 1933. Arsenal's goalscoring legend Cliff Bastin later wrote, with more than a hint of condescension: 'The Third Division footballer may not be a soccer artist, but when it comes to the heavy tackle, he ranks with the best.'

Walsall certainly tackled hard in the game's opening phase, conceding ten free-kicks in as many minutes. But they weathered the storm, went in goalless at half-time, then took the lead when a legend of their own, Gilbert Alsop, headed home from a corner. Arsenal defender Tommy Black then conceded the penalty from which Walsall doubled their lead, and the game was over. Such was the magnitude of the upset (the *Daily Mirror* called it the 'sensation of the century') that an enraged Chapman banned Black from Highbury, and sold him to Plymouth soon after.

If Alsop was Walsall's hero of the pre-war era, Tony Richards assumed the mantle in the Fifties and Sixties, as the club finally roused itself from decades of mediocrity. After he'd completed his National Service in 1954, Richards had trials for Wolves and Birmingham but was rejected by both. Their loss was Walsall's gain. A strong, deft and mobile target-man, Richards went on to score 195 goals in nine years with the club, helping them to the Fourth Division title in 1959/60 and promotion from the Third the following season, when his personal haul was 36 goals. He scored four in a 6–4 win over Port Vale in December 1960, but he was also a team player who ran his heart out for Walsall; during one match at Swindon, he went in goal after the side's 'keeper was injured, saved a penalty, and inspired Walsall to win 3–2.

The swift Cameroonian – Charlie Ntamark

The team survived only two seasons in the Second Division, their crowds too low to support a strengthening of the squad, their football too ambitious for its own good. Richards was sold, and Walsall spent the rest of the Sixties – not to mention the entire Seventies – becalmed in the Third Division.

Allan Clarke briefly rekindled the fans' imagination before moving to Leeds, but it was another graduate of the club's school of goal poaching, Alan Buckley, who was to have a more lasting impact on Walsall. Having spent an initial spell at the club in the early Seventies (during which he scored more than 20 League goals in five successive seasons), Buckley returned from Birmingham in 1979 as player-manager. The club he'd come back to had just been relegated, but Buckley led from the front, inspiring an immediate return to the Third Division and engendering a sense of ambition at long last. He left in 1986, but his legacy continued to be felt and Walsall were promoted to the Second Division under his successor, Tommy Coakley, two years later.

It proved a false dawn, in more ways than one. Buckley's departure had been hastened when Walsall's chairman for 13 years, Ken Wheldon, announced his intention to merge the club with Birmingham, in which he had just acquired a controlling interest. When the fans inevitably rebelled, Wheldon sold out to millionaire Terry Ramsden. A quintessentially Eighties figure, Ramsden was a young London stockbroker who used his financial clout to ensure Walsall's survival as an independent club. The fans lionised him, but the team's promotion season of 1987/88 coincided with the stock-market crash of Black Monday, and within months Ramsden was bankrupt.

Coakley was ordered to sell David Kelly, the Irish striker whose goals had got Wallsall up, to West Ham. When it became clear the club-record £600,000 transfer fee was going to be consumed by Ramsden's debts, Coakley also left. Walsall finished bottom of the Second Division in 1989, and bottom of the Third a year later.

For the supporters, the sense of loss was doubled when Walsall ended the 1989/90 season with their last game at Fellows Park, the club's home since 1896. Ramsden may have gone, but his plan to sell the ground to a supermarket chain and move Walsall to a new stadium on the site of a former sewage works was too far advanced to be abandoned.

So Walsall kicked off the 1990/91 campaign at the Bescot Stadium, a charmless rectangle of sheet metal and blockwork which the fans have been trying to turn into 'home' ever since. Initially the outlook was bleak. The property company which had bought Ramsden's share of Walsall was itself wound up in 1991, having failed to attract any partners to develop the rest of the Bescot site. Local businessman Jeff Bonser became the club's fifth chairman in six years, and while the fans sensed a new

Weather or not – Ray Graydon leads training at a wintry Lilleshall

era of stability, cash was still desperately tight. Kenny Hibbitt, who'd taken over as manager in 1990, put together a mish-mash of a squad that included midfielder Charlie Ntamark, who Walsall had signed from non-League football after watching him play for Cameroon at Italia '90, and who would stay with the club for seven years.

Hibbitt's side made the play-offs in 1993, but it wasn't until his replacement by Chris Nicholl that Walsall finally won promotion. Another bargain import, the Bermudan striker Kyle Lightbourne, then earned the team mid-table respectability for two seasons before being sold to Coventry. He was replaced by Roger Boli, once of RC Lens, but although the fans took the Frenchman and the team's enterprising style to their hearts (and thoroughly enjoyed an FA Cup day out at Old Trafford, despite a 5–1 defeat), Walsall finished the season just four points clear of the relegation zone.

After taking over as manager in 1998, Ray Graydon sold Boli to Dundee United and set about creating a more conventional – though still thoroughly entertaining – English Second Division unit. With Neil Pointon directing defensive traffic and Andy Rammell scoring with almost every sniff of goal, Walsall felt that while they were never going to catch Kevin Keegan's Fulham, they had every chance of filling the second automatic promotion berth. Having pulled away from Preston, Manchester City and the rest, they beat Oldham 3–1 at the Bescot to go up with two fixtures to spare.

Graydon, a former Villa player well-versed in the rivalries of West Midlands football, was named Second Division manager of the season, while a grateful Borough Council laid plans for a civic reception...

Here we go!

The good news is that Bescot Stadium is next to a motorway. The bad news is that said motorway is the M6, and the busiest stretch of it to boot. Until the north Birmingham relief road is built, **motorists** should allow plenty of time to negotiate traffic, from either north or south, particularly before midweek evening kick-offs.

From the south and west, take the M5 beyond Junction 1 then follow signs for Walsall and Wolverhampton as the road divides; this road then joins the northbound M6 and should be followed until the next exit at Junction 9 (signposted Wednesbury). At the roundabout, take the third exit, the A461 toward Walsall. As the road divides, turn right into Wallows Lane, then get into the right-hand lane and go straight across a set of lights. Turn right at the next set into Bescot Crescent – the ground is on your left after the retail park.

From the north, east and south-east, take the M6 and exit at Junction 9, then follow the directions above.

There are separate **car parks** for home and away fans at the ground. Alternatively, save yourself £2 by parking at the retail park instead.

Bescot Stadium has its own eponymously named **train station** just the other side of the M6, served by local trains to and from Birmingham New Street (hourly, no Sunday service). From New Street there are late connections for evening games back to London, Manchester,

Leeds, Derby, Sheffield and Bristol. For the latest timings call ☎0345/484950.

Just the ticket

Visiting fans are accommodated in the William Sharp Stand; enter through turnstiles #21–28 in Bescot Crescent. Ticket prices in 1998/99 were adults £12, juniors and OAPs £8. The stand has seats for 2,000, so you should have no difficulty avoiding one of the Bescot's infamous, view-destroying roof supports. **Disabled supporters** have spaces at the front of the Banks's Brewery Stand, and visiting **families** can also be accommodated here in blocks H and I – book either in advance on ☎01922/622791.

Swift half

The King George V, opposite the *Morrisons* supermarket on Wallows Lane, is a big, friendly place with its own family room and the added attraction of local brew Highgate on draught.

For once, **eating** at the ground makes a modicum of sense, although Walsall's balti pies don't quite live up to the hype that surrounds them. For more substantial fare, why not try the café inside ***Morrisons***? Prices are low and you might just be adding salt to your chips on the site of the old Fellows Park centre-circle.

Club merchandise

There's a **club shop** (open matchdays & Suns only, ☎01922/622791) in the H L Fellows Stand at the ground, and another in Walsall town centre (open Mon–Sat, ☎01922/631072) at Unit 5, The Arcade, Bradford Street. Both outlets have home shirts at £36.99 (children's sizes £26.99), and pint glasses (may as well get your six-packs from from *Morrisons*) at £4.99.

Barmy army

The patience of the Walsall faithful has been tested to breaking point over the past decade, but the fans in the Gilbert Alsop Terrace remain good-natured, all the more so since the 1999 promotion. The Bescot is roofed on all sides, which can make 4,000 sound more like 14,000, and trouble is unheard of – though there may be tension at the local derbies in 1999/2000.

Supermarket sweep – Fellows Park before it became *Morrisons*

In print

The Birmingham-based ***Argus*** and Wolverhampton's ***Star*** both devote a surprising amount of space to Walsall. Both also publish Saturday evening sports editions, available locally from around 6pm. There are no fanzines but there is a fine **programme shop** at the William Sharp end of the ground.

Appropriately, given the club's new status, 1999 will see the publication of a new history of Walsall, ***Saddlers Complete Record*** by Tony Matthews (Breedon, £16.99).

On air

The local BBC station, ***Radio WM*** (95.6 FM) is rated excellent for local football. Alternatives are the independent ***Beacon Radio*** (97.2 FM) and ***Capital Gold*** (1152 AM). Sports phone-ins are very popular in this part of the world – there's sure to be at least one local show on the air-waves as you leave the Bescot.

In the net

There's no need to venture any further than Walsall's **official website** at: www.saddlers.co.uk/. It covers a broad range of subjects from team news to club merchandising, with a smile and a song – we could probably do without the latter.

Watford

Formation	1881 as Watford Rovers
Stadium	Vicarage Road, Watford, WD1 8ER. ☎01923/496000
Ground capacity	22,000
First-choice colours	Yellow, red and black
Major honours	Second Division champions 1998; Third Division champions 1969; Fourth Division champions 1978
Position 1998/99	Fifth in First Division (promoted via play-offs)

For once, Graham Taylor was lost for words. Speaking to his club chairman, Elton John, via a two-way satellite video link, he stood speechless as the the pop singer turned football club saviour intoned platitude after platitude about what a great day it had been, what a magical moment, and so on *ad infinitum*. Of course, Elton couldn't be at Wembley for Watford's play-off final victory over Bolton, as he was on tour in America. But thanks to modern technology he'd seen all the action as it happened, and now, using that same technology, he was thanking his manager the way only pop stars can – lovingly, gushingly, and with no thought as to how many seconds there might be before the next commercial.

Then again, that is what pop star chairmen are for – to encourage from afar, a bit like royalty. Their actual presence is not always required, but they need to be there in spirit. And Watford certainly missed Elton John's spirit during the period he was absent from the club's letterhead, in the early Nineties. Now he's back, and it's like he's never been away – Watford in the top flight, opposition defences cowering at the prospect of another set-piece cross being floated into the box, the Vicarage Road faithful roaring with delight. At a time when so many club chairmen are faceless men in suits who talk purely in terms of business, Elton is special not because of who he is, but because of what he is – a pop star, and a proper fan to boot.

As for Taylor, his world has also come full circle, if anything by an even more tortuous route. True, he didn't have to face the traumatic funerals of Gianni Versace and the Princess of Wales. But standing on the touchline as England lost to Holland in Rotterdam was quite bad enough, thank you very much. At Wembley on 31 May 1999, he was back in his element, like Elton, doing what he does best.

The first coming – Elton at Wembley, 1984

Watford's promotion to the Premiership via the play-offs was either a national

Off the floor – Everton are pressured, 1984

disaster, or a much-needed breath of fresh air, depending on your viewpoint. In the cynics' corner, there are those who believe that the long-ball revolution Taylor preached in the Eighties (and which he used to such devastating non-effect as England boss in the Nineties) effectively hurled our national game back into the dark ages, a period of tactical ignorance and insensitivity from which we have only recently emerged. Also affiliated to this camp are the play-off despisers, who view the current system of promotion as a crass money-making exercise, and want all future movements between the divisions to be decided by League placing alone.

Watford's victory gave powerful ammunition to both groups – they were unashamedly playing the long-ball game (Taylor prefers to call it 'the long pass'), and they finished the 1998/99 season in fifth, nine points behind third-placed Ipswich Town, who didn't even make it as far as Wembley.

On the other hand, it's doubtful whether football – like most team sports – can ever be run on the basis of a simple meritocracy. Its essence lies in its variety and unpredictability, and in this respect, Watford's win was indeed a tonic. There is no more need to fear their tactics than there is to like them. Even if Taylor's side were to make a good go of their Premiership return by 'long passing' it about, it's inconceivable that such a strategy could again become the orthodoxy. Would Ruud Gullit really swap 'sexy football' for Vicarage Road's hit-and hope? Palpably not.

As for the play-offs...every year, supporters of mid-table, lower-division clubs are sustained through their season by the hope, no matter how faint, of reaching them. At a time when it's supposed to be impossible for clubs to take giant strides up the League ladder, the play-offs provide them with a means of doing so. And in taking such rich advantage of them, Watford have done no more than re-affirm the essential fluidity of the game and the fans' opportunity to dream – without which, we may as well let the top four teams in the Premiership play a little tournament of their own, scrap all the other fixtures, and spend the money we've saved down the pub.

If Watford's rise from Second Division to Premiership in two seasons has broken the Nineties rulebook, and their manager's outlook has had coaches dusting off copies of Charles Hughes' *The Winning Formula*, then Taylor's previous spell at the club was, if anything, even more mould-breaking. When he arrived at Vicarage Road in 1977, Watford were in the Fourth Division. Prior to that, their tale had been a study in anonymity, their edge-of-London catchment area a fertile poaching ground for Arsenal and Tottenham, their ground modest and unassuming, their ambition, to all intents and purposes, limited.

Yet, for a part of the world not known for putting down deep football roots, the Watford story starts early. As long ago as 1865, a team called the Hertfordshire Rangers were representing the area in FA Cup matches against some of the leading clubs of the day, and their exploits soon inspired other teams to set up in and around Watford. One of these, Watford

Rovers, first saw the light of day in 1881, and began playing on Vicarage Meadow, not far from Watford FC's current ground. They were forced to move before very long, however, and their search for a more permanent home led to a temporary change of name in 1890, when they were offered use of the new West Herts Sports Club Ground on Cassio Road, on the condition that they play under the name 'West Herts'. This they agreed to do, and the following year, with the best ground in the area at their disposal, West Herts swallowed up the old Hertfordshire Rangers club. When another local rival, Watford St Mary's, was absorbed in 1898, the resulting club forged a new identity as plain Watford FC. As the *de facto* team of the region, Watford then turned professional and joined the Southern League.

In 1909 Watford turned themselves into a limited company in an attempt to become independent of the sports club that owned the West Herts ground. This suited the latter, too, as West Herts members were starting to resent the antics of Watford fans, and the feeling was mutual. Still, Watford didn't leave until after the Southern League had been absorbed into the Third Division of the Football League in 1920, and only then because the local *Benskins* brewery bought the Vicarage Road Recreation Ground, agreed to lease it to the club, then lent Watford £12,000 so that basic stands could be built.

Watford played their first game at Vicarage Road in August 1922, but only 8,000 souls braved pouring rain to attend, and with local interest proving hard to stir, the club came close to receivership on several occasions prior to World War II. Perhaps more money would changed hands at the turnstiles if the football had been better, but muddling along in mid-table was very much Watford's forte until three years before the war, when they moved into the top four in the Third Division (South) and stayed there until the outbreak of fighting.

After the war it was business as usual, with an application for re-election in 1951 (the year a women's toilet was provided at Vicarage Road for the first time), followed by relegation to the newly formed Fourth Division eight years later.

The most gifted Hornet – John Barnes (centre) waves to the crowd, October 1982

Overhead and under the bar – Nick Wright's bicycle kick gives Watford the lead against Bolton

This formed something of a watershed. While the board decided to ditch the club's distinctive but 'unlucky' turquoise shirts in favour of gold, manager Ron Burgess got himself a new strike partnership comprising Dennis Uphill and the former Arsenal centre-forward Cliff Holton. In 1960/61, the two netted 72 goals between them as Watford hauled themselves out of the Fourth Division, albeit only in fourth place.

After Bill McGarry had replaced Burgess and got Watford within a whisker of another promotion in 1964, Ken Furphy took over and succeeded where McGarry had failed, winning the Third Division title in 1969. Furphy's side, with a young Pat Jennings in goal and Tony Currie running the show in midfield, was the best in Watford's history up to this point, and they proved they could live with the elite by knocking Liverpool out of the 1969/70 FA Cup, going all the way to the semi-finals before being humbled 5–1 by Chelsea.

The rot set in when the stars were sold and Furphy himself departed in 1971. Four years later Watford were back in the basement, crowds had fallen, and the club was so heavily in debt that greyhound racing was briefly staged at Vicarage Road to act as an extra source of income.

Within a year, Elton John had bought a controlling interest in Watford and life would never be quite the same again. After a grand scheme to build a new stadium for the club collapsed at the planning stage, the new chairman turned his attentions to the team, and his appointment of Graham Taylor as manager in 1977 proved inspired. The two were a perfect match – Elton the rose-tinted visionary with the resources to make dreams come true; Taylor the rootsy realist whose pioneering work at Lincoln City had shown how a small club could reap the benefits not just of 'direct football' but of forging closer links with its community.

At the end of Taylor's first full season, 1977/78, Watford won the Fourth Division title. Twelve months later they were promoted again. After flirting with relegation from the Second Division in 1979/80, Watford bounced back, and in 1982 were promoted to the top flight for the first time in their history, after finishing second to David Pleat's Luton Town. The really remarkable bit was still to come. Despite (or perhaps because of) an almost total lack of top-division expertise, Taylor's side showed no fear of First Division life. In Ross Jenkins and Luther Blissett they had two of the livliest forwards in the League, and Taylor's system, for all its limitations, also gave free rein to Nigel Callaghan and John Barnes – the son of a Jamaican diplomat who'd been spotted playing parks football – to surge down the flanks with pace and elegance.

The second coming – Taylor, Blissett and John address the press

Jenkins retired after Watford had finished second in the League to Liverpool in 1983, and Blissett was sold to AC Milan for £1million. But Taylor found another energetic young striker in Mo Johnston and, with Barnes still in his pomp and the veteran Kenny Jackett keeping the rest of the team together, Watford reached the 1984 FA Cup final – only to lose 2–0 to Howard Kendall's tough-tackling Everton.

That proved as far as the 'long pass' could take Watford. Blissett returned from Milan, amid persistent reports that the Italians had really wanted Barnes all along, while Barnes himself was sold to Liverpool. Bertie Mee, the former Arsenal manager who had brought vital top-level knowledge to the party, faded from the scene, while Taylor himself was poached by Aston Villa, and without him, Elton John seemed to lose enthusiasm for the project. A brief, disastrous spell under Dave Bassett's management led directly to relegation in 1988, and by the turn of the Nineties, Elton had decided to take a back seat.

The new decade, with its satellite TV deals, its brash marketing and its galaxy of imported stars, was not kind to Watford's homespun wisdom. By 1995 they'd been relegated again, and might have continued to fall had the pop star not been tempted by the prospect of a comeback tour of the Premiership. With Taylor also returning – initially as general manager with Jackett in charge of team affairs, but after May 1997 as manager – the old formula at least had the chance to work its magic.

Few could have predicted, though, that a repeat performance would be engineered so quickly, with such total conviction, and against a footballing backdrop that had changed so dramatically since Watford last rose through the ranks 20 years earlier. Yet rise they did, despite all the criticism, while Taylor completed a remarkable personal transformation from tabloid turnip-head to modern-day media darling.

You can almost see him now, celebrating Watford's triumphant return to Europe (in Rotterdam, perhaps?), greeting a quote-hungry press with the words: 'Do I like yellow.' But only if Elton isn't on the other end of the line.

Here we go!

Watford has the reputation of being a nightmare for **motorists** but it's not really justified – if you get lost, just get back on the ring road (which is very compact) and try again. To get to the town centre, exit the M1 at junction 5 onto the A4008. Keep following signs for Town Centre and park up at one of the multi-storey **car parks**, since street parking around the ground is tricky. From the centre, Vicarage Road is well-signposted. If you don't see any pedestrian signs, follow the motor traffic ones for the A4145 Rickmansworth or the General Hospital.

Watford Junction **train station** is on the West Coast mainline into London Euston, with direct trains from Liverpool, Manchester and Crewe. For the latest timings call ☎0345/484950. At Watford Junction change onto the local service and take this one stop to Watford High Street, which is closer to the ground. From the High Street station, turn left along the ring road, then follow the footpath off to the left, across Wiggenthall Road and on to Vicarage Road – the ground is a little way down on the left.

Just the ticket

Visiting fans are allocated a section of the Vicarage Road (North). Inevitably prices have risen since Watford's promotion and the club is operating a match-category system for 1999/2000 – book any concessions in advance through your own club. **Disabled visitors** are accommodated in the Rookery Stand opposite, booking now advisable on ☎01923/496000.

Swift half

The unofficial away fans' watering hole is ***Mac's Bar*** in Fearnley Street, a left-turning off Vicarage Road if walking back toward the town centre. There's no shortage of alternative options in town, and although pubs some have doormen on matchdays, they will normally let well-behaved, respectable-looking supporters in.

Club merchandise

The ***Hornet Shop*** at the Vicarage Road end (☎01923/496005) has a vast range of yellow, red and black items, from the latest, very traditional home shirt (£40, kids' sizes £33) to Harry or Harriet 'Beanie Buddies' at £8 each. There's no sign of the old turquoise making a comeback just yet, alas.

Barmy army

Trouble has never been a huge problem at Vicarage Road, and things are likely to remain that way unless Luton Town can clamber up to the same level.

In print

The local ***Observer*** is the paper for news and previews but there's no Saturday evening edition. Fanzine information was a bit sketchy at press time but you should find ***Clap Your Hands, Stamp Your Feet*** (9 West Towers, Pinner, HA5 1TZ) on sale at the ground.

Club author Trefor Jones has published both an ***Illustrated Who's Who*** (£8.99) and a ***Season By Season*** guide (£9.99), the latter current to 1998.

On air

BBC Three Counties Radio (630 AM) offers decent matchday coverage including phone-ins after both Saturday and midweek games.

In the net

The **official site** has a neat, fresh feel to it and obligingly offers different versions for fast and slow internet connections – something a lot of other clubs would do well to copy. There's a full news archive, vintage photography and a big e-commerce section at: www.watfordfc.com.

Of the unofficials, the **wfc.net mailing list** site offers links to all other Watford-related sites at: www.wfc.net. Among these, two refreshingly irreverent sites worth visiting are ***Blind, Stupid & Desperate*** at: www.display.co.uk/watford; and ***Cult Of Watford*** at: www.kowalski.demon.co.uk/watford.

West Bromwich Albion

Formation	1878 as West Bromwich Strollers
Stadium	The Hawthorns, Halfords Lane, West Bromwich, B71 4LF. ☎0121/525 8888
Ground capacity	25,400
First-choice colours	Navy-and-white stripes
Major honours	League champions 1920; Second Division champions 1902, 1911; FA Cup winners 1888, 1892, 1931, 1954, 1968; League Cup winners 1966
Position 1998/99	12th in First Division

'I saw this huge gap, the white net and the yellow ball streaking for the corner. It was a fantastic moment. Nothing will ever match it.' Jeff Astle, West Bromwich Albion's winning goalscorer in the 1968 FA Cup final against Everton, was an unusually succinct interviewee. There never was another moment like it for him, and for the club, there has never been another moment like it since.

Going for a song – Jeff Astle at Wembley, 1968

While Astle has since found celebrity status as a novelty singing adjunct to the career of TV comedian Frank Skinner, the sadness for Baggies fans – of whom Skinner is the most famous – is that the club now looks so far from scaling the heights of that sweltering May afternoon more than three decades ago.

Founder members of the Football League, winners of every major domestic trophy the English game has to offer, stout fighters in Europe, West Brom have been out of the top flight since 1986, and have seldom come close to hauling themselves back up since then. Even more galling, to the supporters, is the fact that everyone around them seems to be moving ahead. Yet the Hawthorns, for all its history and its dramatically improved modern facilities, lacks the dynamism of Villa Park's Doug Ellis, the boldness of the Sullivan regime at St Andrew's, or the happy extravagance of Molineux's Jack Hayward. Damnit, even Walsall managed to win promotion to the First Division in 1999.

The limiting factor in West Brom's development was always reckoned to be the club's constitution, under which no one shareholder could own more than 15% of the club. Chairman Tony Hale successfully ended this in the early Nineties, and floated the club as a publicly owned corporation. But while fresh funds have turned the team's immediate environment into a more

Reason to be cheerful – Bobby Robson, 1964

to move repeatedly from ground to ground, Albion had put their first trophy on the table – the Staffordshire Cup, won 3–2 against Stoke in the final. That same year, the FA Cup was entered for the first time – beginning a long association with knockout tournaments which historically have always seemed to be the club's forte. A first FA Cup final was reached in 1886, lost 2–0 to the dominant Blackburn Rovers side of the period after a replay at the Baseball Ground, Derby. Albion repeated the feat a year later, only to lose by the same scoreline to Aston Villa at Kennington Oval. Then, in 1888, it was third time lucky – Preston were beaten 2–1, again at the Oval, with winger Billy Bassett, a newcomer to the side, making the difference between defeat and victory.

A far greater and more symbolic victory for the club, however, was that West Brom's Cup final exploits had pushed them to the forefront of the imagination of the football establishment at the time. It seemed the most natural thing in the world for the Aston Villa president William McGregor to invite Albion to become founder members of his Football League for its inaugural season of 1888/89 – though the prospect of some lucrative local derbies probably also helped West Brom's cause, as it did that of their Black Country neighbours Wolves.

Yet Albion would soon set their pattern of progress in the Cup and frustrating inconsistency in the League. The best they managed in the latter competition before the turn of the century was a fifth-place finish in 1890, but in 1892 they won the Cup again, Bassett again the inspiration behind a satisfying and deeply symbolic 3–0 win over Villa at the Oval. (Villa would gain

pleasant one – with the promise of further improvements to come – life on the pitch has been the same old struggle against inconsistency and in-fighting. One reason why Hale, after all the promises of jam tomorrow, only narrowly won a motion to unseat him in the summer of 1999.

How fans of the Baggies (nobody round these parts seems to use the term 'Throstles') must pine for the earlier, more innocent atmosphere in which the club was formed, back in 1878. The story goes that when workers at the *Salter's Spring Works* in West Bromwich decided to form a football club, they had to send somebody to nearby Wednesbury to purchase a ball, such was the game's rarity value in the town at the time.

The team's first match was played on 13 December 1979 against Black Lake Victoria, and the Strollers won 1–0. However, the name was thought to sound rather casual, and within a year of formation members decided to change it to West Bromwich Albion. By 1883, despite having their revenge three years later, in the first final to be played at Crystal Palace.)

In 1900 Albion finally moved to a ground they could call home – the Hawthorns, so-named by the club's secretary, Frank Heaven, who discovered that the area around the site had been known as the Hawthorn's Estate. The site was a fair distance from the centre of West Bromwich, but the club at that stage hoped to draw additional support from the Birmingham area, and was in sufficiently inspired mood for the ground to be made ready for the 1900/01 season in a little over three months.

Alas, like so many clubs who built new grounds for themselves at the turn of the century, West Brom were in danger of over-reaching themselves. Relegation to the Second Division at the end of that first season at the Hawthorns had a drastic effect on attendances, and only the determination of the club's newly appointed secretary-manager, Fred Everiss, kept both the creditors at bay and pushed the team straight back into the top flight at the first attempt in 1902.

A further relegation and promotion followed in the Edwardian period, culminating in the Second Division title in 1911 and a Cup final the following year, lost 1–0 to 'Battling Barnsley' in a replay at Bramall Lane.

But if the prewar era had been fraught with problems, the postwar one couldn't have got off to a brighter start. Though not without casualties, Everiss' team emerged from World War I with several of its key players still at their posts, including full-backs Jesse 'Peerless' Pennington and Black Country-born Joe Smith. Together with the fresh legs of diminutive wing-half Tommy Magee, they formed the backbone of a side that was too solid for the rest of the League in the first postwar season, and the 1919/20 championship was won in style, with 104 goals scored and a nine-point winning margin from the runners-up, Burnley.

The continuity which was such an asset in 1920, however, would then prove Albion's undoing. As older players such as Pennington hung up their boots, other clubs rebuilt their squads and caught up

From apprentice Baggie to Captain Marvel – Bryan Robson in the thick of it, 1980

with West Brom's fast-paced game. The team sank quickly into mid-table, and by 1927, Albion were playing Second Division football again.

The comeback was a while coming, but worth the wait. In season 1930/31, with Magee still tormenting opposing defenders, captain Tommy Glidden on the opposite flank and Billy Richardson a menacing presence at centre-forward, Albion won promotion from the Second Division and then, just to put the icing on the cake, they beat Birmingham City 2–1 in their first visit to Wembley to regain the FA Cup.

Another Cup final followed in 1935, but was lost 4–2 to Sheffield Wednesday, and once again, Albion were in danger of allowing their Cup exploits to distract them from the serious business of maintaining their top-flight status in the League. They were finally relegated in 1938.

Ten years later, after the interruption of World War II had given the club a chance to take stock, an era came to an end when Fred Everiss decided to cease his involvement with team selection – though he would retain his position on the Hawthorns' board of directors until 1951. Albion were one of the last teams to appoint a full-time manager (Everiss' replacement, Jack Smith) and the change had an immediate effect, with promotion and a run to the FA Cup quarter-finals in 1949.

Much better was to come, though, after Vic Buckingham took charge of team affairs in 1953. With Johnny Nicholls and the immortal Ronnie Allen leading the line, Albion began their 1953/54 First Division campaign with nine straight wins and led the table for much of the season. Later stricken by injuries, they were eventually pipped to the title by Wolves after a 1–0 defeat at the Hawthorns. But, as ever, there was compensation in the FA Cup, where Allen scored twice in a classic final as Tom Finney's Preston were edged out 3–2. Yet while Allen would remain at the Hawthorns for another seven years, Buckingham's team would have only a couple more Cup runs to show for their undoubted flair. The manager himself left in 1959, and although Albion remained a solid top-flight proposition, there would be no more time spent in the spotlight until the mid-Sixties, when a new goalscoring combination of Jeff Astle and Tony Brown propelled the club to further Cup successes. First came the League Cup – a competition which Albion, in common with many leading clubs, had initially refused to enter, but which by 1965/66 had acquired

Winger and a player – the late, great Lawrie Cunningham

From poacher to coach – Cyrille Regis on the Albion bench

enough prestige to persuade them to change their minds. They were glad they did so, for in that first season of participation Albion won the trophy, overcoming a 2–1 deficit against West Ham in a two-leg final by beating the Londoners (replete with the trio of Moore, Peters and Hurst that would win the World Cup for England barely three months later) 4–1 at the Hawthorns.

Two years later, a turgid, stifling FA Cup final against Harry Catterick's Everton appeared to be heading for a goalless draw when, three minutes into extra time, Astle found himself with rare time and space 25 yards out, saw the goal gaping in front of him, and shot unstoppably past Gordon West – 1–0 to Albion, and the only goal of the game.

As it turned out, West Brom's victory against Everton, no matter how memorable, would be the swansong for another side later bedevilled by inconsistency and the absence of squad reinforcement at crucial times. An ill-starred spell in the manager's chair for former Baggies right-back Don Howe led to relegation in 1973, and while the former Leeds midfielder Johnny Giles would bring the club back up as player-manager three years later, it was not until the appointment of Ron Atkinson in 1978 that the Hawthorns regained some its former swagger.

Unlike almost all Albion's postwar managers, Big Ron knew how to play the transfer market and was not afraid to throw inexperienced players into the first team. Thus cheap signings Lawrie Cunningham and Cyrille Regis played off the passing of raw youth products Bryan Robson and Remi Moses in midfield, and West Brom roared back into the public eye, reaching an FA Cup semi-final in Ron's first season and finishing third in 1978/79, the ticket for a return to the European stage the club had first graced a decade earlier.

Sadly, Atkinson left for Manchester United, taking Robson and Moses with him. The transfer fees did wonders for West Brom's bank balance, but the side never recovered its poise, despite a return by Ronnie Allen as manager and, after his sacking at Old Trafford, by Atkinson himself. Relegation in 1986 was followed by the club's darkest hour – a 4–1 home defeat by non-League Woking in the third round of the FA Cup in 1991. Manager Brian Talbot was sacked, but his successor Bobby Gould could not prevent relegation to the Third Division for the first time in Albion history.

Ossie Ardiles managed to get a young side playing their way through the play-offs and back up into what was now the First Division in 1994, but since then, West Brom have been unable to shake off their mid-table malaise. The last incumbent of the manager's chair, Denis Smith, was sacked after chairman Hale won his confidence vote, with only days left before the kick-off to the 199/2000 season. His replacement, Brian Little, faced an unenviable struggle, at a club that used to be the envy of all those around, but is in danger of becoming the ugly duckling.

Here we go!

Motorists have it easy, at least when it comes to finding the ground. From junction 1 of the M5 motorway, simply turn right at the roundabout onto the A41 Birmingham Road. The Hawthorns is about half a mile up ahead, on the right.

There's are **car parks** on Halfords Lane but these are not recommended for a quick getaway. A better bet might be to take the second exit from the motorway roundabout into Kenrick Way, off which there's free street parking and, motorway traffic permitting, a swifter exit. Depending on where you park, allow for a 10–15min walk to the ground from here.

The Hawthorns has its own **train station** served by local services to and from Birmingham Moor Street, across the bullring from the main New Street station. Alternatively fans from London can take train from Marylebone to Birmingham Snow Hill, and catch a Hawthorns service direct from there. See Aston Villa for other connections from New Street, and as usual it pays to check the latest timings on ☎0345/484950.

Just the ticket

Visiting fans are allocated some or all of the Smethwick End of the Hawthorns, the furthest end from Birmingham Road. Tickets in 1998/99 were adults £14, concessions £7.50, though can save a bob or two by booking in advance.

Disabled supporters have plenty of space in front of the Smethwick End. Booking advisable on ☎0121/525 8888.

Swift half

Welcoming pubs are a bit thin on the ground around the Hawthorns. Motorists should explore the centre of West Bromwich, the other side of the motorway roundabout, while those coming by train have a better choice in Birmingham.

Club merchandise

The **club shop** at the ground stocks the expected range of replica kit and leisurewear. Albion have worn the same navy blue-and-white striped shirts since before they joined the League in 1888, but the argument rages on as to whether the term 'Baggies' refers to the players' shorts.

Demolition derby – tempers fray in one of the biennial Black Country clashes with Wolves, 1999

Barmy army

West Brom's hooligan element is small but still very much active, with some incidents pre-arranged with like-minded indivduals from other clubs. As a civilised fan yourself, you should be well out of it so long as you sit in the allocated away fans' section.

In print

The ***Express & Star*** publishes a *Sporting Star* while the ***Argus*** rushes out a *Sports Argus* – take your pick.

The club used to publish its own newspaper, ***Baggies***, but this is now an unofficial publication (apparently the views of the editorial team were a little *risqué*), produced monthly to very high standards. Also look out for the long-established fanzine ***Grorty Dick*** (34 Vicarage Road, Wednesbury, DY10 9BA).

The archives of the *Express & Star* have been very effectively plundered to produce ***Albion Memories – West Bromwich Albion In Pictures*** (Breedon, £16.99), while Glenn Willmore's ***Hawthorns Encyclopedia*** (Mainstream, £7.99) is also worth a look.

On air

BBC Radio WM (95.6 FM) has the ear of the fans with its regular phone-ins after both Saturday afternoon and midweek evening games.

In the net

Albion's **official site** is fairly standard *Planet*-run fare, far too slow to load but quite rewarding once you get there, and with the usual impressive multi-media and e-commerce sections. Find it at: www.wba.co.uk.

Star of the unofficial sites is ***BOING***, an exceptionally wide-ranging effort with great historical, pictorial and multi-media content at: www.baggies.com. Also worth a look is ***Cudden's Baggies Web Page***, which plays the club's *Liquidator* theme tune through your PC speakers at: www.geocities.com/Colosseum/Park/1176.

West Ham United

Formation	1895 as Thames Ironworks FC
Stadium	Boleyn Ground, Upton Park, London, E13 9AZ. ☎0181/548 2748
Ground capacity	26,000
First-choice colours	Claret and sky-blue
Major honours	Second Division champions 1958, 1981; FA Cup winners 1964, 1975, 1980; European Cup-Winners' Cup winners 1965
Position 1998/99	Fifth in Premiership

Fortune's always hiding, so the song says, but the new millennium sees West Ham United mining a rare seam of the stuff. As the players ran out for a UEFA Intertoto Cup game against the Finnish side FC Jokerit in July 1999, the club was celebrating its return to European competition (of a kind) after an absence of 18 years. A fifth-place finish in the Premiership the previous season had been the ticket back to the continent, and it said much about the ambition of the modern-day Upton Park that West Ham accepted the invitation to enter the Intertoto, after earlier hopes of an automatic UEFA Cup place had been dashed. Never mind the slog, the ridicule, the inconvenience, or having to cut short the summer holidays in Florida – if the event's there, it's there to be played for.

The new spirit of endeavour has come as a shot in the arm to Hammers fans, who had become increasingly fed up with the club's image of a noble trier – of a charmingly old-fashioned sporting organisation, to which taking part was more important than winning. Proud as they are of Upton Park's history as a footballing academy, they are no different from any other group of supporters, for all the clichés. They want honours, and they want them sooner rather than later.

Of course, it's as true today as it's ever been that West Ham are capable of throwing away points at times when most other teams would be shutting up shop. Harry Redknapp's squad is littered with prodigious but unpredictable talents, and neither manager nor supporters would have it any other way. Yet the club's *penchant* for adventure on the pitch is mirrored by an extraordinary stability off it – a continuity of administration and management which has given countless generations of West Ham teams a solid platform on which to parade their skills, and which is very much the envy of the club's London rivals, Spurs and Chelsea in particular. With the bare minimum of fuss in the boardroom, the players have been able to get on with their work. So have the team managers, of whom the Hammers have had only eight in the 20th century – a record no other senior English club can match.

To get an idea of how far the club can trace this continuity, you need to go right back to its very formation. The team were the brainchild of Arnold Hills, owner of the biggest shipyard in London's East End docks, the *Thames Ironworks*. He wanted his workers to enjoy leisure pursuits that would keep them fit, and saw football as an obvious choice. In one of the first teams to represent the works was one James Cearns. Today, there is a member of the Cearns family on West Ham's board, as there has been ever since 1900.

Hills' team made their playing debut as Thames Ironworks FC in September 1895, and two years later their mentor laid out a vast new arena for them, complete with cycle and running tracks, to be known as the Memorial Ground. In 1898, the club joined the Southern League, but soon found it necessary to sign professional players in order to keep up with the standard of football. Hills was horrified by this development, and disowned the very club he

Academy pupils (from left) – Ayres, Boyce, Robson, Brooking, Best, Redknapp, Hurst, 1971

had formed. The players were told they could no longer use the Thames Ironworks name and that, furthermore, they would have to leave the Memorial Ground.

So it was that the club was reborn in 1900 as West Ham United, a limited company with James Cearns on its board of directors. But the transformation was not quite complete, and nor, in a sense, would it ever be. The team did not leave the Memorial Ground until their lease expired in 1904, while the two nicknames they had acquired as Thames Ironworks, 'Hammers' and 'Irons', would still be in popular use a century after the club officially ceased to have anything to do with the old industry.

West Ham's new home was to be in the grounds of the Boleyn Castle in Upton Park. The Castle, built in the 16th century and named after Anne Boleyn, was then being used as a school, while the grounds were the home patch of a local amateur side known as Boleyn Castle FC. The latter were soon absorbed by West Ham and the ground (which would come to be known as 'Upton Park' after the surrounding area but which officially remains the Boleyn Ground to this day) was made ready for the first game of the 1904/05 Southern League season, an East End derby against Millwall.

In 1912 West Ham entered the FA Cup for the first time, and after World War I, the club was considered mature enough to merit admission to the Football League, which was expanding both of its divisions by two clubs. The team had little trouble adjusting to their new surroundings, never finishing lower than seventh in the Second Division before winning promotion in 1923. The same year, West Ham reached their first FA Cup final – also the first to be played at Wembley. Once the famous white police horse had helped clear thousands of fans from the pitch, the Hammers pinned their hopes on their normally reliable goalscorer Vic Watson. But he was effectively shackled by the Bolton defence, and West Ham lost 2–0.

After that, the club enjoyed a nine-year spell in the First Division, reaching two FA Cup quarter-finals, before relegation in

1932. This marked the end of the line for Syd King, who'd been team manager for a full three decades. His successor, Charlie Paynter, would have a mere 18 years in the job, all of them in charge of Second Division teams.

Initially Paynter's replacement, Ted Fenton, had no greater success. But piece by piece he assembled a squad of players whose interest in the game would go beyond the mundanities of striving to get West Ham out of the Second Division. Among them were Malcolm Allison, John Bond, Noel Cantwell, Frank O'Farrell, Dave Sexton and Ken Brown – every one of them destined to make his mark in management at the end of his playing career. The club was doing all it could to keep them physically fit for the fight, but with English football having been taught a short, sharp lesson in tactics by Hungary in 1953, the young Hammers felt there must be more to life. Meeting after training in *Cassetari's Café* near the Boleyn Ground, they began planning out possible moves using salt cellars and vinegar bottles – moves which would enable West Ham finally to win promotion as Second Division champions in 1958, and, just as important in the long term, to build its reputation as a footballing academy.

Now, from being dismissed as an irrelevant 'family club' by the mainstream, West Ham had become the place to be – all the more so once Ron Greenwood took over from Fenton in 1961.

By the time Greenwood's side reached the FA Cup final three years after his appointment, most of the original café kids had departed, but not before imparting their wisdom to a new generation. The latter included the trio of players who would go on to win the World Cup with England in 1966 – Bobby Moore, Martin Peters and Geoff Hurst. But there were other, equally influential figures as West Ham strode out at Wembley for the first time in 41 years – notably big midfielder Ronnie Boyce and outside-left John Sissons. Both would score that day in the 3–2 win over Preston (Hurst got the other) that brought silverware back to Upton Park at last, and both would play

Into the black – Premiership action is halted as the lights go out on Upton Park, 1997

Better read than said – the magic of Moore

Young Iron – Bobby at the Boleyn, 1964

West Ham's first scouting report on the schoolboy **Bobby Moore** was none too flattering. Can hold his own, but is never going to set the world on fire. Or words to that effect. And, in a curious way, the prophecy came true. Moore became a household name all over the world as much because of what he didn't do, as what he did. Almost impossible to pass as a central defender, he seldom resorted to rough-house tackling or the vulgarity of shirt-pulling, his ability to read the game preventing such measures from being necessary. Likewise, though a commanding figure among team-mates, he was not the most vocal of players – preferring to have his troops already in position so that he could avoid having to shout.

It was Moore's thirst for knowledge about the game, rather than his innate flair, that most impressed Upton Park on his arrival. Having been taken under the wing of first-team defender **Malcolm Allison**, the teenage Moore would attend extra training sessions on Tuesday and Thursday evenings, listening and learning in the best academy tradition. Already an England youth international, Moore got his big break at West Ham when Allison, ironically, was diagnosed as having tuberculosis in November 1957. In less than a year Moore had replaced him, helping the Hammers to a 3–2 win over Manchester United on his debut.

When **Ron Greenwood** arrived as manager in 1961, he built his new West Ham team around Moore, whose ability to turn the captain's armband into something more than a purely symbolic gesture – a rare quality in the modern game – was gloriously confirmed, also against Manchester United, in the FA Cup semi-final of 1964 which set the club back on the road to silverware.

Greenwood's counterpart **Alf Ramsey** was an eager convert, handing Moore the captaincy of his country when **Jimmy Armfield** was injured before a friendly against Czechoslovakia at Wembley. England won 4–2 – a result that would be repeated at the same venue in the high point of Moore's career, victory over West Germany in the 1966 World Cup final. He would go on to earn 108 England caps (still a record for an outfield player) and play more than 600 matches for the Hammers.

He died in February 1993, at the age of 51, having battled cancer with the same quiet dignity with which he'd worn the claret-and-blue #6 shirt for so many seasons.

a key part in the following season's Cup-Winners' Cup campaign, the club's first-ever in Europe. Boyce scored West Ham's first goal in a competitive game on foreign soil in a 1–0 win over Ghent in Belgium, and after subsequent defeats of Sparta Prague, Lausanne-Sports and Real Zaragoza, the team were fortunate – like Manchester United in the European Cup three years later – that UEFA had pre-ordained that the tournament's final would be held at Wembley. There the West German side TSV Munich 1860, then a bigger club than city rivals Bayern, were beaten

After a fashion – McDowell, Moore, Law and Kidd in classic kits at Old Trafford, 1972

2–0, with both goals coming from Alan Sealey, Sissons' fast-moving opposite number on the right.

As the trophy was paraded around the stadium, it was a fitting tribute to that pioneering work with the condiments at *Cassetari's* – though only Ken Brown, playing alongside Moore at centre-half, remained from the early days. Those East End lads (by no means all of whom, it must be said, were originally from the area) had sought a means of emulating the success of Europeans; now their successors had stuck to the same principles and beaten Johnny Foreigner at his own game.

Oddly, though global recognition still awaited Moore, Peters and Hurst, the club itself had entered a period of gentle decline before the events of the summer of 1966. The defence of the Cup-Winners' Cup ended with a semi-final defeat by Borussia Dortmund, while in the First Division, West Ham were increasingly seen as mid-table fodder – a team whose style was too enterprising for their own good.

The reputation remained unaltered until the turn of the Seventies, when Greenwood stepped up to become general manager and John Lyall, a Hammers full-back whose playing career had been ended prematurely by injury, took charge of first-team affairs. Less attached to the past than his predecessor, Lyall let the old guard move on in a way Greenwood had never allowed, so that by the time West Ham reached another FA Cup final in 1975, they met a Fulham side motivated by Bobby Moore. Now the Hammers had a new motivator of their own, Billy Bonds, ably assisted by intelligent full-backs Frank Lampard and John McDowell, and with a cultured midfield already dominated by a young Trevor Brooking. On the day, however, a player who would have little long-term impact on the club, slightly built striker Alan Taylor, poached both goals in a comfortable 2–0 win.

The following season, 1975/76, West Ham set out on another European adventure, reaching a second Cup-Winners' Cup final. This time, though, the choice of venue would work against them – they were beaten 4–2, in a final characterised by the balanced football of both sides, by the Belgian club, Anderlecht, in Brussels.

It had been a gallant effort by a side whose League form was now edging toward the dangerously inconsistent. By 1978, Lyall's team had been relegated. Yet there was no sense of panic, no mass departure of players, no knee-jerk sacking of the manager. The Hammers rebuilt, and in 1981 won the Second Division title in breathtaking style.

Before that, however, they would return to Wembley for a 1980 FA Cup final appearance against Arsenal. It was a game in which every convention was turned upside-down – when Second Division matched First, when the Hammers outfought the Gunners, when Alvin Martin's expertly marshalled defence never looked like being breached, and when Brooking scored the only goal of the game, with a header of all things.

Another Cup triumph meant another journey into Europe, of course, though this one would be relatively short-lived. In the Cup-Winners' Cup quarter-finals, the Georgian club Dynamo Tblisi came to the East End with a team crammed full of Soviet internationals. They thrashed West Ham 4–1, with a consummate display of counter-attacking football, and were given a standing ovation at the end.

Through the early Eighties, Lyall's team matured into perhaps the most resilient of all modern Hammers teams. With Alan Devonshire playing perfect passes at will and the latest product of the Upton Park youth scheme, Tony Cottee, in effervescent form upfront, West Ham finished third in the League in 1986, the club's highest-ever position.

Yet the stability which had launched that assault on the uncharted territory of the title had its foundation on an ageing side. Lyall, like Greenwood before him, had pinned too much faith in experience. In 1989 West Ham were relegated and, in a

When the Hammers beat the Gunners – Brooking and Lampard with the FA Cup, 1980

break with tradition, Lou Macari was lured from Swindon Town with a brief to overhaul the squad. He did just that, but then resigned in the wake of the Swindon payments scandal, leaving it to a safe pair of Upton Park hands, Billy Bonds, to steer the side Macari had created into the top flight in 1991. They lasted there for only a season, the team's erratic form reflecting a rare sense of unease within the club, as the West Ham board launched an unpopular bond scheme to finance the rebuilding of the Boleyn Ground for the post-Taylor Report era.

Immediate promotion was essential as the Premiership was created in the Hammers' absence, and although 'Bonzo' achieved it at the first attempt, a sense that West Ham was in danger of becoming a yo-yo club led to his being replaced by Harry Redknapp in the 1994 close season. On paper, Redknapp seemed the perfect choice as the man to lead a romantic club successfully through the big-business atmosphere of the mid-Nineties without losing sight of its roots. He had West Ham in his blood, having spent six seasons at the club as a winger during the latter part of the Greenwood era. But he had also gained vital experience of playing the transfer market during an extended career of wheeler-dealing while in charge of Bournemouth. Big-name signings had never really been Upton Park's scene, but now the club needed someone it could trust with its share of Rupert Murdoch's TV cash.

By and large, Redknapp has delivered. Early experiments with various recalcitrant Romanian and Portuguese stars soon gave way to no-nonsense (if expensive) British signings such as Paul Kitson and John Hartson, and the once all-pervading fear of relegation has made way for a different, more optimistic perspective, in which a mid-table finish has come to be seen as a failure, rather than a success.

Meanwhile, though West Ham may win more games 1–0 than they used to, the football is still, as a rule, much as the regulars at *Cassetari's Café* in the Fifties would have envisaged it – courageous, confident, and carefully considered.

Move and pass – Alan Devonshire, the inch-perfect playmaker, makes space for another smart ball

Here we go!

Upton Park is surprisingly easy for **motorists** to find, given its location deep within London's East End suburbs. Parking, on the other hand, isn't so easy, making a spot next to a nearby District Line tube station a popular option.

From all directions except the south, exit the M25 at junction 27 onto the M11 and follow this until it becomes the A406 North Circular Road, heading eastbound. Exit onto the A124 Barking Road toward East Ham. Upton Park (the area, not the ground) is signposted as a right-turn at the junction of Barking Road and Green Street. The ground is a short distance up Green Street on the right hand side.

From the south, exit the M25 at junction 31 (the first junction after the Dartford Tunnel) onto the A13 toward Dagenham. Follow the A13 for about 11 miles, then take the A117 into East Ham. Turn left at the T-junction onto Barking Road, then take this as far as the junction with Green Street (see above).

Bonds' scheme – manager Billy yells a good game

A *London Underground* map will show that Upton Park **tube station** is on the District and Hammersmith & City Lines. However, the latter only runs this far out in peak hours, so unless you're arriving for an evening kick-off, you'll need to change onto the District Line at Aldgate East – simply stay on the platform and wait for a suitable train. Allow 45mins for the whole tube journey from most central London termini.

From Upton Park station, simply turn right onto Green Street and follow the crowds to the ground – a 5min walk.

Just the ticket

Visiting fans are accommodated in a section of the Centenary Stand, which is modern and comfortable but where there's space for only around 2,200 fans. Sellouts and all-ticket games are commonplace, so check with your own club regarding availability before travelling. Ticket prices vary according to the fixture, concessions half price. There are spaces for six **disabled visitors** on the corner of the Centenary and West Stands – book in advance on ☎0181/548 2700.

Swift half

You can get a hot dog and a pint of lager at the **concourse bar** in the Centenary Stand – not a bad bet if you're short of time before the game.

Alternative drinking options are ***The Duke Of Edinburgh*** in Green Street (turn left instead of right as you come out of Upton Park tube, a 2min walk) and ***The Central*** on Barking Road.

For food, ***Cassetari's Café*** is still there at #25 Barking Road, serving an all-day breakfast with coffee for about £4, salt, vinegar and napkins for goals free of charge.

Club merchandise

The old Thames Ironworks team wore an all-blue strip in honour of Arnold Hills' old school,

Harrow, but since then it's been claret-and-blue all the way, with even away strips rarely incorporating any other colour except white. The latest *Fila*-designed shirt does buck tradition, however, in dispensing with blue sleeves.

The main **Hammers Shop** is around the corner from the ground in Barking Road, a stone's throw from *Cassetari's*. You'll find an impressive range of *Fila* leisurewear as well as the replica kit stuff.

Barmy army

The days of the old 'Chicken Run', where thousands of East Enders would sink a pint in the cavernous bar areas, stagger to the front of the terrace and vent their spleen on the team (not to mention the world in general) are sadly long gone, with most noise these days coming from the Bobby Moore Stand, the opposite end from the Centenary Stand. When in the mood, though, the Upton Park can still raise the roof.

Trouble is much rarer than it once was, but the hooligan element is still there, emerging in force for London derbies against Chelsea and Tottenham, in particular. Tread carefully and you should be fine.

In print

There's no Saturday evening paper (this is London, remember), but the ***Evening Standard*** does preview all the big games on a Friday.

The official club magazine, ***Hammers News***, is published monthly and has recently been redesigned – not a bad read if you don't mind getting the official line shoved down your throat all the time. Anyone interested in receiving copies regularly should note that the club was offering a free copy of the book ***Moore Than A Legend*** (see below) to new 12-month subscribers in the summer of 1999. On the fanzine front, the ground-breaking ***Fortune's Always Hiding*** is no more but its spirit lives on in a plethora of drily humorous alternatives. Try ***The Water In Majorca*** (73A Belgrave Road, Ilford, IG1 3AL), ***Over Land And Sea*** (PO Box 26, Dagenham, RM10 8XY) or ***On A Mission*** (PO Box 334, Taverham, NR8 6QF). A new ***Official History Of West Ham United*** by Adam Ward (Hamlyn, £20) was due to be published in autumn 1999, while elsewhere on the bookshelf, Phil Daniels' ***Moore Than A Legend – From Barking To Bogota*** (Goal!, £12.99) is an eloquent tribute to the great man, as offered by those who knew him best – family, friends and team-mates – in more than 100 interviews.

Roar like an Iron – Rio Ferdinand leads the celebrations, 1999

On air

It's the usual London choice of ***GLR*** (94.9 FM) and ***Capital Gold***

(1548 AM), but you could also try the more local ***Millennium Radio*** (106.8 FM).

In the net

West Ham's **official website** is supplied by the ubiquitous *Planet Internet* and is not one of the company's better sites, its homepage overloaded with pointless Java and taking an age to download, even at ISDN2 speeds. If you have the patience, you'll find the usual homage to multimedia and e-commerce, together with squad details and a smattering of informative historical player profiles. Go if you really must to: www.westhamunited.co.uk.

The club's unofficial internet community, appropriately enough, specialises in online East End banter. ***Knees Up Mother Brown*** is typical, a well-conceived site that delivers a wide range of regularly updated content with a wry smile on its face at: easyweb.easynet.co.uk/~graeme.howlett/contents2.htm.

Also worth a look is ***Alf Garnett's Agony Hour***, an online soapbox for Irons fans at: web.ukonline.co.uk/Members/rj.dawkins/index.htm.

Wigan Athletic

Formation	1932
Stadium	JJB Stadium, Robin Park, Wigan, Lancs. ☎01942/244433
Ground capacity	25,000
First-choice colours	Blue, white and green
Major honours	Third Division champions 1997; Auto Windscreens Shield winners 1999; Freight Rover Trophy winners 1985
Position 1998/99	Sixth in Second Division (eliminated in play-off semi-finals)

Wigan Athletic stand as a fine example of what a relatively small football club can achieve, despite being based in a rugby league stronghold, and despite the historical failure of previous attempts to win a slice of the local sporting interest for the round-ball game. Wigan have got where they are today through the sheer determination of their supporters, the commitment of several loyal club servants, and...thanks to an enormous helping hand from a multi-millionaire businessman with as clear a vision of the future of sport in his town as you will find anywhere in the country.

On the edge – Ray Mathias waits in vain

The man in question, Dave Whelan, is the founder of the *JJB Sports* chain of sportswear shops. A former professional player who began his career as a full-back with Wigan Boys' Club before subsequently serving Blackburn and Crewe in the Sixties, Whelan has gone back to his roots with a vengeance, having bought a controlling interest in Wigan Athletic in 1995, and subsequently taken over the local Superleague club, Wigan Warriors. Drawing on all the reserves of courage and evangelical passion with which he helped changed the face of sports retailing in Britain, Whelan has achieved what had locally been considered unthinkable – reconciling the interests of Wigan's football- and rugby-loving publics, to what looks like being the benefit of both.

The most visible outcome is the JJB Stadium, to which Wigan Athletic were due to move in time for the start of the 1999/2000 season, and where the Warriors will begin playing Superleague rugby in 2000. As dramatic a stadium as exists anywhere in Britain, it has been designed to hold an all-seated 25,000 and, even if it were to remain within budget, will have cost in the region of £35million by the time of completion. The contractors, *Alfred McAlpine* (of Huddersfield's McAlpine Stadium fame) finally signed on the dotted line after much deliberation in February 1998, leaving Wigan Athletic with a season and a half more at their historic but sadly crumbling home of Springfield Park. The

Earth summit – fans seek a piece of the Springfield Park turf after the last game, 1999

Warriors, meanwhile, would have a little longer at their Central Park home because of Rupert Murdoch's demands for a summer season for Superleague.

As it turned out, Athletic's last season would be as exciting – and, arguably, as successful – as any in the club's 67-year history. Consistently in the right half of the table throughout the season, the team were scheduled to play their last game at Springfield Park against Chesterfield on 6 May 1999. But a 3–1 win that day earned the old ground a reprieve, since combined with results elsewhere, it proved enough to send Wigan into the play-offs.

Meanwhile, an excellent run in the Auto Windscreens Shield (aka the Associate Members' Cup, an accolade the club had previously won in its Freight Rover Trophy incarnation in 1985) stretched all the way to Wembley and an appearance in the final against Millwall. As they had done throughout the campaign, Wigan's defence held firm, and it was left to Paul Rogers to poach the only goal of the game, three minutes into stoppage time. Within seconds the final whistle had blown, and Wigan's modest travelling army of 8,000 fans (out of a total 55,000) made more noise than had seemed feasible.

The question was whether the team could book a return trip to Wembley in the play-offs. The answer was no – but it was a close call. Springfield Park's final (if not quite finest) hour was a 1–1 draw with Manchester City in the play-off semi-finals. Wigan then lost the second leg 1–0 at Maine Road, amid suspicions that the home side's winning goal had gone in off a hand, and after the visitors had had an excellent penalty appeal turned down.

For Whelan – like all millionaire investors in football clubs, a chairman who perhaps has a right to be impatient – failure could not be tolerated, no matter how marginal. Manager Ray Mathias was sacked within hours of the City defeat, ironically to have his seat taken by a former Maine Road manager, John Benson, former assistant boss at Springfield Park, and a man who'd turned down the manager's job a year earlier after a health scare. Now Benson told

Beginning of the end – Wigan 'keeper Roy Carroll after Manchester City's 'handball' goal, 1999

Whelan he needed £3million to spend on new players. Whelan didn't bat an eyelid.

Such is the determination with which Wigan Athletic are setting their sights on a place in the top half of the Football League. And with such an inspiring backdrop as the JJB Stadium behind them, the odds must be stacked in their favour. Yet if they do make the jump, it will be a remarkable feat for a club that only gained Football League status in 1978, and which has been beset by money problems at regular intervals since.

Inevitably, the story of football in Wigan does not begin with Wigan Athletic. The first attempt at establishing the game in what was already a haven for the Northern Union (later the rugby league) came in 1897, when a club known as Wigan County was established. Using Springfield Park – until now primarily an athletics venue – as their base, the team joined the Lancashire League and played to a decent standard in it, yet went into liquidation after only three seasons, having failed to attract enough business through the turnstiles.

Next up were Wigan United, who were formed in 1901 and who chose to play in the Lancashire Combination. They too were struggling to sustain local interest, and it was no surprise when Springfield Park's management decided to let Wigan rugby league club briefly share the ground with the ailing 'association' side, before the former moved on to Central Park in 1902.

After United folded in 1904, Wigan Town made a go of it, again at Springfield, yet their adventure was to be even more short-lived than the previous two experiments. By 1905, they were no more.

The town then survived 16 years without a senior soccer side of any description, until the formation of Wigan Borough in 1921. Despite a complete lack of a competitive football pedigree, Borough were admitted as founder members of the Third Division (North), the Football League clearly deciding that it was a case of 'now or never' if Wigan's public were going to be won over from rugby. At first the move succeeded. Crowds at Springfield Park (where else?) hovered between 8,000 and 10,000, with a whopping 30,611 turning up to see a third-round FA Cup tie against Sheffield Wednesday in 1929 – the game gallantly lost 3–1 by the local side.

Yet within a few years the Depression was sweeping over Lancashire and Wigan Borough were its first footballing victims, failing to complete the 1931/32 season and folding in a sorry mess of falling crowds, poor management and unpaid wages.

At the end of that unfinished season, Wigan Athletic was born. In an attempt to learn lessons from the Borough episode, the club's board settled initially for competition in local amateur leagues, rather than the professional Third Division. It was a wise decision, for Athletic flourished, first in the Lancashire Combination before and after World War II, then in the Cheshire League, and finally in the newly formed Northern Premier League from 1967.

Having already won the NPL title twice, Athletic completed their 1977/78 campaign with their best-ever record in the competition, and applied for membership of the Football League with confidence. All the club's previous 34 applications had been rejected but now... On Friday 2 June 1978, the League put Wigan's case to the ballot. They received 26 votes, the same as Fourth Division Southport. On the second ballot, Wigan polled 29 votes to Southport's 20. League football was about to return to the town after an absence of 47 years.

Aside from the Freight Rover win and a period of Third Division football (ironically, under Ray Mathias) in the late Eighties, Wigan's League career had been pretty uneventful, pre-Whelan. But all that was to change, as the new chairman provided the funds for three Spanish players (*the Three Amigos* – two of whom are still with the club) to inject fresh life into the football and provide the town with an attractive alternative to rugby league.

Within two years of Whelan's arrival, Athletic had won the (now Third Division) title under John Deehan, and period of change was in full swing.

Now we have the JJB stadium – not just a new home for Wigan's professional football and rugby teams, but the home to a brand-new soccer academy to nurture young talent for the future. All being well, it should a perfect example of Britain's retail revolution not merely putting money in shareholders' pockets, but feeding the grassroots of the game from which it derives its wealth. Which is all very laudable, of

By the seat of his pants – Wembley scorer Paul Rogers

course. But who'd have thought it would happen in a rugby town like Wigan?

Here we go!

The club plans for signposts directing **motorists** to the JJB Stadium to be in place by the start of the 1999/2000 season, at least in Wigan town centre. To reach Wigan, exit the M6 at junction 25 for the A49 if coming from the south or west, or at junction 27 for the B5375 if coming from the north.

There are two **train stations** at Wigan but as Wallgate is for local services only, you will most likely arrive at Wigan North Western, which has direct trains to and from London Euston (hourly, journey time 2hrs 30mins). There are also services for Liverpool Lime Street and (from Wallgate) Manchester Piccadilly. Call ☎0345/484950 for the latest timings.

Just the ticket

Ticket prices are expected to be a flat £12 for anywhere in the stadium, although **visiting supporters** will have their own section allocated. **Disabled visitors** should be able to expect excellent facilities at the new stadium – find out the latest from the club on ☎01942/244433.

Swift half

The JJB Stadium is set to have a 1,000-seat ***Bier Keller*** as part of its final design, though it's not clear whether visiting fans will be admitted.

Club merchandise

After World War II, Wigan Athletic changed from red shirts to blue because that was the only colour in stock. This is unlikely to be the case at the new stadium, where **the biggest *JJB Sports* store in the country** is set to open its doors. Since 1995, Athletic have worn the *JJB* corporate colours of blue, white and green, although the green influence is being reduced for the new 1999/2000 design.

Barmy army

Wigan does have a hooligan element, and there was some unpleasantness with City fans after the play-off semi-final home leg in 1999. It remains to be seen whether the new stadium will calm tempers, but in the meantime, be discreet about your club colours in the town centre.

In print

There's no Wigan-specific sports paper but you may see the *Pink* edition of the ***Manchester Evening News*** if you hang around long enough after a Saturday game.

The fanzine is ***Latic Fanatic*** (186 Hodges Street, Wigan, WN6 7JG).

On air

GMR (95.1 FM) has a smattering of Wigan coverage in among all the Manchester chat, while local station ***Wish FM*** (102.4 FM) fits in what it can around the music.

In the net

Wigan's **official website** went AWOL during the 1998/99 season but there are plenty of unofficial offerings to choose from. Perhaps the best is at: www.geocities.com/Colosseum/Stadium/3294/latics.htmlOnline

Try also another unnamed Wigan site at: www.geocities.com/Colosseum/Arena/1503; and ***Wigan Athletic Springfield Scene*** at: www.btinternet.com/~jon.sanders/index.html.

Wimbledon

Formation	1899 as Wimbledon Old Centrals
Stadium	Selhurst Park, London, SE25 6PY. ☎0181/771 2233
Ground capacity	26,300
First-choice colours	All navy-blue with gold trim
Major honours	Fourth Division champions 1983; FA Cup winners 1988; FA Amateur Cup winners 1963; Southern League champions 1975, 1976, 1977
Position 1998/99	16th in Premiership

Still Crazy after all these years, the Wimbledon Gang began their 14th successive season of top-flight football running the risk of becoming more unpopular than ever. Millwall fans may have coined the phrase 'No-one Likes Us', but it is the supporters of another South London club who now find themselves without friends among the English footballing elite. Despised by followers of bigger clubs because of their no-compromise, knees-and-elbows style; envied by those of less successful teams because of their ability to survive against the odds; and ridiculed by all and sundry for their pitifully low crowds, Wimbledon are used to taking stick. So much so that, if anything, it has helped to build their character.

It's all in the mind – Vinnie Jones, Don extraordinaire

At the end of the 1998/99 season, the club took another step down the road toward social unacceptability by appointing Egil 'Drillo' Olsen as its new team manager. His predecessor, Joe Kinnear, had suffered a heart attack two-thirds of the way through the campaign, and in his absence the team's form had collapsed. Clearly Wimbledon chairman Sam Hammam did not want to take any chances with either Kinnear's health or his resulting commitment to the job.

On his arrival, Olsen joked that 'only Brazil or Wimbledon' could have tempted him away from his native Norway, where he had turned the national team into one of the most feared in the world game, and latterly helped one of the clubs he'd served as a player, Vålerenga, away from the threat of relegation and into Europe. Olsen's appointment, no matter how unlikely, had a beautiful logic. A partial takeover earlier in the previous season had seen an influx of fresh capital from a Norwegian shipping and trading company which also owned a major domestic club, Molde. Wimbledon already had a track record of buying players successfully from Norway and the presence of a manager from that part of the world would only enhance the relationship further. Stylistically, Olsen's devotion to the long-ball game – if anything even more rigid than that of his predecessor Kinnear, who had been showing signs of mellowing in his old age – would ensure there was no culture shock on the training ground, as so many other English clubs had experienced after hiring foreign coaches. And, intriguingly, Olsen had in fact been half-serious when interviewed after his arrival – he was actually a Wimbledon fan, had been for eight years, and was genuinely keen to take up the challenge, regardless of its implications as a career move.

As it turns out, the Dons have many fans in Norway, where football is played scarcely any other way than with a big hoof down the middle, and where the club's rise from the non-League ranks to the pinnacle of the English game has an appealing, fairytale charm.

Wimbledon's problem is that their fans in Oslo, Bergen and points north don't get along to many games. While their presence in Scandinavia offers a potential new source of revenue from the coming era of pay-per-view television, it does nothing to boost attendances at the Dons' adopted home of Selhurst Park, still comfortably the lowest in the Premiership. In absolute terms, Wimbledon's crowds have risen since they moved from their historic Plough Lane home in 1991. But they have not risen fast enough. Despite not enjoying anything like the same continuous membership of the top division, Palace continue to pull in more punters from the immediate area around Selhurst, while Wimbledon's traditional catchment zone, to the west in the borough of Merton, is just far enough away to present a psychological stumbling block to fair-weather fans – of whom South London has more than its fair share.

Strangely, there were more than 25,000 at Selhurst for Wimbledon's first 'home' game there, in 1975, when a fourth-round

When being at home means playing away – only the corner flag says you're 'at Wimbledon'

Magic or tragic – Wimbledon's 1988 FA Cup final victory inspired a wide range of responses

FA Cup replay against Leeds was switched there from Plough Lane. That was when Wimbledon, then a Southern League team, first entered the national consciousness, sparking a two-week frenzy of media activity after holding Leeds to a goalless draw at Elland Road.

Prior to that, the name 'Wimbledon' was generally associated with tennis and the Wombles. Yet the club itself already had a long history of achievement, albeit at relatively low levels of the game.

The story began in 1889, when a group of old boys from the Central School in Camp Road, Wimbledon, decided to form a football team. They called themselves Wimbledon Old Centrals, found a pitch on Wimbledon Common, and used the *Fox & Grapes* pub over the road as their changing rooms. The club entered the Clapham League before switching to the Southern Suburban League in 1902, and three years after that the name was changed to plain Wimbledon FC.

Yet throughout this period Wimbledon were still essentially a parks team, moving from one green space to the next in an attempt to establish a regular following, with decidedly mixed success. By 1910, with no permanent ground or playing strip and precious few supporters, the team stopped playing.

A group of Wimbledon's players and officials, however, then helped to form a new club known as Wimbledon Borough, with a home ground established at the local greyhound stadium in Plough Lane. In 1912, Borough merged with the original Wimbledon club and adopted its name, while plans were laid to move the team to a ground of their own on the site of a former refuse tip, just up the road from the greyhound track – this would become the club's Plough Lane home of legend.

After World War I, chairman Jack Meadows got Wimbledon into the Athenian League, and at the start of the Thirties the team took another step up into the Isthmian League – still an amateur competition, but a much more serious one than had previously been entered. The team were immediately successful, winning the Isthmian League championship four times in six years, before World War II intervened.

The record breaker – biggest-ever signing John Hartson tries to justify his price-tag, 1999

It took a while for the club to rebuild after hostilities had ceased, but new manager Les Henley took Wimbledon to another Isthmian title in 1959, to be followed by three more on the spin from 1962. The 1962/63 season was especially significant, since it also contained a run to the final of the FA Amateur Cup. The Dons had reached this stage twice before, but lost both times. Now, with striker Eddie Reynolds scoring four goals with his head, they beat Sutton United 4–2 at Wembley.

After the last of their trio of Isthmian League titles, Wimbledon successfully applied to join the semi-professional Southern League. They started out in the First Division, but were promoted to the Premier after only a year, and by 1968 had finished as runners-up in the championship.

Yet even at this late stage, players were paid only nominal appearance money and many aspects of the club were still run on an entirely amateur basis. This finally began to change with the arrival of Allen Batsford as manager in 1974. It was Batsford who instituted a proper non-League wage structure, as well as professional training schedules and other elements of senior football. The Dons reaped immediate dividends. A first Southern League title in 1974/75 coincided with a run to the third round of the FA Cup, the furthest the club had ever been. There Wimbledon would be away to Burnley, a respectable top-flight team in those days, and one that had reached the Cup semi-finals themselves only a season earlier. Yet the Dons beat them 1–0 (the first victory by a non-League club away to First Division opposition in 54 years), and the players were still celebrating in the bath when the draw for the fourth round was made and Wimbledon were drawn away to Leeds.

At Elland Road, Batsford's much worked-on defence was holding firm until midway through the second half, when Wimbledon full-back Dave Bassett fouled Eddie Gray in the box. Peter Lorimer stepped up to take the spot-kick, but Dons 'keeper Dickie Guy guessed right and blocked his shot. It finished 0–0. So on to Selhurst Park and the replay, which might also have finished goalless had Bassett not deflected a Johnny Giles shot, which was going wide, past Guy and into his own net.

Wimbledon were out of the Cup, but they would not be out of the limelight for long. Two further Southern League titles followed, not to mention another good Cup run, and on 17 June 1977, after some intensive lobbying by new club chairman Ron Noades, the club was elected to the Football League in place of Workington Town.

The club's first season in the Fourth Division began tentatively, Noades replacing Batsford with his own man, Dario Gradi, midway through the campaign. In 1978/79, after Gradi had insisted that the club shed the last vestiges of the non-League era by offloading all players who would not become full-time professionals, Wimbledon were promoted to the Third Division, only to drop again a year later.

Then, halfway through the 1980/81 season, Noades quit Plough Lane to take over as chairman of Crystal Palace, taking Gradi with him. Control of Wimbledon, meanwhile, passed to Noades' erstwhile fellow board member, Lebanese-born businessman Sam Hammam, who appointed Bassett, by now retired from playing for fear of committing any more penalty-box blunders, as manager.

Thus the foundations of the 'Crazy Gang' were lain. Bassett's approach was as different from Gradi's as the proverbial chalk from cheese. Reasoning that his players were likely to lose possession if they dallied in defence or midfield, the new manager urged his men to pump it forward early. Then, if the ball was lost, it would be lost deep in the opposition half, where no damage could be done. Big strikers Alan Cork and Lawrie Sanchez were the perfect targets for this aerial assault, and if results didn't always go Wimbledon's way, Bassett nurtured a culture of mutual resilience which ensured nobody ever got down in the dumps. At training sessions, he would personally cut up the clothes of each new arrival, telling them when they returned to the dressing room that if they could deal with that, they could handle walking out at Old Trafford in front of 50,000.

Crowds that size weren't quite Wimbledon's scene just yet, but they soon would be. Two successive promotions from 1983 put the club into the top half of the League for the first time, after which the arrival of the impish midfielder Dennis Wise and the intensely physical striker John Fashanu helped to inspire yet another promotion in 1986.

Bassett would remain at the helm for only a single First Division season, his side consolidating in an extraordinary sixth place after being described as the worst top-flight team England had ever seen. It would be left to his successor, Bobby Gould, to scale the final peak, signing former hod carrier Vinnie Jones from Wealdstone in November 1987, then leading his team to the 1988 FA Cup final against Liverpool. Just as against Leeds 13 years earlier, a penalty save would prove crucial – Dave Beasant foiling John Aldridge

Not just any old Joe – Kinnear reflects

after Sanchez had given Wimbledon a first-half lead, glancing in a far-post header from Wise's perfectly delivered free-kick, as the Liverpool defence, Alan Hansen and all, stood like statues.

It finished 1–0 and, if you were to believe the sceptics, it finished English football as a creative force, too. To the *soccerati* Wimbledon's victory over an infinitely more cultured Liverpool side was one of the game's darkest hours. To millions of ordinary TV viewers, it was a classic triumph for David over Goliath, with no great consequences beyond a footnote in the history books.

Both arguments had some validity, but the long-term consequence for Wimbledon was that so many of their players, who were perhaps not quite so uncultured as had been thought, were sold to bigger clubs. The team lost their momentum while comfortably retaining top-flight status, and the transfer fees helped to balance the club's notoriously one-sided books.

At the turn of the Nineties, the problems became almost unbearable. The Taylor Report effectively condemned Plough Lane to the scrapheap, forcing Wimbledon to move in with Crystal Palace 'as a temporary measure'. Meanwhile, brief spells in the manager's seat for Ray Harford and Peter Withe had unsettled the squad, giving the Dons a disjointed look for perhaps the first time since they'd entered the League.

Luckily, in 1992 Hammam appointed Joe Kinnear to the manager's job, and the team never really looked back. A man capable of coaxing towering performances from journeyman players such as Andy Thorn, Robbie Earle and the returning Jones, Kinnear refined the Crazy Gang approach, both on and off the pitch, making the Dons' football more versatile while retaining the old indomitable spirit.

Now his era is over, and Olsen, the poker-playing prophet of the long ball, has taken command. One awkward transition appears to have been managed, but another, Wimbledon's move from Selhurst Park, is still very much on the list of things to do. With Merton apparently a no-go

Drillo and Sam – the Norwegian coach and his Lebanese boss pose for the cameras, 1999

area and a proposed move to Dublin being vetoed by the authorities, the Dons are still homeless chickens, if no longer headless ones. Renting someone else's ground is no place for an aspiring Premiership club to be. But then, the Southern League was no place for an aspiring Premiership club to be coming from, either…

Here we go!

See Crystal Palace.

Just the ticket

In contrast to the situation at Palace home games, **visiting fans** are allocated the whole of the Arthur Wait Stand (entrance in Park Road), with additional seating also available at the Whitehorse Lane end if particularly large numbers are expected. **Disabled supporters** see Crystal Palace.

Swift half

See Crystal Palace.

Club merchandise

Wimbledon maintains a small shop at Selhurst Park, where the latest home shirt (£40, kids' sizes £33) is on sale, alongside *TOFFS* Fifties-style versions (£29.99). The club switched from royal blue to navy in the mid-Nineties in an attempt to carve out a distinctive identity, and it seems to have worked.

Barmy army

Perhaps it's the sheer adversity of their situation that does it, but Wimbledon's hardcore support are among the most amiable and good-humoured you're likely to meet. Nobody can remember when there was last any hooliganism, other than that brought by visiting teams.

In print

There's no Saturday evening paper, of course, but the ***Evening Standard*** previews Dons matches in its Friday edition

There are plenty of fanzines, including the excellent ***Hoof The Ball Up*** (46 Oxford Street, London, W1N 9FJ), ***Route One*** (19 Arundel Avenue, Morden, SM4 4DR) and ***Yidaho*** (23 Ryecroft Avenue, London, SE13 6EZ).

Stephen Crabtree's trilogy of Dons' recent histories is essential reading. Titles are (in chronological order) ***The Dons In The League***, ***The Amazing Journey*** and ***From Wembley To Selhurst***. The books are about £17 each and are available from the club shop.

For a less detailed but all-in-one history try ***Wimbledon: From Southern League To Premiership*** by Clive Leatherdale (Desert Island, £16.99).

On air

It's the usual London choice of ***GLR*** (94.9 FM) and ***Capital Gold*** (1548 AM), though the Dons don't feature much on the latter.

In the net

Wimbledon's **official site** is fairly standard *Planet*-run fare, but does have some interesting historical bits and some fan-run areas, which makes a change. Find it at: www.wimbledon-fc.co.uk.

Of the unofficials, try ***It's A Weird And Wonderful World***, a well-designed and unusually well-written webzine, thoughtfully laid out and delivered with delicious irony. One of the most original one-club football sites on the web at: wkweb5.cableinet.co.uk/wwworld.

For unbiased news and match reports (as opposed to the biased ones on the official site), have a browse through ***Neil's WFC Site*** at: www.thedons.force9.co.uk.

Wolverhampton Wanderers

Formation	1877 as St Luke's/Blakenhall Wanderers
Stadium	Molineux Grounds, Wolverhampton, WV1 4QR. ☎01902/655000
Ground capacity	28,500
First-choice colours	Old gold shirts, black shorts
Major honours	League champions 1954, 1958, 1959; Second Division champions 1932, 1977; Third Division champions 1989; Third Division (North) champions 1924; Fourth Division champions 1988; FA Cup winners 1893, 1908, 1949, 1960; League Cup winners 1974, 1980
Position 1998/99	Seventh in First Division

Can there be another club that sums up the English football experience better than Wolverhampton Wanderers? Founder members of the Football League in 1888, they have won almost everything there is to be won, yet also served time in the very bottom division. Pioneers of European competition and the toast of a nation in the Fifties, by the Eighties they were on the brink of going out of business – not once, but twice. At the turn of the millennium they boast one of the most impressive and inspiring stadia in the country, thanks to a multi-millionaire benefactor who has followed the team since he was a schoolboy – and yet no Wolves fan of school age today has seen his side play top-flight football.

The very name 'Wolves', as someone once put it, 'thunders from the pages of English football history'. Everything about the club, from the sacred tradition of the players' 'old gold' shirts to the spacious elegance of its historic, rebuilt Molineux home, suggests a mighty power in the game. Everything, that is, except Wolves' football itself. Fifteen years since they were relegated from the old First Division, the team have yet to mount a really convincing bid to regain that long-lost status.

That will not deter the faithful from pouring into Molineux in their thousands during the 1999/2000 season, each one of them, hoping, praying, above all *believing* that, with so much already in their favour, Wolves' time will surely come again. Football, alas, doesn't always work that way. And Wolves fans should know that as well as anyone. For although the Molineux honours list is a long one, the club's history is characterised by teams and individuals who seemed destined for immortality, yet achieved only a kind of flawed, fleeting greatness. On more than one occasion, the club has threatened to dominate English football like no other before, only for events to conspire against them – or for Wolves to conspire against themselves.

The story begins as so many English club histories do, with the game's key formative influences – cricket and the church – combining to produce a team capable of riding the football boom of the late 19th century. In 1877, the headmaster of St Luke's school in Blakenhall, Harry Barcroft, presented a football to a group of pupils as their reward for a good year's work. St Luke's FC was born soon after, and two years later, after the team had merged with a local cricket side called Blakenhall Wanderers, the football club became known as Wolverhampton Wanderers.

The team entered the FA Cup for the first time in 1884, and within four years were asked to become founder members of the Football League. While the north-west of England could boast more representatives in the first 12-team competition than any other region, the Black Country had embraced the professional game with the same vigour, and no two original League members were as close geographically as Wolves and West Bromwich Albion – instigating a rivalry that would burn for a century and continues to smoulder today.

Wolves finished third at the end of the inaugural League season of 1888/89 – a decent showing given that the club itself was barely a decade old. Still, 12 points separated them from champions Preston, and Wolves were also beaten 3–0 by the same side in the 1889 FA Cup final at the Kennington Oval.

This inability to live with the *Old Invincibles* from the north-west was compensated for by the fact that the team, after playing at several modest grounds around Wolverhampton, had just found what would become their permanent home at the Molineux Grounds – a pleasure park similar to London's Crystal Palace, and to the Aston Lower Grounds where Wolves' other near-neighbours, Villa, would soon put down roots. Facilities in the park were rudimentary at first, but the Grounds were spacious enough to offer some scope for later expansion.

Over the next few years Wolves maintained a presence in the top six of the Football League, but it was the FA Cup that consistently drew the biggest crowds to Molineux. In 1893, Wolves took advantage of a rather favourable draw to advance to the semi-finals of the Cup, where they beat the favourites Blackburn, 2–1. Their opponents in the final would be Everton, whose rather tougher passage had included a three-match marathon against Preston in the other semi. The Cup final was the only one ever to be played at Fallowfield, Manchester, a venue utterly incapable of accommodating the huge number of fans who turned up for the match. Wolves captain Harry Allen scored the only goal of the game with a speculative long-ranger, but after the final whistle, there was a possibility that crowd disturbances during the 90 minutes would oblige the referee to downgrade the tie to the status of a friendly. After giving the matter some

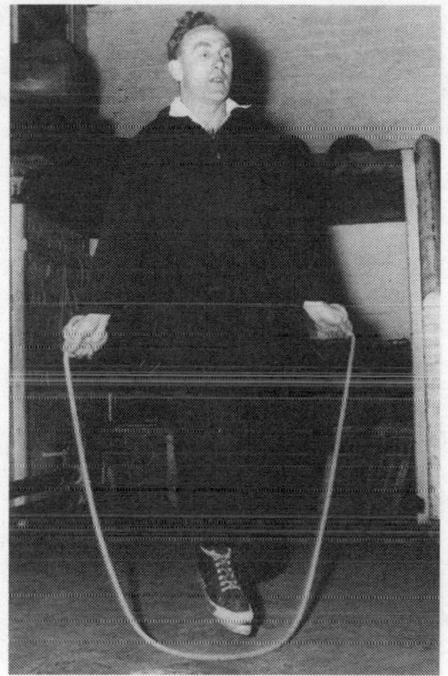

Rope trick – Billy Wright keeps fit, 1958

thought, he decided the two teams had been playing the FA Cup final after all – and Wolverhampton had its first major chunk of footballing silverware.

As well as being a momentous event for the town, Wolves' Cup win was also a personal triumph for the club's secretary-manager John Addenbrooke, whose team – in contrast to many others at the time – was made up entirely of Englishmen, with seven players born within a six-mile radius of Molineux. In time, though, the limitations of Addenbrooke's noble policy would make themselves apparent. After a third Cup final (this one lost 2–1 to Sheffield Wednesday) in 1896, Wolves settled into mid-table anonymity in the League, before finishing bottom and sliding down into the Second Division in 1906.

Two years later, though there was no sign of a League recovery, Addenbrooke coaxed the side to another FA Cup final. As a Second Division side, Wolves were rank outsiders against Newcastle, then one

Gold light in the darkness – the new Molineux

of the top four clubs in the country. But in local lad Kenneth Hunt, Addenbrooke had a player who could turn a game with a touch of magic at right-half. An Oxford undergraduate who refused to sign professional forms, Hunt was studying to be ordained as a priest and could only play for Wolves when his college commitments allowed. He was also being called up regularly to play for the England amateur side, but in early 1908 he chose to forego the chance of an international cap against Wales to play for Wolves against Swindon in the third round of the Cup. It was just as well – an injury to skipper Billy Woodridge obliged Hunt to take over the captain's armband and lead his team to a 2–0 win at Molineux. With Stoke and Southampton accounted for in the next two rounds, Wolves then faced Newcastle in driving April sleet at Crystal Palace. Hunt opened the scoring on the half-hour with one of only two goals he would ever score for Wolves, and the outsiders triumphed 3–1.

The game would become known as the 'H' final because all the scorers' names (Hunt, Hedley and Harrison for Wolves; Howie for Newcastle) began with the same letter, but Hunt would soon have other things on his mind. Later in 1908 he earned his Oxford Blue and also won a gold medal in the Great Britain side that won the Olympic football tournament in London.

Wolves' struggle to regain top-drawer status continued before and after World War I, and another FA Cup final appearance in 1921 was a welcome distraction, even though Spurs took the tie 1–0 at Stamford Bridge. A year later George Jobey took over team affairs from Addenbrooke and within 12 months Wolves had been relegated again, to the Third Division (North) – the first League founders to fall so far. Promotion back to the Second Division was achieved at the first time of asking, but it wasn't until the arrival at Molineux of Major Frank Buckley in 1927 that the club began to regain its position in the front rank of the English game.

Every bit as tough and autocratic as his title suggested (he had served in the Boer War as well as World War I), Buckley was Wolves' first team manager in the modern sense. He brought precious new discipline to the players' training regime and new levels of motivation to the dressing-room. He also shifted the emphasis back to local players after the club had had its fingers singed in the transfer market – and two men who'd been born within a few doors of each other in Wolverhampton, Billy Hartill and Dickie Rhodes, got many of the 115 goals that powered Buckley's side to the Second Division title in 1931/32.

Top-flight consolidation was then the order of the day for the Major, and Wolves did little spectacular in the League until 1937/38, when a side now captained by steely centre-half Stan Cullis were pipped to the title by Arsenal. The following year, Wolves finished as runners-up to Everton in the First Division, then suffered a 4–1 thrashing by Portsmouth in the FA Cup final.

World War II deprived many of Buckley's young discoveries of the best years of their footballing careers, but skipper Cullis, fresh from serving in the army as a PT instructor, returned to Molineux to play through the 1946/47 season. It ended with Wolves needing a point from their last match at home to Liverpool to secure the title, but they were beaten 2–1 and their opponents were crowned champions instead. Cullis, who'd allowed Albert Stubbins to get goal-side of him for Liverpool's winning goal, was criticised for not bringing his man down; his reply was that he didn't want to go down in history as the player who won a League championship medal by 'cheating'.

If that was an old-fashioned sentiment, there was nothing backward about the way Cullis set about remoulding Wolves after taking over as manager from Ted Vizard a year later. Having played under Buckley, Cullis took a leaf out of the old Major's book, fashioning a side that was as committed physically as it was secure organisationally. Cullis evolved a system of 'kick and rush', in which defenders would loft the ball forward while the midfield and attackers joined the rush to get underneath it. The style was unsophisticated but it was always exciting and, unlike some playing patterns of the day, it used the full width of the pitch. It also made very particular demands of players who, in turn, had to be carefully selected by Cullis.

The manager, though still not 35 years old, chose with the expertise of a master. Wingers Johnny Hancocks and Jimmy Mullen were both quick enough to play for their country, while forwards Jessie Pye and Sammy Smyth gleefully snapped up the chances sent them by all that power-play down the flanks. Behind it all, keeping the motor running like a gentle old pro despite limited experience, was Billy Wright, England's best defender of the immediate postwar era and a man who would win 105 caps for his country. Critics complained that the pace of Wolves' midfield and forward lines allowed Wright to conceal his poor distribution; his skill, however, was in being able to turn defence into attack by winning the ball and clearing in one swift movement, his ability to read the game enabling him, if not to hit his target bang-on, then to at least get it there or thereabouts.

In 1949, Wolves' power and passion overwhelmed Leicester City in the FA Cup final at Wembley. Five years later the team finally did what they had been threatening to do since before World War II – lift the League championship for the first time, finishing four points clear of their arch-rivals West Brom.

Like Addenbrooke and Buckley before him, Cullis had won his major honours with a side comprising mainly local players. But he would not stop there, and neither would Wright. After their title win, Wolves invited the crack Hungarian side Honvéd to play a friendly match under Molineux's newly installed floodlights. England's 6–3 and 7–1 maulings at the hands of the *Magical Magyars* in the preceding months had made the country eager for revenge, and there was nothing 'friendly' about the

Reunited – Wright (left) and Puskás admire the view, 1993

atmosphere as Wolves took to the field in front of a Molineux crowd of over 40,000. Though the floodlighting and the home side's luminous orange shirts gave the match a glamorous, almost futuristic feel, the reality was that the cold, muddy conditions gave Wolves a huge advantage. Still, they were 2–0 down at half-time to a side that included a string of Hungarian internationals including the great Ferenc Puskás, and needed a disputed Hancocks penalty to get them back in the game. After that, two goals from Cullis' latest powerhouse attacker, Roy Swinbourne, swung things Wolves' way and the match was won.

A fevered press pronounced Wolves 'world champions', but Cullis was not satisfied. At a time when the FA was doing everything it could to discourage English clubs from meeting European opposition, he invited First Vienna, Real Madrid and two Moscow clubs, Dynamo and Spartak, for further matches to test his team's mettle and keep the local public entertained. Wolves won them all, and after being crowned League champions again in 1958, the team entered the European Cup for the first time.

Wolves were not distracted from their domestic chores, and successfully defended the League championship in 1959. Twelve months later, despite the retirement of Wright, the club was on course to attain the first League and Cup double of the 20th century, before a home defeat by Tottenham on the season's penultimate day allowed Burnley to sneak the title by a point. There was to be no mistake in the Cup, however, Wolves beating Blackburn 3–0 in a bone-crunching final notable for the assured defending of Wright's former colleagues in the half-back line, Bill Slater and Ron Flowers, and by the contribution of inside-forward Norman Deeley, who pressured Rovers' Mick McGrath into scoring an own-goal, netted twice himself, and broke the leg of Blackburn full-back Dave Whelan with a challenge most tactfully described as 'full-blooded'.

In retrospect, that home loss to Spurs at the end of the 1959/60 season would acquire great significance. Tottenham's success in achieving the elusive double 12 months later confirmed the ascendancy of 'push and run' over 'kick and rush', and the Molineux *millieur* was starting to look outmoded. Cullis clung doggedly to his own dogma but, after the team finished in the wrong half of the table in 1963/64, Wolves dispensed with his services. The manager's name continued to be chanted on the terraces, and it would go down in history, after all, in a way that both Cullis and the people of Wolverhampton could be thoroughly proud of. Poor Andy Beattie, who stepped into the great man's shoes, had neither the wit nor the vision to realise the depth of the team's plight, and Wolves were relegated at the end of his only season in the job. Beattie's successor, Ronnie Allen, got the team back up within two years, but it wasn't until the appointment of Bill McGarry as manager in 1968 that Molineux was again given a team worth shouting about.

All too familiar – Dougan in dispute with officialdom, 1972

The strengths of McGarry's side – pace, passion, power – were not dissimilar to those of Cullis', but its style was quite different. The Wolves of

An anachronism in old gold – Steve Bull

On 24 November 1986, a cup-tied Steve Bull sat watching from the stands as Wolves fell to the most ignominious defeat in their history – an FA Cup loss to non-League **Chorley**. The team he had just joined were playing Fourth Division football in front of crowds of 5,000, and had nearly gone to the wall four months earlier. Little did Bull or the club know that his goals would pull Wolves back up the League ladder in double-quick time, or that he would go on to become the most prolific scorer in Molineux history.

Lion in Wolves' clothing – Bully raises a smile

As a teenager playing for his local club Tipton Town, Bull had been spotted by a **West Brom** scout and signed professional forms for Albion in August 1985. He'd played just nine games for them when Wolves manager **Graham Turner** signed him together with left-back Andy Thompson for £65,000.

Despite arriving only halfway through the season, Bull scored 19 goals in a 1986/87 campaign which ended with Wolves missing out on promotion after losing that year's play-off final to Aldershot. The following season he netted 52 goals in all competitions as Wolves won not just the Fourth Division title but also the **Sherpa Van Trophy** at Wembley. When he scored another 50 the following year, it was a feat not performed since the Twenties.

'Bully' was now a fully fledged terrace hero, finding a tailor-made strike partner in **Andy Mutch**, helping Wolves to the Third Division title, and scoring on his England debut against Scotland in May 1989. He went on to win 12 more caps and would surely have won many more had he not resisted all offers to sign for a Premiership club – his loyalty to Wolves as endearingly old-fashioned as his dogged, knockabout approach to the game.

In 1992 Bull broke **John Richards' all-time scoring record** for Wolves, and six years later a stooping header against Bradford City marked his 300th career goal for the club – a record unlikely to be matched this side of the year 2010.

the late Sixties and early Seventies were more comfortable with the ball on the deck, and their approach play was more varied than it had been a decade earlier.

McGarry had inherited a strong squad from Allen. Wolves' defence was well marshalled from right-back by Derek Parkin, Mike Bailey was a formidable but creative presence in midfield, and pacy left-winger David Wagstaffe was a fine crosser of the ball. Star of the show, though, was Derek Dougan, a lanky, Ulster-born forward who had declared himself fit to play for Blackburn against Wolves in the 1960 Cup final, then retired hurt after five minutes. Once dismissed as a restless maverick, Dougan finally found his spiritual home at Molineux, the more abrasive side to his personality smoothed by McGarry.

When centre-forward John Richards arrived in 1969 to turn the team's possession into goals, McGarry's jigsaw puzzle seemed complete. Yet although his team were crowd-pleasers, they were not born

On your marks – Robbie Keane sets off

winners. In 1971/72 Wolves beat Juventus on the way to an all-English UEFA Cup final against Tottenham, lost 3–2 on aggregate. In the League, fourth place was as high as they climbed under McGarry. And though the League Cup was won with a 2–1 defeat of Manchester City at Wembley in 1974, the side were already in decline – Wolves were relegated two years later, and McGarry was edged out.

His replacement, Sammy Chung, led the team straight back up again, and in 1980, with John Barnwell in the manager's seat and Parkin and Richards still in the team, there was more glory in the League Cup with a 1–0 win over Brian Clough's Nottingham Forest. As before, though, the arrival of a trophy disguised problems, and this time they had deeper roots.

Replacing the famous old gold-gabled Molineux Street Stand with a modern all-seater had brought the club to its knees financially, and in 1982, Wolves went into voluntary liquidation. Dougan returned as the frontman for a takeover by the town's infamous Bhatti brothers, embracing the faithful on Molineux's North Bank with the words 'I love you all'.

Wolves bounced straight back up from relegation in 1982, then went down again in 1984 – and didn't stop going down. Two more relegations in successive seasons left the team in the Fourth Division for the first time, and while five managers came and went in four years (including Tommy Docherty and, in a brief and ill-advised return, Bill McGarry), Molineux's remaining wooden stands were closed following the Bradford fire, and the money ran out again.

A consortium comprising the local council, property developers *Gallagher Estates* and the *Asda* supermarket chain saved Wolves from extinction in 1986, but while the no-nonsense management of Graham Turner and addictive goalscoring of Steve Bull (see panel p.587) hauled the team back up to the Second Division, Molineux was still derelict on two sides and the club as a whole had an air of decay.

Enter Jack Hayward, a multi-millionaire businessman who lived as a tax exile in the Bahamas, but who was born 600 yards from Molineux and used to crawl under the turnstiles to watch matches for free as a boy. In 1990, Hayward bought the club from the Gallagher family for £2million. He then spent another £15million on three new stands (the rebuilt Molineux was officially 'opened' with an emotional friendly against Honvéd in 1993, floodlit, of course), installed the club's former goalscoring idol John Richards as managing director and has since lavished further millions on the team.

It hasn't quite paid off – yet. The Wolves managerial careers of Graham Taylor and Mark McGhee both foundered on the rocks of the First Division play-offs, and in 1998/99, despite the prompting of the team's Irish wonder-kid, Robbie Keane, Colin Lee's side failed even to get that far after losing at home to Bradford City on the season's final day.

Here we go!

Molineux is just off Wolverhampton's ring road and is hard to miss. Coming from the north, east or south-east, **motorists** should exit the M6 at junction 10A and take the A449 into Wolverhampton. Approaching the town centre, take the third exit at the Five Ways roundabout into Waterloo Road – the ground is half a mile along here on the left, signposted 'Molineux Centre'.

From the south-west, exit the M5 at junction 2 and take the A4123 into Wolverhampton. Follow this road until the Snow Hill Junction, at which turn right onto the ring road. Molineux is signposted off to the right from this road.

Street parking around the ground is very limited, but there's a choice of **multi-storeys** in Wolverhampton town centre, no more than a 10min walk from Molineux.

Wolverhampton **train station** is served by direct services from London Euston, Liverpool and Manchester, as well as by frequent local services from Birmingham New Street. There are feasible connections via Birmingham to most destinations after a midweek game, but check the latest timings on ☎0345/484950.

From the station, proceed along Lichfield Street, then turn right into Stafford Street, and you will see the ground a little way up on the left, the other side of the ring road.

Just the ticket

Visiting fans are accommodated either in the John Ireland Stand or at one end of the Jack Harris Stand, depending on the fixture. Ticket prices in 1998/99 were £13 in the former, £12 in the latter, concessions £8.50 in both. There is limited space for **disabled visitors** in the Jack Harris Stand – book through your own club.

Swift half

There's no shortage of pubs in the centre of Wolverhampton but relatively few welcome away fans. The ***Great Western*** at the station has real ale on tap and is used to serving a broad-based clientèle, while those travelling by car have a number of welcoming (and family-friendly) pubs to choose from, including ***The Moreton Arms*** on the A449 Stafford Road, and ***The Spread Eagle*** on the A4123.

Club merchandise

The shop built into the Stan Cullis Stand (formerly the North Bank) sells a vast range of surprisingly tasteful clothing, Wolves fans having been among the first to boycott what they saw as unsuitable shirt designs in the early Nineties.

Barmy army

Despite the fact that Molineux's modern stands are all-seated and an unusual distance from the pitch, Wolves is an intimidating place to play – and visit. Serious trouble is rare, however, outside the Black Country derby with West Brom.

In print

The ***Express & Star*** was created by the merger of two separate papers which between them had been reporting on Wolves for decades. The paper continues this rich tradition today, although after the final whistle fans are restricted to the ***Sports Argus***, produced in Birmingham.

Fanzine ***A Load Of Bull*** (PO Box 3483, Birmingham, B17 9SF) is worth half an hour of anyone's time, and has also contributed to the book ***We Are Wolves – The Fans' Story*** by Charlie Ross and Tony Eagle (Juma, £9.95).

Talking With Wolves (Breedon, £16.99) contains vivid recollections of the club's Fifties heyday and later, from many of the players involved, courtesy of the *Express* and *Star* archives.

Kevin Brophy's new book, ***In The Company Of Wolves*** (Mainstream, £9.99), plots the club's more recent attempts to rejoin the elite.

On air

BBC Radio WM (95.6 FM) provides a broader view of West Midlands football than commercial ***X-tra AM*** (1152 AM), but the latter may have live commentary.

In the net

Wolves' **official site** is a *Planet*-run affair, with a plethora of redundant graphics on its homepage concealing a rather lax attitude to site maintenance. That said, excellent history and multi-media areas make it one of the more comprehensive of the company's efforts, and there's a full news service and archive. Find it all at: www.wolves.co.uk.

Lack of proper updating is a recurrent problem with the **unofficial sites**, but Truls Månsson does a good job in Sweden with his site at: home5.swipnet.se/~w-57029/wolves/.

Wrexham

Formation	1872
Stadium	The Racecourse Ground, Mold Road, Wrexham, LL11 2AH. ☎01978/262129
Ground capacity	9,200 (before works during summer 1999)
First-choice colours	Red shirts, white shorts
Major honours	Third Division champions 1978; Welsh Cup winners 23 times
Position 1998/99	17th in Second Division

Location, location, location. The estate agent's mantra has a peculiar resonance for Wrexham AFC. On the one hand, being in North Wales, historically a much more receptive area of the Principality to football than the south, has given the club a solid bedrock of support, as well as the prestige of being the oldest surviving football team in Wales and until fairly recently, the home of the Welsh FA. On the other hand, the close proximity of Everton and Liverpool, both with strong traditions of fielding Welsh players and with resources and a history of big-league success that Wrexham can never hope to match, means that said bedrock of support is only modest in size. While promotion in 1993 helped to make Wrexham the highest-placed Welsh club in the League six years later, there is little the board can do to expand the fan base. The town itself is small and surrounded by farmland, and England is only just down the road. And since when did any Englishmen follow Wrexham?

The mighty Flynn – the long-serving Brian

Actually, English fans did precisely that, and rather avidly too, for much of the Seventies and Eighties, when the club's exploits in the European Cup-Winners' Cup – to which Wrexham had ready access via the Welsh Cup, a trophy they've won on more occasions than anyone else – were regularly featured in the closing 15 minutes or so of *Sportsnight With Coleman*. How a nation (and not just the Welsh nation) trembled on its Draylon settees as the likes of Anderlecht, FC Porto, Hajduk Split and AS Roma travelled to the Racecourse Ground on wet autumn evenings, and returned, if not always with their tails between their legs, then at least chastened by their experience.

Since 1997, a change in UEFA rules has prevented Wrexham, as members of the English Football League, from entering European competition via the Welsh Cup. Similarly, the town no longer hosts fixtures for the Welsh national team, which once provided crucial extra revenue. And, until 1999 anyway, nothing had come to symbolise the club's decline more tragically than the Racecourse Ground itself, much of it abandoned and crumbling, providing the players with a lop-sided theatre in which to play, and supporters with an all-too-potent

Redundant furniture – overgrown terraces at the Racecourse Ground, 1996

reminder of how things used to be, when football was a more innocent game. If the ground had been a residential property, not even the most loquacious estate agent would have been able to find flattering words with which to describe it.

Yet visitors to the ground during the 1999/2000 season are in for a shock – and a pleasant one at that. For the Racecourse Ground is in the course of being dramatically rebuilt, at a cost of some £3.5million. And while the impetus for the restoration is unlikely (the 1999 Rugby World Cup – who'd have thought it?), that hasn't made it unwelcome. At last, that solid bedrock of support will have solid furniture to rest on once again, and perhaps the team will be inspired to greater things, just as the new owners of a restored house might be.

One edifice expected to remain intact through the redevelopment, however, is the *Turf Hotel*, the pub which is so close to the ground as to be almost part of it, and where, in September 1872, members of a cricket club that played in the middle of Wrexham racecourse resolved to form a football section. They would use the same patch for their football matches, reputedly playing their first game against a team of insurance salesmen in early 1873. The two teams fielded 17 players each, but within a couple of years the club had accepted the inviolability of English FA rules, and matches were down to 11-a-side. In 1876, the Welsh FA was formed and Wrexham became founder members, while simultaneously retaining their affiliation to Lancaster Gate – thus instigating the tradition of Welsh clubs playing in both English and Welsh competitions.

In 1883, however, relations with the English turned sour. After the referee had had to be escorted from the pitch during an FA Cup tie against Oswestry, Wrexham were expelled from the English FA and disbanded soon after. Yet by April 1884 a new club known as Wrexham Olympic had been founded and taken up residence at the Racecourse Ground. The new team were immediately admitted to the English FA (remaining solely within the Welsh domain was as unthinkable then as it would

Footsteps in the snow – West Ham come to town and don't like what they see, 1997

be today), and a concilatory game against Oswestry was arranged as a debut fixture. In 1887, the 'Olympic' bit of the club's name was dropped, and it was as if nothing had ever happened.

At the turn of the century, a proper enclosed ground was built for what was now an established football club, though players continued to get changed in the *Turf Hotel* for some years. In 1912, the last races were held on the adjacent course, and once Wrexham had entered the newly formed Third Division (North) of the Football League in 1921, the Racecourse Ground was given over almost exclusively to football.

Wrexham had taken a big step up in class from the Birmingham & District League, yet the team's early results were encouraging. They soon established themselves as a respectable mid-table side, reached the FA Cup quarter-finals in 1925, and finished third in the table (not quite good enough for promotion) in 1929. Four years later they came even closer to promotion, finishing second, only two points behind Hull City, having scored 106 goals.

There would be further narrow scrapes with promotion in the years both before and after World War II, yet when Wrexham finally moved divisions, the direction was down – from the Third to the Fourth in 1960. The remainder of the Sixties would be equally divided between the two, but throughout the Seventies, Wrexham were a solid and often entertaining Third Division side, drawing fresh energy from their European campaigns, from the patient squad-building of their manager John Neal and from their sparkily unpredictable playmaker, Arfon Griffiths.

When Griffiths stepped up to become player-manager in 1977, the stage was set for Wrexham's golden era. With Dai Davies in goal, former Liverpool full-back Joey Jones anchoring the defence, Griffiths rolling back the years in midfield and the prolific Dixie McNeil upfront, Wrexham were crowned Third Division champions in 1978, and threw in a run to the FA Cup quarter-finals for good measure. Three lively seasons of Second Division football followed, but one by one the cast of characters was broken up – Davies went back to Swansea, Jones to Chelsea, McNeil to Lincoln. Griffiths, too, was gone by the time relegation arrived in 1982, to be followed by another only a year later.

The Eighties were grim, spent entirely in the Fourth Division, with only Europe providing occasional light relief. The nadir was reached in 1991, when Wrexham finished bottom of the League, and would have been relegated to the Conference had the remaining League clubs not decided to expand their structure back to its earlier size of 92 teams.

Thus saved, Wrexham prospered again. The board had kept faith with player-manager Brian Flynn who, like Griffiths before him, inspired huge loyalty from his players. All this was repaid in January 1992, when Wrexham knocked Arsenal out of the FA Cup third round, and again 18 months later, when the club finally won promotion to what was now the Second Division.

Since then, Wrexham have been rock-solid, as an estate agent might say, in their retention of a place in the English game's third tier, though a 17th-place finish in 1999 was disappointing. So, too, was Ian Rush's decision not to remain at the Racecouse Ground, despite being offered a position as player-coach.

But Wrexham will get over it, just as they have got over all the other obstacles that have been placed in their way since that very first meeting in the *Turf* all those years ago.

Here we go!

Most **motorists** will approach Wrexham along the A483. After this has become the bypass, take the A541 in toward Wrexham, follow the signs for the town over the next two roundabouts, and you'll see the ground on the left-hand side.

Wrexham General **train station** couldn't be closer to the ground. Simply turn right out of the station and right again along Mold Road, and you're there. Supporters coming from most parts of the country will need to change at Crewe to reach Wrexham. Check the latest times by calling ☎0345/484950.

Just the ticket

There will no longer be any standing accommodation for **visiting fans** in 1999/2000; seats are expected to be allocated in the new Mold Road Stand. Tickets in 1998/99 were adults £11, concessions £8. **Disabled visitors** will have improved accommodation – booking essential on ☎01978/262129.

In a Rush no more – Ian at the Racecourse, 1998

Swift half

The historic ***Turf*** next to the ground is the obvious place for a pre-match pint, but wasn't always serving visiting fans in 1998/99. If you have no joy here, walk into the town centre (down Mold Road past the train station) for a range of alternative options.

Club merchandise

The **club shop** (☎01978/352536) has the expected range of red-and-white items – these are now very much Wrexham's colours despite the fact that the club was still toying with blue as recently as the Fifties.

Barmy army

Local Anglo-Welsh derbies occasionally cause the odd problem, but generally speaking you'll get a warm welcome at the Racecourse.

In print

The local ***Evening Leader*** is the place for Wrexham news and previews, but doesn't publish on Saturday evenings. There are two fanzines – ***The Sleeping Giant*** (21 Dolafon, Pen-y-Bont Fawr, nr Oswestry, SY10 0PA); and ***Red Passion*** (139 Laund Road, Huddersfield, HD1 3DH).

The essential book is ***Wrexham – A Complete Record 1872–1992*** (Breedon, £16.95) by Peter Jones.

On air

BBC Radio Wales (882 AM) and ***Marcher Sound*** (1260 AM).

In the net

There's no **official website** but unofficial offering ***The Webbed Robin*** is one of the best of its kind in the lower divisions, a one-stop resource on the club that's maintained in both English and Welsh languages. You'll find up-to-date news, info on the rebuilt Racecourse Ground and plenty more besides. A fantastic achievement and well worth seeking out at: come.to/webbedrobin.

The ***Red Passion*** fanzine is also online at: www.wrexham-fans.demon.co.uk/.

Wycombe Wanderers

Formation	1884 as North Town Wanderers
Stadium	Adams Park, Hillbottom Road, Sands, High Wycombe, Bucks, HP12 4HJ. ☎01494/472100
Ground capacity	10,000
First-choice colours	Sky blue and navy blue quarters
Major honours	Conference champions 1993; FA Trophy winners 1991, 1993; FA Amateur Cup winners 1931
Position 1998/99	19th in Second Division

Wycombe Wanderers are different. You only have to take one look at them to realise it. Those sky-blue and navy-blue quartered shirts look like something out of the late 19th century – yet the style is so popular that the club faced a boycott from fans when it tried to change it. The surrounding area is different, too, the rolling Chiltern Hills providing League football with one of its most scenic backdrops. There are no belching chimneys, slab-sided office blocks or housing estates here. Even Wycombe's constitution is unusual. There are no shareholders, and no one person has control of the club. Instead, Wanderers are run by their members (anyone who has been a season-ticket holder for three years or more) who in turn elect their chosen board of directors.

A quartet of Quartermen – Wembley, 1993

If all this sounds too good to be true then, in a sense, it is. After making huge strides forward since their admission to the League in 1993, Wanderers have recently come to a bit of a standstill, escaping relegation to the Third Division only on the last day of the 1998/99 season. Crowds at not what they once were, and the board, realising that the current share structure (or lack of one) is acting as a deterrent to would-be outside investors, are asking Wycombe's members to approve a change.

The mere fact that Wycombe still feel they have further to go, however, speaks volumes for just how far they've come in the past 15 years. In 1985 they were still in the Isthmian League, having rejected the idea of turning even semi-professional when offered an invitation to join the Southern League in the early Sixties. Theirs was a quintessentially amateur club, playing for pride rather than profit, and attracting a loyal but miniscule following to its ground at Loakes Park in the centre of High Wycombe. The ground had the inevitable sloping pitch (more than 11ft from one end to the other), and the club owned it outright, having been gifted the deeds by a former team captain, Frank Adams, in 1947 – a selfless gesture very much in keeping with Wycombe's Corinthian image.

Even the club's name, 'Wanderers', has an amateur ring to it. And so it should, for the club apparently decided to adopt it after the original Wanderers, winners of the first FA Cup in 1872 and the antithesis of professionalism, visited the town. There was already a High Wycombe FC in the neighbourhood, but the group of furniture industry workers who got together to form a new team in 1884 would not be deterred. Their club, North Town Wanderers, quickly became the class football act in the area, and in 1887, at a meeting in the *Steam Engine* pub, members decided on a new name – Wycombe Wanderers.

After playing at various grounds, often on an impromptu basis, Wycombe moved to Loakes Park in 1895, and joined the Southern League a year later. The club caught the competition at just the wrong time, though, as it was was becoming increasingly professional in response to the success of the Football League in the north. In 1908, Wycombe withdrew and joined the Great Western Suburban League, where they stayed until World War I. After that they joined the Spartan League, which they won in both years they were members of it.

Feeling that the club needed stiffer competition, in 1921 Frank Adams led Wanderers into the Isthmian League, where the club would maintain a dignified, almost aristocratic presence for decades. Though their team was often studded with amateur internationals, Wycombe seemed content simply to take part (another great amateur ethic) until they finally broke their title duck in 1956.

The following year, Wanderers reached the FA Amateur Cup final. They had won the event before, beating Hayes with a late penalty at Highbury in 1931. But the 1957 tie was the club's first visit to Wembley, and in front of a 90,000 crowd, they were all too easily beaten by Bishop Auckland. Wycombe had also reached the first round of the FA Cup for the first time since World War II in 1956, and from then on until the end of the Sixties, they made regular appearances in the early stages.

The team's Isthmian League form was fading, however, when Brian Lee took charge of the first team in 1969. Lee was the first manager Wycombe had ever had, since prior to his appointment the club had always employed a coach to oversee training and tactics, while the team was selected by a 'match commitee' that met at Loakes Park every Monday morning. During Lee's

Greenery in the scenery – few League grounds provide as idyllic a backdrop as Adams Park

revolutionary seven-year reign, Wycombe would win the Isthmian title four times and finish runners-up twice. In 1973/74, the club broke its duck against League opponents in the FA Cup, beating Newport County in the first round. The following year, Bournemouth were eliminated and Jack Charlton's Middlesbrough, then joint leaders of the First Division, were held to a goalless draw at Loakes Park; 'Boro needed a last-minute goal to win the replay.

Lee stepped up to become chairman in 1976, and it was around this time that he and Frank Adams, who was now the club's patron, began toying with the idea of Wanderers moving house. But when Frank Adams died in 1981 (to be replaced as patron by his son, Jack), Wycombe still hadn't found an alternative location. Neither had they moved on from the Isthmian League – although the development of a unified non-League 'pyramid' with the inception of the Alliance Premier League in 1979 had not gone unnoticed.

The Alliance had become the Gola League by the time the managerial duo of Paul Bence and Alan Gane steered Wycombe into it in 1985. Even now, Wanderers weren't ready – they were relegated after only a season. Gane then guided them to the Isthmian League title in 1987, the club's eighth championship and by far the most convincing, the side scoring 103 goals, winning 32 games and finishing with 101 points. Wycombe hadn't merely bridged the gap between amateur and professional football – they were comfortably the other side of it.

Consolidation in what was now the Conference coincided with the club getting planning application for a new ground, at the 14th attempt. The site, in the Sands district of West Wycombe, may have been in an 'Area Of Outstanding Natural Beauty', but it was also next-door to an industrial estate. Construction duly began early in 1989, and after Loakes Park had been sold to developers, Adams Park (named after Frank Adams, naturally) hosted its first game in August 1990.

At the time, Brian Lee described Adams Park as the biggest gamble in Wanderers' history. Crowds at Loakes Park had seldom risen above 2,000 in the Eighties, yet now the club, traditionally a paragon of caution, was risking its future prosperity on a new arena with a capacity of more than three times that. A group of fans may have revived the team's old turn-of-the-century nickname of 'Chairboys', but the old furniture industry which had given birth to the club no longer dominated the town in the same way. Could contemporary High Wycombe, a comfy halfway house on the hi-tech highway from Oxford to London, be tempted to fall in love with football?

Though he did not know it at the time, Lee had already done much to ensure that it could, by appointing Martin O'Neill as Wanderers' manager five months before the move to Adams Park. Ambitious and articulate, O'Neill made a virtue of his lack of non-League experience by bringing a new professionalism to the club, just as Lee himself had done two decades earlier. At the end of his first full season in charge, Wycombe posted a best-ever Conference finish (fifth) and won the FA Trophy for the first time, beating Kidderminster Harriers in the final at Wembley. Just as important, home gates all but doubled.

In 1991/92, O'Neill's side shattered all Conference records by notching up 30 wins and scoring 94 goals in the process, yet lost the title (and promotion to the League) to Colchester on goal difference. A year later there was no mistake – Wycombe won the Conference by a clear 15 points, and also regained the FA Trophy by beating Runcorn 4–1, with 28,000 fans making the short trip to Wembley to cheer on their Chairboys.

A smaller but still creditable contingent of 1,500 made the 600-mile round trip to see Wycombe's first-ever League game at Carlisle on 14 August 1993, while home crowds over the 1993/94 campaign would average nearly 5,500, bettered only by Carlisle and Preston in the Third Division. As it turned out, these two teams would stand between O'Neill and immediate promotion to the Second Division via the play-offs. The former were beaten 4–1 over two legs, and in the final against the latter at Wembley – rapidly becoming the club's second home – the manager inspired a comeback that saw Wanderers turn a 2–1 half-time deficit into a 4–2 victory.

Bit by bit, Wycombe's first League squad was broken up, with striker Keith Scott and young midfielder Steve Guppy being sold, and veteran defender Glyn Creaser retiring. But O'Neill then brought in Simon Garner, Cyrille Regis and Miguel de Souza to strike fear into Second Division defences, and take the club to within three points of a second play-off adventure. Having turned down approaches from Leicester and Forest because he had 'started something special' at Adams Park, O'Neill finally left for Norwich City in the summer of 1995.

Chairman Ivor Beeks turned to the former Crystal Palace manager Alan Smith as a replacement, but although Wycombe finished a respectable 12th under his guidance in 1995/96, the team had become less attractive to watch and crowd levels dipped as a consequence. This was unfortunate, since the club had just given the go-ahead to the building of a new stand to replace the former Woodlands Terrace, dramatically increasing the amount of seating accommodation at Adams Park and lifting the overall capacity to 10,000.

A poor start to the 1996/97 season saw Smith replaced by John Gregory, but Wanderers remained stuck at the wrong end of the table before a returning Keith Scott helped them take 26 out of their last 30 League points and dodge the drop in style. The loss of Gregory to Aston Villa in February 1998 stopped the team's return to form in its tracks, and Neil Smillie, who stepped into the manager's job after two earlier spells as caretaker boss, was himself dismissed at the start of 1999.

In came Lawrie Sanchez, scorer of the Wimbledon goal that beat Liverpool in the 1988 FA Cup final, and more latterly the Dons' reserve-team boss. With Wycombe in the relegation places on transfer-deadline day, Sanchez sold Scott to Reading and used the money to buy another striker, Sean Devine, from Barnet. Devine's goals helped secure 27 points from 17 games in the latter part of the season, but even so, Wycombe still needed to win at Lincoln on the last day to avoid relegation. The club paid for 30 coaches to take fans up to Sincil Bank, and they were rewarded seven minutes from time when Devine's cross was headed home by Paul Emblen.

If Wycombe have survived to fight another day in the Second Division, you get the impression the board – and the fans – want more than that. And if Sanchez turns out to be another Martin O'Neill in the making, they'll probably get it.

Here we go!

Green the Adams Park valley may be, but it is also a dead end – no matter where they park, **motorists** face a long wait to get out again. To reach the ground, leave the M40 motorway at junction 4 and follow the A4010 toward Aylesbury. Go straight over three roundabouts into New Road, and continue downhill to another mini-roundabout, at which turn sharp left into Lane End Road. At the next mini-roundabout, turn right into Hillbottom Road – Adams Park is at the end of this road.

The club **car park** has spaces for only around 100 cars, but several of the units on the Sands Industrial Estate also offer matchday parking for £1.50 or so. Keep valuables hidden as not all these car parks are patrolled.

The nearest **train station** is High Wycombe, on the line between London Marylebone and Birmingham Snow Hill (hourly, journey 30mins from Marylebone, 2hrs from Snow Hill). There are late trains for midweek matches in both directions. The station is more than 2miles from Adams Park, but the club runs **special buses** (route E) for both afternoon and evening games. Additional buses (route F) also serve **Maidenhead station** which has onward connections for London Paddington, Reading, Bristol, Wales and the West Country. Call ☎0345/484950 for the latest train times, or ☎01494/717818 (*Classic*

Coaches) for bus information. **Return buses** leave Adams Park 15mins after the final whistle.

Just the ticket

The Roger Vere Stand housing **visiting fans** was made all-seater in 1997. Ticket prices in 1998/99 were adults £13, OAPs £12, juniors £11, with discounts for advance booking. **Visiting families** are welcome in the new Servispak Stand, with tickets about £2 less – an excellent deal. There are superb **disabled facilities** in the same stand – book in advance on ☎01494/472100.

Swift half

The ***Centre Spot*** social club at Adams Park welcomes members of visiting supporters' clubs on a reciprocal basis (£1 guest admission, and you'll need to show your card).

The only pub within walking distance (and it's still about a mile away) is ***The Hour Glass*** on Chapel Lane, but this gets very busy on matchdays and the doorman may not let you in. Better try the centre of High Wycombe instead, where if you keep colours out of sight ***The Hobgoblin*** on the High Street offers its own real ale, a beer garden and bar meals.

Those with their own transport can exit the M40 at junction 5 for the ***Fleur de Lys*** in Stokenchurch, where real ale and good food await.

Club merchandise

The ***Cornerflag Shop*** (open matchdays only before and after kick-off, ☎01494/450957) offers the usual replica wear plus a wide range of leisure items. There's also a ***Wanderers In Town*** outlet inside High Wycombe's Octagon Shopping Centre, keeping more regular shop hours.

The latest home shirt is unlikely to be as cheap as the ill-fated 1996 design, which had striped (rather than solid) dark-blue quarters. The club wanted a radical change to quicken the pace of replica sales, but the fans kept their credit cards at home. The stripes lasted barely a season and were then chopped out at £4.99.

Barmy army

Like many of the League's newer sides, Wycombe haven't had the chance to build up heavy rivalries, and trouble is practically unheard of.

In print

The local ***Bucks Free Press*** is the newspaper for Wanderers news and match reports, while the club publishes the magazine ***Quarterman*** every, um, quarter. The Independent Supporters' Club has a fanzine, ***The Wanderer*** (25 Queen Street, High Wycombe, Bucks), and there are two more worth picking up: ***One-One*** (PO Box 589, High Wycombe, HP15 7XL) and ***Tales Of A Chairboy*** (19 Lent Green Lane, Burnham, SL1 7AS).

Wycombe Wanderers History 1887-1996 by Dave Finch and Steve Peart (Yore, £16.95) is the essential book about the club.

On air

Radio High Wycombe (1170 AM) offers live matchday commentary and other club news. Meanwhile, ***Sky TV*** subscribers can keep an ear out for how many times Wanderers director Alan Parry makes reference to his beloved club.

In the net

The **official website** is light on graphics, heavy on proper content, with full news and match-report archives among many other things at: www.wycombewanderers.co.uk. Elsewhere, ***Chairboys On The Net*** have been online since 1995 and, though their site could be on a quicker server, it does include a useful *Rough Guide* to the club, at: www.ndirect.co.uk/~chairboys/.

Chairboys' cheer – Sean Devine is mobbed at Maine Road, 1999

York City

Formation	1903
Stadium	Bootham Crescent, York, YO3 7AQ. ☎01904/624447
Ground capacity	9,500
First-choice colours	All red with navy-blue trim
Major honour	Fourth Division champions 1984
Position 1998/99	21st in Second Division (relegated)

Green and pleasant, picturesque and affluent, the city of York is nobody's idea of a footballing hotbed. Like so many of the country's leading tourist centres (Oxford, Cambridge, Lincoln), York has often seemed, at best, ambivalent toward the game and the local team that play it. Add the rival attraction of rugby league and the decline of the rail industry which once provided the club with much of its support, and you begin to understand why York City fans sometimes regard themselves as members of an oppressed minority.

Lack of achievement on the pitch hasn't helped matters. Though they have often made headlines as Cup giant-killers, City have never graced the top division of the English game and only once, in the mid-Seventies, maintained a presence in the next one down. The current scenario is an achingly familiar one to followers of lower-division football: fans accuse the directors of a lack of ambition, while directors point to low crowds as the limiting factor in any plans to move the club forward.

Nor is this state of affairs anything new. It wasn't until 1903 that it occurred to anyone to start a football club in York, and even then it was an outsider, Darlington-born Ernest Trees, who got the ball rolling. His club effectively folded under the twin pressures of cashflow and World War I, but when a new club was established in 1922, it took Trees' York City name. The team played at Fulfordgate, on the southern edge of the city, and were elected to the Football League in 1929, joining the Third Division (North) in place of Ashington. However, dwindling crowds – the ground could hold 13,000 but was rarely more than a third full – and poor local transport persuaded the club to seek a new, more central home. In 1932 City took over the former Yorkshire County Cricket Club ground at Bootham Crescent, and six years later, more than 28,000 crammed in to see City play Huddersfield in the quarter-finals of the FA Cup. (The game finished goalless, and York lost the replay, 2–1.)

Overall, though, crowds were no higher than they'd been at Fulford, and the team still hadn't finished a League season higher than the sixth place they'd managed in 1930. In an attempt to increase support from workers in the chocolate industry (which, along with the railways, was the town's major employer), the board ordered the team to play in brown and cream striped shirts. But the players complained that the kit clashed too often with that of their opponents, so City went back to wearing red. On the eve of World War II, the club had to apply for re-election.

In the mid-Fifties, things began to look up a bit. Arthur Bottom and Norman Wilkinson, who would net more than 200 goals between them for York, became the most feared strikeforce in the Third Division (North), while goalkeeper Tom Forgan was a formidable barrier at the other end. In 1955, this trio were at the heart of a side that finished fourth in the table and became the first (and only) team from the League's basement to reach the semi-finals of the FA Cup. Blackpool, with Mortensen and Matthews onboard, and Spurs were City's big Cup scalps that season, and in the semi-final against Newcastle at Hillsborough, York forced a 1–1 draw. They were comfortably beaten, 2–0, in the replay at Roker Park.

Yes, Minster – Neil Tolson, Graeme Murty and worshippers after victory over Everton, 1996

A year later Sam Bartram took over as team manager, and when the Fourth Division was formed in 1958/59, York escaped from it at the first attempt. They went back down a year later, though, and Bartram was replaced by Tom Lockie, whose seven-year spell in charge included another season in the Third Division, in 1965/66.

Both Bartram and Lockie were ambitious managers who were frustrated by the club's inability to strengthen its squad for a step up in standard. Tom Johnston, who took over as manager in 1968, felt he had the solution: get the squad right first, then get promoted. Johnston's progress was slow but sure. City finished 21st at the end of his first year in charge, and after dispensing with the services of many older players, he was forced to sell two young strikers, Ted McDougall and Phil Boyer, to Bournemouth in successive seasons. But Paul Aimson, who'd first made his name at Bootham in the early Sixties, returned to lead the line, and with Phil Burrows, Chris Topping and club captain Barry Swallow marshalling the back-line, York won promotion in 1971.

Bit by bit, Johnston was building a side capable of still bigger things: Scotsman Graeme Crawford was the proverbial rock in goal; wingers Barry Lyons and Ian Butler offered more width than most Third Division teams possessed; and Jimmy Seal, Yorkshire through and through, was a qiuck-witted, confident target man.

In 1974 City finished third, and the club began its first and only spell in the Second Division. It wasn't a bad time to be there – Aston Villa, Manchester United, Nottingham Forest and Southampton were among York's opponents, and to celebrate the team's coming of age, Johnston clad his players in a bold, archetypally Seventies shirt of claret with a white 'Y' running down from shoulders to crotch. A crowd of 46,800 saw Johnston's 'Y-fronts' take the field at Old Trafford that season, and though York could not match the fine promotion form of United and Villa, they finished a decent 15th.

Then, much more quickly than it had been built, York's house of cards collapsed. Johnston was poached by Huddersfield

Going, gone – sold striker Richard Cresswell

Town, Swallow retired, and without their guidance the team's confidence evaporated. York were nine points away from safety when they were relegated in 1976.

The bulk of Johnston's side remained intact but former Busby Babe Wilf McGuinness, who had taken over as manager, wanted to bring his own players in, and the Y-fronts were torn apart. York finished the 1976/77 season bottom of the Third Division, and were relegated again. McGuinness departed but his replacement, Charlie Wright, could do no better – the club was forced to seek re-election after finishing third from bottom of the League in 1978. Wright coaxed Barry Lyons back to the club to become its first youth coach, but while that decision would ultimately bear some fruit, the first team were struggling still – Lyons replaced Wright as manager in 1980, and at the end of his first season in charge, York finished bottom of the League.

The turning point came with the recruitment of Denis Smith as manager in 1982. A man who in his own words has 'always liked a challenge', Smith felt there was promise in the York squad that could be fulfilled if some of the old team spirit was restored. He was right. Midfielder Gary Ford and striker John Byrne, who had been living together with Ford's mother since Wilf McGuinness had brought them to York as trainees, would form the nucleus of a side that won the Fourth Division title at a canter in 1984, chalking up a new record of 101 points in the process.

The club couldn't afford to resist QPR's offer of £100,000 for Byrne that summer, but in the hard-working Jamaican Keith Walwyn, Smith had a towering replacement. A last-minute penalty gave York a 1–0 home win over Arsenal in the fourth round of the FA Cup in 1985, and in the same year Liverpool were held 1–1 at Bootham in the League Cup – a result repeated against the same opposition in the FA Cup fifth round the following year.

York had consolidated their position in the Third Division, meanwhile, but just as had happened a decade earlier, the loss of a manager (Smith) proved devastating. In 1988, a year after his departure, the team were relegated back down to the Fourth.

The club returned to its previous existence of treading water in the basement until 1993 when, under John Ward, York beat Crewe 5–3 on penalties to win the Third Division play-off final at Wembley. Twelve months later, with Alan Little at the helm, they reached the Second Division play-offs, losing 1–0 on aggregate to Stockport in the semi-finals.

In 1995, York returned to Old Trafford for the first time since that joyous season in the Second Division, for a League Cup tie. United were pre-occupied by other trophies but even so, Giggs, Beckham, Lee Sharpe and Philip Neville were in the side

Grim up north – the most elegant thing about Bootham Crescent is its floodlights

humiliated 3–0 at home by Little's York. United bounced back to score three goals of their own in the second leg at Bootham Crescent, but Scott Jordan's first-half goal was enough to give York a deserved and hugely symbolic victory.

The team were at it again in the same competition a year later, beating Everton 4–3 on aggregate after a stirring 3–2 win at Bootham in the second leg. In the League, however, the club's progress was stalling. York finished in the wrong half of the Second Division table every year after the win over Everton, and the exodus of playing talent from the club counted Paul Barnes (goalscoring hero of Old Trafford), Nigel Pepper and Graeme Murty among its number.

Alan Little had long since lost the support of fans when he was dismissed as York hovered around the drop zone in March 1999, and the first act of caretaker boss Neil Thompson was to sell the club's greatest asset, striker Richard Cresswell, to Sheffield Wednesday for £1million on transfer deadline day. Even so, Thompson managed to shake things up sufficiently for City to take maximum points from four games during the run-in, and the team were in the relegation places for just seven minutes of the season. Unfortunately, they were the last seven minutes...

Here we go!

The centre of York is a virtual no-go area for cars and most **motorists** should approach the ground from the outer ring road A64 and A1237. Those coming from the north are the exception – simply follow the A19 in toward the centre, take the second exit at the A1237 roundabout onto Shipton Road, go straight across the next set of lights, then turn left into Burton Stone Lane. Take the first right into Grosvenor Road to the ground.

From the south, take the ring road clockwise (signposted York North) until you reach the junction with the A19 Shipton Road, and follow directions as above. Travellers from the east and west can exit the ring road at the same junction and follow the same directions.

There's a small **car park** in Burton Stone Lane, but you could save yourself the price of a pint by finding a street parking space – not normally too difficult as long as you don't set your heart on somewhere within 2mins of the ground.

York's **train station** is on the East Coast main line between London and Edinburgh (half-hourly, journey time 2hrs). It can also be reached by cross-country trains from as far afield as Birmingham, Bristol and Exeter. For the latest timings call ☎0345/484950.

The station is about a mile from the ground, a 20min walk via Station Road, Museum Street, Blake Street, Exhibition Square and Bootham. From Bootham, take the second turning right after the railway line into Bootham Crescent. Aside from departures north to Newcastle, there are no late trains suitable for midweek evening kick-offs.

Just the ticket

Visiting fans are accommodated in the spartan Grosvenor Road terracing; enter through turnstiles #14–23. Ticket prices in 1998/99 were adults £8, concessions £5, and as if they weren't already reasonable enough, for an extra £1 you can usually transfer to the seated (and covered) Popular Stand on the left.

Disabled supporters have 20 spaces in front of the Main Stand, while visiting **families** are welcome in the designated section of the Popular Stand – no need to book for either.

Swift half

Home and away fans mix freely at ***The Burton Stone***, on the corner of Burton Stone Lane and the A19 Clifton. The ***Mansfield Corner House***, also on Burton Stone Lane, is also recommended and might be a better bet for families.

Club merchandise

The **club shop** (open matchdays & Suns only, ☎01922/622791) is adjacent to the Main Stand, to the left of the main entrance in Bootham Crescent. Among the more desirable items is the always popular 'Man United 0, York City 3' T-shirt at £9.99.

Barmy army

Not even low prices and an easily accessible ground can stir the good people of York from their apathy. With average gates of less than 3,000, the faithful in the David Longhurst Stand (named after the York striker who collapsed and died on the pitch in 1990) freely admit that they make more impact away from home.

More atmosphere might be generated when City realise their plans to cover all sides of the ground, but that will have to wait until the club has agreed a ground-sharing agreement with York Wasps rugby league club, who are keen to move back into town from outlying Ryedale.

In print

The locally produced ***Evening Press*** is best for York City news, but doesn't publish a Saturday evening edition. There are no fanzines at present, but ***Citizens & Minstermen – A Who's Who Of York City FC 1922-1997*** (Citizen, £11.99) makes for an informed introduction to the club, diligently penned by Dave Windross and Martin Jarred.

On air

The choice is between ***BBC Radio York*** (103.7 FM) and ***Minster FM*** (104.7 FM). Both offer detailed reporting of City, including after-match phone-ins at 5.30pm.

In the net

There is no official website but York fans do a sterling job keeping their club's internet profile high. The most comprehensive site is ***Blue & Red Net***, at: www.geocities.com/Yosemite/Geyser/9285/. It includes audio interviews with players, a match-report archive and updates on City's youth and reserve teams.

An electronic bulletin board for York fans, ***There's Only One Arthur Bottom***, resides at: pages.hotbot.com/sports/yorkcity/index.html/174,57. Read it and weep.

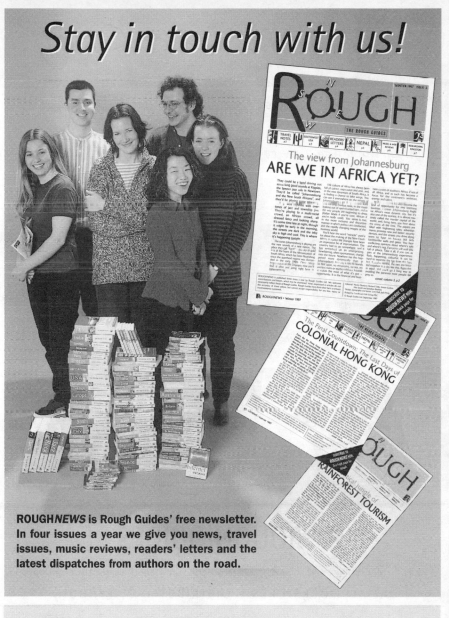

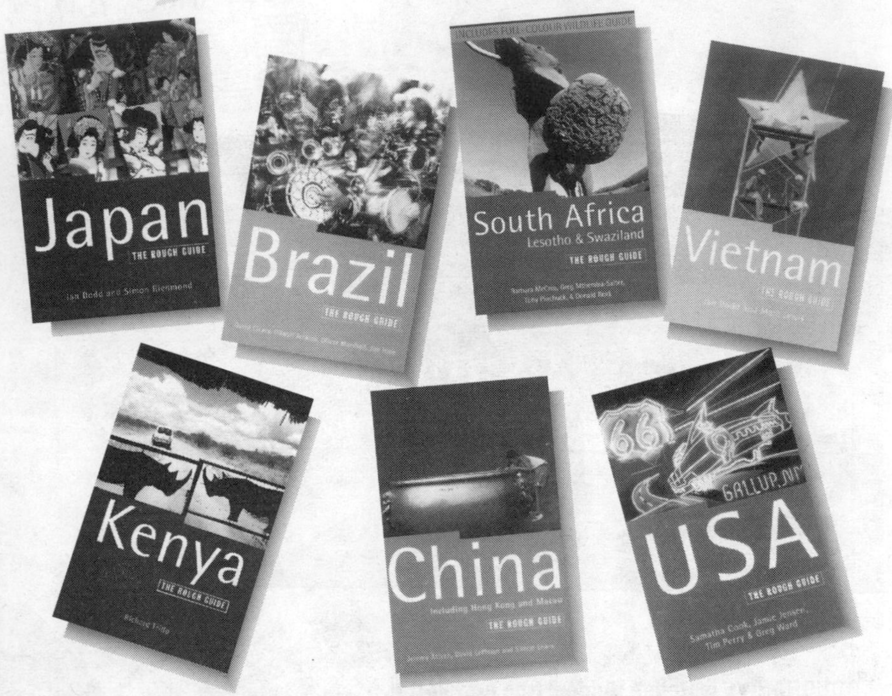

Japan
THE ROUGH GUIDE
Brazil
THE ROUGH GUIDE
South Africa
Lesotho & Swaziland
THE ROUGH GUIDE
Vietnam
Kenya
THE ROUGH GUIDE
China
THE ROUGH GUIDE
GALLUP, NM
USA
THE ROUGH GUIDE